Mission Handbook
1998–2000

U.S. and Canadian
Christian Ministries Overseas

John A. Siewert and Edna G. Valdez, editors

• 17th Edition •

D1088851

a division of World Vision
800 West Chestnut Avenue • Monrovia • California • 91016 • USA

Mission Handbook 1998-2000
(17th Edition)
U.S. and Canadian Christian Ministries Overseas with statistical
data and background essays
John A. Siewert and Edna G. Valdez, editors

ISBN 1-887983-02-3

Published by MARC, a division of World Vision International, 800 West Chestnut
Avenue, Monrovia, California 91016, U.S.A.

Printed in the United States of America. Cover design: Carl Crooks/Crooks Design. "The
New Context of World Mission" section designed by Richard Sears.

The *Mission Handbook* is the successor to a series initiated by the Missionary Research
Library (MRL) in 1953. The 1968 through 1973 editions were published jointly by MRL
and the Mission Advanced Research and Communications Center (MARC). Subsequently
MARC has published the *Mission Handbook*.

All Scripture quotations, unless otherwise indicated, are from the Revised Standard Version of the Bible, copyright © 1946, 1952, 1971 by the Division of Christian Education of
the National Council of Churches of Christ in the USA. Used by permission.

"As one who has looked for answers to questions about missions and the missionary movement almost daily, besides the Bible, the one book that our office could not do without is the *Mission Handbook*. . . . In an age of networking, one of the most helpful tools in the missions arsenal is the *Mission Handbook*."

~**Paul McKaughan**, president and CEO,
Evangelical Fellowship of Mission Agencies

"The *Mission Handbook* is an indispensable resource. I always keep it within easy reach, alongside my dictionary and other desk reference tools. . . . Across the years, the *Mission Handbook* has been a dependable friend."

~**Lois McKinney**, professor of mission,
Trinity Evangelical Divinity School

"The *Mission Handbook* is an essential reference tool for mission executives and scholars. The new edition is better than ever."

~**Gerald H. Anderson**, director,
Overseas Ministries Study Center

Contents

Abbreviations

Admin.	Administrative, administrator	**Lit.**	Literature
Am.	America, American	**Mgr.**	Manager
Apt.	Apartment	**Min(s).**	Ministry(ies)
Assoc.	Association	**Msn.**	Mission
Ave.	Avenue	**Msny(s).**	Missionary(ies)
Bd.	Board	**Mtg.**	Meeting
Blvd.	Boulevard	**N.**	North
Cen.	Central	**NA**	Not Applicable
CEO	Chief Executive Officer	**Natl.**	National
Ch(s).	Church(es)	**NE**	Northeast
Co.	Company	**NR**	Not Reported
Comte.	Committee	**NW**	Northwest
Comm.	Commission	**Ofc.**	Office
Conf.	Conference	**Org.**	Organization
Cong.	Congregational	**Pres.**	President
Conv.	Convention	**P.O.**	Post Office
COO	Chief Operating Officer	**Rsch.**	Research
Coord.	Coordinator	**Rd.**	Road
Ctr.	Center	**Rev.**	Reverend
Dept.	Department	**Rm.**	Room
Dev.	Development	**Rep.**	Republic
Dir.	Director	**S.**	South
Div.	Division	**SE**	Southeast
Dr.	Doctor, Drive	**Secy.**	Secretary
E.	East	**Soc.**	Society
Ed.	Education	**St.**	Saint, Street
Exec.	Executive	**Sta.**	Station
Expy.	Expressway	**Supt.**	Superintendent
Flwshp.	Fellowship	**Ste.**	Suite
Frgn.	Foreign	**Svc(s).**	Service(s)
Gen.	General	**SW**	Southwest
Govt.	Government	**TEE**	Theological Education by
Hdq.	Headquarters		Extension
Hts.	Heights	**Theol.**	Theology, Theological
Hwy.	Highway	**U., Univ.**	University
Inc.	Incorporated	**VP**	Vice President
Inst.	Institute	**W.**	West
Intl.	International	**Wld.**	World
Is(ls).	Island(s)		

Canada

AB	Alberta
BC	British Columbia
MB	Manitoba
NB	New Brunswick
NF	Newfoundland
NS	Nova Scotia
NT	Northwest Territories
ON	Ontario
PE	Prince Edward Island
PQ	Quebec
SK	Saskatchewan
YT	Yukon Territory

United States

AK	Alaska
AL	Alabama
AR	Arkansas
AZ	Arizona
CA	California
CO	Colorado
CT	Connecticut
DE	Delaware
DC	District of Columbia
FL	Florida
GA	Georgia
HI	Hawaii
IA	Iowa
ID	Idaho
IL	Illinois
IN	Indiana
KS	Kansas
KY	Kentucky
LA	Louisiana
MA	Massachusetts
MD	Maryland
ME	Maine
MI	Michigan
MN	Minnesota
MO	Missouri
MS	Mississippi
MT	Montana
NC	North Carolina
ND	North Dakota
NE	Nebraska
NH	New Hampshire
NJ	NewJersey
NM	New Mexico
NV	Nevada
NY	New York
OH	Ohio
OK	Oklahoma
OR	Oregon
PA	Pennsylvania
PR	Puerto Rico
RI	Rhode Island
SC	South Carolina
SD	South Dakota
TN	Tennessee
TX	Texas
UT	Utah
VA	Virginia
VT	Vermont
WA	Washington
WI	Wisconsin
WV	West Virginia
WY	Wyoming

Some Other Countries/Areas

Br Virgin Isls	British Virgin Islands
CIS-Gen	Commonwealth of Independent States (used when an individual state was not specified or to indicate multiple states/republics)
Equat Guinea	Equatorial Guinea
Fr Polynesia	French Polynesia
Neth Antilles	Netherlands Antilles
Papua New Guin	Papua New Guinea
St. Chris-Nevis	St Christopher and Nevis
Trinidad & Tobg	Trinidad & Tobago
Turks & Cai Isl	Turks & Caicos Islands

United Arab Emr   United Arab Emi
rates

Wallis & Fut Is   Wallis & Futuna
Islands

Introduction

The primary purpose of the *Mission Handbook* is to provide the reader with ready access to vital and current information about Christian mission agencies based in the U.S. and Canada that are engaged in overseas ministries (all countries beyond the United States and Canada). As such, it provides the user with the most complete information available today in a single publication.

Please note that the term "agency" is used throughout the *Handbook* in the broad sense, referring to denominational boards and all other kinds of organizations involved in overseas mission.

Chapter 1: The new context of world mission

This chapter by Bryant Myers is both a revision and an expansion of the chapter entitled "The Changing Shape of World Mission" that originally appeared in the 1993-95 *Handbook*. The usefulness and popularity of that original chapter generated requests that led to its publication as a separate booklet.

The separate booklet of this current chapter was published at the end of 1996, as part of the registration materials received by each of the more than 18,000 participants at the InterVarsity Student Mission Convention in Urbana, Illinois. Other organizations and individuals have also taken advantage of the availability of the chapter in booklet and overhead transparency form.

Readers will immediately notice that the chapter is now in full color and has even more concise and well-illustrated information. Besides painting the context in which mission operates today, it also shows mission's historical roots and projections into the twenty-first century.

Chapter 2: Growing local church initiatives

Local churches are becoming more directly involved in sending missionaries overseas. For some churches, this means a complete mission sending program that includes activities formerly carried out by denominational mission boards or other sending agencies. For others, it means a closer relationship between local church mission leaders and a sending agency that goes beyond the traditional one-way support relationship. This chapter provides examples of several churches that model these changes.

Chapter 3: Putting the survey in perspective

This chapter gives a brief description of the survey process with discussion and interpretation of the survey results. Overall, tables show U.S. and Canadian totals for the various categories of personnel serving overseas, U.S.-based ministry and support personnel and income raised for overseas activities.

As in past editions, there are tables ranking the largest 100 U.S. and 20 Canadian agencies by number of overseas personnel and income for overseas ministries. A new feature in this edition are historical graphs of key mission agency indicators from the 1984, 1988, 1992 and 1996 surveys, showing trends into the twenty-first century.

Chapters 4 through 9: U.S. and Canadian Protestant agencies

These chapters present a directory in alphabetical order, indices by church tradition and ministry activity, and a country-by-country listing of the numbers of personnel involved in ministry overseas. A brief introduction at the start of each chapter explains the format, with comments on some of the data.

Chapter 10: U.S. Catholic overseas mission

Tony Gittins, C.S.Sp., a former missionary in Sierra Leone now on the faculty of the Catholic Theological Union in Chicago, identifies five trends in Catholic mission in a well-organized and compact essay.

The U.S. Catholic Mission Association (USCMA) in Washington, D.C., provides an updated country-by-country listing of the U.S. Catholic mission orders involved in overseas work, along with the numbers of the U.S. Catholic mission personnel in each country. This information was compiled by USCMA staff with Executive Director Rosanne Rustemeyer, SSND. We are very grateful for their cooperation in making this information available for publication.

Chapter 11: The Orthodox Christian Mission Center

Dimitrios Couchell, executive director of the Orthodox Christian Mission Center (OCMC) in St. Augustine, Florida, reports on the work of this mission and evangelism agency of the Canonical Orthodox Churches in North America. These are the 10 Eastern Orthodox Churches that are part of a voluntary association, the Standing Conference of Canonical Orthodox Bishops in the Americas.

OCMC coordinates U.S. Orthodox mission assistance in 10 overseas countries and promotes mission involvement among the U.S. Orthodox community (numbering over 5 million adherents) through conferences, retreats and other programs. OCMC participates in cooperative efforts such as the Committee on Common Witness and the InterVarsity Urbana Student Mission Convention. We are very grateful for this report, the first of its kind in the *Handbook*.

A word of caution

Statistics relating to overseas missionary endeavors suffer from the same problems as statistics in general and religious statistics in particular, namely, they may be incomplete, not comparable, or defined in different ways. Even within the same agency some reporting practices may not be consistent from survey to survey because of personnel changes or changes in the agency's practices between surveys.

The reader should exercise extreme caution when comparing statistics between agencies, within the same agency from different years or adding statistics from different agencies. It can be highly inaccurate to draw conclusions about a particular agency, group of agencies or a particular country without being aware of, or securing, additional information that was beyond the scope of the original survey.

Thanks to all

This *Handbook* is the result of the efforts of many individuals and organizations. Special thanks go to those persons in each agency who completed the questionnaires that made the survey possible. For larger agencies this was a collaborative effort involving executives, accountants, researchers and staff from the personnel department.

The computer database and processing modifications needed for this edition were again carried out by our very able consultant, Brett Lamberty. Further steps in simplifying the processing stages were made in meshing the database (FoxPro) and word processing (WordPerfect) software. An interface was created to move selected elements of the database to a spreadsheet (Excel) for the historical and trends analyses.

The questionnaires (initially 1,006 with others added during the process) were sent out and the responses entered into the database and verified by Sherrie Simms. Reminders were then sent when responses were not received and, as a last resort, phone calls were made. Sherrie also assisted with the writing of the introductions to the database chapters, and worked with the computer software needed to extract information from the historical spreadsheet to produce the historical and trends graphs.

Don Brandt provided research assistance for the chapter on "the new context of world mission." We are grateful to Richard Sears for his patience and skill in the design of "the new context of world mission" chapter, and for his design assistance with the interior pages.

RLou Norquist did a whirlwind round of proofreading to ready this book for the printer. Carl Crooks supplied professional expertise with the design of the cover. Dan Roest and Michael Haan at Color House Graphics patiently walked us through the many printing issues that came up as we designed and produced the interior pages. Steve Singley gave skillful marketing guidance and perspective, and JoJo Marano and Bill Johnson kept us informed of the distribution needs of *Handbook* users. Rebecca Russell worked with us on our writing process, and provided gracious support when needed.

We are indebted to Bryant Myers for his thoughtful encouragement and insight into the global mission community, and to John Kenyon for his guidance and steadfast support. Finally, our thanks to Dwayne Sedig for urging us on with humor and understanding, and to our families for continuing to care for us despite our many absences.

John A. Siewert
Edna G. Valdez
October 1997

Chapter 1

The new context of world mission

Bryant L. Myers

Chapter 1

The new context of world mission

Bryant L. Myers

God's world is undergoing profound, rapid, dizzying change at the close of the second millennium since the birth of his Son. Many agree that there have been few periods of history in which individuals, organizations and nations have faced changes on the current scale. Virtually every area of life is being tossed about, seemingly at the whim of forces far beyond our understanding and control. Economics, demographics, technology, the social and spiritual fabric of society, all are undergoing foundational change at a rate almost too fast to follow.

The last decades of this century have witnessed the breaking down of a world order that had been in place since the end of World War II. Early expectations that the post-Cold War period would see reduced levels of conflict and broader economic prosperity have been disappointed. Instead, the end of the second millennium is a time of great uncertainty and fear in many parts of the world. Hope for a better future seems threatened by a combination of spiritual, economic, political, cultural and environmental factors over which people feel little control.

There is some good news. Premier Christian researcher David Barrett points out that the proportion of Christians actively involved in some form of mission is at an all-time high of 36% and most Christian researchers agree that the number of unevangelized people in the world is declining, albeit slowly. There has been an unprecedented wave of human freedom sweeping across many lands. The 1995 United Nations Human Development Report claims that the speed of human development — measured in terms of health, education and economics — in the "developing" countries in the last three decades is three times faster than that of the industrialized world during the nineteenth century.

There is also a lot of disturbing news. There are still over one billion human beings living in places where it is unlikely they will ever hear the good news about Jesus Christ, unless someone goes to tell them. The Christian church continues to decline in places where it was once strong. Too many Christians, stubbornly holding onto the modern dichotomy between the material and the spiritual, limit the lordship of Christ to their inner, private lives. Countries whose populations are overwhelmingly Christian are suffering from corruption, ethnic violence, tolerance for the killing in the womb and unbridled consumption.

The world is a violent place, often inhospitable to human life. There are over 50 ongoing wars taking place as this book is being written. There are almost 50 million uprooted people who have had to flee their homes because of violence, disaster, economics or a failing environment. There are one billion people who do not have access to the basic social services of health care, education, safe drinking water and adequate nutrition. The gap between those with more than enough and those who live on the margins of life is widening. The phenomenon of global economic integration is leaving some people and even some nations permanently on the sidelines.

This chapter provides a brief, easy to read, yet comprehensive description of the world in which Christian mission is to take place as this century closes. For those who make things happen it gives a a bird's-eye view of the context of mission, while preserving some of the complexity of the world.

Because the context of Christian mission is a hurting, conflicted world stubbornly at odds with its Creator, some may feel that this booklet focuses too much on the "secular." But looking at the world needing Christ's mission means looking at the fallen material and spiritual parts of the world — a holistic view. This does not make the view any less Christian or biblical. It is after all God's world — all of it.

Jesus wept for a real Jerusalem, a Jerusalem ruled by Rome and entrapped by religiosity rooted in human rules, a Jerusalem of upper rooms, small shops, lepers, beggars, and rich young rulers, a Jerusalem of Pharisees who came at night, adulteresses and crowds of ordinary people who couldn't make up their minds, a Jerusalem so spiritually blind that it could not recognize the Messiah it longed for even when he stood in their midst. This is the context of Christian mission.

Changing paradigms of mission thinking

Apocalyptic-Early Church

◇ 33–200 AD
◇ Making disciples (Matthew 28:18-19)
◇ Goal of mission is disciples
◇ Apostles and martyrs
◇ Centrality of eschatology
◇ Church as eschatological community

Greek — Patristic Orthodox

◇ 200–500 AD
◇ God so loved the world (John 3:16)
◇ Goal of mission is life
◇ Itinerant evangelists and healers
◇ Centrality of theology
◇ Church as worshipping community

Christendom — Medieval Roman Catholic

◇ 600–1400 AD
◇ Compel them to come in (Luke 14:23)
◇ Goal of mission is expanding Christendom
◇ Monks and conquistadors
◇ Centrality of church, state and culture
◇ Church as powerful institution

| 250 | 500 | 750 | 1000 | 1250 | 1500 |

Adapted from Bosch, *Transforming Mission*, Orbis, 1991

Reformation — Protestant

◇ 1500–1750 AD
◇ The gospel is the power of salvation for everyone who believes (Romans 1:16)
◇ Goal of mission is renewal
◇ Holy Spirit and reformed church
◇ Centrality of Scripture
◇ Church as reforming community

Modern Mission Era

◇ 1750–1950 AD
◇ Come over and help us (Acts 16:9)
◇ Goal is salvation / better life
◇ Volunteers, missionaries
◇ Centrality of mission task
◇ Church as civilizing (Westernizing) community

Emerging mission paradigm at the end of the second millenium

◇ 1950– ?
◇ They preached, drove out demons and healed them (Mark 6:12)
◇ Goal of mission is to call people to faith who then work for social and spiritual transformation
◇ All of the people of God in all of life
◇ Centrality of holism — life, deed, word and sign
◇ Church as pilgrim community

1500   1750   2000

The unfolding of mission history

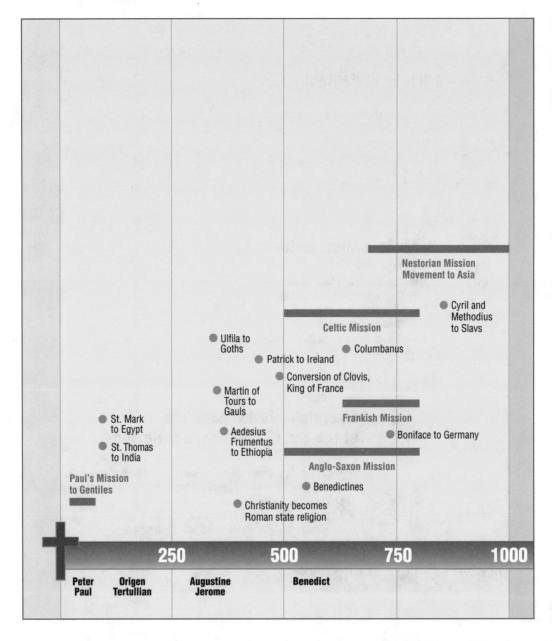

Nestorian Mission
Movement to Asia

● Cyril and
Methodius
to Slavs

Celtic Mission

● Ulfila to
Goths

● Columbanus

● Patrick to Ireland

● Conversion of Clovis,
King of France

● Martin of
Tours to
Gauls

Frankish Mission

● St. Mark
to Egypt

● Aedesius
Frumentus
to Ethiopia

● Boniface to Germany

● St. Thomas
to India

Anglo-Saxon Mission

Paul's Mission
to Gentiles

● Benedictines

● Christianity becomes
Roman state religion

250   500   750   1000

Peter   Origen   Augustine   Benedict
Paul   Tertullian   Jerome

Developed from Neill, *A History of Christian Missions*, Penguin, 1964;
Lapple, *The Catholic Church: A Brief History*, Paulist, 1982

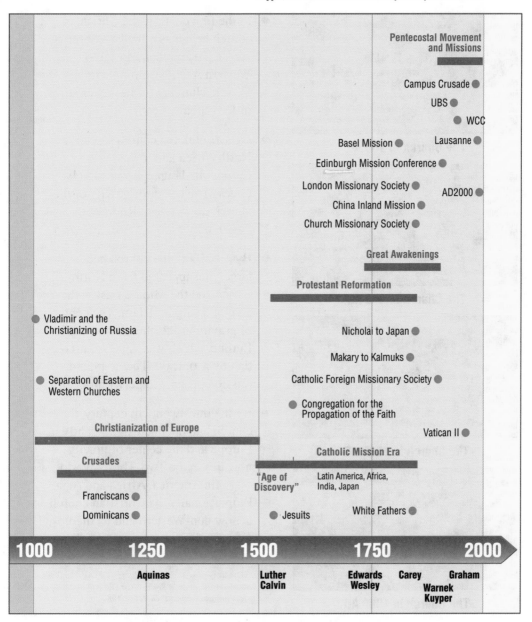

Pentecostal Movement
and Missions

Campus Crusade ●

UBS ●

● WCC

Basel Mission ●   Lausanne ●

Edinburgh Mission Conference ●

London Missionary Society ●   AD2000 ●

China Inland Mission ●

Church Missionary Society ●

Great Awakenings

Protestant Reformation

● Vladimir and the
Christianizing of Russia

Nicholai to Japan ●

Makary to Kalmuks ●

● Separation of Eastern and
Western Churches

Catholic Foreign Missionary Society ●

● Congregation for the
Propagation of the Faith

Christianization of Europe

Vatican II ●

Catholic Mission Era

Crusades

"Age of   Latin America, Africa,
Discovery"   India, Japan

Franciscans ●

Dominicans ●   ● Jesuits   White Fathers ●

1000	1250	1500	1750	2000
	Aquinas	Luther Calvin	Edwards Wesley	Graham
			Carey	
			Warnek	
			Kuyper	

The Christian church grows serially

The Church in 100 AD

The Church in 400 AD

The Church in 1500 AD

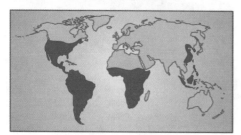

The Church in 1990 AD

◆ In the first century, the Christian church began as a Jewish church in Jerusalem and then moved to Western Asia, becoming a largely Gentile church with its center still in Jerusalem.

◆ By A.D. 600, the church spread to North Africa and to southern Europe. Its language was largely Greek. The center of gravity of the church lay between Rome and Constantinople.

◆ By A.D. 1000, the church had largely disappeared from North Africa and the Middle East in the face of a surging Islam. The center of gravity of the church now lay in Europe, which was largely Christian by A.D. 1500. Theology and mission became largely European.

◆ By the mid-twentieth century, the church had declined significantly in Europe and the center of gravity now lies in the Two-Thirds World — Latin America, Africa and Asia. Proportionally the Christian church is now non-Western and its theology and mission practice are following suit.

Adapted from Andrew Walls, "The Old Age of the Missionary Movement," *IRM*, Jan. 1987

Christianity and Islam: The ebb and flow

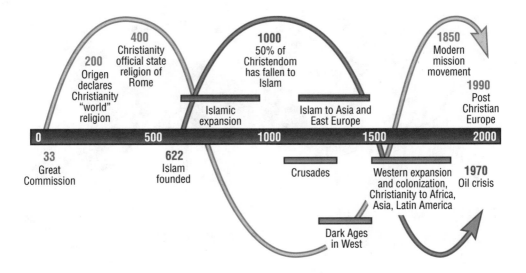

In the ebb and flow of God's history...

◆ By the time Islam arose in the seventh century, Christianity was a world religion and the official religion of the Roman Empire.

◆ Islam expanded serially from Arabia to North Africa and the Middle East, and then into the Caucasus, North Africa and Spain during seventh century.

◆ The classical age of Islam (A.D. 775-1300) roughly corresponded with the Dark Ages in Europe, and was the time that Islam extended its reach to Asia and central Asia.

◆ During the nineteenth and first half of the twentieth century, "Christian Europe" exerted colonial rule over most Muslims.

◆ Until the mid-1980s, there had always been more Muslims than Christians in Africa.

The world by religion

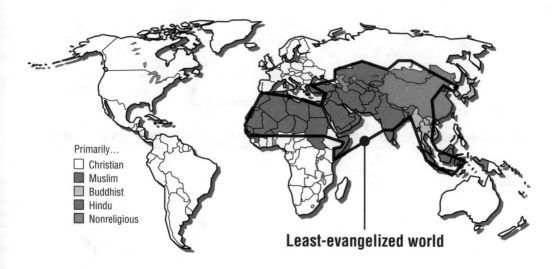

Primarily…
- ☐ Christian
- Muslim
- Buddhist
- Hindu
- Nonreligious

Least-evangelized world

In the year 2000…

◆ There will be 2.1 billion people in the world who identify themselves as members of the Christian church.

◆ There will be 1.2 billion Muslims. Muslims are the fastest growing major religious group, largely as a result of a high birth rate.

◆ There will be over one billion people who are Buddhist or who practice Chinese traditional religion.

◆ There will be 850 million Hindus, largely in India.

◆ There will be 230 million people who identify themselves as atheists.

Source: Barrett, Status of Global Mission, *IBMR,* 1996

The poor and the lost

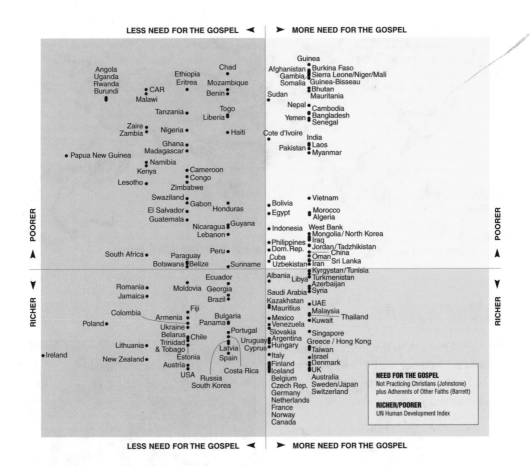

LESS NEED FOR THE GOSPEL ◄ ► MORE NEED FOR THE GOSPEL

In God's world...

◆ A very large proportion of those who have not heard the gospel are also poor.

◆ Eighty-five percent of the world's poorest countries lie within the unevangelized world.

◆ With the demise of Marxism and communism, there is no global ideology which places the poor at the center of its vision for a better human future.

Source: Myers, *The Poor and the Lost*, 1989

How are the children?

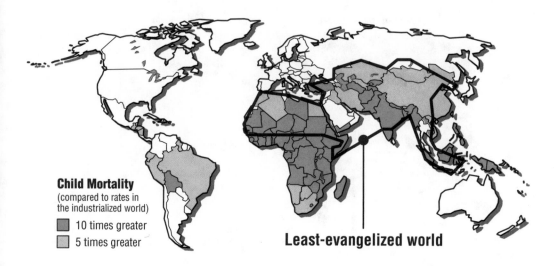

Child Mortality
(compared to rates in the industrialized world)

☐ 10 times greater
☐ 5 times greater

Least-evangelized world

In God's world...

◆ Child mortality, the average number of children per family and primary school enrollment have all improved since 1960.

◆ Yet, 15 million children die every year from preventable causes.

◆ Yet, over 350 million children will be working, instead of being in school, by the year 2000.

◆ Yet, over one million children (90% of them girls) will join the sex trade each year.

Source: "Children at Risk," 1992
The Economist, August 1996.

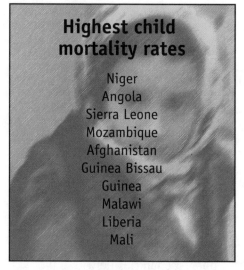

Highest child mortality rates

Niger
Angola
Sierra Leone
Mozambique
Afghanistan
Guinea Bissau
Guinea
Malawi
Liberia
Mali

Source: *State of the World's Children,* 1995

The world's poor

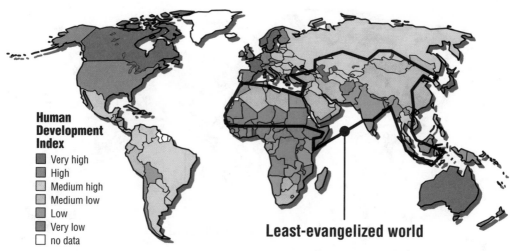

Human Development Index

- Very high
- High
- Medium high
- Medium low
- Low
- Very low
- no data

Least-evangelized world

The Human Development Index approximates knowledge (education), a long healthy life (life expectancy) and a decent standard of living (real GDP).

In God's world…

◆ In the last thirty years, the developing world has improved as much as the industrial world did during the whole of the nineteenth century.

◆ Since 1960, life expectancy in the Two-Thirds World has increased 17 years and infant mortality has dropped by more than half.

◆ Yet, still today one in five — one billion people — do not have access to the basic social services of health care, education, safe drinking water and adequate nutrition.

◆ Women are 70% of the world's poor and two-thirds of the world's illiterates.

Countries with Lowest Human Development Index

Niger	Guinea
Sierra Leone	Mozambique
Mali	Somalia
Ethiopia	Burundi
Burkina Faso	

Source: *Human Development Report 1995*

A world in conflict

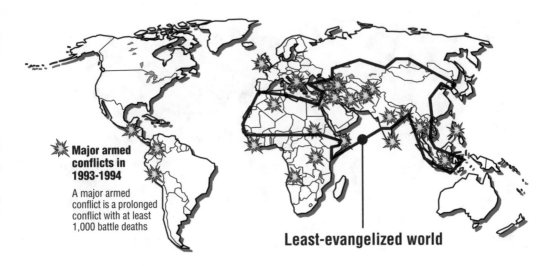

Major armed conflicts in 1993-1994

A major armed conflict is a prolonged conflict with at least 1,000 battle deaths

Least-evangelized world

In God's world...

◆ The number of ongoing wars has risen dramatically from 10 in 1960 to over 50 in 1994.

◆ Twenty-seven countries experienced major armed conflicts: Nine in Asia, six in Africa, five in Europe/Russia, four in the Middle East and three in Latin America

◆ Ninety percent of the casualties in today's armed conflicts are civilians.

Source: *State of the World Conflict Report* 1994-1995 *Human Development Report* 1995; "Complex Emergencies and the Crisis of Developmentalism"

Pollution that kills: Land mines	
Egypt	23 million
Iran	16 million
Angola	15 million
Afghanistan	10 million
Cambodia	10 million
China	10 million
Iraq	10 million
Bosnia Herzegovina	3 million
Croatia	3 million
Mozambique	2 million

Source: *New York Times,* October 5, 1995

People without borders

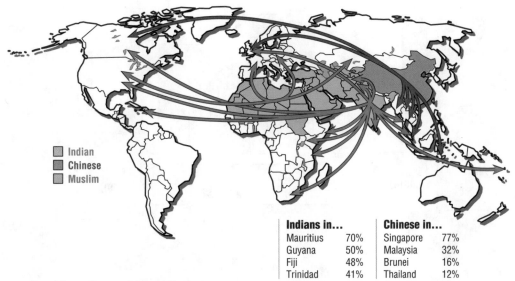

Indian
Chinese
Muslim

Indians in...		Chinese in...	
Mauritius	70%	Singapore	77%
Guyana	50%	Malaysia	32%
Fiji	48%	Brunei	16%
Trinidad	41%	Thailand	12%

In these migrations...

◆ Over 55 million Chinese are living outside of mainland China.

◆ In Indonesia, the Indonesian Chinese (4%) own over 75% of the assets and 17 of the biggest 25 business groups. In Thailand, the Thai Chinese (9%) own 90% of the commercial and manufacturing assets.

◆ The primary economic unit is the extended family.

◆ Today's Muslim missionaries are students, scholars and refugees.

Source: *The Economist.* July 18, 1992

The Chinese Diaspora

Indonesia	7.2 million
Thailand	5.8 million
Malaysia	5.2 million
Singapore	2.0 million
Taiwan	1.8 million
Hong Kong	1.8 million
United States	1.8 million
Myanmar	1.5 million
Philippines	1.0 million
Vietnam	0.8 million

The world by population

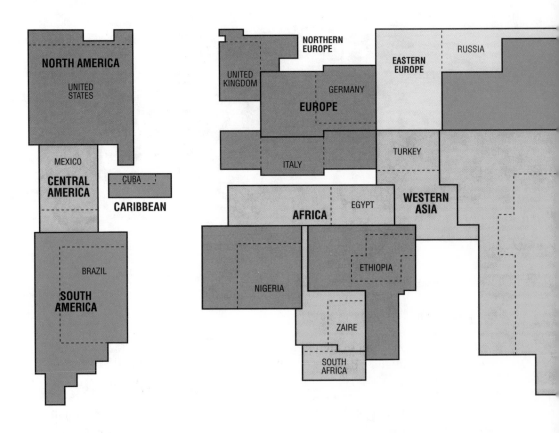

In God's world...

◆ The southern half of the world dwarfs the northern half.

◆ There are over 5.6 billion people and more on the way.

◆ The estimated doubling time for the poorest countries is 31 years.

◆ There is an explosion of the elderly. People over 80 increased from 3 million in 1900 to 53 million in 1993 and are projected at 7% of the world population by the end of the twenty-first century.

Sources: *World Population Data Sheet*, 1995 and Barrett, *AD2000 Global Monitor*, 1993

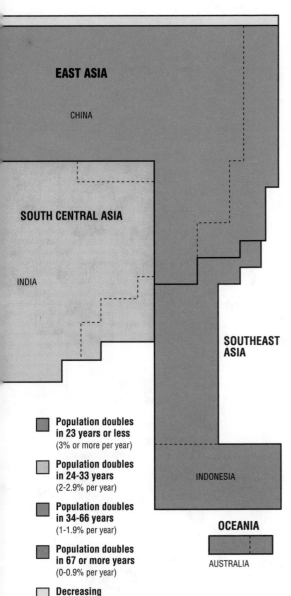

EAST ASIA

CHINA

SOUTH CENTRAL ASIA

INDIA

SOUTHEAST ASIA

INDONESIA

OCEANIA

AUSTRALIA

■ Population doubles in 23 years or less (3% or more per year)

☐ Population doubles in 24-33 years (2-2.9% per year)

■ Population doubles in 34-66 years (1-1.9% per year)

■ Population doubles in 67 or more years (0-0.9% per year)

☐ Decreasing population

Size of Population
(country of largest population indicated in each region)

Population Doubling Time

Fastest

Oman	14 years
Gaza	15 years
Iraq	19 years
Maldives	19 years
Togo	19 years
Yemen	19 years
Cote d'Ivoire	20 years
Comoros	20 years
Syria	20 years
West Bank	20 years

Slowest

Lithuania	6,931 years
Czech Republic	2,310 years
Greece	1,733 years
Slovenia	1,386 years
Sweden	990 years
Portugal	866 years
Denmark	770 years
Spain	578 years
Belgium	578 years
Austria	530 years

The world by income

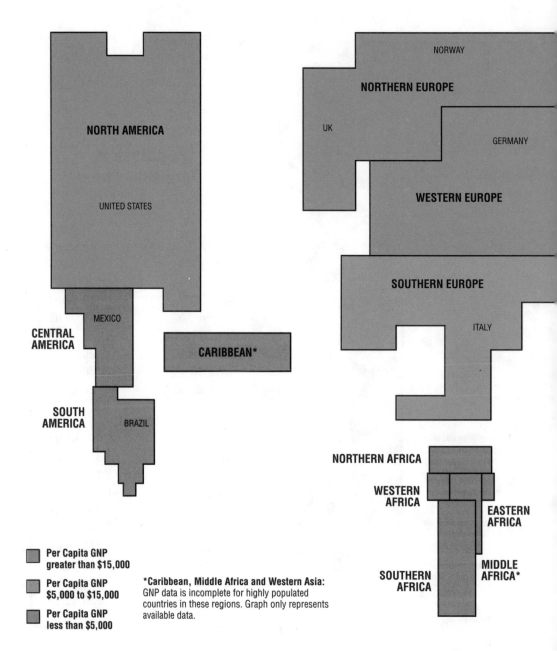

NORWAY

NORTHERN EUROPE

UK

NORTH AMERICA

GERMANY

UNITED STATES

WESTERN EUROPE

MEXICO

CENTRAL
AMERICA

SOUTHERN EUROPE

CARIBBEAN*

ITALY

SOUTH
AMERICA

BRAZIL

NORTHERN AFRICA

WESTERN
AFRICA

EASTERN
AFRICA

Per Capita GNP
greater than $15,000

MIDDLE
AFRICA*

Per Capita GNP
$5,000 to $15,000

*Caribbean, Middle Africa and Western Asia:
GNP data is incomplete for highly populated
countries in these regions. Graph only represents
available data.

SOUTHERN
AFRICA

Per Capita GNP
less than $5,000

Per Capita Gross National Product

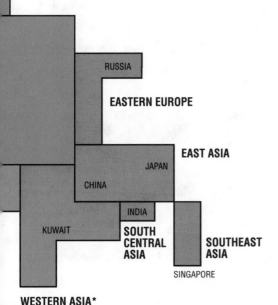

WESTERN ASIA*

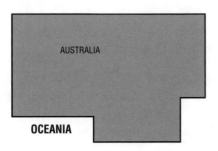

Source: World Population Data Sheet, 1995

In God's world...

- ◆ The northern part of the world dominates the southern part, with North America, Germany and Japan accounting for almost half of the world's income.

- ◆ Almost half the world's families struggle with annual incomes of less than $4,500.

- ◆ Of the 925 million absolute poor in the world, 211 million (or 23%) are Christians.

Sources: Barrett, *Our Globe*, 1990; *New State of the World Atlas*, 1995; World Population Data Sheet, 1995

Gross National Product
(per person)

Highest	Lowest
Switzerland	Mozambique
Luxembourg	Ethiopia
Japan	Tanzania
Denmark	Sierra Leone
Norway	Nepal
Sweden	Bangladesh
United States	Vietnam
Iceland	Burundi
Germany	Uganda
Kuwait	Rwanda
Austria	Chad

Global economic integration

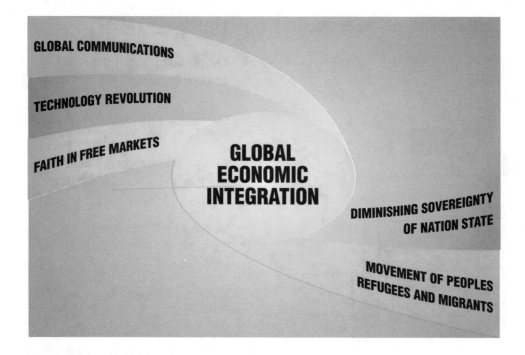

GLOBAL COMMUNICATIONS

TECHNOLOGY REVOLUTION

FAITH IN FREE MARKETS

GLOBAL ECONOMIC INTEGRATION

DIMINISHING SOVEREIGNTY OF NATION STATE

MOVEMENT OF PEOPLES REFUGEES AND MIGRANTS

In God's world...

◆ The world is open for business twenty-four hours a day.

◆ Global communication and the computer revolution mean that nation states are losing control of their currencies, commodity prices and capital markets.

◆ Global economic integration is uneven, leaving some people and nations outside.

◆ The poorest 20% of this world only shared in 1% of global trade and 0.1% of global lending.

◆ The external debt of developing countries rose to $1.8 trillion in the mid-1990s and their debt service was 22% of export earnings.

Source: *Human Development Report 1995*

Global technology and communications

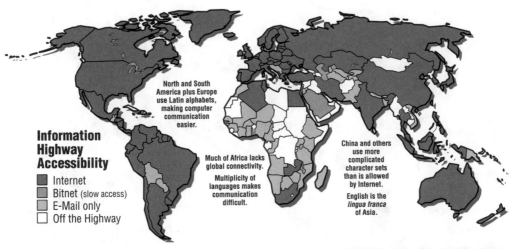

Information Highway Accessibility

North and South America plus Europe use Latin alphabets, making computer communication easier.

Much of Africa lacks global connectivity.

Multiplicity of languages makes communication difficult.

China and others use more complicated character sets than is allowed by Internet.

English is the *lingua franca* of Asia.

- Internet
- Bitnet (slow access)
- E-Mail only
- Off the Highway

In God's world...

◆ News and information is increasingly available all the time all around the world.

◆ A global youth culture — listening to the same music, seeing the same images and wearing the same shoes — is emerging, mediated by Music Television (MTV).

◆ As manipulating information becomes the engine of the global economy, the non-literate, technologically-disconnected poor may find themselves on the outside with no way in.

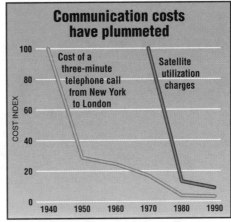

Communication costs have plummeted

COST INDEX

Cost of a three-minute telephone call from New York to London

Satellite utilization charges

Source: *World Development Report 1995*

◆ The cost of telecommunication is increasingly independent of distance.

Sources: Pollack, *New York Times,* August 7, 1995
Cairncross, *The Economist,* September 30, 1995

Economic freedom

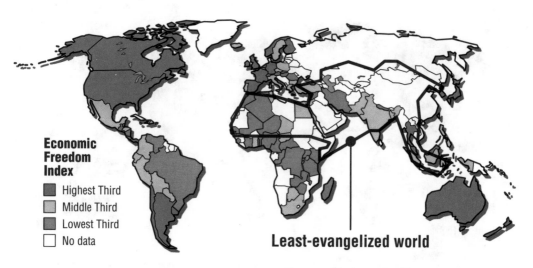

Economic Freedom Index

- ■ Highest Third
- ▨ Middle Third
- ▦ Lowest Third
- □ No data

Least-evangelized world

The **Index of Economic Freedom** is comprised of measures relating to money and inflation, governments and regulations, takings and discriminatory taxation and restrictions on international exchange.

In the last 20 years...

◆ No country with consistently high economic freedom has failed to achieve a high level of income.

◆ All 17 countries where economic freedom most improved have experienced positive growth rates.

◆ Growth rates were consistently negative in countries where economic freedom declined.

◆ There is a high correlation between economic freedom and high consumption.

Source: Gwartney, Lawson and Block, *Economic Freedom of the World 1975-1995*

Economic Freedom

Highest	Lowest
Hong Kong	Zaire
New Zealand	Iran
Singapore	Algeria
United States	Syria
Switzerland	Nicaragua
United Kingdom	Brazil
Canada	Burundi
Ireland	Romania
Australia	Uganda
Japan	Zambia

Structures of sin

Annual estimated cost of "structures of sin"

Financial Crime	$2,000 billion
Military Spending	$950 billion
Fraud	$800 billion
Gambling	$700 billion
Organized Crime	$600 billion
Tax Cheating	$180 billion
Drug Traffic	$150 billion
Shoplifting	$90 billion
Computer Crime	$44 billion
Pornography	$20 billion

In God's world...

◆ Just over 30% of the gross world product is related to the "structures of sin."

◆ The estimated cost of the "structures of sin" every year is $5.5 trillion.

◆ The great majority of the activities that constitute the "structures of sin" are done by the well-off.

◆ The cost of extending basic social services — primary education, clean water and safe sanitation, and health care and nutrition — to people currently in absolute poverty is estimated at $34 billion.

Source: Barrett and Johnson, *Our Globe,* 1990
The Reality of Aid, 1996

The growing human family

In 2025...

◆ Six of every ten people in the world will live in Asia.

◆ Only one of every eight will live in what is now called the West.

◆ Even with today's accelerated mission efforts, one in fourteen — 600 million — will not have heard the gospel.

Sources: *World Population Data Sheet 1995;* Barrett, AD2025 Global Monitor, September, 1995

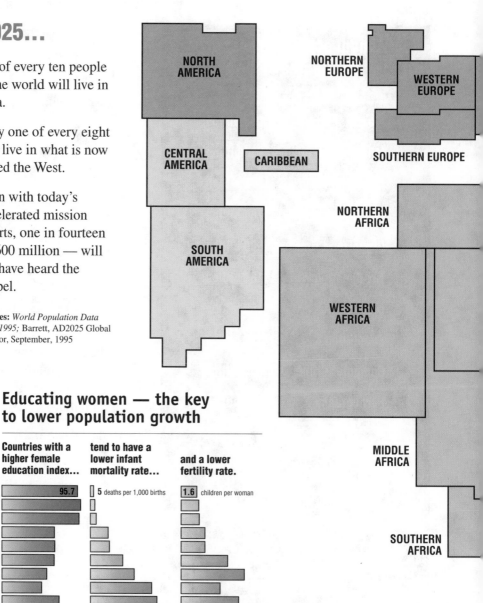

Educating women — the key to lower population growth

Countries with a higher female education index...	tend to have a lower infant mortality rate...	and a lower fertility rate.
Japan — 95.7	5 deaths per 1,000 births	1.6 children per woman
France		
USA		
Thailand		
China		
Zimbabwe		
Kenya		
India		
Namibia		
Rwanda — 50.2	120	8.3

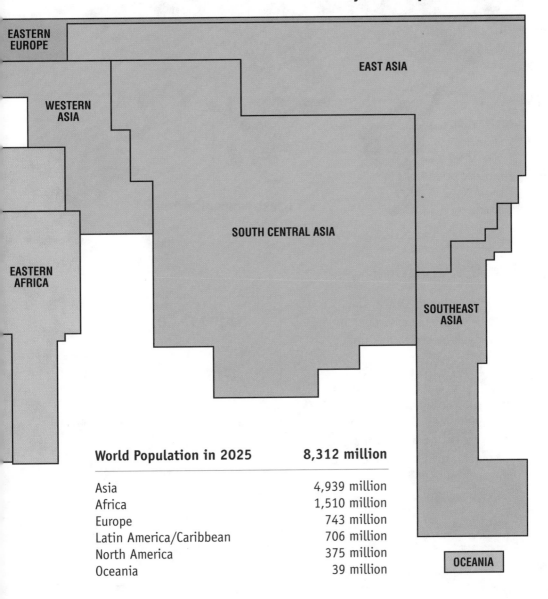

Projected Population in 2025

EASTERN EUROPE

EAST ASIA

WESTERN ASIA

SOUTH CENTRAL ASIA

EASTERN AFRICA

SOUTHEAST ASIA

World Population in 2025	8,312 million
Asia	4,939 million
Africa	1,510 million
Europe	743 million
Latin America/Caribbean	706 million
North America	375 million
Oceania	39 million

OCEANIA

Consuming the earth's resources

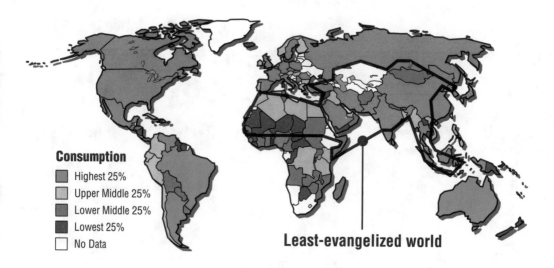

Consumption
- ■ Highest 25%
- ■ Upper Middle 25%
- ■ Lower Middle 25%
- ■ Lowest 25%
- □ No Data

Least-evangelized world

In God's creation...

◆ High population growth adds people where the environment is already stretched to the limit.

◆ Yet, if technology used for production and consumption are extensions of human metabolism when it comes to measuring pressure on the world's energy resources, the greatest pressure on the environment comes from the Northern and Western hemispheres.

Adapted from Mata, Onisto and Vallentyne, "Consumption: The Other Side of Population for Development," 1994

Highest Consumers	
United States	22%
Former USSR	16%
China	9%
Japan	5%
India	4%
Canada	3%
Germany	3%
United Kingdom	2%
France	2%
Brazil	2%

Who has not heard?

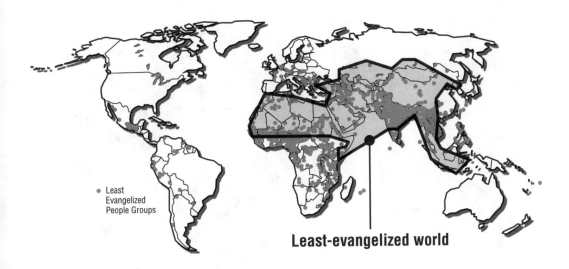

• Least Evangelized People Groups

Least-evangelized world

In the least evangelized part of God's world...

◆ Live 86% of the people groups, of which less than 2% are Christian.

◆ Live over 80% of the world's poorest people.

◆ There are thirty-four Muslim countries, seven Buddhist nations, three Marxist nations and two Hindu countries.

Source: Barrett and Johnson, *Our Globe,* 1990

Countries with the Largest Non-Christian Populations

China

India

Indonesia

Japan

Bangladesh

Pakistan

Nigeria

Turkey

Iran

Shape of the Christian world

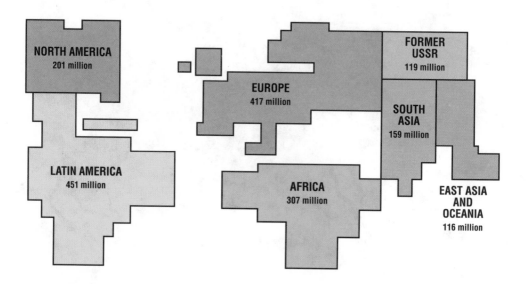

NORTH AMERICA
201 million

FORMER USSR
119 million

EUROPE
417 million

SOUTH ASIA
159 million

LATIN AMERICA
451 million

AFRICA
307 million

EAST ASIA AND OCEANIA
116 million

In God's world...

◆ Over half the Christians live in the Two-Thirds World; nearly 70% of all evangelicals live in the non-Western world.

◆ Over 50% of today's evangelicals are members of Pentecostal and charismatic churches.

◆ Two of every five professing Christians live in poor countries.

◆ Over half the deaths among Christians occur in poor countries.

Sources: Barrett, "Annual Statistical Table on Global Mission: 1995," *IBMR*.
Johnstone, *Operation World*, 1993.

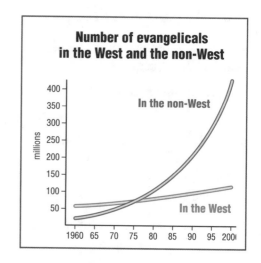

Number of evangelicals in the West and the non-West

millions

In the non-West

In the West

1960 65 70 75 80 85 90 95 2000

State of the Christian church

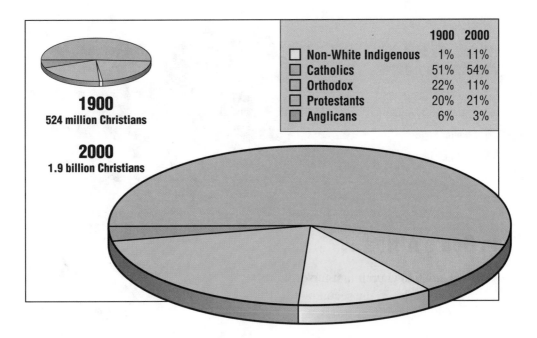

1900
524 million Christians

2000
1.9 billion Christians

	1900	2000
☐ Non-White Indigenous	1%	11%
☐ Catholics	51%	54%
☐ Orthodox	22%	11%
☐ Protestants	20%	21%
☐ Anglicans	6%	3%

During this century in the body of Christ...

◆ The percentage of Christians active in some form of mission today is at an all-time high of 36%.

◆ The non-white indigenous church increased eleven-fold to 11% of all Christians today.

◆ A little over 26% of all Christians are Pentecostals or charismatics. Pentecostals and charismatics increased 130-fold from 3.7 million in 1900 to 480 million today.

◆ The proportion of Roman Catholics among Christians increased to 54%, up from 51% in 1990.

◆ The proportion of Protestants remained unchanged. The proportion of Orthodox and Anglicans declined by half to 11% and 3%, respectively.

Source: Barrett, "Status of Global Mission 1996," *IBMR*.

The church in Africa

Christians and Muslims in Africa

- ■ Christian Minority
- □ Christian Majority
- ■ Muslim Majority
- ■ Areas of Tension

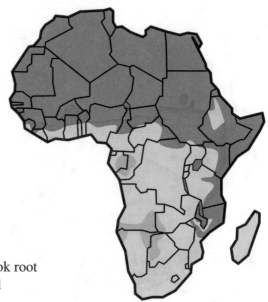

In God's Africa...

◆ The Christian church first took root in North Africa in the second through the fourth centuries.

◆ There were more Muslims than Christians in Africa until the mid-1980s.

◆ Africa is experiencing the fastest church growth of any region.

◆ One third of this region's population does not get enough to eat.

◆ The theological and ministry focus in Africa is on traditional religions and extending the rule of God to ethnic, economic and political life.

Source: Walls, "Significance of Christianity in Africa"
Human Development Report 1995

The Largest Christian Majorities
(among larger countries)

Zaire	92%
Gabon	82%
Lesotho	77%
Congo	76%
Rwanda	76%
Burundi	75%
South Africa	72%
Swaziland	70%
Kenya	70%
Angola	69%

Source: *Operation World,* 1993

The church in Asia

Christians in Asia

- ☐ 0% – 2%
- ☐ 2% – 5%
- ☐ 5% – 10%
- ■ Over 10%

KAZAKHSTAN

MONGOLIA

CHINA

INDIA

INDONESIA

In God's Asia...

◆ The Christian church went to Asia in the second century from the Church of the East in Syria, and again to Asia in the 16th century from Spain and Portugal.

◆ Asian Christians have faced the church's greatest persecutions. Religious discrimination directed toward Christians is once again on the rise.

◆ The theological focus is on uniqueness of Christ in the context of the major world religions. The ministry focus is on Christian witness.

◆ The largest Christian populations are found in the Philippines and China (61 million each), India (33 million) and Indonesia (25 million).

Sources: Moffat, *The History of Christianity in Asia,* 1992; *Operation World,* 1995

The Largest Christian Minorities
(among larger countries)

South Korea	35%
Hong Kong	14%
Indonesia	13%
Singapore	12%
Vietnam	9%
Sri Lanka	8%
Malaysia	7%
Myanmar	6%
People's Republic of China	5%

Source: *Operation World,* 1993

The church in Europe

Nominal Christians in Europe*

- ■ over 90%
- ■ 70% – 90%
- ■ 50% – 70%
- ☐ less than 50%
- ☐ No data

*Proportion of people who profess to be Christian but do not go to church weekly

In God's Europe...

◆ The most religious countries in Europe are Ireland and Poland.

◆ Europe has more nominal Christians than the rest of the world put together.

◆ Animism in the form of magic continues to thrive. The outcome of the conflict between Christianity and modernity may not be secularism, but animism.

Source: Greeley, "Religion Around the World," 1992. Brierley, *UK Christian Handbook 1992-93.*

Magic Index

Proportion who indicate high belief in faith healers, astrology, good luck charms and fortune tellers.

Slovenia	60%
Britain	42%
West Germany	38%
Northern Ireland	37%
Ireland	34%
East Germany	32%

The church in Latin America

Protestants in Latin America

- ▣ over 20%
- ▣ 10% – 20%
- ▣ 5% –10%
- ▣ less than 5%
- ☐ no data

MEXICO

COLOMBIA

BRAZIL

PERU

ARGENTINA

In God's Latin America...

◆ The Christian church came 450 years ago from Spain and Portugal.

◆ The rapid rise of Pentecostal and charismatic churches among the poor and now the middle class is one of the startling new missiological facts of this century.

◆ The largest population of Protestants is in Brazil (32 million).

◆ The income share of the richest 20% is fifteen times that of the poorest 20% in many countries.

◆ The theological and ministry focus is on the struggle to be with and for the poor.

The Largest Protestant Minorities

Chile	28%
Guatemala	24%
El Salvador	20%
Brazil	19%
Nicaragua	18%
Panama	17%
Honduras	11%
Costa Rica	11%
Bolivia	9%
Argentina	8%

Source: *Operation World,* 1993

Source: *Human Development Report* 1995
Operation World, 1995

The status of the Great Commission

Have heard, limited response

Least-evangelized world

Those who call themselves Christians

In the last years of this century...

◆ The percentage of Christians in the world has remained virtually unchanged at 34% since 1900. This has obscured an important sea change.

◆ Since 1975, evangelization has outstripped the increase in non-Christians for the first time in modern mission history.

◆ By the year 2000, one billion people will still have never heard the gospel, but the trend in the number of unevangelized will be decreasing.

Source: Barrett and Johnson, *AD2000 Monitor,* April and July 1994.

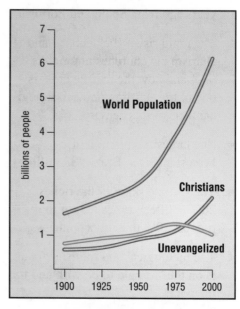

Source: *Operation World,* 1993

Who needs to hear?

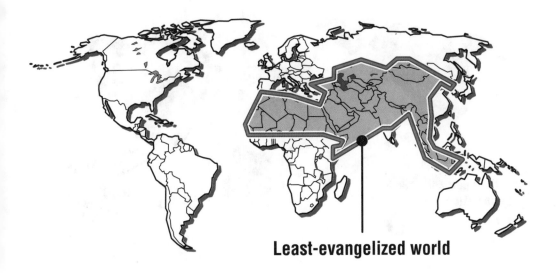

Least-evangelized world

In the least evangelized part of God's world...

◆ Over 1.1 billion people live who have little chance to hear the gospel unless someone goes to tell them.

◆ There are 500 people groups who have never heard the Good News.

◆ The church is deploying only 4,000 of its 332,000 missionaries.

Source: Barrett and Johnson,
AD2000 Global Monitor, October 1994

Largest Least Evangelized	
Bengali (Bangladesh)	120 million
Han groups (China)	97 million
Bhojpuri Bihari (India)	62 million
Punjabi (Pakistan)	57 million
Awadi (India)	53 million
Turks (Turkey)	42 million
Urdu (India)	36 million
Orisi (India)	33 million
Maitili (India)	30 million
Burmese (Myanmar)	29 million

Source: Barrett and Johnson,
AD2000 Monitor, January 1994

Children and youth

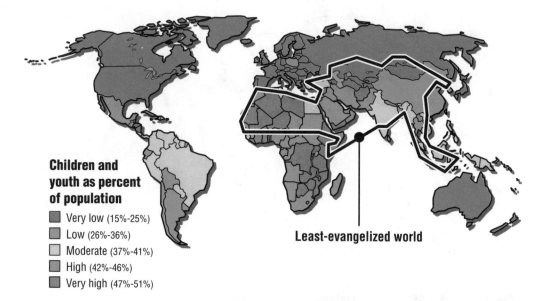

Children and youth as percent of population

- ■ Very low (15%-25%)
- ■ Low (26%-36%)
- ■ Moderate (37%-41%)
- ■ High (42%-46%)
- ■ Very high (47%-51%)

Least-evangelized world

In God's world...

◆ One-third of the world's population is under the age of 15, and 85% of these children and youth live in the Two-Thirds World.

◆ The great majority of people make life-shaping faith decisions before they reach the age of 20.

◆ MARC estimates that over 80% of the world's young people — 1.4 billion — are growing up in non-Christian settings or non-Christian homes.

Source: Myers, "State of the World's Children," *IBMR,* 1993

Highest number of children under the age of 15

China
India
Indonesia
United States
Pakistan
Brazil
Bangladesh
Russia
Mexico

Source: *World Population Data Sheet,* 1994

The growing cities in the south

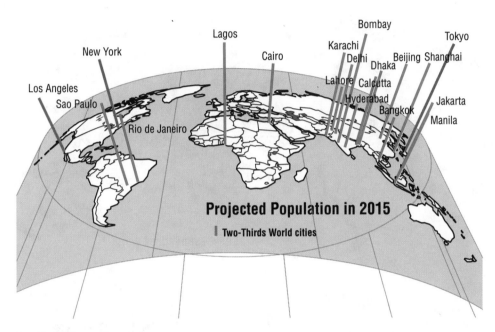

Los Angeles
Sao Paulo
New York
Rio de Janeiro
Lagos
Cairo
Karachi
Bombay
Delhi
Dhaka
Lahore
Calcutta
Hyderabad
Bangkok
Beijing Shanghai
Tokyo
Jakarta
Manila

Projected Population in 2015

Two-Thirds World cities

In God's world...

◆ By 2025, more than one-quarter of the world's population will be poor and living in the squatter settlements of the Two-Thirds World.

◆ 62% of all Christians—over one billion people—live in urban settings.

◆ There are more than 100 million street children in today's world class cities—25% of whom both work and sleep in the streets.

◆ By 2015, seventeen of the twenty-one cities with a population of over 10 million will be in the Two-Thirds World.

Sources: Barrett, "Status of Global Mission 1996," *IBMR*; Linthicum, *Empowering the Poor*

The Muslim world

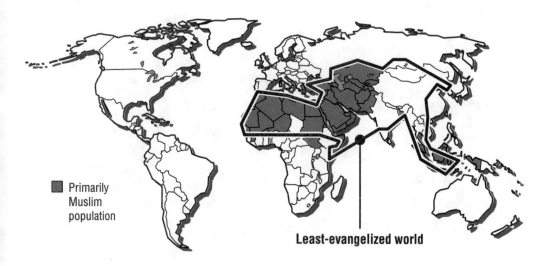

☐ Primarily Muslim population

Least-evangelized world

In God's world...

◆ Over 1.1 billion people in the world are Muslim.

◆ Islam is one of the fastest growing major religious groups, largely as a result of population growth in Asia and Africa.

◆ The majority of Muslims live in South Asia, not the Middle East.

◆ Over 80% of all Muslims have never heard the gospel, yet regard Jesus as a key prophet.

Source: Barrett, "Status of Global Mission 1996," *IBMR*

Countries with largest Muslim populations

Indonesia
Pakistan
India
Bangladesh
Turkey
Iran
Egypt
Nigeria
China
Morocco
Algeria
Uzbekistan

Source: Zwemer Institute, 1992

Allocating our resources for mission

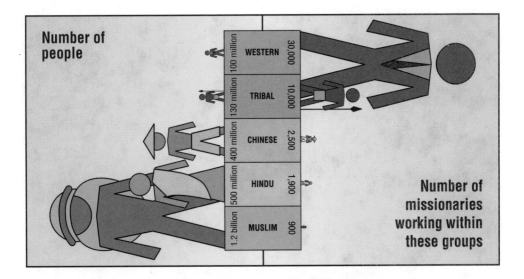

Number of people

WESTERN	100 million	30,000
TRIBAL	130 million	10,000
CHINESE	400 million	2,500
HINDU	500 million	1,900
MUSLIM	1.2 billion	900

Number of missionaries working within these groups

In the unevangelized part of God's world...

◆ Christians are allocating only 1.2% of their mission funding and their foreign missionaries to the 1.1 billion people who live in the unevangelized world.

◆ Only 1% of the Scripture distribution and only 3% of the languages for which the Bible has been translated are directed toward the least evangelized world.

Source: Barrett and Johnson, *AD2000 Global Monitor*, October 1994.

Protestant Missionaries Working in Another Culture

United States	64,378
Asia	23,681
Europe	19,564
Africa	12,829
International	6,457
Pacific	6,211
Latin America	4,482
Other	890
Total	138,492

Source: *Operation World,* 1993

The sinned-against

The sinned-against have no names or faces to most of us.

In God's world...

◆ Over 1.1 billion people live on less than one dollar (US) a day.

◆ Every day, 25,000 people — most of them children — die from the results of dirty drinking water.

◆ One out of four human beings do not have access to any form of health care.

◆ There are 47 million refugees and displaced people.

◆ Half the world's people are unable to vote.

◆ Over 3 billion people are denied the freedom to teach ideas.

Sources: Barrett and Johnson, *Our Globe,* 1990; *World Development Report 1995*

Complex humanitarian emergencies & refugees

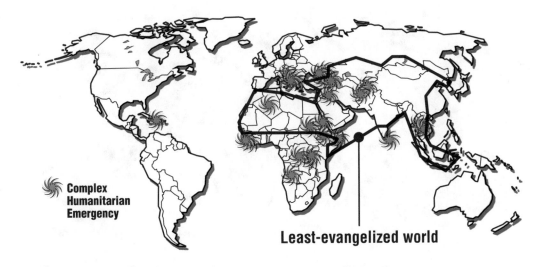

Complex Humanitarian Emergency

Least-evangelized world

A **Complex Humanitarian Emergency** combines internal conflict, large-scale displacement of people, mass famine and fragile or failing economic, political and social institutions

In God's world...

◆ Complex humanitarian emergencies are a relatively new phenomenon. The number of complex humanitarian emergencies has increased from an average of five a year in the early 1980s to 14 in 1984 and 21 in 1994.

◆ The number of refugees has exploded from 3 million in 1970 to 23 million in 1994. Another 27 million are displaced within their own countries.

◆ Over two-thirds of the world's refugees are Muslims.

Source: *State of the World's Refugees 1995*
Medecins sans Frontieres, 1992.
World Refugee Survey, 1995

Largest CHEs and Population at Risk	
Ethiopia	4.3 million
Afghanistan	4.2 million
Rwanda	4.0 million
Angola	3.7 million
Sudan	3.0 million
Bosnia	2.5 million
Liberia	2.1 million
Eritrea	1.6 million
Somalia	1.1 million
Haiti	1.3 million

Source: *Hunger 1996*

The crucial importance of women

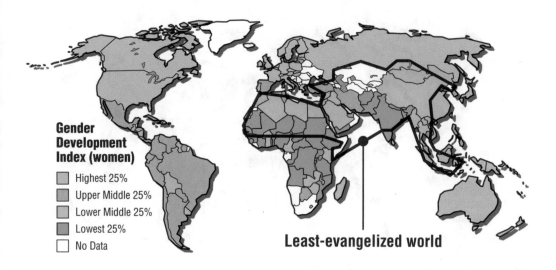

Gender Development Index (women)

- ▨ Highest 25%
- ▨ Upper Middle 25%
- ▨ Lower Middle 25%
- ▨ Lowest 25%
- ☐ No Data

Least-evangelized world

In God's world...

◆ There is a very high correlation between female literacy and positive changes in under-five mortality, fertility rates and economic development.

◆ Yet, the world average for female children reaching the fifth grade is only 68%.

◆ Yet, the proportion of women in all levels of schooling in the Two-Thirds World is only 29%. In the West it is 81%.

Source: *Human Development Report 1995*

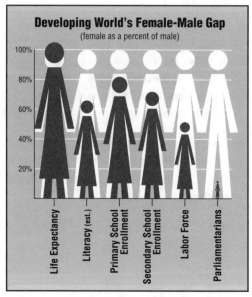

Developing World's Female-Male Gap
(female as a percent of male)

- Life Expectancy
- Literacy (est.)
- Primary School Enrollment
- Secondary School Enrollment
- Labor Force
- Parliamentarians

Source: *Human Development Report*

Promoting equitable human development

Among God's people everywhere...

◆ More than three-fourths of the world's people live in developing countries. The richest 20% of the world enjoy 85% of the global income.

◆ In Asia's high growth economies, the incomes of workers and peasants has grown faster than executives or entrepreneurs.

◆ Recent economic studies suggest that greater income equality is compatible with faster growth.

◆ In less equal societies, concerns for social and political conflict are more likely to lead to government policies which hinder growth.

Sources: *Human Development Report 1995;* Nasar, *New York Times,* January 5, 1995; Persson and Tabellini, *American Economic Review,* 1994.

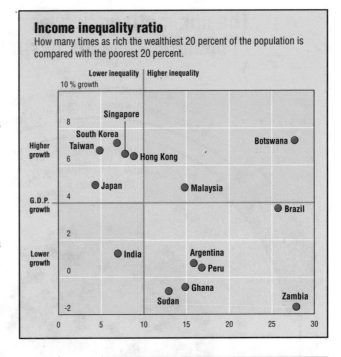

Income inequality ratio
How many times as rich the wealthiest 20 percent of the population is compared with the poorest 20 percent.

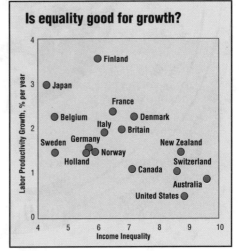

Is equality good for growth?

Caring for creation

The connections between poverty, population and the environment

High child mortality means more children
Low education of women means high fertility rates

Too many young mouths to feed
means no surplus capital

Too many children inheriting means landlessness

POVERTY

POPULATION

No potable water
Poor crop production

Lack of understanding of environmental issues
Inability to meet basic needs leads to overuse

Immigration to crowded urban slums
Increased use of pesticides and fertilizers
Increasing pressure on marginal lands

ENVIRONMENT

Conclusions

Declaring a whole gospel

People are whole beings — body, mind and soul, intertwined in a seamless way. People are not disembodied souls nor spiritless bodies. Furthermore, they live in communities that are physical, social and spiritual.

The pain of this world is the same. Material poverty is also a spiritual problem. The image of God in human form is marred when people are hungry, sick, tormented by demons, or living apart from their Creator. Therefore, our good news for these people must be all the good news.

When Jesus called the twelve disciples, as recorded in Mark, he first called them to "be with him." Being with Jesus is the beginning of life and the beginning of ministry. The disciples were to be with him so that they could preach that people should repent, and so that they could drive out demons and heal the sick. Life, word, sign and deed. Our broken world needs and deserves the whole gospel from whole people.

Good news for the poor

The poor need to hear some good news, if for no other reason than this is what Jesus commands. God's creation is to be productive, made fruitful. We are the ones who are to make it so.

This is not a call for government intervention or redistribution of wealth. It is a call for Christians to go and work alongside those who need support, encouragement, options, access and a little help so that they in turn can make their contribution to God's commandment that all of us be stewards of his creation.

Authentic Christian spirituality

But is our faith up to the task? Christian activists in the inner cities are falling away, burned out by the corrosive influence of sin, size and dynamical relationships confronting those who live in the urban world. Relief workers are collapsing under the weight of too many refugees, horribly abused, their faith eroding in the face of questions about the sovereignty of a God whose creatures commit such horrors.

We cannot transform the world on our own. We do not have the psychological and physical resources in ourselves, or even in our churches. We need to develop a spirituality capable of sustaining us for a lifelong journey in a broken and hostile world.

The rest of the world is also seeking spiritual answers that work. In a postmodern world, the danger is that any spirituality will do. Therefore, our calling demands an authentically Christian spirituality.

A new center of gravity

Everyone knows that the center of gravity of the Christian world has moved to the South into Africa and Latin America and to the East into Asia. Not everyone has adjusted to this fact.

We need to develop an intercontinental conversation that helps identify the gifts God has placed in each continent for the well-being of his global Christian community. Not every continent has the same thing to offer. Yes, the energy and resource for mission is emerging from every continent, and this is good. But when every continent is attempting the same work, this is not so good.

Without all the gifts each continent is uniquely able to offer, the global church is impoverished. Mission work and theological work needs to be done where the church is best able to do it well, on behalf of us all.

Strategic allocation of mission resources

There is enough money for Christian mission in all parts of God's world. However, the way we are allocating our resources for mission continues to be a scandal. The problem is distribution.

Something is wrong when over ninety percent of the church's mission force is working in that part of the world that calls itself Christian. This is not a call to abandon those people groups that are part of the "Christian" world and still have not heard the gospel. It is a call for a more strategic balance. One billion people live where there is little possibility they will ever have a chance to hear about Jesus Christ. They deserve an opportunity to meet a Christian and hear about Christ's claims on their lives.

Twin citizenship

Few today have much faith in the ability of global structures to do anything well that has to be done in local settings. It's simply too far from Colorado Springs, Geneva and Rome to the ministry front lines. No one can see that far.

At the same time, we cannot benefit from economies of scale or the experience of others if our world is limited to the local neighborhood, village, parish or barrio.

Our structures are not keeping up with the changes in the contexts in which they work. The Christian church needs to work away from its hierarchical past and move toward fostering twin citizenship, helping us be citizens of our local churches and their contexts, on the one hand, and citizens of the global church and the world, on the other.

The whole people of God

People are one of the things that have changed most significantly in the last half of this century. People are better educated, and have access to information about their world in ways that were never before possible. More people now have the analytical and conceptual skills to understand what this news means. Many people believe deep inside that their actions can make a difference. People like this are a powerful new force in human history, toppling Marcos, the Berlin wall, the Russian empire and the military dictatorships of Latin America. The list could go on.

This sea change has its parallels in mission work as well. Today, a greater proportion of people are active in mission than ever before. Christian people believe they can make a difference.

Most of these people are volunteers and are not professionally trained in theology or ministry. They are talented, intelligent and committed. Our churches must break with the professional/lay dichotomy and learn how to mobilize and support the whole people of God. These people are our greatest resource and our hope.

A biblical counterpoint

The creation story

By the time Noah was born, God was very unhappy.

God had made a garden, full of animals, fish, plants and trees. He had added something even better, two people made in his own image, the firstborn of creation. Their only job was to enjoy God and tend his garden, to make it productive, to be fruitful, to add a little creativity of their own. Everything in the garden was theirs, except one tree. Apparently, they had not been made to handle the knowledge of good and evil.

But they ate of the one tree they were not given, and God, as a God of justice, had to act. To protect them, they were asked to leave the Garden and were kept from returning on their own. For Adam and Eve, things natural to them became harder and more painful. But, even outside the garden, God remained with them.

Then the story gets sadder. One of their sons killed the other because he could not handle disappointment, apparently unwilling to let God be God. When Cain is asked where his brother is, he says he does not know. God replies, "Your brother's blood cries out to me from the ground."

Again God, who is just, must act. Cain is made a wanderer, a refugee; the ground will not yield its crops to him. Cain is afraid; he is sure he will be killed. Not even God's mark of protection reassures Cain.

The wanderer begins to build cities, permanent places with walls for protection. From his line, we learn of the emergence of livestock, music, metal tools — the hallmarks of emerging civilization. Cain and his descendants are going to take care of themselves. They are still hard at work today, as convinced as ever that they can create a just and peaceful world without God's help.

By the time Noah is born, things have gotten very bad indeed. "Every inclination of their hearts was only evil all the time," said God of humankind. We are told that God was grieved and that his heart was filled with pain. God decided to wipe it all out — humankind, animals, creatures that move along the ground and birds of the air: "I am grieved that I have made them."

It seemed God's creation story was coming to an early, disappointing end. Only then do we learn of Noah, a righteous man. Because God saw this man's righteousness, Noah, his family, and a remnant of all living things, will be saved. The great flood came, destroying everything — all except Noah, his extended family and those God told to join him on the ark.

With that event, this sad story becomes hopeful once again. God decides he will never destroy humankind again, in spite of the fact that human nature has not changed: "Never again will I curse the ground because of man, even though every inclination of his heart is evil from childhood. And never again will I destroy all living creatures."

Grieving the heart of God

Too often this story is read as a legal story, a story of trials and penalties. And it is that to some degree. God has rules, and we are supposed to obey them. When we don't, there are consequences, serious ones. God is a God of justice, after all.

But there is more to the story and we need to hear this part, too. God's reaction was caused by what he felt, not by a list of rules that were broken. His heart was grieved. The flood story is about emotions, about relationships, about feelings. God felt pain. We need to think hard about what it was that grieved God's heart so.

First, God must have felt disappointment that his creation seemed so insistent in turning against his purposes for it. Surely God's pain over this continues today. Today's world is clearly a creation still bent on going its own way, stubbornly seeking to exclude God and the idea of God from its concern.

Even more compelling, the blood of violence cries out to God from the ground. For God, killing is a loud, pain-ful, attention-getting act. The world we've just glimpsed in this booklet is a world full of violence, strife, people being hurt, abused, misused and killed. If God heard the cry of the spilt blood of one innocent man, how much more so must his heart be grieved today?

What can we learn from this story?

First, our God is a relational God before and after he is a just God. In his creation, he created relationships before he established a rule.

Even after his rule was broken, his grace superseded his justice. "If you eat of the tree you will die," he said. But Adam and Eve did not die. Even when Cain had killed and deserved death, God spared him and then offered to guarantee his safety. In a world that fully warranted being wiped out, God found one right-eous man and decided to sustain his creation in spite of its overwhelming failure.

Today we know the rest of the story; grace and relationships take precedence over sin and judgment. If you are in relationship with his Son, your sin is forgiven.

Our Christian mission must build on this truth. Our ministry must be one of restored relationships, of reconciliation. People need to be invited to be reconciled with God, with their inner selves, with their fellow human beings and with the world God created to be their home.

Our ministry must be relational before it is anything else. The only two commandments Christ gave us are both relational: Love your God and love your neighbor. Loving people who do not deserve or attract love must be the basis of Christian mission in today's world.

The second lesson is that there is always at least one righteous person somewhere in the midst of evil. Noah was there. Abraham convinced God to spare Sodom and Gomorrah on the basis of a handful of righteous people. We are all offered life, instead of the death our sin deserves, because there was one who was perfect before God.

Mission at the end of this century takes place in situations where sin and evil appear to have the upper hand. The inner cities of the West, the refugee camps full of those who have seen their loved ones butchered, the women and children who have experienced things too evil to mention.

Many feel as if sin has had the final say. God's story declares that this is not true. Somewhere in the midst of people whose only inclination is evil, we will find a Noah if we look hard enough. In Christian ministry at the end of this century, we need to look for the Noahs and, like God, begin our search for transformation with them.

Finally, we learn that in the end God made a conscious decision not to give up.

After the flood, nothing had changed. Even though he was starting with righteous Noah and his three sons and their families, we are told that every inclination of their hearts is "evil from childhood." Yet God decided to stick it out, to call Abraham, to choose Israel, to exile Israel, to protect a remnant and finally to provide the answer to human sin through the finished work of his Son on the cross.

In our ministry in the midst of a world that must pain and grieve the heart of God no less now than before, we must not give up. God hasn't.

We need to ask God for the faith and spirituality to embrace the pain and injustice of this world, and keep going.

Even when it appears we are making no difference, we must believe that the vision of a world with God and without tears is God's final word.

Bibliography

Barrett, David. "Annual Statistical Tables on Global Mission: 1995," *International Bulletin of Missionary Research.* January 1995.

Barrett, David. "Annual Statistical Tables on Global Mission: 1996," *International Bulletin of Missionary Research.* January 1996.

Barrett, David and Todd Johnson. *AD2000 Global Monitor.* January 1993.

Barrett, David and Todd Johnson. *AD2000 Global Monitor.* January 1994.

Barrett, David and Todd Johnson. *AD2000 Global Monitor.* April 1994.

Barrett, David and Todd Johnson. *AD2000 Global Monitor.* October 1994.

Barrett, David and Todd Johnson. *AD2025 Global Monitor.* September 1995.

Barrett, David and Todd Johnson. *Our Globe and How to Reach It.* Birmingham: New Hope, 1990.

Brierley, Peter. *UK Christian Handbook 1992-93.* London: MARC Europe, 1992.

Bosch, David. *Transforming Mission: Paradigm Shifts in Theology of Mission.* Maryknoll: Orbis, 1991.

Bread for the World. *Hunger 1996: Countries in Crisis.* Silver Spring, MD: Bread for the World, 1995.

Cairncross, Frances. "The Death of Distance: A Survey of Telecommunications," *The Economist.* September 30, 1995.

Carter Center. *State of the World Conflict Report 1994-1995.* Atlanta: The Carter Center, 1995.

Duffield, Mark. "Complex Emergencies and the Crisis of Developmentalism," *IDS Bulletin*, Vol. 25, No. 4, 1994

Economist, The. "Pity the Children." August 31, 1996.

Greeley, Andrew. "Religion Around the World: A Preliminary Report." Chicago: NORC, 1992.

Gwartney, James; Robert Lawson and Walter Block. *Economic Freedom of the World 1975-1995.* Vancouver: Fraser Institute, 1996.

ICVA and Eurostep, *The Reality of Aid: An Independent Review of International Aid.* London: Earthscan Publications, Ltd., 1996.

Johnstone, Patrick. *Operation World.* Grand Rapids: Zondervan, 1993.

Kidron, Michael and Ronald Segal. *The State of the World Atlas.* London: Penguin, 1995.

Lapple, Alfred. *The Catholic Church: A Brief History.* New York: Paulist Press, 1982.

Linthicum, Robert C. *Empowering the Poor.* Monrovia: MARC, 1991.

Mata, Francisco; Larry Onisto and J.R. Vallentyne. "Consumption: The Other Side of Population for Development," paper prepared for the International Conference on Population and Development. Cairo, 1994.

Medecins sans Frontieres. *Populations in Danger.* London: John Libby, 1992.

Myers, Bryant. *The Changing Shape of World Mission.* Monrovia: MARC, 1993.

Myers, Bryant. "State of the World's Children," *International Bulletin of Missionary Research.* July 1994.

Nasar, Sylvia. "Economics of Equality: A New View," *New York Times.* January 5, 1996.

Neill, Stephen. *A History of Christian Missions.* New York: Penguin, 1964.

Parker, John. "Turn Up the Lights: A Survey of Cities," *The Economist.* July 29, 1995.

Persson, Torsten and Guido Tabellini. "Is Inequality Harmful for Growth?" *American Economic Review.* June 1994.

Pollack, Andrew. "A Cyberspace Front in a Multicultural War," *New York Times.* August 7, 1995.

Population Reference Bureau. "1995 World Population Data Sheet." Washington D.C., 1995.

Seager, Joni. *The State of the Earth Atlas.* New York: Touchstone/Simon and Schuster, 1990.

Seager, Joni. *The New State of the Earth Atlas.* New York: Touchstone/Simon and Schuster, 1995.

UNDP, *Human Development Report 1995.* New York: Oxford University Press, 1995.

UNHCR, *The State of the World's Refugees 1995: In Search of Solutions.* New York: Oxford University Press, 1995.

UNICEF, *State of the World's Children 1995.* New York: Oxford University Press, 1995.

Walls, Andrew. "The Old Age of the Missionary Movement." *International Review of Mission.* LXVI Jan. 1987.

Walls, Andrew. "The Significance of Christianity in Africa," public lecture at St. Colm's Education Centre and College, 21 May 1989.

World Resources Institute. *World Resources 1994-1995.* New York: Oxford University Press, 1994.

World Vision UK. "Children At Risk." (Milton Keyes, UK, 1992).

Chapter 2

Growing local church initiatives

John A. Siewert

To what degree are local churches today involved in organizing, sending and directing overseas missionaries? Local churches that directly send missionaries overseas without mission board or agency involvement appear to be increasing. Some churches that may not directly send missionaries are taking a more active role in program planning and missionary deployment decisions with the agencies through which they support missionaries.

The purpose for including this chapter is not to make a case one way or another for the way local churches should support missionaries or programs, but to describe some growing local church initiatives. These initiatives are an increasing part of the world mission effort emanating from North America.

Many local church initiatives are in concert with denominational boards that encourage active local participation or challenge their churches to reclaim their unique role in global mission. This chapter gives examples of churches that

work closely with their denominational boards in long-term efforts but also have strong local initiatives involving short-term programs. Other churches continue to support their denominational programs, but have also expanded their role by setting up an overseas program and sending long-term missionaries directly. Many churches have historically supported missionaries through interdenominational or nondenominational agencies and continue to carry on and expand those working relationships.

A brief history

There is a historical side to this increased direct involvement by local churches in overseas missions. Starting in the 1940s, large numbers of military personnel returning from overseas assignment brought first-hand information back to their home churches about the needs of Christians or lack of a Christian witness in other areas of the world. Such groups as the Navigators, incorporated as a non-profit organization in 1943, encouraged one-to-one discipleship and evangelism among Christian servicemen, which deepened cross-cultural mission awareness. As the U.S. continued to maintain military installations overseas, knowledge of other lands through first-hand contacts continued to grow. U.S. business firms grew more global in nature and with the jet age air travel became less expensive, allowing more and more lay persons and church staff to travel overseas and get a closer view of overseas missions.

In North America events took place that added to the traditional denominational and interdenominational missionary conferences. Other gatherings also further developed overseas mission perspective at the local church level. Such events as the InterVarsity Student Mission Conventions that started in Toronto in 1946, and then moved to the University of Illinois in Urbana, infused new life into the student mission movement. These added to the development of new generations of missionaries, local church clergy and lay leadership with deeper insights regarding the task of world evangelization. The worldwide gatherings of the Baptist World Alliance, World Methodist Council and other worldwide denominational meetings developed international fellowships among pastors and other church leaders. Various world mission congresses

took place, broadening the global perspectives of lay leaders, local church pastors and mission leaders.

More recently, some denominations have organized mission gatherings, such as the "Congregations in Global Mission" conference of the Presbyterian Church (USA), specifically aimed at encouraging the involvement of local congregations in direct global mission experiences. New forms of collaboration among denominational and nondenominational local churches are emerging. An example of this is the Antioch Network, a fellowship of churches that are acting on the challenge to directly send church planting teams to unreached peoples.

The general press has picked up on the trend of direct local church involvement in overseas missions. In April 1997 the U.S. national news magazine *U.S. News & World Report* ran a cover story entitled "Spiritual America." One of the articles described the work of the minister of education of a church in Mississippi. Besides the usual tasks of directing the Sunday school and planning community outreach efforts, her work also involved "traveling as far as Alaska and Singapore on evangelistic missions." Short-term mission trips are a mainstay of local church involvement, but local churches are also involved in directly sending long-term missionaries with years of training and experience in cross-cultural mission.

Two viewpoints

North American Christians view the role of the local church in the overseas missionary enterprise in various ways. At least two of these viewpoints come from distinctively different perspectives.

One viewpoint sees the local church as the valid sending body of missionaries, using the New Testament pattern of the church at Antioch as recorded in Acts 13:1-3 and 14:24-28. This approach continues today with the Brethren Assemblies, Christian Churches, Churches of Christ, independent Baptist churches and others. With this method organizational structures outside the local church exist only as support functions to facilitate, not organize and direct, missionary sending activities.

Another viewpoint sees denominational mission boards as sending agencies on behalf of the local churches for organizing and directing mission efforts, including the selection and placement of missionaries. Most of these boards try to reflect the multiple concerns of their local church constituency as much as possible, but still retain firm control over the selection, placement and ongoing support processes. The local churches pray for the missionaries, contribute

financially and in other ways stay in touch with the overall effort. We find this approach in some, but not all, of the older traditional denominations that formed national missionary arms in the last century, or some of the newer denominations drawn together because of common ethnic backgrounds or other reasons.

Nondenominational mission agencies are for the most part somewhere between these two poles in the matter of church-missionary relationships. A key factor in this is the financial and other support the nondenominational agency missionaries receive from a nondenominational or denominational church. In many of these cases the missionaries are members of the church or are known because of other connections. Interdenominational agencies that are not part of a denomination but work with a variety of denominational and nondenominational churches follow much the same pattern.

Which approach?

Let us note, however, that the local church or separate agency approach is usually not an "either-or" but some mixture of a "both-and" situation. We can see this in the way that proponents of the two approaches have changed over the years. Those who proceed from the local church position have in many cases created agencies to act as clearing houses for financial support, insurance, legal matters, specialized information and other matters where consolidation of similar efforts are beneficial. Examples of this are agencies of the Christian Restoration Movement, Christian Brethren and others. In these cases, however, the major decisions still remain with the local church in terms of the sending, placement and ongoing support functions.

Some denominational boards define their role in terms of assisting local churches to be the primary sending body. We can see this in some of the mission/purpose statements that appear in chapters 4 and 7. For example, the mission statement of one denomination is "to glorify God by helping member churches fulfill Christ's mission for His church in all communities God calls them to serve." This same denomination's publications have attempted for years to keep its constituency as up to date as possible with fresh mission news. The denomination has also strongly encouraged the churches and missionaries to maintain close communication with each other. The board continues using traditional communications media but has also added a Web site, providing quicker access to information. More than this, the board posts the Internet e-mail addresses of missionaries and encourages missionaries to use such information technology when available.

Interdenominational and nondenominational agencies continue to bring opportunities and resources to local churches that in various ways encourage overseas mission involvement. Here again, the mission/purpose quotations in the description sections of the agency listings in chapters 4 and 7 give an idea of such a partnership stance. For example, one interdenominational agency that has existed for less than 20 years but has more than 200 long-term missionaries describes its purpose as an agency that "mobilizes teams to glorify God among unreached peoples by initiating church planting movements in partnership with local churches."

The local churches with growing initiatives in overseas mission outreach do not fit set patterns but show great variety in their approach. They range in size from smaller churches with less than 200 members to larger churches with thousands of members. Some send only short-term personnel from their church, and support long-term personnel by designating financial gifts through an agency. Some have overseas ministries that have taken years to develop, usually through members who have previously served as overseas missionaries, and only have programs designed for long-term commitments.

What follows are short descriptions representing a variety of approaches some local churches have taken to overseas mission work. The purpose is not to show all aspects of a church's involvement but to show the variety of ways churches directly participate in overseas mission support and outreach. The description of the Northside Community Church of Atlanta is more extensive because it represents a case where a local church actively initiated all the elements of a specific mission effort, evolving into a long-term effort that formed strategic alliances with other churches and agencies. The others are brief descriptions of some aspects of their overseas mission involvement.

❧ Northside Community Church (Evangelical Free Church of America), Atlanta, Georgia

Organized in 1985, Northside Community Church now numbers slightly over 400. From the start the church has had a strong outreach orientation, reflecting the style of its pastor, Rev. John Rowell. Members were encouraged to share their faith with those they came into contact with in their daily lives. They helped a small immigrant group that needed church services in their own language become a congrega-

tion of their own. They attended ACMC (Advancing Churches in Missions Commitment) national conferences to hear about what other churches were doing and to expand their vision. From its inception the church supported overseas mission efforts such as the work of a U.S. Campus Crusade staff member in Eastern Europe.

Staff and members became burdened to reach the Muslim world. By reading *Operation World*, Patrick Johnstone's day-by-day prayer guide for the world, they realized in 1990 that Yugoslavia held the least-evangelized Muslim population in Europe. They "adopted" the Bosnian Muslim people group in that land and began to pray regularly for them.

At Northside's annual missions conference in March 1992, the conference brochure outlined some aspects of the potential for sending a short-term team to Sarajevo, Yugoslavia, to plant a church. The next month, however, civil war broke out and the country became further splintered into factions. Many Bosnians had to leave their homes and sought refuge elsewhere. The reports of the erupting civil war on the nightly news appeared to block Northside's plan. But the pastor and others continued to probe the possibilities, including a prayer and vision trip to the region in June.

In the bordering country of Croatia, which had earlier broken away from Yugoslavia, the church came into contact with a refugee camp of more than 3,000 Bosnians. These refugees had fled to Croatia to escape the horrors of the war churning in their homeland. Some of the refugees were from Sarajevo. Also in Croatia was a seminary that had been founded by Dr. Peter Kuzmic. Dr. Kuzmic had been instrumental in organizing the evangelical churches in Croatia into a relief ministry to refugees. These churches had reached the point where they could use some help with their work in the camps. Through prayer and further talks with Dr. Kuzmic, who was then in the U.S. on a teaching assignment, Pastor Rowell and the ministers of Northside saw this as a potential doorway leading to the planting of a church in Sarajevo.

Northside quickly developed a plan to form a strategic partnership with Dr. Kuzmic and the seminary in Croatia. Seminary students would act as interpreters for the church's teams. Northside decided to form short-term (two-week) teams; a longer-term "base team" of three people would stay in Croatia to provide coordination and continuity during the rotations. The two-week period enabled those church members who could not take more time off to be part of this ministry.

Many details were worked out in a relatively short time so that the base team, and then the first 2-week team, were in Croatia by October, about the time freezing weather began and the needs in the refugee camps became even greater. Ideally short-term mission trips are planned for the summer when college students and others usually have more free time. Older church members tend to be the providers of financial help and prayer support. A number of the elders and others who had more flexible schedules decided to volunteer as members of the initial teams. They reasoned that since a major part of their future role would be to uphold in prayer those rotating to Croatia, it would be good for them to have some first-hand knowledge and experience. Thus many of Northside's "older set" formed the initial teams. Eventually one-sixth of Northside Community Church's adults would become directly involved in Croatia.

The short-term teams began their rotations and a trickle of Bosnian refugees became believers. As expected, the teams encountered resistance in various manifestations to their work, and there were some internal conflicts among team members as they had to learn to work together quickly in a radically different setting. But a number of team members had had some cross-cultural experience and most adapted quickly to their new circumstances.

Eventually the peace agreement initialed in Dayton, Ohio, on November 21, 1995, began to take hold in the area. Most of the refugees returned to their homes or were resettled. In conjunction with the leaders of the evangelical churches in the area and some of the new believers, the work of establishing churches began. Some of the short-termers with seminary training or other relevant educational or on-the-job training became candidates for long-term mission work. The work continued through 1996 and 1997 as new forms of outreach, such as conversational English classes, were organized.

The ministry team and Croatia's evangelical church leadership identified 32 cities as prime places to plant churches. As of September 1997, four churches were being planted. There are now six long-term missionaries on the ministry team. U.S. churches from the Antioch Network are taking on the task of planting churches in five of the cities over the next three years. Northside's denominational mission agency, the Evangelical Free Church Mission, has increased its support of this ministry and plans to assist or send teams to fifteen of the cities.

≈ First Baptist Church (Southern Baptist Convention), Montgomery, Alabama

Jay Wolf, pastor at First Baptist Church in Montgomery, Alabama, describes the congregation as "genetically missions-minded." Many of its members feel that God expects each church to be a "world missions strategy center."

In the last five years 17 people from the church have made commitments to vocational Christian service, including a couple who sensed a call to take the gospel to an unreached people group in Africa. Besides the first-hand information the church receives from its members involved in overseas ministries, the church's denominational board provides an array of information in various forms about the global scene. The monthly magazine, *The Commission*, provides fresh feature-length articles with full-color pictures of mission activities from around the world. There is "A Window on the World" section with pithy information and news from a variety of countries and other mission agencies. The "From Our Readers" pages give examples of comments and questions generated by previous articles. Readers are directed to an Internet World Wide Web site for further missions information. Those with Internet e-mail capability can choose from seven different mailing lists to which they can subscribe to get specific up-to-date items.

In 1996 the 3,400-member congregation gave $145,000 to their denomination's annual Christmas offering for international missions. The church continues its Caring Center ministry to the city's downtown area, touching 7,400 lives in 1996 by providing groceries, clothing and other assistance to those in need.

Members can also participate directly in overseas missions through short-term mission activities organized through the church. For example, in May 1997 the church joined with other churches in sending a medical and dental team to northern Kenya to work among the Turkana people. A medical missionary and nurse from the area organized make-shift clinics in conjunction with local believers, who went through the villages telling about the coming of the medical team and assisted in other ways. The clinics were set up outdoors near small scattered desert villages for people who could seldom make into town. It was estimated that up to 90% of the Turkana in such isolated areas have little opportunity to hear the gospel. Commenting on the work of the team missionary Troy Haas, whose long-term assignment includes this area, felt the medical/dental outreach effort

advanced the endeavor to reach the area with the gospel.

New Life Church (nondenominational), Colorado Springs, Colorado

When Pastor Ted Haggard started New Life Church in 1985, it was his desire that it would not only be involved in missions but that it would also be a strategic nerve center for worldwide evangelistic prayer. Today the Christian Information Network (CIN) is a ministry of this charismatic church where 6,000 members worship. The primary purpose of CIN is to serve the United Prayer Track of the AD2000 and Beyond Movement. The United Prayer Track strives "to mobilize existing prayer networks worldwide to direct a significant part of their prayer ministry toward the evangelization of their neighborhoods, cities, nations and the world."

CIN is the primary means for providing churches, mission agencies, other ministries and individuals with information about the month-long prayer emphasis called "Praying through the Window." The "window" is the "10/40 Window," that part of our world between ten degrees and forty degrees north latitude that extends from West Africa to East Asia. Mission researchers have estimated that 95% of the world's least-evangelized people live in this region.

Initially a husband and wife volunteer team from the church formed the staff of CIN, with an estimate that it would take 5 to 10 hours of work per week. The ministry grew quickly and by mid-1997 CIN had a full-time director, two support persons and twenty regular volunteers.

In 1992 a committee of U.S. Christian leaders organized a month-long prayer emphasis focusing on the 10/40 Window. The first emphasis was in October 1993 and focused on the 62 nations of the 10/40 Window. The second initiative took place in October 1995 and focused on 100 "Gateway cities" in the 10/40 Window, seen as the strategic cultural, religious or political centers influencing the spiritual conditions of this area. An estimated 36 million Christians in 102 nations participated in that time of concentrated prayer. Part of the emphasis was to have teams participate in "prayer journeys" and travel to the key cities to pray on site. Reports were that 407 prayer teams participated in 607 prayer journeys. The experiences of many of these teams and other information about the 10/40 Window countries are in the book *Window Watchman II: Millions Prayed . . . God Responded . . . Witness The Impact*, compiled and edited by Beverly Pegus, director of CIN, and published by the New Life Church.

❧ Southeast Christian Church (Christian Churches and Churches of Christ fellowship), Louisville, Kentucky

As a church of the Restoration Movement tradition, Southeast Christian Church has always taken missions initiatives as a local church responsibility. Missionaries may be supported through a facilitating agency, but the local church is still the defining connection.

The church encourages its members to get involved in two-week short-term mission teams. Each year it prints an attractive booklet describing upcoming mission service opportunities and giving the dates of mission trips. Members can choose from a variety of activities available both overseas and in the United States. Over the years church staff and volunteer members have developed outreach endeavors that include basketball camps in Poland, medical work in the Ivory Coast, puppetry and drama in Eastern Europe, assisting in vacation Bible schools, preaching and teaching services and other activities designed to provide witnessing opportunities. Many of these are done in association with missionaries on location or with national churches, schools or organizations. Because most of the participants are from the church, extensive orientation, training and team meetings can take place over a period of time before the short-term overseas trip begins.

Southeast Christian Church participates in an annual national missionary convention of Restoration Movement churches, where all are encouraged to share mission involvement experiences. The 1996 convention challenged church representatives to sign an "Adopt-a-People in Prayer Contract," pledging to pray regularly for one year for one of the 1,739 least-reached people groups for which information was available. Church members also participated in the three-day 1997 National Short-Term Mission Conference, where they and members from other churches shared their short-term mission experiences in training, equipping and mobilizing teams for short-term missions.

The church's Missions Department sees their short-term mission programs as an important aspect of the spiritual growth of its members. Tina Bruner, who heads the department, says: "People initially decide to go on a short-term trip for many reasons. What we pray will happen is that God will meet and exceed the expectations each person places on the trip. It is amazing how much closer we listen for God's voice when we are no longer in the controlled environment of our work and home." Pastor Bob Russell shared with his congregation the

results of his own short-term experience: "My trip to Kenya really broadened my view of world evangelism. It helped me to see the world through different eyes, through God's eyes. I encourage you to get out of your comfort zone and catch the vision of what God is doing through people just like you to reach the lost!"

❧ Cedar Crest Bible Fellowship Church (Bible Fellowship Church), Allentown, Pennsylvania

This church experienced an expanded mission vision that started with prayer for and a vision of reaching one people group where the light of the gospel was dim. It began in 1987, when the youth pastor and senior pastor read an article in an ACMC (Advancing Churches in Missions Commitment) newsletter about churches that focused on a specific people group. The pastors explored this possibility with Africa Inland Mission International, an interdenominational agency. Cedar Crest's youth pastor, Cliff Boone, had earlier participated in a short-term program with the mission.

Cedar Crest decided to focus on the Sandawe people of Tanzania, East Africa. When the bishop of the Africa Inland Church of Tanzania visited the United States, he met with the church leaders and they heard first-hand about the needs in Tanzania. Prayer concern mounted for the Sandawe as the congregation regularly lifted them up to the Lord during the church's Wednesday prayer meetings and at other times. Eventually the church sent the youth pastor and his wife as missionaries to the Sandawe. The congregation began to hear from one of their own how the Sandawe slowly began to turn to Christ. In the ensuing years eight churches in the tri-state area of New York, Pennsylvania and New Jersey linked up in a joint effort with churches in Tanzania and the Africa Inland Mission to work toward the evangelization of the Sandawe.

As has been the case with other churches, Cedar Crest Church grew rapidly in other aspects as the specific mission focus developed. The congregation has grown from about 275 members to over 500 members. The church's financial program has experienced an increase, including over $1,400,000 for building projects. Mission giving increased from $40,000 in 1987 to over $125,000 by 1992. Senior pastor Ron Mahurin has summed up the experience at Cedar Crest this way: "Our mission and building giving doubled, then tripled. Our congregation has grown, and our people have a heart for God's heart for all peoples!"

ᨀ First Baptist Church (American Baptist Churches, USA), Lancaster, California

First Baptist Church in Lancaster, California, formed Mecca Ministries with a focus on equipping and placing small dedicated teams of pioneer evangelists and church planters in cities of the Arab World. The founding core group from the church included missionaries with experience in the Arab Muslim World and other cross-cultural activities. The vision for this work began when these individuals believed that God was calling them to develop teams to work among Arab Muslims in the Middle East.

The ministry developed a strategic plan, part of which called for making the local church one of the central pillars in accomplishing the task. The basis for this view was that the faith community of the local church kindles and feeds the fire for Christian mission in the world. All Mecca Ministries workers must be sent out to do the work by their own local body of believers, and they receive their spiritual support and commitment from that body. When Mecca Ministries began, First Baptist Church committed to facilitate the work as a ministry of the church. Mission workers from other local churches have also become part of this ministry. These local churches also see themselves as the fundamental unit of mission, seeking to share the Good News of Jesus in all of it fullness.

Mecca Ministries' leadership fully realized that larger mission agencies were already working in some parts of the Arab World, and they did not desire to compete with them. The members of Mecca Ministries explained their ministry enterprise in a newsletter. They hope to "assist these agencies by filling a very specialized niche . . . equipping and placing smaller highly focused teams of pioneer evangelist/church planters . . . Once the door is cracked open and the way prepared, the larger and better resourced agencies will be able to capitalize on the new opportunities."

The relatively small percentage of Christian workers in Arab lands is one of the reasons non-traditional mission groups like this have sensed the need to take the gospel to the Arab World. The approach of Mecca Ministries is to place small mobile evangelism/church planting teams of 6-8 adults in target cities "to penetrate pioneer situations and establish a spiritual beachhead."

The first team of two families and two single people were sent to an Arab World city in October 1996. Cliff Huffmire, former pastor of the church's Hispanic congregation, is on the church staff as Outreach Mobilizer for Mecca Ministries. Larry McPherson, a member of the church, is the ministry's Home Director.

❧ Lake Grove Presbyterian Church (Presbyterian Church, USA), Lake Oswego, Oregon

Lake Grove Presbyterian Church started thinking about the Wolof people of Senegal, Africa, in 1994 when they were invited to pray for this people among whom few churches existed. They also heard how a Christian relief and development agency was digging wells for this area, where water was in short supply much of the time.

After much prayer and study, the congregation decided they wanted to know the Wolof in a more personal way. They sent a team to see the people and the land, pray on-site and bring a firsthand report back to the congregation. The team's enthusiasm for the experience sparked a desire in the church community to help the Wolof meet one of their most basic needs: water. On a Pentecost Sunday Pastor Bob Sanders asked his congregation to consider raising the funds to provide a well. The response was amazing—the congregation raised enough money to provide wells for 11 villages.

Lake Grove Church continues to give to the needs of the people through the initial development agency contact, and to a Scripture translation agency working on a Bible for the Wolof. Their partnership with the Wolof, which included several more team visits to Senegal, has grown so close that the Wolof have named their group of villages "Lake Grove Land." The church has seen how their help, combined with that of donors from around the world, has made better health possible among the Wolof even beyond clean water, as children are given immunizations and mothers receive training in health and nutrition. The Wolof have also been true partners in this endeavor. They have not only provided manual labor for the wells, but they also raised $1,000 as their contribution toward the cost of drilling each well, a considerable amount for people with a very limited income.

More information on the local church in mission

In the past decade there has been an increase in quality materials for Christians concerned about world evangelization. Books, videos and now Internet Web sites make information available that in the past was only readily accessible to mission agency leaders. This information, attractively presented and dealing with the core issues of understanding and supporting world missions, has enabled many professional and lay local church leaders to have first-hand involvement in sending and encouraging missionaries, and in many cases gain a first-hand experience of cross-cultural missions.

The following is a list of some materials along these lines. (Most denominations produce these kinds of materials for their specific constituency. Materials listed here are more generic in nature.) The intent is not to present an exhaustive list, but to give an indication of the variety of resources that deal with various aspects of the local church and mission. Some were written specifically with an expanding global outreach of the local church in mind. Others were written for a more general Christian audience, but have also influenced churches to become more directly involved in mission outreach to other countries.

BOOKS

Foundational aspects of the local church in mission:

Borthwick, Paul. *A Mind for Missions*, with further reading list, Colorado Springs, CO: NavPress, 1987. Written by the minister of missions of a local church. Demonstrates the way in which individuals and groups can be sensitized to the needs beyond their borders. 167 pages.

Coleman, Robert E. *The Master Plan of Discipleship*, Old Tappan, NJ: Fleming H. Revell Co., 1987. This companion volume to Coleman's widely-used *The Master Plan of Evangelism* shows how a church can be more effective today by using the pattern of the early church in carrying out Christ's command to "make disciples of all nations." 156 pages.

Douglas, J.D., ed. *Proclaim Christ Until He Comes: Calling the Whole Church to Take the Whole Gospel to the Whole World*, Minneapolis, MN: World Wide Publications, 1989. The official record of the plenary talks, "track" reports, scripts of video presentations and other items from the 1989 International Congress on World Evangelization, Lausanne II, in Manila. 463 pages.

Guder, Darrell L. *Be My Witnesses: The Church's Mission, Message, and Messengers*, Grand Rapids, MI: Wm. B. Eerdmans Publishing Co., 1985. A theology of mission written primarily for those deeply involved in ministry, but not ordained. Designed to stand the test of scholarly review but with very few citations other than Scripture, a minimum of non-English terminology and without footnotes. 237 pages.

Lewis, Jonathan, ed. *World Mission: An Analysis of the World Christian Movement*, second edition, three volumes, with assignments, questions, subject index, and author index, Pasadena, CA: Wm. Carey Library, 1994. A manual that can be used with study groups in a formal or informal educational setting. Compatible with the Perspectives on the World Christian Movement extension course mentioned above. 468 pages.

Piper, John. *Let the Nations Be Glad: The Supremacy of God in Missions*, with Scripture text, person and subject indexes, Grand Rapids, MI: Baker Book House, 1993. Written by a senior pastor to help those reflecting on the relationship between the local church and world mission from the perspective of making God supreme in missions through worship, prayer and suffering. 240 pages.

Van Engen, Charles. *God's Missionary People: Rethinking the Purpose of the Local Church*, with extensive further study resources, wide-ranging bibliography, subject index and Scripture index, Grand Rapids, MI: Baker Book House, 1991. A scholarly study whose thesis is that "as local congregations are built up to reach out in mission to the world, they will become in fact what they already are by faith: God's missionary people." A basic study of the role of the local congregation in the missionary purpose of God.

Winter, Ralph D., Steven C. Hawthorne, eds. *Perspectives on the World Christian Movement: A Reader*, revised edition, with accompanying study guide, Pasadena, CA: Wm. Carey Library, 1992. A selection of ninety-five articles written by mission leaders of this century. Produced for students of the 15-week extension course of the same name and others. Chosen and organized to provide help in understanding the biblical mandate, history, culture and strategy of missions. Includes study questions, glossary, Scripture index and general index. 923 pages.

Organizing the local church for mission:

ACMC (Advancing Churches in Missions Commitment), *Church Missions Policy Handbook*, third edition, Peachtree City, GA: ACMC, 1995. A guide to assist working groups or committees produce a comprehensive written missions policy for their church to help bring focus and continuity to their mission outreach. 77 pages.

Beals, Paul A. *A People for His Name: A Church-Based Missions Strategy*, revised edition, Pasadena, CA: Wm. Carey Library, 1995. An overview of the missions role of the local church, with an emphasis on the practical outworking of relationships with mission agencies, missionary personnel and Christian schools. Includes bibliography, subject index and Scripture index. 259 pages.

Caleb Project. *Life-Changing Encounters*, Littleton, CO: Caleb Project Resources, 1995. A handbook explaining how to form a Joshua Project 2000 or other short-term team for research among unreached peoples. 103 pages.

Caleb Project. *Prayer Journeys: A Leader's How-To Manual*, Littleton, CO: Caleb Project Resources, 1995. A manual designed to help church and other leaders effectively facilitate short-term mission trips, with the primary objective of interceding on-site among unreached people groups. 70 pages.

Camp, Bruce. *Global Access Planner: Steps for Discovering a Strategic Global Evangelism Plan for the Local Church*, with questions and leader's guide, Peachtree City, GA: ACMC, 1996. Describes three paradigms of mission activity in the local church and provides a format for setting and then measuring objectives. 48 pages.

Mays, David. *Building Global Vision: Six Steps to Discovering God's Vision for Your Church*, Peachtree City, GA: ACMC, 1996. A study guide designed for pastoral staff and/or key lay leaders developing their church's vision statement and role in cross-cultural ministry.

Pirolo, Neal. *Serving as Senders*, including group leader's guide and listing of further resources, San Diego, CA: Emmaus Road International, 1991. A study guide designed to help missionaries, churches and church members understand the crucial role of "senders," those at home who commit themselves to provide their missionaries with prayer, logistical, moral and other kinds of support. 207 pages.

Sjogren, Bob, Bill & Amy Stearns. *Run With the Vision: A Remarkable Global Plan for the 21st Century Church*, with listing of further resources, Minneapolis, MN: Bethany House Publishers, 1995. Tells of spiritual breakthrough experiences of individuals and churches in various places around the world and how churches can become active, mobilizing and missionary-sending congregations.

VIDEOTAPES

College Press Publishing Co. *Setting the PACE: Activating Your Local Church and Case Studies in How it is Done*, Joplin MO: College Press, 1996.

College Press Publishing Co. *Perspectives on World Missions: Getting in Step with the God of the Nations*, six lessons on three tapes with participant's reader, Joplin MO: College Press, 1996.

Foreign (now International) Mission Board of the Southern Baptist Convention. *World A: A World Apart*, Richmond, VA: FMB/SBC, 1991.

Middle East Media. *The Real Story: A Christian Guide to the Arab World*, six lessons on one tape with leader's study guide, Lynwood, WA: Middle East Media, 1996.

William Carey Library. *Vision for the Nations*, thirteen lessons on four tapes with leader's guide and participant's guide, Pasadena, CA: Wm. Carey Library, 1996.

World Vision and MARC Publications. *Beyond Duty: A Passion for Christ, A Heart for Mission*, by Tim Dearborn, with leader's guide and study book, Federal Way, WA: World Vision, and Monrovia, CA: MARC Publications, 1997.

Chapter 3

Putting the survey in perspective

John A. Siewert

In the 1996 survey for this *Handbook*, North American mission agencies reported increases in the number of men and women deployed to other countries, as compared to 1992. Gains in most of the categories outweighed slight decreases in others.

Funds raised for overseas ministries also increased, to $2.3 billion for U.S. agencies, an increase of 1.5% in real dollars (adjusted for inflation). Increases in funding for Canadian agencies did not quite keep pace with inflation, so there was a slight real dollar decrease of 0.4%.

The tables in this chapter provide the details of the statistical picture.

A substantial growth in numbers of short-term personnel is reported by North American agencies. Although the survey statistics between 1992 and 1996 are not directly comparable, because the survey questions were changed slightly, it is obvious that short-term service—terms of less than a year—is growing significantly.

Table 3.1 on the next page compares in summary form the totals for personnel and finance reported by U.S. mission agencies in 1992 and 1996. The totals shown were derived from the country-by-country figures reported by U.S. agencies. (See question #12 in the survey questionnaire reproduced in the appendix for further specifics on the origin of the statistics.)

As already noted, for this *Handbook* we have updated and changed the survey questionnaire relating to short-term overseas personnel to better reflect current agency practices. Therefore, direct comparisons for the 2 weeks up to 1 year short-term category between 1992 and 1996 are not applicable.

Personnel from the U.S.	1992	1996	Change
FULLY SUPPORTED U.S. PERSONNEL SERVING OVERSEAS			
Long-Term (Overseas more than 4 years)	32,634	33,074	+1.3%
Short-Term (Overseas from 1 up to 4 years)	5,115	6,562	+28.2%
Nonresidential[1] fully supported	626	507	-19.0%
Total fully supported U.S. personnel serving overseas	*38,375*	*40,143*	*+4.6%*
OTHER U.S. PERSONNEL SERVING OVERSEAS			
Short-term of 2 weeks up to 1 year (1992)	38,968	NA[2]	—
Short-term of 2 weeks up to 1 year (1996)	NA[2]	63,995	—
Bivocational associates[3] sponsored or supervised	1,040	1,336	+28.4%
Nonresidential[1] partially supported	80	215	+168.7%
Non-North American personnel directly supported[4]	**1992**	**1996**	**Change**
Those serving in their home country	NA[2]	28,535	—
Those serving in a country other than their home country	1,898	1,791	-5.6%
U.S. ministry and home office staff	**1992**	**1996**	**Change**
Full-time paid staff	14,694	19,399	+32.0%
Part-time staff/associates	1,742	2,850	+63.6%
Volunteer (ongoing) helpers	37,452	59,332	+58.4%
Financial support raised in the U.S.	**1992**	**1996**	**Change**
Income for overseas ministries	$2,282,787,070[5]	$2,317,196,386	+1.5%

Table 3.1 Comparing U.S. overseas mission statistics, 1992 and 1996.

NOTES FOR TABLE 3.1

1   *Nonresidential* refers to persons
     not living in the country(ies) of
     their ministry, but in the U.S. or
     elsewhere, who travel overseas on
     a regular basis at least 12 weeks
     per year on mission ministry and
     support activities.

2   *NA* indicates that the content or
     other aspect of a particular survey
     question was modified so that a
     direct comparison of survey results
     between years is not applicable.

3   *Bivocational associates,* also
     known as "tentmakers," are persons
     who support themselves partially or
     fully through non-church/mission
     vocations and live overseas for the
     purpose of Christian witness, evan-
     gelism and/or encouraging believ-
     ers.

4   *Non-North American personnel
     directly supported* includes those
     whose financial support from U.S.
     agencies is specifically directed to
     them individually. There are also
     other non-North Americans who
     are beneficiaries of U.S. financial
     support through general support

grants, for which personnel totals
are not available from the agencies.

5   The amount *$2,282,787,070* is the
     1992 income adjusted upward to
     the value of 1996 dollars, based on
     the consumer price index. This
     adjustment for inflation is made to
     provide a more meaningful com-
     parison between 1992 and 1996.

Table 3.2 on the following pages
shows the one hundred largest
agencies ranked by personnel serving overseas for over four years,
including fully-supported nonresidential mission personnel. See the
definition of the nonresidential category in the "Fully supported USA
personnel overseas" section of
chapter 4.

These one hundred agencies
(14% of the grand total) provided
91% of the longer-term personnel
(overseas terms of more than 4
years and nonresidentials) in 1996.
This percentage is the same as it
was in 1992.

Table 3.2 U.S. agencies ranked by number of overseas personnel serving over four years (includes fully supported nonresidential mission personnel).

Rank	Name of Agency	+ 4 Yrs. & NRMs	1 Yr to 4 Yrs	2 Wks to 1 Yr
1	Southern Baptist Convention Intl. Mission Board	3,482	689	15,457
2	Wycliffe Bible Translators USA	2,453	165	99
3	Assemblies of God, Gen. Council	1,569	192	2,746
4	New Tribes Mission	1,434	80	293
5	Christian Churches/Churches of Christ	1,118	44	
6	Churches of Christ	1,014		
7	Baptist Bible Fellowship Intl.	755		
8	Youth With A Mission (YWAM)	736	1,000	5,000
9	TEAM (The Evangelical Alliance Mission)	726	35	70
10	Campus Crusade for Christ, Intl.	665	367	915
11	ABWE (Assoc. of Baptists for World Evangelism)	632	28	130
12	Christian and Missionary Alliance	617	116	92
13	Seventh-day Adventists General Conference	617	37	557
14	Baptist Mid-Missions	614		90
15	Baptist International Missions	530	2	48
16	CBInternational	520	154	225
17	SIM USA	496	22	142
18	Church of the Nazarene, World Mission Division	455		6,221
19	Mission to the World	438	130	2,008
20	Brethren Assemblies	433		
21	Africa Inland Mission International	397	84	66
22	Presbyterian Church (USA), Worldwide Ministries	354	421	150
23	Navigators, U.S. International Ministries Group	346	35	101
24	UFM International	298	19	25
25	Mercy Ships	294		
26	United Methodist Church, Bd. of Global Ministries	282	62	
27	Evangelical Free Church Mission	274	72	500
28	United Pentecostal Church Intl.	267		
29	Gospel Missionary Union	262	73	51
30	Greater Europe Mission	247	14	140
31	OMF International	246		60
32	Mission Aviation Fellowship	237	23	
33	Pioneers	228		70
34	Lutheran Church—Missouri Synod—Bd Msn Svcs	222	127	50

Rank	Name of Agency	+ 4 Yrs. & NRMs	1 Yr to 4 Yrs	2 Wks to 1 Yr
35	Frontiers	221	5	37
36	Evangelical Luth. Ch. in Am., Div. Global Msn.	207	35	151
37	World Gospel Mission	205		527
38	Christian Reformed World Missions	204	49	70
39	International Missions, Inc.	202		2
40	Mennonite Central Committee Intl.	195	186	
41	SEND International	192	10	202
42	HCJB World Radio Missionary Fellowship	176		48
43	World Team	174	1	
44	OMS International, Inc.	172	110	366
45	CAM International	164	9	18
46	Trans World Radio	156	16	
47	Baptist World Mission	150		10
48	Intl. Pentecostal Holiness Church World Missions	141	9	250
49	Operation Mobilization, Inc.	137	144	400
50	Arab World Ministries	137		27
51	Biblical Ministries Worldwide	137		25
52	World Baptist Fellowship Mission Agency	134		
53	OC International, Inc.	124	9	138
54	Gospel Fellowship Association	124		6
55	World Partners - The Missionary Church	122	8	79
56	CMF International	119	6	32
57	Wesleyan World Missions	119		215
58	Word of Life Fellowship	118		25
59	Evangelical Baptist Missions	117	4	22
60	Church of God World Missions	114	7	1,500
61	Evangelical Covenant Church, Bd. of World. Msn.	111	36	
62	Grace Brethren International Missions	110	11	58
63	American Baptist Churches in the USA, Intl. Mins.	109	8	82
64	Calvary International	108		75
65	Macedonia World Baptist Missions	106		
66	Baptist General Conference	104	6	30
67	International Teams, U.S.A.	103	54	126
68	Maranatha Baptist Mission	102		
69	Elim Fellowship, World Missions Department	101	5	
70	Independent Faith Mission	99		6
71	Fellowship International Mission	96		

Rank	Name of Agency	+ 4 Yrs. & NRMs	1 Yr to 4 Yrs	2 Wks to 1 Yr
72	Bethany Fellowship Missions	95		11
73	Latin America Mission	91	46	58
74	Global Outreach Mission	89		59
75	Free Methodist World Missions	88		450
76	South America Mission	87	9	20
77	Free Will Baptist Assoc., Bd. of Foreign Missions	87	3	
78	Reformed Church in America Gen. Synod Council	86		
79	Africa Evangelical Fellowship	83	10	24
80	Mennonite Board of Missions	82		28
81	Eastern Mennonite Missions	80	15	180
82	Team Expansion, Inc.	80		24
83	Child Evangelism Fellowship, Inc.	78		43
84	Mission Society for United Methodists, The	77	21	35
85	World Mission Prayer League	76	6	6
86	Salvation Army, U.S.A.	75	25	37
87	WEC International	71	67	8
88	InterServe/USA	70		23
89	Brazil Gospel Fellowship Mission	69		
90	Wisconsin Evan. Luth. Synod, Bd. for World Msns.	68		7
91	Church of God in Christ, Mennonite Gen. Msn. Bd.	66		
92	Globe Missionary Evangelism	61	33	300
93	Foursquare Missions International	60	2	1,212
94	Pioneer Bible Translators	59		7
95	World Indigenous Missions	57		
96	BCM International	56	9	20
97	United World Mission, Inc.	53	10	86
98	Action International Ministries	52	1	9
99	Rio Grande Bible Institute	51	8	2
100	North American Baptist Conf. Intl. Missions	51	6	

Table 3.3 below shows the one hundred largest agencies ranked by income for overseas ministries, including income received as gifts-in-kind commodities and/or services for overseas activities that were included in their annual financial statement. Not all agencies report gifts-in-kind as income, or include such amounts in their annual financial statement as income.

These one hundred agencies (14% of the grand total) provided 87% of the grand total income reported for overseas ministries in 1996. This percentage is the same as it was in 1992.

Table 3.3 U.S. agencies ranked by income for overseas ministries (in millions of U.S. dollars).

Rank	Name of Agency	Income for Overseas Ministries (in mills. of US$)	Amount of Gifts-in-Kind
1	Southern Baptist Convention Intl. Mission Board	221.1	
2	World Vision	210.7	72.2
3	Assemblies of God, Gen. Council	113.4	
4	MAP International	84.8	77.9
5	Seventh-day Adventists General Conference	77.9	
6	Wycliffe Bible Translators USA	67.3	
7	Compassion International, Inc.	58.3	4.6
8	Campus Crusade for Christ, Intl.	54.2	
9	Presbyterian Church (USA), Worldwide Ministries	40.1	
10	Church of the Nazarene, World Mission Division	38.0	
11	Gideons International, The	35.2	
12	Food for the Hungry	32.7	27.2
13	Mennonite Central Committee Intl.	31.9	9.3
14	United Methodist Church, Board of Global Ministries	30.4	
15	Navigators, U.S. International Ministries Group	25.9	
16	American Bible Society	25.8	
17	Samaritan's Purse	25.4	11.6
18	New Tribes Mission	24.8	
19	Christian Churches/Churches of Christ	24.0	
20	ABWE (Assoc. of Baptists for World Evangelism)	23.2	
21	Evangelical Luth. Ch. in Am., Div. Global. Msn.	23.1	
22	Baptist Bible Fellowship Intl.	22.5	
23	TEAM (The Evangelical Alliance Mission)	22.2	

Rank	Name of Agency	Income for Overseas Ministries (in mills. of US$)	Amount of Gifts-in-Kind
24	Lutheran World Relief	21.8	10.1
25	SIM USA	20.2	
26	Trans World Radio	20.0	
27	Mission to the World	19.7	
28	Christian and Missionary Alliance	18.1	
29	Baptist Mid-Missions	18.0	
30	CBInternational	17.5	
31	Lutheran Church—Missouri Synod, Bd. Msn. Svcs.	17.4	3.5
32	Salvation Army, U.S.A.	17.4	
33	Baptist International Missions	17.0	
34	World Concern	16.3	8.1
35	Interchurch Medical Assistance	16.0	15.3
36	Operation Blessing International	15.9	
37	Mission Aviation Fellowship	15.5	
38	American Baptist Churches in the U.S.A., Intl. Mins.	14.2	
39	OMS International, Inc.	13.7	
40	HCJB World Radio Missionary Fellowship	13.6	
41	Opportunity International	13.0	
42	Christian Broadcasting Network	12.7	
43	Billy Graham Evangelistic Assoc., Intl. Ministries	12.5	
44	Habitat for Humanity International	11.2	
45	United Pentecostal Church Intl.,	11.2	
46	Mercy Ships	11.2	5.7
47	Church of God World Missions	11.1	
48	World Relief Corporation	10.7	
49	Evangelical Free Church Mission	10.4	
50	Episcopal Church, Domestic & Foreign Msn. Society	10.3	
51	Africa Inland Mission International	10.1	
52	Greater Europe Mission	10.1	
53	Childcare International	10.0	8.0
54	UFM International	10.0	
55	Far East Broadcasting Company	9.8	
56	Bible League, The	9.4	0.9
57	United Church Board for World Ministries	9.2	
58	World Gospel Mission	9.2	

Rank	Name of Agency	Income for Overseas Ministries (in mills. of US$)	Amount of Gifts-in-Kind
59	Christian Reformed World Missions	9.0	
60	Wisconsin Evang. Luth. Synod, Bd. for World Msn.	9.0	
61	Gospel Missionary Union	8.2	
62	Operation Mobilization, Inc.	7.9	
63	SEND International	7.9	
64	Pioneers	6.9	
65	OC International, Inc.	6.6	
66	Baptist General Conference	6.5	
67	Foursquare Missions International	6.3	
68	Biblical Ministries Worldwide	6.2	0.2
69	Partners International	6.1	1.3
70	Holt International Children's Services, Inc.	6.1	
71	World Team	6.0	
72	Free Methodist World Missions	5.9	
73	Gospel for Asia	5.9	
74	Christian Aid Ministries	5.8	
75	United Board for Christian Higher Education in Asia	5.7	
76	Word of Life Fellowship	5.7	
77	Blessings International	5.6	5.6
78	Heifer Project International	5.5	0.7
79	International Church Relief Fund	5.5	5.2
80	Every Home for Christ	5.4	
81	CAM International	5.3	
82	Evangelical Covenant Church, Bd. of World Missions	5.3	
83	Wesleyan World Missions	5.2	
84	Mennonite Brethren Missions/ Services	5.1	
85	Reformed Church in America Gen. Synod Council	5.0	
86	Church of God (Anderson, Indiana), Msny. Board	4.9	
87	International Teams, U.S.A.	4.7	
88	OMF International	4.5	
89	Frontiers	4.5	
90	ALM International	4.5	
91	Intl. Pentecostal Holiness Church World Missions	4.4	
92	Baptist World Mission	4.4	
93	International Missions, Inc.	4.4	

Rank	Name of Agency	Income for Overseas Ministries (in mills. of US$)	Amount of Gifts-in-Kind
94	Latin America Mission	4.3	
95	Free Will Baptist Assoc., Bd. of Foreign Missions	3.9	
96	Intl. Lutheran Laymen's League/Lutheran Hour	3.9	
97	Christian Aid Mission	3.7	
98	World Baptist Fellowship Mission Agency	3.7	
99	Slavic Gospel Association	3.5	0.8
100	Christian Reformed World Relief Committee	3.4	

Table 3.4 on the next page shows twenty-six "new" agencies with 1996 income for overseas ministries of $300,000 or more on separate lines. Seventy other new agencies whose individual incomes were under $300,000 are consolidated into a "summary" line.

These ninety-six new agencies (13.6% of the grand total) provided 17.4% of the bivocational, 12.6% of the nonresidential, and 7.2% short-term under one year personnel of the grand totals of those categories in 1996. Their income for overseas ministries was 1.3% of the grand total, and mission personnel serving one or more years was also 1.3%.

Table 3.4 "New" U.S. agencies founded in the last ten years
(in order of 1996 income for overseas ministries).

Agency	Year Founded	$ Income	Per- sonnel 1-4 yrs.	Non- resi- dential	Short- term	Bivoca- tional
Children's Medical Mins.	1988	2,400,000			50	15
World Help	1992	2,308,023		8	245	
Shelter Now Intl.	1989	1,996,000	6		10	25
Christ for the City Intl.	1995	1,912,372	47		645	8
Mission 21 India	1990	1,704,392		1		
P. Deyneka Russian Mins.	1991	1,545,737	3	7		
Advancing Native Missns.	1990	1,400,000	6		40	
Venture Middle East	1986	1,239,037	4		2	4
PAZ International	1986	1,127,000	47		25	5
East-West Ministries Intl.	1993	1,091,832	12		55	10
Global Strategy Msn. Assoc.	1986	1,010,000	50	3	75	4
Intl. Cooperating Mins.	1987	947,000				
AD2000 & Beyond Mvmt.	1989	886,058			14	
Network Intl. Christn. Schs.	1991	657,300	178			18
All God's Children Intl.	1991	568,000		2	4	
Intl. Outreach Mins.	1986	550,000	31	1	6	4
Intl Inst of Chrstn. Studies	1986	531,396	10		36	
RREACH International	1987	458,000			2	
China Ministries Intl.	1987	440,000	3	1		
Global Advance	1990	380,000				
People International	1986	376,000	33			
World Servants	1986	360,000	1	8	1,963	
Big World Ventures, Inc.	1994	358,000		224		
Church Ministries Intl.	1989	350,000	2			
Barnabas International	1986	330,000	4	12	7	
Bezalel World Outreach	1991	300,000		2	17	
70 other "new" agencies		5,089,196	62	44	1,188	140
TOTALS		30,316,173	499	91	4,608	233

Personnel from Canada	1992	1996	Change
FULLY SUPPORTED CANADIAN PERSONNEL SERVING OVERSEAS			
Long-Term (Overseas more than 4 years)	3,075	2,961	-3.7%
Short-Term (Overseas from 1 up to 4 years)	304	416	+36.8%
Nonresidential[1] fully supported	72	120	+66.6%
Total fully supported Canadian personnel serving overseas	*3,451*	*3,497*	*+1.3%*
OTHER CANADIAN PERSONNEL SERVING OVERSEAS			
Short-term of 2 weeks up to 1 year (1992)	1,747	NA[2]	—
Short-term of 2 weeks up to 1 year (1996)	NA[2]	2,470	—
Bivocational associates[3] sponsored or supervised	84	140	+66.6%
Nonresidential[1] partially supported	13	17	+30.7%
Non-North American personnel directly supported[4]	**1992**	**1996**	**Change**
Those serving in their home country	NA[2]	707	—
Those serving in a country other than their home country	36	77	+113.8%
Canadian min. & home office staff	**1992**	**1996**	**Change**
Full-time paid staff	1,412	1,622	+14.8%
Part-time staff/associates	249	389	+56.2%
Volunteer (ongoing) helpers	2,124	3,154	+48.4%
Financial support raised in Canada	**1992**	**1996**	**Change**
Income for overseas ministries	$236,900,455[5]	$235,859,759	-0.4%

Table 3.5 Comparing Canadian overseas mission statistics, 1992 and 1996.

Table 3.5 continues the changes instituted in the 1993-95 *Handbook* about the way overseas personnel are reported and calculated. For fully-supported personnel from Canada and personnel from other countries who are fully or partially-supported from Canada, agencies provide country-by-country figures and an agency's totals are taken from the sum of their country subtotals. See question #12 in the survey questionnaire reproduced in the appendix for specifics.

As already noted, for this *Handbook* we have updated and changed the survey questionnaire relating to short-term overseas personnel to better reflect current agency practices. Therefore, direct comparisons for the 2 weeks up to 1 year short-term category between 1992 and 1996 are not applicable.

NOTES FOR TABLE 3.5

1   *Nonresidential* refers to persons not living in the country(ies) of their ministry, but in Canada or elsewhere, who travel overseas on a regular basis at least 12 weeks per year on mission ministry and support activities.

2   *NA* indicates that the content or other aspect of a particular survey question was modified so that a direct comparison of survey results between years is not applicable.

3   *Bivocational associates*, also known as "tentmakers," are persons who support themselves partially or fully through non-church/mission vocations and live overseas for the purpose of Christian witness, evangelism and/or encouraging believers.

4   *Non-North American personnel directly supported* includes those whose financial support from Canadian agencies is specifically directed to them individually. There are also other non-North Americans who are beneficiaries of Canadian financial support through general support grants, for which personnel totals are not available from the agencies.

5   The amount *$236,900,455* (Canadian dollars) is the 1992 income adjusted upward to the value of 1996 dollars, based on the consumer price index. This adjustment for inflation is made to provide a more meaningful comparison between 1992 and 1996.

Table 3.6 Canadian agencies ranked by overseas personnel serving more than four years (including fully-supported nonresidential mission personnel).

Rank	Name of Agency	+ 4 Yrs. & NRMS	1 Yr to 4 Yrs	2 Wks to 1 Yr
1	Wycliffe Bible Translators of Canada	385	20	30
2	Youth With A Mission (Canada)	350		400
3	Brethren Assemblies (Canada)	209	2	6
4	Christian and Missionary Alliance in Canada, The	191	21	20
5	New Tribes Mission of Canada	171		
6	Pentecostal Assemblies of Canada, Overseas Msns.	167	8	416
7	United Church of Canada, Div. of World Outreach	96		
8	Gospel Missionary Union of Canada	85	27	12
9	Canadian Baptist Ministries	81	26	75
10	FEB International	80	9	12
11	WEC International (Canada)	76		7
12	TEAM - The Evangelical Alliance Msn. of Canada	75	4	9
13	OMF Canada	73	9	58
14	SIM Canada	67	17	63
15	Janz Team Ministries	60	5	9
16	Mission Aviation Fellowship of Canada	59	7	2
17	Africa Inland Mission (Canada)	58	38	31
18	Salvation Army, The	51	6	19
19	World Team	49	11	8
20	Africa Evangelical Fellowship	45	3	7

Table 3.6 above shows the twenty largest agencies ranked by personnel serving overseas for over four years, including fully supported nonresidential mission personnel. See the definition of the nonresidential category in the "Fully supported Canadian personnel overseas" section of chapter 7.

These twenty agencies (16% of the grand total) provided 78% of the longer-term personnel (overseas terms of more than 4 years and fully supported nonresidentials) in 1996. This percentage is the same as it was in 1992.

Table 3.7 Canadian agencies ranked by income for overseas ministries (in millions of Canadian dollars).

Rank	Name of Agency	Income for Overseas Ministries (in mills. of Can$)	Amount of Gifts-in-Kind
1	World Vision Canada	65.2	0.5
2	HOPE International Development Agency	9.5	6.0
3	United Church of Canada, Div. of World Outreach	9.0	
4	Christian and Missionary Alliance in Canada, The	8.3	
5	Pentecostal Assemblies of Canada, Overseas Msns.	8.0	
6	SIM Canada	6.5	
7	Canadian Food for the Hungry	6.4	6.0
8	Salvation Army, The	6.2	
9	Anglican Church of Canada, Partners in Mission	6.0	
10	Compassion Canada	5.6	
11	World Relief Canada	5.6	
12	Canadian Baptist Ministries	5.5	
13	Samaritan's Purse - Canada	5.2	3.3
14	Wycliffe Bible Translators of Canada	5.0	
15	Christian Blind Mission International (Canada)	5.0	0.6
16	Campus Crusade for Christ of Canada	4.4	
17	Christian Reformed World Relief Comm. of Canada	4.1	
18	Canadian Bible Soc./La Societé Biblique Canadienne	4.0	
19	MSC Canada	3.8	
20	Mennonite Brethren Missions/Services	3.3	

Table 3.7 above shows the twenty largest agencies ranked by income for overseas ministries, including income received as gifts-in-kind commodities and/or services for overseas activities that were included in their annual financial statement. Not all agencies report gifts-in-kind as income, or include such amounts in their annual financial statement as income.

These twenty agencies (16% of the grand total) provided 75% of the grand income reported for overseas ministries in 1996. This percentage was 79% in 1992.

Table 3.8 below shows countries in which agencies have reported residential mission personnel from the U.S. and/or Canada. Besides countries, other political units (e.g., American Samoa) are also shown. These may be island territories that are located a significant distance from their related country. The practical realities of preparation, travel and relationships may require that mission agencies sometimes view the world, especially scattered islands, differently from the standard United Nations political subdivisions.

Table 3.8 U.S. and Canadian mission personnel by country.

Country/Area	U.S. Personnel		Canadian Personnel		Total N. American Personnel	
	4+ Yrs.	1-4 Yrs.	4+ Yrs.	1-4 Yrs.	4+ Yrs.	1-4 Yrs.
Afghanistan	20	2			20	2
Albania	96	31	5	1	101	32
American Samoa	6	1			6	1
Andorra	2				2	
Angola	22	9	33	3	55	12
Anguilla	2				2	
Antigua	12	1			12	1
Argentina	370	12	17	3	387	15
Armenia	2	1			2	1
Aruba	2				2	
Australia	269	5	18	2	287	7
Austria	168	59	27	4	195	63
Azerbaijan		2				2
Azores	8				8	
Bahamas	32	2	2	2	34	4
Bahrain	7				7	
Bangladesh	126	17	6	1	132	18
Barbados	8	2	2		10	2
Belarus	14	18			14	18
Belau (Palau)	3	4			3	4
Belgium	154	14	29	6	183	20
Belize	57	18	10		67	18
Benin	59	7	12	5	71	12
Bermuda	4				4	

Country/Area	U.S. Personnel		Canadian Personnel		Total N. American Personnel	
	4+ Yrs.	1-4 Yrs.	4+ Yrs.	1-4 Yrs.	4+ Yrs.	1-4 Yrs.
Bolivia	432	43	66	10	498	53
Bophuthatswana	4				4	
Bosnia-Herzegovina	8	3			8	3
Botswana	72	13	9		81	13
Brazil	1,735	120	109	3	1,844	123
British Virgin Islands	2				2	
Bulgaria	29	11			29	11
Burkina Faso	140	15	23	4	163	19
Burundi	14	7		1	14	8
Cambodia	65	34	3	5	68	39
Cameroon	209	25	28	5	237	30
Canary Islands	11				11	
Cape Verde Islands	2				2	
Caribbean Islands - Gen.	95	19			95	19
Cayman Islands	15				15	
Central African Republic	99	11	2	2	101	13
Chad	69	6	8		77	6
Chile	340	17	22		362	17
China, Peoples Rep.	87	68	2	2	89	70
Colombia	551	37	48	6	599	43
Comoros Islands	9				9	
Congo	40	4	5		45	4
Congo/Zaire	457	56	44	9	501	65
Costa Rica	278	65	15	2	293	67
Cote d'Ivoire	403	75	28	2	431	77
Croatia	32	12		2	32	14
Cuba	7	3	2	1	9	4
Cyprus	36	3			36	3
Czech Republic	109	40		3	109	43
Denmark	11	2			11	2
Djibouti	4	1			4	1
Dominica	9				9	
Dominican Republic	174	21	4		178	21
Ecuador	603	73	58	3	661	76
Egypt	62	23	2		64	23
El Salvador	59	11	2	1	61	12

Country/Area	U.S. Personnel		Canadian Personnel		Total N. American Personnel	
	4+ Yrs.	1-4 Yrs.	4+ Yrs.	1-4 Yrs.	4+ Yrs.	1-4 Yrs.
Equatorial Guinea	15		2		17	
Eritrea	17	4			17	4
Estonia	5	16	2	3	7	19
Ethiopia	193	48	13	6	206	54
Fiji	27	4	3		30	4
Finland	15		7		22	
France	638	31	53	4	691	35
French Guiana	8				8	
French Polynesia	3				3	
Gabon	36	6	10	2	46	8
Gambia	27	10	3		30	10
Gaza	7	2			7	2
Georgia	2				2	
Germany	513	124	68	17	581	141
Ghana	190	17	12	2	202	19
Gibraltar	2				2	
Greece	71	3	5		76	3
Greenland	1		3		4	
Grenada	21		5		26	
Guadeloupe	4				4	
Guam	123	12			123	12
Guatemala	392	152	24	3	416	155
Guinea	116	9	26		142	9
Guinea Bissau	9	7	1		10	7
Guyana	56	5	7	6	63	11
Haiti	262	54	22	7	284	61
Honduras	273	49	2	1	275	50
Hong Kong	366	54	16	3	382	57
Hungary	175	63	9	10	184	73
Iceland	10	2	2		12	2
India	246	53	36	4	282	57
Indonesia	648	68	85	6	733	74
Ireland	166	7	17	1	183	8
Israel	91	23	2		93	23
Italy	216	14	15	4	231	18
Jamaica	113	19	2	1	115	20

Country/Area	U.S. Personnel		Canadian Personnel		Total N. American Personnel	
	4+ Yrs.	1-4 Yrs.	4+ Yrs.	1-4 Yrs.	4+ Yrs.	1-4 Yrs.
Japan	1,106	220	51	9	1,157	229
Jordan	51	9	2		53	9
Kazakhstan	32	16			32	16
Kenya	1,139	173	101	40	1,240	213
Kiribati	2				2	
Korea, South	192	147	2	3	194	150
Kuwait	2				2	
Kyrgyzstan	18	5			18	5
Laos	24	2		1	24	3
Latvia	26	19	5	5	31	24
Lebanon	10		1		11	
Lesotho	41	8	2	4	43	12
Liberia	105	23	3		108	23
Lithuania	25	11			25	11
Luxembourg	6		2		8	
Macao	43	8	2		45	8
Macedonia	15			1	15	1
Madagascar	67	7	2		69	7
Malawi	148	38	16	9	164	47
Malaysia	56	28	7	4	63	32
Maldives	2				2	
Mali	147	21	22		169	21
Malta	6				6	
Marshall Islands	13				13	
Mauritania	2	3			2	3
Mauritius	2		4	2	6	2
Mexico	1,546	155	73	11	1,619	166
Micronesia	30	4			30	4
Moldava	8				8	
Monaco	20				20	
Mongolia	34	11			34	11
Morocco	22				22	
Mozambique	90	21	13	1	103	22
Myanmar/Burma	8	2			8	2
Namibia	38	8	3	2	41	10
Nepal	92	28	7		99	28

Country/Area	U.S. Personnel		Canadian Personnel		Total N. American Personnel	
	4+ Yrs.	1-4 Yrs.	4+ Yrs.	1-4 Yrs.	4+ Yrs.	1-4 Yrs.
Netherlands	112	6	21	2	133	8
Netherlands Antilles	83	7	3		86	7
New Caledonia	8	2			8	2
New Zealand	81	4	10		91	4
Nicaragua	56	35		3	56	38
Niger	118	7	12		130	7
Nigeria	364	38	14	5	378	43
N. Mariana Islands	7	9	1		8	9
Norway	22				22	
Pakistan	152	16	49	4	201	20
Panama	175	14	8		183	14
Papua New Guinea	1,004	150	97	13	1,101	163
Paraguay	220	16	25		245	16
Peru	528	44	43		571	44
Philippines	1,385	118	133	9	1,518	127
Poland	80	14	8	2	88	16
Portugal	143	11	6	5	149	16
Puerto Rico	114	22			114	22
Romania	138	60			138	60
Russian Federation	473	342	5	25	478	367
Rwanda	38	4		3	38	7
Senegal	172	45	25		197	45
Serbia		2				2
Seychelles			2		2	
Sierra Leone	32	5	2		34	5
Singapore	170	20	10		180	20
Slovakia	41	22	2		43	22
Slovenia	17	2			17	2
Solomon Islands	34	1			34	1
Somalia	1	4			1	4
South Africa	422	45	45	7	467	52
Spain	443	28	36		479	28
Sri Lanka	39	5	5		44	5
St Christopher and Nevis	2		2		4	
St Lucia	8				8	
St Vincent	15		1		16	

Country/Area	U.S. Personnel		Canadian Personnel		Total N. American Personnel	
	4+ Yrs.	1-4 Yrs.	4+ Yrs.	1-4 Yrs.	4+ Yrs.	1-4 Yrs.
Sudan	35	10	2	4	37	14
Suriname	100	1	5		105	1
Swaziland	89	10			89	10
Sweden	22		8	2	30	2
Switzerland	31	11	2		33	11
Syria	1	1			1	1
Taiwan, Rep. of China	407	49	24	2	431	51
Tanzania	296	28	24	2	320	30
Thailand	435	118	61	4	496	122
Togo	136	12	1		137	12
Tonga	7				7	
Trinidad &Tobago	63	4	2	2	65	6
Turkey	28	17			28	17
Uganda	104	35	12		116	35
Ukraine	130	120	10	6	140	126
United Arab Emirates	33	4	3	1	36	5
United Kingdom	577	138	24	6	601	144
Uruguay	111	5	9	1	120	6
Uzbekistan	12	15			12	15
Vanuatu	10				10	
Venezuela	489	54	50		539	54
Vietnam	35	11			35	11
Virgin Islands - USA	21				21	
West Bank	8	8			8	8
Western Samoa	2				2	
Yemen	36	7			36	7
Yugoslavia	10				10	
Zambia	200	20	52	3	252	23
Zimbabwe	184	23	29		213	23

Table 3.9 U.S. and Canadian agencies no longer listed.

Name of Agency	Reason No Longer Listed
Adib Eden Evangelistic Missionary Society	Overseas data not available
Amazing Grace Missions	Overseas data not available
American Committee for Keep	Overseas data not available
Apostolic Faith Mission of Portland Oregon	Overseas data not available
Apostolic Overcoming Holy Church of God	Overseas data not available
Bethel Mission of China	Overseas data not available
Bible Pathway Ministries	Overseas data not available
Bible Way Churches of Our Lord	Overseas data not available
Bookmates International, Inc.	Overseas data not available
Chinese for Christ, Inc.	Overseas data not available
Christ is the Answer Crusades	Overseas data not available
Christ's Center Missions	Overseas data not available
Christian Baptist Church of God World Missions	Overseas data not available
Christian Business Men's Committee of Canada	Overseas relationship unknown
Christian Faith Ministries	Overseas data not available
Christian Transportation	Overseas relationship unknown
Church of Bible Understanding	Overseas data not available
Church of Christ Holiness (USA), Foreign Msn. Bd.	Overseas data not available
Church of God at Baden	Overseas data not available
Church Planting World Mission	Overseas data not available
Creative Children's Mins./Share Time Intl.	Overseas data not available
Doulos Vision	Overseas data not available
Ethiopian Outreach Ministry	Overseas data not available
Evangelical Literature League	Overseas data not available
Evangelization Society	Overseas data not available
Faith Partners for Missions	No overseas ministries at present
Fellowship of Faith for the Muslims	Overseas relationship unknown
Good Shepherd Ministries	Disbanded
Gospel Outreach To India	Overseas data not available
Grace Ministries, Inc.	Overseas data not available
Hauge Foreign Missions, Inc.	Overseas data not available
Hope for Africa	Overseas data not available
International Christian Leprosy Mission (Canada)	No office in Canada at present
International Christian Mission	Overseas data not available
International Institute, Inc.	Overseas data not available
International Ministries to Israel	Overseas data not available

Name of Agency	Reason No Longer Listed
Jerry & Jana Lackey Ministries	Overseas data not available
Jewish Voice Broadcasts, Inc.	Overseas data not available
Lutheran Orient Mission Soc.	Overseas data not available
Lutherans for World Evangelization	Overseas data not available
Maranatha South Africa	Overseas data not available
Mexico Inland Mission	Overseas data not available
Ministry of Mission Services	Overseas relationship unknown
Missionary Air Transport	Disbanded
Missionary Evangelistic Fellowship	Overseas data not available
Moody Literature Ministries	Overseas data not available
Order of the Holy Cross	Overseas data not available
Outreach for Christ Intl. - Reach Out Singers	Overseas data not available
P and R Schenck Associates in Evangelism	Overseas data not available
People for Missions	Overseas data not available
R.E.A.P. Mission, Inc.	Overseas relationship unknown
Resurrection Churches and Ministies	Overseas data not available
Share Canada	Overseas data not available
Spanish Evangelical Literature Fellowship, Inc.	No office in USA at present
Sports & Cultural Exchange International	Overseas data not available
Technoserve, Inc.	Now considered non-mission
Totonac Bible Center, Inc.	Overseas data not available
Twenty-Five Hundred Translations	Overseas relationship unknown
Vision Christian Ministries	Overseas relationship unknown
Voice of Calvary Ministries	Overseas relationship unknown
World Christian, Inc.	Disbanded
World Mission Teams/World Film Crusade	Overseas relationship unknown
World Missionary Evangelism	Overseas data not available
World Outreach (USA), Inc.	Overseas data not available
Zwemer Institute of Muslim Studies	Overseas data not available

Mission agency trends 1984-1996

MARC conducted surveys of Protestant mission agencies with overseas ministries in 1984, 1988, 1992 and 1996. New editions of the *Mission Handbook* were published following each survey. See the appendix for the 1996 survey questionnaire.

MARC has created a historical database of statistical data from the fifty largest agencies in the U.S. to facilitate analyses of trends over the 1984-1996 period. These agencies accounted for approximately 66% of the long-term mission personnel and income for overseas ministries in those years. *Handbook* users

refer most often to the information about long-term mission personnel and income for overseas ministries from among the approximately thirty key statistical items gathered in each of these surveys.

The following six figures show the number of long-term overseas mission personnel and income for overseas ministries in relation to three different characteristics of mission agencies. "Long-term" is defined as fully supported personnel with length of service expected to be more than 4 years. These basic charts indicate the occurrence of some definite trends. Most are gradual, however, and in only two

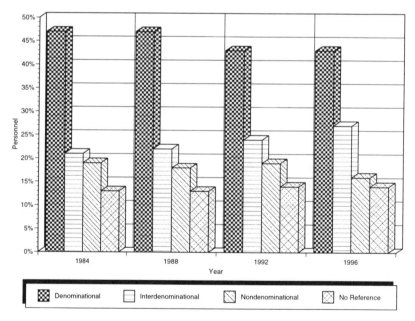

Fig. 3.1 Long-term overseas personnel by denominational orientation of agency.

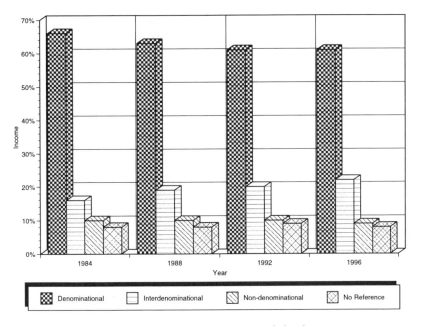

**Fig. 3.2 Income for overseas ministries
by denominational orientation of agency.**

places is there a shift between the categories displayed in the charts.

Figures 3.1 and 3.2 show long-term personnel and financial support for overseas ministries in terms of the denominational orientation of the sending agency. The category "No Reference" shows agencies that preferred not to use the term denomination as a reference in describing themselves. In recent years the survey questionnaire also included "transdenominational" as a category, but none of the larger agencies used that term to describe their denominational orientation.

The two figures show small changes in the percentages for this period, but no shifts between the given categories. A slight trend across the 12 years is a 4% decrease in the percentage of long-term personnel and a 5% decrease in income for overseas ministries for those agencies describing themselves as denominational. The agencies describing themselves as interdenominational picked up the corresponding percentage increases for the most part. However, in 1996 the denominational agencies still led in income for overseas ministries, with 61% to the combined 39% for the other three categories.

Figures 3.3 and 3.4 show long-term personnel and financial support for overseas ministries in terms of the era in which the agency was founded in the U.S. For agencies that are the result of mergers, the founding date of the oldest agency was used. In a few cases where mergers took place during the 12 year period covered by the figure, combined totals of the previously separate agencies were used for the years before the merger. For denominations that may have been formed before their overseas mission program was in operation, the date used was the first year that missionaries were sent overseas.

All of these agencies were founded before 1984 so that statistics were available for all of the survey years for each agency.

The eras used in the charts are those that social historians have noted were times when basic changes took place in U.S. history. These periods are bounded by the U.S. Civil War of the 1860s and the World Wars of the twentieth century. Overseas mission work for the most part stood still or stopped during those wars. After the wars much of the world experienced some basic change and the mission agencies founded after those times of transition tended to reflect the

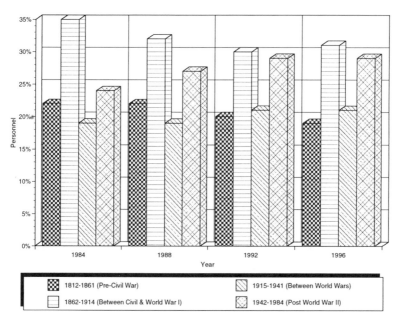

Fig. 3.3 Long-term overseas personnel
by founding era of agency.

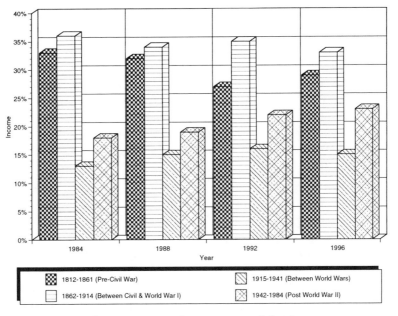

**Fig. 3.4 Income for overseas ministries
by founding era of agency.**

new realities more quickly than those established earlier.

The trends for missionary sending and financial support in Figures 3.3 and 3.4 are identifiable but not markedly distinct. One might expect that the "older" agencies (founded before 1915) might show decreases in the percentage of personnel and financial support compared to the "newer" agencies (founded after 1915). This is the case, but not by great amounts. There was a 7% shift between 1984 and 1996 to the newer agencies in both personnel and financial support. But while the older agencies and newer agencies each had 50% of the long-term personnel in 1996, the older agencies still had a distinct lead in the amount of financial support by 62% to 48%.

Figure 3.3 reveals one of the instances where a basic shift (although small) has taken place. For long-term personnel, the percentage from agencies founded between the World Wars (1915-1941) surpassed the percentage from agencies founded in the pre-Civil War era (1812-1861) by 1% in 1992, increasing to 2% in 1996.

Some statistical aspects of the newest agencies (those founded since 1985) are shown in Table 3.4.

Figures 3.5 and 3.6 show long-term personnel and financial support for overseas ministries in terms of the doctrinal and/or ecclesiastical stance of the agency. Five categories are shown with the remaining summarized under "other."

The 1996 survey questionnaire (see the appendix) lists the twenty-one doctrinal/ecclesiastical groups used in the survey. This list has been refined over time with the core categories remaining the same. There are five generic categories (ecumenical, evangelical, etc.) and sixteen denominational families (Adventist, Baptist, etc.). In cases where agencies indicated more than one category, their primary histori-cal group is used.

The trends for missionary sending and financial support in Figures 3.5 and 3.6 are also identifiable, but not markedly distinct. Figure 3.6 reveals another instance where a basic shift has taken place. Income for overseas ministries among agencies that use the generic term "evangelical" as the primary term describing their traditional doctrinal and/or ecclesiastical stance moved into first place for income in 1992, passing the Baptist denominational family. These agencies already had the largest percentage of long-term personnel in 1984 at 35%, and increased this to 39% by 1996.

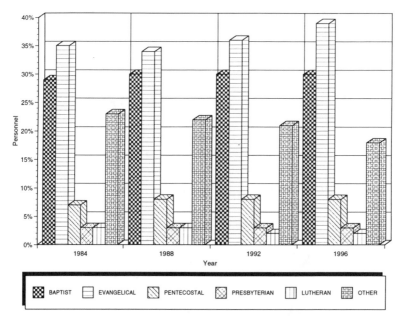

**Fig. 3.5 Long-term overseas personnel
by doctrinal/ecclesiastical stance of agency.**

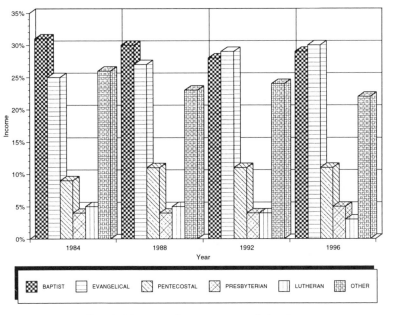

**Fig. 3.6 Income for overseas ministries
by doctrinal/ecclesiastical stance of agency.**

Chapter 4

U.S. Protestant agencies

This chapter is the basic information directory of U.S. Protestant agencies engaged in mission ministries outside the U.S. and Canada. The comprehensive coverage includes the agencies that directly support the work of such ministries or the work of overseas national churches/workers. The agencies supplied the information; the survey questionnaire used to gather the information is reproduced in the appendix.

The *Handbook* covers an agency's overseas ministry and support activities but not its mission work in the U.S. Much cross-cultural mission work takes place in the U.S., but due to the additional complexity of reporting such activities we have not undertaken the task for this publication. Agencies with both overseas and U.S. mission ministries, however, were asked to include U.S.-based ministry personnel in the total that appears in the "Home ministry & office staff" line of the "Other Personnel" section.

Each agency will have at least seven of the basic categories of information listed below, with others included as applicable.

Agency name

Agencies are listed alphabetically. If the article "the" is in an agency's name, it will appear at the end of the name so the agency is in the most commonly referenced alphabetical order. Rare exceptions occur where the Christian public commonly uses the article "the" as the first word in the agency's name.

Agencies that have changed their name since the previous *Handbook* have their prior name listed, with a cross-reference to the current or new name. A subdivision of a larger organization may be listed separately if it is organized to also serve the larger mission community rather than just its parent organization.

Telephone and fax number

The common format of showing the area code in parentheses is used throughout.

E-Mail address

This is the first time electronic mail addresses appear in the directory. The Internet format and emerging standards for capitalization are used. For example, upper case letters are used to the left of the @ sign when meaningful, but all characters to the right are lower case. Acronyms are upper case, and if a second word is also in the name it is all lower case. For example, in this format the address for MARC Publications is MARCpubs@wvi.org.

In some cases, agencies have a general e-mail address, such as Info@xxxx.org. Others have supplied an individual person's address within the organization. In cases where only a Web address is given, it generally means a Web page provides access to several e-mail addresses so an inquiry can be immediately directed to the relevant department or person.

Instead of providing a general e-mail address, an agency may indicate the format to be used to contact individuals within the agency. This usually takes the form of something like Firstname.Lastname@xxxx.org and would be used by the sender when the individual is known.

Mission agencies began to use e-mail on a fairly broad scale by 1995, and over 60 percent of the agencies listed now use e-mail on a regular basis.

Web address

Since 1996 a good number of mission organizations have established a presence on the World Wide Web portion of the Internet. This is the first time a request for a Web address (technically called a uniform resource locator or URL) was included in the survey. Unlike e-mail addresses, Web addresses are case sensitive and must be entered exactly as given.

Because the Web is so new, changes in Web addresses are still taking place as agencies consider different options for a Web presence. Therefore, some addresses may have been added or changed since the *Handbook* database was finalized. The full Web address is given, including the required "http://" prefix, except in cases where including the prefix would have caused the address to spill over to a second line.

Over 30 percent of the agencies provide information about themselves and their work on the Web. A few include audio recordings that can be heard by those with the appropriate sound card and speakers on their personal computers (PCs). Some agencies are starting to include full-motion video clips to take advantage of the Web's multimedia capabilities. This requires a more sophisticated PC and a faster connection to the Internet.

Postal mailing address

A post office box number appears whenever the agency has one, since it is unlikely to change over time.

Chief executive officer

In a few cases where there are multiple primary contacts, two names are listed.

Short descriptive paragraph

A brief description appears based on the denominational orientation and primary activities information supplied by the agency. It always has the same general order so the reader is presented with a format that is consistent across all agencies. Additional specific information, such as name changes, mergers, or other unique aspects may also be included.

Quotation from the agency's mission or purpose statement

This is the first time the survey invited agencies to include their board-adopted short mission or purpose statement in their survey responses. Some of the statements are concise and are shown in their entirety. For most, however, such common or similar phrases as "exists for the purpose of" are replaced by ellipses to present a more concise statement.

Year founded in USA

This is the year the agency or overseas mission component of a larger organization was founded in the USA. In some cases the denomination or organization may have existed earlier in another country.

For some organizations, the founding date of the missionary-sending component may be later than the founding of the larger organization. For denominations and other organizations that have experienced mergers, the founding date is generally that of the oldest component involved in the merger.

Income for overseas ministries

This is the part of an agency's overall income used for ministry activities outside the USA and Canada or in activities that directly facilitate overseas ministries. "NA" indicates that income in this sense is not applicable, and usually applies to specialized service agencies or agencies whose income is reported under a sister or parent organization. "NR" indicates that the agency did not report income for overseas ministries for the survey, but may make this information available on request.

Amount of gifts-in-kind

If applicable, this is the portion of the income that was received in the form of donated gifts-in-kind commodities and/or services used for overseas ministries. Please note that some agencies do not include gifts-in-kind as part of their financial audit process, so the value of such gifts is not included in their income for overseas ministries. Gifts-in-kind amounts that were an insignificant percentage are not shown as a separate item.

Fully supported USA personnel overseas

Not all agencies have overseas personnel in the following categories, so the above heading will not always appear. If applicable, the following lines will appear with the appropriate numbers:

- ◆ "Expecting to serve more than 4 years" for persons from the USA who are fully supported by the agency.
- ◆ "Expecting to serve 1 up to 4 years" for persons from the USA who are fully supported by the agency.
- ◆ "Nonresidential mission personnel" for fully supported USA mission personnel not residing in the country or countries of their ministry, but assigned to work and travel overseas at least 12 weeks per year on operational aspects of the overseas ministry.

Other personnel

If applicable for the agency, the following lines will appear:

- ◆ "Non-USA serving in own/other country" for persons with either citizenship in their country of service or another non-USA country, who are fully or partially sup-

ported from the USA.
- ◆ "Bivocational/Tentmaker from USA" for persons sponsored or supervised by the agency, but who support themselves partially or fully through non-church/mission vocations and live overseas for the purpose of Christian witness, evangelism and/or encouraging believers.
- ◆ "Short-Term less than 1 year from USA" for persons who went on overseas projects or mission trips that lasted less than one year but at least two weeks through the agency, either fully or partially supported, including those raising their own support.
- ◆ "Home ministry and office staff in USA" for persons assigned to ministry and/or office duties in the USA either as full-time or part-time paid staff/associates.

Countries

These are the countries where the agency sends USA personnel or regularly supports national or other non-USA personnel. Following the name of the country is the number of USA personnel with terms of service of one year or more. In some cases a continent or other general area instead of a country is shown. This may be due to several reasons, such as mission personnel whose ministry covers several countries.

Where an agency's work is maintained either by nationals of countries other than the U.S. or Canada, by personnel serving less than one year, or by those serving on a nonresidential basis, the country of activity is listed without a personnel total. Please refer to chapter 6 for detailed country personnel totals of all categories for each agency.

ABWE (Association of Baptists for World Evangelism)

(717)774-7000   Fax: (717)774-1919
E-Mail: ABWE@abwe.org
Web: http://www.abwe.org/
P.O. Box 8585, Harrisburg, PA 17105
Dr. Wendell W. Kempton, President

An independent Baptist sending agency engaged in evangelism, church planting, theological education, leadership development, medical work, Bible translation, and youth programs.

Year Founded in USA	1927
Income for Overseas Ministries	$ 23,175,000

Fully Supported USA Personnel Overseas:
Expecting to serve more than 4 years   . . .   619
Expecting to serve 1 up to 4 years   28
Nonresidential mission personnel   13

Other Personnel:
Bivocational/Tentmaker from USA   10
Short-Term less than 1 year from USA   . .   130
Home ministry & office staff in USA   67

Countries: Argentina 13, Australia 10, Bangladesh 55, Brazil 102, Chile 24, Colombia 16, Europe-E 53, France 10, Gambia 21, Germany 5, Ghana 4, Hong Kong 11, Italy 13, Japan 17, Kenya 4, Mexico 2, Norway 8, Papua New Guin 18, Paraguay 15, Peru 39, Philippines 50, Portugal 31, S Africa 40, Singapore 4, Spain 17, Thailand 2, Togo 52, UK 11.

ACMC (Advancing Churches in Missions Commitment)

(770)631-9900   Fax: (770)631-9470
E-Mail: 76331.2051@compuserve.com
P.O. Box 3929, Peachtree City, GA 30269
Mike Stachura, President

A transdenominational service agency of evangelical tradition engaged in mobilizing churches for mission through conferences, consulting and information services, training, publications, and other activities for church leaders.

"..to help Christian congregations mobilize their resources for effective involvement in world evangelization."

Year Founded in USA	1974
Income for Overseas Ministries	NA

Personnel:
Home ministry & office staff in USA   19

Action International Ministries

(425)485-1967   Fax: (425)486-9477
E-Mail: 75702.31@compuserve.com
Web: http://www.actionintl.org/
P.O. Box 490, Bothell, WA 98041
Doug Nichols, International Director

An interdenominational sending agency of evangelical tradition engaged in street children programs, church planting, development, evangelism, and support of national churches.

"... to reach the masses for Christ, help individual Christians mature, and minister to the 'whole' man, especially the poor..."

Year Founded in USA	1975
Income for Overseas Ministries	$ 1,552,813

Fully Supported USA Personnel Overseas:
Expecting to serve more than 4 years   52
Expecting to serve 1 up to 4 years   1

Other Personnel:
Non-USA serving in own/other country   . . .   4
Short-Term less than 1 year from USA   . . .   9
Home ministry & office staff in USA   14

Countries: Brazil 4, Colombia 4, India 4, Mexico 2, Mongolia 2, Philippines 37.

ACTS International Ministries

(719)282-1247   Fax: (719)282-1139
E-Mail: 73524.1100@compuserve.com
P.O. Box 62725, Colorado Springs, CO 80962
Dr. Alvin Low, President

A transdenominational support agency of evangelical tradition engaged in training, leadership development, and national churches support.

".. equipping national Christian leaders in the least evangelized, economically deprived, and restricted countries of the world..."

Year Founded in USA	1991
Income for Overseas Ministries . .	$ 40,000

Fully Supported USA Personnel Overseas:
Nonresidential mission personnel   1

Other Personnel:
Home ministry & office staff in USA   1

AD2000 & Beyond Movement

(719)567-2000   Fax: (719)567-2685
Web: http://www.ad2000.org/
2860 S Circle #2112, Colorado Springs, CO 80906
Rev. Luis Bush, International Director

A transdenominational support network of evangelical tradition engaged in mobilization for mission, evangelism, and mission-related research and information services for churches and agencies in many countries.

".. to encourage, motivate and network men and women church leaders by inspiring them with the vision of reaching the unreached by AD 2000 through consultations, prayer efforts and communication materials..."

Year Founded in USA 1989
Income for Overseas Ministries . $ 886,058
Personnel:
Short-Term less than 1 year from USA . . . 14
Home ministry & office staff in USA 17

Adopt-A-People Clearinghouse
(719)574-7001   **Fax: (719)574-7005**
E-Mail: AAPC@xc.org
P.O. Box 17490, Colorado Springs, CO 80935
Mr. Keith Butler, Exec. Director

An interdenominational service agency of evangelical tradition engaged in people group information services and orientation for agencies, local churches and small groups.

".. to stimulate and equip Christian Fellow-ships to adopt [at the level of prayer, research, financial support and/or on-site engagement] un-reached people groups for prayer and outreach."

Year Founded in USA 1989
Income for Overseas Ministries . . . . NA
Personnel:
Home ministry & office staff in USA 4

Advancing Indigenous Missions
(830)367-3513   **Fax: (210)734-7620**
P.O. Box 690042, San Antonio, TX 78269
James W. Colley, Exec. Director

A transdenominational support agency of evangelical and charismatic tradition engaged in support of national missions and workers.

"..to mobilize Christian churches, organiza-tions, and individuals for prayer, financial, and logistical support of indigenous missions."

Year Founded in USA 1990
Income for Overseas Ministries . . $ 9,124
Personnel:
Home ministry & office staff in USA 1

Advancing Native Missions
(804)293-8829   **Fax: (804)293-7586**
E-Mail: ANM@adnamis.org
Web: http://www.cstone.net/~adnamis/
P.O. Box 5036, Charlottesville, VA 22905
Carl A. Gordon, President

A transdenominational support agency of evangelical tradition engaged in support of national missions, Bible distribution, funds transmission, leadership development, and mission-related research. Includes 1995 merger of GlobaLink Ministries, Inc.

".. to seek out, evaluate, and support native missions groups .. who are working among unreached people groups..."

Year Founded in USA 1990
Income for Overseas Ministries $ 1,400,000
Fully Supported USA Personnel Overseas:
Expecting to serve more than 4 years 6
Other Personnel:
Non-USA serving in own/other country . . . 6
Short-Term less than 1 year from USA . . . 40
Home ministry & office staff in USA 14
Countries: Asia 5, Indonesia 1.

Advancing Renewal Ministries
(704)846-9355   **Fax: (704)846-9356**
E-Mail: 104273.3130@compuserve.com
11616 Sir Francis Drake Dr., Charlotte, NC 28277
Dr. Arthur M. Vincent, Director

A nondenominational support agency of Lutheran tradition engaged in training national pastors and evangelists, Bible distribution, and literature distribution.

Year Founded in USA 1982
Income for Overseas Ministries . . $ 35,219
Personnel:
Home ministry & office staff in USA 3

Advent Christian World Missions
(704)545-6161   **Fax: (704)573-0712**
P.O. Box 23152, Charlotte, NC 28227
Harold R. Patterson, Director of World Missions
David E. Ross, CEO

A denominational sending agency of Adventist tradition engaged in church planting, theological education, TEE, evangelism, and relief aid.

Year Founded in USA 1865
Income for Overseas Ministries . $ 718,320

Fully Supported USA Personnel Overseas:
Expecting to serve more than 4 years 6
Expecting to serve 1 up to 4 years 7
Other Personnel:
Non-USA serving in own/other country . . . 22
Short-Term less than 1 year from USA . . . 2
Home ministry & office staff in USA 2
Countries: China (PRC), Ghana, Honduras 2, India 2, Japan 5, Liberia, Malaysia, Mexico, New Zealand 2, Nigeria, Philippines 2.

Africa Evangelical Fellowship
(800)934-4176   Fax: (803)548-0885
E-Mail: Administration@aef-usa.com
P.O. Box 411167, Charlotte, NC 28241
Dr. Geoffrey W. Griffith, Exec. Director

An interdenominational sending agency of evangelical tradition engaged in support of national churches, church planting, theological education, evangelism, and medical work.

Year Founded in USA 1906
Income for Overseas Ministries $ 2,268,683
Fully Supported USA Personnel Overseas:
Expecting to serve more than 4 years 83
Expecting to serve 1 up to 4 years 10
Other Personnel:
Short-Term less than 1 year from USA . . . 24
Home ministry & office staff in USA 14
Countries: Angola 9, Botswana 9, Malawi 2, Mozambique 8, Namibia 2, Portugal 2, S Africa 17, Tanzania 2, Zambia 33, Zimbabwe 9.

Africa Inland Mission International
(914)735-4014   Fax: (914)735-1814
E-Mail: Info.AIM@aimint.org
Web: http://www.goshen.net/AIM/
P.O. Box 178, Pearl River, NY 10965
Dr. W. Ted Barnett, U.S. Director

An interdenominational sending agency of evangelical tradition engaged in church planting, theological education, evangelism, leadership development, and medical work.

"..to plant maturing churches .. through the evangelization of unreached people groups and the effective preparation of church leaders."

Year Founded in USA 1895
Income for Overseas Ministries $ 10,131,000
Fully Supported USA Personnel Overseas:
Expecting to serve more than 4 years . . . 393
Expecting to serve 1 up to 4 years 84
Nonresidential mission personnel 4
Other Personnel:

Short-Term less than 1 year from USA . . . 66
Home ministry & office staff in USA 62
Countries: Angola 2, Cen Africa Rep 4, Chad 3, Comoros Isls 9, Congo/Zaire 50, Kenya 312, Lesotho 9, Madagascar 4, Mozambique 21, Namibia 13, S Africa 1, Sudan 1, Tanzania 42, Uganda 6.

Africa Inter-Mennonite Mission
(219)875-5552   Fax: (219)875-6567
E-Mail: 473-3889@mcimail.com
59466 County Rd. 113, Elkhart, IN 46517
Rev. Garry Prieb, Exec. Secretary

A denominational sending agency of Mennonite tradition engaged in church planting, theological ed., leadership development, linguistics, support of national churches, and Bible translation.

".. to build His [Jesus Christ's] church in accordance with His purpose [and] demonstrate Christian love through service ministries."

Year Founded in USA 1912
Income for Overseas Ministries . $ 350,984
Fully Supported USA Personnel Overseas:
Expecting to serve more than 4 years 33
Expecting to serve 1 up to 4 years 3
Other Personnel:
Short-Term less than 1 year from USA . . . 22
Home ministry & office staff in USA 6
Countries: Botswana 10, Burkina Faso 18, Congo/Zaire 4, Lesotho 2, S Africa 2.

African Bible Colleges
(601)352-1791   Fax: (601)924-6353
P.O. Box 103, Clinton, MS 39060
Rev. William L. Mosal, U.S. Director

An interdenominational sending agency of Presbyterian and fundamentalist tradition engaged in Bible college training, correspondence courses, and evangelism.

".. to further evangelical Christian education through establishment and funding of Bible colleges in Africa and the acquisition of Christian teachers for African schools and colleges."

Year Founded in USA 1977
Income for Overseas Ministries . $ 646,754
Fully Supported USA Personnel Overseas:
Expecting to serve more than 4 years 16
Expecting to serve 1 up to 4 years 4
Other Personnel:
Home ministry & office staff in USA 1
Countries: Liberia 4, Malawi 16.

African Christian Mission

(217)948-5486   **Fax: (217)948-5415**
E-Mail: ACMEdBuell@aol.com
P.O. Box 530, Kansas, IL 61933
Edwin D. Buell, Exec. Director

A nondenominational sending agency of Christian (Restoration Movement) tradition engaged in church planting, TEE, leadership development, support of national churches, and Bible translation.

Year Founded in USA 1946
Income for Overseas Ministries . $ 853,206
Fully Supported USA Personnel Overseas:
  Expecting to serve more than 4 years 16
  Expecting to serve 1 up to 4 years 6
Other Personnel:
  Home ministry & office staff in USA 4
Countries: Africa 5, Ethiopia 1, Kenya 5, Mali 7, S Africa 2, Tanzania 2.

African Enterprise, Inc.

(626)357-8811   **Fax: (626)359-2069**
E-Mail: 74507.3114@compuserve.com
P.O. Box 727, Monrovia, CA 91016
Malcolm Graham, Exec. Director

An interdenominational sending agency of evangelical tradition engaged in evangelism, development, leadership development, relief aid, training, and youth programs.

"To evangelise the cities of Africa through Word & Deed in partnership with the Church."

Year Founded in USA 1962
Income for Overseas Ministries . $ 789,000
Fully Supported USA Personnel Overseas:
  Expecting to serve more than 4 years 4
Other Personnel:
  Non-USA serving in own/other country . . 120
  Short-Term less than 1 year from USA . . . 2
  Home ministry & office staff in USA 1
Countries: Ethiopia, Ghana, Kenya, Malawi, Rwanda, S Africa 4, Tanzania, Uganda, Zimbabwe.

African Leadership

(317)889-0456   **Fax: (317)882-8854**
E-Mail: MHAfrica@aol.com
P.O. Box 977, Greenwood, IN 46142
D. Michael Henderson, Director

A transdenominational support agency of evangelical tradition engaged in leadership development, church construction, Christian education, theological education, and TEE.

Year Founded in USA 1990
Income for Overseas Ministries . $ 220,000
Personnel:
  Home ministry & office staff in USA 12

African Methodist Episcopal Church, Dept. of Missions

(212)870-2258   **Fax: (212)870-2242**
P.O. Box 231, New York, NY 10027
Rev. James Blake, Exec. Secy/Treasurer

A denominational support agency of Methodist tradition engaged in Bible distribution, church construction, and childrens programs.

Year Founded in USA 1844
Income for Overseas Ministries . $ 500,000
Personnel:
  Short-Term less than 1 year from USA . . 275

African Methodist Episcopal Zion Church, Dept. of Overseas Msns.

(212)870-2952   **Fax: (212)870-2055**
475 Riverside Dr. Rm. 1935, New York, NY 10115
Rev. K. J. Degraffenreidt, Secretary

A denominational sending agency of Methodist tradition engaged in support of national workers, evangelism, and literature distribution. Statistical data from 1992.

Year Founded in USA 1875
Income for Overseas Ministries . $ 251,000
Fully Supported USA Personnel Overseas:
  Expecting to serve 1 up to 4 years 4
Countries: Ghana 1, Guyana 1, Jamaica 1, Liberia 1.

African Mission Evangelism

(423)579-1467   **Fax: (423)579-2337**
E-Mail: CBridges@ashley.jbc.edu
2313 Bell Dr., Knoxville, TN 37998
Dr. Carl Bridges, President

A nondenominational sending agency of Christian (Restoration Movement) tradition engaged in theological education, church planting, and leadership development.

Year Founded in USA 1968
Income for Overseas Ministries . . $ 85,690
Fully Supported USA Personnel Overseas:
  Expecting to serve more than 4 years 13

Other Personnel:

Non-USA serving in own/other country . . . 5
Short-Term less than 1 year from USA . . . 2

Countries: Ghana 13.

Agape Gospel Mission

(540)562-0322
E-Mail: 104072.747@compuserve.com
P.O. Box 11785, Roanoke, VA 24022
Rev. Rick Whitcomb, Intl. Director

An interdenominational support agency of charismatic tradition engaged in church planting, evangelism, leadership development, and training. Income total from 1992 report.

Year Founded in USA 1983
Income for Overseas Ministries . . $ 60,000
Personnel:

Non-USA serving in own/other country . . . 33
Short-Term less than 1 year from USA . . . 1
Home ministry & office staff in USA 1

Countries: Ghana, Liberia, Niger, Nigeria.

AIMS (Association of International Mission Services)

(757)579-5850   Fax: (757)579-5851
E-Mail: AIMS@cbn.org
P.O. Box 64534, Virginia Beach, VA 23464
Dr. Howard Foltz, President

A consortium of missions-focused churches, agencies, training institutions, vendors, and individuals working cooperatively to make a worldwide impact for Christ.

".. a catalyst to network churches, organizations and individuals in the Holy Spirit Renewal for completion of the Great Commission."

Year Founded in USA 1985
Income for Overseas Ministries . . . . NA

Alberto Mottesi Evangelistic Association

(714)375-0110
P.O. Box 2478, Huntington Bch., CA 92647
Alberto H. Mottesi, President

An interdenominational service agency of evangelical tradition engaged in evangelism, broadcasting, leadership development, and family restoration in 19 Spanish-speaking countries.

Year Founded in USA 1977

Income for Overseas Ministries . . . . NA
Personnel:

Home ministry & office staff in USA 6

Countries: Latin America.

All God's Children International

(503)282-7652   Fax: (503)282-2582
E-Mail: AGCI@aol.com
4114 NE Fremont St. #1, Portland, OR 97212
Ron Beazely, President

A nondenominational service agency of Pentecostal tradition engaged in childcare/adoption programs, literature distribution, providing medical supplies, and relief aid.

Year Founded in USA 1991
Income for Overseas Ministries . $ 568,000
Fully Supported USA Personnel Overseas:

Nonresidential mission personnel 2

Other Personnel:

Non-USA serving in own/other country . . . 5
Short-Term less than 1 year from USA . . . 4
Home ministry & office staff in USA 5

Countries: Bulgaria, China (PRC), Romania.

All Peoples Baptist Mission

(316)682-6545
E-Mail: WoodFBBC@aol.com
1156 N. Oliver St., Wichita, KS 67208
Rev. Richard Wood, Missions Pastor

A denominational support agency of Baptist tradition engaged in funds transmission for closely affiliated missionaries involved in church planting and evangelism. Financial and personnel information from 1992.

Year Founded in USA 1980
Income for Overseas Ministries . $ 278,697
Fully Supported USA Personnel Overseas:

Expecting to serve more than 4 years 8
Expecting to serve 1 up to 4 years 2

Other Personnel:

Bivocational/Tentmaker from USA 1
Short-Term less than 1 year from USA . . . 9

Countries: El Salvador 2, Germany 2, Mexico 6.

Allegheny Wesleyan Methodist Missions

(330)332-0696   Fax: (330)337-9700
E-Mail: AWMC@juno.com
P.O. Box 357, Salem, OH 44460
Rev. William M. Cope, Director

A denominational sending agency of Wesleyan-Arminian and Holiness tradition engaged in evangelism, Bible and literature distribution, church planting, and Christian education.

Year Founded in USA	1969
Income for Overseas Ministries .	$ 215,000

Fully Supported USA Personnel Overseas:

Expecting to serve more than 4 years	14

Other Personnel:

Short-Term less than 1 year from USA . . .	12
Home ministry & office staff in USA	2

Countries: Haiti 9, Peru 2, Ukraine 3.

ALM International

(864)271-7040   **Fax: (864)271-7062**
E-Mail: AmLep@leprosy.org
Web: http://www.leprosy.org
1 ALM Way, Greenville, SC 29601
Mr. Christopher J. Doyle, President

A nondenominational specialized service agency of evangelical tradition engaged in medical work, development, and specialized missionary training. Financial and personnel information from 1992.

Year Founded in USA	1917
Income for Overseas Ministries	$ 4,454,468
Amount of Gifts-In-Kind	$ 19,032

Fully Supported USA Personnel Overseas:

Expecting to serve 1 up to 4 years	3
Nonresidential mission personnel	2

Other Personnel:

Short-Term less than 1 year from USA . . .	2
Home ministry & office staff in USA	30

Countries: Brazil 1, Liberia 2.

Ambassadors for Christ Intl.

(770)980-2020   **Fax: (980)956-8144**
E-Mail: 73440.127@compuserve.com
1355 Terrell Mill Rd. #1484, Marietta, GA 30067
Rev. Allan Gardner, Intl. Director

A nondenominational support agency of evangelical tradition engaged in funds transmission for national worker training and evangelism.

"..to help fulfill the Great Commission through support of national preaching ministries."

Year Founded in USA	1972
Income for Overseas Ministries .	$ 624,747

Personnel:

Non-USA serving in own/other country . .	119
Home ministry & office staff in USA	6

Countries: Dominica, Egypt, Fiji, Ghana, Guadeloupe, India, Indonesia, Kenya, Myanmar/Burma, Nigeria, Pakistan, Philippines, S Africa, Singapore, Spain, St Vincent, Sudan, Tonga, UK, Zambia.

Ambassadors for Christ, Inc.

(717)687-8564   **Fax: (717)687-8891**
E-Mail: AFC@afcinc.org
Web: http://www.idsonline.com/afc/
P.O. Box 0280, Paradise, PA 17562
Ron Harper, Jr., Development Manager

An interdenominational support agency of evangelical tradition engaged in student evangelism and mobilization for mission.

Year Founded in USA	1963
Income for Overseas Ministries	NA

Personnel:

Home ministry & office staff in USA	22

American Association of Lutheran Churches - Commission for World Missions

(520)287-7042
E-Mail: Esco3229@aol.com
10800 Lyndale S., #120, Minneapolis, MN 55420
Rev. Louis A. Escobedo, Chair

A denominational agency of Lutheran tradition supporting evangelism and agricultural programs.

Year Founded in USA	1987
Income for Overseas Ministries . .	$ 62,000

American Baptist Association Missionary Committee

(903)792-2312   **Fax: (903)794-1290**
Web: http://www.abaptist.org/
P.O. Box 1050, Texarkana, TX 75504
Randy Cloud, Secretary/Treasurer

A denominational support agency of Baptist tradition engaged in evangelism and church planting. Statistical information from 1992.

Year Founded in USA	1924
Income for Overseas Ministries .	$ 450,000

Fully Supported USA Personnel Overseas:

Expecting to serve more than 4 years	16

Countries: Am Samoa 2, Australia 1, Colombia 1, Costa Rica 3, France 1, Germany 1, Japan 1, Kenya 3, New Zealand 2, Solomon Isls 1.

American Baptist Churches in the U.S.A., International Ministries

(610)768-2201   **Fax: (610)768-2088**
E-Mail: 102262.713@compuserve.com
Web: http://www.abc-usa.org/
P.O. Box 851, Valley Forge, PA 19482
Dr. John A. Sundquist, Exec. Director

A denominational sending board of Baptist tradition engaged in support of national churches, development, theological education, evangelism, leadership development, and medical work.

Year Founded in USA 1814
Income for Overseas Ministries $ 14,217,311
Fully Supported USA Personnel Overseas:
    Expecting to serve more than 4 years . . . 107
    Expecting to serve 1 up to 4 years 8
    Nonresidential mission personnel 2
Other Personnel:
    Non-USA serving in own/other country . . . 8
    Bivocational/Tentmaker from USA 2
    Short-Term less than 1 year from USA . . . 82
    Home ministry & office staff in USA 44
Countries: Austria 2, Bangladesh 1, Bolivia 5, Chile 2, China (PRC) 1, Congo/Zaire 13, Costa Rica 2, Czech Rep 2, Dominican Rep 3, El Salvador 1, Haiti 14, Hong Kong 2, India 8, Japan 12, Mexico 6, Nicaragua 7, Philippines 3, Russia 2, S Africa 2, Thailand 27.

American Bible Society

(212)408-1200   **Fax: (212)408-1512**
E-Mail: mmaus@americanbible.org
Web: http://www.americanbible.org
1865 Broadway, New York, NY 10023
Dr. Eugene B. Habecker, President

An interdenominational specialized service agency engaged in Scripture translation, publication and distribution in fellowship with 135 members of the United Bible Societies and other Bible agencies distributing Scriptures in approximately 200 countries and territories.

".. to provide the Holy Scriptures to every man, woman and child in a language and form each can readily understand, and at a price each can easily afford."

Year Founded in USA 1816
Income for Overseas Ministries $ 25,800,000

American Missionary Fellowship

(610)527-4439   **Fax: (610)527-4720**
E-Mail: AMFGerhart@aol.com
Web: http://www.sonic.net/~mfergie/amf/
P.O. Box 368, Villanova, PA 19085
Dr. Donald C. Palmer, Gen. Director

A nondenominational support agency of evangelical tradition with 55 missionaries engaged in cross-cultural ministry of church planting and other activities in North America.

".. seeking to evangelize, disciple, and congregate the yet unreached peoples of the U.S..."

Year Founded in USA 1817
Income for Overseas Ministries . . . . NA
Personnel:
    Home ministry & office staff in USA 74

American Tract Society

(972)276-9408   **Fax: (972)272-9642**
E-Mail: 72672.770@compuserve.com
Web: www.goshen.net/AmericanTractSociety/
P.O. Box 462008, Garland, TX 75046
Mr. Douglas Salser, Sr. Vice President

An interdenominational service agency of independent tradition engaged in literature publication/distribution through individuals, churches and mission groups. Income report from 1992.

Year Founded in USA 1825
Income for Overseas Ministries . . $ 41,000
Personnel:
    Home ministry & office staff in USA 28

American Waldensian Society

(610)432-9569   **Fax: (610)432-9518**
E-Mail: Waldensi@ptd.net
183 Shiloh Ct., Whitehall, PA 18052
Revs. Ruth & Edward Santana-Grace, Co-Dirs.

An interdenominational support agency of ecumenical tradition engaged in support of national churches, and literature production.

Year Founded in USA 1906
Income for Overseas Ministries . $ 407,444
Personnel:
    Short-Term less than 1 year from USA . . . 30
    Home ministry & office staff in USA 3
Countries: Argentina, Italy, Uruguay.

AmeriTribes

(520)526-0875   Fax: (520)526-0872
E-Mail: Challeng@ameritribes.org
Web: http://www.ameritribes.org/ask/
P.O. Box 3717, Flagstaff, AZ 86003
Timothy C. Brown, Exec. Director

An interdenominational support agency of evangelical tradition engaged in church planting, providing medical supplies, and support of national workers with most of the work in the USA.

".. to establish and strengthen clusters of viable, reproducing, indigenous churches within .. unreached Indian tribes in the Americas..."

Year Founded in USA	1944
Income for Overseas Ministries . .	$ 15,750

Personnel:

Non-USA serving in own/other country . . .	6
Home ministry & office staff in USA	2

Countries: Mexico.

AMF International

(708)418-0020   Fax: (708)418-0132
E-Mail: 103752.1361@compuserve.com
Web: http://www.goshen.net/amf/
P.O. Box 5470, Lansing, IL 60438
Mr. Wesley N. Taber, Exec. Director

An interdenominational sending agency of evangelical tradition engaged in evangelism, literature distribution, and training focused on Jewish outreach.

Year Founded in USA	1887
Income for Overseas Ministries .	$ 116,300

Fully Supported USA Personnel Overseas:

Expecting to serve more than 4 years	2

Other Personnel:

Non-USA serving in own/other country . . .	4
Short-Term less than 1 year from USA . . .	16
Home ministry & office staff in USA	28

Countries: Israel 2, Mexico.

AMG International

(423)894-6060   Fax: (423)894-6863
E-Mail: AMGIntl@aol.com
Web: http://www.goshen.net/amg/
P.O. Box 22000, Chattanooga, TN 37422
Dr. Spiros Zodhiates, President

An interdenominational sending agency of evangelical tradition engaged in Bible distribution, church planting, childrens programs, correspondence courses, theological education, and support of national workers.

Year Founded in USA	1942
Income for Overseas Ministries	$ 2,053,000

Fully Supported USA Personnel Overseas:

Expecting to serve more than 4 years	25

Other Personnel:

Non-USA serving in own/other country . .	613
Bivocational/Tentmaker from USA	3
Short-Term less than 1 year from USA . . .	30
Home ministry & office staff in USA	20

Countries: Albania 2, Bahamas 2, Bulgaria, Cyprus 4, Greece 2, Guatemala 2, India, Indonesia, Mexico 4, Peru 2, Philippines, Romania, Russia, Spain 7, Sri Lanka, Thailand, Uganda.

AMOR Ministries

(619)662-1200   Fax: (619)662-1295
1664 Precision Park Lane, San Diego, CA 92713
Scott & Gayla Congdon, Presidents/Founders

A nondenominational sending agency of evangelical tradition engaged in development, church construction, short-term programs, and training.

Year Founded in USA	1980
Income for Overseas Ministries	$ 1,118,379

Fully Supported USA Personnel Overseas:

Expecting to serve more than 4 years	11

Other Personnel:

Non-USA serving in own/other country . . .	5
Short-Term less than 1 year from USA . . .	16
Home ministry & office staff in USA	7

Countries: Mexico 11.

Anglican Frontier Missions

(804)355-8468   Fax: (804)355-8260
E-Mail: AFM@xc.org
Web: http://www.episcopalian.org/afm/
P.O. Box 18024, Richmond, VA 23226
Rev. E. A. de Bordenave, Director

A denominational sending agency of Anglican and ecumenical tradition engaged in evangelism and church planting.

Year Founded in USA	1993
Income for Overseas Ministries .	$ 130,000

Fully Supported USA Personnel Overseas:

Expecting to serve more than 4 years	15

Countries: Asia 6, China (PRC) 5, Nepal 2, Singapore 2.

Countries: Australia 2, Brazil 23, Japan 2, Mexico 1, Papua New Guin 9, Paraguay 1, Puerto Rico 2.

Anglican Orthodox Church

(704)873-8365   Fax: (704)873-8948
P.O. Box 128, Statesville, NC 28687
Bishop Robert J. Godfrey, Exec. Officer

A denominational support agency of Anglican tradition engaged in support of national church workers, Christian education, and evangelism.

Year Founded in USA 1963
Income for Overseas Ministries . . . . NR
Personnel:
    Non-USA serving in own/other country . . . 11
    Home ministry & office staff in USA 6
Countries: Fiji, India, Japan, Kenya, Liberia, Madagascar, Pakistan, Philippines.

Anis Shorrosh Evangelistic Association, Inc.

(334)626-1124   Fax: (334)621-0507
P.O. Box 7577, Spanish Fort, AL 36577
Dr. Anis Shorrosh, Evangelist

An interdenominational support agency of Baptist and evangelical tradition engaged in evangelism and literature distribution.

Year Founded in USA 1970
Income for Overseas Ministries . . $ 24,000
Personnel:
    Short-Term less than 1 year from USA . . . 14
    Home ministry & office staff in USA 3

Apostolic Christian Church Foundation, Inc.

(314)821-1866   Fax: (314)821-1865
E-Mail: Custer@mo.net
620 Meadowridge Lane, St. Louis, MO 63122
Ted Custer, Missionary Committee Chair
Jimmy Hodges, Exec. Director

A denominational sending agency of Ana-baptist tradition engaged in funds transmission, church construction, support of national workers, and relief aid. Statistical information from 1992.

Year Founded in USA 1953
Income for Overseas Ministries . $ 507,974
Fully Supported USA Personnel Overseas:
    Expecting to serve more than 4 years 36
    Expecting to serve 1 up to 4 years 4
Other Personnel:
    Short-Term less than 1 year from USA . . . 45
    Home ministry & office staff in USA 2

Apostolic Team Ministries, Intl.

(419)867-3645   Fax: (419)865-5468
6045 W. Bancroft St., Toledo, OH 43615
Mr. Ronald G. King, Admin. Director

A nondenominational support agency of charismatic tradition engaged in church planting and missionary training. Statistics from 1992.

Year Founded in USA 1980
Income for Overseas Ministries . . $ 50,000
Fully Supported USA Personnel Overseas:
    Expecting to serve more than 4 years 4
    Expecting to serve 1 up to 4 years 3
Other Personnel:
    Home ministry & office staff in USA 3
Countries: Bolivia 2, France 2, Mexico 1, UK 2.

Arab World Ministries

(800)447-3566   Fax: (610)352-2652
Web: http://www.awm.com
P.O. Box 96, Upper Darby, PA 19082
Rev. Dennis Brice, Candidate Director
Mr. William D. Bell, Assoc. Director

A nondenominational sending agency of evangelical tradition engaged in evangelism, broadcasting, correspondence courses, TEE, and literature distribution.

Year Founded in USA 1952
Income for Overseas Ministries . $ 3,346,215
Fully Supported USA Personnel Overseas:
    Expecting to serve more than 4 years . . . 137
Other Personnel:
    Bivocational/Tentmaker from USA 30
    Short-Term less than 1 year from USA . . . 27
    Home ministry & office staff in USA 15
Countries: Africa 29, Asia 20, Egypt 9, France 39, Germany 3, Israel 4, Jordan 14, Spain 4, UK 15.

Arabic Communication Center

(626)291-2866   Fax: (626)286-3149
E-Mail: 74224.1634@compuserve.com
P.O. Box 1124, Temple City, CA 91780
Dr. Hisham S. Kamel, President

A nondenominational service agency of Presbyterian and Reformed tradition engaged in radio and TV broadcasting, evangelism, and literature production.

Year Founded in USA	1992
Income for Overseas Ministries . .	$ 20,000
Amount of Gifts-In-Kind	$ 9,000

Personnel:
Home ministry & office staff in USA 4

ARISE International

(301)613-2180   Fax: (301)598-4839
E-Mail: CKim@capaccess.org
P.O. Box 3221, Silver Spring, MD 20918
Rev. C. Daniel Kim, Director

A nondenominational support agency of evangelical tradition engaged in mobilization for mission, and support of national workers.

Year Founded in USA	1990
Income for Overseas Ministries . .	$ 50,000
Amount of Gifts-In-Kind	$ 7,000

Personnel:
Non-USA serving in own/other country . . . 3
Short-Term less than 1 year from USA . . . 5
Home ministry & office staff in USA 2
Countries: Ghana, India, Japan, Niger, Uzbekistan.

Armenian Missionary Association of America, Inc.

(201)265-2607   Fax: (201)265-6015
140 Forest Ave., Paramus, NJ 07652
The Rev. Moses B. Janbazian, Exec. Director

A nondenominational service agency of evangelical tradition engaged in orphanage programs, Bible distribution, camping programs, church construction, and theological education.

Year Founded in USA	1918
Income for Overseas Ministries	$ 1,200,000
Amount of Gifts-In-Kind . . .	$ 120,000

Fully Supported USA Personnel Overseas:
Nonresidential mission personnel 2
Other Personnel:
Non-USA serving in own/other country . . . 31
Short-Term less than 1 year from USA . . . 60
Home ministry & office staff in USA 13
Countries: Armenia.

Artists In Christian Testimony

(615)591-2598   Fax: (615)591-2599
E-Mail: 105222.3223@compuserve.com
Box 395, Franklin, TN 37065
Rev. Byron L. Spradlin, Director

An interdenominational support agency of evangelical tradition engaged in mission mobilization and training with other agencies.

"Discovering & developing Christian communicators -many from music and arts backgrounds- who will lead the Church into evangelism and worship appropriate to the communities around them."

Year Founded in USA	1973
Income for Overseas Ministries . .	$ 50,000

Personnel:
Short-Term less than 1 year from USA . . . 10
Home ministry & office staff in USA 5

Asian Outreach U.S.A.

(714)557-2742   Fax: (714)557-2742
E-Mail: JR2135@aol.com
3941 S. Bristol St. #67, Santa Ana, CA 92704
Rev. James R. Swanson, Exec. Director

An interdenominational support agency of evangelical tradition engaged in literature distribution, Bible distribution, broadcasting, literature production, and support of national churches.

Year Founded in USA	1960
Income for Overseas Ministries	$ 1,078,000
Amount of Gifts-In-Kind . . .	$ 1,000,000

Fully Supported USA Personnel Overseas:
Expecting to serve more than 4 years 1
Expecting to serve 1 up to 4 years 5
Other Personnel:
Non-USA serving in own/other country . . . 3
Short-Term less than 1 year from USA . . . 8
Home ministry & office staff in USA 1
Countries: Asia 2, Hong Kong 3, Japan 1, Mongolia.

Assemblies of God, Gen. Council Division of Foreign Missions

(417)862-2781   Fax: (417)862-0978
E-Mail: DFM@ag.org
Web: http://www.ag.org/
1445 Boonville Ave., Springfield, MO 65802
Rev. Loren Triplett, Exec. Director

A denominational sending agency of Pentecostal tradition engaged in church planting, correspondence courses, theological education, literature production, and video/film production and distribution.

".. to .. evangelize the spiritually lost .. establish indigenous churches .. train national believers .. show compassion for the suffering..."

Year Founded in USA 1914
Income for Overseas Ministries $ 113,357,227
Fully Supported USA Personnel Overseas:
 Expecting to serve more than 4 years . . 1,569
 Expecting to serve 1 up to 4 years 192
Other Personnel:
 Short-Term less than 1 year from USA . . 2,746
 Home ministry & office staff in USA . . . 103

Countries: Africa 64, Albania 10, Am Samoa 2, Angola 4, Argentina 20, Asia 137, Austria 6, Bahamas 6, Belau(Palau) 2, Belgium 19, Belize 8, Benin 4, Bolivia 16, Bosnia, Botswana 4, Brazil 15, Burkina Faso 10, Cambodia 20, Cameroon 4, Canary Isls 10, Caribbean Isls 10, Cayman Isls 2, Central Asia 16, Chile 29, Colombia 25, Congo 6, Congo/Zaire 12, Costa Rica 27, Cote d'Ivoire 2, Croatia 5, Czech Rep 6, Dominican Rep 11, Ecuador 20, El Salvador 12, Equat Guinea 9, Ethiopia 8, Europe 153, Fiji 8, France 11, Germany 35, Ghana 4, Greece 10, Greenland, Guam 3, Guatemala 11, Guinea Bissau 4, Guyana 2, Haiti 4, Honduras 17, Hong Kong 26, Hungary 4, Iceland 2, Indonesia 34, Ireland 6, Italy 4, Jamaica 14, Japan 42, Kenya 29, Korea-S 5, Laos 3, Latin America 51, Lesotho 2, Liberia 8, Luxembourg 2, Madagascar 6, Malawi 10, Malaysia 2, Mali 8, Malta 2, Marshall Isls 5, Mexico 68, Mongolia 14, Mozambique 8, Namibia 4, Netherlands 4, New Caledonia 2, Nicaragua 8, Niger 6, Nigeria 8, Oceania 4, Panama 10, Paraguay 23, Peru 13, Philippines 54, Portugal 11, Romania 12, Rwanda 2, S Africa 28, Senegal 10, Sierra Leone 2, Singapore 15, Slovakia 4, Slovenia 4, Solomon Isls 4, Spain 33, Sudan 2, Suriname 2, Swaziland 10, Taiwan (ROC) 13, Tanzania 16, Thailand 26, Togo 11, Tonga 2, Unspecified 192, Uruguay 14, Vanuatu 4, Venezuela 17, Vietnam 9, Zimbabwe 4.

ASSIST - Aid to Special Saints in Strategic Times

(714)530-6598 **Fax: (714)636-7351**
E-Mail: 74152.337@compuserve.com
P.O. Box 2126, Garden Grove, CA 92642
Dan Wooding, President

A nondenominational service agency of evangelical tradition engaged in mission information services and Bible/literature distribution.

".. encourages and supports believers who, for religious, political, or economic reasons, are unable to worship and witness freely for their faith."

Year Founded in USA 1989
Income for Overseas Ministries . . $ 27,000

Fully Supported USA Personnel Overseas:
 Nonresidential mission personnel 1
Other Personnel:
 Short-Term less than 1 year from USA . . . 6
 Home ministry & office staff in USA 2

Associate Reformed Presbyterian Church - World Witness
See: World Witness

Association of Baptists for World Evangelism
See: ABWE

Association of Free Lutheran Congregations World Missions

(612)545-6472 **Fax: (612)545-0079**
E-Mail: HQmail@aflc.org
Web: http://www.Minn.Net/aflc.org/worldmis.html
3110 E Medicine Lk. Blvd, Minneapolis, MN 55441
Rev. Eugene Enderlein, Missions Director

A denominational sending agency of Lutheran and evangelical tradition engaged in church planting, childcare/orphanage programs, Christian education, theological education, and support of national churches and workers.

Year Founded in USA 1963
Income for Overseas Ministries . $ 482,454
Fully Supported USA Personnel Overseas:
 Expecting to serve more than 4 years 17
Other Personnel:
 Non-USA serving in own/other country . . . 45
 Short-Term less than 1 year from USA . . . 59
 Home ministry & office staff in USA 2

Countries: Brazil 9, Czech Rep 2, India, Mexico 6.

Association of International Mission Services
See: AIMS

Audio Scripture Ministries

(616)396-5291 **Fax: (616)396-5294**
E-Mail: ASM-MI@xc.org
Web: http://www.goshen.net/AudioScriptures/
760 Waverly Rd., Holland, MI 49423
Ron Berry, President

An interdenominational specialized service agency of Reformed and evangelical tradition engaged in audio recording/distribution in over 150 languages. Previously know as PRM International and Audio Scriptures International.

Year Founded in USA 1989
Income for Overseas Ministries . . . . NR
Personnel:
Home ministry & office staff in USA 2

Back to the Bible International
(402)464-7200   Fax: (402)464-7474
E-Mail: Info@backtothebible.org
Web: http://www.backtothebible.org/
P.O. Box 82808, Lincoln, NE 68501
Dr. Woodrow Kroll, President

A nondenominational service agency of evangelical tradition engaged in broadcasting, audio recording/distribution, funds transmission, literature production/distribution, and support of national workers.

".. to lead believers into spiritual maturity and active service .. and to reach unbelievers with the Gospel .. by teaching the Bible through media."

Year Founded in USA 1939
Income for Overseas Ministries $ 1,897,213
Personnel:
Non-USA serving in own/other country . . 127
Home ministry & office staff in USA . . . 111
Countries: Australia, Ecuador, India, Italy, Jamaica, Philippines, Poland, Sri Lanka, UK.

BALL World Missions
(314)789-4368   Fax: (314)797-2266
E-Mail: 74347.420@compuserve.com
4450 Outreach Dr., Hillsboro, MO 63050
Rev. Norman L. Knudsen, Exec. Director

An interdenominational sending agency of charismatic and evangelical tradition engaged in evangelism, church planting, literature distribution, and support of national workers. Financial and personnel information from 1992.

Year Founded in USA 1973
Income for Overseas Ministries . $ 878,433
Fully Supported USA Personnel Overseas:
Expecting to serve more than 4 years 2
Expecting to serve 1 up to 4 years 8
Nonresidential mission personnel 4
Other Personnel:

Short-Term less than 1 year from USA . . . 41
Home ministry & office staff in USA 7
Countries: Guatemala 4, Hong Kong 2, Kenya 4.

Baptist Bible Fellowship Intl.
(417)862-5001   Fax: (417)865-0794
E-Mail: 76043.2702@compuserve.com
Web: http://www.bbfi.org/
P.O. Box 191, Springfield, MO 65801
Dr. Bob Baird, Mission Director

An independent sending agency of Baptist tradition engaged in church planting, theological education, evangelism, support of national churches, and missionary training.

Year Founded in USA 1950
Income for Overseas Ministries $ 22,531,653
Fully Supported USA Personnel Overseas:
Expecting to serve more than 4 years . . . 755
Other Personnel:
Home ministry & office staff in USA 49
Countries: Albania 2, Argentina 26, Australia 35, Azores 2, Belgium 6, Belize 6, Bolivia 2, Brazil 37, Bulgaria 2, Burkina Faso 2, Canary Isls 1, Chile 19, China (PRC) 2, Colombia 4, Congo/Zaire 8, Costa Rica 16, Cote d'Ivoire 4, Cuba 2, Dominican Rep 2, Ecuador 14, Ethiopia 6, Fiji 2, Fr Polynesia 2, France 8, Georgia 2, Germany 24, Greece 2, Guyana 4, Haiti 3, Honduras 1, Hong Kong 11, Hungary 10, India 7, Indonesia 6, Ireland 6, Italy 2, Jamaica 8, Japan 26, Kenya 41, Korea-S 21, Lithuania 4, Malta 2, Mexico 62, Micronesia 2, Netherlands 2, New Zealand 12, Nigeria 4, Pakistan 4, Panama 9, Papua New Guin 16, Paraguay 6, Peru 11, Philippines 52, Portugal 4, Puerto Rico 6, Romania 14, Russia 14, S Africa 18, Singapore 4, Spain 18, Sri Lanka 2, Switzerland 2, Taiwan (ROC) 14, Tanzania 14, Thailand 8, UK 46, Uganda 2, Uruguay 2, Venezuela 4, Zambia 13.

Baptist Faith Missions
(614)532-8747
51 County Rd. #7, Ironton, OH 45638
Pastor Jim Orrick, Exec. Secretary

A denominational sending agency of Baptist tradition engaged in church planting, camping programs, Christian education, and evangelism. Income total from 1992 report.

Year Founded in USA 1923
Income for Overseas Ministries . $ 535,000
Fully Supported USA Personnel Overseas:
Expecting to serve more than 4 years 20
Expecting to serve 1 up to 4 years 2

Countries: Brazil 18, Kenya 2, Peru 2.

Baptist General Conference, Church Planting and Enrichment

(847)228-0200   **Fax: (847)228-5376**
Web: http://www.bgc.bethel.edu/
2002 S. Arlington Hts. Rd, Arlington Hts., IL 60193
Bob Ricker, President
Ron Larson, VP C.P.   John Dickau, VP C.E.

A denominational sending agency of Baptist and evangelical tradition engaged in church planting, extension education, theological education, evangelism, leadership development, and support of national churches.

".. helping member churches fulfill Christ's mission for His church in all communities God calls them to serve."

Year Founded in USA 1944
Income for Overseas Ministries $ 6,503,300
Fully Supported USA Personnel Overseas:
   Expecting to serve more than 4 years . . . 104
   Expecting to serve 1 up to 4 years 6
Other Personnel:
   Non-USA serving in own/other country . . . 5
   Short-Term less than 1 year from USA . . . 30
   Home ministry & office staff in USA 9
Countries: Argentina 14, Asia 2, Brazil 8, Bulgaria 1, Cameroon 7, Central Asia 2, Cote d'Ivoire 8, Ethiopia 5, France 5, India, Japan 16, Mexico 13, Philippines 20, Slovakia 2, Thailand 3, Uruguay 4.

Baptist International Missions

(423)344-5050   **Fax: (423)344-4774**
E-Mail: 73122.1321@compuserve.com
P.O. Box 9215, Chattanooga, TN 37412
Dr. Don Sisk, President/Gen. Director

An independent Baptist sending agency of fundamental tradition engaged in church planting, Bible distribution, broadcasting, correspondence courses, theological education, and literature distribution.

Year Founded in USA 1960
Income for Overseas Ministries $ 17,000,000
Fully Supported USA Personnel Overseas:
   Expecting to serve more than 4 years . . . 530
   Expecting to serve 1 up to 4 years 2
Other Personnel:
   Non-USA serving in own/other country . . . 28
   Short-Term less than 1 year from USA . . . 48
   Home ministry & office staff in USA 30

Countries: Albania 2, Anguilla 2, Antigua 6, Argentina 6, Australia 21, Austria 4, Bahamas 7, Belarus 3, Belgium 2, Bolivia 5, Brazil 36, Cambodia 2, Cayman Isls 6, Chile 2, China (PRC) 12, Colombia 4, Costa Rica 8, Cote d'Ivoire 14, Cuba, Czech Rep 2, Dominican Rep 12, Ecuador 5, Fiji 4, France 4, Germany 8, Ghana, Grenada 2, Guatemala 5, Guyana 1, Haiti 4, Honduras 10, Hungary 4, India 2, Indonesia 2, Ireland 14, Italy 1, Jamaica 4, Japan 35, Kenya 6, Liberia, Malawi 4, Mexico 44, Micronesia 4, Moldava 2, New Caledonia 2, New Zealand 4, Nicaragua 2, Niger 2, Nigeria 12, Norway 1, Panama 2, Papua New Guin 10, Peru 9, Philippines 32, Poland 2, Puerto Rico 16, Romania 10, Russia 22, S Africa 15, Senegal 4, Singapore 4, Spain 4, St Chris-Nevis 2, Thailand 2, Trinidad & Tobg, UK 26, Uganda 10, Ukraine 2, Venezuela 10, Virgin Isls USA 6.

Baptist Mid-Missions

(216)826-3930   **Fax: (216)826-4457**
E-Mail: Info@bmm.org
P.O. Box 308011, Cleveland, OH 44130
Dr. Gary L. Anderson, President

An independent sending agency of Baptist and fundamentalist tradition engaged in church planting, camping programs, correspondence courses, theological education, evangelism, literature production, literacy work, and Bible translation.

Year Founded in USA 1920
Income for Overseas Ministries $ 18,000,000
Fully Supported USA Personnel Overseas:
   Expecting to serve more than 4 years . . . 606
   Nonresidential mission personnel 8
Other Personnel:
   Non-USA serving in own/other country . . . 21
   Short-Term less than 1 year from USA . . . 90
   Home ministry & office staff in USA . . . 314
Countries: Argentina 4, Australia 22, Austria 2, Bangladesh 3, Belarus 2, Brazil 177, Cen Africa Rep 41, Chad 6, Chile 6, China (PRC) 4, Cote d'Ivoire 8, Cuba 2, Ecuador 15, Ethiopia 1, Finland 2, France 26, Germany 19, Ghana 18, Guyana 8, Haiti 11, Honduras 8, Hong Kong 1, India 6, Ireland 6, Italy 6, Jamaica 2, Japan 26, Liberia 17, Mexico 20, Micronesia 4, Netherlands 6, New Zealand 8, Peru 34, Poland 2, Puerto Rico 6, Romania 2, Russia 9, Singapore 4, Slovakia 4, Spain 8, St Vincent 7, Taiwan (ROC) 6, UK 18, Venezuela 5, Vietnam 2, Zambia 10, Zimbabwe 2.

Baptist Missionary Association of America

(501)455-4977   **Fax: (501)455-3636**
P.O. Box 193920, Little Rock, AR 72219
Rev. Don Collins, Exec. Director

A denominational sending agency of Baptist tradition engaged in church planting, Bible distribution, theological education, and evangelism. Income and personnel totals from 1992 report.

Year Founded in USA 1950
Income for Overseas Ministries $ 2,100,000
Fully Supported USA Personnel Overseas:
Expecting to serve more than 4 years 28
Countries: Bolivia 3, Brazil 2, Costa Rica 2, Czech Rep 1, Guatemala 3, Honduras 4, Japan 1, Mexico 5, Philippines 5, Taiwan (ROC) 1, Uruguay 1.

Baptist Missions to Forgotten Peoples

(904)783-4007   **Fax: (904)783-0402**
E-Mail: 102077.274@compuserve.com
Web: http://www.wrldnet.net/~parson/bmfp.html
P.O. Box 37043, Jacksonville, FL 32236
Dr. Gene Burge, Exec. Director

A nondenominational sending agency of Baptist tradition engaged in church planting and evangelism.

".. to serve the local church by providing a faith-missions ministry committed to strategic church planting .. among the unevangelized people groups of the world."

Income for Overseas Ministries . . . . NA
Fully Supported USA Personnel Overseas:
Expecting to serve more than 4 years 44
Countries: Azores 2, Colombia 2, Europe-E 4, Germany 11, Grenada 2, Iceland 2, Italy 2, Mexico 2, Nigeria 2, Philippines 2, Romania 2, Russia 3, S Africa 2, Trinidad & Tobg 2, UK 2, Ukraine 2.

Baptist World Mission

(205)353-2221   **Fax: (205)353-2266**
E-Mail: 103273.3262@compuserve.com
P.O. Box 1463, Decatur, AL 35602
Dr. Fred Moritz, Exec. Director

An independent sending agency of Baptist and fundamental tradition engaged in church planting, theological ed., evangelism, and national churches support. Personnel totals from 1992.

Year Founded in USA 1961
Income for Overseas Ministries $ 4,400,000
Fully Supported USA Personnel Overseas:
Expecting to serve more than 4 years . . . 150
Other Personnel:

Short-Term less than 1 year from USA . . . 10
Home ministry & office staff in USA 10
Countries: Africa 7, Argentina 4, Australia 10, Brazil 13, Europe-E 17, France 6, Haiti 4, Hungary 2, India 2, Ireland 2, Israel 4, Italy 2, Japan 14, Korea-S 2, Latin America 4, Mexico 13, Myanmar/Burma 2, New Zealand 3, Nigeria 2, Papua New Guin 2, Portugal 2, Puerto Rico 4, Romania 2, Singapore 2, Spain 4, Thailand 4, UK 12, Uruguay 5.

Barnabas International

(815)395-1335   **Fax: (815)395-1385**
E-Mail: Barnabas_Int@compuserve.com
Web: http://www.barnabas.org/
P.O. Box 11211, Rockford, IL 61126
Dr. Lareau Lindquist, Exec. Director

A nondenominational sending agency of evangelical tradition engaged in missionary pastoral care, leadership development, support of national churches, and psychological counseling.

".. to edify, enrich, encourage, and strengthen [missionaries, pastors, national church leaders and their families] ... through personal, small group, and conference ministries."

Year Founded in USA 1986
Income for Overseas Ministries . $ 330,830
Fully Supported USA Personnel Overseas:
Expecting to serve more than 4 years 4
Nonresidential mission personnel 12
Other Personnel:
Short-Term less than 1 year from USA . . . 7
Home ministry & office staff in USA 2
Countries: Philippines 2, Ukraine 2.

Barnabas Ministries, Inc.

(209)526-8872
P.O. Box 578892, Modesto, CA 95357
Raymond E. Benson, M.D., President

An interdenominational support agency of evangelical tradition engaged in evangelism, orphanage and childrens programs, Christian education, and medical work.

Year Founded in USA 1993
Income for Overseas Ministries . . $ 22,500
Personnel:
Non-USA serving in own/other country . . . 8
Short-Term less than 1 year from USA . . . 4
Home ministry & office staff in USA 1
Countries: Haiti.

BCM International

(610)352-7177   Fax: (610)352-5561
E-Mail: 103046.613@compuserve.com
237 Fairfield Ave., Upper Darby, PA 19082
Rev. Thomas R. Koch, Gen. Director

An interdenominational sending agency of
evangelical tradition engaged in Christian
education, camping programs, evangelism,
literature production, and missionary training.

".. making disciples of all age groups .. so that
churches may be strengthened and/or established"

Year Founded in USA	1936
Income for Overseas Ministries	$ 3,075,012

Fully Supported USA Personnel Overseas:
Expecting to serve more than 4 years   30
Expecting to serve 1 up to 4 years   9
Nonresidential mission personnel   26
Other Personnel:
Non-USA serving in own/other country   . . 366
Short-Term less than 1 year from USA   . . . 20
Home ministry & office staff in USA   49

Countries: Africa, Argentina, Asia, Australia, Austria 1,
Brazil, Caribbean Isls, Colombia, Finland, France 4,
Germany 4, Ghana 3, Greece, Hungary, India, Ireland
6, Italy 4, Korea-S, Latin America, Mexico,
Myanmar/Burma, Nepal, Netherlands 3, Pakistan 1,
Peru, Philippines, Poland 1, Russia 1, Spain 3, Sri
Lanka, UK 6, Ukraine 2.

Berean Mission, Inc.

(314)773-0110   Fax: (314)773-7062
E-Mail: 74133.3601@compuserve.com
Web: http://ourworld.compuserve.com/homepages/
     Berean/
3536 Russell Blvd., St. Louis, MO 63104
Dr. Kenneth A. Epp, Gen. Director

An independent sending agency of fundamentalist tradition engaged in church planting,
TEE, evangelism, leadership development, and
medical work. Income from 1992 report.

".. presenting the Gospel of Jesus Christ to
non-Christian and spiritually neglected peoples
both in the United States and abroad."

Year Founded in USA	1937
Income for Overseas Ministries .	$ 526,000

Fully Supported USA Personnel Overseas:
Expecting to serve more than 4 years   49
Expecting to serve 1 up to 4 years   7
Other Personnel:
Non-USA serving in own/other country   . . . 4

Short-Term less than 1 year from USA   . . 149
Home ministry & office staff in USA   16
Countries: Brazil 9, Congo/Zaire 12, Dominica 5,
Ecuador 17, Grenada 3, New Zealand 2, Philippines 2,
UK 6.

Bethany Fellowship Missions

(612)829-2492   Fax: (612)829-2753
E-Mail: 105063.2561@compuserve
Web: ourworld.compuserve.com/homepages/bfm/
6820 Auto Club Rd., Bloomington, MN 55438
Mr. Tim Freeman, Director

An interdenominational sending agency of
evangelical tradition engaged in missionary
training, church planting, literature production/
distribution, and mobilizing for mission.

".. to witness, to train and send missionaries, to
plant churches, to publish Christian literature,
and to establish creative resource ventures for the
expansion of Christ's Kingdom."

Year Founded in USA	1963
Income for Overseas Ministries	$ 1,130,115

Fully Supported USA Personnel Overseas:
Expecting to serve more than 4 years   95
Other Personnel:
Non-USA serving in own/other country   . . . 16
Bivocational/Tentmaker from USA   4
Short-Term less than 1 year from USA   . . . 11
Home ministry & office staff in USA   19

Countries: Africa 2, Albania 3, Asia 9, Brazil 33,
Dominican Rep 2, Europe 1, France 7, Ghana 2,
Indonesia 3, Japan 2, Mexico 18, Philippines 7,
Slovenia 4, Spain 2.

Bethany Home, Inc.

(716)381-1196   Fax: (716)248-2074
P.O. Box 10356, Rochester, NY 14610
Dr. James Dumm, President

A nondenominational support agency of
evangelical tradition engaged in childcare/
orphanage programs and Christian education.

Year Founded in USA	1946
Income for Overseas Ministries .	$ 165,310

Fully Supported USA Personnel Overseas:
Expecting to serve more than 4 years   1
Nonresidential mission personnel   1
Other Personnel:
Short-Term less than 1 year from USA   . . . 2
Home ministry & office staff in USA   1
Countries: Philippines 1.

Bethany Missionary Association
(562)433-5771   Fax: (562)433-1462
2209 E. 6th St., Long Beach, CA 90814
Pastor David Copp, Director

An interdenominational sending agency of independent tradition engaged in Christian education, and missionary training. Personnel and income information from 1992.

Year Founded in USA 1953
Income for Overseas Ministries . . $ 72,000
Fully Supported USA Personnel Overseas:
Expecting to serve more than 4 years 9
Other Personnel:
Short-Term less than 1 year from USA . . . 2
Home ministry & office staff in USA 5
Countries: Denmark 1, Japan 4, Mexico 4.

Bethel Pentecostal Temple
(206)441-0444   Fax: (206)443-9752
2033 Second Ave., Seattle, WA 98121
Rev. Daniel W. Peterson, Senior Pastor

A nondenominational sending agency of Pentecostal tradition engaged in church planting, evangelism, and literature distribution. Personnel and income information from 1992.

Year Founded in USA 1914
Income for Overseas Ministries . . $ 38,500
Fully Supported USA Personnel Overseas:
Expecting to serve more than 4 years 6
Countries: Indonesia 2, Japan 4.

Bezalel World Outreach / Galcom International
(813)933-8111   Fax: (813)933-8886
E-Mail: GalcomUSA@aol.com
Box 270956, Tampa, FL 33688
Gary Nelson, U.S. Administrator

A nondenominational support agency of charismatic tradition engaged in supplying communications equipment and technical assistance.

Year Founded in USA 1991
Income for Overseas Ministries . $ 300,000
Personnel:
Short-Term less than 1 year from USA . . . 17
Home ministry & office staff in USA 1

Bible Alliance Mission, Inc.
(914)746-2572   Fax: (914)748-2625
P.O. Box 1549, Bradenton, FL 34206
Rev. James E. Pike, Director of Missions

An independent support agency of evangelical tradition engaged in church planting, evangelism, leadership development, and literature programs.

Year Founded in USA 1978
Income for Overseas Ministries . $ 133,000
Fully Supported USA Personnel Overseas:
Expecting to serve more than 4 years 2
Other Personnel:
Non-USA serving in own/other country . . . 6
Home ministry & office staff in USA 2
Countries: Italy 2.

Bible League, The
(708)331-2094   Fax: (708)331-7172
E-Mail: BibleLeague@xc.org
Web: http://www.bibleleague.org/
16801 Van Dam Rd., South Holland, IL 60473
Rev. Dennis M. Mulder, President

A nondenominational specialized service agency of evangelical tradition engaged in Bible distribution through indigenous churches and evangelistic organizations in over 90 countries. Information from 1992 report.

Year Founded in USA 1938
Income for Overseas Ministries $ 9,448,070
Amount of Gifts-In-Kind . . . $ 931,370
Personnel:
Home ministry & office staff in USA 70

Bible Literature International
(614)267-3116   Fax: (614)267-7110
E-Mail: 70712.1412@compuserve.com
Web: http://www.bli.org/home.html
P.O. Box 477, Columbus, OH 43216
Mr. James R. Falkenberg, Intl. President

An interdenominational service agency of evangelical tradition engaged in Bible and literature distribution, evangelism, and funds transmission working in partnership with mission organizations and national workers.

".. to help individuals around the world find new life in Christ through God's Word..."

Year Founded in USA 1923

Income for Overseas Ministries $ 1,768,327
Personnel:
Home ministry & office staff in USA 23

Bible Missionary Church
(208)337-3873   Fax: (208)337-3860
P.O. Box 2030, Homedale, ID 83628
Rev. Don Bowman, Gen. Foreign Missions Secy.

A denominational sending agency of Holiness tradition engaged in church planting, Bible distribution, theological education, evangelism, literature distribution, and support of natl. churches.

Year Founded in USA 1956
Income for Overseas Ministries . $ 500,000
Fully Supported USA Personnel Overseas:
Expecting to serve more than 4 years 32
Countries: Barbados, Germany 2, Ghana 2, Guyana 4, Japan 2, Mexico 2, Nepal, Nigeria 2, Papua New Guin 8, Peru 2, Philippines 2, Russia 4, St Vincent, Venezuela 2.

Bibles For The World
(630)668-7733   Fax: (630)668-6348
P.O. Box 805, Wheaton, IL 60189
Dr. Rochunga Pudaite, President

A nondenominational support agency of evangelical tradition engaged in Bible distribution, Christian education, medical work, and support of natl. workers. Financial totals from 1992.

Year Founded in USA 1972
Income for Overseas Ministries . $ 520,962
Amount of Gifts-In-Kind .... $ 12,044
Personnel:
Home ministry & office staff in USA 20
Countries: India.

Biblical Literature Fellowship
(630)858-0348   Fax: (630)858-1946
E-Mail: BiblicalLF@aol.com
P.O. Box 629, Wheaton, IL 60189
Richard L. Gibson, Exec. Director

A nondenominational specialized service agency of evangelical tradition engaged in literature production, Bible distribution, and translation work.

".. publishing and distributing quality Christian literature for evangelism, church planting and Christian growth."

Year Founded in USA 1958
Income for Overseas Ministries . $ 529,463
Fully Supported USA Personnel Overseas:
Expecting to serve more than 4 years 7
Expecting to serve 1 up to 4 years 2
Other Personnel:
Short-Term less than 1 year from USA ... 80
Home ministry & office staff in USA 5
Countries: Belgium 9.

Biblical Ministries Worldwide
(770)339-3500   Fax: (770)513-1254
E-Mail: 75534.546@compuserve.com
1595 Harrington Rd., Lawrenceville, GA 30243
Rev. Paul G. Seger, Gen. Director

A nondenominational sending agency of fundamentalist and independent tradition engaged in church planting, theological education, and leadership development.

".. to function as a missionary arm of the local church in the planting of autonomous, reproducing churches through administrating, equipping, and overseeing missionaries..."

Year Founded in USA 1948
Income for Overseas Ministries $ 6,200,000
Amount of Gifts-In-Kind ... $ 200,000
Fully Supported USA Personnel Overseas:
Expecting to serve more than 4 years ... 135
Nonresidential mission personnel 2
Other Personnel:
Non-USA serving in own/other country ... 4
Bivocational/Tentmaker from USA 1
Short-Term less than 1 year from USA ... 25
Home ministry & office staff in USA 13
Countries: Argentina 9, Australia 2, Austria 2, Cyprus 4, Fiji 2, Germany 11, Guam 4, Honduras 8, Hong Kong 4, Ireland 11, Italy 9, Japan 2, Luxembourg 2, Mexico 11, Netherlands 7, New Zealand 8, Puerto Rico 2, S Africa 15, Spain 6, Suriname 2, UK 2, Uruguay 12.

Big World Ventures Inc.
(800)599-8778   Fax: (918)481-5257
E-Mail: Venture@galaxt.galstar.com
P.O. Box 703203, Tulsa, OK 74170
Steve Goley, President

An interdenominational support agency of charismatic tradition engaged in youth programs, evangelism, leadership development, short-term programs, and technical assistance.

Year Founded in USA 1994
Income for Overseas Ministries . $ 358,000
Personnel:
  Short-Term less than 1 year from USA . . 224
  Home ministry & office staff in USA 8

BILD International
(515)292-7012   **Fax: (515)292-6838**
E-Mail: BILD@ames.net
Web: http://www.BILD.net
4911 W. Lincoln Way, Ames, IA 50014
Donald L. Erickson, Chairman/Acting Director

A transdenominational support agency of
evangelical tradition engaged in leadership
development, TEE, and support of national
workers. Income total from 1992 report.

Year Founded in USA 1986
Income for Overseas Ministries . $ 128,945
Countries: India, Nepal.

Billy Graham Center, The
(630)752-5157   **Fax: (630)752-5916**
E-Mail: BGCadm@wheaton.edu
Web: http://www.wheaton.edu/bgc/bgc.html
500 College Ave., Wheaton, IL 60187
Dr. Kenneth D. Gill, Acting Director

A nondenominational service agency of
evangelical tradition supporting world evangelization through research, correspondence courses,
missionary education, information services,
leadership development, and video distribution.

".. to develop strategies and skills for communicating the gospel... through leadership training,
research, networking, and strategic planning."

Year Founded in USA 1975
Income for Overseas Ministries . . . . NA
Personnel:
  Home ministry & office staff in USA 36

Billy Graham Evangelistic Association, International Ministries
(612)338-0500   **Fax: (612)335-1289**
Web: http://www.graham-assn.org/
P.O. Box 779, Minneapolis, MN 55440
John R. Corts, President & CEO
Robert L. Williams, Director of Intl. Ministries

An interdenominational evangelistic
association of evangelical tradition engaged in
evangelism, radio/TV broadcasting, evangelism
training, and video/film production/distribution
in many countries. Income for overseas ministries
from 1992.

".. to present the message of Jesus Christ to
people around the world by every available
means, in cooperation with the local church, by
supporting the evangelistic call and tradition of
ministry of Billy Graham."

Year Founded in USA 1950
Income for Overseas Ministries $ 12,500,000

Blessings International
(918)250-8101   **Fax: (918)250-1281**
E-Mail: 75554.3572@compuserve.com
5881 S. Garnett St., Tulsa, OK 74146
Dr. Harold C. Harder, President

A nondenominational support agency of
charismatic and evangelical tradition engaged in
shipping pharmaceutical and medical supplies to
61 countries.

Year Founded in USA 1981
Income for Overseas Ministries $ 5,587,167
Amount of Gifts-In-Kind . . . $ 5,582,542
Personnel:
  Short-Term less than 1 year from USA . . . 2
  Home ministry & office staff in USA 5

Blossoming Rose
(616)696-3435   **Fax: (616)696-8280**
360 W. Pine St., Cedar Springs, MI 49319
Dr. DeWayne Coxon, President

A nondenominational service agency of
evangelical tradition engaged in coordinating
short-term programs.

".. sponsoring projects in Israel which
encourage peace, are restorative in nature..."

Year Founded in USA 1984
Income for Overseas Ministries . · $ 150,000
Personnel:
  Short-Term less than 1 year from USA . . . 60

Brazil Gospel Fellowship Mission

(217)523-7176   Fax: (217)523-7186
121 N. Glenwood, Springfield, IL 62702
Rev. Larry Lipka, Exec. Secretary

An independent sending agency of
fundamentalist tradition engaged in church
planting, camping programs, evangelism, and
literature distribution.

Year Founded in USA 1939
Income for Overseas Ministries . $ 772,197
Fully Supported USA Personnel Overseas:
Expecting to serve more than 4 years 69
Other Personnel:
Home ministry & office staff in USA 3
Countries: Brazil 69.

Bread for the World

(301)608-2400   Fax: (301)608-2401
E-Mail: Bread@igc.apc.org
Web: http://www.bread.org/
1100 Wayne Ave. #1000, Silver Spring, MD 20910
Rev. David Beckmann, President

An interdenominational Christian citizen's
movement of many traditions helping citizens be
active in public-policy issues important to the
reduction of hunger.

"..seeking justice for the world's hungry people
by lobbying our nation's decision makers."

Year Founded in USA 1974
Income for Overseas Ministries . . . . NA
Personnel:
Home ministry & office staff in USA 49

Brethren Assemblies

(No central office)

The Brethren Assemblies are also known as
"Christian Brethren" or "Plymouth Brethren".
Missionaries are sent from each local assembly
(church) and not through a central agency.
Personnel totals are summaries from the
Handbook published by the Christian Missions in
Many Lands service agency.

Income for Overseas Ministries . . . . NA
Fully Supported USA Personnel Overseas:
Expecting to serve more than 4 years . . . 426
Nonresidential mission personnel 7
Other Personnel:
Bivocational/Tentmaker from USA 2

Countries: Albania 6, Argentina 10, Austria 7, Barbados
1, Bolivia 17, Brazil 14, Burundi 7, Chad 1, Chile 6,
Colombia 20, Congo/Zaire 13, Dominican Rep 2,
Ecuador 17, El Salvador 4, Estonia 2, France 18,
French Guiana 2, Germany 4, Greece 4, Guatemala 6,
Honduras 8, Hong Kong 2, Hungary 1, India 9,
Indonesia 3, Ireland 12, Italy 7, Jamaica 6, Japan 11,
Korea-S 2, Mexico 32, Mozambique 2, Netherlands 4,
Nigeria 6, Papua New Guin 6, Paraguay 14, Peru 16,
Philippines 18, Portugal 4, Puerto Rico 2, Romania 4,
S Africa 7, Senegal 3, Spain 8, Taiwan (ROC) 2,
Uganda 2, Unspecified 40, Uruguay 1, Venezuela 1,
Virgin Isls USA 2, Zambia 25, Zimbabwe 5.

Brethren Church Missionary Bd.

(419)289-1708   Fax: (419)281-0450
E-Mail: BrethrenCh@aol.com
524 College Ave., Ashland, OH 44805
Rev. Reilly R. Smith, Exec. Director

A denominational sending agency of Brethren
tradition engaged in evangelism, church planting,
childcare programs, leadership development,
medical work, and support of national churches.

Year Founded in USA 1892
Income for Overseas Ministries . $ 636,752
Fully Supported USA Personnel Overseas:
Expecting to serve more than 4 years 3
Other Personnel:
Non-USA serving in own/other country . . . 4
Home ministry & office staff in USA 4
Countries: Argentina 1, India, Malaysia, Mexico 2.

Brethren in Christ World Missions

(717)697-2634   Fax: (717)691-6053
E-Mail: BICmissions@mcis.messiah.edu
P.O. Box 390, Grantham, PA 17027
Rev. Jack McClane, Exec. Director

A denominational sending agency of Wesleyan
tradition engaged in church planting, theological
education, TEE, evangelism, medical work, and
support of national churches. Income from 1992.

Year Founded in USA 1895
Income for Overseas Ministries $ 1,527,004
Fully Supported USA Personnel Overseas:
Expecting to serve more than 4 years 33
Expecting to serve 1 up to 4 years 12
Other Personnel:
Non-USA serving in own/other country . . . 4
Bivocational/Tentmaker from USA 7
Short-Term less than 1 year from USA . . . 50
Home ministry & office staff in USA 9

Countries: Asia 7, Colombia 6, Honduras 2, India, Malawi 2, Mexico 2, Nicaragua 2, Spain 2, UK 2, Venezuela 3, Zambia 9, Zimbabwe 8.

Bridge Builders International
(541)929-5627   Fax: (541)929-5628
123 N. 18th St., Suite A, Philomath, OR 97370
Charles D. Kelley, Exec. Director

A transdenominational support agency of evangelical tradition engaged in support of national workers, mobilization for mission, and short-term programs coordination.

Year Founded in USA	1994
Income for Overseas Ministries . .	$ 19,739

Personnel:
Short-Term less than 1 year from USA . . . 20
Home ministry & office staff in USA 3

Bright Hope International
(847)526-5566   Fax: (847)526-0073
E-Mail: BrightHope@aol.com
1000 Brown Street #207, Wavconda, IL 60084
Mr. Craig H. Dyer, President

A nondenominational service agency of evangelical tradition engaged in development including alternative trade organizations and jobs, Bible distribution, support of national workers, and relief aid.

Year Founded in USA 1968
Income for Overseas Ministries . $ 276,973
Personnel:
Non-USA serving in own/other country . . . 53
Short-Term less than 1 year from USA . . . 4
Home ministry & office staff in USA 7
Countries: China (PRC), Guatemala, Kenya, Romania, Russia, Uzbekistan, Vietnam, Yugoslavia.

Cadence International
(303)762-1400   Fax: (303)788-0661
E-Mail: Admin@cadence.mhs.compuserve.com
P.O. Box 1268, Englewood, CO 80150
Mr. David Schroeder, Gen. Director

A nondenominational service agency of evangelical tradition engaged in evangelism and youth programs. Statistical information from 1992.

Year Founded in USA 1954
Income for Overseas Ministries $ 1,081,500
Fully Supported USA Personnel Overseas:
Expecting to serve more than 4 years 26

Expecting to serve 1 up to 4 years 62
Other Personnel:
Short-Term less than 1 year from USA . . . 21
Home ministry & office staff in USA 53
Countries: Germany 61, Italy 4, Japan 9, Korea-S 4, Panama 2, Philippines 2, Spain 2, UK 4.

Caleb Project
(303)730-4170   Fax: (303)730-4177
E-Mail: Info@cproject.com
Web: http://www.calebproject.org/
#10 W. Dry Creek Circle, Littleton, CO 80120
Mr. Gregory E. Fritz, President

An interdenominational service agency of evangelical tradition engaged in mobilization for mission, services for other agencies, short-term teams coordination, missionary training, and video production/distribution.

".. serves churches, mission agencies, and campus ministries throughout the United States by educating, assisting, and challenging them to complete their part in the goal of evangelizing the people groups of the world."

Year Founded in USA 1980
Income for Overseas Ministries . . $ 18,318
Personnel:
Short-Term less than 1 year from USA . . . 25
Home ministry & office staff in USA 53

Calvary Commission, Inc.
(903)882-5501   Fax: (903)882-7282
E-Mail: 102651.401@compuserve.com
P.O. Box 100, Lindale, TX 75771
Rev. Joe L. Fauss, Intl. Director

An interdenominational sending agency of charismatic tradition engaged in training, church planting, and evangelism. Statistical data from 1991.

Year Founded in USA 1977
Income for Overseas Ministries . . $ 52,000
Amount of Gifts-In-Kind . . . . $ 2,000
Fully Supported USA Personnel Overseas:
Expecting to serve more than 4 years 8
Expecting to serve 1 up to 4 years 4
Nonresidential mission personnel 1
Other Personnel:
Short-Term less than 1 year from USA . . . 14
Countries: Belize 2, Mexico 10, Romania.

Calvary Evangelistic Mission (WIVV & WBMJ Radio)

(787)724-2727   **Fax: (787)723-9633**
E-Mail: 104743.1413@compuserve.com
P.O. Box 367000, San Juan, PR 00936
Mrs. Ruth Luttrell, President

An interdenominational sending agency of Baptist tradition engaged in radio broadcasting, Bible distribution, correspondence courses, evangelism, and literature distribution.

".. winning, challenging, training and motivating people to work for Jesus..."

Year Founded in USA	1953
Income for Overseas Ministries	$ 1,019,005
Amount of Gifts-In-Kind . . .	$ 107,261

Fully Supported USA Personnel Overseas:
Expecting to serve more than 4 years 10
Expecting to serve 1 up to 4 years 6
Other Personnel:
Non-USA serving in own/other country . . . 32
Bivocational/Tentmaker from USA 2
Short-Term less than 1 year from USA . . . 85
Countries: Caribbean Isls 16.

Calvary International

(904)398-6559   **Fax: (904)398-6840**
E-Mail: CalTeam@juno.com
P.O. Box 10305, Jacksonville, FL 32247
Dr. Daniel W. Williams, President

A transdenominational sending agency of charismatic tradition engaged in church planting, orphanage work, development, theological ed., short-term programs coordination, and training.

".. to help mobilize and network the body of Christ worldwide so that in our generation the gospel of Jesus Christ is preached and disciples are made in every nation."

Year Founded in USA	1981
Income for Overseas Ministries	$ 2,150,201

Fully Supported USA Personnel Overseas:
Expecting to serve more than 4 years . . . 104
Nonresidential mission personnel 4
Other Personnel:
Non-USA serving in own/other country . . . 7
Bivocational/Tentmaker from USA 2
Short-Term less than 1 year from USA . . 75
Home ministry & office staff in USA 14
Countries: Belize 1, Colombia 3, Costa Rica 6, Cote d'Ivoire 2, Ecuador 8, Guatemala 15, India 1, Jordan 2,
Latvia 12, Mexico 12, Nigeria 5, Philippines 14, Romania 2, Russia 15, S Africa 2, Turkey 2, UK 2.

CAM International

(214)327-8206   **Fax: (214)327-8201**
E-Mail: 75142.2016@compuserve.com
Web: http://www.bible.org/cam/welcome.htm
8625 La Prada Dr., Dallas, TX 75228
Dr. J. Ronald Blue, President

A nondenominational sending agency of evangelical and fundamental tradition engaged in church planting, Bible distribution, broadcasting, theological education, evangelism, and literature production. Includes CAM's Practical Missionary Training ministry previously listed separately.

"..to bring the inhabitants of Spanish-speaking areas of the world to a saving knowledge of the love of God in Christ, to establish indigenous churches, and to assist doctrinally compatible churches in their ..worldwide missions outreach."

Year Founded in USA	1890
Income for Overseas Ministries	$ 5,313,538

Fully Supported USA Personnel Overseas:
Expecting to serve more than 4 years . . . 164
Expecting to serve 1 up to 4 years 9
Other Personnel:
Non-USA serving in own/other country . . . 19
Short-Term less than 1 year from USA . . . 18
Home ministry & office staff in USA 76
Countries: Costa Rica 20, El Salvador 9, Guatemala 50, Honduras 20, Mexico 51, Panama 7, Spain 16.

Campus Crusade for Christ, Intl.

(407)826-2000   **Fax: (407)826-2851**
E-Mail: Postmaster@ccci.org
Web: http://www.ccci.org
100 Sunport Lane, Orlando, FL 32809
Dr. William R. Bright, President & CEO
Dr. E. Bailey Marks, VP for Intl. Ministries

An interdenominational sending agency of evangelical tradition engaged in evangelism, training, video/film production and distribution, youth programs, and small group discipleship. Includes The JESUS Film Project and other overseas ministries.

Year Founded in USA	1951
Income for Overseas Ministries	$ 54,198,000

Fully Supported USA Personnel Overseas:
Expecting to serve more than 4 years . . . 665
Expecting to serve 1 up to 4 years 367

Other Personnel:
Short-Term less than 1 year from USA   .   915
Home ministry & office staff in USA   .   . 5,021

Countries: Albania 27, Am Samoa, Angola, Argentina 5, Armenia, Asia 92, Australia 6, Austria 4, Azerbaijan, Bangladesh, Barbados, Belarus 18, Belau(Palau), Belgium, Belize, Benin, Bhutan, Bolivia 1, Bosnia, Botswana, Brazil 12, Brunei, Bulgaria 15, Burkina Faso, Burundi, Cambodia 2, Cameroon, Cen Africa Rep 2, Chile 8, Colombia, Congo, Congo/Zaire, Costa Rica 10, Cote d'Ivoire 2, Croatia 13, Cuba, Cyprus 2, Czech Rep 15, Dominican Rep, Ecuador 2, Egypt 7, El Salvador, Eritrea, Estonia 17, Ethiopia, Fiji, Finland, France 31, Gabon, Gambia, Georgia, Germany 30, Ghana, Greece 3, Guam, Guatemala, Guinea 2, Guyana, Haiti, Honduras, Hong Kong 7, Hungary 82, India, Indonesia 2, Ireland, Italy 2, Jamaica, Japan 30, Kazakhstan 10, Kenya 43, Korea-S, Kyrgyzstan 8, Laos, Latvia 16, Lebanon, Lesotho 8, Liberia, Lithuania 10, Macao, Madagascar, Malawi, Malaysia 2, Mali 2, Marshall Isls, Mexico 4, Micronesia, Moldava, Mongolia 5, Nepal, Neth Antilles, Netherlands, New Zealand 6, Nicaragua, Niger, Nigeria 11, Norway, Pakistan, Panama, Papua New Guin, Paraguay, Peru, Philippines 47, Poland 14, Portugal, Puerto Rico, Romania 20, Russia 184, Rwanda, S Africa 8, Senegal 4, Sierra Leone, Singapore 14, Slovakia 15, Slovenia, Solomon Isls 2, Spain 4, Sri Lanka, Suriname, Swaziland 4, Sweden, Taiwan (ROC) 6, Tanzania 7, Thailand 8, Togo, Tonga, Trinidad & Tobg 2, UK 20, Uganda 3, Ukraine 66, Uruguay, Uzbekistan 14, Vanuatu, Venezuela, Vietnam, Yugoslavia 6, Zambia 2, Zimbabwe 8.

Carpenter's Tools
(320)235-0155   **Fax: (320)235-0185**
E-Mail: CarToolsInt@willmar.com
P.O. Box 100, Willmar, MN 56201
Mr. David Lien, President

An interdenominational support agency of evangelical tradition engaged in youth concerts and evangelism in developing and other countries. An associate ministry of Youth for Christ International.

Year Founded in USA   1988
Income for Overseas Ministries . $ 150,000
Personnel:
Short-Term less than 1 year from USA   . . 56
Home ministry & office staff in USA   . . . 6

Carver Foreign Missions, Inc.
(770)482-7592
Morris Brown Sta., Box 92091, Atlanta, GA 30314
Rev. Glenn Mason, Director

An interdenominational sending agency of Baptist tradition engaged in Christian education, literature distribution, literacy work, and support of national workers.

Year Founded in USA   1955
Income for Overseas Ministries . $ 160,500
Amount of Gifts-In-Kind   . . . $ 55,000
Fully Supported USA Personnel Overseas:
Expecting to serve more than 4 years   . . . 1
Expecting to serve 1 up to 4 years   8
Other Personnel:
Non-USA serving in own/other country   . . 7
Short-Term less than 1 year from USA   . . 14
Home ministry & office staff in USA   .   . 2
Countries: Liberia 9.

CAS International
See: Muslim Hope

CBInternational
(630)260-3800   **Fax: (630)665-1418**
E-Mail: CBI@cb.usa.com
Web: http://www.cbi.org/
P.O. Box 5, Wheaton, IL 60189
Dr. Hans Finzel, Exec. Director

A evangelical sending agency of Baptist tradition engaged in church planting, evangelism, leadership development, TEE, and literature production/distribution.

"In vital partnership with churches at home and abroad, .. be a pioneering force in fulfilling Christ's commission."

Year Founded in USA   1943
Income for Overseas Ministries $ 17,500,000
Fully Supported USA Personnel Overseas:
Expecting to serve more than 4 years   . . 518
Expecting to serve 1 up to 4 years   . . . 154
Nonresidential mission personnel   2
Other Personnel:
Bivocational/Tentmaker from USA   11
Short-Term less than 1 year from USA   . . 225
Home ministry & office staff in USA   . . . 81
Countries: Africa 7, Albania 5, Argentina 18, Asia 7, Austria 31, Belgium 10, Brazil 39, Cen Africa Rep 22, Central Asia 5, Congo/Zaire 14, Cote d'Ivoire 80, Czech

Rep 8, France 22, Hong Kong 8, Hungary 18, India 8, Indonesia 15, Ireland 2, Italy 25, Japan 9, Jordan 10, Kenya 23, Lithuania 3, Macao 8, Madagascar 8, Netherlands 5, Pakistan 18, Philippines 69, Poland 12, Portugal 7, Romania 13, Russia 3, Rwanda 7, Senegal 26, Singapore 2, Slovenia 5, Spain 9, Taiwan (ROC) 38, UK 2, Uganda 13, Ukraine 17, Venezuela 19, Zambia 2.

Cedar Lane Missionary Homes
(609)783-6525   Fax: (609)783-8538
E-Mail: Cedarlane@juno.com
103 Cedar Lane, Laurel Springs, NJ 08021
Rev. Russell Baker, Director

A nondenominational support agency of Baptist and evangelical tradition engaged in furloughed missionary support.

".. providing restful homes and otherwise assisting missionaries on furlough."

Year Founded in USA 1949
Income for Overseas Ministries . . . . NA
Personnel:
Home ministry & office staff in USA 3

CEIFA Ministries International
(618)377-0579
E-Mail: CEIFA@aol.com
729 Albers Lane, Bethalto, IL 62010
Rev. David W. Runyan, President

An interdenominational service agency of evangelical tradition engaged in evangelism, literature distribution, and relief aid.

"To proclaim and demonstrate, through word and deed, the gospel of Jesus Christ in neglected world areas in cooperation with the Church."

Year Founded in USA 1991
Income for Overseas Ministries . $ 120,000
Fully Supported USA Personnel Overseas:
Expecting to serve 1 up to 4 years 1
Other Personnel:
Non-USA serving in own/other country . . . 15
Bivocational/Tentmaker from USA 2
Short-Term less than 1 year from USA . . 150
Home ministry & office staff in USA 2
Countries: Albania, Austria, Moldava, Portugal, Romania 1, Russia.

Celebrant Singers
(209)740-4000   Fax: (209)740-4040
E-Mail: Celebrants@celebrants.com
Web: http://www.celebrants.com/
P.O. Box 1416, Visalia, CA 93279
Mr. Jon F. Stemkoski, President

An interdenominational service agency of charismatic and ecumenical tradition engaged in evangelism through musical concert teams and crusades in over 30 countries.

Year Founded in USA 1977
Income for Overseas Ministries $ 1,200,000
Fully Supported USA Personnel Overseas:
Nonresidential mission personnel 8
Other Personnel:
Short-Term less than 1 year from USA . . 175
Home ministry & office staff in USA 32

Central Yearly Meeting of Friends Missions
(317)896-5082
P.O. Box 542, Westfield, IN 46074
Rev. Joseph A. Enyart, President

A denominational sending agency of Friends tradition engaged in church planting, Bible distribution, TEE, and evangelism.

Year Founded in USA 1925
Income for Overseas Ministries . . $ 28,899
Fully Supported USA Personnel Overseas:
Expecting to serve more than 4 years 5
Expecting to serve 1 up to 4 years 2
Other Personnel:
Short-Term less than 1 year from USA . . . 17
Countries: Bolivia 7.

Child Evangelism Fellowship, Inc
(314)456-4321   Fax: (314)456-5000
P.O. Box 348, Warrenton, MO 63383
Mr. Reese R. Kauffman, President

An interdenominational sending agency of evangelical tradition engaged in evangelism, camping programs, support of national workers, and training.

".. to evangelize boys and girls .. and establish them in the Word of God and the local church..."

Year Founded in USA 1937
Income for Overseas Ministries $ 3,280,000

Fully Supported USA Personnel Overseas:
Expecting to serve more than 4 years 70
Nonresidential mission personnel 8
Other Personnel:
Non-USA serving in own/other country . . 1,232
Short-Term less than 1 year from USA . . . 43
Home ministry & office staff in USA . . . 770
Countries: Albania, Argentina, Asia, Australia 4, Austria 1, Belgium 2, Benin, Bolivia, Botswana 1, Brazil 2, Bulgaria, Burkina Faso, Burundi, Cambodia 2, Cameroon, Cen Africa Rep, Chile, Colombia, Congo/Zaire, Cote d'Ivoire, Croatia, Cyprus 6, Czech Rep 1, Denmark 2, Dominican Rep, Ecuador, Estonia, Fiji 2, Finland, France 2, Gabon, Gambia, Germany 4, Ghana, Greece, Guatemala, Haiti 2, Honduras 1, Hong Kong 1, Hungary 1, India, Indonesia, Ireland, Israel 2, Italy, Jamaica, Japan, Jordan 2, Kenya 7, Korea-S, Lebanon, Liberia, Macedonia, Madagascar, Malawi, Mali, Mauritius, Mexico 1, Micronesia 2, Myanmar/Burma, Namibia, Nepal, Neth Antilles 2, Netherlands 2, New Zealand, Nicaragua, Nigeria, Norway, Papua New Guin, Paraguay, Philippines, Poland, Portugal, Puerto Rico, Romania, Russia 2, Rwanda, S Africa 1, Sierra Leone, Singapore, Slovakia, Solomon Isls, Spain, Sweden, Switzerland 4, Taiwan (ROC) 2, Thailand, Togo, UK 4, Uganda, Ukraine 1, Venezuela, Yugoslavia 4, Zambia, Zimbabwe.

Childcare International
(360)647-2283   Fax: (360)647-2392
E-Mail: CCIbham@aol.com
P.O. Box W, Bellingham, WA 98227
Dr. Max Lange, President

A nondenominational service agency of Baptist tradition engaged in childcare programs, church planting, relief aid, short-term programs coordination, and training.

Year Founded in USA 1981
Income for Overseas Ministries $ 10,000,000
Amount of Gifts-In-Kind . . . $ 8,000,000
Personnel:
Non-USA serving in own/other country . . 144
Short-Term less than 1 year from USA . . 100
Home ministry & office staff in USA 12
Countries: Belarus, Haiti, India, Kenya, Mexico, Peru, Philippines, Sri Lanka, Uganda.

Children International
(816)942-2000   Fax: (816)942-3714
E-Mail: Children@cikc.org
2000 E. Red Bridge Rd., Kansas City, MO 64131
Mr. James R. Cook, President/CEO

A nondenominational service agency of independent tradition engaged in childcare/orphanage programs and medical work. Personnel data from 1992.

Year Founded in USA 1936
Income for Overseas Ministries . . . . NR
Fully Supported USA Personnel Overseas:
Expecting to serve more than 4 years 4
Other Personnel:
Non-USA serving in own/other country . . 437
Home ministry & office staff in USA . . . 102
Countries: Unspecified 4.

Children of India Foundation
(401)596-0846
P.O. Box 354, Westerly, RI 02891
Dr. Janna L. Runge, Exec. Director

A nondenominational support agency of Pentecostal tradition engaged in childcare programs, funds transmission, and providing medical supplies. Income amount from 1992 report.

Year Founded in USA 1977
Income for Overseas Ministries . . $ 19,540
Personnel:
Non-USA serving in own/other country . . . 2
Countries: India.

Children's Haven International
(956)787-7378   Fax: (956)783-4637
400 E. Minnesota Rd., Pharr, TX 78577
Rev. Tim Kliewer, Chairman

A nondenominational service agency of Mennonite tradition engaged in childcare programs. Financial and personnel data from 1992.

Year Founded in USA 1972
Income for Overseas Ministries . $ 322,500
Fully Supported USA Personnel Overseas:
Expecting to serve 1 up to 4 years 3
Other Personnel:
Short-Term less than 1 year from USA . . . 2
Home ministry & office staff in USA 6
Countries: Mexico 3.

Children's Medical Ministries
(301)261-3211   Fax: (301)888-2533
E-Mail: ChildMedMinistries@charitiesusa.com
P.O. Box 3382, Crofton, MD 21114
Bill K. Collins, Founder/CEO

A nondenominational support agency of Baptist tradition engaged in medical work, childrens programs, literature distribution, relief aid, and technical assistance in 20 countries.

Year Founded in USA 1988
Income for Overseas Ministries $ 2,400,000
Amount of Gifts-In-Kind . . . $ 2,000,000
Personnel:
   Bivocational/Tentmaker from USA 15
   Short-Term less than 1 year from USA . . . 50

China Ministries International
(626)398-0145   **Fax: (626)398-2361**
E-Mail: 104435.2547@compuserve.com
P.O. Box 40489, Pasadena, CA 91104
Rev. Ronald Yu, U.S. Director
Dr. Jonathan Chao, Founder and President

A nondenominational support agency of evangelical and Reformed tradition engaged in theological education, Bible distribution, funds transmission, leadership development, mission-related research, and missionary training.

".. for the evangelization of China, the strengthening of the Chinese Church .. by engaging in ministries of research, training of workers, and sending them to the harvest field..."

Year Founded in USA 1987
Income for Overseas Ministries . $ 440,000
Fully Supported USA Personnel Overseas:
   Expecting to serve more than 4 years 2
   Expecting to serve 1 up to 4 years 1
   Nonresidential mission personnel 1
Other Personnel:
   Non-USA serving in own/other country . . . 50
   Home ministry & office staff in USA 3
Countries: Australia, Hong Kong 1, Korea-S, Philippines, Taiwan (ROC) 2, UK.

China Outreach Ministries
(703)273-3500   **Fax: (703)273-3500**
P.O. Box 310, Fairfax, VA 22030
Rev. Earnest W. Hummer, President

A nondenominational support agency of evangelical tradition engaged in evangelism, broadcasting, and literature distribution.

Year Founded in USA 1969
Income for Overseas Ministries . . . . NA
Personnel:
   Home ministry & office staff in USA 20

China Service Coordinating Office
(630)752-5951   **Fax: (630)752-5916**
E-Mail: China@xc.org
Institute for China Studies, Wheaton College, Wheaton, IL 60187
Brent Fulton, Managing Director

A nondenominational specialized service agency of Reformed tradition engaged in mission mobilization, information services, and research.

".. mobilizing in N America for effective China involvement and assisting agencies, churches, organizations, and individuals involved in China to network and communicate more effectively."

Year Founded in USA 1995
Income for Overseas Ministries . . . . NA
Personnel:
   Home ministry & office staff in USA 3

Chinese Christian Mission, Inc.
(707)762-1314   **Fax: (707)762-1713**
E-Mail: CCMUSA@ix.netcom.com
P.O. Box 750759, Petaluma, CA 94975
Kitty Ma, Administrative Executive

An interdenominational sending agency of evangelical tradition engaged in evangelism, church planting, literature production, and mobilization for mission. Statistical data from 1992.

Year Founded in USA 1961
Income for Overseas Ministries . $ 917,440
Fully Supported USA Personnel Overseas:
   Expecting to serve more than 4 years 10
   Nonresidential mission personnel 2
Other Personnel:
   Non-USA serving in own/other country . . . 4
   Short-Term less than 1 year from USA . . . 7
   Home ministry & office staff in USA 33
Countries: Argentina 1, Costa Rica, Hong Kong 5, Macao 4, Thailand.

Chosen People Ministries
(704)357-9000   **Fax: (704)357-6359**
E-Mail: missiondirector@chosen-people.com
Web: http://www.chosen-people.com
1300 Cross Beam Dr., Charlotte, NC 28217
Mitch Glaser, President & CEO

A nondenominational service agency of independent and evangelical tradition engaged in evangelism, literature distribution, and missionary training. Statistical data from 1992.

Year Founded in USA 1894
Income for Overseas Ministries . $ 182,493
Personnel:
  Non-USA serving in own/other country . . . 9
  Home ministry & office staff in USA 94
Countries: Argentina, Israel, Russia.

CHOSEN, Inc.
(814)833-3023   **Fax: (814)833-4091**
3642 W. 26th St., Erie, PA 16506
Mr. Carl Eldred, Exec. Director

An interdenominational specialized service agency of evangelical tradition engaged in providing medical supplies, equipment, and technical assistance to Christian medical facilities.

Year Founded in USA 1969
Income for Overseas Ministries $ 1,276,938
Amount of Gifts-In-Kind . . . $ 1,078,072
Personnel:
  Short-Term less than 1 year from USA . . . 4
  Home ministry & office staff in USA 5

Christ Community Church
(847)746-1411   **Fax: (847)746-1452**
E-Mail: CCCZion@aol.com
2500 Dowie Memorial Dr., Zion, IL 60099
Ken Langley, Senior Pastor

A sending ministry of evangelical tradition engaged in support of national churches, church planting, and evangelism. Statistical data from 1992. Name changed from Christian Catholic Church (Evangelical Protestant) in 1995.

Year Founded in USA 1896
Income for Overseas Ministries . $ 174,805
Fully Supported USA Personnel Overseas:
  Expecting to serve more than 4 years 10
Countries: Angola 2, Egypt 2, Japan 2, S Africa 4.

Christ for India Ministries
(803)794-5504   **Fax: (803)794-5504**
E-Mail: CFI@csrnet.org
P.O. Box 210765, Columbia, SC 29221
Dr. Jim Stallings, President

A nondenominational support agency of evangelical tradition engaged in support of national workers for literature distribution.

Year Founded in USA 1978
Income for Overseas Ministries . $ 321,000

Christ for India, Inc.
(972)771-7221   **Fax: (972)771-4021**
P.O. Box 271086, Dallas, TX 75227
Dr. P. J. Titus, Founder/President
Arlene Phelps, Admin. Secretary

A nondenominational service agency of charismatic tradition engaged in church planting, training, corres. courses, evangelism, literature distribution, and support of national workers.

"... to 'make ready a people, prepared for the coming of the Lord'."

Year Founded in USA 1981
Income for Overseas Ministries . $ 187,254
Personnel:
  Non-USA serving in own/other country . . 500
  Short-Term less than 1 year from USA . . . 30
  Home ministry & office staff in USA 1
Countries: India.

Christ for the City International
(402)592-8332
E-Mail: InfoCFC@aol.com
P.O. Box 241827, Omaha, NE 68124
J. Paul Landrey, President

A transdenominational sending agency of evangelical tradition engaged in evangelism, church planting, childrens programs, leadership development, short-term programs coordination.

"To multiply 'open churches' in strategic population centers and inspire, equip and encourage every believer in these 'open churches' to influence their world for Christ."

Year Founded in USA 1995
Income for Overseas Ministries $ 1,912,372
Fully Supported USA Personnel Overseas:
  Expecting to serve more than 4 years 31
  Expecting to serve 1 up to 4 years 16
Other Personnel:
  Non-USA serving in own/other country . . . 60
  Bivocational/Tentmaker from USA 8
  Short-Term less than 1 year from USA . . 645
  Home ministry & office staff in USA 7
Countries: Argentina 2, Brazil 2, Colombia 8, Costa Rica 18, Mexico 14, Peru 1, Spain 2, Switzerland.

Christ for the Island World
(910)855-0656   Fax: (910)854-1555
P.O. Box 18962, Greensboro, NC 27419
Rev. Ken Taylor, President

An interdenominational support agency of
evangelical tradition engaged in support of
national workers, church planting, and
evangelism.

Year Founded in USA 1983
Income for Overseas Ministries . . $ 50,000
Personnel:
Non-USA serving in own/other country . . 111
Home ministry & office staff in USA 2
Countries: Brazil, Indonesia, Russia.

Christ for the Nations, Inc.
(214)376-1711   Fax: (214)302-6228
E-Mail: Info@cfni.org
Web: http://www.cfni.org/
P.O. Box 769000, Dallas, TX 75376
Rev. Dennis Lindsay, President/CEO

An interdenominational support agency and
Bible school of charismatic tradition engaged in
literature distribution, church construction,
missionary education, and funds transmission.

Year Founded in USA 1948
Income for Overseas Ministries $ 1,143,863
Fully Supported USA Personnel Overseas:
Expecting to serve more than 4 years 3
Nonresidential mission personnel 3
Other Personnel:
Non-USA serving in own/other country . . . 11
Short-Term less than 1 year from USA . . 300
Home ministry & office staff in USA . . . 210
Countries: Belarus 2, Israel 1, Jamaica, Romania.

Christian Advance International
(713)981-9033   Fax: (713)981-9033
P.O. Box 741427, Houston, TX 77274
Rev. Chris G. Jones, President

An interdenominational sending agency of
charismatic and Pentecostal tradition engaged in
childrens programs, evangelism, providing medical supplies, and support of national workers.

Year Founded in USA 1984
Income for Overseas Ministries . $ 617,000
Amount of Gifts-In-Kind . . . $ 120,000
Fully Supported USA Personnel Overseas:

Expecting to serve more than 4 years 4
Expecting to serve 1 up to 4 years 2
Other Personnel:
Non-USA serving in own/other country . . . 29
Short-Term less than 1 year from USA . . 335
Home ministry & office staff in USA 4
Countries: Belize 2, Mexico 4.

Christian Aid Ministries
(330)893-2428   Fax: (330)893-2305
P.O. Box 360, Berlin, OH 44610
Mr. David N. Troyer, Gen. Director

An interdenominational service agency of
Mennonite tradition engaged in relief aid, Bible
distribution, church construction, and providing
medical supplies. Statistical data from 1992.

Year Founded in USA 1981
Income for Overseas Ministries $ 5,793,868
Fully Supported USA Personnel Overseas:
Expecting to serve 1 up to 4 years 4
Other Personnel:
Home ministry & office staff in USA 17
Countries: Haiti 2, Romania 2.

Christian Aid Mission
(804)977-5650   Fax: (804)295-6814
E-Mail: CAidInfo@christianaid.org
Web: http://www.christianaid.org/   P.O.   9037
3045 Ivy Road, Charlottesville, VA 22903   22906
Dr. Robert V. Finley, Chairman

A nondenominational service agency of
evangelical tradition raising financial support for
indigenous mission boards and Bible institutes
involved in church planting, evangelism,
literature distribution, and missionary training.

Year Founded in USA 1953
Income for Overseas Ministries $ 3,663,916
Fully Supported USA Personnel Overseas:
Nonresidential mission personnel 8
Other Personnel:
Non-USA serving in own/other country . . 2,333
Home ministry & office staff in USA 20
Countries: Albania, Argentina, Armenia, Bangladesh,
Bolivia, Brazil, Cambodia, China (PRC), Colombia,
Costa Rica, Croatia, Cuba, Dominican Rep, Egypt,
Gambia, Ghana, Guatemala, Haiti, Honduras, India,
Indonesia, Jordan, Kazakhstan, Kenya, Kyrgyzstan,
Laos, Macedonia, Malawi, Mexico, Mongolia,
Myanmar/Burma, Nepal, Nigeria, Pakistan, Papua New
Guin, Paraguay, Peru, Philippines, Poland, Romania,
Russia, Rwanda, Sierra Leone, Sri Lanka, Syria,

Tanzania, Thailand, Turkey, Uganda, Ukraine, Uruguay, Uzbekistan, Vietnam, West Bank, Zimbabwe.

Christian and Missionary Alliance
(719)599-5999   Fax: (719)599-8346
E-Mail: 70570.3457@compuserve.com
Web: http://cma-world.com
P.O. Box 35000, Colorado Springs, CO 80935
Dr. Peter Nanfelt, VP Overseas Division
Dr. Paul Bubna, President

A denominational sending agency of evangelical tradition engaged in church planting, theological and missionary education, TEE, evangelism, natl. church support, and relief aid.

".. committed to world missions, stressing the fullness of Christ in personal experiences, building the Church and preaching the Gospel to the ends of the earth."

Year Founded in USA 1887
Income for Overseas Ministries $ 18,066,769
Fully Supported USA Personnel Overseas:
   Expecting to serve more than 4 years . . . 617
   Expecting to serve 1 up to 4 years 116
Other Personnel:
   Bivocational/Tentmaker from USA 60
   Short-Term less than 1 year from USA . . 92
   Home ministry & office staff in USA . . . 120
Countries: Argentina 20, Australia 2, Brazil 22, Burkina Faso 27, Cambodia 21, Chile 25, China (PRC) 2, Colombia 23, Congo 9, Congo/Zaire 2, Cote d'Ivoire 59, Dominican Rep 13, Ecuador 68, France 17, Gabon 38, Guatemala 2, Guinea 2, Hong Kong 14, Indonesia 58, Israel 8, Japan 10, Jordan 2, Laos 8, Lebanon 2, Malaysia 36, Mali 33, Mexico 10, New Zealand 1, Nigeria 2, Peru 20, Philippines 49, Poland 4, Russia 30, Spain 8, Suriname 2, Taiwan (ROC) 18, Thailand 32, UK 8, Unspecified 8, Venezuela 13, Vietnam 2.

Christian Associates International
(818)865-1816   Fax: (818)865-0317
1534 N. Moorpark Rd. #356, Thousand Oaks, CA 91360
Dr. Linus Morris, Director

A transdenominational sending agency of evangelical tradition engaged in church planting, and support of national churches.

".. to establish high-impact churches that help fulfill the Great Commission of making disciples of all people."

Year Founded in USA 1968

Income for Overseas Ministries . $ 991,177
Fully Supported USA Personnel Overseas:
   Expecting to serve more than 4 years 16
Other Personnel:
   Non-USA serving in own/other country . . . 8
   Short-Term less than 1 year from USA . . . 32
   Home ministry & office staff in USA . . . 12
Countries: Ireland 4, Latvia, Netherlands 6, Russia 1, Spain 4, Sweden 1.

Christian Blind Mission Intl.
(864)239-0065   Fax: (864)239-0069
E-Mail: 102070.3266@compuserve.com
P.O. Box 19000, Greenville, SC 29602
Alan Harkey, U.S. President

An interdenominational service agency of evangelical tradition engaged in disability assistance programs, providing medical supplies, and technical assistance. Financial and personnel information from 1992.

Year Founded in USA 1976
Income for Overseas Ministries . $ 422,874
Fully Supported USA Personnel Overseas:
   Expecting to serve more than 4 years 9
   Expecting to serve 1 up to 4 years 26
Other Personnel:
   Home ministry & office staff in USA 7
Countries: Botswana 1, Burkina Faso 1, Cen Africa Rep 2, China (PRC) 2, Ethiopia 2, Jamaica 2, Kenya 5, Mali 2, Nepal 2, Philippines 1, Sierra Leone 4, Tanzania 4, Togo 4, Uganda 2, Zimbabwe 1.

Christian Brethren
See: Brethren Assemblies

Christian Broadcasting Network
(757)579-7000   Fax: (757)579-2017
Web: http://www.cbn.org/cbn/cbn.html
977 Centerville Turnpk., Virginia Beach, VA 23463
Pat Robertson, Chairman & CEO
Michael D. Little, President & COO

An interdenominational support agency of evangelical tradition engaged in TV broadcasting, Bible distribution, literature distribution, and video production/distribution for evangelism efforts in 70 countries of Africa, Asia, Europe, and Latin America. See also Operation Blessing International, an affiliate organization of CBN.

".. to prepare the world for the Second Coming of Jesus Christ and the establishment of the everlasting kingdom of God on earth."

Year Founded in USA 1960
Income for Overseas Ministries $ 12,688,500
Fully Supported USA Personnel Overseas:
    Nonresidential mission personnel 14

Christian Business Men's Committee of USA

(423)698-4444 **Fax: (423)629-4434**
E-Mail: dferrel@voyageronline.net
Web: http://www.cmbc.com
P.O. Box 3308, Chattanooga, TN 37404
Mr. Phil Downer, President

An interdenominational fellowship of evangelical tradition encouraging its members to witness personally and through informally organized overseas teams.

".. saturating the business and professional community with the Gospel .. by establishing, equipping and mobilizing teams where we work and live that yield spiritual reproducers."

Year Founded in USA 1950
Income for Overseas Ministries . . . . NA

Christian Catholic Church (Evangelical Protestant)
See: Christ Community Church

Christian Church (Disciples of Christ), Div.of Overseas Ministries
(317)635-3100 **Fax: (317)635-4323**
P.O. Box 1986, Indianapolis, IN 46206
Rev. Patricia Tucker Spier, President

A denominational support agency of Christian (Restoration Movement) and ecumenical tradition engaged in support of national churches.

Year Founded in USA 1849
Income for Overseas Ministries . . . . NR

Christian Church of North America Missions
(412)962-3501 **Fax: (412)962-1766**
E-Mail: CCNA@nauticom.net
1294 Rutledge Rd., Transfer, PA 16154
Rev. John DelTurco, Gen. Overseer

A denominational sending agency of Pentecostal tradition engaged in evangelism, broadcasting, church establishing and construction, orphanages, and medical work.

Year Founded in USA 1907
Income for Overseas Ministries . $ 800,000
Fully Supported USA Personnel Overseas:
    Expecting to serve more than 4 years 12
Other Personnel:
    Short-Term less than 1 year from USA . . . 19
    Home ministry & office staff in USA 2
Countries: Africa 2, Argentina, Brazil, Chile, Colombia 1, Europe 2, India 4, Italy 1, Paraguay, Philippines 2, Uruguay, Venezuela.

Christian Churches / Churches of Christ
(No central office)

A body of autonomous congregations and agencies of the Christian "Restoration Movement" (using instrumental music in worship) which sends and supports missionaries directly from local congregations. Personnel totals compiled in 1992 by Mission Services Association. Income figure is a 1988 estimation.

Income for Overseas Ministries $ 24,000,000
Fully Supported USA Personnel Overseas:
    Expecting to serve more than 4 years . . 1,110
    Expecting to serve 1 up to 4 years 44
    Nonresidential mission personnel 8
Countries: Albania, Argentina 6, Australia 14, Austria 2, Bahamas 2, Bangladesh 2, Barbados 2, Belgium 2, Benin 4, Bophuthatswana 4, Botswana 2, Brazil 49, Cayman Isls 5, Chile 32, China (PRC) 5, Colombia 14, Congo/Zaire 34, Costa Rica 6, Cote d'Ivoire 10, Denmark 2, Dominican Rep 6, Ecuador 6, France 6, Germany 10, Ghana 7, Grenada 4, Guatemala 6, Guinea 1, Guyana 2, Haiti 29, Honduras 7, Hong Kong 18, India 23, Indonesia 24, Ireland 4, Israel 2, Italy 7, Jamaica 9, Japan 45, Kenya 69, Korea-S 4, Liberia 1, Malawi 7, Mali 2, Mexico 53, Mozambique 6, New Zealand 2, Nigeria 2, Panama 4, Papua New Guin 28, Philippines 46, Poland, Portugal 5, Puerto Rico 30, Russia 2, S Africa 24, Singapore 6, Spain 1, St Vincent 6, Taiwan (ROC) 10, Thailand 47, UK 57, Ukraine 4,

Unspecified 228, Uruguay 8, Venezuela 10, Virgin Isls USA 2, Zambia 16, Zimbabwe 59.

Christian Dental Society

(800)237-7368   **Fax: (319)578-8843**
Box 177, Sumner, IA 50674
Dr. Richard C. Haw, Secy./Treasurer

An interdenominational specialized service agency of evangelical tradition engaged in medical work, purchasing services, and supplying services and equipment for other agencies.

Year Founded in USA	1962
Income for Overseas Ministries .	$ 457,409
Amount of Gifts-In-Kind . . .	$ 300,480

Personnel:
Bivocational/Tentmaker from USA 5
Short-Term less than 1 year from USA . . . 27

Christian Dynamics

(602)878-6892
10878 N. 57th Ave., Glendale, AZ 85304
Dr. Harvey M. Lifsey, President

A transdenominational service agency of evangelical tradition engaged in support of national workers, orphanage work, corres. courses, evangelism, and literacy work.

".. to support National workers who will penetrate with the Gospel into unreached areas and establish indigenous churches."

Year Founded in USA	1976
Income for Overseas Ministries .	$ 100,000
Amount of Gifts-In-Kind	$ 90,000

Fully Supported USA Personnel Overseas:
Nonresidential mission personnel 1
Other Personnel:
Non-USA serving in own/other country . . . 48
Short-Term less than 1 year from USA . . . 2
Home ministry & office staff in USA 1
Countries: Cambodia, India.

Christian Fellowship Union

(512)686-5886
E-Mail: 76765.2323@compuserve.com
P.O. Box 909, McAllen, TX 78502
Rev. Steven P. Johnson, Gen. Director

An interdenominational sending agency of charismatic and evangelical tradition engaged in church planting, church construction, evangelism, and support of national churches.

Year Founded in USA	1945
Income for Overseas Ministries . .	$ 82,000

Fully Supported USA Personnel Overseas:
Expecting to serve more than 4 years 2
Nonresidential mission personnel 4
Other Personnel:
Home ministry & office staff in USA 8
Countries: Mexico 2.

Christian Information Service, Inc. Missions Division

(804)973-8439   **Fax: (804)973-7470**
P.O. Box 6511, Charlottesville, VA 22906
William T. Bray, President

A transdenominational support agency of evangelical tradition engaged in services for other agencies, and mobilization for mission.

Year Founded in USA	1972
Income for Overseas Ministries . .	$ 45,890

Fully Supported USA Personnel Overseas:
Nonresidential mission personnel 2
Other Personnel:
Short-Term less than 1 year from USA . . . 10
Home ministry & office staff in USA 2

Christian Laymen's Missionary Evangelism Association

(509)786-3178   **Fax: (509)786-1000**
826 Ford St., Prosser, WA 99350
Larry Taylor, President

A nondenominational support agency of Pentecostal and charismatic tradition engaged in evangelism using the JESUS film; Bible and literature distribution.

"To raise up laymen for world evangelism."

Year Founded in USA	1977
Income for Overseas Ministries . .	$ 7,715

Personnel:
Bivocational/Tentmaker from USA 1
Short-Term less than 1 year from USA . . . 2

Home ministry & office staff in USA   2

Christian Leadership Development, Inc.

(502)821-0699   **Fax: (502)825-7310**
E-Mail: Ftsdcld@vci.net
P.O. Box 402, Madisonville, KY 42431
Mr. Randall Wittig, Gen. Director

An interdenominational service agency of evangelical tradition engaged in leadership development, literature distribution, literature production, and training.

".. to provide teaching, encouragement and counseling ... to Christian leaders, particularly those of limited resources who do not have other means of of spiritual development available..."

Year Founded in USA   1978
Income for Overseas Ministries . $ 146,000
Fully Supported USA Personnel Overseas:
  Expecting to serve more than 4 years   3
Other Personnel:
  Non-USA serving in own/other country   . . .   5
Countries: Costa Rica 3, Peru.

Christian Life Missions

(407)333-4618   **Fax: (407)333-4675**
P.O. Box 952248, Lake Mary, FL 32795
Mrs. Dottie McBroom, Exec. Director

A nondenominational support agency of evangelical tradition engaged in funds transmission, Bible distribution, correspondence courses, and literature distribution.

Year Founded in USA   1956
Income for Overseas Ministries . $ 100,000
Personnel:
  Home ministry & office staff in USA   2

Christian Literacy Associates

(412)364-3777
E-Mail: DRLiteracy@aol.com
311 Cumberland Rd., Pittsburgh, PA 15237
Dr. William E. Kofmehl Jr., President

An interdenominational specialized service agency of ecumenical tradition engaged in literacy development and training.

Year Founded in USA   1976
Income for Overseas Ministries . . $ 10,000
Personnel:
  Short-Term less than 1 year from USA   . . .   2

Christian Literature & Bible Center

(706)886-7734
1006 Oak Cliff Dr., Toccoa, GA 30577
Rev. Dr. Andrew J. Losier, Founder/President

A nondenominational support agency of independent tradition engaged in literature distribution and correspondence courses with materials shipped to 16 countries.

Year Founded in USA   1952
Income for Overseas Ministries . . $ 32,000
Amount of Gifts-In-Kind   . . . . $ 25,000
Personnel:
  Short-Term less than 1 year from USA   . . .   1

Christian Literature Crusade

(215)542-1244   **Fax: (215)542-7580**
E-Mail: 76043.3053@compuserve.com
701 Pennsylvania Ave, Ft. Washington, PA 19034
William M. Almack, President

An interdenominational sending agency of evangelical tradition engaged in literature distribution/production, Bible distribution, correspondence courses, and linguistics.

Year Founded in USA   1957
Income for Overseas Ministries . $ 207,000
Fully Supported USA Personnel Overseas:
  Expecting to serve more than 4 years   8
Countries: Colombia 2, Hong Kong 2, Italy 2, UK 2.

Christian Literature International

(503)266-9734   **Fax: (503)266-1143**
E-Mail: Christian@canby.com
P.O. Box 777, Canby, OR 97013
Gleason H. Ledyard, President

A nondenominational support agency of evangelical tradition engaged in Bible and literature distribution. Publishers of the 850 word limited-vocabulary NEW LIFE version Bible.

Year Founded in USA   1967
Income for Overseas Ministries . . . .   NA

Christian Medical & Dental Society
(423)844-1000   **Fax: (423)844-1005**
E-Mail: 75364.331@compuserve.com
Web: http://www.gocin.com/CMDS
P.O. Box 5, Bristol, TN 37621
David Stevens, MD, Exec. Director

A nondenominational professional society of physicians and dentists engaged in medical work, continuing education, and evangelism through coordination of short-term programs in Africa, Asia, Latin America, and North America.

".. living out our faith through our professions in .. opportunities for ministry afforded by medicine and dentistry, from whole person health care to missions around the world..."

Year Founded in USA 1931
Income for Overseas Ministries $ 1,239,381
Personnel:
   Short-Term less than 1 year from USA   . . 1,000
   Home ministry & office staff in USA   42

Christian Methodist Episcopal Church, Board of Missions
(404)522-2736
201 Ashby St. NW, Suite 212, Atlanta, GA 30314
Dr. Raymond Williams, Gen. Secretary

A denominational support agency of Wesleyan tradition engaged in Christian education and support of national churches. Financial and personnel information from 1992.

Year Founded in USA 1870
Income for Overseas Ministries . . $ 50,000
Fully Supported USA Personnel Overseas:
   Expecting to serve more than 4 years   1
Other Personnel:
   Home ministry & office staff in USA   1
Countries: Haiti, Jamaica, Nigeria 1.

Christian Mission for the Deaf
(313)933-1424   **Fax: (313)933-1424**
E-Mail: CMDeaf@aol.com
P.O. Box 28005, Detroit, MI 48228
Mrs. Berta Foster, Admin. Secretary

A denominational support agency of Plymouth Brethren tradition engaged in disability assistance programs, Christian education, evangelism, funds transmission, and training.

Year Founded in USA 1956
Income for Overseas Ministries . . $ 36,600
Personnel:
   Non-USA serving in own/other country   . . . 4
   Home ministry & office staff in USA   2
Countries: Nigeria, Sierra Leone.

Christian Missionary Fellowship
See: CMF International

Christian Missions in Many Lands
(732)449-8880   **Fax: (732)974-0888**
P.O. Box 13, Spring Lake, NJ 07762
Mr. Samuel E. Robinson, President
Mr. John G. Jeffers, Treasurer

A denominational service agency of Christian/Plymouth Brethren tradition engaged in funds transmission and various other services for assembly-commended missionaries. Overseas personnel included under Brethren Assemblies.

".. to provide necessary services which are difficult or impossible for the individual missionary or assembly to provide."

Year Founded in USA 1921
Income for Overseas Ministries . . . . NA
Personnel:
   Home ministry & office staff in USA   11

Christian Outreach International
(561)778-0571   **Fax: (561)778-6781**
E-Mail: COIhq@sprynet.com
P.O. Box 2823, Vero Beach, FL 32961
Mr. Jack Isleib, Exec. Director

An interdenominational service agency of evangelical tradition engaged in short-term programs coordination, evangelism, support of national workers, and mobilization for mission.

Year Founded in USA 1984
Income for Overseas Ministries $ 1,400,000
Fully Supported USA Personnel Overseas:
   Expecting to serve more than 4 years   1
   Expecting to serve 1 up to 4 years   26
Other Personnel:
   Non-USA serving in own/other country   . . . 11
   Short-Term less than 1 year from USA   . . 500
   Home ministry & office staff in USA   12
Countries: Czech Rep 7, France 1, Ukraine 9, Venezuela 10.

Christian Pilots Association

(626)962-0381   Fax: (909)606-0759
P.O. Box 603, West Covina, CA 91793
Howard Payne, President

An interdenominational specialized service
agency of evangelical tradition engaged in
providing medical supplies and aviation services.

Year Founded in USA	1972
Income for Overseas Ministries . .	$ 25,000
Amount of Gifts-In-Kind	$ 25,000

Christian Printing Mission

(330)895-3801   Fax: (330)895-3656
P.O. Box 210, Minerva, OH 44657
Pastor Jerald Hiebert, Director

A denominational support agency of Mennonite tradition engaged in literature production/
distribution, Bible distribution, and providing
medical supplies. Statistical data from 1992.

Year Founded in USA	1988
Income for Overseas Ministries .	$ 111,109
Personnel:	
Short-Term less than 1 year from USA . . .	3
Home ministry & office staff in USA	6

Christian Reformed World Missions

(616)224-0700   Fax: (616)224-0834
2850 Kalamazoo Av SE, Grand Rapids, MI 49560
Rev. William Van Tol, Intl. Director

A denominational sending agency of Reformed
and evangelical tradition engaged in establishing
churches, Christian education, theological
education, evangelism, leadership development,
and support of national churches.

Year Founded in USA	1888
Income for Overseas Ministries	$ 9,000,000
Fully Supported USA Personnel Overseas:	
Expecting to serve more than 4 years . . .	201
Expecting to serve 1 up to 4 years	49
Nonresidential mission personnel	3
Other Personnel:	
Non-USA serving in own/other country . . .	8
Bivocational/Tentmaker from USA	4
Short-Term less than 1 year from USA . . .	70
Home ministry & office staff in USA	21

Countries: Belize 1, China (PRC) 26, Costa Rica 15,
Dominican Rep 27, Ecuador 1, France 1, Guam 4,
Guinea 10, Haiti 7, Honduras 15, Hungary 6, Japan 22,
Kenya 1, Liberia 2, Mali 8, Mexico 13, Nigeria 43,
Pakistan 2, Philippines 33, Romania 3, Russia 1, Sierra
Leone 4, Taiwan (ROC) 5.

Christian Reformed World Relief Committee

(616)246-0740   Fax: (616)246-0806
E-Mail: CRWRC@crcnet.mhs.compuserve.com
2850 Kalamazoo Av. SE, Grand Rapids, MI 49560
Mr. John DeHaan, U.S. Director

A denominational service agency of Reformed
tradition engaged in relief aid, development, agricultural programs, literacy, and medical work.

"Showing God's love to people in need by
working with them and their communities to
create positive permanent change..."

Year Founded in USA	1962
Income for Overseas Ministries	$ 3,385,881
Fully Supported USA Personnel Overseas:	
Expecting to serve more than 4 years	21

Countries: Africa 3, Asia 2, Bangladesh 2, Dominican
Rep 1, Ecuador 1, El Salvador 1, Guinea 1, Honduras
1, Kenya 2, Malawi 1, Mozambique 1, Nicaragua 1,
Nigeria 2, Uganda 1, Zambia 1.

Christian Salvage Mission

(517)223-3193   Fax: (517)223-7668
P.O. Box 356, Fowlerville, MI 48836
Mr. Bruce E. Craft, Director

A nondenominational specialized service
agency of evangelical tradition engaged in
literature distribution by sending overseas surplus
and reusable Christian literature and Bibles.

Year Founded in USA	1956
Income for Overseas Ministries .	$ 150,000
Personnel:	
Home ministry & office staff in USA	10

Christian Services, Inc.

(612)944-7898   Fax: (612)944-7898
E-Mail: 105453.1637@compuserve.com
P.O. Box 39276, Minneapolis, MN 55439
Barbara Moore, Gen. Director

A nondenominational service agency of
evangelical tradition engaged in Christian
education, funds transmission, management
consulting/training, and youth programs. Income

and personnel information from 1992.

Year Founded in USA 1973
Income for Overseas Ministries . . $ 66,000
Fully Supported USA Personnel Overseas:
Expecting to serve more than 4 years 2
Other Personnel:
Short-Term less than 1 year from USA . . . 1
Home ministry & office staff in USA 10
Countries: Kenya 1, Liberia 1.

Christian Union Mission
(419)533-4166
P.O. Box 454, Liberty Center, OH 43532
Mr. Gareld Spiess, Director

A denominational sending agency of independent tradition engaged in evangelism, church construction, literature production/distribution, and youth programs.

Year Founded in USA 1864
Income for Overseas Ministries . $ 120,000
Fully Supported USA Personnel Overseas:
Expecting to serve more than 4 years 5
Other Personnel:
Short-Term less than 1 year from USA . . . 10
Home ministry & office staff in USA 1
Countries: Liberia 3, Mexico 2.

Christian World Publishers
(510)689-9944   **Fax: (510)689-1538**
101 Gregory Lane #42, Pleasant Hill, CA 94523
Mr. Peter Cunliffe, President

A nondenominational specialized service agency of evangelical tradition engaged in literature production and distribution.

Year Founded in USA 1974
Income for Overseas Ministries . $ 105,000
Fully Supported USA Personnel Overseas:
Expecting to serve more than 4 years 2
Other Personnel:
Home ministry & office staff in USA 1
Countries: France 2.

Christians In Action, Inc.
(209)564-3762   **Fax: (209)564-1231**
E-Mail: 73612.3633@compuserve.com
P.O. Box 728, Woodlake, CA 93286
Rev. Elgin Taylor, Intl. Director

An interdenominational sending agency of evangelical tradition engaged in evangelism, church planting, support of national churches, and missionary training.

Year Founded in USA 1957
Income for Overseas Ministries . $ 666,692
Fully Supported USA Personnel Overseas:
Expecting to serve more than 4 years 32
Expecting to serve 1 up to 4 years 72
Nonresidential mission personnel 3
Other Personnel:
Non-USA serving in own/other country . . 179
Short-Term less than 1 year from USA . . . 22
Home ministry & office staff in USA 15
Countries: Brazil 4, Colombia 3, Ecuador 2, Germany 3, Ghana 1, Guatemala 71, Guinea Bissau 2, India, Japan 6, Macao 2, Mexico 2, Peru 2, Philippines 2, Sierra Leone, Taiwan (ROC) 2, UK 2.

Church Ministries International
(972)772-3406   **Fax: (972)722-0012**
E-Mail: Church_Ministries@compuserve.com
500 Turtle Cove Blvd. #101, Rockwall, TX 75087
Mr. Jim Murray, Exec. Director

An interdenominational support agency of evangelical tradition engaged in church construction, missionary education, and evangelism.

".. serving as a catalyst to established mission teams and churches for strategic planning and implementation of programs that address the goal of evangelizing and discipling an entire nation."

Year Founded in USA 1989
Income for Overseas Ministries . $ 350,000
Fully Supported USA Personnel Overseas:
Expecting to serve more than 4 years 2
Other Personnel:
Home ministry & office staff in USA 4
Countries: Latin America 2.

Church of God (Anderson, Indiana), Missionary Board
(765)642-0258   **Fax: (765)642-5652**
E-Mail: MBChoGofc@aol.com
P.O. Box 2498, Anderson, IN 46018
Dr. Norman S. Patton, President

A nondenominational sending agency of Holiness movement tradition engaged in leadership development, church planting, TEE, support of national workers, and short-term programs co-ordination. Overseas personnel totals from 1992.

Year Founded in USA 1909
Income for Overseas Ministries $ 4,929,524
Fully Supported USA Personnel Overseas:
  Expecting to serve more than 4 years 48
  Nonresidential mission personnel 3
Other Personnel:
  Short-Term less than 1 year from USA . . . 72
  Home ministry & office staff in USA 18
Countries: Argentina 2, Bermuda 2, Bolivia 2, Brazil 2, Costa Rica 2, Cyprus 1, Egypt 4, Hong Kong 2, Japan 6, Kenya 8, Rwanda 2, Tanzania 6, Uganda 3, Uruguay 2, Venezuela 2, Zambia 2.

Church of God (Holiness), World Mission Board

(913)432-0303   Fax: (913)722-0351
E-Mail: WLHayton@aol.com
P.O. Box 4711, Overland Park, KS 66204
Rev. William L. Hayton, Exec. Secretary

A nondenominational sending agency of Holiness and independent tradition engaged in support of national churches and workers, church planting, theological education and evangelism.

Year Founded in USA 1917
Income for Overseas Ministries . $ 236,979
Fully Supported USA Personnel Overseas:
  Expecting to serve more than 4 years 7
  Expecting to serve 1 up to 4 years 2
Other Personnel:
  Non-USA serving in own/other country . . . 11
  Home ministry & office staff in USA 2
Countries: Bolivia 3, Cayman Isls 2, Nigeria 2, Ukraine 2.

Church of God (Seventh Day) Gen. Conference, Missions Abroad

(303)452-7973
P.O. Box 33677, Denver, CO 80233
Mr. Victor Burford, Director

A denominational support agency of evangelical tradition engaged in funds transmission, Bible and literature distribution, and support of national churches in 16 countries.

Year Founded in USA 1860
Income for Overseas Ministries . . $ 70,000
Personnel:
  Short-Term less than 1 year from USA . . . 4
  Home ministry & office staff in USA 1

Church of God in Christ, Mennonite General Mission Board

(316)345-2532   Fax: (316)345-2582
P.O. Box 230, Moundridge, KS 67107
Dale Koehn

A denominational sending agency of Mennonite tradition engaged in evangelism, church planting, Christian education, and medical work. Income and personnel data from 1992.

Year Founded in USA 1933
Income for Overseas Ministries $ 1,407,014
Fully Supported USA Personnel Overseas:
  Expecting to serve more than 4 years 66
Countries: Unspecified 66.

Church of God of Apostolic Faith

(918)437-7652   Fax: (918)437-7652
P.O. Box 691745, Tulsa, OK 74169
Rev. Joe L. Edmonson, Gen. Superintendent

A denominational sending agency of Pente-costal tradition engaged in theological education, Bible distribution, church construction, and literature distribution. Income from 1992 report.

Year Founded in USA 1951
Income for Overseas Ministries . . $ 39,500
Fully Supported USA Personnel Overseas:
  Expecting to serve more than 4 years 2
  Expecting to serve 1 up to 4 years 2
Other Personnel:
  Home ministry & office staff in USA 2
Countries: Mexico 4.

Church of God of Prophecy

(423)559-5336   Fax: (423)472-5037
E-Mail: WMCOGOP@aol.com
Web: http://www.COGOP.org
P.O. Box 2910, Cleveland, TN 37320
Mr. Randy Howard, Global Outreach Director
Mr. Billy Murray, General Overseer

A denominational sending agency of Holiness and Pentecostal tradition engaged in evangelism, church planting, childcare/orphanage programs, and missionary training.

Year Founded in USA 1903
Income for Overseas Ministries $ 2,800,000
Fully Supported USA Personnel Overseas:
  Expecting to serve more than 4 years 13
  Expecting to serve 1 up to 4 years 5

Other Personnel:
Non-USA serving in own/other country . . . 86
Bivocational/Tentmaker from USA 7
Short-Term less than 1 year from USA . . . 36
Home ministry & office staff in USA 4
Countries: Argentina, Australia 2, Belarus, Belgium, Belize, Benin, Bolivia, Botswana, Brazil, Bulgaria, Burkina Faso, Cameroon, Chile, Colombia, Congo/Zaire, Costa Rica, Cuba, Cyprus, Ecuador, Egypt, Ethiopia, Fiji, Finland, France, French Guiana, Germany 5, Ghana, Greece 3, Guyana, Haiti, India, Indonesia, Israel, Italy, Jamaica, Japan 2, Kazakhstan, Kenya, Liberia, Malawi, Malaysia, Nigeria, Pakistan, Panama, Paraguay, Philippines, Portugal, Rwanda, S Africa, Spain, Suriname, Swaziland, Tanzania, Thailand, Togo, Trinidad & Tobg, Uganda, Ukraine 2, Uruguay, Venezuela 2, W Samoa 2, Zimbabwe.

Church of God World Missions
(423)478-7190   Fax: (423)478-7155
P.O. Box 8016, Cleveland, TN 37320
Gene Rice, Gen. Director

A denominational sending agency of Pentecostal tradition engaged in church planting, church construction, Christian education, literature distribution, medical work, and support of national workers.

".. to help unchurched or nominal Christians become committed disciples of Christ and non-Christian people become Christians..."

Year Founded in USA 1910
Income for Overseas Ministries $ 11,069,852
Fully Supported USA Personnel Overseas:
Expecting to serve more than 4 years . . . 109
Expecting to serve 1 up to 4 years 7
Nonresidential mission personnel 5
Other Personnel:
Non-USA serving in own/other country . . 180
Bivocational/Tentmaker from USA 41
Short-Term less than 1 year from USA . . 1,500
Home ministry & office staff in USA 51
Countries: Africa 2, Albania, Angola, Aruba 2, Asia 4, Australia 2, Austria, Bahamas 2, Bahrain, Barbados, Belgium 4, Belize, Bolivia, Botswana 2, Brazil 6, Bulgaria 1, Cameroon, Caribbean Isls 1, Chad, Chile 2, China (PRC), Colombia, Congo/Zaire, Costa Rica, Cote d'Ivoire 2, Cyprus, Czech Rep, Djibouti, Dominican Rep, Ecuador 6, Egypt, El Salvador, Ethiopia, Europe 6, Fiji, France, Germany 6, Ghana, Greece, Guatemala 2, Haiti 4, Honduras 8, Hong Kong, India, Indonesia 2, Israel 5, Italy 2, Kenya 10, Korea-S 2, Latin America 2, Liberia, Malawi, Mexico 2, Myanmar/Burma, Nepal, Netherlands, New Zealand, Nicaragua 2, Nigeria, Oceania, Pakistan, Panama, Paraguay 2, Peru,

Philippines 9, Poland, Portugal, Puerto Rico, Romania, Russia 3, Rwanda, Serbia, Singapore, Spain 3, Suriname, Taiwan (ROC), Tanzania, Thailand, Togo, Trinidad & Tobg, UK 4, Uganda, Ukraine, United Arab Emr, Uruguay 2, Venezuela, Virgin Isls USA 2, W Samoa, Zambia 2.

Church of God, The
(502)622-3900
P.O. Box 525, Scottsville, KY 42164
Bishop Danny R. Patrick, General Overseer

A denominational support agency of Pentecostal tradition engaged in support of natl. churches.

Year Founded in USA 1903
Income for Overseas Ministries . . . . NR
Countries: Ghana, Haiti, Jamaica.

Church of the Brethren
(847)742-5100   Fax: (847)742-6103
E-Mail: cod_africa_me_rep.parti@ecunet.org
1451 Dundee Ave., Elgin, IL 60120
Mervin Keeney, Dir. Global Msn. Partnership

A denominational sending agency of Brethren tradition engaged in support of national churches, development, TEE, and relief aid. Personnel information from 1992.

Year Founded in USA 1884
Income for Overseas Ministries . . . . NR
Fully Supported USA Personnel Overseas:
Expecting to serve more than 4 years 2
Expecting to serve 1 up to 4 years 37
Other Personnel:
Short-Term less than 1 year from USA . . . 5
Countries: China (PRC) 2, Germany 5, Haiti 2, Israel 4, Japan 2, Netherlands 2, Nigeria 8, Poland 2, Sudan 4, Switzerland 2, UK 6.

Church of the Nazarene, World Mission Division
(816)333-7000   Fax: (816)363-3100
Web: http://www.nazarene.org/wm/
6401 The Paseo, Kansas City, MO 64131
Dr. Louie E. Bustle, Director

A denominational sending agency of Holiness and Wesleyan tradition engaged in church planting, theological education, TEE, evangelism, leadership development, and literature distribution.

".. to respond to the Great Commission of Christ to 'go and make disciples of all nations.' .. to advance God's Kingdom by the preservation and propagation of Christian Holiness..."

Year Founded in USA 1895
Income for Overseas Ministries $ 38,000,000
Fully Supported USA Personnel Overseas:
    Expecting to serve more than 4 years . . . 455
Other Personnel:
    Non-USA serving in own/other country . . . 61
    Bivocational/Tentmaker from USA 6
    Short-Term less than 1 year from USA . . 6,221
    Home ministry & office staff in USA 45
Countries: Africa 4, Albania 4, Am Samoa 2, Argentina 6, Australia 2, Belize 1, Bolivia 4, Botswana 2, Brazil 12, Cambodia, Cape Verde Isls 2, Chile 6, Costa Rica 15, Cote d'Ivoire 9, Dominican Rep 6, Ecuador 15, Ethiopia 2, Fiji 2, France 4, French Guiana 2, Germany 18, Ghana 4, Guam 1, Guatemala 15, Haiti 8, Honduras 2, Hong Kong 6, India 4, Indonesia 8, Ireland, Israel 2, Japan 15, Jordan 4, Kenya 20, Korea-S 6, Lesotho 2, Liberia, Madagascar 6, Malawi 13, Mexico 10, Mozambique 6, Namibia 2, Nicaragua 2, Nigeria 3, Papua New Guin 48, Peru 9, Philippines 34, Portugal 5, Puerto Rico 2, Romania 4, Russia 10, Rwanda 2, S Africa 21, Spain 2, Suriname 2, Swaziland 21, Switzerland 3, Taiwan (ROC) 2, Tanzania 4, Thailand 8, Trinidad & Tobg 4, Ukraine 2, Venezuela 4, Vietnam 3, Zambia 4, Zimbabwe 4.

Church of the United Brethren in Christ, Department of Missions
(219)356-2312   **Fax: (219)356-4730**
E-Mail: KMcQuill@huntcol.edu
302 Lake St., Huntington, IN 46750
Rev. Kyle W. McQuillen, Jr., Dir. of Missions

A denominational sending agency of evangelical tradition engaged in support of national workers, church planting, Christian education, theological education, medical work, and support of national churches.

".. to grow and multiply churches through worship, evangelism, discipleship and social concern by actively seeking and winning the lost..."

Year Founded in USA 1853
Income for Overseas Ministries $ 1,050,550
Fully Supported USA Personnel Overseas:
    Expecting to serve more than 4 years 3
    Expecting to serve 1 up to 4 years 5
Other Personnel:
    Non-USA serving in own/other country . . . 2
    Short-Term less than 1 year from USA . . 145

Home ministry & office staff in USA 4
Countries: Honduras, Hong Kong, India 1, Jamaica, Macao 7, Nicaragua, Sierra Leone.

Church Planting International
(904)444-9889   **Fax: (904)444-9979**
P.O. Box 12268, Pensacola, FL 32581
Rev. Don A. Dunkerley, Missionary at Large

An interdenominational support agency of Reformed and Presbyterian tradition engaged in church planting, evangelism, and support of national churches. Name changed from World Outreach Committee in 1997.

Year Founded in USA 1994
Income for Overseas Ministries . $ 156,870
Fully Supported USA Personnel Overseas:
    Nonresidential mission personnel 1
Other Personnel:
    Home ministry & office staff in USA 1
Countries: Myanmar/Burma, Philippines, Uganda.

Church Resource Ministries
(714)779-0370   **Fax: (714)779-0189**
E-Mail: CRM@crmnet.org
Web: http://www.crmnet.org/
1240 N. Lakeview Ave. #120, Anaheim, CA 92807
Dr. Samuel F. Metcalf, President

A transdenominational sending agency of evangelical tradition engaged in leadership development and church planting.

".. to develop leaders to strengthen and start churches worldwide."

Year Founded in USA 1980
Income for Overseas Ministries . . . . NR
Fully Supported USA Personnel Overseas:
    Expecting to serve more than 4 years 46
    Nonresidential mission personnel 4
Other Personnel:
    Non-USA serving in own/other country . . . 3
    Short-Term less than 1 year from USA . . . 3
    Home ministry & office staff in USA 7
Countries: Australia 2, Cambodia 4, Hungary 13, Poland 4, Romania 6, Russia 13, Venezuela 4.

Church World Service & Witness, Unit of the National Council of the Churches of Christ in the U.S.A.

(212)870-3004   Fax: (212)870-3523
Web: http://www.ncccusa.org
475 Riverside Dr., Rm. 678, New York, NY 10115
The Rev. Dr. Rodney Page, Exec. Director

An interdenominational service agency of ecumenical tradition engaged in relief aid, agricultural programs, long-term development, and assistance to refugees with partner agencies in the USA and more than 70 other countries.

"... meets basic needs of people in peril, works for justice and dignity with the poor and vulnerable, promotes peace and understanding among people of different faiths, races, and nations, and affirms and preserves the diversity and integrity of God's creation."

Year Founded in USA 1946
Income for Overseas Ministries . . . . NR
Fully Supported USA Personnel Overseas:
  Expecting to serve more than 4 years 17
Other Personnel:
  Non-USA serving in own/other country . . . 24
Countries: Unspecified 17.

Churches of Christ

(No central missions office)

A body of autonomous congregations and agencies of the Christian "Restoration Movement" (not using instrumental music in worship) which sends and supports missionaries directly from local congregations. Overseas personnel totals from 1994 Abilene Christian Univ. survey.

Income for Overseas Ministries . . . . NA
Fully Supported USA Personnel Overseas:
  Expecting to serve more than 4 years . . 1,014
Countries: Africa 229, Asia 148, Europe 303, Latin America 273, Oceania 61.

Churches of Christ in Christian Union - General Missionary Dept.

(614)477-7714   Fax: (614)477-7766
P.O. Box 30, Circleville, OH 43113
Dr. David Lattimer, Missionary Supt.

A denominational sending agency of Holiness tradition engaged in evangelism, church planting, support of natl. churches, and Bible translation.

Year Founded in USA 1909
Income for Overseas Ministries . $ 669,999
Fully Supported USA Personnel Overseas:
  Expecting to serve more than 4 years 8
Other Personnel:
  Home ministry & office staff in USA 3
Countries: Dominica 2, Papua New Guin 6.

Churches of God General Conference, Commission on Cross-Cultural Ministries

(419)424-1961   Fax: (419)424-3433
E-Mail: DDD@bright.net
P.O. Box 926, Findlay, OH 45839
Don Dennison, Associate

A denominational sending agency of evangelical tradition engaged in church planting, correspondence courses, Christian education, and evangelism.

Year Founded in USA 1825
Income for Overseas Ministries . $ 397,257
Fully Supported USA Personnel Overseas:
  Expecting to serve more than 4 years 3
  Expecting to serve 1 up to 4 years 4
Other Personnel:
  Non-USA serving in own/other country . . . 1
  Home ministry & office staff in USA 1
Countries: Brazil 2, Haiti 5, India.

Cities for Christ Worldwide

(760)489-1812   Fax: (760)489-1813
E-Mail: 76132.170@compuserve.com
P.O. Box 301032, Escondido, CA 92030
Timothy Monsma, Exec. Director

A transdenominational support agency of evangelical tradition providing information and training focused on developing-world cities.

Year Founded in USA 1985
Income for Overseas Ministries . . . . NA
Fully Supported USA Personnel Overseas:
  Expecting to serve 1 up to 4 years 2
Countries: Malawi 2.

CityTeam Ministries

(408)232-5600   **Fax: (408)428-9505**
E-Mail: CityTeam@cityteam.org
Web: http://www.goshen.net/CityTeam/
2302 Zanker Rd. #206, San Jose, CA 95131
Patrick J. Robertson, President

A transdenominational support agency of evangelical tradition engaged in evangelism, camping programs, leadership development, missionary training, and youth programs.

".. serving people in need, proclaiming the gospel, and establishing disciples among disadvantaged people of cities."

Year Founded in USA 1957
Income for Overseas Ministries . . . . NA
Personnel:
    Short-Term less than 1 year from USA . . . 4
    Home ministry & office staff in USA . . . 102

CMF International

(317)578-2700   **Fax: (317)578-2827**
E-Mail: 76534.244@compuserve.com
P.O. Box 501020, Indianapolis, IN 46250
Dr. Doug Priest, Gen. Director

A nondenominational sending agency of Christian (Restoration Movement) and evangelical tradition engaged in church planting, broadcasting, development, leadership development, literacy work, and medical work.

".. to serve Jesus Christ and His Church in world evangelization .. in partnership with Christians around the world through teams that make disciples and establish church-planting movements among unreached people."

Year Founded in USA 1949
Income for Overseas Ministries $ 3,382,475
Fully Supported USA Personnel Overseas:
    Expecting to serve more than 4 years . . . 119
    Expecting to serve 1 up to 4 years 6
Other Personnel:
    Short-Term less than 1 year from USA . . . 32
    Home ministry & office staff in USA 21
Countries: Benin 4, Brazil 11, Chile 10, Ethiopia 9, Indonesia 10, Kenya 45, Mexico 8, Singapore 2, Thailand 6, UK 16, Ukraine 4.

ComCare International

(914)679-3250   **Fax: (914)679-3250**
E-Mail: ComCareInt@aol.com
701 Zena Highwoods Rd., Kingston, NY 12401
Dieter W. Walter, Exec. Director

A nondenominational service agency of evangelical tradition engaged in disability assistance programs, evangelism, and medical work.

".. to bring necessary hearing care to needy people all over the world."

Year Founded in USA 1989
Income for Overseas Ministries . $ 111,500
Amount of Gifts-In-Kind . . . . $ 36,500
Personnel:
    Short-Term less than 1 year from USA . . . 11

Compassion International, Inc.

(719)594-9900   **Fax: (719)594-6271**
E-Mail: CIInfo@us.ci.org
Web: http://www.ci.org
P.O. Box 7000, Colorado Springs, CO 80933
Dr. Wesley K. Stafford, President

A nondenominational service agency of evangelical tradition engaged in child development programs, Bible distribution, Christian education, providing medical supplies, and youth programs.

".. an advocate for children to release them from their spiritual, economic, social and physical poverty and enable them to become responsible and fulfilled Christian adults."

Year Founded in USA 1952
Income for Overseas Ministries $ 58,270,837
Amount of Gifts-In-Kind . . . $ 4,584,311
Fully Supported USA Personnel Overseas:
    Expecting to serve more than 4 years 2
    Expecting to serve 1 up to 4 years 4
    Nonresidential mission personnel 4
Other Personnel:
    Non-USA serving in own/other country . . . 4
    Home ministry & office staff in USA . . . 200
Countries: Asia 2, Indonesia 2, Kenya 2.

Concordia Gospel Outreach

(314)268-1363
P.O. Box 201, St. Louis, MO 63166
Mr. Kenneth Wunderlich, Manager

A denominational specialized service agency of Lutheran tradition supplying Christian literature and Bibles for distribution in 50 countries for evangelism and Christian education.

Year Founded in USA 1958
Income for Overseas Ministries . . $ 86,000
Personnel:
Home ministry & office staff in USA 3

Congregational Christian Churches, National Assoc. of

(414)764-1620 **Fax: (414)764-0319**
8473 S. Howell Ave., Milwaukee, WI 53154
Dr. Michael Halcomb, Missions Secretary

A denominational support agency of Congregational tradition engaged in support of national churches, church planting, childrens programs, Christian education, and youth programs.

"To encourage and assist local churches in their development of vibrant and effective witnesses to Christ in Congregational ways."

Year Founded in USA 1953
Income for Overseas Ministries . $ 297,568
Personnel:
Non-USA serving in own/other country . . . 12
Bivocational/Tentmaker from USA 2
Short-Term less than 1 year from USA . . . 13
Home ministry & office staff in USA 13
Countries: Greece, Honduras, Hong Kong, India, Mexico, Nigeria, Philippines.

Congregational Holiness Church World Missions

(770)228-4833 **Fax: (770)228-1177**
3888 Fayetteville Hwy., Griffin, GA 30223
Rev. Billy Anderson, Supt. of World Missions

A denominational support agency of Pentecostal and Holiness tradition engaged in support of national churches and workers, Bible distribution, and church construction. Income figure from 1991 report.

Year Founded in USA 1921
Income for Overseas Ministries . $ 390,099
Personnel:
Short-Term less than 1 year from USA . . 100
Countries: India, Latin America.

Congregational Methodist Church, Division of Mission Ministries

(601)845-8787 **Fax: (601)845-8788**
E-Mail: CMChdq@aol.com
P.O. Box 9, Florence, MS 39073
Rev. Billy Harrell, Director

A denominational sending agency of Wesleyan tradition engaged in church planting, theological education, and evangelism. Income and personnel information from 1992.

Year Founded in USA 1945
Income for Overseas Ministries . $ 242,033
Fully Supported USA Personnel Overseas:
Expecting to serve more than 4 years 14
Other Personnel:
Home ministry & office staff in USA 2
Countries: Honduras 3, Mexico 9, Paraguay 2.

Conservative Baptist Foreign Mission Society (CBFMS)
See: CBInternational

Conservative Baptist Home Mission Society (CBHMS)
See: Mission to the Americas

Conservative Congregational Christian Conference

(612)739-1474 **Fax: (612)739-0750**
7582 Currell Blvd. #108, St. Paul, MN 55125
Rev. Clifford R. Christensen, Conf. Minister

A denominational support agency of Congregational and evangelical tradition engaged in support of national churches and short-term programs coordination.

Year Founded in USA 1948
Income for Overseas Ministries . $ 107,805
Fully Supported USA Personnel Overseas:
Expecting to serve more than 4 years 2
Expecting to serve 1 up to 4 years 2
Other Personnel:
Home ministry & office staff in USA 3
Countries: Micronesia 4.

Cook Communications Ministries International
(847)741-2400   **Fax: (847)741-2444**
Web: http://www.cookministries.com/internat.htm
850 N. Grove Ave., Elgin, IL 60120
Mr. David Mehlis, President

An interdenominational service agency of evangelical tradition engaged in training Christian publishers and literature distributors.

".. to empower Christians worldwide to build self-sufficient communications organizations..."

Year Founded in USA 1944
Income for Overseas Ministries . $ 990,000

Cooperative Baptist Fellowship
(770)220-1600   **Fax: (770)220-1680**
Web: http://www.cbfonline.org/
P.O. Box 450329, Atlanta, GA 31145
Dr. R. Keith Parks, Global Missions Coordinator

A denominational sending agency of Baptist tradition engaged in church planting, evangelism, and mission-related research.

".. to network, empower, and mobilize Baptist Christians and churches for effective missions and ministry in the name of Christ."

Year Founded in USA 1992
Income for Overseas Ministries . . . . NR
Personnel:
Home ministry & office staff in USA 5

Cornerstone, The
(606)858-4578   **Fax: (606)858-4578**
E-Mail: 103220.3636@compuserve.com
P.O. Box 192, Wilmore, KY 40390
Mr. E. Duane Jones, Director

A nondenominational sending agency of Wesleyan and charismatic tradition engaged in evangelism, Bible distribution, church planting, and youth programs.

"..to evangelize and disciple .. [in] partnership with local churches in the launching of short-term and career missionaries."

Year Founded in USA 1972
Income for Overseas Ministries . . $ 90,000
Fully Supported USA Personnel Overseas:
Expecting to serve more than 4 years 4

Other Personnel:
Short-Term less than 1 year from USA . . . 1
Home ministry & office staff in USA 2
Countries: France 2, S Africa 2.

Correll Missionary Ministries
(540)362-5196   **Fax: (540)366-7630**
P.O. Box 12182, Roanoke, VA 24023
Rev. Michael R. Correll, President

An interdenominational service agency of evangelical tradition engaged in support of national workers, Christian education, and medical work.

Year Founded in USA 1978
Income for Overseas Ministries . . $ 77,542
Personnel:
Non-USA serving in own/other country . . . 75
Home ministry & office staff in USA 3
Countries: Bolivia, Guatemala, India, Philippines, Portugal, Spain.

Covenant Celebration Church Global Outreach
(253)475-6454   **Fax: (253)473-7515**
E-Mail: CCC@kgc.com
1819 E. 72nd St., Tacoma, WA 98404
Ms. Jo Kling, Missions Coordinator

A nondenominational ministry of evangelical and charismatic tradition engaged in support of national churches and workers for evangelism.

".. [to] pursue the Great Commission both mono-culturally and cross-culturally through aggressive action in .. evangelism and missions."

Year Founded in USA 1981
Income for Overseas Ministries . . $ 60,000
Personnel:
Non-USA serving in own/other country . . . 7
Bivocational/Tentmaker from USA 3
Short-Term less than 1 year from USA . . . 8
Home ministry & office staff in USA 1
Countries: Bulgaria, Philippines, Thailand, Vietnam.

Crossover Communications Intl.
(800)845-2721   **Fax: (803)786-4209**
E-Mail: CrossoverC@juno.com
P.O. Box 2200, Stone Mountain, GA 30086
Dr. William H. Jones, President

A transdenominational service agency of Baptist tradition engaged in evangelism, leadership development, and mobilization for mission. Financial and personnel information from 1992.

Year Founded in USA 1987
Income for Overseas Ministries . . $ 35,000
Fully Supported USA Personnel Overseas:
Nonresidential mission personnel 1
Other Personnel:
Short-Term less than 1 year from USA . . . 63
Home ministry & office staff in USA 1

CSI Ministries

(765)286-0711   **Fax: (765)286-5773**
804 W. McGalliard Rd., Muncie, IN 47303
Mr. Eddy Cline, President

A nondenominational service agency of evangelical and fundamentalist tradition engaged in church construction, evangelism, funds transmission, and short-term teams coordination.

Year Founded in USA 1963
Income for Overseas Ministries . $ 800,000
Fully Supported USA Personnel Overseas:
Expecting to serve more than 4 years 5
Other Personnel:
Short-Term less than 1 year from USA . . 836
Home ministry & office staff in USA 7
Countries: Haiti 2, Jamaica 3.

Cumberland Presbyterian Church Board of Missions

(901)276-4572   **Fax: (901)276-4578**
1978 Union Ave., Memphis, TN 38104
Rev. Jack Barker, Exec. Director

A denominational sending board of Presbyterian and evangelical tradition engaged in church planting, evangelism, leadership development, and support of national and workers.

Year Founded in USA 1908
Income for Overseas Ministries . $ 500,000
Amount of Gifts-In-Kind . . . $ 100,000
Fully Supported USA Personnel Overseas:
Expecting to serve more than 4 years 5
Expecting to serve 1 up to 4 years 2
Other Personnel:
Bivocational/Tentmaker from USA 2
Short-Term less than 1 year from USA . . . 2
Home ministry & office staff in USA 1
Countries: Brazil 3, Colombia 3, Hong Kong 1.

David Livingstone Missionary Foundation

(918)494-9902   **Fax: (918)496-2873**
E-Mail: 103460.3661@compuserve.com
P.O. Box 232, Tulsa, OK 74102
Mr. Lonnie Rex, President

A nondenominational service agency of independent tradition engaged in support of national workers.

Year Founded in USA 1969
Income for Overseas Ministries $ 1,948,100
Amount of Gifts-In-Kind . . . $ 755,000
Fully Supported USA Personnel Overseas:
Nonresidential mission personnel 1
Other Personnel:
Home ministry & office staff in USA 7

DAWN Ministries

(719)548-7460   **Fax: (719)548-7475**
7899 Lexington Dr., Suite 200B
Colorado Springs, CO 80920
Dr. James H. Montgomery, President
Dr. Stephen D. Steele, CEO

A transdenominational service agency of evangelical tradition engaged in mobilizing the whole Body of Christ in whole nations.

".. to see saturation church planting become the generally accepted and fervently practiced strategy for completing the task of making disciples of all peoples in our generation."

Year Founded in USA 1985
Income for Overseas Ministries . $ 711,315
Fully Supported USA Personnel Overseas:
Nonresidential mission personnel 9
Other Personnel:
Home ministry & office staff in USA 4

Dayspring Enterprises Intl.

(757)428-1092   **Fax: (757)428-0257**
1062 Laskin Rd. #21A, Virginia Beach, VA 23451
Rev. John E. Gilman, President

A nondenominational support agency of evangelical tradition engaged in video/film production/distribution for evangelism and church planting through support of national workers.

Year Founded in USA 1979
Income for Overseas Ministries . $ 878,255

Personnel:
Home ministry & office staff in USA 8
Countries: India.

Daystar U.S.
(612)928-2550   **Fax: (612)928-2551**
E-Mail: 74461.414@compuserve.com
5701 Normandale Rd. #343, Edina, MN 55424
Dr. Robert J. Oehrig, Exec. Director

A nondenominational sending agency of evangelical tradition providing support for Daystar Univ. in Nairobi, extension training of church leaders, and research for planning/programming.

"To expand God's Kingdom in Africa by equipping Christian servant leaders through B.A./M.A. programs, short courses and research services."

Year Founded in USA 1963
Income for Overseas Ministries $ 2,022,000
Fully Supported USA Personnel Overseas:
Expecting to serve more than 4 years 7
Other Personnel:
Non-USA serving in own/other country . . . 3
Short-Term less than 1 year from USA . . . 40
Home ministry & office staff in USA 4
Countries: Kenya 7.

Deaf Missions International
(813)530-3020   **Fax: (813)530-3020**
P.O. Box 8514, Clearwater, FL 34618
M. Eldeny Hale, Director

A transdenominational service agency of evangelical tradition engaged in ministry to those with hearing disabilities through mission projects including missionary orientation and training.

Year Founded in USA 1967
Income for Overseas Ministries . $ 160,000
Fully Supported USA Personnel Overseas:
Expecting to serve more than 4 years 1
Nonresidential mission personnel 1
Other Personnel:
Non-USA serving in own/other country . . . 5
Home ministry & office staff in USA 1
Countries: Colombia 1, Costa Rica, Honduras.

Derek Prince Ministries, Intl.
(704)357-3556   **Fax: (704)357-1413**
E-Mail: 76520.3105@compuserve.com
Web: http://www.derekprince.com
P.O. Box 19501, Charlotte, NC 28219
Mr. David Selby, Intl. Director

A nondenominational agency engaged in the translation, production and distribution of Bible teaching books, audios and videos in conjunction with teaching conferences and radio broadcasting in 13 languages.

Year Founded in USA 1963
Income for Overseas Ministries . $ 929,907
Personnel:
Home ministry & office staff in USA 22

Door of Hope International
(626)799-6940   **Fax: (626)799-9521**
E-Mail: 75471.57@compuserve.com
P.O. Box 10460, Glendale, CA 91209
Rev. Paul H. Popov, President

An interdenominational service agency of evangelical tradition promoting religious freedom through support of national workers, services for other agencies, and youth programs.

Year Founded in USA 1972
Income for Overseas Ministries . $ 101,109
Fully Supported USA Personnel Overseas:
Expecting to serve more than 4 years 6
Other Personnel:
Non-USA serving in own/other country . . . 10
Short-Term less than 1 year from USA . . . 2
Home ministry & office staff in USA 4
Countries: Albania 4, Bulgaria, Macedonia 2, Russia.

Dorcas Aid International USA
(616)261-2080   **Fax: (616)454-3456**
E-Mail: DorcasAid@aol.com
6475 28th St. SE, #233, Grand Rapids, MI 49546
Mr. Ken Sweers, Chief Exec. Officer

An interdenominational support agency of Reformed tradition engaged in development, agricultural programs, and relief aid. Income and personnel information from 1992.

Year Founded in USA 1987
Income for Overseas Ministries . $ 297,750
Amount of Gifts-In-Kind . . . $ 262,750
Personnel:

Short-Term less than 1 year from USA   . . .   4

East West Ministries

(612)462-5404   Fax: (612)462-5404
E-Mail: SJ33W1@aol.com
P.O. Box 120171, St. Paul, MN 55112
Dr. Samuel V. Jones, President

A service agency of evangelical tradition engaged in funds transmission in support of national workers involved in church planting, childrens programs, and evangelism.

".. helping develop national workers in areas where foreign missionaries cannot go..supporting ministries already established by nationals."

Year Founded in USA 1993
Income for Overseas Ministries . . $ 48,000
Personnel:
   Short-Term less than 1 year from USA   . . .   2
   Home ministry & office staff in USA   1

East West Missionary Service

(562)697-7143   Fax: (562)691-3468
E-Mail: 74553.546@compuserve.com
P.O. Box 2191, La Habra, CA 90632
Mr. Robert T. Seelye, President

A nondenominational support agency of evangelical tradition engaged in services for existing agencies and missionaries through funds transmission and prayer letter services.

Year Founded in USA 1978
Income for Overseas Ministries . $ 425,250
Personnel:
   Home ministry & office staff in USA   4

East-West Ministries International

(214)265-8300   Fax: (214)373-8571
E-Mail: 74264.2624@compuserve.com
10310 N. Central Expressway, Bldg. 3 - Suite 500, Dallas, TX 75231
John Maisel, President

A nondenominational sending agency of evangelical tradition engaged in church planting, evangelism, leadership development, support of national churches, and training.

".. to provide church planting training and coordination of evangelistic resources to help

plant churches that are doctrinally sound, spiritually alive, grace oriented and multiplying..."

Year Founded in USA 1993
Income for Overseas Ministries $ 1,091,832
Fully Supported USA Personnel Overseas:
   Expecting to serve more than 4 years   12
Other Personnel:
   Bivocational/Tentmaker from USA   10
   Short-Term less than 1 year from USA   . . .   55
   Home ministry & office staff in USA   5
Countries: Kazakhstan 4, Russia 8.

Eastern European Bible Mission

(719)577-4450   Fax: (719)577-4453
P.O. Box 110, Colorado Sprgs, CO 80901
Mr. Hank Paulson, Founder & President

A nondenominational support agency of evangelical tradition engaged in youth and programs, evangelism, and literature distribution through support of national workers.

Year Founded in USA 1972
Income for Overseas Ministries . $ 484,000
Fully Supported USA Personnel Overseas:
   Nonresidential mission personnel   1
Other Personnel:
   Non-USA serving in own/other country   . . .   68
   Short-Term less than 1 year from USA   . . .   60
   Home ministry & office staff in USA   6
Countries: Czech Rep, Romania, Slovakia, Ukraine.

Eastern European Outreach, Inc.

(909)696-5244   Fax: (909)696-5247
E-Mail: EEO@pe.net
Web: http://www.EEO.org
P.O. Box 685, Murrieta, CA 92564
Jeff L. Thompson, Exec. Director

A nondenominational service agency of evangelical tradition engaged in evangelism, church planting, support of national workers, relief aid, and short-term programs coordination.

Year Founded in USA 1980
Income for Overseas Ministries . $ 615,000
Amount of Gifts-In-Kind . . . $ 250,000
Fully Supported USA Personnel Overseas:
   Expecting to serve 1 up to 4 years   19
   Nonresidential mission personnel   4
Other Personnel:
   Short-Term less than 1 year from USA   . .   145
   Home ministry & office staff in USA   6

Countries: Bulgaria 3, Romania 6, Russia 7, Ukraine 3.

Eastern Mennonite Missions
(717)898-2251   **Fax: (717)898-8092**
E-Mail: 75020.2662@compuserve.com
P.O. Box 628, Salunga, PA 17538
Mr. Richard Showalter, President

A denominational sending agency of Mennonite tradition engaged in support of national churches, church planting, development, theological education, and evangelism. Personnel information from 1992.

Year Founded in USA	1914
Income for Overseas Ministries	$ 3,000,000

Fully Supported USA Personnel Overseas:
Expecting to serve more than 4 years	80
Expecting to serve 1 up to 4 years	15

Other Personnel:
Non-USA serving in own/other country . . .	10
Bivocational/Tentmaker from USA	2
Short-Term less than 1 year from USA . .	180
Home ministry & office staff in USA	54

Countries: Asia 2, Australia 2, China (PRC) 3, Djibouti 5, Egypt 2, Ethiopia 4, France, Germany 3, Greece 2, Guatemala 13, Honduras 2, Hong Kong 5, Kenya 10, Peru 8, Philippines 2, S Africa 1, Somalia 1, Swaziland 2, Tanzania 24, Venezuela 4.

ECHO (Educational Concerns for Hunger Organization)
(941)543-3246   **Fax: (941)543-5317**
E-Mail: ECHO@xc.org
Web: http://www.xc.org/echo
17430 Durance Rd., N. Ft Myers, FL 33917
Dr. Martin L. Price, Exec. Director

An interdenominational service agency of evangelical tradition engaged in agricultural programs, services for other agencies, technical assistance, and training.

".. linking technical knowledge and practical solutions for subsistence farmers and gardeners primarily in the Third World."

Year Founded in USA	1973
Income for Overseas Ministries .	$ 487,744
Amount of Gifts-In-Kind	$ 49,195

Fully Supported USA Personnel Overseas:
Expecting to serve 1 up to 4 years	1

Other Personnel:
Short-Term less than 1 year from USA . . .	6
Home ministry & office staff in USA	10

Countries: Haiti 1.

EFMA (Evangelical Fellowship of Mission Agencies)
(770)457-6677   **Fax: (770)457-0037**
E-Mail: EFMA@xc.org
4201 N. Peachtree Rd. #300, Atlanta, GA 30341
Rev. Paul E. McKaughan, President & CEO

A confederation of mission agencies which serves for the exchange of ideas and building of supportive relationships.

".. to increase the effectiveness of the evangelical missions agencies and their leaders in worldwide cross-cultural mission..."

Year Founded in USA	1945
Income for Overseas Ministries	NA

Personnel:
Home ministry & office staff in USA	4

Elim Fellowship, World Missions Department
(716)582-2790   **Fax: (716)624-1229**
E-Mail: 102155.2620@compuserve.com
Web: http://www.frontiernet.net/~elim/
7245 College St., Lima, NY 14485
Thomas Brazell, Director

A nondenominational sending agency of Pentecostal and charismatic tradition engaged in church planting, theological education, missionary education, and leadership development. See Teen World Outreach for short-term program.

Year Founded in USA	1947
Income for Overseas Ministries	$ 1,322,000

Fully Supported USA Personnel Overseas:
Expecting to serve more than 4 years . . .	101
Expecting to serve 1 up to 4 years	5

Other Personnel:
Home ministry & office staff in USA	3

Countries: Andorra 2, Argentina 2, Australia 2, Austria 1, Belgium 1, Cambodia 1, Colombia 6, Denmark 2, Ethiopia 1, Europe-E 2, Haiti 2, Hong Kong 4, Israel 2, Kenya 25, Kiribati 2, Malaysia 2, Mexico 15, Mozambique 2, New Zealand 2, Niger 2, Nigeria 3, Peru 2, S Africa 1, Spain 4, Tanzania 12, UK 2, Uganda 3, Zimbabwe 1.

Emmanuel Intl. Mission (U.S.)
(905)640-2111   Fax: (905)640-2186
E-Mail: 105466.1550@compuserve.com
P.O. Box 8082, Port Huron, MI 48061
Joe Richardson, Director, U.S. Operations

An interdenominational service agency of evangelical tradition engaged in support of national churches, evangelism, and missionary training. Statistical information from 1992.

Year Founded in USA 1976
Income for Overseas Ministries . . $ 63,000
Fully Supported USA Personnel Overseas:
Expecting to serve more than 4 years 1
Countries: Philippines 1.

Emmaus Road, International
(619)292-7020   Fax: (619)292-7020
E-Mail: Emmaus-Road@eri.org
Web: http://www.eri.org
7150 Tanner Court, San Diego, CA 92111
Neal Pirolo, Director

A transdenominational service agency engaged in missionary training, audio and video recording/distribution, mobilization for mission, and short-term programs coordination.

".. to benefit the churches, mission agencies, cross-cultural teams, national ministries and any individual who wants to take the 'next step' .. in cross-cultural outreach ministry."

Year Founded in USA 1983
Income for Overseas Ministries . . $ 92,000
Fully Supported USA Personnel Overseas:
Nonresidential mission personnel 2
Other Personnel:
Short-Term less than 1 year from USA . . . 35

Engineering Ministries Intl.
(719)633-2078   Fax: (719)633-2970
E-Mail: EMIusa@aol.com
Web: http://members.aol.com/emiusa/website/
emipage.htm
110 S. Weber St., Suite 104, Colorado Springs, CO 80903
Mr. Michael T. Orsillo, Exec. Director

An interdenominational specialized service agency of evangelical tradition engaged in technical assistance for church construction, medical facilities and other development projects.

".. supporting the work of spreading the gospel by providing free professional design assistance to Christian Ministries in the Third world."

Year Founded in USA 1981
Income for Overseas Ministries . $ 594,000
Amount of Gifts-In-Kind . . . $ 311,000
Personnel:
Short-Term less than 1 year from USA . . . 57
Home ministry & office staff in USA 1

Enterprise Development Intl.
(703)243-9500   Fax: (703)243-1681
E-Mail: EDI1@ix.netcom.com
Web: http://logos.ghn.org/ENTERPRISE
1730 N. Lynn St, Suite 500, Arlington, VA 22209
Mr. Stephen A. Rosenburgh, President & CEO

A transdenominational service agency engaged in management consulting, training, and technical assistance for partner implementing agencies.

".. enabling the poor in developing nations to become productive, self supporting citizens."

Year Founded in USA 1985
Income for Overseas Ministries . $ 904,930
Fully Supported USA Personnel Overseas:
Expecting to serve more than 4 years 2
Expecting to serve 1 up to 4 years 1
Other Personnel:
Non-USA serving in own/other country . . . 1
Short-Term less than 1 year from USA . . . 1
Home ministry & office staff in USA 6
Countries: Colombia, Nicaragua 1, Philippines 2.

Episcopal Church Missionary Community
(412)266-2810   Fax: (412)266-6773
E-Mail: 102350.3234@compuserve.com
Web: http://www.episcopalian.org/ecms/
Box 278, Ambridge, PA 15003
Sharon Stockdale, Director

A denominational support agency of Episcopal and evangelical tradition engaged in missionary training, missions information services, and mobilization for mission.

".. to enable Episcopalians to be more knowledgeable, active and effective in world missions."

Year Founded in USA 1974
Income for Overseas Ministries . . $ 18,000

Episcopal Church, Domestic & Foreign Missionary Society

(212)922-5198   Fax: (212)490-6684
Web: http://www.dfms.org/
815 Second Ave., New York, NY 10017
Ms. Sonia J. Francis, Senior Exec. for Programs

A denominational sending agency of Episcopal tradition engaged in support of national churches, leadership development, community development, and providing medical supplies in Latin America, Africa, Asia and Europe.

Year Founded in USA 1821
Income for Overseas Ministries $ 10,322,549
Fully Supported USA Personnel Overseas:
   Expecting to serve more than 4 years 21
   Expecting to serve 1 up to 4 years 32
Countries: Unspecified 53.

Episcopal World Mission

(704)248-1377   Fax: (704)248-2482
E-Mail: EWM@rfci.net
P.O. Box 490, Forest City, NC 28043
The Rev. J. Eugene Horn, President

A denominational sending agency of Episcopal tradition engaged in evangelism, support of national churches, and mobilization for mission. Financial and personnel information from 1992.

Year Founded in USA 1982
Income for Overseas Ministries . $ 399,409
Fully Supported USA Personnel Overseas:
   Expecting to serve more than 4 years 11
Other Personnel:
   Non-USA serving in own/other country . . . 5
   Home ministry & office staff in USA 6
Countries: Congo/Zaire 3, Cyprus, Israel 2, Madagascar 2, Pakistan 2, Solomon Isls 2.

Equipping the Saints

(540)234-6222
E-Mail: ETS@rica.net
1254 Keezletown Road, Weyers Cave, VA 24486
Rev. Keith A. Jones, Exec. Director

A nondenominational service agency of evangelical tradition engaged in purchasing services and supplying equipment.

"..to enhance the outreach of indigenous evangelical ministries .. by providing appropriate human, material and financial resources."

Year Founded in USA 1991
Income for Overseas Ministries . . $ 24,000
Amount of Gifts-In-Kind . . . . $ 22,000
Personnel:
   Home ministry & office staff in USA 4

European Christian Mission

(604)943-0211   Fax: (604)943-0212
E-Mail: 74663.3176@compuserve.com
P.O. Box 1006, Point Roberts, WA 98281
Rev. Vincent Price, Director for N. America

An interdenominational sending agency of evangelical tradition engaged in evangelism, broadcasting, and literature distribution. Financial and personnel information from 1992.

Year Founded in USA 1960
Income for Overseas Ministries . $ 466,149
Fully Supported USA Personnel Overseas:
   Expecting to serve more than 4 years 35
Other Personnel:
   Bivocational/Tentmaker from USA 2
   Short-Term less than 1 year from USA . . . 18
Countries: Europe-E 15, Greece 7, Ireland 1, Italy 2, Spain 8, UK 2.

European Evangelistic Society

(404)344-7458
P.O. Drawer 90150, East Point, GA 30364
Mr. James L. Evans, Exec. Director

A nondenominational sending agency of Christian (Restoration Movement) tradition engaged in theological education, church planting, evangelism, and mission-related research.

Year Founded in USA 1932
Income for Overseas Ministries . $ 146,540
Fully Supported USA Personnel Overseas:
   Expecting to serve more than 4 years 4
Other Personnel:
   Non-USA serving in own/other country . . . 2
   Home ministry & office staff in USA 2
Countries: Germany 2, Lithuania 2.

European Missions Outreach

(804)973-7999   Fax: (804)978-4535
P.O. Box 6937, Charlottesville, VA 22906
Robert M. Baxter, President

A nondenominational sending agency of evangelical and charismatic tradition engaged in funds transmission, audio recording/distribution, church planting, and translation work.

"[to] train and equip European leadership, establish and support local churches, reach tomorrow's leaders by evangelizing today's youth."

Year Founded in USA	1990
Income for Overseas Ministries . .	$ 70,000

Fully Supported USA Personnel Overseas:

Expecting to serve more than 4 years	4

Other Personnel:

Non-USA serving in own/other country . . .	2
Short-Term less than 1 year from USA . . .	4
Home ministry & office staff in USA	1

Countries: France 2, Ireland, Netherlands 2.

Evangel Bible Translators

(972)722-2140   Fax: (972)722-1721
P.O. Box 669, Rockwall, TX 75087
Rev. H. Syvelle Phillips, President

A transdenominational support agency of charismatic and Pentecostal tradition engaged in Bible translation and Bible/literature distribution.

Year Founded in USA	1976
Income for Overseas Ministries	NR

Personnel:

Home ministry & office staff in USA	6

Evangelical Baptist Missions

(765)453-4488   Fax: (765)455-0889
E-Mail: 75053.3553@compuserve.com
P.O. Box 2225, Kokomo, IN 46904
Dr. W. Paul Jackson, Gen. Director

An independent Baptist sending agency engaged in church planting, childrens programs, extension education, evangelism, Bible translation, and video/film production and distribution. Income amount from 1992 report.

Year Founded in USA	1928
Income for Overseas Ministries	$ 2,696,762

Fully Supported USA Personnel Overseas:

Expecting to serve more than 4 years . . .	117
Expecting to serve 1 up to 4 years	4

Other Personnel:

Non-USA serving in own/other country . . .	2
Short-Term less than 1 year from USA . . .	22
Home ministry & office staff in USA . . .	12

Countries: Argentina 8, Benin 1, Cote d'Ivoire 12, France 26, Germany 6, Italy 4, Japan 4, Mali 18, Niger 10, Nigeria, Romania 4, Russia 4, S Africa 14, Sweden 4, UK 6.

Evangelical Bible Mission

(352)245-2560   Fax: (352)245-7783
E-Mail: EBMission@aol.com
P.O. Drawer 189, Summerfield, FL 34492
Rev. V. O. Agan, Chairman

An interdenominational sending agency of Holiness tradition engaged in church planting, Bible distribution, evangelism, literature distribution, and supplying equipment. Overseas personnel totals from 1992.

Year Founded in USA	1939
Income for Overseas Ministries	$ 1,700,000

Fully Supported USA Personnel Overseas:

Expecting to serve 1 up to 4 years	65
Nonresidential mission personnel	2

Other Personnel:

Home ministry & office staff in USA	5

Countries: Brazil 4, Haiti 6, Papua New Guin 55.

Evangelical Congregational Church, Division of Missions

(717)866-7584   Fax: (717)866-7383
E-Mail: ECdom@nbn.net
P.O. Box 186, Myerstown, PA 17067
Dr. John P. Ragsdale, Director

A denominational service agency of Wesleyan tradition engaged in church planting and support of national churches and workers. Financial and personnel information from 1988.

Year Founded in USA	1922
Income for Overseas Ministries .	$ 521,210

Fully Supported USA Personnel Overseas:

Expecting to serve more than 4 years	30
Expecting to serve 1 up to 4 years	4

Other Personnel:

Home ministry & office staff in USA	3

Countries: India, Kenya, Mexico, Unspecified 34.

Evangelical Covenant Church, Board of World Missions

(773)784-3000   Fax: (773)784-4366
E-Mail: 105502.1470@compuserve.com
5101 N. Francisco Ave., Chicago, IL 60625
Rev. Raymond L. Dahlberg, Exec. Director

A denominational sending agency of evangelical and Congregational tradition engaged in church planting, development, evangelism, medical work, support of national churches, and missionary training. Statistical data from 1992.

Year Founded in USA 1885
Income for Overseas Ministries $ 5,283,980
Fully Supported USA Personnel Overseas:
   Expecting to serve more than 4 years . . . 111
   Expecting to serve 1 up to 4 years 36
Other Personnel:
   Home ministry & office staff in USA 9
Countries: Colombia 9, Congo/Zaire 67, Ecuador 13, Germany 2, Japan 18, Mexico 21, Taiwan (ROC) 9, Thailand 8.

Evangelical Fellowship of Mission Agencies

See: EFMA

Evangelical Free Church Mission

(612)854-1300   **Fax: (612)853-8474**
E-Mail: 72220.2577@compuserve.com
901 E. 78th St., Minneapolis, MN 55420
Dr. Ben Sawatsky, Exec. Director

A denominational sending agency of evangelical tradition engaged in church planting, theological education, TEE, evangelism, leadership development, and short-term programs.

".. making disciples of Jesus Christ and incorporating them into congregations with the same purpose."

Year Founded in USA 1887
Income for Overseas Ministries $ 10,399,940
Fully Supported USA Personnel Overseas:
   Expecting to serve more than 4 years . . . 274
   Expecting to serve 1 up to 4 years 72
Other Personnel:
   Bivocational/Tentmaker from USA 6
   Short-Term less than 1 year from USA . . 500
   Home ministry & office staff in USA 34
Countries: Africa 2, Asia 13, Austria 3, Belgium 21, Brazil 4, Central Asia 3, Congo/Zaire 35, Czech Rep 18, Europe 2, France 12, Germany 21, Haiti 2, Hong Kong 12, India 4, Japan 22, Latin America 7, Macao 3, Mexico 7, Mongolia 6, Peru 8, Philippines 28, Poland 6, Romania 31, Russia 8, Singapore 11, Spain 4, Tanzania 2, UK 5, Ukraine 6, Venezuela 40.

Evangelical Friends Mission

(303)421-8100   **Fax: (303)431-6455**
E-Mail: 74152.1211@compuserve.com
P.O. Box 525, Arvada, CO 80001
Dr. Norval Hadley, Exec. Director

A denominational sending agency of Friends and evangelical tradition engaged in church planting, Christian education, TEE, evangelism, leadership development, and support of national workers.

Year Founded in USA 1978
Income for Overseas Ministries . $ 668,000
Fully Supported USA Personnel Overseas:
   Expecting to serve more than 4 years 12
Other Personnel:
   Non-USA serving in own/other country . . . 7
   Bivocational/Tentmaker from USA 2
   Short-Term less than 1 year from USA . . . 3
   Home ministry & office staff in USA 5
Countries: Bolivia, India 2, Mexico 4, Nepal, Philippines, Rwanda 6.

Evangelical Lutheran Church in America, Div. for Global Mission

(773)380-2650   **Fax: (773)380-2410**
Web: http://www.elca.org/dgm/
8765 W. Higgins Road, Chicago, IL 60631
Rev. Bonnie Jensen, Exec. Director

A denominational sending agency of Lutheran tradition engaged in support of national churches, community development, theological education, leadership development, short-term programs coordination, and missionary training.

Year Founded in USA 1842
Income for Overseas Ministries $ 23,057,000
Fully Supported USA Personnel Overseas:
   Expecting to serve more than 4 years . . . 199
   Expecting to serve 1 up to 4 years 35
   Nonresidential mission personnel 8
Other Personnel:
   Bivocational/Tentmaker from USA 104
   Short-Term less than 1 year from USA . . 151
   Home ministry & office staff in USA 44
Countries: Argentina 1, Bangladesh 4, Brazil 4, Cameroon 22, Cen Africa Rep 8, China (PRC) 10, Colombia 2, Denmark 1, Egypt 3, El Salvador 1, Ethiopia 2, Finland 1, Germany 2, Ghana 2, Guam, Guatemala 1, Hong Kong 6, India 4, Indonesia 5, Israel 5, Jamaica 2, Japan 25, Kenya 2, Korea-S 2, Latvia 2, Liberia 2, Madagascar 17, Mexico 2, Namibia 4, Nepal 2, Nicaragua 4, Nigeria 5, Norway 2, Panama 2, Papua

New Guin 7, Peru 1, Poland 2, Puerto Rico 2, S Africa 3, Senegal 11, Singapore 8, Slovakia 6, Taiwan (ROC) 5, Tanzania 27, Thailand 3, UK 1, West Bank 2.

Evangelical Lutheran Synod

(507)386-5356   Fax: (507)386-5376
E-Mail: ELSoffice@aol.com
6 Browns Court, Mankato, MN 56001
Rev. George M. Orvick, President

A denominational sending agency of Lutheran tradition engaged in evangelism, church planting, theological education, and literature production. Income and personnel totals from 1992.

Year Founded in USA 1918
Income for Overseas Ministries . $ 215,000
Fully Supported USA Personnel Overseas:
Expecting to serve more than 4 years 10
Countries: Chile 2, Czech Rep 3, Peru 3, Ukraine 2.

Evangelical Mennonite Church - International Ministries

(219)423-3649   Fax: (219)420-1905
E-Mail: EMCIntlMin@aol.com
1420 Kerrway Court, Fort Wayne, IN 46805
Dr. Harry L. Hyde, Exec. Director

A denominational sending agency of Mennonite and evangelical tradition engaged in church planting, Christian education, theological education, TEE, evangelism, and leadership development.

Year Founded in USA 1947
Income for Overseas Ministries . $ 670,575
Fully Supported USA Personnel Overseas:
Expecting to serve more than 4 years 25
Countries: Albania 2, Botswana 2, Burkina Faso 2, Congo/Zaire 2, Hong Kong 2, Ireland 2, Maldives 2, Mexico 1, Spain 2, Turkey 2, Venezuela 6.

Evangelical Methodist Church, Board of Missions

(317)780-8017   Fax: (317)780-8078
P.O. Box 17070, Indianapolis, IN 46217
Rev. Vernon W. Perkins, Gen. Conf. Secy.-Treas.

A denominational sending agency of Wesleyan and evangelical tradition engaged in evangelism, church planting, theological education, and medical work.

Year Founded in USA 1946

Income for Overseas Ministries . $ 239,000
Fully Supported USA Personnel Overseas:
Expecting to serve more than 4 years 6
Other Personnel:
Home ministry & office staff in USA 2
Countries: Bolivia 4, Mexico 2.

Evangelical Missions Information Service

(630)653-2158   Fax: (630)653-0520
E-Mail: PulseNews@aol.com
P.O. Box 794, Wheaton, IL 60189
Gary Corwin, Interim Director

An interdenominational agency of evangelical tradition providing information for missionaries, mission executives, church leaders and mission professors through the publications *Evangelical Missions Quarterly* and *World Pulse*. A cooperative office sponsored by the EFMA and IFMA.

Year Founded in USA 1964
Income for Overseas Ministries . . . . NA
Personnel:
Home ministry & office staff in USA 6

Evangelical Presbyterian Church

(313)261-2001   Fax: (313)261-3282
E-Mail: 76155.3570@compuserve.com
29140 Buckingham Ave. #5, Livonia, MI 48154
Richard Oestreicher, World Outreach Director

A denominational sending agency of Presbyterian and Reformed tradition engaged in church planting, evangelism, leadership development, linguistics, support of national churches/workers.

Year Founded in USA 1981
Income for Overseas Ministries . $ 903,768
Fully Supported USA Personnel Overseas:
Expecting to serve more than 4 years 21
Nonresidential mission personnel 2
Other Personnel:
Non-USA serving in own/other country . . . 19
Bivocational/Tentmaker from USA 11
Home ministry & office staff in USA 3
Countries: Argentina 3, Asia, France 2, India 2, Japan 2, Kazakhstan 4, Kenya 2, Mexico 2, Russia 2, Taiwan (ROC) 2.

Evangelism Explosion III Intl.
(954)491-6100   Fax: (954)771-2256
E-Mail: 102336.426@compuserve.com
P.O. Box 23820, Ft. Lauderdale, FL 33307
Dr. D. James Kennedy, Founder and President

An interdenominational support agency of evangelical tradition engaged in evangelism, literature production, training, and youth programs.

".. equipping the Body of Christ worldwide for friendship, evangelism, discipleship and healthy growth."

Year Founded in USA	1962
Income for Overseas Ministries .	$ 937,901

Personnel:
Home ministry & office staff in USA 24

Evangelism Resources
(606)858-3530   Fax: (606)858-3596
E-Mail: 203-6731@mcimail.com
P.O. Box 5, Wilmore, KY 40390
Dr. Willys K. Braun, President

An interdenominational sending agency of evangelical tradition engaged in leadership development, church planting, theological education, evangelism, and support of national workers.

Year Founded in USA	1976
Income for Overseas Ministries .	$ 552,221

Fully Supported USA Personnel Overseas:
Expecting to serve more than 4 years 8
Other Personnel:
Non-USA serving in own/other country . . . 31
Home ministry & office staff in USA 4
Countries: Congo/Zaire 6, India 2, Nigeria, Russia.

Evangelistic Faith Missions
(812)275-7531   Fax: (812)275-7532
P.O. Box 609, Bedford, IN 47421
Rev. J. Stevan Manley, President & Director

An interdenominational sending agency of Wesleyan and Holiness tradition engaged in evangelism, church planting, TEE, literature distribution, and support of national workers.

Year Founded in USA	1905
Income for Overseas Ministries .	$ 595,381

Fully Supported USA Personnel Overseas:
Expecting to serve 1 up to 4 years 9

Other Personnel:
Non-USA serving in own/other country . . . 48
Short-Term less than 1 year from USA . . . 30
Countries: Bolivia 2, Egypt, El Salvador, Eritrea 2, Guatemala 2, Honduras 3, Korea-S.

Evangelize China Fellowship, Inc.
(626)288-8828   Fax: (626)288-6727
P.O. Box 418, Pasadena, CA 91102
Dr. Paul C. C. Szeto, Gen. Director

An nondenominational service agency of independent tradition engaged in evangelism, church planting, education, and literature distribution. Statistical information from 1992.

Year Founded in USA	1947
Income for Overseas Ministries .	$ 161,337

Personnel:
Short-Term less than 1 year from USA . . . 3
Home ministry & office staff in USA 9
Countries: Asia, China (PRC).

Every Child Ministries, Inc.
(219)996-4201
P.O. Box 810, Hebron, IN 46341
Mr. Floyd C. Bertsch, Exec. Director

A nondenominational sending agency of evangelical tradition engaged in training, church planting, theological education, and support of national churches.

Year Founded in USA	1985
Income for Overseas Ministries . .	$ 82,983

Fully Supported USA Personnel Overseas:
Expecting to serve more than 4 years 2
Nonresidential mission personnel 2
Other Personnel:
Non-USA serving in own/other country . . . 8
Short-Term less than 1 year from USA . . . 3
Countries: Congo/Zaire 2.

Every Home for Christ
(719)260-8888   Fax: (719)260-7408
E-Mail: Wes@ehc.org
Web: http://www.sni.net/ehc/
P.O. Box 35930, Colorado Springs, CO 80935
Dr. Dick Eastman, President
Rev. Wesley R. Wilson, VP Intl. Administration

A transdenominational service agency of evangelical tradition engaged in literature distribution/production, church planting, evangelism, and support of national churches.

".. to serve, mobilize and train the Church to pray and actively participate in the systematic personal presentation of a printed or repeatable message of the Gospel of Jesus Christ to every home in the whole world..."

Year Founded in USA 1946
Income for Overseas Ministries $ 5,369,897
Personnel:
Non-USA serving in own/other country . . 1,111
Short-Term less than 1 year from USA . . . 4
Home ministry & office staff in USA . . . 55

Countries: Albania, Argentina, Bangladesh, Belarus, Benin, Bolivia, Brazil, Bulgaria, Burkina Faso, Cambodia, China (PRC), Congo, Congo/Zaire, Costa Rica, Cote d'Ivoire, Cuba, Czech Rep, El Salvador, Equat Guinea, Estonia, Ethiopia, France, Ghana, Greece, Honduras, India, Indonesia, Kazakhstan, Korea-S, Kyrgyzstan, Lebanon, Malawi, Malaysia, Mexico, Myanmar/Burma, Namibia, Nepal, Nicaragua, Nigeria, Panama, Papua New Guin, Paraguay, Peru, Philippines, Poland, Russia, Sierra Leone, Solomon Isls, Spain, Sri Lanka, Thailand, Togo, Ukraine, Uruguay, Uzbekistan, Zambia, Zimbabwe.

Faith Christian Fellowship Intl.
(918)492-5800   Fax: (918)492-6140
P.O. Box 35443, Tulsa, OK 74153
Dr. Doyle Harrison, President

A nondenominational support agency of charismatic tradition engaged in evangelism, church planting, Christian education, and funds transmission. Statistical information from 1992.

Year Founded in USA 1978
Income for Overseas Ministries . . . . NR
Fully Supported USA Personnel Overseas:
Expecting to serve more than 4 years 48
Other Personnel:
Home ministry & office staff in USA 2

Countries: Botswana 2, Costa Rica 2, Finland 2, Germany 4, Guatemala 4, Hungary 2, India 2, Jamaica 4, Nigeria, Philippines 8, Sweden 2, UK 16.

Far East Broadcasting Company
(562)947-4651   Fax: (562)943-0160
E-Mail: FEBC@febc.org
Web: http://www.febc.org/
P.O. Box 1, La Mirada, CA 90637
Mr. Jim Bowman, President

A nondenominational sending agency of evangelical tradition engaged in broadcasting, TEE, and evangelism.

".. bringing the gospel of Jesus Christ to the world by radio..."

Year Founded in USA 1945
Income for Overseas Ministries $ 9,750,673
Fully Supported USA Personnel Overseas:
Expecting to serve 1 up to 4 years 20
Other Personnel:
Non-USA serving in own/other country . . . 5
Home ministry & office staff in USA 56

Countries: Korea-S 2, N Mariana Isls 7, Philippines 11.

Farms International, Inc.
(218)834-2676   Fax: (218)834-2676
E-Mail: 102554.3305@compuserve.com
Web: www.gospelcom.net/mnn/media/farms.html
P.O. Box 270, Knife River, MN 55609
Mr. Joseph E. Richter, Exec. Director

An interdenominational service agency of evangelical tradition engaged in development, agricultural programs, evangelism, and technical assistance.

".. serving the church by equipping families in poverty with the means for self-support..[to help] ..families find a biblical path out of poverty."

Year Founded in USA 1961
Income for Overseas Ministries . . $ 93,000
Personnel:
Non-USA serving in own/other country . . . 7
Home ministry & office staff in USA 2

Countries: Bangladesh, India, Philippines, Sri Lanka.

Fellowship International Mission
(610)435-9099   Fax: (610)435-2641
E-Mail: 74434.2344@compuserve.com
555 S. 24th St., Allentown, PA 18104
Rev. Richard R. Ruth, Exec. Director

A nondenominational sending agency of fundamentalist and independent tradition engaged in church planting, camping programs, evangelism, leadership development, and youth programs.

Year Founded in USA 1950
Income for Overseas Ministries $ 1,580,000
Fully Supported USA Personnel Overseas:
Expecting to serve more than 4 years 96
Other Personnel:

Non-USA serving in own/other country . . . 8
Home ministry & office staff in USA 7
Countries: Australia 8, Belgium 1, Brazil 30, Colombia 2, Ecuador 4, Fiji 1, France 1, Germany 2, Japan 3, Mexico 8, Morocco 8, New Zealand 2, Niger 3, Nigeria 4, Poland 1, Spain 3, Suriname 2, Sweden 3, UK 4, Uganda, Ukraine 2, Venezuela 4.

Fellowship of Associates of Medical Evangelism

(812)379-4351   Fax: (812)379-1105
P.O. Box 688, Columbus, IN 47202
Dr. Robert E. Reeves, Exec. Director

A denominational support agency of Christian (Restoration Movement) tradition engaged in medical work, evangelism, funds transmission, and short-term programs coordination.

Year Founded in USA 1970
Income for Overseas Ministries . $ 1,055,000
Personnel:
  Bivocational/Tentmaker from USA 2
  Short-Term less than 1 year from USA . . 250
  Home ministry & office staff in USA 3

Fellowship of Missions
See: FOM

Floresta USA, Inc.

(800)633-5319   Fax: (619)274-3728
E-Mail: Floresta@xc.org
Web: http://www.floresta.org/
4903 Morena Blvd. #1215, San Diego, CA 92117
Scott C. Sabin, Exec. Director

A nondenominational support agency of ecumenical and evangelical tradition engaged in environmental, agricultural, and economic development programs.

".. to address, .. out of love and compassion for others as a Christian witness, the basic economic problems resulting from serious deforestation..."

Year Founded in USA 1984
Income for Overseas Ministries . $ 102,450
Personnel:
  Non-USA serving in own/other country . . . 15
  Home ministry & office staff in USA 3
Countries: Dominican Rep.

Flying Doctors of America

(770)451-3068   Fax: (770)457-6302
E-Mail: FDOAmerica@aol.com
Web: http://home.navisoft.com/vip/flyingdoctorsof america.htm
1951 Airport Rd. Suite #203, Atlanta, GA 30341
Allan M. Gathercoal, President/Founder

A nondenominational service agency of ecumenical tradition engaged in medical work, providing medical supplies, and rehabilitation assistance through short-term medical missions in 8 countries. A div. of Medical Mercy Missions Inc.

".. to help people, help people...[by].. creating a network of God's love that reaches into the farthest corners of the world and the human heart."

Year Founded in USA 1990
Income for Overseas Ministries . $ 200,513
Personnel:
  Short-Term less than 1 year from USA . . 204
  Home ministry & office staff in USA 6

FOCAS (Foundation of Compassionate American Samaritans)

(513)791-0181   Fax: (513)791-0181
E-Mail: FOCAS@aol.com
P.O. Box 428760, Cincinnati, OH 45242
Richard P. Taylor, President

A transdenominational service agency of Pentecostal tradition engaged in childrens programs, Christian education, evangelism, and support of national workers.

".. to see specific groups of the poor saved, discipled, helped in crucial physical needs, and equipped for a productive and godly life."

Year Founded in USA 1986
Income for Overseas Ministries . $ 100,000
Amount of Gifts-In-Kind . . . . $ 20,000
Personnel:
  Non-USA serving in own/other country . . . 25
  Short-Term less than 1 year from USA . . . 2
  Home ministry & office staff in USA 5
Countries: Haiti.

FOM (Fellowship of Missions)

(302)378-1525   Fax: (302)378-1525
E-Mail: 75541.21@compuserve.com
904 S. Broad St., Middletown, DE 19709
Rev. Henry J. Heijermans, President

A nondenominational inter-mission service agency of fundamental tradition acting as an accrediting agency for its constituents and encouraging the formation of missionary and church fellowships.

Year Founded in USA 1969
Income for Overseas Ministries . . . . NA
Personnel:
    Short-Term less than 1 year from USA . . . 2
    Home ministry & office staff in USA 2

Food for the Hungry
(602)998-3100   **Fax: (602)443-1420**
E-Mail: Hunger@fh.org
Web: http://www.fh.org
7729 E. Greenway Rd., Scottsdale, AZ 85260
Dr. Tetsunao Yamamori, President

A nondenominational service agency of evangelical tradition engaged in relief aid, development, and evangelism. Income and personnel information from 1992.

Year Founded in USA 1971
Income for Overseas Ministries $ 32,745,000
Amount of Gifts-In-Kind . . $ 27,200,000
Fully Supported USA Personnel Overseas:
    Expecting to serve more than 4 years 11
    Expecting to serve 1 up to 4 years 30
Other Personnel:
    Short-Term less than 1 year from USA . . . 30
    Home ministry & office staff in USA 44
Countries: Bolivia 8, Dominican Rep 1, Japan 10, Kenya 7, Laos 4, Peru 4, Romania 2, Thailand 5.

For Haiti with Love Inc.
(813)938-3245   **Fax: (813)942-6945**
E-Mail: ForHaiti@aol.com
P.O. Box 1017, Palm Harbor, FL 34683
Eva DeHart, Secretary-Treasurer

A transdenominational service agency of Messianic Methodist tradition engaged in development, evangelism, providing medical supplies, and relief aid.

Year Founded in USA 1982
Income for Overseas Ministries . $ 250,944
Amount of Gifts-In-Kind . . . . $ 71,183
Personnel:
    Non-USA serving in own/other country . . . 12
Countries: Haiti.

Forward Edge International
(360)574-3343   **Fax: (360)574-2118**
E-Mail: 76761.2706@compuserve.com
15121-A NE 72nd Ave., Vancouver, WA 98686
Rev. Joseph Anfuso, Director

A transdenominational service agency of charismatic tradition engaged in short-term programs coordination in support of national churches in evangelism.

".. to mobilize 'ordinary' Christians to .. reach into all the world with the gospel..through action-oriented training and short-term mission teams .."

Year Founded in USA 1983
Income for Overseas Ministries . $ 200,000
Personnel:
    Short-Term less than 1 year from USA . . 425
    Home ministry & office staff in USA 7

Foundation For His Ministry
(818)834-4734   **Fax: (818)834-4724**
P.O. Box 9803, N. Hollywood, CA 91609
Chuck & Charla Pereau, Founders

An interdenominational service agency of charismatic and independent tradition engaged in orphanage programs, church planting, medical work, and relief aid.

Year Founded in USA 1967
Income for Overseas Ministries . $ 702,402
Fully Supported USA Personnel Overseas:
    Nonresidential mission personnel 25
Other Personnel:
    Bivocational/Tentmaker from USA 15
    Short-Term less than 1 year from USA . . . 30
    Home ministry & office staff in USA 4
Countries: Mexico.

Foursquare Missions International
(213)484-2400   **Fax: (213)483-5863**
E-Mail: fmi@foursquare.org
Web: http://www.foursquare.org
P.O. Box 26902, Los Angeles, CA 90026
Rev. James A. Tolle, Director

A denominational sending agency of Pentecostal and evangelical tradition engaged in church planting, TEE, evangelism, leadership development, and support of national churches.

".. to glorify God and advance His kingdom in obedience to Jesus Christ's mandate to preach the gospel and make disciples of all nations/peoples."

Year Founded in USA 1923
Income for Overseas Ministries $ 6,259,464
Fully Supported USA Personnel Overseas:
    Expecting to serve more than 4 years 50
    Expecting to serve 1 up to 4 years 2
    Nonresidential mission personnel 10
Other Personnel:
    Non-USA serving in own/other country . . . 2
    Short-Term less than 1 year from USA . . 1,212
    Home ministry & office staff in USA 19
Countries: Africa, Asia 4, Belize 2, Benin 2, Bolivia 2, Brazil 4, Caribbean Isls, Chile 1, Costa Rica 2, Ecuador 2, El Salvador 2, Europe 4, Germany 2, Ghana 2, Haiti 2, Honduras 2, Kenya 2, Latin America, Malawi 2, Nepal 2, Panama 2, Papua New Guin 2, Philippines 2, S Africa 2, Singapore 2, Sri Lanka 1, Taiwan (ROC) 2.

Franconia Mennonite Conference
(215)723-5513   **Fax: (215)723-1211**
E-Mail: Franco@becnet.com
P.O. Box 116, Souderton, PA 18964
Walter Sawatzky, Director of Missions

A denominational sending agency of Mennonite tradition engaged in church planting and evangelism in Mexico.

Year Founded in USA 1917
Income for Overseas Ministries . $ 140,000
Personnel:
    Home ministry & office staff in USA 1

Free Gospel Church, Missions Department
(412)327-5454   **Fax: (412)327-3419**
E-Mail: cbeam@usaor.net
P.O. Box 477, Export, PA 15632
Rev. Chester H. Heath, Gen. Superintendent

A denominational sending agency of Pentecostal tradition engaged in support of national churches, church construction, and evangelism. Income and personnel information from 1992.

Year Founded in USA 1916
Income for Overseas Ministries . $ 175,000
Fully Supported USA Personnel Overseas:
    Expecting to serve more than 4 years 11
Countries: Philippines 5, Sierra Leone 6.

Free Methodist World Missions
(317)244-3660   **Fax: (317)241-1248**
E-Mail: 73517.1063@compuserve.com
P.O. Box 535002, Indianapolis, IN 46253
Larry Houck, Gen. Director

A denominational sending agency of Holiness and evangelical tradition engaged in leadership development, church planting, orphanage programs, Christian education, and evangelism.

".. to make known to people everywhere God's call to wholeness through forgiveness and holiness in Jesus Christ and to invite into membership and equip for ministry all who respond..."

Year Founded in USA 1885
Income for Overseas Ministries $ 5,917,617
Fully Supported USA Personnel Overseas:
    Expecting to serve more than 4 years 88
Other Personnel:
    Bivocational/Tentmaker from USA 6
    Short-Term less than 1 year from USA . . 450
    Home ministry & office staff in USA . . . 17
Countries: Africa 32, Asia 18, Caribbean Isls, Hungary 5, Latin America 33.

Free Will Baptist Association, Board of Foreign Missions
(615)731-6812   **Fax: (615)731-5345**
5233 Mt. View Rd., Antioch, TN 37013
Rev. R. Eugene Waddell, Gen. Director

A denominational sending board of Baptist tradition engaged in church planting, audio recording/distribution, church construction, missionary education, evangelism, and medical work.

Year Founded in USA 1935
Income for Overseas Ministries $ 3,920,420
Fully Supported USA Personnel Overseas:
    Expecting to serve more than 4 years 87
    Expecting to serve 1 up to 4 years 3
Other Personnel:
    Home ministry & office staff in USA 12
Countries: Brazil 20, Cote d'Ivoire 27, France 9, India 2, Japan 14, Panama 6, Spain 5, Uruguay 7.

French International Mission
(904)944-6753
2600 Michigan Ave. #86B, Pensacola, FL 32526
Mr. John C. Lawrence, Gen. Director

A denominational sending agency of independent Baptist tradition engaged in support of national churches and workers, church planting, evangelism, and literature distribution.

Year Founded in USA 1989
Income for Overseas Ministries . . $ 32,000
Fully Supported USA Personnel Overseas:
  Expecting to serve more than 4 years 2
Other Personnel:
  Non-USA serving in own/other country . . . 3
Countries: France 2.

Friends Church Southwest Yearly Meeting

(562)947-2883 **Fax: (562)947-9385**
E-Mail: Donfcsw@aol.com
Web: http://www.friendschurchsw.org
P.O. Box 1607, Whittier, CA 90609
Dr. Charles Mylander, Gen. Supt.

A denominational sending agency of evangelical Friends tradition engaged in church planting, theological education, TEE, evangelism, and support of national workers.

Year Founded in USA 1895
Income for Overseas Ministries . $ 263,425
Fully Supported USA Personnel Overseas:
  Expecting to serve more than 4 years 6
  Nonresidential mission personnel 6
Other Personnel:
  Short-Term less than 1 year from USA . . . 18
  Home ministry & office staff in USA 2
Countries: Guatemala 4, Honduras 2.

Friends for Missions, Inc.

(404)305-8299
P.O. Box 10942, Atlanta, GA 30310
Mrs. Mary E. Sawyer Goodwin, Exec. Director

An interdenominational support agency of evangelical tradition engaged in funds transmission for Bible distribution, Christian education, and providing medical supplies.

Year Founded in USA 1968
Income for Overseas Ministries . $ 108,472
Fully Supported USA Personnel Overseas:
  Expecting to serve more than 4 years 1
Other Personnel:
  Non-USA serving in own/other country . . . 15
  Short-Term less than 1 year from USA . . . 4

Countries: Haiti 1.

Friends in the West

(360)435-8983 **Fax: (360)435-6334**
E-Mail: Info@fitw.com
Web: http://www.fitw.com/acc
P.O. Box 250, Arlington, WA 98223
Rev. Raymond R. Barnett, President

An interdenominational service agency of evangelical tradition engaged in childcare/ orphanage programs, camping programs, and relief aid. Statistical information from 1992.

Year Founded in USA 1972
Income for Overseas Ministries . $ 810,267
Amount of Gifts-In-Kind . . . . $ 46,332
Fully Supported USA Personnel Overseas:
  Expecting to serve 1 up to 4 years 5
  Nonresidential mission personnel 2
Other Personnel:
  Non-USA serving in own/other country . . . 59
  Short-Term less than 1 year from USA . . . 28
  Home ministry & office staff in USA 11
Countries: Kenya, Romania 1, Uganda 4.

Friends of Israel Gospel Ministry

(609)853-5590 **Fax: (609)853-9565**
E-Mail: Daniel_n_p@msn.com
Web: http://www.foigm.org
P.O. Box 908, Bellmawr, NJ 08099
Dr. Elwood McQuaid, Exec. Director

A nondenominational service agency of evangelical tradition engaged in evangelism, broadcasting, correspondence courses, and literature production/distribution in Israel and 6 other countries.

Year Founded in USA 1938
Income for Overseas Ministries . $ 522,393
Personnel:
  Home ministry & office staff in USA 78

Friends of Turkey
See: Turkish World Outreach

Friends United Meeting, World Ministries

(765)962-7573 **Fax: (765)966-1293**
101 Quaker Hill Dr., Richmond, IN 47374
Retha McCutchen, Assoc. Secretary

A denominational sending agency of Friends tradition engaged in support of national churches, church planting, theological education, leadership development, and medical work.

".. to energize and equip Friends through the power of the Holy Spirit to gather people into fellowships where Jesus Christ is known..."

Year Founded in USA 1894
Income for Overseas Ministries . $ 402,000
Fully Supported USA Personnel Overseas:
    Expecting to serve more than 4 years 2
    Expecting to serve 1 up to 4 years 6
Other Personnel:
    Short-Term less than 1 year from USA . . . 10
    Home ministry & office staff in USA 4
Countries: Belize 1, Kenya 4, Romania 1, Uganda 1, West Bank 1.

Friendship International
(719)386-8808   **Fax: (719)633-9994**
E-Mail: FrInt@aol.com
Box 50884, Colorado Sprgs, CO 80949
Rev. Del Huff, Exec. Director

An interdenominational service agency of evangelical tradition engaged in evangelism, camping programs, literature distribution, and youth programs. Statistical data from 1992.

Year Founded in USA 1990
Income for Overseas Ministries . . $ 17,269
Fully Supported USA Personnel Overseas:
    Expecting to serve 1 up to 4 years 2
Other Personnel:
    Short-Term less than 1 year from USA . . . 35
    Home ministry & office staff in USA 2
Countries: Hungary 2.

Friendship Ministries
(425)823-1405
Totem Lake P.O. Box 8387, Kirkland, WA 98034
Denise C. Johnson, President & Founder

An interdenominational support agency of evangelical and ecumenical tradition engaged in support of national churches, Christian education, and psychological counseling.

".. to access and mobilize resources for the support of mission teams and to establish, encourage and develop friendships to answer and meet the needs in the Eastern European Church."

Year Founded in USA 1988
Income for Overseas Ministries . . $ 15,000
Fully Supported USA Personnel Overseas:
    Expecting to serve 1 up to 4 years 2
Other Personnel:
    Bivocational/Tentmaker from USA 2
    Short-Term less than 1 year from USA . . . 2
Countries: Poland 2.

Frontiers
(602)834-1500   **Fax: (602)834-1974**
E-Mail: Info@us.frontiers.org
Web: http://www.us.frontiers.org/
325 N. Stapley Dr., Mesa, AZ 85203
Dr. Richard D. Love, II, President

A sending agency of evangelical tradition engaged in church planting, evangelism, and mobilization for mission.

".. working in close cooperation with local churches to see vital, worshiping witnessing churches established..."

Year Founded in USA 1982
Income for Overseas Ministries $ 4,500,000
Fully Supported USA Personnel Overseas:
    Expecting to serve more than 4 years . . . 220
    Expecting to serve 1 up to 4 years 5
    Nonresidential mission personnel 1
Other Personnel:
    Non-USA serving in own/other country . . . 25
    Short-Term less than 1 year from USA . . . 37
    Home ministry & office staff in USA 33
Countries: Africa 43, Asia 133, Europe 49.

Full Gospel Evangelistic Assoc.
(281)447-5342   **Fax: (281)931-1883**
11503 Tomball Pkwy, Houston, TX 77086
Rev. Earl Pruitt, President

An interdenominational support agency of Pentecostal tradition supporting national churches engaged in evangelism, literature distribution, and church planting.

Year Founded in USA 1951
Income for Overseas Ministries . . $ 51,949
Personnel:
    Short-Term less than 1 year from USA . . . 4
    Home ministry & office staff in USA 5

Full Gospel Grace Fellowship

(918)224-7837
P.O. Box 4564, Tulsa, OK 74159
Rev. F. W. Peck, President

A nondenominational sending agency of Pentecostal tradition engaged in church planting and evangelism. Financial and personnel information from 1992.

Year Founded in USA 1970
Income for Overseas Ministries . . $ 52,821
Fully Supported USA Personnel Overseas:
    Expecting to serve more than 4 years 11
Countries: Argentina 3, Ghana 1, Indonesia 1, Mexico 2, Paraguay 2, Suriname 2.

Fundamental Baptist Mission of Trinidad & Tobago

(304)744-6443
762 Echo Rd., S. Charleston, WV 25303
Mr. Ted R. Smith, U.S. Director

A sending agency of Baptist and fundamental tradition engaged in church planting, evangelism, and support of national workers.

Year Founded in USA 1921
Income for Overseas Ministries . $ 102,000
Fully Supported USA Personnel Overseas:
    Expecting to serve more than 4 years 7
Other Personnel:
    Non-USA serving in own/other country . . . 10
    Short-Term less than 1 year from USA . . . 11
    Home ministry & office staff in USA 1
Countries: Trinidad & Tobg 7.

Fundamental Bible Missions

(609)881-5516
P.O. Box 43, Glassboro, NJ 08028
Rev. Harold E. Haines, Director

A denominational sending agency of fundamentalist tradition engaged in evangelism, church planting, and Christian education. Financial and personnel information from 1992.

Year Founded in USA 1940
Income for Overseas Ministries . . $ 60,000
Fully Supported USA Personnel Overseas:
    Expecting to serve more than 4 years 2
Countries: Japan 2.

General Association of Regular Baptist Churches

(847)843-1600   Fax: (847)843-3757
E-Mail: GRBC@grbc.org
1300 N. Meacham Rd., Schaumburg, IL 60173
John Greening, Natl. Representative

A denominational agency of Baptist tradition providing information for its associated churches relative to cooperating mission agencies.

Year Founded in USA 1932
Income for Overseas Ministries . . . . NA

General Baptists International

(573)785-7746   Fax: (573)785-0564
100 Stinson Dr., Poplar Bluff, MO 63901
Rev. Jack Eberhardt, Exec. Director

A denominational sending agency of Baptist tradition engaged in church planting, agricultural programs, literacy work, medical work, and support of national churches and workers.

"... to assist [local associations and churches of General Baptists] in the task of winning people to Christ at home and abroad..."

Year Founded in USA 1903
Income for Overseas Ministries . $ 520,661
Fully Supported USA Personnel Overseas:
    Expecting to serve 1 up to 4 years 11
    Nonresidential mission personnel 2
Other Personnel:
    Short-Term less than 1 year from USA . . . 50
    Home ministry & office staff in USA 3
Countries: Honduras 4, N Mariana Isls 2, Philippines 5.

General Conf. Mennonite Church, Commission on Overseas Mission

(316)283-5100   Fax: (316)283-0454
E-Mail: COM@gcmc.org
P.O. Box 347, Newton, KS 67114
Rev. Glendon Klaassen, Exec. Secretary

A denominational sending agency of Mennonite tradition engaged in evangelism, church planting, development, theological education, and support of national churches.

Year Founded in USA 1891
Income for Overseas Ministries . . $ 2,630,742
Fully Supported USA Personnel Overseas:
    Expecting to serve more than 4 years 42

Expecting to serve 1 up to 4 years 2
Other Personnel:
Non-USA serving in own/other country . . . 52
Bivocational/Tentmaker from USA 41
Short-Term less than 1 year from USA . . . 18
Home ministry & office staff in USA 9
Countries: Botswana 3, Brazil 1, Burkina Faso 3, China (PRC) 2, Colombia 2, Congo/Zaire 1, France 2, Gambia 2, Germany, Hong Kong 2, Hungary 2, India 2, Israel 2, Japan 3, Kenya 4, Mexico, Mozambique 2, Nepal 2, Paraguay 2, Russia, S Africa 2, Taiwan (ROC) 5.

Gideons International, The
(615)883-8533
2900 Lebanon Road, Nashville, TN 37214
Mr. Wendell McClinton, Exec. Director

An international Christian professional men's association of evangelical tradition engaged in Bible distribution and evangelism. Active in 156 countries with 45,000 overseas members.

Year Founded in USA 1899
Income for Overseas Ministries $ 35,200,000
Fully Supported USA Personnel Overseas:
Expecting to serve more than 4 years 5
Other Personnel:
Home ministry & office staff in USA 56
Countries: Unspecified 5.

GLINT International
See: Gospel Literature Intl.

Global Advance
(972)771-9042   **Fax: (972)771-3315**
E-Mail: GlobalAdv@earthlink.net
P.O. Box 742077, Dallas, TX 75374
Dr. David Shibley, President

An interdenominational service agency of evangelical tradition engaged in leadership development, literature distribution, support of national churches, and missionary training.

".. to help fulfill the Great Commission .. by empowering national leaders to evangelize and disciple their own and surrounding nations..."

Year Founded in USA 1990
Income for Overseas Ministries . $ 380,000
Personnel:
Home ministry & office staff in USA 5

Global Evangelization Movement & World Evangelization Research Center
(804)355-1646   **Fax: (804)355-2016**
E-Mail: GEM@xc.org
Web: http://www.gem-werc.org/
P.O. Box 6628, Richmond, VA 23230
David B. Barrett, President & Director

A multi-denominational specialized service agency initiating, promoting, publishing, and disseminating research related to all varieties of global Christian evangelization and mission.

".. to document world Christianity and its progress in completing the Great Commission, communicate this information to the global body of Christ, and advocate the unevangelized as the leading priority of world mission."

Year Founded in USA 1965
Income for Overseas Ministries . . . . NA
Personnel:
Home ministry & office staff in USA 8

Global Harvest Ministries
(719)262-9922   **Fax: (818)262-9920**
E-Mail: 74114.570@compuserve.com
P.O. Box 63060, Colorado Springs, CO 80962
Dr. C. Peter Wagner, President
Doris Wagner, Exec. Director

A transdenominational support agency of evangelical tradition engaged in training and informational literature production.

".. to unite existing national and international prayer networks to focus prayer power on world evangelization, especially the '10/40 window'..."

Year Founded in USA 1991
Income for Overseas Ministries . . . . NA
Personnel:
Home ministry & office staff in USA 6

Global Mapping International
(719)531-3599   **Fax: (719)548-7459**
E-Mail: Info@gmi.org
Web: http://www.gmi.org
7899 Lexington Dr. Suite 200A, Colorado Springs, CO 80920
Mr. Michael O'Rear, President

An interdenominational specialized service agency of evangelical tradition providing services for other organizations through technical assistance and training, computer mapping, and CD-ROM and other electronic publishing.

Year Founded in USA	1983
Income for Overseas Ministries . .	$ 30,000
Personnel:	
Home ministry & office staff in USA	11

Global Opportunities
(626)398-2393   **Fax: (626)398-2396**
1600 Elizabeth St., Pasadena, CA 91104
Mr. David E. English, Exec. Director

A nondenominational specialized service agency of evangelical tradition engaged in training, and mobilization for mission.

".. to mobilize and equip missions-committed Christians to serve abroad as effective tentmakers, especially in countries of greatest spiritual need."

Year Founded in USA	1984
Income for Overseas Ministries	NA
Personnel:	
Home ministry & office staff in USA	3

Global Outreach Mission
(716)688-5048   **Fax: (716)688-5049**
P.O. Box 711, Buffalo, NY 14240
Dr. James O. Blackwood, President

An interdenominational sending agency of evangelical tradition engaged in evangelism, broadcasting, and medical work.

Year Founded in USA	1943
Income for Overseas Ministries	$ 1,532,688
Fully Supported USA Personnel Overseas:	
Expecting to serve more than 4 years	89
Other Personnel:	
Non-USA serving in own/other country . . .	2
Short-Term less than 1 year from USA . . .	59
Home ministry & office staff in USA	16

Countries: Australia 2, Austria 1, Bahamas 1, Belgium 4, Brazil 2, Congo 2, Denmark 2, France 29, Germany 7, Ghana, Greece 2, Honduras 2, Ireland 17, Micronesia 2, Neth Antilles 2, Paraguay 2, Russia 2, UK 10.

Global Outreach, Ltd.
(601)842-4615   **Fax: (601)842-4620**
E-Mail: world@berean.net
Web: http://www.globaloutreach.org
P.O. Box 1, Tupelo, MS 38802
Dr. Sammy Simpson, Exec. Director

A nondenominational sending agency of evangelical tradition engaged in development, evangelism, and medical work. Financial and personnel information from 1992.

Year Founded in USA	1970
Income for Overseas Ministries .	$ 924,121
Fully Supported USA Personnel Overseas:	
Expecting to serve more than 4 years	2
Expecting to serve 1 up to 4 years	27
Other Personnel:	
Short-Term less than 1 year from USA . . .	59

Countries: Asia 1, Belgium 5, Brazil 1, Chile 2, Ecuador 2, Haiti 4, Honduras 5, Uganda 9.

Global Reach
(510)462-4884   **Fax: (510)462-3199**
P.O. Box 234, Pleasanton, CA 94566
Dr. Jay Lykins, President

A nondenominational support agency of evangelical tradition engaged in development, management training, and services for other agencies.

".. working in partnership with churches and missions organizations to start small businesses..[that]..provide jobs for needy people and build local sources of support for ministries..."

Year Founded in USA	1982
Income for Overseas Ministries	NA
Personnel:	
Bivocational/Tentmaker from USA	15
Home ministry & office staff in USA	9

Global Strategy Mission Assoc.
(504)536-3000   **Fax: (504)536-6550**
E-Mail: GSMA@compuserve.com
Web: http://www.cajunnet2.cajunnet.com/~gsma/
P.O. Box 2800, Reserve, LA 70084
Rev. Dick Bashta, Field Director

A nondenominational sending agency of charismatic tradition engaged in church planting, evangelism, funds transmission, mobilization for mission, and missionary training.

Year Founded in USA 1986
Income for Overseas Ministries $ 1,010,000
Fully Supported USA Personnel Overseas:
  Expecting to serve more than 4 years 10
  Expecting to serve 1 up to 4 years 40
  Nonresidential mission personnel 1
Other Personnel:
  Non-USA serving in own/other country . . . 2
  Bivocational/Tentmaker from USA 4
  Short-Term less than 1 year from USA . . . 75
  Home ministry & office staff in USA 9
Countries: China (PRC) 4, Haiti 2, Japan 2, Mexico 5, Russia 35, Singapore 2.

GlobaLink Ministries, Inc.

See: Advancing Native Missions

Globe Missionary Evangelism

(904)453-3453   **Fax: (904)456-6001**
E-Mail: 76263.1426@compuserve.com
P.O. Box 3040, Pensacola, FL 32516
Mr. J. Robert Bishop, President

A nondenominational sending agency of charismatic tradition engaged in church planting, Bible distribution, theological education, evangelism, leadership development, and relief aid.

Year Founded in USA 1973
Income for Overseas Ministries $ 1,795,806
Fully Supported USA Personnel Overseas:
  Expecting to serve more than 4 years 60
  Expecting to serve 1 up to 4 years 33
  Nonresidential mission personnel 1
Other Personnel:
  Non-USA serving in own/other country . . . 32
  Short-Term less than 1 year from USA . . 300
  Home ministry & office staff in USA 10
Countries: Albania 4, Bangladesh 2, Costa Rica 2, Germany 2, Guatemala 14, Haiti 4, Honduras 2, Iceland 2, India 3, Indonesia 2, Kenya 6, Malaysia 2, Mexico 16, Pakistan 2, Philippines 4, Russia 5, Thailand 6, UK 10, Ukraine 4, Uruguay 1.

Go International

(606)858-3171   **Fax: (606)858-4324**
P.O. Box 123, Wilmore, KY 40390
Rev. Larry G. Cochran, President

An interdenominational support agency of Wesleyan tradition engaged in mobilization for mission, Bible distribution, childrens programs, evangelism, and short-term teams coordination.

".. [to] collaborate with indigenous ministries [and] give Christians in the USA the opportunity to become directly involved in the life and ministry of the church in the Two-Thirds World..."

Year Founded in USA 1968
Income for Overseas Ministries . $ 878,989
Amount of Gifts-In-Kind . . . $ 138,797
Fully Supported USA Personnel Overseas:
  Expecting to serve 1 up to 4 years 2
Other Personnel:
  Short-Term less than 1 year from USA . . . 10
  Home ministry & office staff in USA 4
Countries: Kenya 2.

Go Ye Fellowship

(626)398-2305   **Fax: (626)797-5576**
E-Mail: 73324.3411@compuserve.com
P.O. Box 40039, Pasadena, CA 91114
Mr. William H. Gustafson, President

An interdenominational support agency of evangelical tradition engaged in funds transmission services.

".. enabling missionaries to pursue their God-given call and vision by serving as the link between missionaries and those who send them."

Year Founded in USA 1944
Income for Overseas Ministries . $ 422,889
Fully Supported USA Personnel Overseas:
  Expecting to serve more than 4 years 15
  Nonresidential mission personnel 4
Other Personnel:
  Non-USA serving in own/other country . . . 2
  Bivocational/Tentmaker from USA 4
  Home ministry & office staff in USA 3
Countries: Argentina 2, Asia 2, Brazil 3, Central Asia 4, Germany 2, Indonesia 1, Taiwan (ROC) 1.

Good News Productions Intl.

(417)782-0060   **Fax: (417)782-3999**
E-Mail: GNPI@xc.org
P.O. Box 222, Joplin, MO 64802
Mr. Ziden L. Nutt, Exec. Director

A nondenominational specialized service agency of Christian (Restoration Movement) tradition engaged in video production/ distribution and broadcasting. Financial and personnel information from 1992.

Year Founded in USA 1976
Income for Overseas Ministries . $ 700,000

Personnel:
Short-Term less than 1 year from USA . . . 6
Home ministry & office staff in USA 21

Gospel Fellowship Association

(864)242-1598   Fax: (864)242-1598
E-Mail: GFA@bju.edu
1430 Wade Hampton Blvd. #205, Greenville, SC
29609
Mr. Mark Batory, Director of Missions

A nondenominational sending agency of
fundamental tradition engaged in church
planting, evangelism, theological education, and
camping programs.

Year Founded in USA 1961
Income for Overseas Ministries . . . . NR
Fully Supported USA Personnel Overseas:
Expecting to serve more than 4 years . . . 122
Nonresidential mission personnel 2
Other Personnel:
Short-Term less than 1 year from USA . . . 6
Home ministry & office staff in USA 6
Countries: Australia 6, Azores 4, Brazil 10, Cameroon
4, Chile 6, Costa Rica 2, Dominica 2, Germany 18, Italy
2, Japan 4, Korea-S 6, Marshall Isls 4, Mexico 14,
Philippines 14, Puerto Rico 4, S Africa 4, Spain 4,
Taiwan (ROC) 2, UK 12.

Gospel for Asia

(972)416-0340   Fax: (972)416-6131
E-Mail: info@gfa.org
Web: http://www.gfa.org
1932 Walnut Plaza, Carrollton, TX 75006
Rev. K. P. Yohannan, President

A nondenominational service agency of evangelical tradition engaged in missionary training,
evangelism, broadcasting, church planting, leadership development, and support of natl. workers.

Year Founded in USA 1979
Income for Overseas Ministries $ 5,901,816
Fully Supported USA Personnel Overseas:
Nonresidential mission personnel 2
Other Personnel:
Non-USA serving in own/other country . . 6,439
Short-Term less than 1 year from USA . . . 28
Home ministry & office staff in USA 27
Countries: Bhutan, China (PRC), India,
Myanmar/Burma, Nepal, Pakistan, Philippines, Russia,
Sri Lanka, Thailand, Vietnam.

Gospel Furthering Fellowship

(717)272-7702
E-Mail: GFF@paonline.com
315 N. 8th St., Lebanon, PA 17042
Rev. Bruce Busch, Gen. Director

A nondenominational sending agency of
fundamentalist and Baptist tradition engaged in
church planting, theological education,
evangelism, and support of national churches.

Year Founded in USA 1935
Income for Overseas Ministries . $ 230,000
Fully Supported USA Personnel Overseas:
Expecting to serve more than 4 years 7
Other Personnel:
Non-USA serving in own/other country . . . 3
Home ministry & office staff in USA 17
Countries: Kenya 3, Spain 2, Tanzania 2.

Gospel Literature International, Inc. (GLINT)

(909)481-5222   Fax: (909)481-5216
E-Mail: GLINT@glint.org
Web: http://www.glint.org/
2910 Inland Empire Blvd.#104, Ontario, CA 91764
Georgalyn B. Wilkinson, President

A nondenominational service agency of
evangelical tradition providing copyrighted
English Christian education curriculum and
literature for adaptation, translation and
publication into other languages.

".. to provide indigenous Church leaders in
nations where Christian literature and training
materials are limited with Bible teaching
resources and books in national languages."

Year Founded in USA 1961
Income for Overseas Ministries . . . . NA
Personnel:
Home ministry & office staff in USA 7

Gospel Mission of South America

(954)587-2975
1401 SW 21st Ave., Fort Lauderdale, FL 33312
Rev. Terry Thompson, Gen. Director

A nondenominational sending agency of
Baptist and fundamentalist tradition engaged in
church planting, broadcasting, theological
education, and literature production/distribution.

"..[for] the evangelization of the peoples of South America by means of itinerant and localized work resulting in establishing and developing local national churches."

Year Founded in USA	1923
Income for Overseas Ministries .	$ 752,148

Fully Supported USA Personnel Overseas:
Expecting to serve more than 4 years	34
Expecting to serve 1 up to 4 years	1

Other Personnel:
Non-USA serving in own/other country . . .	4
Home ministry & office staff in USA	5

Countries: Argentina 6, Chile 23, Uruguay 6.

Gospel Missionary Union
(816)734-8500   Fax: (816)734-4601
E-Mail: DWeaver@gmu-kc.mhs.compuserve.com
10000 N. Oak Trafficway, Kansas City, MO 64155
Dr. Carl McMindes, President

An interdenominational sending agency of evangelical and Baptist tradition engaged in church planting, evangelism, broadcasting, camping programs, correspondence courses, theological education, and TEE.

Year Founded in USA	1892
Income for Overseas Ministries	$ 8,173,914

Fully Supported USA Personnel Overseas:
Expecting to serve more than 4 years . . .	260
Expecting to serve 1 up to 4 years	73
Nonresidential mission personnel	2

Other Personnel:
Non-USA serving in own/other country . . .	37
Short-Term less than 1 year from USA . . .	51
Home ministry & office staff in USA	33

Countries: Argentina 13, Austria 4, Bahamas 6, Belgium 7, Belize 4, Bolivia 31, Brazil 29, CIS 54, Colombia 8, Ecuador 54, Europe-E 8, France 14, Germany 13, Greece 6, Italy 7, Mali 20, Mexico 5, Panama 8, Spain 13, UK 8, Unspecified 21.

Gospel Outreach
(707)445-2135   Fax: (707)445-8914
E-Mail: GO@htan.org
P.O. Box 1022, Eureka, CA 95502
Pastor Dave Sczepanski, Director

A nondenominational support agency of charismatic tradition engaged in church planting and Christian education. Financial information from 1992.

Year Founded in USA	1971

Income for Overseas Ministries .	$ 180,000

Countries: Brazil, Ecuador, Guatemala, Nicaragua.

Gospel Outreach Ministries Intl.
(314)789-2160   Fax: (314)789-2789
4478 Goldman Spur Rd., Hillsboro, MO 63050
Dr. Sam Paul Gokanakonda, Founder/CEO

A nondenominational support agency of charismatic and evangelical tradition engaged in evangelism, church planting, support of national workers, and mission-related research.

Year Founded in USA	1988
Income for Overseas Ministries . .	$ 91,704

Fully Supported USA Personnel Overseas:
Nonresidential mission personnel	1

Other Personnel:
Non-USA serving in own/other country . .	250
Short-Term less than 1 year from USA . . .	6
Home ministry & office staff in USA	3

Countries: India.

Gospel Recordings USA
(213)250-0207   Fax: (213)250-0136
E-Mail: GloReNet@aol.com
Web: http://users.aol.com/glorenet
122 Glendale Blvd., Los Angeles, CA 90026
Mr. Colin Stott, Exec. Director

An interdenominational specialized service agency of evangelical tradition engaged in audio recording/distribution, evangelism, support of national workers, mission-related research, services for other agencies, and technical assistance.

Year Founded in USA	1939
Income for Overseas Ministries .	$ 225,514

Fully Supported USA Personnel Overseas:
Expecting to serve 1 up to 4 years	8
Nonresidential mission personnel	8

Other Personnel:
Non-USA serving in own/other country . . .	25
Short-Term less than 1 year from USA . . .	10
Home ministry & office staff in USA	37

Countries: Burkina Faso, CIS 2, Cameroon, Chad, Ghana, Guatemala 2, Liberia, Mexico 2, Nepal, Philippines, Sierra Leone, Singapore, UK 2.

Gospel Revival Ministries

(616)798-7373   **Fax: (616)798-4274**
E-Mail: GRMglobal@novagate.com
Web: http://www.novagate.com/~grmglobal/
P.O. Box 315, Fruitport, MI 49415
John Musser, President/Evangelist

A nondenominational agency of evangelical tradition supporting national workers involved in Bible distribution, church planting, and literature distribution.

Year Founded in USA 1980
Income for Overseas Ministries . . $ 63,325
Personnel:
  Non-USA serving in own/other country . . . 16
  Short-Term less than 1 year from USA . . . 3
  Home ministry & office staff in USA 7
Countries: Ghana, India, Nigeria, Philippines.

Grace and Truth, Inc.

(217)442-1120   **Fax: (217)443-1163**
E-Mail: GTPress@soltec.com
Web: http://www.soltec.com/~gtpress
210 Chestnut St., Danville, IL 61832
Mr. Sam O. Hadley, Exec. Officer

A nondenominational support agency of Christian/Plymouth Brethren tradition engaged in literature production/production in 11 languages and prison correspondence courses.

Year Founded in USA 1931
Income for Overseas Ministries . . . . NR

Grace Brethren International Missions

(219)267-5161   **Fax: (219)269-4066**
E-Mail: 17555.1160@compuserve.com
Web: http://www.grace.edu/gbim/gbim.htm
P.O. Box 588, Winona Lake, IN 46590
Dr. Tom Julien, Exec. Director

A denominational sending agency of Brethren tradition engaged in church planting, theological education, evangelism, leadership development, literacy work, and medical work.

"To partner with Grace Brethren Churches world-wide in order to call out a people for His name and gather them together in churches that are authentic expressions of the New Testament pattern."

Year Founded in USA 1900
Income for Overseas Ministries . . . . NR
Fully Supported USA Personnel Overseas:
  Expecting to serve more than 4 years . . . 110
  Expecting to serve 1 up to 4 years 11
Other Personnel:
  Non-USA serving in own/other country . . . 2
  Short-Term less than 1 year from USA . . . 58
  Home ministry & office staff in USA 17
Countries: Argentina 7, Brazil 9, Cen Africa Rep 21, Chad 2, Czech Rep 4, France 23, Germany 12, Japan 6, Mexico 9, Philippines 9, Portugal 5, Russia 4, Spain 4, UK 6.

Grace Ministries International

(616)241-5666   **Fax: (616)241-2542**
E-Mail: GraceMin@aol.com
P.O. Box 9405, Grand Rapids, MI 49509
Dr. Samuel R. Vinton, Jr., Exec. Director

A nondenominational sending agency of evangelical tradition engaged in church planting, Christian education, theological education, TEE, leadership development, and providing medical supplies.

Year Founded in USA 1939
Income for Overseas Ministries $ 1,432,035
Fully Supported USA Personnel Overseas:
  Expecting to serve more than 4 years 51
  Expecting to serve 1 up to 4 years 4
Other Personnel:
  Short-Term less than 1 year from USA . . . 42
  Home ministry & office staff in USA 6
Countries: Australia 6, Bolivia 6, Brazil 2, Congo/Zaire 13, Costa Rica 4, India, Neth Antilles, Philippines 6, Puerto Rico 6, Tanzania 12, Uruguay.

Grand Old Gospel Fellowship

(215)361-8111   **Fax: (215)643-2288**
160 E. Main St., Lansdale, PA 19446
Dr. B. Sam Hart, President

A nondenominational agency of Christian/Plymouth Brethren tradition engaged in radio broadcasting and literature distribution.

Year Founded in USA 1962
Income for Overseas Ministries . . $ 5,000
Personnel:
  Short-Term less than 1 year from USA . . . 2
  Home ministry & office staff in USA 3

Greater Europe Mission
(719)488-8008   Fax: (719)488-8018
E-Mail: 71327.1617@compuserve.com
Web: http://www.gospelcom.net/gem
18950 Base Camp Rd., Monument, CO 80132
Rev. John Graham, U.S. Director
Rev. Ted Noble, President

A nondenominational sending agency of
evangelical tradition engaged in church planting,
evangelism, theological education, and camping
programs. Short-Term and home staff totals from
1992 report.

Year Founded in USA 1949
Income for Overseas Ministries $ 10,105,000
Fully Supported USA Personnel Overseas:
   Expecting to serve more than 4 years . . . 247
   Expecting to serve 1 up to 4 years 14
Other Personnel:
   Non-USA serving in own/other country . . . 20
   Short-Term less than 1 year from USA . . 140
   Home ministry & office staff in USA . . . 35
Countries: Albania 1, Austria 18, Belgium 39, Bulgaria
   3, Croatia 6, France 34, Germany 22, Greece 15,
   Hungary 10, Iceland 4, Ireland 26, Italy 5, Latvia 6,
   Luxembourg 2, Netherlands 10, Poland 2, Portugal 13,
   Romania 4, Russia 1, Slovakia 8, Spain 27, Sweden 1,
   Ukraine 4.

Greater Grace World Outreach
(410)483-3700   Fax: (410)483-3708
E-Mail: missions@ggwo.smart.net
Web: http://www.ggwo.org
P.O. Box 18715, Baltimore, MD 21206
Guy V. Duff, Missions Director
Carl H. Stevens, Senior Pastor

A nondenominational support agency of
evangelical tradition engaged in evangelism,
church planting, and Christian education through
bi-vocational mission workers.

Year Founded in USA 1986
Income for Overseas Ministries . . . . NA
Personnel:
   Bivocational/Tentmaker from USA 65
   Short-Term less than 1 year from USA . . . 70

Gulf States Mission Agency
See: Global Strategy Mission Assoc.

Habitat for Humanity International
(912)924-6935   Fax: (912)924-6541
E-Mail: Info@habitat.org
Web: http://www.habitat.org/
121 Habitat St., Americus, GA 31709
Dr. Millard D. Fuller, President

An interdenominational specialized service
agency of ecumenical tradition engaged in
community development, funds transmission,
short-term programs coordination, training, and
supplying equipment and technical assistance.

".. to develop communities with God's people
in need by building and renovating houses .. in
which people can live and grow into all that God
intended."

Year Founded in USA 1976
Income for Overseas Ministries $ 11,239,834
Fully Supported USA Personnel Overseas:
   Expecting to serve more than 4 years 11
   Expecting to serve 1 up to 4 years 108
Other Personnel:
   Non-USA serving in own/other country . . 538
   Short-Term less than 1 year from USA . . . 30
   Home ministry & office staff in USA . . . 381
Countries: Antigua 1, Australia 1, Bolivia 2, Botswana 6,
   Brazil 2, Cen Africa Rep 3, Colombia 3, Congo/Zaire
   1, Costa Rica 3, Dominican Rep 4, Egypt 1, El
   Salvador, Ethiopia 5, Fiji 4, Ghana 3, Guatemala 2,
   Guyana 4, Haiti 3, Honduras 3, Hungary 3, India 3,
   Ireland 1, Jamaica 1, Kenya 4, Korea-S 1, Kyrgyzstan
   1, Malawi 6, Mexico 5, Netherlands 1, New Zealand,
   Nicaragua 2, Papua New Guin 9, Paraguay 2, Peru 2,
   Philippines 2, Poland 1, Romania 2, S Africa 2,
   Slovenia 1, Sri Lanka 2, Tanzania 4, Trinidad & Tobg
   2, UK 3, Uganda 3, Zambia 2, Zimbabwe 4.

Haiti Gospel Mission
(330)848-8742   Fax: (330)848-8744
4530 Butterbridge Rd NW, North Lawrence, OH
44666
W. John Hawthorn, Director

An interdenominational service agency of
Wesleyan and Holiness tradition engaged in
evangelism, orphanage programs, Christian
education, and relief feeding programs.

Year Founded in USA 1972
Income for Overseas Ministries . $ 120,000
Fully Supported USA Personnel Overseas:
   Expecting to serve more than 4 years 1
Other Personnel:

Non-USA serving in own/other country . . . 68
Short-Term less than 1 year from USA   . . . 1
Countries: Haiti 1.

Handclasp International, Inc.
(909)337-1894   **Fax: (909)336-1674**
E-Mail: DanHenrich@xc.org
Web: http://home.sprynet.com/sprynet/danhenri/
hpage.htm
P.O. Box 159, Crest Park, CA 92326
Mr. Daniel J. Henrich, President

A transdenominational service agency of evangelical and Baptist tradition engaged in video/film production, extension education, mission-related research, and services for other agencies.

Year Founded in USA 1970
Income for Overseas Ministries . $ 175,000
Amount of Gifts-In-Kind . . . $ 160,000
Fully Supported USA Personnel Overseas:
Expecting to serve more than 4 years 2
Other Personnel:
Non-USA serving in own/other country . . . 5
Short-Term less than 1 year from USA . . . 2
Countries: Kenya 2.

Harvest
(602)968-2600   **Fax: (602)894-6599**
E-Mail: 70153.1444@compuserve.com
1979 E. Broadway Rd. #2, Tempe, AZ 85282
Mr. Robert C. Moffitt, Exec. Director

An interdenominational service agency of evangelical tradition engaged in leadership development and training. Income amount from 1992.

Year Founded in USA 1981
Income for Overseas Ministries . . $ 69,987
Fully Supported USA Personnel Overseas:
Expecting to serve 1 up to 4 years 1
Nonresidential mission personnel 2
Other Personnel:
Non-USA serving in own/other country . . . 8
Home ministry & office staff in USA 4
Countries: Dominican Rep, Haiti, Honduras, India, Philippines 1, Venezuela.

Harvest Evangelism, Inc.
(408)927-9052   **Fax: (408)927-9830**
P.O. Box 20310, San Jose, CA 95160
Rev. Ed Silvoso, President

An interdenominational specialized service agency of evangelical tradition engaged in prayer evangelism training in support of evangelism and church planting.

"..to help the Church of the city, comprised of its various congregations, implement a comprehensive strategy to effectively saturate the city with the Good News of the gospel..."

Year Founded in USA 1980
Income for Overseas Ministries . $ 200,000
Fully Supported USA Personnel Overseas:
Expecting to serve more than 4 years 2
Nonresidential mission personnel 1
Other Personnel:
Bivocational/Tentmaker from USA 2
Short-Term less than 1 year from USA . . 400
Home ministry & office staff in USA 15
Countries: Argentina 2.

Harvest International Christian Outreach / Target Teams
(800)840-4426   **Fax: (402)330-5067**
E-Mail: TargetTeam@aol.com
P.O. Box 37656, Omaha, NE 68137
Michael Darr, Director

An interdenominational service agency of evangelical tradition engaged in short-term programs coordination, mission mobilization and training for literature distribution, evangelism, and church construction.

"Mobilizing churches into missions through short term mission experiences."

Year Founded in USA . . . . . . $ 1992
Income for Overseas Ministries . . $ 58,000
Fully Supported USA Personnel Overseas:
Nonresidential mission personnel 2
Other Personnel:
Short-Term less than 1 year from USA . . . 80
Home ministry & office staff in USA 6

Harvestime International Network
(209)661-1126
18911 Shore Dr., Madera, CA 93638
Rev. Argis D. Hulsey, President

An interdenominational support agency of charismatic tradition engaged in literature distribution in 60 countries, correspondence courses, and prison ministry.

".. to recruit, train, motivate, and mobilize a
network of international harvesters capable of ..
intercession, articulation, and demonstration of
the principles of spiritual harvest..."

Year Founded in USA 1983
Income for Overseas Ministries . . $ 14,000

Harvesting In Spanish

(503)226-2310   Fax: (503)226-0382
E-Mail: Harvest@es.com.sv
P.O. Box 025364, Miami, FL 33102
Rev. Donald W. Benner, President

An interdenominational sending agency of
independent tradition engaged in childcare/
orphanage programs, agricultural programs, Bible
distribution, church planting, Christian
education, and literature distribution.

Year Founded in USA 1980
Income for Overseas Ministries . $ 180,000
Fully Supported USA Personnel Overseas:
    Expecting to serve 1 up to 4 years 3
Other Personnel:
    Short-Term less than 1 year from USA . . 190
Countries: El Salvador 3.

Have Christ Will Travel Ministries

(215)438-6308   Fax: (215)438-6308
528 E. Church Lane, Philadelphia, PA 19144
Rev. Joseph C. Jeter, Director/President

An interdenominational support agency of
fundamental tradition engaged in Christian education, evangelism, support of national workers,
and youth programs. Income from 1988 report.

Year Founded in USA 1965
Income for Overseas Ministries . . $ 87,969
Personnel:
    Non-USA serving in own/other country . . . 67
    Short-Term less than 1 year from USA . . . 22
Countries: Haiti, India, Liberia.

HBI Global Partners

(704)286-8317   Fax: (704)287-0580
E-Mail: 103207.2556@compuserve.com
P.O. Box 245, Union Mills, NC 28167
John Gupta, U.S. Chair

A nondenominational sending agency of evangelical tradition engaged in mobilization for mission, church planting, and missionary training.

".. enabling the North American Church to
develop partnerships with national movements to
reach the unreached in India and beyond."

Year Founded in USA 1950
Income for Overseas Ministries . $ 316,000
Fully Supported USA Personnel Overseas:
    Expecting to serve more than 4 years 8
Other Personnel:
    Home ministry & office staff in USA 2
Countries: India 8.

HCJB World Radio Missionary Fellowship

(719)590-9800   Fax: (719)590-9801
E-Mail: PTolles@mhs.wrmf.org
Web: http://www.hcjb.org.ec/
P.O. Box 39800, Colorado Sprgs, CO 80949
Dr. Ronald A. Cline, President

An interdenominational service agency of
evangelical tradition engaged in radio and TV
broadcasting, medical work, technical assistance,
and video/film production and distribution.

"To communicate the gospel of Jesus Christ to
all nations so that people are transformed and become an active, vital part of the Body of Christ."

Year Founded in USA 1931
Income for Overseas Ministries $ 13,648,538
Fully Supported USA Personnel Overseas:
    Expecting to serve more than 4 years . . . 176
Other Personnel:
    Non-USA serving in own/other country . . . 74
    Short-Term less than 1 year from USA . . . 48
    Home ministry & office staff in USA 49
Countries: Australia, Brazil, Czech Rep 2, Ecuador 170,
Panama 2, Sweden, UK, Ukraine 2.

Health Teams International

(918)481-1115   Fax: (918)481-1115
E-Mail: 76265.3374@compuserve.com
7518 S. Evanston Ave., Tulsa, OK 74136
Dr. Robert W. Miller, President

An interdenominational service agency of
ecumenical tradition engaged in medical work,
evangelism, services for other agencies, and
short-term programs coordination.

"..to assist in the evangelization of the
unreached people groups of the world through

the ministrations of short term Christian health care teams."

Year Founded in USA 1986
Income for Overseas Ministries . . $ 42,800
Personnel:
    Short-Term less than 1 year from USA . . . 50
    Home ministry & office staff in USA 1

Heart to Heart Intl. Ministries
(760)789-8798   Fax: (760)789-8798
E-Mail: Sorrels@adnc.com
P.O. Box 1832, Ramona, CA 92065
Thomas Sorrels, Gen. Director

A nondenominational support agency of evangelical tradition engaged in childrens programs, evangelism, and Bible/literature distribution.

".. to evangelize and build up believers where the church has been greatly hampered by oppression and where there are few or no indigenous churches..."

Year Founded in USA 1994
Income for Overseas Ministries . . $ 75,700
Fully Supported USA Personnel Overseas:
    Expecting to serve 1 up to 4 years 4
    Nonresidential mission personnel 2
Other Personnel:
    Non-USA serving in own/other country . . . 1
    Short-Term less than 1 year from USA . . . 10
Countries: Hungary 1, Romania 3.

Heifer Project International
(501)376-6836   Fax: (501)376-8906
E-Mail: 74222.1542@compuserve.com
Web: http://www.intellinet.com/Heifer
1015 Louisiana Street, Little Rock, AR 72202
Jo Luck, Exec. Director

An interdenominational support agency of ecumenical tradition engaged in agricultural programs, development, extension education, technical assistance, and training.

Year Founded in USA 1944
Income for Overseas Ministries $ 5,500,000
Amount of Gifts-In-Kind . . . $ 715,000
Fully Supported USA Personnel Overseas:
    Expecting to serve more than 4 years 2
    Expecting to serve 1 up to 4 years 1
Other Personnel:
    Non-USA serving in own/other country . . 90
    Short-Term less than 1 year from USA . . . 6

Home ministry & office staff in USA . . . 100
Countries: Bolivia, Cameroon, China (PRC), Dominican Rep, Ecuador, Europe, Guatemala, Honduras, India, Kenya, Mexico, Mozambique 1, Peru, Philippines, Tanzania 2, Thailand, Uganda, Zimbabwe.

Hellenic Ministries
(630)462-7088   Fax: (630)462-3740
E-Mail: 100666.1532@compuserve.com
P.O. Box 726, Wheaton, IL 60189
Trevor Eby, Candidate Secretary

A nondenominational sending agency of evangelical tradition engaged in church planting, evangelism, and youth programs.

Year Founded in USA 1986
Income for Overseas Ministries . . $ 29,191
Fully Supported USA Personnel Overseas:
    Expecting to serve more than 4 years 7
Other Personnel:
    Non-USA serving in own/other country . . . 9
    Short-Term less than 1 year from USA . . . 4
    Home ministry & office staff in USA 1
Countries: Greece 7.

Help for Christian Nationals, Inc.
(972)780-5909
P.O. Box 381006, Duncanville, TX 75137
Dr. John Jauchen, Director

A transdenominational sending agency of evangelical tradition engaged in leadership development, extension education, literature distribution, support of national churches and workers, and training.

".. serving Christian national workers through economic and educational assistance, equipping them to be more effective in reaching their own people for Jesus Christ."

Year Founded in USA 1982
Income for Overseas Ministries . $ 225,000
Fully Supported USA Personnel Overseas:
    Expecting to serve more than 4 years 1
    Nonresidential mission personnel 1
Other Personnel:
    Non-USA serving in own/other country . . . 9
    Home ministry & office staff in USA 1
Countries: Guatemala, Honduras, India, Philippines, Russia, Spain 1.

Helps International Ministries
(704)253-2899   Fax: (704)253-2253
E-Mail: HIM@xc.org
Web: http://www.xc.org/helpintl/
P.O. Box 1640, Asheville, NC 28802
Rev. David Summey, Exec. Director

An interdenominational specialized service
agency of evangelical and Baptist tradition
engaged in technical assistance and services for
other agencies.

".. providing technical assistance to Christian
mission agencies and mission related organizations throughout the world..to assist, strengthen
and better equip evangelical ministries..."

Year Founded in USA 1976
Income for Overseas Ministries . . $ 95,885
Fully Supported USA Personnel Overseas:
  Expecting to serve more than 4 years 12
Other Personnel:
  Short-Term less than 1 year from USA . . . 8
  Home ministry & office staff in USA 1
Countries: Ethiopia 4, Israel 2, UK 6.

Hermano Pablo Ministries
(714)645-0676   Fax: (714)645-0374
P.O. Box 100, Costa Mesa, CA 92628
Rev. Paul Finkenbinder, Chairman of the Board
Rev. Charles Stewart, President

An interdenominational agency of evangelical
tradition broadcasting on 2,0000 radio stations in
27 countries in Latin America and Europe.

Year Founded in USA 1964
Income for Overseas Ministries . $ 396,000
Personnel:
  Home ministry & office staff in USA 5

High Adventure Ministries / Voice of Hope Broadcasting Network
(805)520-9460   Fax: (805)520-7823
Web: http://www.highadventure.org/
P.O. Box 100, Simi Valley, CA 93062
George Otis, President

An interdenominational service agency of
charismatic and evangelical tradition engaged in
radio broadcasting and audio/video production/
distribution in support of evangelism.

Year Founded in USA 1972

Income for Overseas Ministries . $ 388,511
Fully Supported USA Personnel Overseas:
  Expecting to serve more than 4 years 2
Other Personnel:
  Non-USA serving in own/other country . . . 28
  Short-Term less than 1 year from USA . . . 3
  Home ministry & office staff in USA 33
Countries: Belau(Palau) 1, Israel 1.

High School Evangelism Fellowship, Inc.
(201)387-1750   Fax: (201)387-1348
E-Mail: HIBA@carroll.com
P.O. Box 7, Bergenfield, NJ 07621
Mr. Andy Nelson, Intl. Director

A nondenominational sending agency of evangelical tradition engaged in youth programs and
camping programs for evangelism and discipleship, and short-term programs coordination.

".. to evangelize high school students by
discipling Christian students in their spiritual
growth and training them to share Christ..."

Year Founded in USA 1938
Income for Overseas Ministries . $ 400,000
Fully Supported USA Personnel Overseas:
  Expecting to serve more than 4 years 7
Other Personnel:
  Non-USA serving in own/other country . . . 17
  Short-Term less than 1 year from USA . . . 14
  Home ministry & office staff in USA 10
Countries: Japan 6, Russia 1.

Hinduism International Ministries
(847)872-7022   Fax: (847)872-7022
E-Mail: Singhal@cs.uwp.edu
P.O. Box 602, Zion, IL 60099
Dr. Mahendra P. Singhal, Chairman

A nondenominational support agency of
independent tradition engaged in evangelism,
leadership development, and training. Financial
information from 1992 report.

Year Founded in USA 1986
Income for Overseas Ministries . . $ 7,500
Personnel:
  Short-Term less than 1 year from USA . . . 20
  Home ministry & office staff in USA 2

Hindustan Bible Institute
See: HBI Global Partners

His Word To The Nations
(770)271-4140   Fax: (770)271-7890
E-Mail: the-revs@worldnet.att.net
3475 Maple Terrace Dr., Suwanee, GA 30174
Rev. June L. Schmidt, President

A transdenominational service agency of
Pentecostal tradition engaged in leadership development, church planting, Christian education,
evangelism, and support of national churches.

Year Founded in USA 1984
Income for Overseas Ministries . . $ 10,000
Amount of Gifts-In-Kind . . . . $ 2,000
Personnel:
  Non-USA serving in own/other country . . . 3
  Short-Term less than 1 year from USA . . . 2
  Home ministry & office staff in USA 1
Countries: Trinidad & Tobg, UK.

Holt International Children's Services, Inc.
(541)687-2202   Fax: (541)683-6175
E-Mail: Info@holtintl.attmail.com
P.O. Box 2880, Eugene, OR 97402
Mr. John L. Williams, Exec. Director

An interdenominational service agency of
evangelical tradition serving the needs of
homeless children and families at risk through
childcare, medical, and camping programs.

".. to carry out God's plan for every child to
have a permanent loving home through reuniting
birth families, in-country adoption, or
international adoption."

Year Founded in USA 1956
Income for Overseas Ministries . $ 6,094,101
Fully Supported USA Personnel Overseas:
  Expecting to serve 1 up to 4 years 6
Other Personnel:
  Non-USA serving in own/other country . . 552
  Short-Term less than 1 year from USA . . . 5
  Home ministry & office staff in USA . . . 120
Countries: China (PRC), Ecuador, Guatemala, Hong
  Kong 1, India, Korea-S, Philippines, Romania 2,
  Thailand, Vietnam 3.

HOPE Bible Mission, Inc.
(973)543-4492   Fax: (973)543-4492
P.O. Box 161, Morristown, NJ 07963
Mr. Rick Carey, Director

A nondenominational support agency of
evangelical tradition engaged in Bible distribution, evangelism, and support of natl. workers.

Year Founded in USA 1950
Income for Overseas Ministries . . . . NR
Personnel:
  Short-Term less than 1 year from USA . . . 6
Countries: Haiti, Spain.

Hope for the Hungry
(254)939-0124   Fax: (254)939-0882
E-Mail: HHungry@sage.net
Web: http://www.sage.net/~hhungry/index.htm
P.O. Box 786, Belton, TX 76513
Rev. Dan Kirkley, President

An interdenominational sending agency of
charismatic and evangelical tradition engaged in
evangelism, childcare/orphanage programs, and
youth programs. Statistical data from 1992.

Year Founded in USA 1982
Income for Overseas Ministries . $ 381,588
Fully Supported USA Personnel Overseas:
  Expecting to serve more than 4 years 2
  Expecting to serve 1 up to 4 years 19
Countries: Belize 4, Costa Rica 2, Czech Rep 2, France
  2, Haiti 5, Italy 2, Jamaica 2, Mexico 2.

Hosanna
(505)881-3321   Fax: (505)881-1681
E-Mail: 74212.3202@compuserve.com
2421 Aztec Rd. NE, Albuquerque, NM 87107
Mr. Jerry Jackson, President

An interdenominational service agency of ecumenical tradition serving as a repository of Bible
recordings in all available languages in addition
to providing training, equipment, funding for
recordings, and support of national workers.

Year Founded in USA 1972
Income for Overseas Ministries . . $ 86,992
Fully Supported USA Personnel Overseas:
  Nonresidential mission personnel 1
Other Personnel:
  Short-Term less than 1 year from USA . . . 6
  Home ministry & office staff in USA 92

ICI University

(972)751-1111   **Fax: (972)714-8185**
E-Mail: Info@ici.edu
Web: http://www.ici.edu/
6300 N. Belt Line Rd., Irving, TX 75063
Dr. George Flattery, President

A denominational service agency of Pentecostal and evangelical tradition engaged in extension theological education and literature production in support of national churches.

Year Founded in USA 1967
Income for Overseas Ministries $ 1,500,000
Personnel:
   Home ministry & office staff in USA   32

Icthus International

(626)359-7916   **Fax: (626)359-2069**
E-Mail: Don@Icthus.sheperd.com
P.O. Box 177, Monrovia, CA 91016
Mr. Don Weisbrod, Board Chair

An interdenominational service agency of evangelical tradition engaged in evangelism, Bible memorization and camping programs for children, youth and families in 14 countries of Latin America.

Year Founded in USA 1985
Income for Overseas Ministries . . $ 42,149
Personnel:
   Short-Term less than 1 year from USA   . . . 6
   Home ministry & office staff in USA   1

IDEA/PROLADES

(714)666-1906   **Fax: (714)666-1906**
E-Mail: CLHolland@xc.org
P.O. Box 3406, Orange, CA 92857
Mr. Clifton L. Holland, Exec. Director

A nondenominational service agency of evangelical tradition engaged in missiological research, leadership development, and providing technical assistance to others in these areas.

".. to produce or facilitate the development of in-depth evangelization, authentic Christian discipleship, and integral church growth..."

Year Founded in USA 1982
Income for Overseas Ministries . . $ 75,000
Fully Supported USA Personnel Overseas:
   Expecting to serve more than 4 years   2

Other Personnel:
   Home ministry & office staff in USA   2
Countries: Costa Rica 2.

IFMA (Interdenominational Foreign Mission Association)

(630)682-9270   **Fax: (630)682-9278**
E-Mail: IFMA@aol.com
P.O. Box 0398, Wheaton, IL 60189
Dr. John H. Orme, Exec. Director

An association of mission agencies without denominational affiliation organized for the purpose of strengthening the effectiveness and outreach of interdenominational missions.

Year Founded in USA 1917
Income for Overseas Ministries . . . . NA

Impact International

(561)338-7515   **Fax: (561)338-7516**
P.O. Box 2530, Boca Raton, FL 33427
Rev. Bruce Woodman, Exec. Director

An interdenominational service agency of evangelical tradition engaged in evangelism, radio broadcasting, and church planting. Personnel and income totals from 1992 report.

Year Founded in USA 1959
Income for Overseas Ministries . $ 272,898
Fully Supported USA Personnel Overseas:
   Nonresidential mission personnel   2
Other Personnel:
   Non-USA serving in own/other country   . . . 17
   Home ministry & office staff in USA   2
Countries: Argentina, Colombia, Guatemala, Honduras, Mexico, Venezuela.

In Touch Mission International

(602)968-4100   **Fax: (602)968-5462**
E-Mail: 75222.2215@compuserve.com
P.O. Box 28240, Tempe, AZ 85285
Bill Bathman, Director

An interdenominational sending agency of Baptist tradition engaged in support of national workers, Bible distribution, evangelism, and providing medical supplies.

Year Founded in USA 1981
Income for Overseas Ministries . $ 151,000
Fully Supported USA Personnel Overseas:
   Expecting to serve more than 4 years   2

Other Personnel:
Non-USA serving in own/other country . . . 7
Home ministry & office staff in USA 4
Countries: Europe-E 2, Mexico.

In-Depth Evangelism Associates
See: IDEA/PROLADES

Independent Board for Presbyterian Foreign Missions
(215)438-0511   Fax: (215)438-0560
246 W. Walnut Lane, Philadelphia, PA 19144
Dr. William R. LeRoy, Exec. Director

An interdenominational support agency of fundamentalist and Presbyterian tradition engaged in evangelism, Bible distribution, church planting, and theological education. Income from 1992.

Year Founded in USA 1933
Income for Overseas Ministries . $ 403,670

Independent Faith Mission
(910)292-1255
P.O. Box 7791, Greensboro, NC 27417
Rev. Robert F. Kurtz, Exec. Director

A nondenominational service agency of Baptist tradition providing various services to local churches sending missionaries engaged in church planting and evangelism. Financial and personnel information from 1992.

Year Founded in USA 1950
Income for Overseas Ministries $ 1,800,000
Fully Supported USA Personnel Overseas:
Expecting to serve more than 4 years 99
Other Personnel:
Short-Term less than 1 year from USA . . . 6
Countries: Antigua 4, Congo/Zaire 15, Italy 7, Kenya 16, Mexico 4, Micronesia 2, Philippines 2, S Africa 11, Suriname 21, UK 2, Unspecified 12, Zimbabwe 3.

Independent Gospel Missions
(412)342-1090   Fax: (412)342-1371
327 Stambaugh Ave., Sharon, PA 16146
Dr. D. L. Bovard, Founder/Director

A nondenominational agency of Baptist tradition supporting national churches and workers for church planting and evangelism.

Year Founded in USA 1968

Income for Overseas Ministries . $ 720,000

India Evangelical Mission, Inc.
(714)739-8068   Fax: (714)739-8068
P.O. Box 1633, Lakewood, CA 90716
Dr. G. V. Mathai, President

A nondenominational service agency of Brethren tradition engaged in support of national workers, church planting, correspondence courses, evangelism, literature distribution, and medical work.

Year Founded in USA 1966
Income for Overseas Ministries . $ 189,000
Fully Supported USA Personnel Overseas:
Nonresidential mission personnel 1
Other Personnel:
Non-USA serving in own/other country . . 100
Short-Term less than 1 year from USA . . . 4
Home ministry & office staff in USA 1
Countries: India.

India Gospel Outreach
(909)948-2404   Fax: (909)948-2406
E-Mail: 103417.3401@compuserve.com
Web: http://igo.ncsa.com/igo/
P.O. Box 550, Rancho Cucamong, CA 91729
Rev. T. Valson Abraham, Founder/Director

A transdenominational service agency of charismatic and evangelical tradition partnering with national churches and workers in India engaged in church planting, theological education, evangelism, and leadership development.

".. planting dynamic churches in all 3,000 castes and tribes .. and establishing Bible training centers in all states of India .. by the year 2000."

Year Founded in USA 1984
Income for Overseas Ministries . $ 360,000
Personnel:
Short-Term less than 1 year from USA . . . 8
Home ministry & office staff in USA 7
Countries: India.

India National Inland Mission
(818)241-4010
P.O. Box 652, Verdugo City, CA 91046
Mr. Paul C. Nelson, Treasurer

A nondenominational support agency of evangelical tradition engaged in funds transmission, church planting, childcare/orphanage programs, theological education, and literature distribution through partners in India.

Year Founded in USA 1964
Income for Overseas Ministries . $ 768,989
Countries: India.

India Rural Evangelical Fellowship
(847)680-6767
E-Mail: IREF4US@aol.com
P.O. Box 1332, Park Ridge, IL 60068
Mr. Emmanuel Rebba, President

An interdenominational agency of evangelical tradition supporting national churches involved in church planting, orphanage/schools programs, Christian education, and evangelism.

Year Founded in USA 1985
Income for Overseas Ministries . $ 290,220
Personnel:
    Non-USA serving in own/other country . . 127
    Home ministry & office staff in USA 1
Countries: India.

Institute for International Christian Communication
(503)234-1639   **Fax: (503)234-1639**
E-Mail: 73143.2050@compuserve.com
6012 SE Yamhill St., Portland, OR 97215
Dr. Donald K. & Mrs. Faye Smith, Directors

A transdenominational service agency of Baptist tradition supporting the leadership of Third World churches by forging meaningful collaborations that result in sharing resources of research, education, personnel, and materials.

Year Founded in USA 1967
Income for Overseas Ministries . . $ 5,410
Amount of Gifts-In-Kind . . . . $ 2,545
Personnel:
    Home ministry & office staff in USA 7

Institute of Chinese Studies
(626)398-2320   **Fax: (626)398-2492**
1605 Elizabeth St., Pasadena, CA 91104
Rev. James Ziervogel, Founder/Sr. Rsch. Fellow
Rev. Jim Nickel, Exec. Director

An interdenominational service agency of evangelical tradition engaged in services for other

agencies, literature production, mission-related research, and video/film production/distribution.

".. forming strategy profiles of the world's unevangelized Chinese people groups [and] communicating [these] to the Body of Christ..."

Year Founded in USA 1977
Income for Overseas Ministries . . . . NA
Personnel:
    Short-Term less than 1 year from USA . . . 2
    Home ministry & office staff in USA 5

Institute of Hindu Studies
(626)398-2314   **Fax: (626)398-2263**
1605 Elizabeth St., Pasadena, CA 91104
Miss Henrietta Watson, Director

An interdenominational service agency of evangelical tradition engaged in missionary training, mobilization for mission, and mission-related research.

Year Founded in USA 1976
Income for Overseas Ministries . . . . NA
Personnel:
    Short-Term less than 1 year from USA . . . 2
    Home ministry & office staff in USA 2

Institute of Japanese Studies
See: Japanese Evangelization Center

Inter-Mission International
(626)797-1260   **Fax: (626)797-1260**
P.O. Box 40288, Pasadena, CA 91104
Dr. David J. Cho, International Chair

A nondenominational support agency of evangelical tradition engaged in services for Third World mission agencies to enhance leadership and information networking.

Year Founded in USA 1968
Income for Overseas Ministries . . . . NA
Personnel:
    Short-Term less than 1 year from USA . . . 3
    Home ministry & office staff in USA 2

InterAct Ministries

(503)668-5571   **Fax: (503)668-6814**
E-Mail: InterActMn@aol.com
Web: http://www.interactministries.org
31000 SE Kelso Rd., Boring, OR 97009
Rev. Gary Brumbelow, Gen. Director

An interdenominational sending agency of evangelical tradition engaged in church planting, evangelism, leadership development, support of national churches, and training.

".. to see local culturally relevant evangelical churches established and led by indigenous leaders committed to further missionary outreach."

Year Founded in USA 1951
Income for Overseas Ministries . $ 190,000
Fully Supported USA Personnel Overseas:
  Expecting to serve more than 4 years 8
Other Personnel:
  Non-USA serving in own/other country . . . 1
  Home ministry & office staff in USA 3
Countries: Russia 8.

Interchurch Medical Assistance

(410)635-8720   **Fax: (410)635-8726**
E-Mail: IMA@ecunet.org
Web: http://www.interchurch.org
P.O. Box 429, New Windsor, MD 21776
Paul Derstine, Exec. Director

An interdenominational support agency of ecumenical tradition distributing medical supplies to health care facilities in 53 countries affiliated with Member and associate organizations.

"..to provide essential products and services for emergency, health and development programs of interest to Members, which serve people in need with preference given to the poorest of the poor.."

Year Founded in USA 1960
Income for Overseas Ministries $ 16,008,711
Amount of Gifts-In-Kind . . $ 15,303,391
Fully Supported USA Personnel Overseas:
  Nonresidential mission personnel 2
Other Personnel:
  Home ministry & office staff in USA 8

INTERCOMM

(219)267-5834
E-Mail: 71430.3002@compuserve.com
1520 E. Winona Ave., Warsaw, IN 46580
Chuck Roost, Exec. Director

A nondenominational equipping agency of evangelical tradition engaged in video/film production/distribution, training, and translation for evangelism through national workers. A ministry of Ken Anderson Films.

".. to equip National Christian leaders with culturally-appropriate media tools."

Year Founded in USA 1990
Income for Overseas Ministries . . $ 33,500
Amount of Gifts-In-Kind . . . . $ 2,500
Personnel:
  Bivocational/Tentmaker from USA 1
  Short-Term less than 1 year from USA . . . 3
  Home ministry & office staff in USA 1

Intercristo

(800)251-7740   **Fax: (206)546-7375**
E-Mail: DLH@crista.org
Web: http://www.halcyon.com/ico/
19303 Fremont Ave., N., Seattle, WA 98133
Ann Brooks, Exec. Director

An interdenominational service agency of evangelical tradition providing assistance and information to mission agencies in locating qualified personnel for positions at home and abroad.

Year Founded in USA 1967
Income for Overseas Ministries . . . . NA
Personnel:
  Home ministry & office staff in USA 12

Interdenominational Foreign Mission Association
See: IFMA

INTERDEV

(425)775-8330   **Fax: (425)775-8326**
E-Mail: INTERDEV-US@xc.org
P.O. Box 3883, Seattle, WA 98124
Mr. Phillip W. Butler, President

An interdenominational service agency of evangelical tradition engaged in partnership development and services for other agencies.

".. to serve the Church in accelerating the Great Commission by facilitating the development, formation, and long-term effective operation of international partnerships for evangelism among the world's unreached people."

Year Founded in USA	1974
Income for Overseas Ministries .	$ 862,205

Fully Supported USA Personnel Overseas:
Expecting to serve more than 4 years 6
Nonresidential mission personnel 8
Other Personnel:
Home ministry & office staff in USA 9
Countries: Africa 2, Asia 2, UK 2.

International Aid, Inc.
(616)846-7490   **Fax: (616)846-3842**
E-Mail: IntlAid@xc.org
17011 W. Hickory St., Spring Lake, MI 49456
Rev. Ralph E. Plumb, President/CEO

A nondenominational specialized service agency of evangelical tradition engaged in providing relief and development assistance in 166 countries. The income total does not include an estimated $41.7 million of donated medicines, medical equipment/supplies, food, vitamins, etc.

Year Founded in USA	1980
Income for Overseas Ministries	$ 2,822,374

Personnel:
Home ministry & office staff in USA 60

International Bible Institute
(562)907-5555   **Fax: (562)907-5552**
P.O. Box 2473, Santa Fe Sprgs., CA 90670
Dr. Earle E. Williams, President

A nondenominational service agency of evangelical tradition establishing extension Bible institutes in local churches using audio tapes, printed materials and other means.

Year Founded in USA	1971
Income for Overseas Ministries . .	$ 40,000

Personnel:
Non-USA serving in own/other country . . . 1
Short-Term less than 1 year from USA . . . 3
Home ministry & office staff in USA 4
Countries: Ghana, Philippines, S Africa.

International Bible Society
(719)488-9200   **Fax: (719)488-3840**
E-Mail: IBS@gospelcom.net
Web: http://www.gospelcom.net/ibs
1820 Jet Stream Dr., Colorado Sprgs, CO 80921
Dr. Lars Dunberg, Intl. President

A transdenominational service agency of evangelical tradition engaged in Bible distribution, literature production, services for other agencies, and Bible translation. Financial information from 1992.

Year Founded in USA	1809
Income for Overseas Ministries	$ 2,426,000

Personnel:
Home ministry & office staff in USA . . . 123

International Board of Jewish Missions, Inc.
(423)698-3417   **Fax: (423)698-3418**
P.O. Box 3307, Chattanooga, TN 37404
Dr. Orman L. Norwood, President

An independent Baptist sending board engaged in evangelism, broadcasting, literature production/distribution, and video distribution.

Year Founded in USA	1949
Income for Overseas Ministries	NR

Personnel:
Short-Term less than 1 year from USA . . . 30
Home ministry & office staff in USA 15

International Child Care
(614)447-9952   **Fax: (614)447-1123**
E-Mail: 103220.473@compuserve.com
P.O. Box 14485, Columbus, OH 43214
Dr. John Yates, Exec. Director

An interdenominational service agency of evangelical tradition engaged in medical work, development, disability assistance programs, providing medical supplies, and technical assistance.

Year Founded in USA	1965
Income for Overseas Ministries .	$ 354,456

Fully Supported USA Personnel Overseas:
Expecting to serve more than 4 years 2
Other Personnel:
Non-USA serving in own/other country . . 288
Home ministry & office staff in USA 4
Countries: Dominican Rep, Haiti 2.

International Children's Care

(360)573-0429   Fax: (360)573-0491
P.O. Box 4406, Vancouver, WA 98662
Mr. Rick Fleck, President

A nondenominational service agency of
Adventist tradition engaged in childcare and
orphanage programs. Financial and personnel
information from 1992.

Year Founded in USA 1978
Income for Overseas Ministries . $ 901,104
Fully Supported USA Personnel Overseas:
   Expecting to serve 1 up to 4 years 10
   Nonresidential mission personnel 1
Other Personnel:
   Short-Term less than 1 year from USA . . . 3
   Home ministry & office staff in USA 10
Countries: Costa Rica 1, Dominican Rep 2, Guatemala
6, Romania 1.

International Christian Leprosy Mission, Inc. (USA)

(503)244-5935   Fax: (503)244-5935
P.O. Box 23353, Portland, OR 97281
Mr. Lauritz Pillers, President

A nondenominational support agency engaged
in providing medical supplies and support of
national medical workers.

Year Founded in USA 1943
Income for Overseas Ministries . . $ 24,000
Personnel:
   Home ministry & office staff in USA 1
Countries: India, Philippines.

International Christian Literature Distributors, Inc.

(612)920-4687
P.O. Box 8295, Minneapolis, MN 55408
Mr. E. Michael Ondov, President

An interdenominational support agency of
evangelical tradition recycling Christian literature
to overseas countries.

Year Founded in USA 1961
Income for Overseas Ministries . . $ 72,000
Personnel:
   Short-Term less than 1 year from USA . . . 7

International Church Relief Fund

(707)528-8000   Fax: (707)525-1310
E-Mail: ICRF@sonic.net
182 Farmers Lane, #200, Santa Rosa, CA 95405
Kathleen Macall, Vice President
Colonel V. Doner, Chairman

A nondenominational service agency of
evangelical tradition engaged in relief aid and
development. Income report from 1992.

Year Founded in USA 1976
Income for Overseas Ministries $ 5,479,803
Amount of Gifts-In-Kind . . . $ 5,156,650

International Cooperating Ministries

(757)827-6704   Fax: (757)838-6486
606 Aberdeen Rd., Hampton, VA 23661
Dois I. Rosser, Jr., Chairman

An interdenominational support agency of
evangelical tradition engaged in church construction, broadcasting, and literature distri-
bution/production through national workers.

"To encourage the growth of the national
indigenous church without making that church
dependent on outside resources..."

Year Founded in USA 1987
Income for Overseas Ministries . $ 947,000
Personnel:
   Home ministry & office staff in USA 5
Countries: India, Russia, Vietnam, Zimbabwe.

International Crusades, Inc.

(214)747-1444   Fax: (214)747-1417
E-Mail: IntCrusade@aol.com
Web: members.aol.com/intcrusade/ichome.htm
500 S. Ervay St., #409, Dallas, TX 75201
Rev. Gary Baird, President

A denominational service agency of Baptist
tradition engaged in short-term programs
coordination and training in support of
evangelism. Income figure from 1992.

".. working with Southern Baptist Churches in
the U.S. to facilitate partnership mission crusades
with Baptist churches overseas..."

Year Founded in USA 1971
Income for Overseas Ministries . $ 500,000

Personnel:

Short-Term less than 1 year from USA . . 521
Home ministry & office staff in USA 18

International Discipleship Mission

(714)990-2738
P.O. Box 655, Brea, CA 92822
Mr. Emil Aanderud, Director

A nondenominational sending agency of Baptist and fundamentalist tradition engaged in evangelism and literature distribution. Financial and personnel information from 1992.

Year Founded in USA 1951
Income for Overseas Ministries . . $ 73,000
Fully Supported USA Personnel Overseas:
Expecting to serve more than 4 years 4
Countries: Germany 2, Mexico 2.

International Family Missions

(303)665-7927   Fax: (303)661-0733
P.O. Box 309, Lafayette, CO 80026
Rev. Joseph Hart, Minister/Director

A transdenominational sending agency of evangelical tradition engaged in short-term programs coordination, evangelism, and training.

Year Founded in USA 1987
Income for Overseas Ministries . . $ 95,000
Fully Supported USA Personnel Overseas:
Expecting to serve more than 4 years 4
Nonresidential mission personnel 2
Other Personnel:
Bivocational/Tentmaker from USA 2
Short-Term less than 1 year from USA . . . 80
Home ministry & office staff in USA 22
Countries: Mexico 4.

International Fellowship of Evangelical Students - USA

See: InterVarsity Mission

International Films, Inc.

(626)797-5462   Fax: (626)797-7524
P.O. Box 40400, Pasadena, CA 91114
Mr. C. Ray Carlson, President

A nondenominational specialized service agency of evangelical tradition engaged in video/film production/distribution, technical

assistance for others, and training.

Year Founded in USA 1963
Income for Overseas Ministries . . . . NA

International Foundation for EWHA Woman's University

(212)864-5759   Fax: (212)864-2552
475 Riverside Dr. Rm. 1221, New York, NY 10115
Ms. Miran Kim, Exec. Director

An interdenominational support agency of ecumenical tradition providing financial and other support to EWHA University in South Korea. Financial information from 1992.

Year Founded in USA 1969
Income for Overseas Ministries . $ 400,000

International Gospel League

(626)304-9233   Fax: (626)304-9233
P.O. Box 519, Pasadena, CA 91102
Dr. Howard T. Lewis, President

A nondenominational sending agency of evangelical tradition engaged in evangelism, literature distribution, and support of national workers. Statistical information from 1992.

Year Founded in USA 1906
Income for Overseas Ministries $ 1,000,000
Fully Supported USA Personnel Overseas:
Expecting to serve more than 4 years 10
Countries: Kenya 5, Uganda 5.

International Gospel Outreach

(334)645-2117   Fax: (334)645-2118
E-Mail: IntGospl@maf.mobile.al.us
P.O. Drawer 1008, Semmes, AL 36575
Mr. Bertist Rouse, President
Mr. David Fackler, Director

An interdenominational sending agency of charismatic and Wesleyan tradition engaged in support of national churches, church planting, theological education, and evangelism.

Year Founded in USA 1973
Income for Overseas Ministries . $ 192,673
Fully Supported USA Personnel Overseas:
Expecting to serve more than 4 years 4
Expecting to serve 1 up to 4 years 8
Other Personnel:
Non-USA serving in own/other country . . . 12

Bivocational/Tentmaker from USA 2
Home ministry & office staff in USA 26
Countries: Belize 2, Chile, Honduras 1, India, Kenya 3, Mexico 2, Russia 2, Singapore 2.

International Institute for Christian Studies

(913)642-1166 **Fax: (913)642-1280**
E-Mail: 73754.1132@compuserve.com
Web: http://www.goshen.net/iics
P.O. Box 12147, Overland Park, KS 66282
Dr. Daryl McCarthy, CEO

A nondenominational service agency of evangelical tradition engaged in teaching Christian truth in public universities, evangelism, and leadership development.

Year Founded in USA 1986
Income for Overseas Ministries . $ 531,396
Fully Supported USA Personnel Overseas:
Expecting to serve more than 4 years 7
Expecting to serve 1 up to 4 years 3
Other Personnel:
Non-USA serving in own/other country . . . 2
Short-Term less than 1 year from USA . . . 36
Home ministry & office staff in USA 4
Countries: Asia 2, Belarus 2, Czech Rep 1, Nigeria 2, Romania 2, Russia 1.

International Leadership Seminars

(716)624-9660 **Fax: (716)624-9129**
P.O. Box 56A, Lima, NY 14485
Dr. Costa S. Deir, Exec. Director

A nondenominational service agency of charismatic and Pentecostal tradition engaged in leadership development through seminars and publications. Overseas income from 1992 report.

Year Founded in USA 1973
Income for Overseas Ministries . . $ 85,000
Personnel:
Short-Term less than 1 year from USA . . . 1
Home ministry & office staff in USA 4

International Lutheran Laymen's League / Lutheran Hour Ministries

(314)951-4100 **Fax: (314)951-4295**
Web: http://www.lhm.org
2185 Hampton Ave., St. Louis, MO 63139
Mr. Laurence Lumpe, Gifts Planning Counselor

A denominational service agency of Lutheran tradition engaged in broadcasting and correspondence courses. Financial and personnel information from 1992.

Year Founded in USA 1917
Income for Overseas Ministries $ 3,875,990
Fully Supported USA Personnel Overseas:
Expecting to serve more than 4 years 1
Countries: Korea-S 1.

International Messengers

(515)357-6700 **Fax: (515)357-6791**
E-Mail: Messengers@netins.net
P.O. Box R, Clearlake, IA 50428
Mr. Robert P. Rasmusson, President

A transdenominational sending agency of evangelical tradition engaged in evangelism, camping programs, church planting, mobilization for mission, short-term programs coordination, and missionary training.

"To develop a partnership with local churches which facilitates a greater level of personal involvement and responsibility by the local church in the task of world mission."

Year Founded in USA 1984
Income for Overseas Ministries . $ 504,502
Fully Supported USA Personnel Overseas:
Expecting to serve more than 4 years 17
Expecting to serve 1 up to 4 years 1
Nonresidential mission personnel 3
Other Personnel:
Non-USA serving in own/other country . . . 29
Short-Term less than 1 year from USA . . . 150
Home ministry & office staff in USA 12
Countries: Czech Rep 2, Hungary 2, Latvia 2, Poland 7, Romania 1, Slovakia 2, Ukraine 2.

International Missions, Inc.

(610)375-0300 **Fax: (610)375-6862**
E-Mail: Info@imi.org
Web: http://www.intermissions.org
P.O. Box 14866, Reading, PA 19612
Dr. Patrick O. Cate, Gen. Director

A nondenominational sending agency of evangelical tradition engaged in church planting, correspondence courses, evangelism, and literature distribution. Statistical information from 1992.

" To .. proclaim the Gospel .. and establish local indigenous churches, primarily among unreached Asian communities worldwide."

Year Founded in USA 1930
Income for Overseas Ministries $ 4,399,648
Fully Supported USA Personnel Overseas:
Expecting to serve more than 4 years . . . 202
Other Personnel:
Bivocational/Tentmaker from USA 15
Short-Term less than 1 year from USA . . . 2
Home ministry & office staff in USA 9
Countries: Africa 19, Asia 52, France 6, Germany 4, Hong Kong 8, India 17, Japan 19, Kenya 23, Netherlands 3, Pakistan 10, Philippines 24, Suriname 7, UK 10.

International Needs - USA
(360)354-1991   **Fax: (360)354-1991**
E-Mail: 102006.2256@compuserve.com
Web: http://ualberta.ca/~dharapnu/intlneed/
P.O. Box 977, Lynden, WA 98264
Mr. David Culross, Exec. Director

A transdenominational service agency of evangelical tradition engaged in support of national workers, childcare programs, evangelism, leadership development, and literature distribution.

Year Founded in USA 1974
Income for Overseas Ministries . $ 508,882
Personnel:
Non-USA serving in own/other country . . 420
Short-Term less than 1 year from USA . . . 28
Home ministry & office staff in USA 7
Countries: Africa, Asia, Bangladesh, Colombia, Croatia, Czech Rep, Eritrea, Ethiopia, Fiji, Ghana, Hong Kong, India, Indonesia, Korea-S, Nepal, Philippines, Romania, Slovakia, Sri Lanka, Uganda, Vietnam, Zambia.

International Outreach Ministries
(334)633-7171   **Fax: (334)639-0489**
E-Mail: IOM@zegra.net
P.O. Box 850066, Mobile, AL 36685
Rev. Gary Henley, Coordinator

A nondenominational sending agency of Reformed and charismatic tradition engaged in church planting, Christian education, leadership development, and literature production.

Year Founded in USA 1986
Income for Overseas Ministries . $ 550,000
Fully Supported USA Personnel Overseas:
Expecting to serve more than 4 years 29

Expecting to serve 1 up to 4 years 2
Nonresidential mission personnel 1
Other Personnel:
Non-USA serving in own/other country . . . 7
Bivocational/Tentmaker from USA 4
Short-Term less than 1 year from USA . . . 6
Home ministry & office staff in USA 2
Countries: Argentina 2, Belgium 5, Colombia 1, Congo/Zaire 6, Costa Rica 2, Jamaica 2, Kenya 4, Mexico 2, Papua New Guin 2, Russia 1, S Africa 2, Uzbekistan 2.

International Partnership Ministries, Inc.
(717)637-7388   **Fax: (717)637-1618**
E-Mail: IPM@sun-link.com
P.O. Box 41, Hanover, PA 17331
Dr. Timothy B. Shorb, President

A nondenominational agency of Baptist tradition supporting, in partnership with Two-Thirds World mission agencies, national workers involved in leadership development.

Year Founded in USA 1982
Income for Overseas Ministries . $ 520,532
Fully Supported USA Personnel Overseas:
Expecting to serve more than 4 years 2
Other Personnel:
Non-USA serving in own/other country . . . 89
Short-Term less than 1 year from USA . . . 15
Home ministry & office staff in USA 4
Countries: Chile, Ghana, Haiti, India, Mexico, Paraguay, Togo 2.

International Pentecostal Church of Christ, Global Missions Dept.
(404)627-2681   **Fax: (404)627-0702**
P.O. Box 18145, Atlanta, GA 30316
Dr. James B. Keiller, Director

A denominational sending agency of Pentecostal tradition engaged in evangelism, Bible distribution, orphanage work, theological education, and literature distribution.

Year Founded in USA 1917
Income for Overseas Ministries . $ 186,504
Fully Supported USA Personnel Overseas:
Expecting to serve more than 4 years 5
Other Personnel:
Short-Term less than 1 year from USA . . . 10
Home ministry & office staff in USA 1
Countries: India 1, Kenya 3, Mexico 1.

International Pentecostal Holiness Church World Missions

(405)787-7110   **Fax: (405)787-7729**
E-Mail: 103114.2476@compuserve.com
Web: http://www.iphc.org
P.O. Box 12609, Oklahoma City, OK 73157
Rev. Jesse D. Simmons, Exec. Director

A denominational sending agency of Pentecostal and Holiness tradition engaged in church planting, theological education, evangelism, leadership development, support of national churches, and mobilization for mission.

Year Founded in USA 1911
Income for Overseas Ministries $ 4,409,487
Fully Supported USA Personnel Overseas:
    Expecting to serve more than 4 years . . . 141
    Expecting to serve 1 up to 4 years 9
Other Personnel:
    Non-USA serving in own/other country . . . 7
    Short-Term less than 1 year from USA . . 250
    Home ministry & office staff in USA 14
Countries: Africa 4, Asia 2, Australia 4, Botswana 2, China (PRC) 3, Congo/Zaire 2, Costa Rica 2, Cote d'Ivoire 4, Ethiopia 2, France 2, Germany 4, Ghana 3, Guatemala 2, Haiti 5, Honduras 2, Hong Kong 3, Hungary 2, India 4, Italy 2, Japan 4, Kenya 11, Malawi 6, Malaysia 4, Malta 2, Mexico 2, Norway 2, Philippines 4, Russia 2, S Africa 16, Singapore 2, Spain 2, Trinidad & Tobg 2, UK 7, Ukraine 2, Unspecified 23, Venezuela 2, Zambia 4, Zimbabwe 1.

International Street Kids Outreach Ministries

(800)265-1970
P.O. Box 272446, Tampa, FL 33688
Rev. John M. Schmidt, President

A nondenominational support agency of evangelical tradition engaged in youth programs, camping programs, and evangelism.

Year Founded in USA 1995
Income for Overseas Ministries . . $ 98,000
Fully Supported USA Personnel Overseas:
    Expecting to serve more than 4 years 1
Other Personnel:
    Short-Term less than 1 year from USA . . . 5
    Home ministry & office staff in USA 1
Countries: Brazil 1.

International Students, Inc

(719)576-2700   **Fax: (719)576-5363**
E-Mail: ISIteam@aol.com
Web: http://www.isionline.org
P.O. Box C, Colorado Springs, CO 80901
Mr. Tom K. Phillips, President

A transdenominational sending agency of evangelical and ecumenical tradition engaged in evangelism, camping programs, and training. Financial and personnel information from 1992.

Year Founded in USA 1953
Income for Overseas Ministries . . $ 22,169
Fully Supported USA Personnel Overseas:
    Expecting to serve more than 4 years 2
    Nonresidential mission personnel 2
Other Personnel:
    Home ministry & office staff in USA . . . 140
Countries: Japan 2.

International Teams, U.S.A.

(847)870-3800   **Fax: (847)870-3399**
E-Mail: Info@itusa.org
Web: http://www.iteams.org/
P.O. Box 203, Prospect Hts., IL 60070
Mr. Stephen Freed, President

A nondenominational sending agency of evangelical tradition engaged in evangelism, church planting, development, leadership development, mobilization for mission, and training.

Year Founded in USA 1960
Income for Overseas Ministries $ 4,730,040
Fully Supported USA Personnel Overseas:
    Expecting to serve more than 4 years . . . 103
    Expecting to serve 1 up to 4 years 54
Other Personnel:
    Non-USA serving in own/other country . . . 41
    Short-Term less than 1 year from USA . . 126
    Home ministry & office staff in USA 73
Countries: Albania 2, Asia 2, Austria 43, Bulgaria 3, Colombia 2, Costa Rica 2, Czech Rep 10, France 20, Germany 3, Greece 5, Hungary 3, Italy 4, Kazakhstan 3, Mexico 5, Philippines 7, Poland 3, Romania 6, Russia 5, Spain 4, UK 21, Ukraine 2, Vietnam 2.

International Urban Associates

(773)275-9260   **Fax: (773)275-9969**
E-Mail: IUA1@ais.net
Web: http://www.cl.ais.net:80/iua1/
5151 N. Clark St., 2nd Floor, Chicago, IL 60640
Dr. Ray Bakke, Sr. Associate

A transdenominational information and service agency of evangelical tradition engaged in urban leadership development through church consultations, and theological/mission education.

"..to empower God's people in the largest cities of the world by means of leadership consultations that generate vision, partnerships, motivations and resources, so that the 'whole church can take the whole gospel to the whole city'."

Year Founded in USA 1989
Income for Overseas Ministries . $ 200,000
Fully Supported USA Personnel Overseas:
  Nonresidential mission personnel 1
Other Personnel:
  Home ministry & office staff in USA 5

InterServe/USA

(610)352-0581   **Fax: (610)352-4394**
E-Mail: 72400.2234@compuserve.com
Web: http://www.interserve.org/
P.O. Box 418, Upper Darby, PA 19082
Dr. Ralph W. Eckardt, Jr., Exec. Director

An interdenominational support agency of e-vangelical tradition whose personnel/partners are engaged in medical work, development, Christian education, and support of national churches.

Year Founded in USA 1964
Income for Overseas Ministries $ 1,644,331
Fully Supported USA Personnel Overseas:
  Expecting to serve more than 4 years 66
  Nonresidential mission personnel 4
Other Personnel:
  Bivocational/Tentmaker from USA 14
  Short-Term less than 1 year from USA . . . 23
  Home ministry & office staff in USA 10
Countries: Afghanistan 15, Asia 12, Bangladesh 3, Central Asia 14, Cyprus 2, India 3, Nepal 8, Pakistan 7, Yemen 2.

InterVarsity Mission

(608)274-9001   **Fax: (608)274-9680**
E-Mail: LINK@ivcf.org
Web: http://www.ivcf.org/missions/
P.O. Box 7895, Madison, WI 53707
John M. Criswell, Director of InterVarsity LINK

A department of InterVarsity (IV) Christian Fellowship engaged in student evangelism, leadership development, mission mobilization, and training. IV is a member movement of the International Fellowship of Evangelical Students (IFES) which has national movements in 136 countries. The triennial IV Urbana Student Mission Convention enables students to investigate mission opportunities through seminars, workshops, and a "job fair" with 200+ mission agencies. IV Global Projects provides short-term overseas opportunities specifically designed for college students. IV LINK provides recent graduates and IV staff opportunities to serve in IFES overseas settings.

Year Founded in USA 1941
Income for Overseas Ministries $ 2,811,000
Fully Supported USA Personnel Overseas:
  Expecting to serve more than 4 years 10
  Expecting to serve 1 up to 4 years 51
Other Personnel:
  Short-Term less than 1 year from USA . . 316
  Home ministry & office staff in USA 24
Countries: Austria 4, Belarus 1, Brazil 2, Bulgaria 1, Czech Rep 3, Ecuador 2, France 2, Gabon 2, Israel 1, Italy 3, Jordan 1, Kazakhstan 5, Kenya 3, Nigeria 1, Poland 2, Puerto Rico 2, Romania 4, Russia 14, Slovakia 2, Spain 2, Switzerland 1, Ukraine 3.

Iranian Christians International

(719)596-0010   **Fax: (719)574-1141**
E-Mail: ICI@farisnet.com
Web: http://www.farsinet.com/ici/
P.O. Box 25607, Colorado Sprgs, CO 80936
Mr. Ebrahim (Abe) Ghaffari, Exec. Director

An interdenominational agency of evangelical tradition engaged in support of national churches, evangelism, literature production/distribution and training focused on Persian speaking peoples.

Year Founded in USA 1981
Income for Overseas Ministries . . $ 35,000
Personnel:
  Home ministry & office staff in USA 3

Ireland Outreach International Inc.
(319)277-8883
P.O. Box 1772, Waterloo, IA 50704
Mr. James W. Gillett, President

A nondenominational sending agency of Christian/Plymouth Brethren tradition engaged in evangelism, Bible distribution, church planting, correspondence courses, and lit. distribution.

Year Founded in USA	1981
Income for Overseas Ministries	NR

Fully Supported USA Personnel Overseas:
Expecting to serve more than 4 years 3
Expecting to serve 1 up to 4 years 1
Other Personnel:
Non-USA serving in own/other country . . . 11
Countries: Ireland 4, Nigeria.

Island Missionary Society
(717)566-2708　　　**Fax: (717)892-7078**
P.O. Box 725, Ephrata, PA 17522
Rev. Mac Eifert, Chairman

A nondenominational sending agency of evangelical tradition engaged in church planting, evangelism, and support of national churches.

Year Founded in USA	1937
Income for Overseas Ministries .	$ 181,000

Fully Supported USA Personnel Overseas:
Expecting to serve more than 4 years 4
Countries: Jamaica 4.

ISOH/Impact
(419)878-8546　　　**Fax: (419)878-2869**
905 Farnsworth Rd., Waterville, OH 43566
Dr. Linda A. Green, Administrator

An interdenominational service agency of ecumenical tradition engaged in providing medical supplies, childrens programs, and medical work. Personnel and financial totals from 1992 report.

Year Founded in USA	1982
Income for Overseas Ministries .	$ 968,091
Amount of Gifts-In-Kind . . .	$ 896,710

Fully Supported USA Personnel Overseas:
Expecting to serve 1 up to 4 years 2
Other Personnel:
Short-Term less than 1 year from USA . . . 10
Countries: Bolivia 1, Haiti 1.

Issachar Frontier Missions Strategies
(253)318-8777　　　**Fax: (253)474-0317**
E-Mail: IssacharHQ@aol.com
3906A S. 74th St., Suite 103, Tacoma, WA 98409
Andrew Y. Low, President

A transdenominational service agency of evangelical tradition engaged in missions information services and research, mobilization for mission, and services for other agencies.

".. seeks to empower, train, and coach North American local churches to effectively activate their business and professional people for strategic impact among unreached people groups..."

Year Founded in USA	1981
Income for Overseas Ministries .	$ 200,000

JAARS, Inc.
(704)843-6000　　　**Fax: (704)843-6200**
E-Mail: Info@jaars.org
Web: http://www.jaars.org/
P.O. Box 248, Waxhaw, NC 28173
Mr. Jim Akovenko, Exec. Director

A nondenominational agency of evangelical tradition serving Wycliffe Bible translators with various technical support services including aviation and radio. Financial data from 1992.

"..to provide high quality technical support services to its sister organizations, Wycliffe Bible Translators and the Summer Inst. of Linguistics."

Year Founded in USA	1947
Income for Overseas Ministries .	$ 325,000

JAF Ministries
(818)707-5664　　　**Fax: (818)707-2391**
E-Mail: JAFMin@jafministries.com
Web: http://www.jafministries.com
P.O. Box 3333, Agoura, CA 91301
Joni Eareckson Tada, President
L. Michael Lynch, Exec. Director

A nondenominational service agency of evangelical tradition engaged in disability assistance programs, broadcasting, technical assistance, and training. Name changed from Joni and Friends.

".. to continue being a light, leading the way, and guiding the Christian community to reach out to persons with disabilities..."

Year Founded in USA		1979
Income for Overseas Ministries .		$ 100,000
Personnel:		
Short-Term less than 1 year from USA	. . .	35
Home ministry & office staff in USA	. . . .	25

Japan - North American Commission on Cooperative Mission

(212)870-2021   Fax: (212)870-2055
475 Riverside Dr., Rm. 618, New York, NY 10115
Ms. Patricia J. Patterson, Coordinator

An interdenominational ecumenical forum for cooperative Christian mission in and between two denominations in Japan, two in Canada, and five in the USA. Income amount from 1992.

Year Founded in USA		1973
Income for Overseas Ministries .		$ 500,000
Countries: Japan.		

Japanese Evangelical Missionary Society

(213)613-0022   Fax: (213)613-0211
948 E. Second St., Los Angeles, CA 90012
Rev. Sam Tonomura, Exec. Director

An interdenominational service agency of evangelical tradition engaged in support of national churches, evangelism, short-term programs coordination, and missionary training.

Year Founded in USA		1950
Income for Overseas Ministries .		$ 300,000
Fully Supported USA Personnel Overseas:		
Expecting to serve more than 4 years	. . . .	1
Expecting to serve 1 up to 4 years	. . . .	2
Nonresidential mission personnel	. . . . .	7
Other Personnel:		
Non-USA serving in own/other country	. . .	6
Short-Term less than 1 year from USA	. . .	24
Home ministry & office staff in USA	. . . .	8
Countries: Brazil 1, Japan 2.		

Japanese Evangelization Center

(626)794-4400
1605 Elizabeth St., Pasadena, CA 91104
Dr. John Mizuki, Exec. Director

A nondenominational agency of evangelical tradition engaged in mission-related research in support of evangelism and church planting.

Year Founded in USA		1981
Income for Overseas Ministries		NA

JESUS Film Project, The
See: Campus Crusade for Christ

Jews for Jesus

(415)864-2600   Fax: (415)552-8325
E-Mail: JFJ@jews-for-jesus.org
Web: http://www.jews-for-jesus.org/
60 Haight St., San Francisco, CA 94102
David Brickner, Exec. Director

A nondenominational support agency of evangelical tradition engaged in evangelism, literature distribution, and training.

Year Founded in USA		1973
Income for Overseas Ministries .		$ 948,432
Personnel:		
Non-USA serving in own/other country	. . .	15
Short-Term less than 1 year from USA	. . .	3
Home ministry & office staff in USA	. . . .	56
Countries: France, Israel, Russia, S Africa, UK.		

John Milton Society for the Blind

(212)870-3335   Fax: (212)870-3229
475 Riverside Dr., Rm. 455, New York, NY 10115
Darcy Quigley, Managing Director/Editor

A nondenominational service agency of ecumenical tradition publishing audio recordings and Braille and large-type Christian education materials for those with visual disabilities.

".. providing Christian nurture in a worldwide service to persons who cannot see regular print."

Year Founded in USA		1928
Income for Overseas Ministries		NR
Personnel:		
Home ministry & office staff in USA	. . . .	4

Joni and Friends
See: JAF Ministries

Key Communications

(503)233-7680   Fax: (503)236-0733
P.O. Box 13620, Portland, OR 97213
Mr. Bryan L. Turner, Director

A nondenominational service agency of Christian (Restoration Movement) tradition engaged in radio broadcasting, Bible distribution, and literature distribution.

Year Founded in USA 1978
Income for Overseas Ministries . . $ 25,311
Personnel:
Non-USA serving in own/other country . . . 2
Countries: Pakistan.

Kids Alive International

(219)464-9035   Fax: (219)462-5611
2507 Cumberland Dr., Valparaiso, IN 46383
Mr. Alfred Lackey, President

A nondenominational sending agency of evangelical tradition engaged in childcare, disability assistance, and Christian education programs for children and youth.

".. meeting the spiritual, physical, educational, and emotional needs of children and youth who have no other reasonable means of support..."

Year Founded in USA 1916
Income for Overseas Ministries . $ 622,300
Fully Supported USA Personnel Overseas:
Expecting to serve more than 4 years 10
Expecting to serve 1 up to 4 years 3
Nonresidential mission personnel 1
Other Personnel:
Non-USA serving in own/other country . . . 14
Short-Term less than 1 year from USA . . . 86
Home ministry & office staff in USA 12
Countries: Dominican Rep 3, Guatemala 2, Hong Kong 2, Lebanon, Mexico, Papua New Guin 1, Peru 3, Taiwan (ROC) 2, West Bank.

Kingdom Building Ministries

(303)745-8191   Fax: (303)745-4196
E-Mail: Missions@KBM.org
Web: http://www.KBM.org/
14140 E. Evans Ave., Denver, CO 80014
Dwight Robertson, President

An interdenominational support agency of evangelical tradition engaged in mobilization for mission, leadership development, mission-related research, short-term programs, and training.

".. to raise up new generations of laborers for Kingdom service world-wide."

Year Founded in USA 1986
Income for Overseas Ministries . $ 212,000
Personnel:
Short-Term less than 1 year from USA . . 100
Home ministry & office staff in USA 21

Korea Gospel Mission

(602)266-4637
P.O. Box 20044, Phoenix, AZ 85036
Mr. Paul Van Liew, President

An interdenominational of Baptist tradition engaged in Christian education, and evangelism. Income amount from 1992 report.

Year Founded in USA 1952
Income for Overseas Ministries . . $ 24,000

Larry Jones International Ministries (Feed the Children)

(405)942-0228   Fax: (405)945-4177
Web: http://www.feedthechildren.org
P.O. Box 36, Oklahoma City, OK 73101
Dr. Larry W. Jones, President

An interdenominational service agency of evangelical tradition engaged in food aid, evangelism, and other assistance in over 20 countries. Personnel information from 1992.

".. providing food, clothing, educational supplies, medical equipment and other necessities to people who lack these essentials because of famine, drought, flood, war or other calamities."

Year Founded in USA 1964
Income for Overseas Ministries . . . . NR
Fully Supported USA Personnel Overseas:
Nonresidential mission personnel 5
Other Personnel:
Home ministry & office staff in USA . . . 136

Latin America Assistance, Inc.

(800)925-6359   Fax: (805)899-3432
E-Mail: lamapent@sol.racsa.co.cr
P.O. Box 4082, Santa Barbara, CA 93140
Mr. Joseph B. Pent, Director

A nondenominational service agency of evangelical tradition engaged in agricultural programs, evangelism, and youth programs. Financial and personnel information from 1992.

Year Founded in USA 1976
Income for Overseas Ministries . $ 150,000
Fully Supported USA Personnel Overseas:
Expecting to serve more than 4 years 2
Other Personnel:
Non-USA serving in own/other country . . . 4
Countries: Costa Rica 1, Nicaragua 1.

Latin America Lutheran Mission
(956)722-4047   **Fax: (956)722-4047**
3519 Salinas Ave., Laredo, TX 78041
Mr. V. Gary Olson, Director

A denominational sending agency of Lutheran tradition engaged in support of national churches, church planting, evangelism, support of national workers, and coordinating short-term programs.

".. to encourage Bible study and discipleship, and to train and equip the Mexican people to fulfill Christ's 'Great Commission'."

Year Founded in USA 1936
Income for Overseas Ministries . $ 258,405
Personnel:
Short-Term less than 1 year from USA . . 600
Home ministry & office staff in USA 1
Countries: Mexico.

Latin America Mission
(305)884-8400   **Fax: (305)885-8649**
E-Mail: info@lam.org
Web: http://www.lam.org
P.O. Box 52-7900, Miami, FL 33152
Dr. David M. Howard, President

An interdenominational sending agency of evangelical tradition engaged in evangelism, church planting, theological education, leadership development, and literature distribution.

".. to encourage, assist and participate with the Latin church in the task of building the church of Jesus Christ in the Latin world and beyond."

Year Founded in USA 1921
Income for Overseas Ministries $ 4,299,335
Fully Supported USA Personnel Overseas:
Expecting to serve more than 4 years 91

Expecting to serve 1 up to 4 years 46
Other Personnel:
Non-USA serving in own/other country . . . 39
Short-Term less than 1 year from USA . . . 58
Home ministry & office staff in USA . . . 28
Countries: Argentina 6, Bolivia 1, Brazil 2, Colombia 13, Costa Rica 73, Ecuador 1, Guatemala 2, Mexico 27, Panama, Peru 2, Spain 4, Venezuela 6.

Liberia Christian Mission
(217)498-7014
E-Mail: 71242.2321@compuserve.com
P.O. Box 383, Rochester, IL 62563
Mr. Ken Vogel, President

A nondenominational sending agency of Christian (Restoration Movement) tradition engaged in support of national churches, broadcasting, Christian education, and TEE.

Year Founded in USA 1982
Income for Overseas Ministries . . $ 50,000
Fully Supported USA Personnel Overseas:
Expecting to serve more than 4 years 2
Other Personnel:
Home ministry & office staff in USA 1
Countries: Cote d'Ivoire 2.

Liberty Baptist Mission
(804)582-2841   **Fax: (804)582-2589**
P.O. Box 20000, Lynchburg, VA 24506
Mr. Wes Tuttle, Coordinator

A denominational sending agency of Baptist and fundamentalist tradition engaged in evangelism, church planting, Christian education, and theological education.

Year Founded in USA 1978
Income for Overseas Ministries . . . . NR
Fully Supported USA Personnel Overseas:
Expecting to serve more than 4 years 10
Countries: Australia 4, Czech Rep 2, Mexico 2, Taiwan (ROC) 2.

Liberty Corner Mission
(908)647-1777   **Fax: (908)647-4117**
P.O. Box 204, Liberty Corner, NJ 07938
Rev. E. E. Achenbach, President

An interdenominational sending agency of Holiness and evangelical tradition engaged in evangelism and support of national churches.

Year Founded in USA 1933
Income for Overseas Ministries . $ 170,736
Fully Supported USA Personnel Overseas:
    Expecting to serve more than 4 years 4
Other Personnel:
    Non-USA serving in own/other country . . . 16
    Short-Term less than 1 year from USA . . . 1
    Home ministry & office staff in USA 1
Countries: Japan 2, Taiwan (ROC) 2.

Liebenzell Mission USA
(908)852-3044   Fax: (908)852-4531
E-Mail: Liebenzell_usa@compuserve.com
Web: http://ourworld.compuserve.com/homepages/
    liebenzell_usa/
P.O. Box 66, Schooley's Mtn., NJ 07870
Rev. Larry C. Mills, Exec. Director

An interdenominational sending agency of
evangelical tradition engaged in church planting,
theological education, evangelism, and
missionary training. Statistical data from 1992.

Year Founded in USA 1941
Income for Overseas Ministries . $ 399,000
Fully Supported USA Personnel Overseas:
    Expecting to serve more than 4 years 19
    Expecting to serve 1 up to 4 years 6
Other Personnel:
    Bivocational/Tentmaker from USA 2
    Home ministry & office staff in USA 8
Countries: Belau(Palau) 4, Germany 2, Guam 8,
    Micronesia 5, Papua New Guin 6.

LIFE Ministries
(909)599-8491   Fax: (909)592-3946
E-Mail: 71561.1373@compuserve.com
Web: http://ourworld.compuserve.com/homepages/
    LIFE_Ministries
P.O. Box 200, San Dimas, CA 91773
Rev. S. Douglas Birdsall, President

An interdenominational sending agency of
evangelical tradition engaged in evangelism,
church planting, Christian education, leadership
development, and support of national churches.

".. to strengthen and start Japanese churches in
partnership with visionary pastors and
congregations through innovation in evangelism
and leadership training."

Year Founded in USA 1967
Income for Overseas Ministries . $ 3,110,990
Fully Supported USA Personnel Overseas:

Expecting to serve more than 4 years 34
Expecting to serve 1 up to 4 years 19
Other Personnel:
    Non-USA serving in own/other country . . . 15
    Short-Term less than 1 year from USA . . . 40
    Home ministry & office staff in USA 12
Countries: Japan 53.

Lifewater International
(626)962-4187   Fax: (626)962-6786
E-Mail: Lifewater@xc.org
Web: http://www.lifewater.org
15854 Business Center Dr., Irwindale, CA 91706
Mr. William A. Ashe, Director

A nondenominational service agency of evangelical tradition engaged in technical assistance,
development, supplying equipment, and training.

"To .. help disadvantaged people of the world
meet their needs for safe drinking water, sanitation, and self-sufficiency, [and] help .. meet spiritual needs by demonstrating the gospel in action."

Year Founded in USA 1979
Income for Overseas Ministries . $ 144,494
Personnel:
    Short-Term less than 1 year from USA . . . 27
    Home ministry & office staff in USA 2

LIGHT International, Inc.
(916)467-3686   Fax: (916)467-3686
E-Mail: 72642.2115@compuserve.com
P.O. Box 368, Etna, CA 96027
Mr. Robert H. Waymire, President

A nondenominational specialized service
agency of evangelical tradition engaged in
mission-related research/information services and
training. Financial and personnel data from 1992.

Year Founded in USA 1991
Income for Overseas Ministries . . $ 85,000
Personnel:
    Home ministry & office staff in USA 4

Link Care Center
(209)439-5920   Fax: (209)439-2214
E-Mail: 75027.2265@compuserve.com
1734 W. Shaw Ave., Fresno, CA 93711
Dr. Brent Lindquist, President

An interdenominational support agency of
evangelical tradition engaged in psychological

counseling, linguistics, mission-related research, and missionary training.

Year Founded in USA 1965
Income for Overseas Ministries . . $ 22,000
Personnel:
    Short-Term less than 1 year from USA . . . 3
    Home ministry & office staff in USA 30

Lion and Lamb Outreach
(970)223-4350   **Fax: (970)221-3428**
E-Mail: 74267.1676@compuserve.com
P.O. Box 271037, Fort Collins, CO 80527
Rev. Richard C. Borgman, President

A nondenominational sending agency of charismatic tradition engaged in leadership development, support of national workers, and missionary training.

Year Founded in USA 1972
Income for Overseas Ministries . . $ 52,480
Fully Supported USA Personnel Overseas:
    Expecting to serve more than 4 years 3
Other Personnel:
    Non-USA serving in own/other country . . . 9
    Short-Term less than 1 year from USA . . . 15
Countries: Cote d'Ivoire 1, France 2.

Literacy & Evangelism Intl.
(918)585-3826   **Fax: (918)585-3224**
E-Mail: 75313.2613@compuserve.com
1800 S. Jackson Ave., Tulsa, OK 74107
Rev. John C. Taylor, Director

An interdenominational sending agency of evangelical and Presbyterian tradition engaged in literacy work, missionary education, literature production, and services for other agencies.

Year Founded in USA 1967
Income for Overseas Ministries . $ 264,167
Fully Supported USA Personnel Overseas:
    Expecting to serve more than 4 years . . . 7
Other Personnel:
    Non-USA serving in own/other country . . . 1
    Short-Term less than 1 year from USA . . . 4
    Home ministry & office staff in USA 4
Countries: Asia 1, Brazil, Congo/Zaire 2, Ghana, India, Indonesia, Kenya, Pakistan 2, Peru, Philippines, Uganda 2.

Living Water Teaching Intl.
(903)527-4160   **Fax: (903)527-2134**
E-Mail: LWTcaddo@aol.com
P.O. Box 1190, Caddo Mills, TX 75135
Dr. James L. Zirkle, Founder/President

An interdenominational sending agency of charismatic and evangelical tradition engaged in theological education, evangelism, funds transmission, and missionary training.

Year Founded in USA 1979
Income for Overseas Ministries $ 1,444,697
Fully Supported USA Personnel Overseas:
    Expecting to serve more than 4 years 18
    Expecting to serve 1 up to 4 years 19
Other Personnel:
    Non-USA serving in own/other country . . . 15
    Short-Term less than 1 year from USA . . . 15
    Home ministry & office staff in USA 11
Countries: Belize, Costa Rica, El Salvador 4, Guatemala 26, Honduras 5, Mexico, Nicaragua, Paraguay 2.

LOGOI/FLET
(305)232-5880   **Fax: (305)232-3592**
E-Mail: LOGOI@aol.com
14540 SW 136th St., Suite 200, Miami, FL 33186
Rev. Leslie J. Thompson, President

A transdenominational service agency of Reformed tradition engaged in non-formal theological education and publishing print and video materials used in all Spanish speaking countries.

Year Founded in USA 1968
Income for Overseas Ministries . $ 827,550
Personnel:
    Home ministry & office staff in USA 12

Lott Carey Baptist Mission Conv.
(202)667-8493   **Fax: (202)483-8626**
1501 11th St. NW, Washington, DC 20001
Dr. David E. Goatley, Exec. Director

A denominational service agency of Baptist tradition engaged in Christian ed., providing medical supplies, and support of natl. workers.

Year Founded in USA 1897
Income for Overseas Ministries . . . . NR

Ludhiana Christian Medical College Board, USA, Inc.

(717)561-0990
900 S Arlington Av Rm 221, Harrisburg, PA 17109
Rev. Roberta K. Jones, Exec. Director

An interdenominational service board of ecumenical tradition engaged in medical/dental work, education, and supplies provision.

Year Founded in USA 1906
Income for Overseas Ministries . $ 505,133
Amount of Gifts-In-Kind . . . $ 405,133
Personnel:
    Short-Term less than 1 year from USA . . . 2
    Home ministry & office staff in USA 5

Luis Palau Evangelistic Assoc.

(503)614-1500   **Fax: (503)614-1599**
E-Mail: LPEA@palau.org
Web: http://www.gospelcom.net/lpea
P.O. Box 1173, Portland, OR 97207
Dr. Luis Palau, President

A nondenominational evangelistic association of evangelical tradition engaged in evangelism, radio/TV broadcasting, leadership development, and literature production.

".. to win .. people .. to Jesus Christ throughout the world, proclaiming His Good News by all available means...to stimulate, revive, train and mobilize the Church to continuous, effective evangelism, follow-up, and church growth... raising up a new generation of godly leaders..."

Year Founded in USA 1978
Income for Overseas Ministries $ 1,400,000
Fully Supported USA Personnel Overseas:
    Expecting to serve more than 4 years 6
Other Personnel:
    Non-USA serving in own/other country . . . 5
    Home ministry & office staff in USA 50
Countries: Europe 3, Latin America 3.

Luke Society, The

(601)638-1629   **Fax: (601)636-6711**
E-Mail: LukeSoc@juno.com
P.O. Box 349, Vicksburg, MS 39181
Peter A. Boelens, M.D., Exec. Director

An interdenominational service agency of Reformed and charismatic tradition engaged in

medical work, development, evangelism, and support of national workers.

Year Founded in USA 1964
Income for Overseas Ministries . $ 568,765
Personnel:
    Non-USA serving in own/other country . . . 22
    Short-Term less than 1 year from USA . . . 70
    Home ministry & office staff in USA 8
Countries: Dominican Rep, Ghana, Honduras, India, Peru, Philippines, Romania, Uganda, Ukraine.

Lutheran Bible Translators

(630)897-0660   **Fax: (630)897-3567**
E-Mail: LBT@xc.org
Web: http://www.lbt.org/
P.O. Box 2050, Aurora, IL 60507
Rev. Robert Roegner, Exec. Director

A denominational sending agency of Lutheran tradition engaged in Bible translation, linguistics, print and non-print media, literacy work, and missionary training.

".. to help people come to faith .. specifically through Bible translation and literacy work."

Year Founded in USA 1964
Income for Overseas Ministries $ 2,183,608
Fully Supported USA Personnel Overseas:
    Expecting to serve more than 4 years 41
    Expecting to serve 1 up to 4 years 3
    Nonresidential mission personnel 3
Other Personnel:
    Non-USA serving in own/other country . . . 63
    Short-Term less than 1 year from USA . . . 20
    Home ministry & office staff in USA 21
Countries: Botswana 5, Cameroon 6, Ecuador 3, Guatemala 10, Kazakhstan 1, Liberia 11, Namibia 3, Russia 1, Sierra Leone 4, Togo.

Lutheran Braille Workers, Inc.

(909)795-8977   **Fax: (909)795-8970**
E-Mail: LBWBraille@aol.com
P.O. Box 5000, Yucaipa, CA 92399
Mr. LeRoy Delafosse, Exec. Director

A denominational specialized service agency of Lutheran tradition engaged in literature distribution/production and Bible distribution for the blind and visually impaired.

Year Founded in USA 1944
Income for Overseas Ministries . . . . NR

Lutheran Brethren World Missions

(218)739-3336   **Fax: (218)739-2346**
E-Mail: LBWM@mcimail.com
P.O. Box 655, Fergus Falls, MN 56538
Rev. Matthew Rogness, Exec. Director

A denominational sending agency of Lutheran
and evangelical tradition engaged in church
planting, theological education, TEE, literature
production/distribution, and literacy work.

".. serving the congregations of the Church of
the Lutheran Brethren to facilitate their task of
fulfilling the Great Commission..."

Year Founded in USA 1900
Income for Overseas Ministries . $ 850,000
Fully Supported USA Personnel Overseas:
   Expecting to serve more than 4 years 28
   Expecting to serve 1 up to 4 years 9
Other Personnel:
   Home ministry & office staff in USA 7
Countries: Cameroon 8, Chad 6, Japan 16, Taiwan
(ROC) 7.

Lutheran Church--Missouri Synod, Board for Mission Services

(314)965-9000   **Fax: (314)965-0959**
Web: http://www.lcms.org
1333 S. Kirkwood Rd., St. Louis, MO 63122
Dr. Glenn O'Shoney, Exec. Director

A denominational sending board of Lutheran
tradition engaged in church planting, leadership
development, theological education, and
evangelism. Also partners in projects with LCMS
World Relief and Lutheran Bible Translators.

Year Founded in USA 1893
Income for Overseas Ministries $ 17,432,620
Amount of Gifts-In-Kind . . . $ 3,480,000
Fully Supported USA Personnel Overseas:
   Expecting to serve more than 4 years . . . 222
   Expecting to serve 1 up to 4 years 127
Other Personnel:
   Non-USA serving in own/other country . . . 2
   Short-Term less than 1 year from USA . . . 50
   Home ministry & office staff in USA 57
Countries: Botswana 4, Brazil 1, China (PRC) 10, Cote
d'Ivoire 8, Eritrea 2, Europe-E 3, Ghana 16, Guatemala
13, Guinea 2, Honduras 2, Hong Kong 40, Hungary 5,
India 1, Jamaica 4, Japan 31, Kazakhstan 7, Korea-S 6,
Liberia 2, Macao 4, Mexico 6, Nigeria 24, Panama 12,
Papua New Guin 17, Paraguay 2, Peru 2, Philippines 7,
Puerto Rico 4, Russia 33, S Africa 2, Slovakia 7, Sri

Lanka 2, Taiwan (ROC) 20, Thailand 12, Togo 9,
Venezuela 27, Vietnam 2.

Lutheran Literature Society for the Chinese

(218)724-1068
1827 Woodland Ave., Duluth, MN 55803
Rev. Jerome Elness, President

An interdenominational support agency of
Lutheran tradition engaged in literature
production/distribution and Bible distribution.

".. to promote evangelism among the Chinese ..
by supporting .. Christian literature .. and by creating wider interest in these goals among the
members of Lutheran Churches in N. America."

Year Founded in USA 1942
Income for Overseas Ministries . . $ 25,135

Lutheran World Relief

(212)532-6350   **Fax: (212)213-6081**
E-Mail: LWR@lwr.org
Web: http://www.lwr.org
390 Park Ave. So., New York, NY 10016
Dr. Kathryn F. Wolford, President

A denominational service agency of Lutheran
tradition engaged in relief aid, agricultural
programs, community development, and
leadership development.

".. to alleviate suffering caused by natural disaster, conflict or poverty; through development
efforts to enable marginalized people to realize
more fully their God-given potential; and through
education and advocacy efforts to promote a
peaceful, just and sustainable global community."

Year Founded in USA 1945
Income for Overseas Ministries $ 21,814,333
Amount of Gifts-In-Kind . . $ 10,083,216
Fully Supported USA Personnel Overseas:
   Expecting to serve more than 4 years 4
Other Personnel:
   Non-USA serving in own/other country . . . 1
   Short-Term less than 1 year from USA . . . 1
   Home ministry & office staff in USA 23
Countries: Kenya 2, Niger 2, Peru.

Lutheran Youth Encounter

(612)789-3556   Fax: (612)789-6027
2500-39th Ave. NE, #222, Minneapolis, MN 55421
Rev. Larry Dean Johnson, President

A denominational service agency of Lutheran tradition engaged in youth programs, audio recording/distribution, and missionary training. Financial and personnel information from 1993.

Year Founded in USA 1965
Income for Overseas Ministries . $ 167,600
Personnel:
    Short-Term less than 1 year from USA . . . 15
    Home ministry & office staff in USA 43

M/E International

(714)630-2000   Fax: (714)630-5279
E-Mail: JFord767@aol.com
1061-D N. Shepard St., Anaheim, CA 92806
Mr. James R. Ford, President

An interdenominational service agency of evangelical tradition engaged in audio recording/distribution and technical assistance. Financial and personnel information from 1992.

Year Founded in USA 1948
Income for Overseas Ministries . . $ 30,000
Fully Supported USA Personnel Overseas:
    Expecting to serve more than 4 years 2
Other Personnel:
    Home ministry & office staff in USA 3
Countries: Kenya 2.

Macedonia World Baptist Missions

(770)963-9079   Fax: (770)963-3090
E-Mail: 75402.3212@compuserve.com
P.O. Box 551, Lawrenceville, GA 30246
Dr. Thurman Wade, Gen. Director

An independent sending agency of Baptist tradition engaged in church planting, aviation services, theological education, evangelism, and literature production/distribution.

Year Founded in USA 1967
Income for Overseas Ministries $ 3,000,562
Fully Supported USA Personnel Overseas:
    Expecting to serve more than 4 years . . . 106
Other Personnel:
    Bivocational/Tentmaker from USA 3
    Home ministry & office staff in USA 6

Countries: Belize 2, Brazil 14, Caribbean Isls 2, Chile 2, China (PRC) 6, Colombia 2, Costa Rica 2, Cote d'Ivoire 2, Cyprus 2, Germany 4, Grenada 2, Haiti 2, Indonesia 2, Jamaica 6, Japan 2, Mexico 10, Moldava 6, N Mariana Isls 2, Peru 12, Puerto Rico 14, Romania 2, St Lucia 2, Taiwan (ROC) 2, United Arab Emr 2, Uzbekistan 2.

Macedonian Missionary Service

(941)984-4060   Fax: (941)984-4505
E-Mail: HaroldWilliams@juno.com
P.O. Box 91237, Lakeland, FL 33804
Dr. Harold R. Williams, Chairman

A denominational support agency of Baptist tradition engaged in short-term programs coordination, broadcasting, church construction, correspondence courses, and missionary training.

Year Founded in USA 1973
Income for Overseas Ministries . $ 150,000
Personnel:
    Short-Term less than 1 year from USA . . 200
    Home ministry & office staff in USA 3

Mahesh Chavda Ministries Intl.

(704)543-7272   Fax: (704)541-5300
E-Mail: Info@watchofthelord.com
Web: http://www.watchofthelord.com
P.O. Box 472009, Charlotte, NC 28247
Rev. Mahesh Chavda, Founder/President

A nondenominational service agency of charismatic tradition engaged in evangelism, audio recording/distribution, support of national churches, and training.

Year Founded in USA 1985
Income for Overseas Ministries . . $ 65,928
Personnel:
    Home ministry & office staff in USA 7

Mailbox Club International

(912)244-6812   Fax: (912)245-8977
404 Eager Rd., Valdosta, GA 31602
Mr. John Mark Eager, Director

An interdenominational support agency of evangelical tradition producing correspondence courses for children in 13 languages.

Year Founded in USA 1965
Income for Overseas Ministries . . $ 65,920
Personnel:
    Home ministry & office staff in USA 8

MAP International

(912)265-6010   **Fax: (912)265-6170**
E-Mail: MAPUS@map.org
Web: http://www.map.org/
P.O. Box 215000, Brunswick, GA 31521
Paul B. Thompson, President and CEO

A nondenominational service agency providing medicines and supplies for medical work, health development and emergency relief.

".. to provide enabling services which promote total health care for needy people in the developing world."

Year Founded in USA	1954
Income for Overseas Ministries	$ 84,795,519
Amount of Gifts-In-Kind . .	$ 77,919,826

Fully Supported USA Personnel Overseas:
Expecting to serve more than 4 years 6
Expecting to serve 1 up to 4 years 1
Nonresidential mission personnel 2
Other Personnel:
Non-USA serving in own/other country . . . 8
Home ministry & office staff in USA 81
Countries: Bolivia, Cote d'Ivoire, Ecuador 4, Kenya 3.

Maranatha Baptist Mission

(601)442-0141   **Fax: (601)446-5105**
P.O. Drawer 1425, Natchez, MS 39121
Dr. James W. Crumpton, President

A nondenominational sending agency of Baptist tradition engaged in funds transmission for missionaries involved in church planting. Financial and personnel information from 1992.

Year Founded in USA	1961
Income for Overseas Ministries	$ 2,800,000

Fully Supported USA Personnel Overseas:
Expecting to serve more than 4 years . . . 102
Countries: Argentina 4, Australia 8, Bolivia 8, Brazil 8, Chile 4, Colombia 4, France 8, Germany 4, Grenada 2, Guatemala 2, Israel 2, Japan 2, Mexico 12, Norway 2, Papua New Guin 4, Peru 2, Puerto Rico 2, S Africa 2, Solomon Isls 2, Spain 2, UK 11, Venezuela 7.

MARC (Mission Advanced Research & Communications Ctr.)

(626)303-8811   **Fax: (626)301-7786**
E-Mail: MARC@wvi.org
Web: http://www.wvi.org/marc
800 W. Chestnut Ave., Monrovia, CA 91016
Bryant L. Myers, Exec. Director

A nondenominational service agency of evangelical and ecumenical tradition engaged in holistic mission research, publications, and strategic thinking. A division of World Vision Intl.

".. inspiring vision and empowering holistic mission among those who are extending the whole gospel to the whole world."

Year Founded in USA	1966
Income for Overseas Ministries	NA

Personnel:
Home ministry & office staff in USA 10

Marriage Ministries International

(303)933-3331   **Fax: (303)933-2153**
E-Mail: MichaelP@marriage.org
Web: http://www.marriage.org
P.O. Box 1040, Littleton, CO 80160
Rev. Michael E. Phillipps, Director

An interdenominational service agency of charismatic tradition providing training materials in 8 languages for strengthening married couples for evangelism and other ministries.

Year Founded in USA	1983
Income for Overseas Ministries .	$ 150,000

Personnel:
Bivocational/Tentmaker from USA 24
Short-Term less than 1 year from USA . . . 80
Home ministry & office staff in USA 22

Mazahua Mission

(419)352-7919
16011 W. Poe Rd., Bowling Green, OH 43402
Mr. Barry Milliron, Co-Chairperson

A nondenominational support agency of Congregational and evangelical tradition engaged in support of national churches, agricultural programs, and funds transmission. Financial and personnel information from 1992.

Year Founded in USA	1986
Income for Overseas Ministries . .	$ 35,808

Fully Supported USA Personnel Overseas:
Expecting to serve more than 4 years 1
Nonresidential mission personnel 1
Countries: Mexico 1.

Media Associates International
(630)893-1977   Fax: (630)893-1141
P.O. Box 218, Bloomingdale, IL 60108
Mr. Robert B. Reekie, President
Mr. John Maust, Director of Training

A nondenominational service agency of evangelical tradition engaged in training personnel to become skilled communicators of the Gospel through books, magazines and other publications. Also publishing and consulting for missions and national agencies in the Two-Thirds World.

Year Founded in USA 1985
Income for Overseas Ministries . $ 144,245
Fully Supported USA Personnel Overseas:
Nonresidential mission personnel 2
Other Personnel:
Short-Term less than 1 year from USA . . . 1
Home ministry & office staff in USA 2

Medical Ambassadors Intl.
(209)524-0600   Fax: (209)571-3538
E-Mail: MedAmb@ix.netcom.com
P.O. Box 576645, Modesto, CA 95357
Dr. Paul Calhoun, M.D., Exec. Director

An interdenominational specialized service agency of evangelical tradition engaged in medical work in support of evangelism, development projects, and national workers.

".. recruits, trains and supports national leaders among developing peoples .. to reach their own people physically and spiritually..."

Year Founded in USA 1974
Income for Overseas Ministries $ 1,201,958
Fully Supported USA Personnel Overseas:
Expecting to serve more than 4 years 3
Expecting to serve 1 up to 4 years 1
Nonresidential mission personnel 3
Other Personnel:
Non-USA serving in own/other country . . 293
Short-Term less than 1 year from USA . . . 37
Home ministry & office staff in USA 10
Countries: Albania, Argentina, Bangladesh, Congo/Zaire, Dominican Rep, El Salvador, Ethiopia, Gabon, Guatemala, Haiti 1, India, Kenya, Mexico 1, Nepal, Philippines 2, Tanzania, Uganda, Venezuela.

Medical Missions Philippines
(209)527-7466
P.O. Box 3656, Modesto, CA 95352
Mr. Richard G. Hagerty, President

A nondenominational support agency of Baptist tradition engaged in funds transmission, evangelism, and providing medical supplies.

Year Founded in USA 1987
Income for Overseas Ministries . . $ 55,400
Personnel:
Short-Term less than 1 year from USA . . . 5

Men for Missions International
(317)881-6752   Fax: (317)865-1076
P.O. Box A, Greenwood, IN 46142
Mr. Warren Hardig, Exec. Director

A nondenominational support agency of evangelical tradition engaged in overseas missionary housing construction, literature production, and providing other technical assistance as a short-term arm of OMS Intl.

Year Founded in USA 1954
Income for Overseas Ministries . . . . NA
Personnel:
Short-Term less than 1 year from USA . . 200
Home ministry & office staff in USA 9

Mennonite Board of Missions
(219)294-7523   Fax: (219)294-8669
P.O. Box 370, Elkhart, IN 46515
Stanley W. Green, President

A denominational sending agency of Mennonite tradition engaged in leadership development, theological education, literature production, medical work, and missionary training. Financial and personnel information from 1992.

Year Founded in USA 1906
Income for Overseas Ministries $ 2,104,000
Fully Supported USA Personnel Overseas:
Expecting to serve more than 4 years 80
Nonresidential mission personnel 2
Other Personnel:
Non-USA serving in own/other country . . . 5
Bivocational/Tentmaker from USA 33
Short-Term less than 1 year from USA . . . 28
Home ministry & office staff in USA 5
Countries: Argentina 8, Asia 2, Belgium 2, Benin 4, Brazil 7, Chile 2, China (PRC) 2, France 3, Ghana 6,

India 4, Ireland 2, Israel 4, Japan 8, Liberia 3, Nepal 12, Puerto Rico 2, Spain 2, Suriname 2, UK 5.

Mennonite Brethren Missions/ Services

(209)456-4600   **Fax: (209)251-1432**
E-Mail: MBMS@compuserve.com
Web: http://www.mobynet.com/mbms/mbms.html
4867 E. Townsend Ave., Fresno, CA 93727
Rev. Harold Ens, General Director

A denominational sending agency of Mennonite and Brethren tradition engaged in church planting, church construction, evangelism, leadership development, and support of national workers.

".. to participate in making disciples of all people groups, sharing the gospel cross-culturally and globally, in Spirit-empowered obedience to Christ's great Commission and in partnership with local Mennonite Brethren Churches."

Year Founded in USA 1878
Income for Overseas Ministries $ 5,100,000
Fully Supported USA Personnel Overseas:
   Expecting to serve more than 4 years 35
   Expecting to serve 1 up to 4 years 42
Other Personnel:
   Non-USA serving in own/other country . . 131
   Bivocational/Tentmaker from USA 2
   Short-Term less than 1 year from USA . . 286
   Home ministry & office staff in USA . . 15
Countries: Afghanistan 2, Angola, Austria 4, Botswana 2, Brazil 6, China (PRC), Colombia 7, Ethiopia, Germany 12, Guatemala, India, Indonesia, Japan 4, Kazakhstan, Kyrgyzstan 1, Lithuania 8, Mexico 7, Pakistan 2, Panama, Paraguay, Peru 8, Portugal 4, Russia 2, Thailand 4, Uruguay 2, Venezuela 2.

Mennonite Central Committee Intl.

(717)859-1151   **Fax: (717)859-2171**
E-Mail: MailBox@mcc.org
Web: http://www.mennonitecc.ca/mcc/
P.O. Box M, Akron, PA 17501
Dr. John A. Lapp, Exec. Secretary

A binational denominational service agency of Mennonite tradition engaged in community development, agricultural programs, extension ed., medical work, relief aid, technical assistance, training, and youth programs. Financial and overseas personnel totals are for the U.S. and Canada.

".. to demonstrate God's love through committed women and men who work among people suffering from poverty, conflict, oppression and natural disaster."

Year Founded in USA 1920
Income for Overseas Ministries $ 31,943,548
Amount of Gifts-In-Kind . . . $ 9,290,437
Fully Supported USA Personnel Overseas:
   Expecting to serve more than 4 years . . . 195
   Expecting to serve 1 up to 4 years 186
Other Personnel:
   Home ministry & office staff in USA . . . 286
Countries: Bangladesh 18, Bolivia 26, Botswana 8, Brazil 14, Burkina Faso 12, Burundi 6, Cambodia 12, Chad 8, China (PRC) 8, Congo/Zaire 7, Costa Rica 2, Croatia 1, Egypt 18, El Salvador 11, Ethiopia 2, Germany 2, Guatemala 6, Haiti 16, Honduras 6, India 4, Indonesia 19, Ireland 2, Jamaica 14, Jordan 2, Kenya 10, Laos 2, Lebanon 2, Lesotho 6, Lithuania 1, Mexico 12, Mozambique 10, Nepal 8, Nicaragua 10, Nigeria 8, Paraguay 5, Philippines 7, Russia 5, S Africa 6, Serbia 2, Somalia 1, Sudan 8, Swaziland 6, Switzerland 7, Syria 2, Tanzania 3, Thailand 1, Uganda 8, Ukraine 1, Vietnam 8, West Bank 8, Zambia 9, Zimbabwe 1.

Mercy Ships

(903)882-0887   **Fax: (903)882-0336**
E-Mail: Info@mercyships.org
Web: http://www.mercyships.org/
P.O. Box 2020, Lindale, TX 75771
Don K. Stephens, President/CEO

An interdenominational service agency of evangelical tradition engaged in medical work, evangelism, relief aid, training, and development. The maritime arm of Youth With A Mission.

".. to bring physical and spiritual healing to the poor and needy in port cities around the world..."

Year Founded in USA 1978
Income for Overseas Ministries $ 11,177,682
Amount of Gifts-In-Kind . . . $ 5,745,612
Fully Supported USA Personnel Overseas:
   Expecting to serve more than 4 years . . . 294
Countries: Unspecified 294.

Message of Life, Inc.

(209)683-7028   **Fax: (209)683-7028**
E-Mail: mensjevida@aol.com
58607 Rd. 601, Ahwahnee, CA 93601
Mr. Ezequiel Mantilla, Gen. Manager

An interdenominational service agency of evangelical tradition engaged in literature production and distribution.

Year Founded in USA	1961
Income for Overseas Ministries	$ 60,000

Messenger Films, Inc.

(757)631-1442 **Fax: (757)631-1442**
E-Mail: MsngrFilms@aol.com
P.O. Box 65003, Virginia Beach, VA 23467
Christopher Krusen, President/Founder

A nondenominational service agency of evangelical tradition engaged in video/film production/distribution in support of mass evangelism in South Africa and Latin America.

Year Founded in USA	1988
Income for Overseas Ministries	NA

Metropolitan Church Association

(414)248-6786
323 Broad St., Lake Geneva, WI 53147
Rev. Warren Bitzer, President

A denominational sending agency of Holiness tradition engaged in evangelism, church planting, and support of national workers. Financial and personnel information from 1992.

Year Founded in USA	1894
Income for Overseas Ministries	$ 86,572
Fully Supported USA Personnel Overseas:	
Expecting to serve more than 4 years	4

Countries: Mexico 1, S Africa 1, Swaziland 2.

Mexican Border Missions

(956)838-2895
P.O. Box 2138, Brownsville, TX 78522
Rev. Robert Blodget, President

A nondenominational sending agency of independent tradition engaged in church planting, church construction, evangelism, and support of national workers.

Year Founded in USA	1961
Income for Overseas Ministries	$ 47,485
Fully Supported USA Personnel Overseas:	
Expecting to serve more than 4 years	2
Other Personnel:	
Non-USA serving in own/other country	5

Countries: Mexico 2.

Mexican Christian Mission

(800)658-1600
P.O. Box 1757, La Mesa, CA 91944
Mr. Stephen P. Sammons, Exec. Director

A nondenominational sending agency of independent tradition engaged in church planting, evangelism, literature distribution, and support of national workers.

Year Founded in USA	1956
Income for Overseas Ministries	$ 142,500
Fully Supported USA Personnel Overseas:	
Expecting to serve more than 4 years	4
Other Personnel:	
Non-USA serving in own/other country	5
Bivocational/Tentmaker from USA	1

Countries: Mexico 4.

Mexican Medical, Inc.

(619)660-1106 **Fax: (619)660-1223**
E-Mail: MexMedHQ@mexicanmedical.com
2520 Sweetwater Springs Blvd., Spring Valley, CA 91978
Rev. Melvin Peabody

A nondenominational service agency of evangelical tradition engaged in medical work, agricultural programs, and childcare programs. Includes the former Missions of Baja organization.

Year Founded in USA	1967
Income for Overseas Ministries	NR
Fully Supported USA Personnel Overseas:	
Expecting to serve more than 4 years	2
Expecting to serve 1 up to 4 years	2

Countries: Mexico 4.

Mexican Mission Ministries

(512)787-3543
P.O. Box 636, Pharr, TX 78577
Rev. Linden Ray Unruh, President

An interdenominational sending agency of Baptist and evangelical tradition engaged in church planting, church construction, childrens programs, theological education, literature distribution, and youth programs.

Year Founded in USA	1954
Income for Overseas Ministries	$ 488,500
Fully Supported USA Personnel Overseas:	
Expecting to serve more than 4 years	10

Other Personnel:
Non-USA serving in own/other country   . . .   12
Home ministry & office staff in USA   9
Countries: Mexico 10.

Middle East Christian Outreach

(218)236-5963   Fax: (218)236-5963
E-Mail: 75227.633@compuserve.com
P.O. Box 1008, Moorhead, MN 56561
Rev. James R. Smith, U.S. Director

An interdenominational sending agency of
evangelical tradition engaged in support of
national churches, evangelism, print and video
production/distribution, and medical work.

Year Founded in USA   1978
Income for Overseas Ministries   . $ 995,000
Fully Supported USA Personnel Overseas:
Expecting to serve more than 4 years   3
Other Personnel:
Non-USA serving in own/other country   . . .   1
Bivocational/Tentmaker from USA   2
Home ministry & office staff in USA   1
Countries: Asia 3.

Middle East Media - USA

(425)778-0752   Fax: (425)778-0752
E-Mail: 73004.645@compuserve.com
P.O. Box 359, Lynnwood, WA 98046
Ronald J. Ensminger, President & CEO

A transdenominational sending agency of
evangelical tradition engaged in evangelism,
audio recording/distribution, Bible distribution,
TV broadcasting, literature distribution, and
video/film production/distribution.

Year Founded in USA   1976
Income for Overseas Ministries   . $ 399,800
Fully Supported USA Personnel Overseas:
Expecting to serve more than 4 years   4
Other Personnel:
Non-USA serving in own/other country   . . .   4
Short-Term less than 1 year from USA   . . .   10
Home ministry & office staff in USA   3
Countries: Asia 4.

Ministries In Action

(305)234-7855   Fax: (305)234-7825
P.O. Box 140325, Coral Gables, FL 33114
Rev. E. Walford Thompson, President

An interdenominational sending agency of
evangelical tradition engaged in evangelism,
extension education, and support of national
churches. Statistical information from 1992.

Year Founded in USA   1961
Income for Overseas Ministries   . $ 474,000
Fully Supported USA Personnel Overseas:
Expecting to serve more than 4 years   3
Other Personnel:
Home ministry & office staff in USA   9
Countries: Haiti 3.

Ministry of Jesus, Inc.

(410)875-9111   Fax: (410)635-2929
2017 W. Old Liberty Rd., Westminster, MD 21157
Rev. Thomas W. Beak, President

A service agency of independent tradition
engaged in church planting, agricultural
programs, primary health education, and
Christian education.

Year Founded in USA   1984
Income for Overseas Ministries   . $ 187,000
Fully Supported USA Personnel Overseas:
Expecting to serve more than 4 years   6
Other Personnel:
Non-USA serving in own/other country   . . .   35
Short-Term less than 1 year from USA   . . .   8
Home ministry & office staff in USA   1
Countries: Togo 6.

Ministry to Eastern Europe

(804)320-6456   Fax: (804)320-6456
E-Mail: MTEE@erols.com
10301 Edgebrook Ct., Richmond, VA 23235
Dr. John F. McGeorge,, Jr., President

An interdenominational sending agency of
charismatic tradition engaged in theological
education, literature production, national worker
support, training, and translation work.

Year Founded in USA   1983
Income for Overseas Ministries   . $ 115,000
Fully Supported USA Personnel Overseas:
Nonresidential mission personnel   5
Other Personnel:
Non-USA serving in own/other country   . . .   18
Short-Term less than 1 year from USA   . . .   40
Home ministry & office staff in USA   2
Countries: Bulgaria, Poland, Romania, Slovakia.

Mission 21 India

(616)453-8855   **Fax: (616)791-9926**
E-Mail: M21India@alliance.net
Web: http://www.missionindia.org/
P.O. Box 141312, Grand Rapids, MI 49514
Rev. John F. DeVries, President

An interdenominational support agency of evangelical tradition partnering with national organizations engaged in church planting, Bible distribution, childrens programs, development, literature distribution, and literacy work.

"...to motivate, train, and assist national Indian denominations and missions to plant one new house church for every 1,000 persons."

Year Founded in USA 1990
Income for Overseas Ministries $ 1,704,392
Amount of Gifts-In-Kind . . . $ 203,866
Fully Supported USA Personnel Overseas:
  Nonresidential mission personnel 1
Other Personnel:
  Home ministry & office staff in USA 13
Countries: India.

Mission Advanced Research and Communications Center

See: MARC

Mission Aides, Inc.

(626)355-3346   **Fax: (626)355-8689**
E-Mail: MisCom@aol.com
P.O. Box 1, Sierra Madre, CA 91025
Mr. Hugh S. Bell, Jr., President

A nondenominational service agency of evangelical tradition engaged in technical assistance and broadcasting.

Year Founded in USA 1954
Income for Overseas Ministries . . $ 20,000
Personnel:
  Bivocational/Tentmaker from USA 2
  Home ministry & office staff in USA 1

Mission Aviation Fellowship

(909)794-1151   **Fax: (909)794-3016**
E-Mail: MAF-US@maf.org
Web: http://www.maf.org/
P.O. Box 3202, Redlands, CA 92374
Gary L. Bishop, President & CEO

A nondenominational specialized service agency of evangelical tradition engaged in aviation, electronic communication, purchasing, and other technical assistance services in support of evangelism, relief aid, and other ministries.

".. to multiply the effectiveness of the Church using aviation and other strategic technologies to reach the world for Christ."

Year Founded in USA 1945
Income for Overseas Ministries $ 15,499,861
Fully Supported USA Personnel Overseas:
  Expecting to serve more than 4 years . . . 237
  Expecting to serve 1 up to 4 years 23
Other Personnel:
  Non-USA serving in own/other country . . . 16
  Home ministry & office staff in USA . . . 112
Countries: Africa 2, Albania 4, Asia 2, Brazil 7, Congo/Zaire 47, Ecuador 25, Guatemala 10, Haiti 5, Honduras 12, Indonesia 85, Lesotho 12, Mali 10, Mexico 3, Mozambique 2, Nicaragua 4, Russia 4, Suriname 8, Venezuela 8, Zambia 4, Zimbabwe 6.

Mission Connection, The

(210)272-2100   **Fax: (210)696-3833**
E-Mail: TMC96@juno.com
4203 Gardendale, #218, San Antonio, TX 78229
Helen Hunter, Director

A placement service agency engaged in mobilization for mission and missions information services to link individuals with sending agencies.

Year Founded in USA 1995
Income for Overseas Ministries . . . . NA
Personnel:
  Home ministry & office staff in USA 2

Mission Ministries, Inc.

(714)722-1304
P.O. Box 10044, Costa Mesa, CA 92627
Dr. John A. Lindvall, Director

A nondenominational sending agency of Congregational and evangelical tradition engaged in childrens programs, church planting, Christian education, evangelism, and relief aid.

Year Founded in USA 1980
Income for Overseas Ministries . $ 175,776
Fully Supported USA Personnel Overseas:
  Expecting to serve more than 4 years 5
Other Personnel:

Non-USA serving in own/other country   . . .   5
Bivocational/Tentmaker from USA   5
Short-Term less than 1 year from USA   . . .   1
Home ministry & office staff in USA   3
Countries: Asia, Mexico 2, Philippines, Uganda, Venezuela 3.

Mission O.N.E., Inc.
(615)672-9504   **Fax: (615)672-9513**
E-Mail: MissionWun@aol.com
P.O. Box 70, White House, TN 37188
Bob Schlinder, President

An interdenominational support agency of Baptist and evangelical tradition engaged in training and support of national workers for evangelism and church planting.

".. to mobilize the Church for the support of national missionaries, primarily among unreached people groups in developing nations."

Year Founded in USA   1991
Income for Overseas Ministries   . . $ 74,781
Personnel:
Non-USA serving in own/other country   . .   151
Short-Term less than 1 year from USA   . . .   10
Home ministry & office staff in USA   3
Countries: China (PRC), Ethiopia, India, Indonesia, Kenya, Laos, Myanmar/Burma, Nepal, Pakistan, Sudan, Thailand, Uganda, Zambia.

Mission of Mercy
(719)593-0099   **Fax: (719)531-6820**
P.O. Box 62600, Colorado Springs, CO 80962
Mr. Donald D. Beard, President

A nondenominational support agency of charismatic and evangelical tradition engaged in church construction, providing medical supplies, and relief aid. Financial information from 1992.

Year Founded in USA   1977
Income for Overseas Ministries $ 2,000,000
Personnel:
Home ministry & office staff in USA   10

Mission Possible
(561)465-0373   **Fax: (561)465-0639**
E-Mail: 103167.2325@compuserve.com
Web: http://www.odyssey.on.ca/~missionpossible/
P.O. Box 520, Fort Pierce, FL 34954
Mr. George E. Wadsworth, President

A nondenominational service agency of evangelical tradition engaged in evangelism, Christian ed., support of national workers, and relief aid.

Year Founded in USA   1979
Income for Overseas Ministries   . $ 495,414
Amount of Gifts-In-Kind   . . . . $ 51,414
Fully Supported USA Personnel Overseas:
Expecting to serve more than 4 years   4
Expecting to serve 1 up to 4 years   2
Other Personnel:
Non-USA serving in own/other country   . . .   91
Short-Term less than 1 year from USA   . . .   5
Home ministry & office staff in USA   4
Countries: Dominican Rep 1, Haiti 5.

Mission Possible Foundation, Inc.
(940)382-1508   **Fax: (940)566-1875**
E-Mail: MP@xc.org
Web: http://www.mp.org/
P.O. Box 2014, Denton, TX 76202
Dr. W. Ralph Mann, President/CEO

A nondenominational sending agency of independent tradition engaged in extension education, leadership development, literature production and support of national churches to enable evangelism and church planting.

".. to serve local national churches and enable them to evangelize unbelievers and disciple new believers..."

Year Founded in USA   1974
Income for Overseas Ministries   . $ 779,005
Amount of Gifts-In-Kind   . . . $ 172,610
Fully Supported USA Personnel Overseas:
Expecting to serve more than 4 years   4
Expecting to serve 1 up to 4 years   3
Other Personnel:
Non-USA serving in own/other country   . . .   2
Short-Term less than 1 year from USA   . . .   6
Home ministry & office staff in USA   8
Countries: Finland 2, Germany 3, Ukraine 2.

Mission Safety International
(423)542-8892   **Fax: (423)542-8892**
E-Mail: 103404.337@compuserve.com
P.O. Box 1632, Elizabethton, TN 37644
Mr. Joe Hopkins, President

A nondenominational specialized service agency of evangelical tradition engaged in aviation safety services for other agencies.

".. to provide educational and consulting services to assist missions and related agencies in realizing their [aircraft operations] objectives effectively and efficiently."

Year Founded in USA 1983
Income for Overseas Ministries . . . . NA

Mission Services Association

(423)577-9740   **Fax: (423)577-9743**
E-Mail: 102774.1772@compuserve.com
P.O. Box 2427, Knoxville, TN 37901
W. Reggie Hundley, Exec. Director

A nondenominational support agency of Christian (Restoration Movement) tradition engaged in services for missionaries and local churches including mission research, video distribution, and newsletter printing/mailing.

Year Founded in USA 1946
Income for Overseas Ministries . . . . NA

Mission Society for United Methodists, The

(770)446-1381   **Fax: (770)446-3044**
Web: http://www.lightpath.com/msum/
P.O. Box 922637, Norcross, GA 30092
Dr. Alvern L. Vom Steeg, President

A denominational sending agency of Methodist tradition engaged in evangelism, church planting, medical work/supplies, support of national churches, and missionary training.

Year Founded in USA 1984
Income for Overseas Ministries $ 2,210,433
Amount of Gifts-In-Kind . . . $ 287,082
Fully Supported USA Personnel Overseas:
  Expecting to serve more than 4 years 77
  Expecting to serve 1 up to 4 years 21
Other Personnel:
  Non-USA serving in own/other country . . . 2
  Short-Term less than 1 year from USA . . . 35
  Home ministry & office staff in USA 18
Countries: Africa 6, China (PRC) 1, Costa Rica 8, France 6, Ghana 8, Guatemala 2, Guinea 2, Haiti 1, Honduras 2, Hungary 2, India 2, Indonesia 2, Japan 2, Kenya 5, Mexico 4, Papua New Guin 2, Paraguay 6, Philippines 2, Russia 25, Singapore 2, Solomon Isls 2, Spain 2, UK 2, Vietnam 2.

Mission to the Americas

(630)260-3800   **Fax: (630)653-4936**
P.O. Box 828, Wheaton, IL 60189
Rev. Rick Miller, Exec. Director

An evangelical sending agency of Baptist tradition engaged in church planting, broadcasting, theological ed., evangelism, leadership development, and support of national churches in N. and S. America, including USA and Canadian cross-cultural ministries. Formerly known as Conservative Baptist Home Mission Society (CBHMS).

Year Founded in USA 1950
Income for Overseas Ministries $ 1,642,950
Fully Supported USA Personnel Overseas:
  Expecting to serve more than 4 years 25
Other Personnel:
  Non-USA serving in own/other country . . . 40
  Short-Term less than 1 year from USA . . . 10
  Home ministry & office staff in USA 15
Countries: Belize 2, Costa Rica 2, Dominican Rep 1, Guam 2, Guatemala, Haiti 2, Honduras 8, Mexico 8.

Mission to the World

(404)320-3373   **Fax: (404)325-5974**
E-Mail: Postmaster@mtw.org
P.O. Box 29765, Atlanta, GA 30359
Dr. Paul D. Kooistra, Exec. Director

A denominational sending agency of the Presbyterian Church in America engaged in church planting, evangelism, and support of national workers.

"To reach the world's unreached responsive peoples with God's Good News through the testimony of church-planting teams and strategic technical and support personnel..."

Year Founded in USA 1973
Income for Overseas Ministries $ 19,746,919
Fully Supported USA Personnel Overseas:
  Expecting to serve more than 4 years . . . 438
  Expecting to serve 1 up to 4 years 130
Other Personnel:
  Bivocational/Tentmaker from USA 2
  Short-Term less than 1 year from USA . . 2,008
  Home ministry & office staff in USA 50
Countries: Africa 32, Angola 2, Argentina 2, Australia 16, Austria 6, Bangladesh 1, Br Virgin Isls 2, Brazil 3, Bulgaria 2, Burkina Faso 2, Chile 21, China (PRC) 2, Colombia 23, Congo/Zaire 2, Cote d'Ivoire 16, Czech Rep 13, Ecuador 24, Ethiopia 4, France 29, Germany 9, Ghana 2, Haiti 2, Hong Kong 2, Hungary 6, India 9,

Indonesia 10, Ireland 3, Italy 4, Jamaica 3, Japan 45, Kazakhstan 10, Kenya 22, Korea-S 6, Malawi 2, Mexico 48, Micronesia 2, Mongolia 1, Niger 2, Nigeria 8, Papua New Guin 6, Peru 22, Philippines 17, Poland 2, Portugal 9, Romania 2, Russia 3, S Africa 2, Senegal 9, Spain 14, Taiwan (ROC) 9, Tanzania 6, UK 3, Uganda 1, Ukraine 46, Unspecified 17, Zimbabwe 2.

Mission To Unreached Peoples

(206)781-3151   Fax: (206)781-3182
E-Mail: MUPinfo@mup.org
Web: http://www.mup.org/mupinfo/
P.O. Box 45880, Seattle, WA 98145
Mr. David M. Hupp, U.S. Director

An interdenominational sending agency of evangelical tradition engaged in technical assistance, church planting, evangelism, support of national churches, and mobilization for mission.

Year Founded in USA 1982
Income for Overseas Ministries . $ 744,000
Fully Supported USA Personnel Overseas:
  Expecting to serve 1 up to 4 years 32
Other Personnel:
  Bivocational/Tentmaker from USA 43
  Short-Term less than 1 year from USA . . . 2
  Home ministry & office staff in USA 8
Countries: Cambodia 6, China (PRC) 2, Hong Kong 2, India 2, Indonesia 2, Japan 2, Nepal 2, Philippines 2, Poland 2, Russia 4, Singapore 2, Thailand 4.

Mission Training and Resource Center

(626)797-7903   Fax: (626)797-7906
E-Mail: PhilElkins@aol.com
3800 Canon Blvd., Altadena, CA 91001
Phillip Elkins, President

A nondenominational service agency of evangelical tradition engaged in missionary training, missions information service, and mission-related research.

Year Founded in USA 1979
Income for Overseas Ministries . . . . NA

Mission Training International

(719)594-0687   Fax: (719)594-4682
E-Mail: MIntern@aol.com
Web: http://www.mti.org
P.O. Box 50110, Colorado Springs, CO 80949
Mr. Paul E. Nelson, President

A nondenominational specialized service agency of evangelical tradition engaged in missionary training, furloughed missionary support, and research/information services, for others. Name changed from Missionary Internship.

"Working together with churches and mission agencies to train and nurture Christians for effective intercultural service."

Year Founded in USA 1954
Income for Overseas Ministries . . . . NA
Personnel:
  Home ministry & office staff in USA 10

Mission: Moving Mountains

(612)884-8450   Fax: (612)884-8456
E-Mail: MMM@xc.org
Web: http://www.movingmountains.org
10800 Lyndale Ave. S. #100, Bloomington, MN 55420
Dr. Gary T. Hipp, President & CEO

An interdenominational sending agency of Baptist tradition engaged in wholistic community dev., discipleship, and agricultural programs.

".. to facilitate the physical and spiritual well-being of impoverished people in developing countries."

Year Founded in USA 1978
Income for Overseas Ministries . $ 1,500,000
Fully Supported USA Personnel Overseas:
  Expecting to serve more than 4 years 36
  Expecting to serve 1 up to 4 years 9
Other Personnel:
  Non-USA serving in own/other country . . . 6
  Home ministry & office staff in USA 11
Countries: Ethiopia 7, Kenya 16, Senegal 6, Tanzania 13, Uganda 3.

Missionaire International

(308)235-4147   Fax: (308)235-4147
P.O. Box 474, Kimball, NE 69145
Jon Foote, Director of Operations

An interdenominational service agency of evangelical tradition engaged in aviation services, support of national workers, and services for other agencies.

Year Founded in USA 1988
Income for Overseas Ministries . . $ 24,900
Personnel:

Non-USA serving in own/other country . . . 4
Bivocational/Tentmaker from USA 2
Short-Term less than 1 year from USA . . . 6
Home ministry & office staff in USA 6
Countries: Congo/Zaire, Russia.

Missionary Action, Inc.

(941)739-1700   Fax: (941)739-1700
E-Mail: MAflame@juno.com
P.O. Box 1027, Bradenton, FL 34206
Dr. Lee Roy, President

An interdenominational support agency of
Pentecostal tradition engaged in mobilization for
mission, evangelism, and natl. worker support.

Year Founded in USA 1982
Income for Overseas Ministries . . $ 69,193
Personnel:
Non-USA serving in own/other country . . . 2
Home ministry & office staff in USA 1
Countries: Nicaragua.

Missionary Athletes International

(719)528-1636   Fax: (719)528-1638
E-Mail: 103016.1115@compuserve.com
P.O. Box 25010, Colorado Springs, CO 80936
Mr. Timothy A. Conrad, President

An interdenominational service agency of
evangelical and fundamental tradition engaged in
sports evangelism, Bible distribution, and
short-term programs coordination.

Year Founded in USA 1983
Income for Overseas Ministries . $ 200,000
Fully Supported USA Personnel Overseas:
Expecting to serve more than 4 years 9
Expecting to serve 1 up to 4 years 5
Other Personnel:
Non-USA serving in own/other country . . . 2
Short-Term less than 1 year from USA . . . 60
Home ministry & office staff in USA 14
Countries: Czech Rep 5, UK 9.

Missionary Auto-Truck Service Inc

(513)677-1234   Fax: (513)677-1238
E-Mail: MATS@tso.cin.ix.net
6925 Glenellyn Dr., Loveland, OH 45140
Mr. Charles R. Schroth, Exec. Director

A nondenominational support agency of evangelical tradition providing a purchasing service

for vehicles used abroad and in the USA by
mission agencies, churches, and other ministries.

Year Founded in USA 1977
Income for Overseas Ministries . . . . NA

Missionary Crusader, Inc.

(806)799-1040   Fax: (806)799-0092
2451 34th St., Lubbock, TX 79411
Mark Duncan, Exec. Director
Rev. Homer Duncan, Founding Director

A nondenominational service agency of
independent tradition engaged in literature
distribution and production.

Year Founded in USA 1943
Income for Overseas Ministries . . $ 30,000
Personnel:
Home ministry & office staff in USA 3

Missionary Dentists

(425)771-3241   Fax: (425)775-5155
P.O. Box 7002, Seattle, WA 98133
Dr. John P. Loney, Director

An interdenominational specialized service
agency of evangelical tradition engaged in
medical work, evangelism, and providing medical
supplies and equipment in several countries.

Year Founded in USA 1950
Income for Overseas Ministries . . $ 92,000
Amount of Gifts-In-Kind . . . . $ 67,000
Fully Supported USA Personnel Overseas:
Nonresidential mission personnel 2
Other Personnel:
Short-Term less than 1 year from USA . . . 15
Home ministry & office staff in USA 5

Missionary Flights International

(561)686-2488   Fax: (561)697-4882
P.O. Box 15665, West Palm Beach, FL 33406
Richard Snook, President

A nondenominational support agency of
Baptist tradition engaged in aviation and other
services for mission efforts.

Year Founded in USA 1964
Income for Overseas Ministries $ 1,300,000
Personnel:
Home ministry & office staff in USA 8
Countries: Haiti.

Missionary Gospel Fellowship
(209)634-8575
264 West Main Street, Turlock, CA 95380
Mr. John L. Harvey, Director

An interdenominational support agency of evangelical tradition engaged in evangelism, Bible distribution, church planting, and support of national workers in the USA and Mexico.

"..to share the Gospel and to disciple various ethnic or unreached groups of people in or near the USA."

Year Founded in USA	1939
Income for Overseas Ministries	NR

Personnel:
Non-USA serving in own/other country . . .	4
Short-Term less than 1 year from USA . . .	2
Home ministry & office staff in USA	45

Countries: Mexico.

Missionary Information Exchange
(248)541-3688
23225 Berkley, Oak Park, MI 48237
Mr. Robert B. Hicks, Director

A nondenominational support agency of charismatic and Holiness tradition engaged in mission-related information services.

Year Founded in USA	1967
Income for Overseas Ministries	NA

Missionary Maintenance Services
(614)622-6848   **Fax: (614)622-8277**
E-Mail: MMS@sota-oh.com
Web: http://tims.net/mms/
P.O. Box 1118, Coshocton, OH 43812
Mr. Dwight Jarboe, Gen. Director

A nondenominational support agency of evangelical tradition providing technical assistance and training in mission aviation for others.

".. to train individuals in aviation maintenance and prepare them for service in the Christian mission aviation community."

Year Founded in USA	1975
Income for Overseas Ministries	NA

Personnel:
Short-Term less than 1 year from USA . . .	4
Home ministry & office staff in USA	14

Missionary Retreat Fellowship Inc.
(717)689-2984   **Fax: (717)689-2984**
E-Mail: GMcbr10310@aol.com
R.R. #4, Box 303, Lake Ariel, PA 18436
Rev. Gene McBride, Exec. Director

An interdenominational support agency of evangelical and independent tradition engaged in furloughed missionary support.

".. to provide the furloughing missionary with fully furnished housing .. at subsidized rates."

Year Founded in USA	1965
Income for Overseas Ministries	NA

Missionary Revival Crusade
(956)722-2646
102 E. Lyon St., Laredo, TX 78040
Rev. Roger J. West, President

An interdenominational support agency of charismatic and evangelical tradition engaged in church planting, broadcasting, evangelism, and funds transmission.

Year Founded in USA	1959
Income for Overseas Ministries	$ 1,000,000

Fully Supported USA Personnel Overseas:
Expecting to serve more than 4 years	31

Other Personnel:
Non-USA serving in own/other country . . .	2

Countries: Argentina 3, Colombia 4, Mexico 24.

Missionary TECH Team
(903)757-4530   **Fax: (903)758-2799**
E-Mail: MTTEAM@aol.com
25 FRJ Dr., Longview, TX 75602
Mr. Birne D. Wiley, President

A nondenominational service agency of fundamentalist tradition engaged in technical assistance, furloughed missionary support, and services for other agencies.

".. providing technical assistance, 'know-how', and support services to mission organizations around the world."

Year Founded in USA	1969
Income for Overseas Ministries .	$ 500,000

Fully Supported USA Personnel Overseas:
Nonresidential mission personnel	3

Other Personnel:
Short-Term less than 1 year from USA . . .	10

Home ministry & office staff in USA 26

Missions of Baja
See: Mexican Medical, Inc.

Missions Outreach International
(816)425-2277 **Fax: (816)425-2279**
P.O. Box 73, Bethany, MO 64424
Bob & Sharon Johnson, Directors

An interdenominational service agency of evangelical tradition engaged in short-term programs coordination, church construction, and mobilization for mission. Financial and personnel information from 1992.

".. to serve the local evangelical church for the purpose of discipleship training through cross-cultural team ministries..."

Year Founded in USA 1976
Income for Overseas Ministries . $ 337,000
Personnel:
   Short-Term less than 1 year from USA . . 190
   Home ministry & office staff in USA 1

Missions Resource Center
(513)522-2847 **Fax: (513)522-2846**
E-Mail: 71005.1031@compuserve.com
Web: http://www.ccmrc.org/
9452 Winton Road, Cincinnati, OH 45231
Marvin D. Grooms, Director

A nondenominational specialized service agency of Christian (Restoration Movement) tradition engaged in missions information services and research.

"..to collect, store and disseminate to the local church and its support agencies, data related to the world wide fulfillment of the mission of God..."

Year Founded in USA 1991
Income for Overseas Ministries . . . . NA

Missions To Japan, Inc.
(408)998-1768
P.O. Box 1203, Campbell, CA 95009
Rev. Joe Weigand, President

A nondenominational support agency of evangelical tradition engaged in support of national churches, Christian education, and evangelism.

".. to promote fellowship, cooperation, protection, recognition and the propagation of, the Christian Gospel at home and abroad..."

Year Founded in USA 1959
Income for Overseas Ministries . . $ 19,224
Personnel:
   Non-USA serving in own/other country . . . 5
   Home ministry & office staff in USA 3
Countries: China (PRC), Philippines.

Moody Institute of Science
Division of Moody Bible Institute
(800)647-6909 **Fax: (800)647-6910**
820 N. LaSalle Dr., Chicago, IL 60610
Ms. Barbara Goodwin, Vice President

A nondenominational service agency of evangelical tradition engaged in video/film production/distribution for evangelism and Christian education.

Year Founded in USA 1945
Income for Overseas Ministries . . . . NR

Moravian Church in North America, Board of World Mission
(610)868-1732 **Fax: (610)866-9223**
E-Mail: EHMorgan@enter.net
Web: http://www.moravian.org
P.O Box 1245, Bethlehem, PA 18016
Rev. E. Hampton Morgan, Exec. Director

A denominational sending board of Moravian tradition engaged in support of national churches, theological education, TEE, evangelism, and medical work.

Year Founded in USA 1949
Income for Overseas Ministries . $ 513,087
Fully Supported USA Personnel Overseas:
   Expecting to serve more than 4 years 2
   Expecting to serve 1 up to 4 years 3
Other Personnel:
   Non-USA serving in own/other country . . . 1
   Home ministry & office staff in USA 4
Countries: Asia 2, Honduras 3.

Morelli Ministries International

(918)664-2552   Fax: (918)628-0084
Box 700026, Tulsa, OK 74170
Michael Morelli, Founder-President

An interdenominational support agency of evangelical tradition engaged in evangelism, literature distribution, and national church support.

Year Founded in USA 1995
Income for Overseas Ministries . . $ 11,000
Personnel:
Non-USA serving in own/other country . . . 2
Short-Term less than 1 year from USA . . . 1
Home ministry & office staff in USA 2
Countries: Honduras, Uganda.

Muslim Hope

(513)932-8121   Fax: (513)932-8121
1000 Franklin Road, Lebanon, OH 45036
Mr. Donald S. Tingle, Director of Ministries
Marty Egelston, Co-ordinator

A nondenominational service agency of Christian (Restoration Movement) tradition engaged in evangelism, Bible and literature distribution, and relief aid. Reorganization of CAS International.

Year Founded in USA 1996
Income for Overseas Ministries . . $ 45,000
Fully Supported USA Personnel Overseas:
Expecting to serve more than 4 years 3
Other Personnel:
Non-USA serving in own/other country . . . 2
Bivocational/Tentmaker from USA 4
Short-Term less than 1 year from USA . . . 6
Home ministry & office staff in USA 3
Countries: Asia 1, Ukraine 2.

Mustard Seed, Inc.

(626)791-5123   Fax: (626)398-2392
E-Mail: mseedinc@wavenet.com
P.O. Box 400, Pasadena, CA 91114
Rev. Garry O. Parker, President

An interdenominational support agency of evangelical tradition partnering with churches and ministries engaged in Christian education, agricultural programs, church planting, childcare programs, medical work, and relief aid.

"... to assist in the task of world evangelization by means of compassionate services and verbal

witness among tribal peoples, particularly those having to learn to cope with modernity..."

Year Founded in USA 1948
Income for Overseas Ministries . $ 795,298
Fully Supported USA Personnel Overseas:
Expecting to serve 1 up to 4 years 1
Other Personnel:
Non-USA serving in own/other country . . 320
Short-Term less than 1 year from USA . . . 1
Home ministry & office staff in USA 7
Countries: Indonesia, Papua New Guin 1, Taiwan (ROC).

Mutual Faith Ministries Intl.

(818)830-6392   Fax: (818)830-8685
P.O. Box 3788, Granada Hills, CA 91394
Keith Hershey, President/Founder

A nondenominational support agency of charismatic tradition engaged in short-term programs coordination for evangelism teams in Central America.

Year Founded in USA 1984
Income for Overseas Ministries . . . . NR
Personnel:
Short-Term less than 1 year from USA . . . 40
Home ministry & office staff in USA 4

Narramore Christian Foundation

(626)821-8400   Fax: (626)821-8409
P.O. Box 661900, Arcadia, CA 91066
Dr. Clyde M. Narramore, President

A nondenominational specialized service agency of evangelical tradition providing crisis counseling and seminars for missionaries on location throughout the world.

Year Founded in USA 1955
Income for Overseas Ministries . . . . NA

National Baptist Convention of America, Foreign Mission Board

(214)942-3311   Fax: (214)943-4924
P.O. Box 223665, Dallas, TX 75222
Rev. N. Andrew Allen, Exec. Director

A denominational support agency of Baptist tradition engaged in evangelism, church construction, Christian education, funds transmission, and support of national workers.

Year Founded in USA 1915

Income for Overseas Ministries . $ 390,000
Personnel:
Home ministry & office staff in USA 4
Countries: Ghana, Haiti, Jamaica.

National Baptist Convention USA, Inc., Foreign Mission Board

(215)735-7868 **Fax: (215)735-1721**
P.O. Box 3873, Station D, Philadelphia, PA 19146
Dr. William J. Harvey III, Exec. Secretary

A denominational sending board of Baptist tradition engaged in church planting, church construction, Christian education, and providing medical supplies.

Year Founded in USA 1880
Income for Overseas Ministries $ 1,746,418
Fully Supported USA Personnel Overseas:
Expecting to serve more than 4 years 12
Expecting to serve 1 up to 4 years 10
Nonresidential mission personnel 5
Other Personnel:
Non-USA serving in own/other country . . 381
Short-Term less than 1 year from USA . . . 14
Countries: Bahamas 2, Barbados 2, Guinea 2, Lesotho 2, Liberia 2, Malawi 2, Nicaragua 2, S Africa 2, Sierra Leone 2, Swaziland 2, Zambia 2.

National Religious Broadcasters

(703)330-7000 **Fax: (703)330-7100**
E-Mail: mkisha@nrb.com
Web: http://www.nrb.com/
7839 Ashton Ave., Manassas, VA 20109
Dr. E. Brandt Gustavson, President

An interdenominational association of radio and television stations, program producers, and related organizations, including a Caribbean chapter and International Committee.

Year Founded in USA 1944
Income for Overseas Ministries . . $ 3,953

Navajo Gospel Mission

See: AmeriTribes

Navigators, U.S. International Ministries Group

(719)598-1212 **Fax: (719)260-0479**
E-Mail: Navs@gospelcom.net
Web: http://www.gospelcom.net/navs/usimg/
3820 N. 30th St., Colorado Springs, CO 80904
Dr. Terry Taylor, U.S. Director
Rod Beidler, Group Director

An interdenominational sending agency of evangelical tradition engaged in discipleship training, camping programs, evangelism, literature production, and missionary training.

"To reach, disciple, and equip people to know Christ and to make Him known through successive generations."

Year Founded in USA 1949
Income for Overseas Ministries $ 25,883,000
Fully Supported USA Personnel Overseas:
Expecting to serve more than 4 years . . . 346
Expecting to serve 1 up to 4 years 35
Other Personnel:
Bivocational/Tentmaker from USA 34
Short-Term less than 1 year from USA . . 101
Home ministry & office staff in USA . . . 1,211
Countries: Argentina 4, Asia 141, Australia 10, Austria 7, Brazil 6, Cameroon 4, Chile 4, Congo/Zaire 4, Costa Rica 2, Cote d'Ivoire 8, Croatia 2, Europe 8, Finland 4, France 10, Ghana 7, Hungary 4, Iceland 2, Indonesia 10, Italy 2, Japan 30, Kenya 5, Korea-S 2, Latin America 7, Latvia 2, Lithuania 2, Malawi 4, Mexico 4, New Zealand 2, Nigeria 2, Philippines 10, Romania 3, S Africa 6, Singapore 2, Slovakia 4, Slovenia 5, Spain 10, Taiwan (ROC) 8, Tanzania 2, Uganda 4, Unspecified 19, Venezuela 6, Zambia 3.

Nazarene Church World Mission

See: Church of the Nazarene

NEED, Inc.

(602)992-1321
P.O. Box 54541, Phoenix, AZ 85078
Mr. Dulal C. Borpujari, Intl. President

A nondenominational support agency of evangelical tradition engaged in funds transmission, Christian education, medical work, and relief aid in India and Vietnam.

Year Founded in USA 1985
Income for Overseas Ministries . $ 203,782
Amount of Gifts-In-Kind . . . . $ 80,060

Fully Supported USA Personnel Overseas:
Nonresidential mission personnel   1
Other Personnel:
Short-Term less than 1 year from USA   . . . 8
Home ministry & office staff in USA   1

Network of International Christian Schools

(901)276-8377   **Fax: (901)276-8389**
E-Mail: 74604.1703@compuserve.com
Web: http://goshen.net/NICS/
P.O. Box 18151, Memphis, TN 38181
Rev. Dave Fleming, U.S. Administrator
Dr. Joe Hale, Exec. Director

A nondenominational service agency of evangelical and independent tradition engaged in Christian education and evangelism.

Year Founded in USA   1991
Income for Overseas Ministries . $ 657,300
Fully Supported USA Personnel Overseas:
Expecting to serve 1 up to 4 years   . . . 178
Other Personnel:
Bivocational/Tentmaker from USA   18
Home ministry & office staff in USA   . . . 5
Countries: Austria 2, Indonesia 11, Korea-S 110, Singapore 7, Thailand 48.

New Life League International

(602)650-2203   **Fax: (602)650-2215**
E-Mail: NLLI@ix.netcom.com
P.O. Box 16030, Phoenix, AZ 85011
Rev. Stanley Runnels, President

An interdenominational service agency of evangelical tradition engaged in literature production/distribution through national workers.

Year Founded in USA   1954
Income for Overseas Ministries . . . NA
Personnel:
Non-USA serving in own/other country   . . 92
Bivocational/Tentmaker from USA   2
Home ministry & office staff in USA   4
Countries: Guatemala, Japan.

New Missions in Haiti

(407)240-4058
E-Mail: YesHaiti@aol.com
Web: http://www.newmissions.org
P.O. Box 2727, Orlando, FL 32802
Mr. George DeTellis, Jr., U.S. Exec. Director

A nondenominational sending agency of charismatic tradition engaged in Christian education and childcare/orphanage programs.

Year Founded in USA   1983
Income for Overseas Ministries . . $ 10,000
Fully Supported USA Personnel Overseas:
Expecting to serve 1 up to 4 years   6
Nonresidential mission personnel   2
Other Personnel:
Short-Term less than 1 year from USA   . . 30
Home ministry & office staff in USA   . . . 5
Countries: Haiti 6.

New Tribes Mission

(407)323-3430   **Fax: (407)330-0376**
Web: http://ntm.org/
1000 E. First St., Sanford, FL 32771
Dave Calderwood, Chairman

A nondenominational sending agency of fundamental and independent tradition engaged in church planting, theological ed., linguistics, literacy work, short-term programs coordination, Bible translation, and missionary training.

".. to assist the ministry of the local church through mobilizing, equipping, and coordinating of missionaries to evangelize unreached people groups, translate the Scriptures, and see indigenous New Testament churches established..."

Year Founded in USA   1942
Income for Overseas Ministries $ 24,822,163
Fully Supported USA Personnel Overseas:
Expecting to serve more than 4 years   . 1,434
Expecting to serve 1 up to 4 years   . . . 80
Other Personnel:
Non-USA serving in own/other country   . 174
Short-Term less than 1 year from USA   . 293
Home ministry & office staff in USA   . 441
Countries: Bolivia 105, Brazil 165, Colombia 57, Cote d'Ivoire 68, Germany 2, Greenland 1, Guinea 41, India 1, Indonesia 70, Japan 2, Korea-S 2, Malaysia, Mexico 84, Mongolia 7, Panama 81, Papua New Guin 374, Paraguay 69, Philippines 108, Russia 18, Senegal 71, Singapore 4, Thailand 67, Venezuela 117.

Next Towns Crusade, Inc.

(210)344-7467   **Fax: (210)344-6745**
3015 Gainesborough St., San Antonio, TX 78230
Pastor John M. Bell, Exec. Officer

A nondenominational sending agency of charismatic tradition engaged in church planting,

Bible distribution, childrens programs, leadership development, support of national churches, and missionary training. Income from 1992 report.

Year Founded in USA 1957
Income for Overseas Ministries . $ 300,000
Fully Supported USA Personnel Overseas:
    Expecting to serve more than 4 years 5
    Expecting to serve 1 up to 4 years 1
Other Personnel:
    Bivocational/Tentmaker from USA 2
    Short-Term less than 1 year from USA . . . 5
    Home ministry & office staff in USA 2
Countries: Japan 2, Mexico 4.

No Greater Love Ministries, Inc.
(618)542-4503   **Fax: (618)542-4503**
P.O. Box 263, DuQuoin, IL 62832
Rev. Fred L. Bishop

A transdenominational service agency of evangelical tradition engaged in evangelism and short-term programs coordination/orientation.

Year Founded in USA 1975
Income for Overseas Ministries . . $ 14,000
Personnel:
    Short-Term less than 1 year from USA . . . 45
    Home ministry & office staff in USA 2

North American Baptist Conf. International Missions Dept.
(630)495-2000   **Fax: (630)495-3301**
1 S. 210 Summit Ave., Oakbrook Terrace, IL 60181
Mr. Ronald D. Salzman, Intl. Missions Director

A denominational sending agency of Baptist tradition engaged in church planting, theological education, TEE, evangelism, and medical work.

Year Founded in USA 1891
Income for Overseas Ministries $ 3,105,575
Fully Supported USA Personnel Overseas:
    Expecting to serve more than 4 years 51
    Expecting to serve 1 up to 4 years 6
Other Personnel:
    Home ministry & office staff in USA 9
Countries: Brazil 8, Cameroon 22, Japan 11, Mexico 6, Nigeria 4, Philippines 6.

OC International, Inc.
(719)592-9292   **Fax: (719)592-0693**
E-Mail: 103130.3660@compuserve.com
Web: http://www.oci.org/
P.O. Box 36900, Colorado Springs, CO 80936
Dr. Lawrence E. Keyes, President

An interdenominational sending agency of evangelical tradition engaged in leadership development/training, church planting, evangelism, support of national churches, and research.

".. to assist the Body of Christ to make disciples of all peoples..."

Year Founded in USA 1950
Income for Overseas Ministries $ 6,566,453
Fully Supported USA Personnel Overseas:
    Expecting to serve more than 4 years . . . 124
    Expecting to serve 1 up to 4 years 9
Other Personnel:
    Non-USA serving in own/other country . . . 22
    Short-Term less than 1 year from USA . . 138
    Home ministry & office staff in USA 56
Countries: Argentina 4, Brazil 17, Colombia 1, France 8, Germany 10, Greece 2, Guatemala 16, Hong Kong 2, India, Indonesia 20, Japan 6, Kenya 8, Mexico 4, Philippines 12, Singapore 6, Swaziland 9, Taiwan (ROC) 8.

Omega World Missions
(760)241-2287
P.O. Box 1423, Victorville, CA 92393
Rev. Frank Brasel, President

A transdenominational sending agency of charismatic tradition engaged in support of national workers, church planting, leadership development, and literacy work.

Year Founded in USA 1980
Income for Overseas Ministries . $ 166,000
Fully Supported USA Personnel Overseas:
    Expecting to serve more than 4 years 7
Other Personnel:
    Non-USA serving in own/other country . . . 15
Countries: Indonesia 2, Philippines 5.

OMF International
(303)730-4160   **Fax: (303)730-4165**
E-Mail: OMF@xc.org
Web: http://www.omf.org/
10 W. Dry Creek Circle, Littleton, CO 80120
Dr. Daniel W. Bacon, U.S. Natl. Director

An interdenominational sending agency of evangelical tradition engaged in church planting, theological education, evangelism, leadership development, literature production, and support of national churches.

"To glorify God by the urgent evangelization of East Asia's millions."

Year Founded in USA 1888
Income for Overseas Ministries $ 4,522,466
Fully Supported USA Personnel Overseas:
    Expecting to serve more than 4 years . . . 240
    Nonresidential mission personnel 6
Other Personnel:
    Non-USA serving in own/other country . . 534
    Bivocational/Tentmaker from USA 24
    Short-Term less than 1 year from USA . . . 60
    Home ministry & office staff in USA 58
Countries: Asia 24, Hong Kong 16, Indonesia 19, Japan 42, Korea-S 6, Macao, Malaysia 1, Pakistan 2, Philippines 33, Singapore 12, Taiwan (ROC) 23, Thailand 62.

OMS International, Inc.
(317)881-6751   Fax: (317)888-5275
E-Mail: 74741.3507@compuserve.com
941 Fry Rd., Greenwood, IN 46142
Dr. J. B. Crouse, Jr., President

A nondenominational sending agency of Holiness and evangelical tradition engaged in church planting and construction, general Christian and theological education, evangelism, and support of national churches.

".. to reach around the world with the good news of Jesus Christ...in cooperation with national churches..."

Year Founded in USA 1901
Income for Overseas Ministries $ 13,678,210
Fully Supported USA Personnel Overseas:
    Expecting to serve more than 4 years . . . 168
    Expecting to serve 1 up to 4 years 110
    Nonresidential mission personnel 4
Other Personnel:
    Non-USA serving in own/other country . . 185
    Bivocational/Tentmaker from USA 30
    Short-Term less than 1 year from USA . . 366
    Home ministry & office staff in USA . . . 117
Countries: Brazil 7, Colombia 14, Ecuador 28, Haiti 17, Hong Kong 15, Hungary 14, India 2, Indonesia 13, Japan 13, Korea-S 7, Mexico 18, Mozambique 3, Philippines 6, Russia 83, Spain 8, Taiwan (ROC) 20, Unspecified 10.

On The Go Ministries / Keith Cook Evangelistic Association
(615)382-7929   Fax: (615)382-1344
P.O. Box 963, Springfield, TN 37172
Rev. Keith Cook, President

A transdenominational support agency of evangelical tradition engaged in evangelism and leadership development in several countries.

Year Founded in USA 1980
Income for Overseas Ministries . $ 100,000
Personnel:
    Short-Term less than 1 year from USA . . 350
    Home ministry & office staff in USA 17

Open Air Campaigners
(561)692-4283   Fax: (561)692-4712
P.O. Box 2542, Stuart, FL 34995
Rev. David Wilson, Overseas Ministries Director

An interdenominational service agency of evangelical tradition engaged in evangelism and church planting. Overseas ministries are now autonomous.

Year Founded in USA 1956
Income for Overseas Ministries . . . . NR
Fully Supported USA Personnel Overseas:
    Nonresidential mission personnel 1
Other Personnel:
    Home ministry & office staff in USA 2

Open Bible Ministries
(717)253-1544
P.O. Box 148, Honesdale, PA 18431
Mr. Bruce R. Burke, Director

A nondenominational sending agency of fundamentalist tradition engaged in church planting, Bible distribution, evangelism, and literature distribution.

Year Founded in USA 1971
Income for Overseas Ministries . . $ 40,000
Fully Supported USA Personnel Overseas:
    Expecting to serve more than 4 years 2
Other Personnel:
    Short-Term less than 1 year from USA . . . 3
Countries: S Africa 2.

Open Bible Standard Churches, Dept. of International Ministries

(515)288-6761   Fax: (515)288-2510
2020 Bell Ave., Des Moines, IA 50315
Rev. Paul V. Canfield, Exec. Director

A denominational sending agency of Pentecostal and evangelical tradition engaged in church planting, theological education, TEE, evangelism, and literature distribution.

Year Founded in USA 1935
Income for Overseas Ministries $ 1,070,611
Fully Supported USA Personnel Overseas:
   Expecting to serve more than 4 years 16
Other Personnel:
   Home ministry & office staff in USA 4
Countries: Chile 2, Guinea 2, Kenya 2, Mexico 3, Papua New Guin 2, Philippines 5, Romania.

Open Doors with Brother Andrew

(714)752-6600   Fax: (714)752-6442
P.O. Box 27001, Santa Ana, CA 92799
Mr. Michael Yoder, Communications Director

A nondenominational support agency of evangelical tradition engaged in Bible distribution, audio recording/distribution, broadcasting, and literature distribution. Financial and personnel information from 1992.

Year Founded in USA 1973
Income for Overseas Ministries $ 2,024,000
Amount of Gifts-In-Kind . . . . $ 97,231
Personnel:
   Short-Term less than 1 year from USA . . 160
   Home ministry & office staff in USA 34

Operation Blessing International

(757)579-3400   Fax: (757)579-3411
Web: http://www.ob.org/
977 Centerville Turnpk., Virginia Beach, VA 23463
Michael D. Little, President

An interdenominational specialized service agency of evangelical tradition engaged in relief aid, evangelism, mobilizing medical teams, and providing medical supplies. An affiliate of the Christian Broadcasting Network.

".. to demonstrate God's love by alleviating human need and suffering in the United States and throughout the world."

Year Founded in USA 1978
Income for Overseas Ministries $ 15,893,169
Fully Supported USA Personnel Overseas:
   Expecting to serve more than 4 years 1
Other Personnel:
   Non-USA serving in own/other country . . . 12
   Bivocational/Tentmaker from USA 5
   Short-Term less than 1 year from USA . . 236
   Home ministry & office staff in USA 43
Countries: Chile, Congo/Zaire 1, El Salvador, Guatemala, Romania, Ukraine.

Operation Mobilization, Inc.

(770)631-0432   Fax: (770)631-0439
E-Mail: Info@omusa.om.org
Web: http://www.om.org
P.O. Box 444, Tyrone, GA 30290
Dr. Rick Hicks, President

An interdenominational sending agency of evangelical tradition engaged in evangelism, church planting, literature distribution, mobilization for mission, and training.

".. to motivate, develop and equip people for world evangelization, and to strengthen and help plant churches, especially among the unreached in the Middle East, South and Central Asia, and Europe."

Year Founded in USA 1957
Income for Overseas Ministries $ 7,866,961
Fully Supported USA Personnel Overseas:
   Expecting to serve more than 4 years . . . 137
   Expecting to serve 1 up to 4 years 144
Other Personnel:
   Bivocational/Tentmaker from USA 10
   Short-Term less than 1 year from USA . . 400
   Home ministry & office staff in USA 83
Countries: Africa 16, Asia 66, Austria 3, Belgium 9, Brazil 1, Central Asia 31, Europe 48, France 1, Germany 4, India 5, Ireland 2, Mexico 6, Mozambique 2, Papua New Guin 2, S Africa 1, Spain 4, Sweden 1, UK 38, Unspecified 41.

Opportunity International

(800)793-9455   Fax: (630)279-3107
Web: http://www.opportunity.org/
P.O. Box 3695, Oak Brook, IL 60522
Eric Thurman, President

A service organization "motivated by Jesus Christ's call to serve the poor", engaged in microenterprise development in 27 countries.

".. to provide opportunities for people in chronic poverty to transform their lives."

Year Founded in USA 1971
Income for Overseas Ministries $ 13,000,000
Fully Supported USA Personnel Overseas:
   Expecting to serve 1 up to 4 years 18
Other Personnel:
   Short-Term less than 1 year from USA . . . 4
   Home ministry & office staff in USA 27
Countries: Africa 2, Asia 5, Europe-E 7, Latin America 4.

ORA International

(757)497-9320   **Fax: (757)497-9352**
E-Mail: ORA@infi.net
P.O. Box 64154, Virginia Beach, VA 23467
Dr. James Lee, Director

An interdenominational support agency of evangelical tradition engaged in evangelism, Bible distribution, and missionary training.

Year Founded in USA 1981
Income for Overseas Ministries . $ 150,000

Oriental Missionary Crusade

(714)582-5041
P.O. Box 6336, Laguna Niguel, CA 92607
Rev. Ernest A. Reb, President

An interdenominational sending agency of charismatic tradition engaged in church construction, literature distribution, and training.

Year Founded in USA 1958
Income for Overseas Ministries . . $ 99,000
Fully Supported USA Personnel Overseas:
   Expecting to serve more than 4 years 2
Other Personnel:
   Home ministry & office staff in USA 3
Countries: Philippines 2.

Orthodox Presbyterian Church, Committee on Foreign Missions

(215)830-0900   **Fax: (215)830-0350**
E-Mail: Info@opc.org
Web: http://www.opc.org
P.O. Box P, Willow Grove, PA 19090
Mr. Mark T. Bube, Gen. Secretary

A denominational sending agency of Presbyterian tradition engaged in evangelism, church

planting, theological education, and literature distribution. Statistical information from 1992.

Year Founded in USA 1937
Income for Overseas Ministries . $ 769,836
Fully Supported USA Personnel Overseas:
   Expecting to serve more than 4 years 17
Other Personnel:
   Bivocational/Tentmaker from USA 10
   Short-Term less than 1 year from USA . . . 3
Countries: Cyprus 2, Japan 7, Kenya 2, Korea-S 2, Suriname 4.

Outreach To Asia Nationals

(540)665-6418   **Fax: (540)665-0793**
E-Mail: 102045.2310@compuserve.com
P.O. Box 1909, Winchester, VA 22604
Mr. Otis S. Goodwin, Director

A nondenominational support agency of Baptist tradition supporting national workers engaged in Bible distribution, evangelism, and literature distribution.

Year Founded in USA 1986
Income for Overseas Ministries . $ 250,000
Personnel:
   Non-USA serving in own/other country . . 169
   Short-Term less than 1 year from USA . . . 10
   Home ministry & office staff in USA 3
Countries: Asia.

Outreach, Inc.

(616)363-7817   **Fax: (616)363-7880**
E-Mail: OutreachIn@aol.com
3140 3 Mile Rd. NE, Grand Rapids, MI 49505
Mr. Carl H. Smith, Exec. Director

A nondenominational support agency of Reformed tradition engaged in theological education and funds transmission.

".. to assist in the theological education of individuals preparing for Church leadership and cross-cultural ministry."

Year Founded in USA 1966
Income for Overseas Ministries . $ 375,000
Amount of Gifts-In-Kind . . . . $ 35,000
Personnel:
   Home ministry & office staff in USA 3

Overcomer Press, Inc.

(517)723-8277   Fax: (517)725-3103
P.O. Box 248, Owosso, MI 48867
Mr. Gordon H. Bennett, President

A nondenominational specialized service agency of Christian/Plymouth Brethren tradition engaged in print and audio publications in English and Spanish, and missions information services.

Year Founded in USA 1963
Income for Overseas Ministries . . . . NA

Overseas Council for Theological Education & Missions, Inc.

(317)788-7250   Fax: (317)788-7257
E-Mail: 76517.2770@compuserve.com
P.O. Box 17368, Indianapolis, IN 46217
Dr. John C. Bennett, President

A transdenominational support agency of evangelical tradition engaged in leadership development, theological education, TEE, funds transmission, and mission-related research in 15 key regions of the Two-Thirds World.

"... helping national seminaries and Bible colleges train their own people to become evangelists, teachers, pastors and missionaries..."

Year Founded in USA 1974
Income for Overseas Ministries $ 1,770,571
Fully Supported USA Personnel Overseas:
Nonresidential mission personnel 2
Other Personnel:
Home ministry & office staff in USA 18

Overseas Ministries Study Center

(203)624-6672   Fax: (203)865-2857
E-Mail: mailbox@omsc.org
Web: http://www.omsc.org
490 Prospect St., New Haven, CT 06511
Dr. Gerald H. Anderson, Director

A nondenominational study center of evangelical and ecumenical tradition providing continuing education and related activities. Publishes the *International Bulletin of Missionary Research.*

".. to strengthen the Christian world mission by providing residential programs for the renewal of missionaries and overseas church leaders, continuing education in cross-cultural Christian

ministries, and advancement of mission scholarship through research and publication."

Year Founded in USA 1922
Income for Overseas Ministries . . . . NA
Personnel:
Home ministry & office staff in USA 13

Overseas Missionary Fellowship
See: OMF International

Overseas Radio & Television, Inc.

(206)634-1919   Fax: (206)547-0400
Web: http://www.ortv.com.tw
P.O. Box 118, Seattle, WA 98118
Sharon Chiang, Chinese Ministries Coordinator

An interdenominational support agency of evangelical and charismatic tradition engaged in broadcasting, audio recording/distribution, evangelism, and video production/distribution.

Year Founded in USA 1960
Income for Overseas Ministries . . . . NR
Personnel:
Bivocational/Tentmaker from USA 10
Home ministry & office staff in USA 5
Countries: Taiwan (ROC).

Pacific Northwest Mennonite Conf Evangelism & Missions Comte.

(503)452-2563   Fax: (503)452-2563
6976 SW Pine, Tigard, OR 97223
Dr. John M. Miller, Missions Minister

A denominational agency of Mennonite tradition engaged in support of national churches for church planting and evangelism.

Year Founded in USA 1906
Income for Overseas Ministries . . $ 34,000

Pan American Missions

(619)444-3077
P.O. Box 2636, El Cajon, CA 92021
Mr. Fred Jappe, President

An interdenominational support agency of Baptist tradition engaged in video/film/literature distribution and evangelism in Mexico.

Year Founded in USA 1960
Income for Overseas Ministries . . . . NR

Fully Supported USA Personnel Overseas:
Nonresidential mission personnel 1
Other Personnel:
Bivocational/Tentmaker from USA 1
Short-Term less than 1 year from USA . . . 1
Home ministry & office staff in USA 1

Paraclete Mission Group, Inc.
(719)590-7777   Fax: (719)590-7902
E-Mail: 74262.3071@compuserve.com
P.O. Box 49367, Colorado Springs, CO 80949
Phillip W. Elkins, CEO
Keith Butler, COO

A nondenominational support agency of evangelical tradition engaged in missionary training, church planting, management consulting/training, research, and technical assistance.

".. to serve mission agencies and churches in their efforts to effectively plant churches among unreached people groups."

Year Founded in USA 1988
Income for Overseas Ministries . . $ 68,700
Fully Supported USA Personnel Overseas:
Expecting to serve more than 4 years 4
Nonresidential mission personnel 4
Other Personnel:
Bivocational/Tentmaker from USA 2
Home ministry & office staff in USA 17
Countries: Albania 2, Vietnam 2.

Partners in Asian Missions
(205)854-8418   Fax: (205)879-2407
E-Mail: JFSharpe@bham.mindspring.com
Web: http://www.mindspring.com/~jfsharpe
P.O. Box 531011, Birmingham, AL 35253
Rev. Jerry F. Sharpe, Intl. Director

A nondenominational support agency of evangelical tradition engaged in leadership development, evangelism, and national worker support.

".. establishes strategic-level alliances with key regional leaders in order to develop cooperative projects and share evangelism training materials."

Year Founded in USA 1972
Income for Overseas Ministries . . $ 60,000
Fully Supported USA Personnel Overseas:
Nonresidential mission personnel 1
Other Personnel:
Non-USA serving in own/other country . . . 50

Countries: Asia.

Partners International
(408)453-3800   Fax: (408)437-9708
E-Mail: Info@partnersintl.org
Web: http://www.partnersintl.org/
P.O. Box 15025, San Jose, CA 95115
Mr. Chuck Bennett, President

A nondenominational support agency of evangelical tradition engaged in support of national workers, church planting, leadership development, and management consulting/training.

".. to multiply the effectiveness of indigenous Christian ministries who are taking Christ to neglected peoples around the world."

Year Founded in USA 1943
Income for Overseas Ministries $ 6,109,852
Amount of Gifts-In-Kind . . . $ 1,274,718
Fully Supported USA Personnel Overseas:
Expecting to serve more than 4 years 8
Other Personnel:
Non-USA serving in own/other country . . 3,500
Short-Term less than 1 year from USA . . . 34
Countries: Africa, Asia 2, Bangladesh, Bolivia, Brazil, Bulgaria, Cambodia, China (PRC), Congo/Zaire, Cuba, El Salvador 2, France, Ghana, Guatemala, Hong Kong 2, India, Indonesia, Jamaica, Kenya, Korea-S, Laos, Liberia, Macao, Macedonia, Malaysia, Mexico, Myanmar/Burma, Nigeria, Pakistan, Philippines, Russia, S Africa, Singapore 2, Sudan, Taiwan (ROC), Tanzania, Thailand, Unspecified, Vietnam.

Pass the Torch Ministries
(701)223-6117   Fax: (701)223-6117
P.O. Box 7392, Bismarck, ND 58507
Greg Runyon, President

An interdenominational service agency of charismatic tradition engaged in training, evangelism, and literature distribution.

Year Founded in USA 1987
Income for Overseas Ministries . . $ 12,000
Personnel:
Non-USA serving in own/other country . . . 12
Short-Term less than 1 year from USA . . . 6
Home ministry & office staff in USA 2
Countries: Myanmar/Burma, Philippines, Thailand.

PAZ International

(309)263-2299   **Fax: (309)263-2299**
E-Mail: PazInter@heartland.bradley.edu
P.O. Box 913, Morton, IL 61550
Mr. Brian Donais, Chairman of the Board

A nondenominational sending agency of evangelical tradition engaged in church planting, evangelism, medical work, support of national churches and workers, and missionary training.

".. developing nationally led church planting movements, focusing on the Amazon Basin and extending around the world."

Year Founded in USA 1986
Income for Overseas Ministries $ 1,127,000
Amount of Gifts-In-Kind . . . . $ 10,000
Fully Supported USA Personnel Overseas:
   Expecting to serve more than 4 years 40
   Expecting to serve 1 up to 4 years 7
Other Personnel:
   Non-USA serving in own/other country . . . 36
   Bivocational/Tentmaker from USA 5
   Short-Term less than 1 year from USA . . . 25
Countries: Brazil 40, Japan 7, Mozambique, Portugal.

Pentecostal Church of God, World Missions Department

(417)624-7050   **Fax: (417)624-7102**
E-Mail: WM@pcg.org
Web: http://www.pcg.org
P.O. Box 2248, Joplin, MO 64803
Dr. James D. Gee, Gen. Superintendent

A denominational sending agency of Pentecostal tradition engaged in church planting, Bible distribution, church construction, and literature distribution. Statistical information from 1992.

Year Founded in USA 1919
Income for Overseas Ministries . $ 851,394
Fully Supported USA Personnel Overseas:
   Expecting to serve more than 4 years 3
Other Personnel:
   Home ministry & office staff in USA 4
Countries: Africa 1, Asia 1, Latin America 1.

Pentecostal Free Will Baptist Church, World Witness Dept.

(910)892-4161   **Fax: (910)892-6876**
P.O. Box 1568, Dunn, NC 28334
Rev. David A. Taylor, Director

A denominational sending agency of Pentecostal and Holiness tradition engaged in church planting, church construction, evangelism, and support of national churches.

Year Founded in USA 1959
Income for Overseas Ministries . $ 160,000
Fully Supported USA Personnel Overseas:
   Expecting to serve 1 up to 4 years 4
   Nonresidential mission personnel 1
Other Personnel:
   Non-USA serving in own/other country . . . 16
   Bivocational/Tentmaker from USA 1
   Home ministry & office staff in USA 2
Countries: Costa Rica, El Salvador, Guatemala 2, Mexico, Nicaragua, Nigeria, Philippines, Venezuela 2.

Pentecostal Holiness Church

See: Intl. Pentecostal Holiness Ch.

People International

(253)884-1933   **Fax: (253)884-1934**
E-Mail: 110156.3265@compuserve.com
P.O. Box 158, Vaughn, WA 98394
Rev. Mark Struck, U.S. Director

An interdenominational sending agency of evangelical tradition engaged in church planting, development, evangelism, and research.

".. to evangelize people groups ... and see believers in local churches where they can be built up in the faith and made effective in service..."

Year Founded in USA 1986
Income for Overseas Ministries . $ 376,000
Fully Supported USA Personnel Overseas:
   Expecting to serve more than 4 years 33
Other Personnel:
   Home ministry & office staff in USA 2
Countries: Asia 33.

Peoples Mission International

(510)793-6919   **Fax: (510)793-6919**
E-Mail: 74404.447@compuserve.com
P.O. Box 66, Fremont, CA 94537
Dr. Larry D. Pate, President

A transdenominational support agency of evangelical tradition engaged in missionary orientation, training and strategy development focusing on Christians in the non-Western world.

Year Founded in USA 1992

Income for Overseas Ministries . . $ 14,880
Personnel:
    Non-USA serving in own/other country . . . 1
    Home ministry & office staff in USA 2
Countries: Congo/Zaire.

Peter Deyneka Russian Ministries
(630)462-1739   Fax: (630)690-2976
E-Mail: RMUSA@mcimail.com
Web: http://shoga.wwa.com/~strtegy/
P.O. Box 496, Wheaton, IL 60189
Dr. Peter Deyneka, President

An interdenominational support agency of evangelical tradition engaged in Bible and literature distribution, support of national workers, and mission-related research.

"To promote indigenous evangelism and church growth in the former Soviet Union by developing creative and strategic partnerships between nationals and Western Christians."

Year Founded in USA 1991
Income for Overseas Ministries $ 1,545,737
Fully Supported USA Personnel Overseas:
    Expecting to serve more than 4 years 2
    Expecting to serve 1 up to 4 years 1
    Nonresidential mission personnel 7
Other Personnel:
    Non-USA serving in own/other country . . . 28
    Home ministry & office staff in USA 11
Countries: Russia 3.

Pilgrim Fellowship, Inc.
(717)867-1767   Fax: (717)867-1767
P.O. Box 557, Lebanon, PA 17042
Mr. William Martindale, Board President

A nondenominational support agency of fundamentalist tradition engaged in funds transmission for mission workers involved in audio recording/distribution, and church planting.

Year Founded in USA 1943
Income for Overseas Ministries . $ 173,700
Personnel:
    Non-USA serving in own/other country . . . 3
    Home ministry & office staff in USA 1
Countries: Asia, Belgium, Brazil.

Pillar of Fire Missions Intl.
(303)430-8260
3455 W. 83rd Ave., Westminster, CO 80030
Rev. Arlene Konkel, Director

A sending agency of Holiness tradition engaged in support of national churches, childrens programs, and elementary education.

Year Founded in USA 1960
Income for Overseas Ministries . $ 165,806
Fully Supported USA Personnel Overseas:
    Expecting to serve 1 up to 4 years 5
Other Personnel:
    Home ministry & office staff in USA 1
Countries: UK 5.

Pioneer Bible Translators
(972)709-2460   Fax: (972)709-2463
E-Mail: PBT@xc.org
7500 W. Camp Wisdom Rd., Dallas, TX 75236
Dr. Rondal B. Smith, President

A nondenominational sending agency of Christian (Restoration Movement) tradition engaged in Bible translation, church planting, linguistics, literacy work, and training.

".. translating of the Word of God for the world's peoples who do not yet have access to it in their own language."

Year Founded in USA 1975
Income for Overseas Ministries $ 1,330,000
Fully Supported USA Personnel Overseas:
    Expecting to serve more than 4 years 59
Other Personnel:
    Non-USA serving in own/other country . . . 41
    Short-Term less than 1 year from USA . . . 7
    Home ministry & office staff in USA 18
Countries: Congo/Zaire 6, Cote d'Ivoire 2, Equat Guinea 2, Guinea 20, Papua New Guin 29.

Pioneer Clubs
(630)293-1600   Fax: (630)293-3053
P.O. Box 788, Wheaton, IL 60189
Judy Bryson, President

An interdenominational service agency of evangelical tradition engaged in youth and camping programs others have adapted to their culture.

".. to work with churches in helping children and youth put Christ in every phase of life by recognizing him as Savior and Lord and developing a lifestyle based on biblical values."

Year Founded in USA 1939
Income for Overseas Ministries . . . NR
Personnel:
    Home ministry & office staff in USA 39

Pioneers

(407)382-6000   **Fax: (407)382-1008**
E-Mail: 74511.1250@compuserve.com
Web: http://www.pioneers.org
12343 Narcoossee Rd., Orlando, FL 32827
Rev. John E. Fletcher, Exec. Director

An interdenominational sending agency of evangelical tradition engaged in church planting, evangelism, discipleship, leadership develop-ment, and short-term programs coordination.

".. mobilizes teams to glorify God among unreached peoples by initiating church planting movements in partnership with local churches."

Year Founded in USA 1979
Income for Overseas Ministries $ 6,882,572
Fully Supported USA Personnel Overseas:
    Expecting to serve more than 4 years . . . 228
Other Personnel:
    Non-USA serving in own/other country . . . 13
    Bivocational/Tentmaker from USA 147
    Short-Term less than 1 year from USA . . . 70
    Home ministry & office staff in USA 25
Countries: Albania 11, Asia 70, Belize 4, Bolivia 8, Bosnia 5, Croatia 8, Ghana, Guyana 1, Hungary 2, Indonesia 57, Japan 6, Kyrgyzstan 7, Macedonia 2, Mali, N Mariana Isls 1, Nepal 2, Nigeria, Papua New Guin 14, Russia 6, Senegal 6, Thailand 9, Turkey 3, Uzbekistan 4, Zambia 2.

Plymouth Brethren
See: Brethren Assemblies

Pocket Testament League

(717)626-1919   **Fax: (717)626-5553**
E-Mail: TPTL@prolog.net
P.O. Box 800, Lititz, PA 17543
Rev. Michael J. McCaskey, Exec. Director

An interdenominational service agency of evangelical tradition engaged in Scripture distribution, broadcasting, church establishing, evangelism, and training.

"To assist and equip Christians worldwide in the effective proclamation of the Gospel of Jesus Christ through a coordinated program of Scripture distribution and evangelism."

Year Founded in USA 1908
Income for Overseas Ministries . $ 370,722
Fully Supported USA Personnel Overseas:
    Expecting to serve more than 4 years 2
Other Personnel:
    Non-USA serving in own/other country . . 150
    Home ministry & office staff in USA 12
Countries: Austria 1, Brazil, France, Germany 1, India, Indonesia, Korea-S, Mexico, Philippines, Poland, Portugal, Spain, Thailand, Yugoslavia.

Practical Missionary Training
See: CAM International

Prakash Association USA

(408)722-2244   **Fax: (408)662-8851**
9081 Soquel Dr., Aptos, CA 95003
Mr. Vern Hart, Exec. Director

An interdenominational agency of Baptist tra-dition supporting national workers, Christian education, and agricultural programs for evan-gelism, Bible distribution, and church planting.

".. to support the training of nationals to become Christian businessmen and spiritual leaders ... and carry out personal evangelism..."

Year Founded in USA 1969
Income for Overseas Ministries . $ 149,919
Fully Supported USA Personnel Overseas:
    Nonresidential mission personnel 1
Other Personnel:
    Non-USA serving in own/other country . . . 35
    Home ministry & office staff in USA 1
Countries: India.

Precious Seed Ministries

(956)585-9966   **Fax: (956)585-9966**
Rte. 8, Box 763, Mission, TX 78572
Wyman Pylant, President

A nondenominational support agency of charismatic tradition engaged in support of national workers, church planting, childcare programs, and evangelism.

Year Founded in USA 1985
Income for Overseas Ministries . . $ 28,000

Personnel:
Non-USA serving in own/other country   . . .   8
Home ministry & office staff in USA   3
Countries: Mexico.

Presbyterian Center for Mission Studies

(626)398-2468   Fax: (626)398-2391
E-Mail: PCMS.parti@ecunet.org
1605 Elizabeth St., Pasadena, CA 91104
Michael Boyland, Exec. Director

A denominational support agency of Presbyterian and evangelical tradition engaged in mobilization for mission, mission-related research, and services for other agencies.

"..to greatly multiply the mission efforts of individuals, congregations, and the Presbyterian Church (USA) toward completing the task of world evangelization."

Year Founded in USA 1972
Income for Overseas Ministries . . . . NA
Personnel:
Home ministry & office staff in USA   4

Presbyterian Church (USA), Worldwide Ministries

(502)569-5000   Fax: (502)569-8039
Web: http://www.pcusa.org/pcusa/wmd/
100 Witherspoon St., Louisville, KY 40202
Dr. Marian McClure, Director

A denominational sending agency of Presbyterian tradition engaged in support of national churches, church planting, development, theological education, evangelism, leadership development, and medical work.

Year Founded in USA 1837
Income for Overseas Ministries $ 40,107,046
Fully Supported USA Personnel Overseas:
Expecting to serve more than 4 years   . . . 354
Expecting to serve 1 up to 4 years   421
Other Personnel:
Bivocational/Tentmaker from USA   60
Short-Term less than 1 year from USA   . . 150
Home ministry & office staff in USA   81
Countries: Albania 7, Argentina 13, Australia 2, Bangladesh 6, Belgium 3, Brazil 44, Cameroon 4, Chile 7, China (PRC) 24, Colombia 7, Congo/Zaire 22, Costa Rica 14, Croatia 2, Cuba 3, Dominican Rep 3, Egypt 23, Ethiopia 24, Fiji 2, France 2, Germany 10, Ghana 4,

Guatemala 34, Haiti 6, Honduras 9, Hong Kong 9, India 21, Indonesia 14, Israel 4, Italy 2, Jamaica 5, Japan 38, Kazakhstan 4, Kenya 21, Korea-S 25, Kyrgyzstan 6, Lebanon 3, Lesotho 2, Lithuania 2, Madagascar 3, Malawi 29, Mauritius 2, Mexico 34, Mozambique 2, Nepal 23, New Zealand 4, Nicaragua 15, Pakistan 20, Papua New Guin 3, Philippines 18, Poland 2, Portugal 2, Romania 5, Russia 7, S Africa 6, Slovakia 4, Spain 4, Sri Lanka 2, Sudan 15, Taiwan (ROC) 9, Thailand 30, Turkey 2, UK 79, Uzbekistan 3, Venezuela 10, Vietnam 4, Zambia 5, Zimbabwe 2.

Presbyterian Church in America
See: Mission to the World

Presbyterian Evangelistic Fellowship

(404)244-0740   Fax: (404)244-0914
P.O. Box 1890, Decatur, GA 30031
Dr. Al Herrington, Exec. Director

An interdenominational sending agency of Presbyterian and Reformed tradition engaged in evangelism, church planting, leadership development, and support of national workers.

"..to practice, train and equip God's people to do Biblical evangelism..."

Year Founded in USA 1958
Income for Overseas Ministries . $ 800,000
Fully Supported USA Personnel Overseas:
Expecting to serve more than 4 years   10
Other Personnel:
Non-USA serving in own/other country   . . . 21
Bivocational/Tentmaker from USA   2
Short-Term less than 1 year from USA   . . .   4
Home ministry & office staff in USA   9
Countries: Bulgaria, Chile 3, Indonesia 1, Japan 1, Kenya, Liberia, Mexico 4, Nigeria 1, Uganda.

Presbyterian Missionary Union

(615)228-4465   Fax: (615)227-0224
E-Mail: MacPMU@aol.com
P.O. Box 160070, Nashville, TN 37216
Dr. Robert W. Anderson, President

A denominational sending agency of Presbyterian and Reformed tradition engaged in support of national churches, Bible distribution, funds transmission, and literature distribution.

Year Founded in USA 1985
Income for Overseas Ministries . . $ 50,400

Fully Supported USA Personnel Overseas:
Expecting to serve more than 4 years 2
Nonresidential mission personnel 2
Other Personnel:
Home ministry & office staff in USA 2
Countries: Kenya 2.

Presbyterian Order for World Evangelization

(626)794-5544   Fax: (626)794-6655
1469 Bresee Ave., Pasadena, CA 91104
Dr. Ralph D. Winter, Assoc. Gen. Director

A denominational support agency of evangelical tradition engaged in evangelism, agricultural programs, church planting, and providing medical supplies.

Year Founded in USA 1974
Income for Overseas Ministries . . $ 95,000
Fully Supported USA Personnel Overseas:
Expecting to serve more than 4 years 2
Nonresidential mission personnel 2
Countries: Asia 2.

Primitive Methodist Church in the USA, International Mission Board

(330)726-2643
E-Mail: 76622.2237@compuserve.com
7872 Glenwood Ave., Youngstown, OH 44512
Rev. William L. Vasey, Gen. Director

A denominational sending board of Wesleyan and Methodist tradition engaged in church planting, theological education, TEE, medical work, and support of national churches.

Year Founded in USA 1922
Income for Overseas Ministries . $ 382,933
Fully Supported USA Personnel Overseas:
Expecting to serve more than 4 years 11
Other Personnel:
Non-USA serving in own/other country . . . 11
Countries: Bolivia 2, Guatemala 4, Mexico 2, Spain 3.

Priority One International

(972)423-3800   Fax: (972)422-7535
E-Mail: TotalTV@gte.net
Web: http://www.total-tv.com
555 Republic Dr. #510, Plano, TX 75074
Marty Mosley, President

A nondenominational service agency of evangelical and Baptist tradition producing mission-related videos for mobilization and offering video production services to mission agencies.

".. bringing awareness, focus and vision to the cause of world missions within the local church in order to mobilize Christian young people and adults for missionary service."

Year Founded in USA 1979
Income for Overseas Ministries . $ 300,000
Personnel:
Home ministry & office staff in USA 63

Prison Fellowship International

(703)481-0000   Fax: (703)481-0003
E-Mail: Info@pfi.org
Web: http://www.prisonfellowshipintl.org/
P.O. Box 17434, Washington, DC 20041
Mr. Ronald W. Nikkel, President

A transdenominational specialized service agency of evangelical and ecumenical tradition providing ministry development training and services to national PFs in 74 countries.

"To mobilize and empower national PF ministries ... to be a movement of reconciliation and restoration ... to prisoners, ex-prisoners, victims and their families; and advance biblical standards of justice in the criminal justice system."

Year Founded in USA 1979
Income for Overseas Ministries $ 2,400,000
Amount of Gifts-In-Kind . . . $ 100,000
Personnel:
Bivocational/Tentmaker from USA 2
Short-Term less than 1 year from USA . . . 25

Prison Mission Association

(360)876-0918
P.O. Box 1587, Port Orchard, WA 98366
Rev. Vernon G. Bigelow, Exec. Secretary

A nondenominational support agency of fundamental and Reformed tradition engaged in correspondence courses, evangelism, and literature distribution to prison inmates and others.

Year Founded in USA 1955
Income for Overseas Ministries . . $ 10,050
Personnel:
Non-USA serving in own/other country . . . 1
Bivocational/Tentmaker from USA 1

Home ministry & office staff in USA 4
Countries: Cameroon.

PRM International

See: Audio Scripture Ministries

Progressive National Baptist Conv USA, Global Mission Bureau

(215)474-3939

163 N. 60th St., Philadelphia, PA 19139
Dr. Ronald K. Hill, Exec. Director

A denominational support agency of Baptist tradition engaged in supplying equipment, Bible distribution, church construction, and childrens programs in 16 countries.

Year Founded in USA 1962
Income for Overseas Ministries . . . . NR

Progressive Vision

(714)498-4800   **Fax: (714)498-4839**
E-Mail: 76612.2302@compuserve.com
Web: http://www.dcr.org
P.O. Box 5854, San Clemente, CA 92674
Marcus Vegh, President

A transdenominational service agency of ecumenical tradition providing biblically based multilingual interactive video training materials.

".. to develop and distribute holistic training media tools for equipping Christian nationals, .. establishing a network of 'Digital Circuit Riders' to carry the curriculum and presentation system.."

Year Founded in USA 1995
Income for Overseas Ministries . . . . NA
Personnel:
Home ministry & office staff in USA 3

Project Care

(206)937-4458   **Fax: (206)870-4374**
E-Mail: ProjectCare@xc.org
7103 35th Ave. SW, Seattle, WA 98126
Chuck Schukar, Director

A nondenominational agency of evangelical tradition supporting national workers and others involved in evangelism and discipleship.

Year Founded in USA 1991
Income for Overseas Ministries . . $ 25,000

Personnel:
Non-USA serving in own/other country . . . 2
Short-Term less than 1 year from USA . . . 2
Countries: Europe-E, Poland.

Project Christ International

(718)845-6992   **Fax: (718)845-6992**
124-08 Linden Blvd., So. Ozone Park, NY 11420
Rev. S. Samraj, President

A nondenominational support agency of evangelical tradition engaged in missionary training, Bible distribution, church planting, and correspondence courses. Income amount from 1992.

Year Founded in USA 1984
Income for Overseas Ministries . . $ 32,947
Personnel:
Short-Term less than 1 year from USA . . . 2

Project Mercy, Inc.

(219)747-2559   **Fax: (219)478-1361**
E-Mail: ProMer@gte.net
7011 Ardmore Ave., Fort Wayne, IN 46809
Marta Gabre-Tsadick, Exec. Director

A nondenominational support agency of evangelical tradition engaged in relief aid, support of national churches, and technical assistance. Financial information from 1992.

Year Founded in USA 1977
Income for Overseas Ministries . $ 339,321
Amount of Gifts-In-Kind . . . . $ 73,947
Personnel:
Home ministry & office staff in USA 4

Project Partner with Christ

(513)425-0938   **Fax: (513)425-6628**
E-Mail: PrjctPtr@wspin.com
P.O. Box 610, Springboro, OH 45066
Rev. Donna S. Thomas, President

A transdenominational support agency of evangelical tradition linking overseas nationals with USA sources for funds transmission to further evangelism and church planting.

Year Founded in USA 1969
Income for Overseas Ministries . $ 381,584
Personnel:
Non-USA serving in own/other country . . . 4
Short-Term less than 1 year from USA . . . 1

Countries: China (PRC), India, Mexico, Russia.

Providence Mission Homes, Inc.
(626)293-1752
P.O. Box 40727, Pasadena, CA 91114
Robert J. Gerry, Exec. Director
Mr. Peter Geddes, Jr., President

An interdenominational support agency of evangelical tradition engaged in furloughed missionary support.

Year Founded in USA 1973
Income for Overseas Ministries . . . . NA

Radio Bible Class
(616)942-6770   Fax: (616)957-5741
E-Mail: RBC@rbc.net
Web: http://www.rbc.net
Grand Rapids, MI 49555
Howard Liverance, Manager of Intl. Ministries

A nondenominational service agency of evangelical tradition engaged in broadcasting in over 10 countries and producing literature in over 30 languages. Financial information from 1992.

Year Founded in USA 1938
Income for Overseas Ministries $ 1,800,000
Personnel:
Home ministry & office staff in USA . . . 160

Ramabai Mukti Mission
(908)735-8770
P.O. Box 4912, Clinton, NJ 08809
Rev. David L. Scott, Exec. Director

An interdenominational support agency of evangelical tradition engaged in orphanage programs, evangelism, medical work, and support of national workers.

Year Founded in USA 1929
Income for Overseas Ministries . $ 178,000
Amount of Gifts-In-Kind . . . . $ 7,600
Personnel:
Non-USA serving in own/other country . . . 45
Short-Term less than 1 year from USA . . . 2
Home ministry & office staff in USA 3
Countries: India.

RBMU International
See: World Team

Reach Ministries International
(562)690-4252   Fax: (562)690-5612
P.O. Box 842, La Habra, CA 90631
Mr. Gene Tabor, Board Chairman

A nondenominational sending agency of evangelical tradition engaged in evangelism, childrens programs, literature production, support of national workers, and missionary training.

Year Founded in USA 1976
Income for Overseas Ministries . $ 153,873
Fully Supported USA Personnel Overseas:
Expecting to serve more than 4 years 5
Other Personnel:
Non-USA serving in own/other country . . . 5
Short-Term less than 1 year from USA . . . 2
Home ministry & office staff in USA 3
Countries: Hong Kong 1, India 2, Mexico 2, Philippines.

REAP/International Aid, Inc.
See: International Aid, Inc.

Reciprocal Ministries International
(305)233-9903   Fax: (305)233-9907
E-Mail: RMIMIA@aol.com
14540 SW 136th St., Suite #208, Miami, FL 33186
Rev. Herbert L. Shoemaker, President

An interdenominational sending agency of evangelical tradition engaged in support of national churches, church construction, Christian education, funds transmission, and training.

Year Founded in USA 1988
Income for Overseas Ministries . $ 218,670
Fully Supported USA Personnel Overseas:
Expecting to serve more than 4 years 3
Other Personnel:
Non-USA serving in own/other country . . . 3
Home ministry & office staff in USA 5
Countries: Haiti 2, Jamaica 1.

Red Sea Mission Team
(408)257-2948   Fax: (408)257-5231
P.O. Box 3331, Saratoga, CA 95070
Rev. Kenneth E. Churchill, U.S. Home Director

An interdenominational support agency of evangelical tradition engaged in evangelism, agricultural programs, funds transmission and

Bible distribution in Africa and Asia.

Year Founded in USA 1953
Income for Overseas Ministries . . $ 82,110
Fully Supported USA Personnel Overseas:
Nonresidential mission personnel 3
Other Personnel:
Short-Term less than 1 year from USA . . . 1

Reformation Translation Flwshp.
(812)339-1922
302 E. 1st St., Bloomington, IN 47401
Rev. William Roberts, American Representative

A nondenominational service agency of Reformed tradition engaged in translation work and literature distribution/production.

Year Founded in USA 1950
Income for Overseas Ministries . . $ 79,691

Reformed Baptist Mission Svcs.
(717)249-7473   Fax: (717)258-0614
E-Mail: 75721.2116@compuserve.com
P.O. Box 289, Carlisle, PA 17013
Rev. David K. Straub, Mission Coord.

A denominational sending agency of Baptist tradition engaged in church planting, missions information services, and literature production.

".. to provide to churches that hold to the London Confession of 1689, those services that will assist them in promoting gospel missions..."

Year Founded in USA 1985
Income for Overseas Ministries . . $ 301,517
Fully Supported USA Personnel Overseas:
Expecting to serve more than 4 years 10
Other Personnel:
Non-USA serving in own/other country 4
Short-Term less than 1 year from USA . . . 2
Home ministry & office staff in USA 2
Countries: Asia 2, Colombia 2, France 2, Israel, Jamaica, Kenya 2, UK 2.

Reformed Church in America Gen. Synod Council, Mission Services
(616)698-7071   Fax: (616)698-6606
Web: http://www.rca.org/
4500 - 60th St, S.E., Grand Rapids, MI 49512
Rev. Bruce Menning, Director Mission Services

A denominational sending agency of Reformed tradition engaged in church planting, agricultural programs, Christian education, evangelism, and medical work.

Year Founded in USA 1857
Income for Overseas Ministries $ 5,000,000
Fully Supported USA Personnel Overseas:
Expecting to serve more than 4 years 86
Countries: Bahrain 7, Cambodia 1, Estonia 2, Ethiopia 6, Honduras 3, Hong Kong 2, Hungary 2, India 3, Japan 11, Kenya 10, Kuwait 2, Mexico 10, Nicaragua 1, Philippines 4, Singapore 2, Sudan 3, Taiwan (ROC) 3, Ukraine 1, Unspecified 9, Venezuela 4.

Reformed Episcopal Board of Foreign Missions
(212)755-0995
317 E. 50th St., New York, NY 10022
Dr. Barbara West, President

A denominational sending agency of Anglican tradition engaged in church planting, medical work, and Bible translation.

Year Founded in USA 1892
Income for Overseas Ministries . $ 150,000
Fully Supported USA Personnel Overseas:
Expecting to serve more than 4 years 8
Other Personnel:
Non-USA serving in own/other country . . . 13
Short-Term less than 1 year from USA . . . 13
Home ministry & office staff in USA 2
Countries: Brazil 1, France 2, Germany 3, India, Liberia, Uganda 2.

Reformed Presbyterian Church, Board of Foreign Missions
(812)378-4190   Fax: (812)378-3890
E-Mail: 74114.1513@compuserve.com
3711 Premier Dr., Columbus, IN 47203
Rev. Robert A. Henning, Exec. Secretary

A denominational sending board of Reformed tradition engaged in church planting, evangelism, and literature distribution.

Year Founded in USA 1856
Income for Overseas Ministries . $ 313,552
Fully Supported USA Personnel Overseas:
Expecting to serve more than 4 years 5
Other Personnel:
Bivocational/Tentmaker from USA 2
Short-Term less than 1 year from USA . . . 8

Countries: Cyprus, Japan 5.

Rehoboth Ministries, Inc
(910)630-3730
333 Hilliard Dr., Fayetteville, NC 28311
Lucia A. Adams, Secretary-Treasurer
Rev. Pritchard Adams, III, President

A transdenominational sending agency of charismatic and Pentecostal tradition engaged in evangelism, general Christian and theological education, and leadership development.

Year Founded in USA 1985
Income for Overseas Ministries . . $ 63,270
Fully Supported USA Personnel Overseas:
  Expecting to serve more than 4 years 2
Countries: Haiti 2.

Rio Grande Bible Institute
(956)380-8100   Fax: (956)380-8101
E-Mail: RGBIMail@juno.com
4300 S. Business Ave. #281, Edinburg, TX 78539
Dr. Russell J. Hobbs, President

An interdenominational service agency of evangelical tradition engaged in theological education, correspondence courses, missionary education, and video production/distribution.

"..serving the Hispanic church through equipping leaders, edifying believers, and evangelizing the lost."

Year Founded in USA 1946
Income for Overseas Ministries . . . . NA
Fully Supported USA Personnel Overseas:
  Expecting to serve more than 4 years 51
  Expecting to serve 1 up to 4 years 8
Other Personnel:
  Bivocational/Tentmaker from USA 5
  Short-Term less than 1 year from USA . . . 2
  Home ministry & office staff in USA 59
Countries: Mexico 59.

Ripe for Harvest, Inc.
(619)637-8778
P.O. Box 19160, San Diego, CA 92159
Dr. Tim Smith, President

A nondenominational sending agency of evangelical and independent tradition engaged in funds transmission, Bible distribution, evangelism, and support of national churches.

Year Founded in USA 1979
Income for Overseas Ministries . $ 208,500
Fully Supported USA Personnel Overseas:
  Expecting to serve more than 4 years 4
  Expecting to serve 1 up to 4 years 12
Other Personnel:
  Bivocational/Tentmaker from USA 15
  Home ministry & office staff in USA 8
Countries: El Salvador 1, Honduras 5, Hungary 1, India 2, Japan 2, Mexico 1, Russia 4.

Romanian Mission of Chicago
(773)764-5991   Fax: (773)764-9445
1411 W. Farwell, Chicago, IL 60626
Rev. Iosif J. Isfan, Director/Founder

An interdenominational service agency of Pentecostal tradition engaged in relief and/or rehabilitation, Bible distribution, church construction, childrens programs, literature distribution, and support of national workers.

Year Founded in USA 1990
Income for Overseas Ministries . . $ 85,199
Countries: Albania, Romania.

Romanian Missionary Society
(630)665-6503   Fax: (630)665-6538
P.O. Box 527, Wheaton, IL 60189
Dr. Darrel Anderson, Exec. Director

A nondenominational sending agency of Baptist tradition engaged in theological education, broadcasting, leadership development, literature production/distribution, and Bible translation.

Year Founded in USA 1968
Income for Overseas Ministries . $ 757,179
Fully Supported USA Personnel Overseas:
  Expecting to serve more than 4 years 4
Other Personnel:
  Non-USA serving in own/other country . . . 4
  Home ministry & office staff in USA 9
Countries: Romania 4.

Rosedale Mennonite Missions
(614)857-1366   Fax: (614)857-1605
9920 Rosedale Milford Ctr. Rd., Irwin, OH 43029
Mr. Nathan Miller, President

A denominational sending agency of Mennonite tradition engaged in church planting, evangelism, and youth programs.

Year Founded in USA 1919
Income for Overseas Ministries . $ 316,000
Fully Supported USA Personnel Overseas:
  Expecting to serve more than 4 years 15
  Expecting to serve 1 up to 4 years 14
Other Personnel:
  Non-USA serving in own/other country . . . 2
  Bivocational/Tentmaker from USA 15
  Short-Term less than 1 year from USA . . . 70
  Home ministry & office staff in USA 13
Countries: Asia 3, Bangladesh 1, Costa Rica 4, Ecuador 10, Germany 2, Nicaragua 1, Turkey 8.

RREACH International
(972)702-0303
E-Mail: RREACHint@aol.com
6350 LBJ Freeway #250, Dallas, TX 75240
Dr. Ramesh Richard, President

A nondenominational support agency of evangelical tradition engaged in leadership development, TV/radio broadcasting, theological education, funds transmission, and training.

".. to reach weaker economies for the Lord Jesus Christ by evangelizing their opinion leaders and strengthening their pastoral leaders."

Year Founded in USA 1987
Income for Overseas Ministries . $ 458,000
Personnel:
  Short-Term less than 1 year from USA . . . 2
  Home ministry & office staff in USA 7

Russian Bible Society, Inc.
(704)252-8896   **Fax: (704)252-8891**
P.O. Box 6068, Asheville, NC 28816
Dr. Robert Doom, Director

An interdenominational specialized service agency of Baptist and fundamentalist tradition engaged in Bible translation and distribution.

"..to continue providing the 'Synodal Translation' of the Russian Bible .. and its translation into many of the minority languages [of Russia]."

Year Founded in USA 1944
Income for Overseas Ministries . $ 200,000
Personnel:
  Short-Term less than 1 year from USA . . . 10
  Home ministry & office staff in USA 1

Salvation Army, U.S.A.
(703)684-5500   **Fax: (703)684-3478**
Web: http://www.salvationarmy.org/
P.O. Box 269, Alexandria, VA 22313
Commissioner Robert Watson, Natl. Commander

A denominational sending agency of Holiness tradition engaged in evangelism, literacy work, medical work, support of national workers, and training in just over 100 countries.

".. to preach the Gospel of Jesus Christ and to meet human needs in His name without discrimination."

Year Founded in USA 1880
Income for Overseas Ministries $ 17,393,615
Fully Supported USA Personnel Overseas:
  Expecting to serve more than 4 years 75
  Expecting to serve 1 up to 4 years 25
Other Personnel:
  Short-Term less than 1 year from USA . . . 37
Countries: Argentina 6, Australia 2, Bahamas 4, Bolivia 1, Brazil 4, Chile 8, Congo/Zaire 3, Costa Rica 2, Czech Rep 2, Germany 2, Ghana 2, Hong Kong 2, India 2, Jamaica 5, Japan 2, Kenya 1, Korea-S 2, Mexico 3, Philippines 1, Russia 23, S Africa 2, Spain 2, Sweden 1, UK 9, Uruguay 2, Zambia 2, Zimbabwe 5.

Samaritan's Purse
(704)262-1980   **Fax: (704)262-1796**
E-Mail: USA@samaritan.org
Web: http://www.samaritan.org/
P.O. Box 3000, Boone, NC 28607
Franklin Graham, President

A nondenominational specialized service agency of evangelical tradition engaged in relief aid, childrens programs, evangelism, support of national workers, and supplying equipment. On Jan. 1, 1996, World Medical Mission merged into Samaritan's Purse as an operating division.

".. specializing in meeting the needs of victims of war, poverty, natural disasters, and disease while sharing the Good News of Jesus Christ."

Year Founded in USA 1970
Income for Overseas Ministries $ 25,352,451
Amount of Gifts-In-Kind . . $ 11,612,132
Personnel:
  Short-Term less than 1 year from USA . . 331
Countries: Angola, Bangladesh, Belarus, Bosnia, Brazil, Cambodia, Cameroon, China (PRC), Congo/Zaire, Costa Rica, Cote d'Ivoire, Ecuador, Egypt, Eritrea,

Ethiopia, Guatemala, Haiti, Honduras, India, Indonesia, Japan, Kenya, Madagascar, Mexico, Nicaragua, Niger, Nigeria, Pakistan, Papua New Guin, Philippines, Portugal, Romania, Russia, Rwanda, Thailand, Ukraine, United Arab Emr, Vietnam, Zambia, Zimbabwe.

SAND Institutes International
(815)889-4613
P.O. Box 21, Milford, IL 60953
Don & Lois Sobkoviak

An interdenominational support agency of evangelical and charismatic tradition engaged in training mission and development workers, agricultural programs, and technical assistance.

Year Founded in USA 1982
Income for Overseas Ministries . . $ 10,000

Schwenkfelder Church in the USA, Board of Missions
(215)679-3103   **Fax: (215)679-8175**
105 Seminary St., Pennsburg, PA 18073
Mrs. Doris Haygood, President

A denominational support agency of Brethren and evangelical tradition engaged in support of national workers and Christian education. Financial information from 1992.

Year Founded in USA 1895
Income for Overseas Ministries . . $ 10,800

Scripture Union (USA)
(610)341-0830   **Fax: (610)341-0836**
E-Mail: BlankSU@aol.com
P.O. Box 6720, Wayne, PA 19087
Whitney Kuniholm, President

An interdenominational service agency of evangelical tradition engaged in literature production/distribution, training, and youth programs. Statistical information from 1992.

Year Founded in USA 1959
Income for Overseas Ministries . $ 274,373
Fully Supported USA Personnel Overseas:
  Expecting to serve more than 4 years 3
Other Personnel:
  Non-USA serving in own/other country . . . 2
  Home ministry & office staff in USA 9
Countries: Kenya 1, Liberia, Peru 2.

Seed Company, The
(714)969-4697   **Fax: (714)969-4661**
E-Mail: Seed_Co@wycliffe.org
Web: http://www.wycliffe.org/seedco
P.O. Box 2727, Huntington Beach, CA 92647
Roger Garland, Director

A nondenominational support agency of evangelical tradition engaged in funds transmission for Bible translation/distribution, literacy work, and support of national workers. A ministry of Wycliffe Bible Translators.

".. to recruit and nurture prayer and financial partners in support of translation projects which will be managed by national translators or in which they will play a central role."

Year Founded in USA 1993
Income for Overseas Ministries . $ 269,000
Personnel:
  Home ministry & office staff in USA 1

Self-Help Foundation
(319)352-4040   **Fax: (319)352-4040**
E-Mail: selfhelp@sbt.net
Web: http://www.sbt.net/selfhelp/
805 W. Bremer Ave., Waverly, IA 50677
Mr. Llewellyn Hille, Exec. Director

An interdenominational service agency of Methodist tradition engaged in rural development through agricultural programs, technical assistance, and training.

"..to increase productivity, profitability and the quality of life in rural communities of developing countries."

Year Founded in USA 1959
Income for Overseas Ministries . $ 111,000
Fully Supported USA Personnel Overseas:
  Expecting to serve more than 4 years 1
Other Personnel:
  Non-USA serving in own/other country . . . 1
  Short-Term less than 1 year from USA . . . 5
  Home ministry & office staff in USA 5
Countries: Ghana 1.

SEND International

(248)477-4210   **Fax: (248)477-4232**
E-Mail: 75763.2333@compuserve.com
Web: http://www.send.org/
P.O. Box 513, Farmington, MI 48332
Dr. Frank M. Severn, Gen. Director

An interdenominational sending agency of evangelical tradition engaged in church planting, broadcasting, TEE, evangelism, leadership development, and support of national churches.

".. to make disciples through evangelism, nurturing new believers and developing leaders while planting the church where it does not exist and serving it where it does."

Year Founded in USA 1947
Income for Overseas Ministries $ 7,861,796
Fully Supported USA Personnel Overseas:
   Expecting to serve more than 4 years . . . 189
   Expecting to serve 1 up to 4 years 10
   Nonresidential mission personnel 3
Other Personnel:
   Non-USA serving in own/other country . . . 9
   Short-Term less than 1 year from USA . . 202
   Home ministry & office staff in USA . . 49
Countries: Albania 8, Bulgaria 3, Czech Rep 6, Europe-W 2, Germany 3, Hungary 4, Japan 46, Macedonia 11, Philippines 35, Poland 12, Romania 2, Russia 23, Spain 7, Taiwan (ROC) 19, Ukraine 18.

Sentinel Group, The

(425)672-2989   **Fax: (425)672-3028**
P.O. Box 6334, Lynnwood, WA 98036
George K. Otis, Jr., President & CEO

A nondenominational support agency of evangelical and charismatic tradition engaged in mission-related research, services for other agencies, and training.

".. to facilitate the evangelization of the world's most severely under-serviced mission frontiers."

Year Founded in USA 1990
Income for Overseas Ministries . $ 140,000
Personnel:
   Home ministry & office staff in USA 10

Servants in Faith & Technology

(205)396-2017   **Fax: (205)396-2501**
E-Mail: Info@sifat.org
Web: http://www.sifat.org
2944 County Rd. 113, Lineville, AL 36266
Mrs. Sarah Corson, Exec. Director

An interdenominational service agency of Methodist tradition engaged in training, development, technical assistance, and video production.

".. teaching appropriate technology as a means of promoting self-help .. to people in need."

Year Founded in USA 1979
Income for Overseas Ministries . . . . NR
Personnel:
   Non-USA serving in own/other country . . . 20
   Short-Term less than 1 year from USA . . 650
   Home ministry & office staff in USA 9
Countries: Bolivia, Ecuador, Venezuela.

Seventh Day Baptist Missionary Society

(401)596-4326   **Fax: (401)596-4326**
119 Main St., Westerly, RI 02891
Mr. G. Kirk Looper, Exec. Director

A denominational support agency of Baptist tradition engaged in funds transmission for support of national churches.

Year Founded in USA 1842
Income for Overseas Ministries . . $ 29,000
Personnel:
   Home ministry & office staff in USA 1

Seventh-day Adventists General Conference

(301)680-6000   **Fax: (301)680-6090**
E-Mail: 74431.1570@compuserve.com
12501 Old Columbia Pike, Silver Spring, MD 20904
Elder Robert S. Folkenberg, President

A denominational sending agency of Adventist tradition engaged in evangelism, broadcasting, church planting, theological education, medical work, and relief aid.

Year Founded in USA 1874
Income for Overseas Ministries $ 77,858,400
Fully Supported USA Personnel Overseas:
   Expecting to serve more than 4 years . . . 617

Expecting to serve 1 up to 4 years 37
Other Personnel:
Non-USA serving in own/other country . . 447
Short-Term less than 1 year from USA . . 557
Countries: Albania, Angola, Antigua 2, Argentina 2, Armenia 2, Australia 6, Bangladesh 13, Bolivia 2, Botswana, Brazil 6, Burkina Faso, Burundi, Cambodia 6, Cameroon 6, Cape Verde Isls, Chile 4, Colombia, Congo, Congo/Zaire 10, Costa Rica 11, Cote d'Ivoire 5, Cyprus 9, Czech Rep 2, Djibouti, Dominican Rep 2, Ecuador, Egypt 4, Ethiopia 7, Fiji, Fr Polynesia, French Guiana, Gabon 2, Germany, Ghana 3, Guam 77, Guinea 2, Guinea Bissau, Guyana, Haiti 6, Honduras 4, Hong Kong 39, India 10, Indonesia 6, Ireland 2, Israel 2, Italy 2, Jamaica 11, Japan 16, Kenya 43, Korea-S 8, Laos 2, Lebanon, Liberia 2, Madagascar 4, Malawi 22, Malaysia 4, Mali 2, Marshall Isls 4, Mexico 27, Myanmar/Burma 4, N Mariana Isls 2, Nepal, Neth Antilles 2, Nicaragua 3, Niger 4, Nigeria, Norway 2, Pakistan 12, Papua New Guin 2, Paraguay, Peru, Philippines 20, Puerto Rico 16, Russia 28, Rwanda 16, S Africa 12, Senegal, Sierra Leone 2, Singapore 30, Sri Lanka 8, Sudan 6, Suriname, Switzerland 2, Taiwan (ROC) 8, Tanzania 8, Thailand 14, Togo 2, Trinidad & Tobg 14, Turkey, UK 10, Uganda, Uruguay, Venezuela 2, Vietnam 2, Zambia 8, Zimbabwe 16.

SGM International
(407)365-2265   **Fax: (407)365-2399**
E-Mail: USA@sgm.org
Web: http://members.aol.com/sgmint/index.htm
P.O. Box 195575, Winter Spring, FL 32719
Rev. David Whitfield, Exec. Director

An interdenominational support agency of evangelical tradition engaged in Bible and literature production/production for evangelism.

Year Founded in USA 1915
Income for Overseas Ministries . . . . NR
Personnel:
Home ministry & office staff in USA 2

Share International
(515)292-9134   **Fax: (515)232-6280**
P.O. Box 1651, Ames, IA 50014
Sammy Murimi, President

An interdenominational support agency of evangelical tradition engaged in support of natl. workers, mobilization for mission, and training.

Year Founded in USA 1989
Income for Overseas Ministries . . $ 5,000
Personnel:
Non-USA serving in own/other country . . . 2

Countries: Kenya.

Shelter Now International, Inc.
(920)426-1207   **Fax: (920)426-4321**
E-Mail: Thor@shelter.org
Web: http://www.shelter.org
P.O. Box 1306, Oshkosh, WI 54902
Mr. Thor Armstrong, Exec. Director

A nondenominational support agency of independent tradition engaged in relief and/or rehabilitation, agricultural programs, development, services for other agencies, and training.

Year Founded in USA 1989
Income for Overseas Ministries $ 1,996,000
Amount of Gifts-In-Kind . . . $ 358,000
Fully Supported USA Personnel Overseas:
Expecting to serve more than 4 years 3
Expecting to serve 1 up to 4 years 3
Other Personnel:
Non-USA serving in own/other country . . . 9
Bivocational/Tentmaker from USA 25
Short-Term less than 1 year from USA . . . 10
Home ministry & office staff in USA 6
Countries: Asia 6, Central Asia.

Shield of Faith Ministries
(254)939-0124
P.O. Box 786, Belton, TX 76513
Mr. Rocky J. Malloy, Director

A nondenominational support agency of independent tradition engaged in church planting, evangelism, and mobilization for mission.

Year Founded in USA 1990
Income for Overseas Ministries . . $ 10,000
Fully Supported USA Personnel Overseas:
Nonresidential mission personnel 5
Other Personnel:
Bivocational/Tentmaker from USA 1
Short-Term less than 1 year from USA . . . 50

Shield of Faith Mission Intl.
(541)382-7081   **Fax: (541)382-4471**
P.O. Box 144, Bend, OR 97709
Mr. Larry Montgomery, President

A nondenominational sending agency of evangelical tradition engaged in evangelism, church planting, and missionary training.

Year Founded in USA 1953
Income for Overseas Ministries . $ 126,045

Fully Supported USA Personnel Overseas:
Expecting to serve more than 4 years 17
Other Personnel:
Non-USA serving in own/other country . . . 4
Bivocational/Tentmaker from USA 3
Home ministry & office staff in USA 2
Countries: Brazil 2, Cote d'Ivoire 2, Mexico 7, Pakistan 1, Romania 2, Russia 2, Turkey 1.

SIM USA
(704)588-4300   **Fax: (704)587-1518**
E-Mail: Info@sim.org
Web: http://www.sim.org/sim.html
P.O. Box 7900, Charlotte, NC 28241
Dr. Larry D. Fehl, U.S. Director

An interdenominational sending agency of evangelical tradition engaged in church planting, broadcasting, development, theological ed., medical work, and support of national churches.

".. evangelizing the unreached, ministering to human need, discipling believers into churches equipped to fulfill Christ's commission."

Year Founded in USA 1893
Income for Overseas Ministries $ 20,237,406
Fully Supported USA Personnel Overseas:
Expecting to serve more than 4 years . . . 496
Expecting to serve 1 up to 4 years 22
Other Personnel:
Bivocational/Tentmaker from USA 4
Short-Term less than 1 year from USA . . 142
Home ministry & office staff in USA . . . 204
Countries: Bangladesh 10, Benin 18, Bolivia 53, Brazil 2, Burkina Faso 21, Cen Africa Rep 1, Chile 9, Cote d'Ivoire 15, Ecuador 4, Eritrea 5, Ethiopia 95, Ghana 17, Guinea 19, India 7, Italy 2, Kenya 23, Liberia 28, Nepal 2, Niger 67, Nigeria 74, Pakistan 2, Paraguay 15, Peru 7, Philippines 5, S Africa 1, Senegal 8, Sudan 6, Uruguay 2.

Slavic Gospel Association
(815)282-8900   **Fax: (815)282-8901**
E-Mail: SGA@sga.org
Web: http://www.goshen.net/sga/sga.html
6151 Commonwealth Dr., Loves Park, IL 61111
Dr. Robert W. Provost, President

An interdenominational sending agency of evangelical tradition engaged in training, Bible distribution, evangelism, support of national churches, and relief aid.

"To help the evangelical churches reach the lands of Russia."

Year Founded in USA 1934
Income for Overseas Ministries $ 3,545,299
Amount of Gifts-In-Kind . . . $ 834,959
Fully Supported USA Personnel Overseas:
Nonresidential mission personnel 2
Other Personnel:
Non-USA serving in own/other country . . . 91
Home ministry & office staff in USA 42
Countries: Belarus, Kazakhstan, Russia, Ukraine.

Slavic Missionary Service
(732)873-8981   **Fax: (732)873-1625**
P.O. Box 307, South River, NJ 08882
Rev. Alex Leonovich, Exec. Director

An interdenominational agency of evangelical tradition supporting national churches for church planting, broadcasting, and literature distribution.

Year Founded in USA 1933
Income for Overseas Ministries . . . . NR
Personnel:
Short-Term less than 1 year from USA . . . 3
Home ministry & office staff in USA 9

Society for Europe's Evangelization
(941)747-6870   **Fax: (941)750-8701**
P.O. Box 1868, Bradenton, FL 34206
Rev. Don E. Hudson, President

A denominational sending agency of Baptist tradition engaged in evangelism leading to church planting, Bible distribution, theological education, and leadership development.

Year Founded in USA 1956
Income for Overseas Ministries . $ 117,333
Fully Supported USA Personnel Overseas:
Expecting to serve more than 4 years 5
Other Personnel:
Non-USA serving in own/other country . . . 13
Short-Term less than 1 year from USA . . . 3
Home ministry & office staff in USA 3
Countries: France 5.

Society of St. Margaret
(617)445-8961
17 Highland Park St., Boston, MA 02119
Sister Adele Marie, Mother Superior

A denominational support agency of Episcopal tradition engaged in Christian education and providing medical supplies.

Year Founded in USA 1873
Income for Overseas Ministries . . . . NR
Fully Supported USA Personnel Overseas:
  Expecting to serve more than 4 years 2
Other Personnel:
  Non-USA serving in own/other country . . . 4
Countries: Haiti 2.

Son Shine Ministries International
(817)444-3777   Fax: (817)270-0199
P.O. Box 456, Azle, TX 76098
Rev. Lewis F. Shaffer, Co-Director

An interdenominational sending agency of evangelical tradition engaged in evangelism, correspondence courses, and Christian education. Income and personnel information from 1992.

Year Founded in USA 1977
Income for Overseas Ministries . . $ 42,000
Fully Supported USA Personnel Overseas:
  Expecting to serve more than 4 years 4
Countries: Germany 2, UK 2.

Source of Light Ministries Intl.
(706)342-0397   Fax: (706)342-9072
E-Mail: SOL1usa@aol.com
Web: http://www.sourcelight.org/
1011 Mission Rd., Madison, GA 30650
Mr. Glenn E. Dix, Gen. Director

A nondenominational sending agency of evangelical and fundamentalist tradition engaged in literature production/distribution, correspondence courses, and evangelism. Information from 1992.

Year Founded in USA 1953
Income for Overseas Ministries . $ 550,000
Fully Supported USA Personnel Overseas:
  Expecting to serve more than 4 years 6
Other Personnel:
  Home ministry & office staff in USA 65
Countries: Kenya 1, Liberia 2, Mexico 2, Romania 1.

South America Mission
(561)965-1833   Fax: (561)439-8950
E-Mail: 74010.1731@compuserve.com
5217 S. Military Trail, Lake Worth, FL 33463
Rev. William K. Ogden, Exec. Director

An interdenominational sending agency of evangelical tradition engaged in church planting, aviation services, theological education, evangelism, and support of national churches.

".. to establish the church of Jesus Christ in South America by planting and nurturing churches, training church leaders, [and] developing church associations."

Year Founded in USA 1914
Income for Overseas Ministries $ 2,955,152
Fully Supported USA Personnel Overseas:
  Expecting to serve more than 4 years 84
  Expecting to serve 1 up to 4 years 9
  Nonresidential mission personnel 3
Other Personnel:
  Non-USA serving in own/other country . . . 8
  Short-Term less than 1 year from USA . . . 20
  Home ministry & office staff in USA 11
Countries: Bolivia 34, Brazil 15, Colombia 12, Paraguay 7, Peru 25.

South American Missionary Society of the Episcopal Church
(412)266-0669   Fax: (412)266-5681
E-Mail: SAMS@episcopalian.org
Web: www.episcopalian.org/sams-usa/main.htm
P.O. Box 399, Ambridge, PA 15003
Rev. Thomas M. Prichard, Exec. Director

A denominational sending agency of Episcopal tradition engaged in church planting, Christian education, evangelism, leadership development, and support of national churches.

"To be witnesses and make disciples for Jesus Christ in fellowship with the Episcopal/Anglican Church in Latin America."

Year Founded in USA 1976
Income for Overseas Ministries . $ 802,395
Fully Supported USA Personnel Overseas:
  Expecting to serve more than 4 years 27
Other Personnel:
  Non-USA serving in own/other country . . . 5
  Short-Term less than 1 year from USA . . . 6
  Home ministry & office staff in USA 14
Countries: Chile 3, Costa Rica, Dominican Rep 4, Honduras 14, Peru 2, Spain 2, Uruguay 2.

Southern Baptist Convention International Mission Board

(804)353-0151   Fax: **(804)254-8970**
E-Mail: Info@imb.org
Web: http://www.imb.org
P.O. Box 6767, Richmond, VA 23230
Dr. Jerry Rankin, President

A denominational sending board of Baptist tradition engaged in church planting, theological education, evangelism, medical work, relief aid, support of national churches, mission-related research and all other mission activities. Name changed from Foreign Mission Board to International Mission Board in June of 1997.

".. to lead Southern Baptists in international missions efforts to evangelize the lost, disciple believers, develop churches and minister to people in need..."

Year Founded in USA 1845
Income for Overseas Ministries $ 221,125,889
Fully Supported USA Personnel Overseas:
   Expecting to serve more than 4 years . . 3,482
   Expecting to serve 1 up to 4 years 689
Other Personnel:
   Short-Term less than 1 year from USA . 15,457
   Home ministry & office staff in USA 36
Countries: Africa 72, Angola 4, Argentina 81, Asia 512, Australia 7, Bangladesh 11, Belize 17, Benin 21, Bermuda 2, Bolivia 27, Botswana 16, Brazil 267, Burkina Faso 30, Burundi 4, CIS 98, Caribbean Isls 71, Chad 6, Chile 62, Colombia 42, Costa Rica 36, Cote d'Ivoire 33, Dominican Rep 31, Ecuador 65, Egypt 10, El Salvador 9, Equat Guinea 4, Eritrea 12, Ethiopia 25, Europe 115, France 55, French Guiana 4, Gambia 12, Gaza 9, Germany 65, Ghana 30, Guatemala 49, Guinea 12, Guinea Bissau 4, Guyana 11, Haiti 6, Honduras 42, Hong Kong 88, India 11, Indonesia 79, Israel 50, Italy 18, Japan 166, Jordan 23, Kenya 103, Korea-S 79, Latin America 31, Liberia 13, Macao 20, Madagascar 14, Malawi 41, Malaysia 19, Mali 26, Mexico 101, Morocco 12, Mozambique 13, Namibia 16, Nepal 8, Neth Antilles 6, New Zealand 2, Nicaragua 13, Niger 16, Nigeria 95, Oceania 16, Pakistan 4, Panama 27, Paraguay 41, Peru 63, Philippines 144, Portugal 23, Rwanda 3, S Africa 76, Senegal 33, Sierra Leone 8, Singapore 11, Spain 54, Sri Lanka 4, Suriname 8, Swaziland 14, Taiwan (ROC) 90, Tanzania 86, Thailand 73, Togo 38, Trinidad & Tobg 12, UK 26, Uganda 28, Unspecified 30, Uruguay 39, Venezuela 76, West Bank 5, Yemen 41, Zambia 23, Zimbabwe 23.

Sowers International, The

(310)325-0950   Fax: **(310)325-9593**
E-Mail: GwynnL@ix.netcom.com
Web: http://www.w3s.com/sowers
26347 Governor Ave., Harbor City, CA 90710
Mr. Gwynn Lewis, Exec. Director

A transdenominational support agency of evangelical tradition engaged in funds transmission for support of national and short-term workers engaged in evangelism, development, and childrens ministries.

Year Founded in USA 1992
Income for Overseas Ministries . $ 180,000
Amount of Gifts-In-Kind . . . . $ 10,000
Personnel:
   Non-USA serving in own/other country . . . 7
   Bivocational/Tentmaker from USA 1
   Short-Term less than 1 year from USA . . . 45
   Home ministry & office staff in USA 2
Countries: Colombia, Guatemala, Philippines, Taiwan (ROC).

Spanish World Gospel Mission

(219)267-8821   Fax: **(219)267-3524**
P.O. Box 542, Winona Lake, IN 46590
Mr. Cornelius Rivera, Exec. Director

An interdenominational service agency of Baptist and independent tradition engaged in broadcasting, Bible and literature distribution, evangelism, and support of national workers.

Year Founded in USA 1959
Income for Overseas Ministries . $ 120,000
Personnel:
   Non-USA serving in own/other country . . . 19
   Home ministry & office staff in USA 5
Countries: Argentina, Chile, Colombia, Honduras, Mexico, Peru, Spain, Venezuela.

Spiritual Growth Resources, Inc.

(209)536-1544   Fax: **(408)818-4198**
P.O. Box 1014, Downey, CA 90240
Rev. Royal L. Peck, President

An interdenominational sending agency of Baptist and Brethren tradition engaged in evangelism, funds transmission, and literature production. Financial and personnel data from 1992.

Year Founded in USA 1984
Income for Overseas Ministries . $ 100,000

Fully Supported USA Personnel Overseas:
Expecting to serve more than 4 years 2
Other Personnel:
Home ministry & office staff in USA 1
Countries: Italy 2.

Spiritual Overseers Service International Corp.

(707)451-9830   Fax: (707)451-2827
E-Mail: SOSIntl@community.net
P.O. Box 2756, Vacaville, CA 95696
Rev. Henry E. Jones, President

An interdenominational agency of evangelical tradition engaged in leadership development and evangelism. Financial data from 1992.

Year Founded in USA 1979
Income for Overseas Ministries . $ 327,373
Personnel:
Home ministry & office staff in USA 3

STEER, Inc.

(701)258-4911   Fax: (701)258-7684
P.O. Box 1236, Bismarck, ND 58502
Rev. LaRue Goetz, Exec. Director

An interdenominational support agency of evangelical tradition engaged in funds transmission, agricultural programs, and services for other agencies.

".. raising money to help existing missionary societies get the Gospel to the ends of the earth in the shortest possible time..."

Year Founded in USA 1957
Income for Overseas Ministries . $ 476,968
Personnel:
Home ministry & office staff in USA 8

STEM (Short-Term Evangelical Mission) Ministries

(612)535-2944   Fax: (612)535-0022
E-Mail: STEMMin@aol.com
Web: http://www.goshen.net/STEM/
P.O. Box 290066, Minneapolis, MN 55429
Rev. Roger P. Peterson, Exec. Director

A nondenominational support agency of evangelical tradition engaged in short-term programs, Bible distribution, church construction, evangelism, and mission-related research.

".. [to] encourage Christians to discover God's purpose for the world and fulfill their strategic role in His global plan."

Year Founded in USA 1984
Income for Overseas Ministries . $ 341,539
Fully Supported USA Personnel Overseas:
Expecting to serve 1 up to 4 years 2
Other Personnel:
Short-Term less than 1 year from USA . . 321
Home ministry & office staff in USA 7
Countries: Cuba, Dominican Rep, Haiti 2, Jamaica, Paraguay, Trinidad & Tobg.

Strategic Ventures Network

(719)687-6818   Fax: (719)687-3694
E-Mail: 74211.2162@compuserve.com
P.O. Box 220, Woodland Park, CO 80866
Mr. Gary Taylor, President

A nondenominational service agency of evangelical tradition engaged in mobilization for mission through entrepreneurial tentmaking.

Year Founded in USA 1986
Income for Overseas Ministries . . . . NA
Personnel:
Bivocational/Tentmaker from USA 54
Home ministry & office staff in USA 2

TAM-ICCC (The Associated Missions of the International Council of Christian Churches)

(609)858-7175
1115 Haddon Ave., Collingswood, NJ 08108
Dr. Earl White, President

An inter-mission service agency of fundamental tradition serving its constituents in the International Council of Christian Churches.

Year Founded in USA 1948
Income for Overseas Ministries . . . . NA

TCM International

(317)299-0333   Fax: (317)290-8607
P.O. Box 24560, Indianapolis, IN 46224
Dr. Tony Twist, President

A nondenominational sending agency of Christian (Restoration Movement) tradition engaged in theological education, Bible distribution, and support of national churches.

Income and personnel information from 1992.

Year Founded in USA 1957
Income for Overseas Ministries . $ 916,410
Fully Supported USA Personnel Overseas:
  Expecting to serve more than 4 years 10
Other Personnel:
  Non-USA serving in own/other country . . . 6
Countries: Europe-E 10.

TEAM (The Evangelical Alliance Mission)

(630)653-5300   Fax: (630)653-1826
Web: http://www.teamworld.org/
P.O. Box 969, Wheaton, IL 60189
Dr. George W. Murray, Gen. Director

A nondenominational sending agency of evangelical tradition engaged in evangelism, church planting, TEE, linguistics, medical work, and short-term programs coordination. Includes merger of Bible Christian Union in 1994.

".. to help churches send missionaries to plant reproducing churches in other nations."

Year Founded in USA 1890
Income for Overseas Ministries $ 22,190,000
Fully Supported USA Personnel Overseas:
  Expecting to serve more than 4 years . . . 726
  Expecting to serve 1 up to 4 years 35
Other Personnel:
  Non-USA serving in own/other country . . . 6
  Short-Term less than 1 year from USA . . . 70
  Home ministry & office staff in USA 54
Countries: Austria 25, Brazil 6, Chad 19, Colombia 26, Czech Rep 13, France 53, Germany 19, Hong Kong 4, India 2, Indonesia 32, Italy 29, Japan 110, Korea-S 5, Macao 3, Mexico 13, Mozambique, Nepal 17, Neth Antilles 10, Pakistan 50, Peru 10, Philippines 21, Portugal 17, Russia 18, S Africa 29, Spain 28, Sri Lanka 2, Taiwan (ROC) 37, Trinidad & Tobg 10, Turkey 2, United Arab Emr 35, Venezuela 94, Zimbabwe 22.

Team Expansion, Inc.

(800)447-0800
Web: http://www.teamexpansion.org/
3700 Hopewell Road, Louisville, KY 40299
Mr. Doug Lucas, Coordinator of Intl. Services

An independent sending agency of Christian (Restoration Movement) tradition engaged in church planting, Bible distribution, evangelism,

leadership development, mobilization for mission, and missionary training.

".. to pioneer with local churches to send and sustain teams of interdependent missionaries to plant indigenous churches among unreached people groups worldwide."

Year Founded in USA 1978
Income for Overseas Ministries . . . . NR
Fully Supported USA Personnel Overseas:
  Expecting to serve more than 4 years 80
Other Personnel:
  Short-Term less than 1 year from USA . . . 24
  Home ministry & office staff in USA 5
Countries: Albania 6, Argentina 4, Colombia 2, Ecuador 12, France 2, Hungary 6, Ireland 7, Taiwan (ROC) 8, Tanzania 10, Ukraine 16, Venezuela 7.

Teen Missions International

(407)453-0350   Fax: (407)452-7988
E-Mail: TMI@cape.net
Web: http://www.teenmissions.goshen.net
885 East Hall Rd., Merritt Island, FL 32953
Rev. Robert M. Bland, Director

An interdenominational sending agency of evangelical tradition engaged in short-term camping programs, evangelism, literature production, missionary training, and youth programs.

".. providing North American teenagers and adults the opportunity to work in cross-cultural environments for up to six weeks..."

Year Founded in USA 1970
Income for Overseas Ministries . $ 419,348
Fully Supported USA Personnel Overseas:
  Expecting to serve more than 4 years 2
  Expecting to serve 1 up to 4 years 14
  Nonresidential mission personnel 18
Other Personnel:
  Non-USA serving in own/other country . . . 26
  Bivocational/Tentmaker from USA 8
  Short-Term less than 1 year from USA . . 1,425
  Home ministry & office staff in USA 60
Countries: Australia, Brazil 4, Honduras 5, Malawi 4, Mozambique, New Zealand, Philippines 1, Tanzania, Uganda, Zambia, Zimbabwe 2.

Teen World Outreach

(716)582-2790   Fax: (716)624-1229
Web: http://www.frontiernet.net/~elim/twopage.htm
7245 College St., Lima, NY 14485
Rev. James Porter, Director

A nondenominational service agency of Pentecostal and charismatic tradition engaged in short-term programs coordination, church construction, evangelism, and youth programs. The short-term program division of the Elim Fellowship World Missions Department.

Year Founded in USA 1981
Income for Overseas Ministries . $ 750,000
Fully Supported USA Personnel Overseas:
Nonresidential mission personnel 2
Other Personnel:
Short-Term less than 1 year from USA . . 300
Home ministry & office staff in USA 8

Tele-Missions International, Inc.
(914)268-3000   Fax: (914)268-9407
P.O. Drawer J, Valley Cottage, NY 10989
Dr. Gordon S. Anderson, Exec. Director

A nondenominational service agency of evangelical tradition engaged in evangelism, literature distribution, and video production/distribution. Financial information from 1992.

Year Founded in USA 1954
Income for Overseas Ministries . . $ 21,000
Personnel:
Short-Term less than 1 year from USA . . . 2
Home ministry & office staff in USA 8

The Evangelical Alliance Mission
See: TEAM

The Master's Harvest
(956)782-0316   Fax: (956)782-1864
E-Mail: Harvestbdr@aol.com
P.O. Box 955, Alamo, TX 78516
Mr. Kenny Ingram, Director

An interdenominational sending agency of Baptist and charismatic tradition engaged in church planting, Bible distribution, Christian education, and evangelism.

Year Founded in USA 1992
Income for Overseas Ministries . . $ 47,500
Fully Supported USA Personnel Overseas:
Expecting to serve more than 4 years 4
Expecting to serve 1 up to 4 years 2
Other Personnel:
Home ministry & office staff in USA 2

Countries: Belize 4, Mexico 2.

The Master's Mission, Inc.
(704)479-6873   Fax: (704)479-2471
Web: http://www.novagate.com/~solascriptura/tmm_home.html
P.O. Box 547, Robbinsville, NC 28771
Rev. Paul Teasdale, Exec. Director

An interdenominational sending agency of Baptist and evangelical tradition engaged in missionary ed. and specialized training, church planting, medical work, and technical assistance.

Year Founded in USA 1980
Income for Overseas Ministries . $ 730,000
Fully Supported USA Personnel Overseas:
Expecting to serve more than 4 years 20
Other Personnel:
Non-USA serving in own/other country . . . 9
Short-Term less than 1 year from USA . . . 3
Home ministry & office staff in USA 12

Countries: Congo/Zaire 2, Kenya 16, Mexico 2, Nigeria.

Things To Come Mission, Inc
(317)262-8806   Fax: (317)262-8852
E-Mail: 10215.3467@compuserve.com
Web: http://150.161.6.35/sistelos/index.html
2200 English Ave., Indianapolis, IN 46201
Rev. Joseph W. Watkins, Exec. Director

A nondenominational sending agency of evangelical and fundamentalist tradition engaged in church planting, correspondence courses, theological education, and evangelism. Financial and personnel information from 1992.

Year Founded in USA 1955
Income for Overseas Ministries . $ 410,996
Fully Supported USA Personnel Overseas:
Expecting to serve more than 4 years 21
Nonresidential mission personnel 2
Other Personnel:
Short-Term less than 1 year from USA . . . 2
Home ministry & office staff in USA 5

Countries: Brazil 8, Indonesia 2, Kenya 7, Philippines 2, UK 2.

TMA Ministries
(901)367-2677   Fax: (901)367-2677
E-Mail: 74241.332@compuserve.com
P.O. Box 38366, Memphis, TN 38183
Rev. John L. Langston, III, President

A nondenominational service agency of evangelical tradition engaged in technical assistance, evangelism, and services for others.

".. to use professional experience in the field of architecture and design to support the work of the body of Christ, worldwide .. as part of the team effort of world evangelism,.."

Year Founded in USA	1982
Income for Overseas Ministries . .	$ 12,000
Amount of Gifts-In-Kind	$ 1,000

Fully Supported USA Personnel Overseas:

Expecting to serve 1 up to 4 years	5
Nonresidential mission personnel	1

Other Personnel:

Short-Term less than 1 year from USA . . .	2
Home ministry & office staff in USA	3

Countries: Belize 2, Europe 1, Europe-E 1, India 1.

Training Evangelistic Leadership
(940)382-8365
P.O. Drawer E, Denton, TX 76202
Rev. Roy Robertson, International Director

A nondenominational sending agency of evangelical tradition engaged in training national evangelists, evangelism, literature distribution, and support of national churches.

Year Founded in USA	1970
Income for Overseas Ministries .	$ 180,000

Fully Supported USA Personnel Overseas:

Expecting to serve more than 4 years	8
Nonresidential mission personnel	1

Other Personnel:

Non-USA serving in own/other country . . .	2
Bivocational/Tentmaker from USA	4
Short-Term less than 1 year from USA . . .	35
Home ministry & office staff in USA . . .	2

Countries: China (PRC) 3, Hong Kong 4, Indonesia 1.

Trans World Missions
(818)762-4231   Fax: (818)762-5872
P.O. Box 10, Glendale, CA 91209
Rev. Luis R. Mejia, President

An interdenominational service agency of evangelical tradition engaged in church planting, Bible distribution, childrens programs, evangelism, and support of national workers.

".. ministering to the whole man spiritually, physically, emotionally, and mentally..."

Year Founded in USA	1949

Income for Overseas Ministries .	$ 302,734

Personnel:

Non-USA serving in own/other country . . .	83
Home ministry & office staff in USA	5

Countries: El Salvador, Honduras, Mexico, Nicaragua, Panama, Unspecified.

Trans World Radio
(919)460-3700   Fax: (919)460-3702
E-Mail: Info@twr.org
Web: http://www.twr.org/
P.O. Box 8700, Cary, NC 27512
Mr. Thomas J. Lowell, President

An interdenominational service agency of evangelical tradition engaged in broadcasting, correspondence courses, and evangelism. Financial and personnel information from 1992.

Year Founded in USA	1952
Income for Overseas Ministries	$ 20,000,000

Fully Supported USA Personnel Overseas:

Expecting to serve more than 4 years . . .	155
Expecting to serve 1 up to 4 years	16
Nonresidential mission personnel	1

Other Personnel:

Non-USA serving in own/other country . . .	59
Home ministry & office staff in USA . . .	106

Countries: Austria, Ecuador 2, Germany 1, Guam 35, Monaco 18, Neth Antilles 64, Netherlands 4, Singapore 5, Sri Lanka 20, Swaziland 18, UK 4.

Tribes and Nations Outreach, USA
(310)828-4858   Fax: (310)828-8084
P.O. Box 3139, Santa Monica, CA 90408
Marion Wu, USA Director
Brother Joseph, International Director

A nondenominational support agency of evangelical and independent tradition engaged in training and Bible distribution.

".. to build the body of Christ in Asia through training of nationals and provision of Bibles."

Year Founded in USA	1985
Income for Overseas Ministries	NR

Personnel:

Non-USA serving in own/other country . . .	14
Short-Term less than 1 year from USA . . .	25

Countries: Cambodia, China (PRC), Indonesia, Laos, Myanmar/Burma, Nepal, Philippines, Thailand, Vietnam.

Trinity Intl. Baptist Mission

(210)648-2601
P.O. Box 201213, San Antonio, TX 78220
Roy Johns, Director

A denominational sending agency of Baptist and fundamentalist tradition engaged in evangelism, Bible distribution, and literature distribution. Statistical information from 1992.

Year Founded in USA 1975
Income for Overseas Ministries . . $ 20,697
Fully Supported USA Personnel Overseas:
  Expecting to serve more than 4 years 2
Other Personnel:
  Home ministry & office staff in USA 2
Countries: Mexico 2.

Turkish World Outreach

(970)434-1942   **Fax: (970)434-1461**
E-Mail: TWO@onlinecol.com
508 Fruitvale Court, Grand Junction, CO 81504
Rev. Steven E. Hagerman, U.S. Director

A nondenominational sending agency of Christian (Restoration Movement) tradition engaged in literature distribution, Bible distribution, church planting, and evangelism. Name changed from Friends of Turkey in 1996.

Year Founded in USA 1969
Income for Overseas Ministries . $ 120,000
Fully Supported USA Personnel Overseas:
  Expecting to serve more than 4 years 10
  Nonresidential mission personnel 2
Other Personnel:
  Bivocational/Tentmaker from USA 10
  Home ministry & office staff in USA 8
Countries: Germany 2, Turkey 8.

UFM International

(610)667-7660   **Fax: (610)660-9068**
E-Mail: Bala@ufm.mhs.compuserve.com
Web: http://www.ufm.org/
P.O. Box 306, Bala-Cynwyd, PA 19004
Dr. James H. Nesbitt, Gen. Director

A nondenominational sending agency of evangelical tradition engaged in church planting, theological education, TEE, evangelism, leadership development, and medical work.

Year Founded in USA 1931
Income for Overseas Ministries $ 10,000,000

Fully Supported USA Personnel Overseas:
  Expecting to serve more than 4 years . . . 298
  Expecting to serve 1 up to 4 years 19
Other Personnel:
  Bivocational/Tentmaker from USA 5
  Short-Term less than 1 year from USA . . . 25
  Home ministry & office staff in USA 24
Countries: Austria 8, Belgium 1, Brazil 66, Caribbean Isls 2, Congo/Zaire 8, Czech Rep 2, Dominican Rep 20, France 27, Germany 23, Guyana 10, Haiti 35, Indonesia 20, Ireland 11, Italy 19, Mexico 14, Monaco 2, Philippines 15, Puerto Rico 2, Romania 4, Russia 6, S Africa 5, Slovakia 5, Spain 10, Sweden 2.

UIM International

(520)774-0651   **Fax: (520)779-3052**
E-Mail: Info@uim.org
Web: http://www.primenet.com/~uim/
P.O. Box 3600, Flagstaff, AZ 86003
Rev. Warren Cheek, Gen. Director

A nondenominational sending agency of fundamental and independent tradition engaged in church planting, camping programs, evangelism, and literature production/distribution.

Year Founded in USA 1956
Income for Overseas Ministries . . . . NR
Amount of Gifts-In-Kind . . . . $ 10,000
Fully Supported USA Personnel Overseas:
  Expecting to serve more than 4 years 20
Other Personnel:
  Bivocational/Tentmaker from USA 6
  Short-Term less than 1 year from USA . . . 2
  Home ministry & office staff in USA 84
Countries: Mexico 20.

United Board for Christian Higher Education in Asia

(212)870-2609   **Fax: (212)870-2322**
E-Mail: staff@ubchea.org
475 Riverside Dr. Rm. 1221, New York, NY 10115
Dr. David W. Vikner, President

An interdenominational cooperative service agency of ecumenical tradition engaged in leadership development and other assistance.

".. to contribute to higher education and to the exchange of resources in and with Asia for the pursuit of truth and knowledge .. and full human development understood from the perspective of Christian faith."

Year Founded in USA 1932

Income for Overseas Ministries $ 5,700,000
Personnel:
   Short-Term less than 1 year from USA   . . . 38
   Home ministry & office staff in USA   11
Countries: Asia.

United Church Board for World Ministries

(216)736-3202   **Fax: (216)736-3259**
700 Prospect Ave. E., Cleveland, OH 44115
Rev. Dr. David Hirano, Exec. V.P.

A denominational sending board of
Congregational, Reformed, and ecumenical
tradition engaged in support of national churches,
development, general Christian and theological
education, leadership development, and medical
work. Personnel information from 1992.
Financial figures from 1988.

Year Founded in USA   1812
Income for Overseas Ministries $ 9,242,604
Fully Supported USA Personnel Overseas:
   Expecting to serve more than 4 years   15
   Expecting to serve 1 up to 4 years   84
Other Personnel:
   Non-USA serving in own/other country   . . . 6
   Home ministry & office staff in USA   48
Countries: Brazil 2, China (PRC) 1, Dominican Rep 1,
Ecuador 1, El Salvador 2, Ghana 1, Honduras 1, Hong
Kong 4, India 8, Indonesia 4, Jamaica 1, Japan 21,
Kenya 3, Korea-S 2, Lesotho 3, Micronesia 2,
Mozambique 3, Nepal 3, Nicaragua 2, Poland 2, S
Africa 3, Sri Lanka 1, Taiwan (ROC) 4, Thailand 4,
Turkey 13, Zambia 2, Zimbabwe 5.

United Evangelical Churches

(800)228-2289   **Fax: (408)757-2006**
P.O. Box 1000, S. Juan Batista, CA 95045
Dr. Charles J. Hardin, President

A transdenominational sending agency of
charismatic tradition engaged in evangelism,
church planting, and Christian education.
Financial and personnel information from 1992.

Year Founded in USA   1964
Income for Overseas Ministries . . $ 42,000
Fully Supported USA Personnel Overseas:
   Expecting to serve more than 4 years   12
Countries: Australia 1, Austria 1, Bolivia 2, Mexico 2,
Philippines 6.

United Methodist Church, Board of Global Ministries

(212)870-3606   **Fax: (212)870-3748**
Web: http://gbgm-umc.org/
475 Riverside Dr. Rm. 1400, New York, NY 10115
Dr. Randolph Nugent, Gen. Secretary

A denominational sending agency of
Methodist and ecumencal tradition responding to
program and personnel needs through relationships to overseas partner Churches and ecumenical organizations with a wide range of activities
including evangelism, community development,
Christian education, and leadership development.

Year Founded in USA   1820
Income for Overseas Ministries $ 30,396,998
Fully Supported USA Personnel Overseas:
   Expecting to serve more than 4 years   . . . 246
   Expecting to serve 1 up to 4 years   62
   Nonresidential mission personnel   36
Other Personnel:
   Home ministry & office staff in USA   . . . 554
Countries: Afghanistan 2, Africa 36, Angola 1,
Argentina 3, Austria 2, Bolivia 9, Botswana 2, Brazil 7,
Bulgaria 2, Chile 4, China (PRC) 13, Congo/Zaire 25,
Costa Rica 3, Cote d'Ivoire 1, Cuba 2, Europe 31,
Germany 2, Ghana 2, Guatemala 2, Guyana 2, Haiti 2,
Honduras 2, India 10, Indonesia 2, Ireland 2, Israel 2,
Jamaica 3, Japan 21, Kenya 11, Korea-S 11, Liberia 7,
Lithuania 4, Malaysia 1, Mexico 7, Mozambique 2,
Nepal 6, Nicaragua 2, Nigeria 9, Panama 3, Philippines
8, Russia 11, Senegal 6, Singapore 2, Spain 2,
Switzerland 1, Taiwan (ROC) 4, Uganda 2, Uruguay 2,
Zimbabwe 12.

United Methodist Committee on Relief

See: United Methodist Church

United Pentecostal Church Intl., Foreign Missions Division

(314)837-7300   **Fax: (314)837-2387**
E-Mail: FMDUPCI@stlnet.com
Web: http://www.upci.org/maintemp
8855 Dunn Rd., Hazelwood, MO 63042
Rev. Harry E. Scism, Gen. Director

A denominational sending agency of Pentecostal tradition engaged in evangelism, Bible
distribution, church planting, and theological education. Financial and personnel data from 1992.

Year Founded in USA 1924
Income for Overseas Ministries $ 11,227,696
Fully Supported USA Personnel Overseas:
Expecting to serve more than 4 years . . . 267
Countries: Argentina 8, Asia 15, Australia 4, Austria 4, Bahamas 2, Belgium 2, Belize 2, Bolivia 4, Botswana 2, Brazil 12, CIS 2, Cameroon 2, Chile 6, Colombia 4, Costa Rica 2, Cote d'Ivoire 2, Dominican Rep 6, Ecuador 4, Egypt 2, El Salvador 4, Europe-E 4, Finland 2, France 4, Germany 4, Ghana 5, Greece 4, Guatemala 2, Haiti 4, Honduras 4, Hong Kong 4, Hungary 2, Indonesia 4, Japan 2, Kenya 6, Korea-S 3, Liberia 2, Madagascar 10, Malawi 4, Malaysia 2, Mexico 12, Micronesia 4, Namibia 2, Neth Antilles 4, Netherlands 2, New Zealand 2, Nigeria 6, Norway 2, Oceania 6, Pakistan 4, Panama 4, Paraguay 2, Peru 4, Philippines 8, Portugal 2, Puerto Rico 2, S Africa 2, Sierra Leone 2, Singapore 2, Spain 2, Swaziland 6, Taiwan (ROC) 4, Tanzania 6, Trinidad & Tobg 2, UK 4, Uruguay 2, Venezuela 4, Zambia 4.

United States Center for World Mission
(626)797-1111   **Fax: (626)398-2263**
E-Mail: Firstname.Lastname@uscwm.org
Web: http://www.uscwm.org/
1605 E Elizabeth St., Pasadena, CA 91104
Dr. Ralph D. Winter, Founder
Rev. Greg H. Parsons, Exec. Director

An interdenominational support agency of evangelical tradition engaged in mobilization for mission, extension missionary education, and missions research and information services.

"To stimulate and encourage the growth of a movement for frontier missions throughout the United States and the world..."

Year Founded in USA 1976
Income for Overseas Ministries . $ 180,563
Fully Supported USA Personnel Overseas:
Expecting to serve more than 4 years 2
Expecting to serve 1 up to 4 years 2
Other Personnel:
Home ministry & office staff in USA 98
Countries: India 2, Morocco 2.

United World Mission, Inc.
(704)287-8996   **Fax: (704)287-0580**
E-Mail: 73410.1740@compuserve.com
Web: http://uwm.org
6494 Hudlow Rd., Union Mills, NC 28167
Rev. Eugene W. Phillips, Jr., President

A nondenominational sending agency of evangelical tradition engaged in church planting, theological education, leadership development, support of national churches, and missionary training. Financial and personnel data from 1992.

Year Founded in USA 1946
Income for Overseas Ministries $ 1,812,226
Fully Supported USA Personnel Overseas:
Expecting to serve more than 4 years 53
Expecting to serve 1 up to 4 years 10
Other Personnel:
Non-USA serving in own/other country . . . 9
Short-Term less than 1 year from USA . . . 86
Home ministry & office staff in USA 57
Countries: Belgium 5, Bolivia 11, Brazil 2, Congo 6, Guatemala 4, Mali 5, Nigeria 2, Romania 1, Senegal 15, Spain 2, UK 6, Venezuela 4.

University Language Service
(918)495-7045   **Fax: (918)495-6050**
E-Mail: ULS@oru.edu
P.O. Box 701984, Tulsa, OK 74170
Dr. Hallett Hullinger, Director

A transdenominational service agency of charismatic and evangelical tradition providing training to overseas mission-related personnel in teaching English as a second language.

Year Founded in USA 1984
Income for Overseas Ministries . $ 100,000
Personnel:
Bivocational/Tentmaker from USA 91

VELA Ministries International
(408)232-5663   **Fax: (408)944-0466**
Web: http://www.gospelcom.net/vela/
2302 Zanker Rd., Suite 129, San Jose, CA 95131
Galo Vasquez, President

An interdenominational support agency of evangelical tradition engaged in leadership development, funds transmission, support of national workers, mobilization for mission, mission-related research, and training.

Year Founded in USA 1990
Income for Overseas Ministries . $ 200,000
Fully Supported USA Personnel Overseas:
Expecting to serve more than 4 years 1
Nonresidential mission personnel 1
Other Personnel:
Non-USA serving in own/other country . . . 9

Home ministry & office staff in USA   3
Countries: Mexico 1.

Vellore Christian Medical College Board (USA), Inc.

(212)870-2640   **Fax: (212)870-2173**
E-Mail: 103507.755@compuserve.com
Web: http://www.vellorecmc.org/
475 Riverside Dr. Rm. 243, New York, NY 10115
Dr. Robert H. Carman, Exec. Director

An interdenominational support agency of
ecumenical tradition engaged in medical work,
purchasing services, mobilization for mission,
and supplying equipment.

".. to provide support through fund raising and
interpretive programs for the wide range of
educational, health care and community outreach
programs of Vellore Christian Medical College
and Hospital (India)."

Year Founded in USA   1948
Income for Overseas Ministries . $ 942,698
Amount of Gifts-In-Kind   . . . $ 356,340
Personnel:
    Short-Term less than 1 year from USA   . . . 20
    Home ministry & office staff in USA   4
Countries: India.

Venture Middle East

(800)421-2159   **Fax: (206)729-8011**
E-Mail: 74512.3725@compuserve.com
P.O. Box 15313, Seattle, WA 98115
Mr. Leonard Rogers, President

An interdenominational service agency of
evangelical tradition engaged in support of
national churches, evangelism, leadership development, management consulting, and relief aid.

Year Founded in USA   1986
Income for Overseas Ministries $ 1,239,037
Amount of Gifts-In-Kind   . . . $ 1,014,500
Fully Supported USA Personnel Overseas:
    Expecting to serve more than 4 years   4
Other Personnel:
    Non-USA serving in own/other country   . . .   8
    Bivocational/Tentmaker from USA   4
    Short-Term less than 1 year from USA   . . .   2
    Home ministry & office staff in USA   5
Countries: Cyprus 4, Egypt, Kyrgyzstan, Lebanon.

Virginia Mennonite Board of Missions

(540)434-9727   **Fax: (540)434-7627**
901 Parkwood Dr, Harrisonburg, VA 22801
Mr. David D. Yoder, President

An interdenominational sending agency of
Mennonite tradition engaged in leadership
development, theological education, evangelism,
linguistics, and support of national churches.

".. [to] meet human needs, extend an invitation
to a relationship with Jesus Christ, promote
communities of faith that continue God's work in
the world..."

Year Founded in USA   1919
Income for Overseas Ministries . $ 670,449
Fully Supported USA Personnel Overseas:
    Expecting to serve more than 4 years   9
    Expecting to serve 1 up to 4 years   4
Other Personnel:
    Non-USA serving in own/other country   . . .   2
    Short-Term less than 1 year from USA   . . .   9
    Home ministry & office staff in USA   11
Countries: Albania 2, Guyana, Italy 8, Trinidad & Tobg
3.

Voice of China and Asia Missionary Society, Inc.

(626)441-0640   **Fax: (626)441-8124**
P.O. Box 15, Pasadena, CA 91102
Dr. Robert B. Hammond, President

An interdenominational sending agency of
evangelical and fundamentalist tradition engaged
in support of national workers, Christian
education, and evangelism.

Year Founded in USA   1946
Income for Overseas Ministries . . . .   NR
Fully Supported USA Personnel Overseas:
    Expecting to serve more than 4 years   1
    Nonresidential mission personnel   1
Other Personnel:
    Non-USA serving in own/other country   . . 200
    Home ministry & office staff in USA   7
Countries: Korea-S 1, Taiwan (ROC).

Voice of the Martyrs, The

(918)337-8015 **Fax: (918)337-9287**
E-Mail: VOMUSA@ix.netcom.com
Web: http://www.iclnet.org/pub/resources/text/
vom/vom.html
P.O. Box 443, Bartlesville, OK 74005
Rev. Richard Wurmbrand, Founder & President
Mr. Tom White, USA Director

An interdenominational support agency of
evangelical tradition engaged in the distribution
of Bibles, Christian literature, and humanitarian
aid to families in countries where Christians are
currently in prison for their faith.

Year Founded in USA 1967
Income for Overseas Ministries $ 1,355,466

Walk Thru The Bible Ministries

(770)458-9300 **Fax: (770)454-9313**
E-Mail: 74721.1535@compuserve.com
Web: http://www.walkthru.com
4201 N. Peachtree Rd., Atlanta, GA 30341
Rev. John W. Hoover, VP Intl. Ministries

A transdenominational service agency of
evangelical tradition engaged in Christian ed.,
leadership development, literature production/
distribution, and video production/distribution.

".. to contribute to the spiritual growth of
Christians worldwide through Bible teaching,
tools, and training."

Year Founded in USA 1977
Income for Overseas Ministries $ 1,000,000
Personnel:
  Non-USA serving in own/other country . . 1,520
  Short-Term less than 1 year from USA . . 110
  Home ministry & office staff in USA 85
Countries: Argentina, Australia, Belarus, Brazil, Costa
Rica, Cote d'Ivoire, Ecuador, El Salvador, Estonia,
France, Germany, Greece, Guatemala, Guyana, Hong
Kong, India, Indonesia, Ireland, Kazakhstan, Kenya,
Korea-S, Kyrgyzstan, Latvia, Lithuania, Mali, Mexico,
Moldava, Netherlands, New Zealand, Nigeria, Norway,
Papua New Guin, Philippines, Poland, Romania,
Russia, S Africa, Senegal, Singapore, Spain, Sweden,
Taiwan (ROC), Tanzania, Thailand, UK, Uganda,
Ukraine, Uruguay, Uzbekistan, Zambia.

WEC International

(215)646-2322 **Fax: (215)646-6202**
E-Mail: 76145.1774@compuserve.com
P.O. Box 1707, Fort Washington, PA 19034
Dr. Thomas I. Marks,, Jr., Director

An interdenominational sending agency of
evangelical tradition engaged in evangelism,
church planting, correspondence courses, literacy
work, medical work, and Bible translation.

".. [to] see viable churches formed among
unreached peoples and to disciple, train and
equip believers for evangelism, church planting
and involvement in worldwide mission..."

Year Founded in USA 1939
Income for Overseas Ministries $ 2,044,269
Fully Supported USA Personnel Overseas:
  Expecting to serve more than 4 years 69
  Expecting to serve 1 up to 4 years 67
  Nonresidential mission personnel 2
Other Personnel:
  Non-USA serving in own/other country . . 9
  Short-Term less than 1 year from USA . . 8
  Home ministry & office staff in USA 35
Countries: Asia 59, Brazil 4, Cambodia 1, Chad 2, Cote
d'Ivoire 14, France 1; Gambia 2, Germany 1, Guinea 1,
Guinea Bissau 5, India 2, Indonesia 9, Italy 4, Japan 1,
Mexico 9, Portugal 1, Senegal 1, Spain 6, Thailand 6,
UK 5, Venezuela 2.

Wesleyan World Missions

(317)595-4160 **Fax: (317)841-1125**
E-Mail: WWM@wesleyan.org
Web: http://www.iquest.net/wesleyan/wwm/
P.O. Box 50434, Indianapolis, IN 46250
Dr. Donald L. Bray, Gen. Director

A denominational sending agency of Wesleyan
tradition engaged in church planting, Christian
education, theological education, evangelism,
medical work, and support of national churches.

".. calling Wesleyans to evangelism, church
planting, leadership development, and ministries
of compassion for the establishing of a
flourishing international church."

Year Founded in USA 1889
Income for Overseas Ministries $ 5,195,620
Fully Supported USA Personnel Overseas:
  Expecting to serve more than 4 years . . . 119
Other Personnel:
  Non-USA serving in own/other country . . . 9

Short-Term less than 1 year from USA   . .   215
Home ministry & office staff in USA   21

Countries: Albania 2, Australia 4, Brazil 6, Cambodia 2, Colombia 4, Croatia 2, Czech Rep 4, Germany 2, Guyana 1, Haiti 11, Honduras 2, Indonesia 5, Japan 2, Mexico 5, Mozambique 2, Nepal 1, Pakistan, Papua New Guin 9, Peru 6, Philippines 2, Puerto Rico 4, Russia 8, S Africa 14, Sri Lanka, Suriname 2, Swaziland 4, Zambia 15.

Westminister Biblical Missions
(916)273-4673
E-Mail: Mathatas@nccn.net
Web: http://www.nccn.net/~wbminc
17355 Alexandra Way, Grass Valley, CA 95949
Rev. Dennis E. Roe, Gen. Secretary

A transdenominational sending agency of Presbyterian tradition engaged in theological education, literature production, and support of national churches.

Year Founded in USA   1974
Income for Overseas Ministries   . $ 200,000
Fully Supported USA Personnel Overseas:
Expecting to serve more than 4 years   5
Nonresidential mission personnel   2
Other Personnel:
Non-USA serving in own/other country   . . .   1
Short-Term less than 1 year from USA   . . .   3
Home ministry & office staff in USA   5
Countries: Hungary 1, Korea-S 1, Mexico 1, Pakistan 2.

Wisconsin Evangelical Lutheran Synod, Board for World Missions
(414)256-3233   **Fax: (414)256-0136**
E-Mail: WELSworld@aol.com
2929 N. Mayfair Road, Milwaukee, WI 53222
Rev. Duane K. Tomhave, Administrator

A denominational sending board of Lutheran tradition engaged in church planting, broadcasting, theological education, missionary education, literature production, and national church support.

".. to make disciples throughout the world .., using the gospel to win the lost for Christ and to nurture believers for lives of Christian service..."

Year Founded in USA   1955
Income for Overseas Ministries $ 9,000,000
Fully Supported USA Personnel Overseas:
Expecting to serve more than 4 years   67
Nonresidential mission personnel   1

Other Personnel:
Short-Term less than 1 year from USA   . . .   7
Home ministry & office staff in USA   5
Countries: Albania 2, Brazil 4, Bulgaria 4, Cameroon 2, Colombia 3, Cuba 1, Dominican Rep 2, Hong Kong 4, India 1, Indonesia 1, Japan 6, Malawi 7, Mexico 2, Puerto Rico 4, Russia 5, Taiwan (ROC) 3, Thailand 2, Zambia 14.

Witnessing Ministries of Christ
(209)226-7349   **Fax: (209)226-0558**
4717 N. Barton Ave., Fresno, CA 93726
Rev. Philip A. Prasad, President

An interdenominational service agency of Presbyterian tradition engaged in church planting, Christian education, leadership development, literacy work, and medical work.

Year Founded in USA   1983
Income for Overseas Ministries   . $ 535,640
Personnel:
Non-USA serving in own/other country   . .   287
Short-Term less than 1 year from USA   . . .   4
Home ministry & office staff in USA   2
Countries: India.

Word of Life Fellowship
(518)532-7111   **Fax: (518)532-7421**
Web: http://www.gospelcom.net/wol/
P.O. Box 600, Schroon Lake, NY 12870
Rev. Paul L. Bubar, Exec. Dir. of Overseas Mins.

A nondenominational sending agency of independent tradition engaged in evangelism, broadcasting, and youth camping in 34 countries.

Year Founded in USA   1940
Income for Overseas Ministries $ 5,700,000
Fully Supported USA Personnel Overseas:
Expecting to serve more than 4 years   . . .   118
Other Personnel:
Non-USA serving in own/other country   . .   543
Short-Term less than 1 year from USA   . . .   25
Home ministry & office staff in USA   . . .   507
Countries: Unspecified 118.

Word To Russia
(916)372-4610   **Fax: (916)371-2077**
P.O. Box 846, West Sacramento, CA 95605
Mr. Michael D. Lokteff, President

A nondenominational support agency of Baptist and evangelical tradition engaged in radio broadcasting, audio cassette recording and distribution, and literature distribution.

Year Founded in USA 1972
Income for Overseas Ministries . . $ 66,450
Personnel:
  Short-Term less than 1 year from USA . . . 2
  Home ministry & office staff in USA 5
Countries: Russia.

World Baptist Fellowship Mission Agency

(817)274-7161   Fax: (817)861-1992
E-Mail: WBFraley@onramp.net
P.O. Box 13459, Arlington, TX 76094
Rev. Thomas M. Raley, Missions Director

A denominational sending agency of Baptist and fundamental tradition engaged in church planting, evangelism, funds transmission, and literature distribution.

Year Founded in USA 1928
Income for Overseas Ministries $ 3,650,964
Fully Supported USA Personnel Overseas:
  Expecting to serve more than 4 years . . . 134
Other Personnel:
  Home ministry & office staff in USA 9
Countries: Australia 2, Belarus 4, Belgium 2, Brazil 33, Caribbean Isls 10, Colombia 6, Ecuador 16, France 2, Guatemala 2, Honduras 8, Indonesia 7, Ireland 2, Latvia 2, Mexico 26, New Zealand 4, Singapore 2, Spain 4, UK 2.

World Bible Translation Center

(817)595-1664   Fax: (817)589-7013
E-Mail: 71033.200@compuserve.com
P.O. Box 820648, Fort Worth, TX 76182
Mr. Dale Randolph, President

A nondenominational agency of evangelical tradition supporting Bible translation and distribution in 16 languages. Income figure from 1992.

Year Founded in USA 1973
Income for Overseas Ministries . $ 800,000
Personnel:
  Short-Term less than 1 year from USA . . . 5
  Home ministry & office staff in USA 13

World Concern

(206)546-7201   Fax: (206)546-7317
Web: http://www.worldconcern.org/
P.O. Box 33000, Seattle, WA 98133
Mr. Paul Kennell, President

A nondenominational sending agency of evangelical tradition engaged in development, agricultural programs, medical programs, relief/rehabilitation, and training. A ministry of CRISTA.

Year Founded in USA 1973
Income for Overseas Ministries $ 16,349,096
Amount of Gifts-In-Kind . . . $ 8,133,513
Fully Supported USA Personnel Overseas:
  Expecting to serve more than 4 years 31
  Expecting to serve 1 up to 4 years 35
  Nonresidential mission personnel 1
Other Personnel:
  Non-USA serving in own/other country . . 602
  Short-Term less than 1 year from USA . . . 35
  Home ministry & office staff in USA 35
Countries: Bangladesh, Bolivia 2, Cambodia 9, Ethiopia 2, Haiti 4, Kenya 11, Laos 4, Mongolia 6, Myanmar/Burma 2, Nepal 8, Peru 1, Rwanda 1, Somalia 3, Thailand 4, Uganda 6, Ukraine, Uzbekistan 2, Vietnam 1.

World Evangelization Research Center

See: Global Evangelization Movement

World Gospel Mission

(765)664-7331   Fax: (765)662-3278
E-Mail: 103164.2306@compuserve.com
Web: http://www.wgm.org/
P.O. Box 948, Marion, IN 46952
Dr. Thomas H. Hermiz, President

An interdenominational sending agency of Wesleyan and Holiness tradition engaged in church planting, theological education, TEE, evangelism, and medical work.

".. to lead men and women into a personal relationship with Christ as Savior and Lord; to gather converts into self-propagating, self-supporting, and self-governing congregations; and to lead them into a lifestyle of Christian holiness..."

Year Founded in USA 1910
Income for Overseas Ministries $ 9,177,905
Fully Supported USA Personnel Overseas:

Expecting to serve more than 4 years . . . 205
Other Personnel:
Non-USA serving in own/other country . . . 5
Short-Term less than 1 year from USA . . . 527
Home ministry & office staff in USA 92
Countries: Argentina 13, Bolivia 40, Burundi 3, Haiti 2, Honduras 31, Hungary 5, India 2, Japan 4, Kenya 67, Mexico 15, Paraguay 8, Taiwan (ROC) 2, Tanzania 8, Uganda 5.

World Harvest Mission
(215)885-1811   Fax: (215)885-4762
E-Mail: 75402.2654@compuserve.com
222 Pennsylvania Ave., Oreland, PA 19075
Mr. Josiah Bancroft, U.S. Director

A nondenominational sending agency of Presbyterian and Reformed tradition engaged in church planting, evangelism, support of national churches, and mobilization for mission.

".. [to see] local churches revived, mobilized and .. sending teams of trained men and women to plant churches overseas."

Year Founded in USA 1983
Income for Overseas Ministries $ 1,483,000
Fully Supported USA Personnel Overseas:
Expecting to serve more than 4 years 15
Expecting to serve 1 up to 4 years 11
Other Personnel:
Non-USA serving in own/other country . . . 2
Short-Term less than 1 year from USA . . 110
Home ministry & office staff in USA 16
Countries: Ireland 4, Netherlands 7, UK 8, Uganda 7.

World Help
(804)525-4657   Fax: (804)525-4727
E-Mail: WorldHp@aol.com
P.O. Box 501, Forest, VA 24551
Vernon Brewer, President

An interdenominational service agency of evangelical tradition engaged in Bible distribution, church planting, evangelism, and providing medical supplies.

Year Founded in USA 1992
Income for Overseas Ministries $ 2,308,023
Amount of Gifts-In-Kind . . . $ 1,814,946
Fully Supported USA Personnel Overseas:
Nonresidential mission personnel 6
Other Personnel:
Non-USA serving in own/other country . . . 4
Short-Term less than 1 year from USA . . 245

Home ministry & office staff in USA 23
Countries: China (PRC), Cuba, Hungary, India, Kazakhstan, Lithuania, Romania, Russia.

World Horizons
(804)353-9155   Fax: (804)266-8825
E-Mail: Admin@whorizons.org
Web: http://www.whorizons.org
P.O. Box 17721, Richmond, VA 23226
Andrew Fuller, Operations Director

A transdenominational support agency of charismatic and evangelical tradition engaged in church planting and support, mobilization for mission, and short-term programs coordination.

Year Founded in USA 1992
Income for Overseas Ministries . . $ 69,644
Fully Supported USA Personnel Overseas:
Expecting to serve more than 4 years 2
Other Personnel:
Bivocational/Tentmaker from USA 4
Short-Term less than 1 year from USA . . . 46
Countries: Turkey 2.

World In Need - USA
(708)524-9474   Fax: (708)524-9119
E-Mail: WorldIN@juno.com
237 Harrison, Oak Park, IL 60603
Mr. Larry Kendrick, USA Director

An interdenominational support agency of evangelical tradition engaged in literature production and mobilization for mission through the World In Need international office in Singapore.

Year Founded in USA 1992
Income for Overseas Ministries . . . . NR
Personnel:
Short-Term less than 1 year from USA . . . 2
Home ministry & office staff in USA 2

World Indigenous Missions
(830)629-0863   Fax: (830)629-0357
E-Mail: WIMplant@sat.net
P.O. Box 310627, New Braunfels, TX 78131
Mr. Mark R. Balderson, President

A nondenominational sending agency of charismatic tradition engaged in church planting, evangelism, support of national churches, mobilization for mission, and missionary training.

Year Founded in USA 1981

Income for Overseas Ministries $ 1,051,000
Fully Supported USA Personnel Overseas:
Expecting to serve more than 4 years 57
Other Personnel:
Bivocational/Tentmaker from USA 2
Home ministry & office staff in USA 3
Countries: Bolivia 4, Dominican Rep 2, Indonesia 2, Mexico 35, Philippines 6, Puerto Rico 2, Russia 4, Spain 2.

World Medical Mission
See: Samaritan's Purse

World Mission Associates
(717)898-2281 **Fax: (717)898-3993**
E-Mail: GlennSchwartz@xc.org
825 Darby Lane, Lancaster, PA 17601
Rev. Glenn J. Schwartz, Exec. Director

A nondenominational service agency of evangelical tradition engaged in national church support and mobilization for mission through seminars, training, and video production/distribution.

Year Founded in USA 1983
Income for Overseas Ministries . . $ 98,000
Fully Supported USA Personnel Overseas:
Expecting to serve more than 4 years 2
Other Personnel:
Bivocational/Tentmaker from USA 1
Home ministry & office staff in USA 2
Countries: Kenya 2.

World Mission Prayer League
(612)871-6843 **Fax: (612)871-6844**
E-Mail: WMPL@aol.com
232 Clifton Ave., Minneapolis, MN 55403
Mr. Robert Andrews, Gen. Director

A denominational sending agency of Lutheran tradition engaged in church planting, development, theological education, evangelism, medical work, and support of national churches.

Year Founded in USA 1937
Income for Overseas Ministries $ 1,484,900
Fully Supported USA Personnel Overseas:
Expecting to serve more than 4 years 76
Expecting to serve 1 up to 4 years 6
Other Personnel:
Non-USA serving in own/other country . . . 81
Bivocational/Tentmaker from USA 1
Short-Term less than 1 year from USA . . . 6

Home ministry & office staff in USA 20
Countries: Afghanistan 3, Asia 3, Bangladesh 10, Bolivia 9, Ecuador 13, India 2, Kenya 12, Mexico 5, Mongolia 4, Nepal 9, Pakistan 3, Peru 3, Philippines 4, Romania 2.

World Missionary Press, Inc.
(219)831-2111 **Fax: (219)831-2161**
E-Mail: 74357.3222@compuserve.com
Web: http://www.WMPress.org
P.O. Box 120, New Paris, IN 46553
Mr. Jay Benson, President

A nondenominational specialized service agency of evangelical tradition engaged in production/distribution of free topical Scripture and Bible study booklets in 280 languages.

Year Founded in USA 1961
Income for Overseas Ministries $ 1,700,000
Personnel:
Home ministry & office staff in USA 45

World Missions Far Corners
(562)402-4400 **Fax: (562)402-9039**
P.O. Box 2611, Long Beach, CA 90801
Dr. J. Leonard Bell, President/Director

A nondenominational service agency of evangelical tradition providing receipting, mailing, and other services for missionaries and national workers engaged in evangelism, church planting, and other activities in 15 countries.

Year Founded in USA 1958
Income for Overseas Ministries . $ 700,000
Fully Supported USA Personnel Overseas:
Expecting to serve more than 4 years 40
Other Personnel:
Home ministry & office staff in USA 10
Countries: Unspecified 40.

World Missions Fellowship
(503)655-5152 **Fax: (503)557-2338**
E-Mail: WMF@teleport.com
P.O. Box 5148, Oregon City, OR 97045
George A. Bradley, Gen. Director

An interdenominational sending agency of evangelical and independent tradition engaged in church planting, camping programs, orphanages, evangelism, support of national churches, and short-term programs.

Year Founded in USA 1946
Income for Overseas Ministries . $ 231,150
Fully Supported USA Personnel Overseas:
   Expecting to serve more than 4 years 10
   Expecting to serve 1 up to 4 years 4
Other Personnel:
   Non-USA serving in own/other country . . . 8
   Short-Term less than 1 year from USA . . . 11
   Home ministry & office staff in USA 4
Countries: Austria 4, India 4, Ireland 6, Japan.

World Neighbors

(405)752-9700   **Fax: (405)752-9393**
4127 NW 122nd St., Oklahoma City, OK 73120
Mr. William S. Brackett, Chief Exec. Officer

A nondenominational service agency of evangelical tradition engaged in community development and agricultural programs. Income and personnel totals from 1992.

Year Founded in USA 1951
Income for Overseas Ministries $ 1,370,878
Fully Supported USA Personnel Overseas:
   Expecting to serve more than 4 years 4
Countries: Asia 2, Latin America 2.

World Opportunities International

(213)466-7187   **Fax: (213)871-1546**
E-Mail: WorldOp@msn.com
1415 Cahuenga Blvd., Hollywood, CA 90028
Dr. Roy B. McKeown, President

An interdenominational service agency of evangelical tradition engaged in relief aid, childcare programs, and literature distribution. Income report from 1992.

Year Founded in USA 1961
Income for Overseas Ministries $ 1,000,000

World Outreach Committee

See: Church Planting International

World Outreach Ministries

(770)424-1545   **Fax: (770)424-1545**
P.O. Box B, Marietta, GA 30061
Jason R. Peebles, Founder/President

An interdenominational support agency of charismatic and evangelical tradition performing a variety of home office duties for independent missionaries engaged in evangelism, church planting and other activities.

Year Founded in USA 1979
Income for Overseas Ministries $ 1,200,000

World Partners - The Missionary Church

(219)747-2027   **Fax: (219)747-5331**
E-Mail: 72754.613@compuserve.com
P.O. Box 9127, Fort Wayne, IN 46899
Rev. Paul DeMerchant, Director

A denominational sending agency of evangelical tradition engaged in church planting, extension and theological education, evangelism, leadership development, and national church support.

".. [to] communicate the gospel to under-evangelized peoples and establish the converts ... in a mature national church in a continuing process of world outreach..."

Year Founded in USA 1969
Income for Overseas Ministries $ 3,223,985
Fully Supported USA Personnel Overseas:
   Expecting to serve more than 4 years . . . 116
   Expecting to serve 1 up to 4 years 8
   Nonresidential mission personnel 6
Other Personnel:
   Bivocational/Tentmaker from USA 2
   Short-Term less than 1 year from USA . . . 79
   Home ministry & office staff in USA 9
Countries: Asia 17, Brazil 11, Dominican Rep 6, Ecuador 17, Europe 14, France 8, Guinea 6, Haiti, India, Jamaica 4, Mexico 1, Nigeria 14, Portugal 4, Sierra Leone 2, Spain 14, Thailand 6.

World Radio Missionary Flwshp.

See: HCJB World Radio Msny. Flwshp.

World Reach, Inc.

(205)979-2400   **Fax: (205)979-6289**
E-Mail: 70451.236@compuserve.com
P.O. Box 26155, Birmingham, AL 35260
Rev. Timothy Q. Prewitt, Gen. Director

An interdenominational sending agency of evangelical tradition engaged in church planting, correspondence courses, evangelism, leadership development, and medical work.

".. targeting unreached peoples in both remote and urban areas for the purpose of evangelizing and discipling."

Year Founded in USA	1982
Income for Overseas Ministries .	$ 660,000

Fully Supported USA Personnel Overseas:
Expecting to serve more than 4 years 16
Nonresidential mission personnel 1

Other Personnel:
Non-USA serving in own/other country . . . 31
Short-Term less than 1 year from USA . . . 4
Home ministry & office staff in USA 5

Countries: El Salvador 2, Germany 4, Honduras 6, Kenya, Russia 4.

World Relief Corporation
(630)665-0235   Fax: (630)665-4473
E-Mail: WorldRelief@xc.org
Web: http://www.worldrelief.org/
P.O. Box WRC, Wheaton, IL 60189
Dr. Clive Calver, President

An interdenominational service agency of evangelical tradition engaged in relief, rehabilitation, development, agricultural programs, medical work, and technical assistance. An arm of the National Assoc. of Evangelicals, USA.

".. to work with the church in alleviating human suffering worldwide in the name of Christ."

Year Founded in USA	1944
Income for Overseas Ministries	$ 10,685,652

Fully Supported USA Personnel Overseas:
Expecting to serve more than 4 years 5
Expecting to serve 1 up to 4 years 5
Nonresidential mission personnel 4

Other Personnel:
Non-USA serving in own/other country . . . 2
Bivocational/Tentmaker from USA 1
Home ministry & office staff in USA . . . 292

Countries: Cambodia 3, Liberia 2, Nicaragua 1, Pakistan 1, Rwanda 1, Swaziland 1, Vietnam 1.

World Salt Foundation
(941)422-9191   Fax: (941)422-9191
P.O. Box 2209, Haines City, FL 33845
Mr. Roger G. Heim, President

An interdenominational service agency of charismatic tradition engaged in evangelism, Bible distribution, and church planting. Financial and personnel information from 1992.

Year Founded in USA	1978

Income for Overseas Ministries	$ 381,000

Fully Supported USA Personnel Overseas:
Expecting to serve more than 4 years 20
Expecting to serve 1 up to 4 years 6

Other Personnel:
Short-Term less than 1 year from USA . . . 43
Home ministry & office staff in USA 5

Countries: Argentina 2, Belize 2, Bosnia 2, Croatia 2, Gibraltar 2, Jamaica 2, Kenya 2, Mexico 6, Paraguay 2, Spain 2, UK 2.

World Servants
(612)866-0010   Fax: (612)866-0078
E-Mail: WorldServant@worldservants.org
7130 Portland Ave. S., Richfield, MN 55423
Rev. Timothy N. Gibson, Exec. Director

An interdenominational support agency of evangelical tradition engaged in short-term programs coordination, support of national churches, mobilization for mission, missionary orientation, and youth programs.

Year Founded in USA	1986
Income for Overseas Ministries .	$ 360,000

Fully Supported USA Personnel Overseas:
Expecting to serve more than 4 years 1
Nonresidential mission personnel 6

Other Personnel:
Non-USA serving in own/other country . . . 12
Short-Term less than 1 year from USA . . 1,963
Home ministry & office staff in USA 20

Countries: Dominican Rep, Ecuador 1, Jamaica, Kenya, Mexico, Russia.

World Team
(215)491-4900   Fax: (215)491-4910
E-Mail: 75553.3610@compuserve.com
Web: http://www.worldteam.org/
1431 Stuckert Rd., Warrington, PA 18976
Rev. Lee Maliska, USA Director
Rev. Albert Ehmann, Intl. President

A nondenominational sending agency of evangelical tradition engaged in church planting, evangelism, leadership development, support of national churches, mobilization for mission, and missionary training. Merger of WorldTeam and RBMU Interntional in 1995.

Year Founded in USA	1928
Income for Overseas Ministries	$ 6,036,455

Fully Supported USA Personnel Overseas:
Expecting to serve more than 4 years . . . 174

Expecting to serve 1 up to 4 years 1
Other Personnel:
Non-USA serving in own/other country . . . 56
Bivocational/Tentmaker from USA 7
Home ministry & office staff in USA 19
Countries: Brazil 12, Cameroon 17, Chile 5, Dominican
Rep 4, Europe-E 4, France 12, Guadeloupe 4, Haiti 9,
Indonesia 24, Italy 4, Mexico 1, Peru 10, Philippines
18, Russia 14, Spain 15, St Vincent 2, Suriname 9,
Trinidad & Tobg 7, UK 4.

World Thrust, Inc.

(770)939-5215   Fax: (770)493-7215
P.O. Box 450105, Atlanta, GA 31145
Rev Bill Boerop, President

A nondenominational support agency of
evangelical tradition engaged in mobilization for
mission and leadership development with
seminars or conferences in over 30 countries.

".. to serve .. as a catalyst to help mobilize the
local church toward a more effective involvement
in the evangelization of the world."

Year Founded in USA 1984
Income for Overseas Ministries . . $ 22,000
Personnel:
Non-USA serving in own/other country . . . 3
Home ministry & office staff in USA 4
Countries: S Africa.

World Vision

(253)815-1000   Fax: (253)815-3447
Web: http://www.worldvision.org/
P.O. Box 9716, Federal Way, WA 98063
Bob Seiple, President

A transdenominational service agency of
evangelical and ecumenical tradition engaged in
relief, rehabilitation, childcare programs,
development, Christian education, evangelism,
and technical assistance.

".. working with the poor and oppressed to
promote human transformation, seek justice and
bear witness to the good news of the Kingdom of
God."

Year Founded in USA 1950
Income for Overseas Ministries $ 210,722,000
Amount of Gifts-In-Kind . . $ 72,236,000
Fully Supported USA Personnel Overseas:
Expecting to serve more than 4 years 8
Expecting to serve 1 up to 4 years 42
Other Personnel:

Home ministry & office staff in USA . . . 581
Countries: Angola 7, Armenia 1, Azerbaijan 2,
Bangladesh, Belarus, Bolivia, Bosnia 4, Botswana,
Brazil, Burundi 1, Cambodia 5, Chad, Chile, China
(PRC), Colombia, Congo/Zaire 2, Costa Rica, Croatia,
Cyprus, Dominican Rep, Ecuador, Egypt, El Salvador,
Eritrea, Ethiopia, Fiji, Gaza, Georgia, Ghana,
Guatemala, Haiti, Honduras, Hungary, India, Indonesia,
Israel 1, Jamaica, Jordan, Kenya, Laos 3, Lebanon,
Lesotho, Liberia 1, Malawi, Mali 2, Mauritania 5,
Mexico, Mongolia, Mozambique 5, Myanmar/Burma,
Nepal, Nicaragua, Niger 1, Nigeria, Panama, Peru,
Philippines, Romania 2, Russia 1, Rwanda 2, S Africa
1, Senegal, Sierra Leone 1, Solomon Isls, Somalia, Sri
Lanka, Sudan, Suriname, Swaziland, Tanzania,
Thailand, Tonga, Turkey, Uganda, Ukraine, Vietnam 3,
West Bank, Zambia, Zimbabwe.

World Vision International

(626)303-8811   Fax: (626)301-7786
Web: http://www.wvi.org/
800 W. Chestnut Ave., Monrovia, CA 91016
Dean R. Hirsch, International President

The international coordination office for the 4
regional offices, 46 national offices, and other
entities of the World Vision Partnership engaged
in childcare programs, community development,
evangelism, leadership development, medical
work, relief aid, and training. North American
personnel serving overseas, income for overseas
ministries, and countries of activity shown under
World Vision (USA) and World Vision Canada.

".. working with the poor and oppressed to
promote human transformation, seek justice and
bear witness to the good news of the Kingdom of
God."

Year Founded in USA 1978
Income for Overseas Ministries . . . . NA
Personnel:
Home ministry & office staff in USA . . . 150

World Witness - Associate Reformed Presbyterian Church Board of Foreign Missions

(864)233-5226   Fax: (864)233-5326
E-Mail: 74152.372@compuserve.com
One Cleveland St. #220, Greenville, SC 29601
Mr. John E. Mariner, Exec. Director

A denominational sending board of
Presbyterian and Reformed tradition engaged in

church planting, TEE, evangelism, medical work, support of national workers, and youth programs.

"To glorify God through Jesus Christ through evangelism among unreached peoples, urban church planting, and a demonstration of the compassion of Jesus Christ..."

Year Founded in USA 1839
Income for Overseas Ministries $ 2,683,736
Amount of Gifts-In-Kind . . . $ 332,227
Fully Supported USA Personnel Overseas:
   Expecting to serve more than 4 years 42
   Expecting to serve 1 up to 4 years 1
   Nonresidential mission personnel 4
Other Personnel:
   Non-USA serving in own/other country . . 500
   Short-Term less than 1 year from USA . . . 12
   Home ministry & office staff in USA . . . 6
Countries: Asia 4, Germany 3, Mexico 13, Pakistan 17, Russia 4, Turkey 2.

World-Wide Missions
(909)793-2009   **Fax: (909)793-6880**
P.O. Box 2300, Redlands, CA 92373
Rev. Fred M. Johnson, Exec. Director

An interdenominational support agency of evangelical tradition engaged in support of national workers, church planting, childcare/orphanage programs, Christian education, funds transmission, and medical work.

Year Founded in USA 1950
Income for Overseas Ministries $ 1,010,543
Amount of Gifts-In-Kind . . . $ 341,540
Fully Supported USA Personnel Overseas:
   Expecting to serve more than 4 years 4
   Expecting to serve 1 up to 4 years 2
Other Personnel:
   Non-USA serving in own/other country . . 112
Countries: Bolivia, Brazil 2, Congo/Zaire 1, Haiti 2, India, Kenya, Korea-S, Liberia, Mexico, Nepal 1, Philippines, Turkey.

Worldwide Discipleship Assoc.
(770)460-1337   **Fax: (770)460-1339**
E-Mail: Headquarters@wdausa.org
110 Carnegie Place #100, Fayetteville, GA 30214
Rev. Carl W. Wilson, President

An interdenominational support agency of evangelical and Presbyterian tradition engaged in discipleship training, evangelism, and missions information services.

Year Founded in USA 1974
Income for Overseas Ministries . $ 134,126
Fully Supported USA Personnel Overseas:
   Expecting to serve more than 4 years 4
   Nonresidential mission personnel 2
Other Personnel:
   Short-Term less than 1 year from USA . . . 18
   Home ministry & office staff in USA 8
Countries: Korea-S 3, Romania 1.

Wycliffe Associates, Inc.
(714)639-9950   **Fax: (714)771-5262**
E-Mail: WA@wycliffe.org
P.O. Box 2000, Orange, CA 92669
Alan Bergstedt, CEO
Martin Huyett, President

A nondenominational service agency of evangelical tradition engaged in short-term programs coordination and mobilization for mission.

".. to support the work of Wycliffe Bible Translators, Inc., by providing programs and services to encourage and allow lay people to become directly involved in Bible translation."

Year Founded in USA 1967
Income for Overseas Ministries $ 1,900,000
Fully Supported USA Personnel Overseas:
   Expecting to serve 1 up to 4 years 1
Other Personnel:
   Short-Term less than 1 year from USA . . 125
   Home ministry & office staff in USA 61
Countries: UK 1.

Wycliffe Bible Translators International
(972)709-2400   **Fax: (972)709-3350**
Web: http://www.wycliffe.org
7500 W. Camp Wisdom Rd., Dallas, TX 75236
Mr. Steven N. Sheldon, Exec. Director

An interdenominational agency of evangelical tradition that is the international coordination center for 24 Wycliffe national sending agencies from around the world. Wycliffe is engaged in Bible translation, linguistics, literacy work and all other activities needed to support these primary ministries. Income and overseas personnel totals from the USA and Canada shown under Wycliffe USA and Wycliffe Canada.

Year Founded in USA 1934
Income for Overseas Ministries . . . . NA

Wycliffe Bible Translators USA

(714)969-4600   **Fax: (714)969-4661**
E-Mail: Info.USA@wycliffe.org
Web: http://www.wycliffe.org
P.O. Box 2727, Huntington Beach., CA 92647
Roy Peterson, Exec. Director

An interdenominational agency of evangelical tradition engaged in Bible translation, linguistics, literacy work, technical assistance, and training. Sister organizations in the USA include Wycliffe Bible Translators Intl., JAARS, Inc., and Wycliffe Associates.

".. to integrate Scripture translation, scholarship and service so that all people will have access to God's Word in their own language."

Year Founded in USA 1934
Income for Overseas Ministries $ 67,286,647
Fully Supported USA Personnel Overseas:
Expecting to serve more than 4 years . . 2,453
Expecting to serve 1 up to 4 years 165
Other Personnel:
Short-Term less than 1 year from USA . . . 99
Home ministry & office staff in USA . . . 955
Countries: Africa 75, Asia 346, Australia 16, Benin 8, Brazil 130, Burkina Faso 27, Cameroon 126, Caribbean Isls 2, Cen Africa Rep 6, Chad 22, Colombia 173, Congo 21, Congo/Zaire 56, Cote d'Ivoire 56, Ethiopia 17, Europe 75, Ghana 31, Guatemala 97, Guyana 5, Kenya 84, Latin America 11, Mali 21, Mexico 209, Mozambique 9, New Caledonia 4, Niger 9, Nigeria 25, Panama 5, Papua New Guin 452, Paraguay 4, Peru 196, Philippines 215, Solomon Isls 22, St Lucia 6, Suriname 28, Togo 21, Uganda 2, Vanuatu 6.

Young Life

(719)381-1800   **Fax: (719)381-1750**
Web: http://www.YoungLife.com/
P.O. Box 520, Colorado Springs, CO 80901
Mr. Denny Rydberg, President

A nondenominational sending agency of evangelical tradition engaged in evangelism, camping programs, and youth programs. Financial and personnel information from 1992.

Year Founded in USA 1941
Income for Overseas Ministries $ 1,628,500
Fully Supported USA Personnel Overseas:
Expecting to serve more than 4 years 34
Expecting to serve 1 up to 4 years 29
Other Personnel:

Bivocational/Tentmaker from USA 12
Short-Term less than 1 year from USA . . . 2
Countries: Austria 15, Belgium 3, Czech Rep 4, Dominican Rep 4, Germany 17, Hungary 2, Kenya 6, Nicaragua 3, Poland 1, Russia 4, S Africa 4.

Youth for Christ / USA, World Outreach Division

(303)843-9000   **Fax: (303)843-6793**
E-Mail: 75462.21@compuserve.com
Web: http://www.yfc.org/worldoutreach
P.O. Box 228822, Denver, CO 80222
Mr. Lawrence Russell, Division Director

A nondenominational sending agency of evangelical tradition engaged in evangelism and youth programs. Statistical information from 1992.

Year Founded in USA 1945
Income for Overseas Ministries $ 2,460,910
Fully Supported USA Personnel Overseas:
Expecting to serve more than 4 years 38
Expecting to serve 1 up to 4 years 21
Other Personnel:
Short-Term less than 1 year from USA . . 1,780
Home ministry & office staff in USA 9
Countries: Am Samoa 1, Austria 1, Brazil 5, Colombia 2, Cyprus 2, Ecuador 2, France 1, Kenya 2, Lebanon 2, Liberia 2, Mexico 2, Myanmar/Burma 2, Portugal 3, S Africa 11, Singapore 3, Spain 2, Sweden 1, Switzerland 8, UK 4, Uganda 1, Zimbabwe 2.

Youth With A Mission (YWAM), North American Office

(503)364-3837   **Fax: (503)378-7026**
E-Mail: 76604.235@compuserve.com
Web: http://www.ywam.org/
7085 Battlecreek Rd. SE, Salem, OR 97301
Loren Cunningham, Intl. Director
Peter Iliyn, Natl. Director

An interdenominational sending agency of evangelical tradition engaged in evangelism, church planting, relief aid, missionary training, and youth programs. See also Mercy Ships.

Year Founded in USA 1960
Income for Overseas Ministries . . . . NA
Fully Supported USA Personnel Overseas:
Expecting to serve more than 4 years . . . 736
Expecting to serve 1 up to 4 years 1,000
Other Personnel:
Short-Term less than 1 year from USA . . 5,000
Home ministry & office staff in USA . . . 1,611

Countries: Albania 9, Argentina 3, Australia 25, Austria 8, Bangladesh 1, Barbados 5, Belgium 4, Belize 6, Bolivia 4, Brazil 29, Cambodia 2, Chile 6, Colombia 5, Costa Rica 2, Croatia 3, Cyprus 1, Czech Rep 7, Denmark 3, Dominican Rep 13, Fiji 4, Finland 2, Fr Polynesia 1, France 9, Germany 15, Ghana 2, Grenada 6, Guam 1, Guatemala 17, Guinea Bissau 1, Guyana 5, Haiti 10, Honduras 3, Hong Kong 8, Hungary 9, India 37, Ireland 6, Italy 1, Jamaica 9, Japan 50, Kenya 9, Latvia 4, Lebanon 1, Lesotho 1, Liberia 1, Malaysia 11, Mali 2, Mexico 19, Micronesia 1, Mozambique 1, N Mariana Isls 2, Netherlands 48, New Caledonia 2, New Zealand 12, Nicaragua 2, Niger 1, Norway 3, Panama 3, Papua New Guin 4, Paraguay 2, Peru 2, Philippines 12, Poland 6, Russia 33, S Africa 4, Senegal 4, Singapore 10, Spain 12, Sweden 6, Switzerland 12, Taiwan (ROC) 15, Thailand 12, Togo 3, Tonga 5, UK 62, Uganda 1, Ukraine 14, Unspecified 1051, Virgin Isls USA 9, Zambia 2.

YUGO Ministries

(909)592-6621   **Fax: (909)394-1210**

E-Mail: Outreach@yugo.org
Web: http://www.yugo.org
P.O. Box 25, San Dimas, CA 91773
Mr. Leonard K. Janssen, Exec. Director

A nondenominational sending agency of evangelical tradition engaged in short-term programs coordination, church planting, evangelism, and youth programs.

Year Founded in USA   1964
Income for Overseas Ministries . $ 721,506
Fully Supported USA Personnel Overseas:
    Expecting to serve more than 4 years   13
    Nonresidential mission personnel   2
Other Personnel:
    Non-USA serving in own/other country   . . .   12
    Short-Term less than 1 year from USA   . . .   5
    Home ministry & office staff in USA   13
Countries: Mexico 13.

Chapter 5

Indices to
U.S. Protestant agencies

Many *Handbook* users find it valuable to locate agencies by particular categories of church tradition or ministry activity. This chapter provides the user with those indices. Agency responses on the *Mission Handbook* survey questionnaire helped define the categories that are listed. The organizations in each category appear in alphabetical order by organization name.

Index by church tradition

If an agency needed more than one generic or denominational category to describe its traditional doctrinal and/or ecclesiastical stance, the agency may appear under as many as two of the given categories. We have arranged the list alphabetically by category and within each category by agency name. See question #7 of the survey questionnaire reproduced in the appendix for the actual wording of the question and the check-off list of choices.

Index by ministry activity

Almost all agencies are involved

in several types of ministry activities. Each agency may be listed under as many as six primary categories of activity. We asked those with more than six primary activities to indicate the six activities toward which they had committed the largest amount of resources. The very largest agencies could indicate more activities if they desired.

We have divided the broad activities of education and evangelism into subcategories. For example, the evangelism category appears as "evangelism, mass" and "evangelism, student," and so on. See question #8 of the survey questionnaire in the appendix for the actual wording of the question and the check-off list of activities.

Agencies often convey new categories under the "other" choice in the previous survey, so we usually add or reword three or four categories for the new survey. Sometimes we drop categories because of lack of use. The most used categories, however, have remained the same over the years.

ADVENTIST

Advent Christian World Msns.
International Children's Care
Seventh-day Adventists

ANGLICAN

Anglican Frontier Missions
Anglican Orthodox Church
Reformed Episcopal Bd Missions

BAPTIST

ABWE
All Peoples Baptist Mission
American Baptist Association
American Baptist Churches USA
Anis Shorrosh Evang. Assoc.
Baptist Bible Fellowship Intl.
Baptist Faith Missions
Baptist General Conference
Baptist International Missions
Baptist Mid-Missions
Baptist Missionary Assoc.
Baptist Missions to Forgotten
Baptist World Mission
Calvary Evangelistic Mission
Carver Foreign Missions, Inc.
CBInternational
Cedar Lane Missionary Homes
Childcare International
Children's Medical Ministries
Cooperative Baptist Fellowship
Crossover Communications Intl.
Evangelical Baptist Missions
Free Will Baptist Association
French International Mission
Fundamental Bapt. Msn Trinidad
General Assoc Regular Baptists
General Baptists International
Gospel Furthering Fellowship
Gospel Mission of S. America
Gospel Missionary Union
Handclasp International, Inc.
Helps International Ministries
In Touch Mission Intl.
Independent Faith Mission

Independent Gospel Missions
Institute Intl Christian Comm
International Crusades, Inc.
International Partnership Mins
Intl. Board of Jewish Missions
Intl. Discipleship Mission
Korea Gospel Mission
Liberty Baptist Mission
Lott Carey Baptist Mission
Macedonia World Baptist Msns.
Macedonian Missionary Service
Maranatha Baptist Mission
Medical Missions Philippines
Mexican Mission Ministries
Mission O.N.E., Inc.
Mission to the Americas
Mission: Moving Mountains
Missionary Flights Intl.
National Baptist Conv. of Am.
National Baptist Conv. USA
North American Baptist Conf.
Outreach To Asia Nationals
Pan American Missions
Prakash Association USA
Priority One International
Progressive Natl Bapt Conv USA
Reformed Baptist Mission Svcs.
Romanian Missionary Society
Russian Bible Society, Inc.
Seventh Day Baptist Msny. Soc.
Society for Europe's Evang.
Southern Baptist Intl. Mission
Spanish World Gospel Mission
Spiritual Growth Resources
The Master's Harvest
The Master's Mission, Inc.
Trinity Intl. Baptist Mission
Word To Russia
World Baptist Fellowship Msn

BRETHREN

Brethren Church Missionary Bd.
Church of The Brethren
Grace Brethren Intl. Missions
India Evangelical Mission
Mennonite Brethren Msns/Svcs
Schwenkfelder Church in USA

Spiritual Growth Resources

CHARISMATIC

Advancing Indigenous Missions
Agape Gospel Mission
Apostolic Team Ministries Intl
BALL World Missions
Bezalel World Outreach/Galcom
Big World Ventures Inc.
Blessings International
Calvary Commission, Inc.
Calvary International
Celebrant Singers
Christ for India, Inc.
Christ for the Nations, Inc.
Christian Advance Intl.
Christian Fellowship Union
Christian Laymen's Msny Evang
Cornerstone, The
Covenant Celebration Church
Elim Fellowship World Missions
European Missions Outreach
Evangel Bible Translators
Faith Christian Fellowship
Forward Edge International
Foundation For His Ministry
Global Strategy Mission Assoc.
Globe Missionary Evangelism
Gospel Outreach
Gospel Outreach Mins. Intl.
Harvestime Intl. Network
High Adventure Ministries
Hope for the Hungry
India Gospel Outreach
International Gospel Outreach
International Leadership Smnrs
International Outreach Mins.
Lion and Lamb Outreach
Living Water Teaching Intl.
Luke Society, The
Mahesh Chavda Ministries Intl.
Marriage Ministries Intl.
Ministry to Eastern Europe
Mission of Mercy
Missionary Information Exch.
Missionary Revival Crusade
Mutual Faith Ministries Intl.

New Missions in Haiti
Next Towns Crusade, Inc.
Omega World Missions
Oriental Missionary Crusade
Overseas Radio & Television
Pass the Torch Ministries
Precious Seed Ministries
Rehoboth Ministries, Inc
SAND Institutes International
Sentinel Group, The
Teen World Outreach
The Master's Harvest
United Evangelical Churches
University Language Service
World Horizons
World Indigenous Missions
World Outreach Ministries
World Salt Foundation

CHRISTIAN (RESTORATION MOVEMENT)

African Christian Mission
African Mission Evangelism
Christian Chs. /Chs. of Christ
Christian Church (Disciples)
Churches of Christ
CMF International
European Evangelistic Society
Fellowship of Assoc. Medical
Good News Productions Intl.
Key Communications
Liberia Christian Mission
Mission Services Association
Missions Resource Center
Muslim Hope
Pioneer Bible Translators
TCM International
Team Expansion, Inc.
Turkish World Outreach

CHRISTIAN/PLYMOUTH BRETHREN

Brethren Assemblies
Christian Mission for the Deaf
Christian Msns. in Many Lands
Grace and Truth, Inc.
Grand Old Gospel Fellowship
Ireland Outreach Intl., Inc.

Overcomer Press, Inc.

CONGREGATIONAL

Congregational Christian Chs.
Conservative Cong. Christian
Evangelical Covenant Church
Mazahua Mission
Mission Ministries, Inc.
United Church Board World Mins

ECUMENICAL

American Waldensian Society
Anglican Frontier Missions
Bread for the World
Celebrant Singers
Christian Church (Disciples)
Christian Literacy Associates
Christian Medical & Dental Soc
Church World Service & Witness
Floresta USA, Inc.
Flying Doctors of America
Friendship Ministries
Habitat for Humanity Intl
Health Teams International
Heifer Project International
Hosanna
Interchurch Medical Assistance
International Students, Inc
Intl. Foundation for EWHA
ISOH/Impact
Japan - North American Comm
John Milton Society for Blind
Ludhiana Christian Medical Col
MARC
Overseas Ministries Study Ctr.
Prison Fellowship Intl.
Progressive Vision
United Board for Christian Ed.
United Church Board World Mins
United Methodist Church
Vellore Christian Medical Col.
World Vision

EPISCOPAL

Episcopal Church Msnry Commun.
Episcopal Church, Msny. Soc.

Episcopal World Mission
Society of St. Margaret
South American Missionary Soc.

EVANGELICAL

ACMC
Action International Mins.
ACTS International Ministries
AD2000 & Beyond Movement
Adopt-A-People Clearinghouse
Advancing Indigenous Missions
Advancing Native Missions
Africa Evangelical Fellowship
Africa Inland Mission Intl
African Enterprise, Inc.
African Leadership
Alberto Mottesi Evang Assoc
ALM International
Ambassadors for Christ Intl.
Ambassadors for Christ, Inc.
American Missionary Fellowship
AmeriTribes
AMF International
AMG International
AMOR Ministries
Anis Shorrosh Evang. Assoc.
Arab World Ministries
ARISE International
Armenian Misssionary Assoc.
Artists In Christian Testimony
Asian Outreach U.S.A.
ASSIST - Aid to Special Saints
Assoc of Free Lutheran Congs
Audio Scripture Ministries
Back to the Bible Intl.
BALL World Missions
Baptist General Conference
Barnabas International
Barnabas Ministries, Inc.
BCM International
Bethany Fellowship Missions
Bethany Home, Inc.
Bible Alliance Mission, Inc.
Bible League, The
Bible Literature International
Bibles For The World
Biblical Literature Fellowship

BILD International
Billy Graham Center, The
Billy Graham Evang. Assoc.
Blessings International
Blossoming Rose
Bridge Builders International
Bright Hope International
Cadence International
Caleb Project
CAM International
Campus Crusade for Christ
Carpenter's Tools
Cedar Lane Missionary Homes
CEIFA Ministries International
Child Evangelism Fellowship
China Ministries International
China Outreach Ministries
Chinese Christian Mission, Inc
Chosen People Ministries
CHOSEN, Inc.
Christ Community Church
Christ for India Ministries
Christ for the City Intl.
Christ for the Island World
Christian Aid Mission
Christian and Msny. Alliance
Christian Associates Intl.
Christian Blind Mission Intl.
Christian Broadcasting Network
Christian Business Men's Comte
Christian Dental Society
Christian Dynamics
Christian Fellowship Union
Christian Information Service
Christian Leadership Dev.
Christian Life Missions
Christian Literature Crusade
Christian Literature Intl.
Christian Medical & Dental Soc
Christian Outreach Intl.
Christian Pilots Association
Christian Reformed World Msns.
Christian Salvage Mission
Christian Services, Inc.
Christian World Publishers
Christians In Action, Inc.
Church Ministries Intl.
Church of God (Anderson, IN)

Church of God (Seventh Day)
Church of the United Brethren
Church Resource Ministries
Churches of God General Conf.
Cities for Christ Worldwide
CityTeam Ministries
CMF International
ComCare International
Compassion International, Inc.
Conservative Cong. Christian
Cook Communications Ministries
Correll Missionary Ministries
Covenant Celebration Church
CSI Ministries
Cumberland Presbyterian Church
DAWN Ministries
Dayspring Enterprises Intl.
Daystar U.S.
Deaf Missions International
Door of Hope International
East West Ministries
East West Missionary Service
East-West Ministries Intl.
Eastern European Bible Mission
Eastern European Outreach
ECHO
EFMA
Emmanuel Intl. Mission (U.S.)
Engineering Ministries Intl.
Episcopal Church Msnry Commun.
Equipping the Saints
European Christian Mission
European Missions Outreach
Evangelical Covenant Church
Evangelical Free Church Msn.
Evangelical Friends Mission
Evangelical Mennonite Church
Evangelical Methodist Church
Evangelical Missions Info Serv
Evangelism Explosion III Intl.
Evangelism Resources
Every Child Ministries, Inc.
Every Home for Christ
Far East Broadcasting Company
Farms International, Inc.
Floresta USA, Inc.
Food for the Hungry
Foursquare Missions Intl.

Free Methodist World Missions
Friends Church Southwest
Friends for Missions, Inc.
Friends in the West
Friends of Israel Gospel Min.
Friendship International
Friendship Ministries
Frontiers
Gideons International, The
Global Advance
Global Harvest Ministries
Global Mapping International
Global Opportunities
Global Outreach Mission
Global Outreach, Ltd.
Global Reach
Go Ye Fellowship
Gospel for Asia
Gospel Literature Intl.
Gospel Missionary Union
Gospel Outreach Mins. Intl.
Gospel Recordings USA
Gospel Revival Ministries
Grace Ministries International
Greater Europe Mission
Greater Grace World Outreach
Handclasp International, Inc.
Harvest
Harvest Evangelism, Inc.
Harvest Intl. Christian Outrch
HBI Global Partners
HCJB World Radio Msny. Flwshp.
Heart to Heart Intl Ministries
Hellenic Ministries
Help for Christian Nationals
Helps International Ministries
Hermano Pablo Ministries
High Adventure Ministries
High School Evangelism Flwshp.
Holt Intl. Children's Services
HOPE Bible Mission, Inc.
Hope for the Hungry
ICI University
Icthus International
IDEA/PROLADES
Impact International
India Gospel Outreach
India National Inland Mission

India Rural Evangelical Flwshp
Institute of Chinese Studies
Institute of Hindu Studies
Inter-Mission International
InterAct Ministries
INTERCOMM
Intercristo
INTERDEV
International Aid, Inc.
International Bible Institute
International Bible Society
International Child Care
International Cooperating Mins
International Family Missions
International Films, Inc.
International Gospel League
International Messengers
International Missions, Inc.
International Needs - USA
International Street Kids Mins
International Students, Inc
International Teams, U.S.A.
International Urban Associates
InterServe/USA
InterVarsity Mission
Intl. Christian Lit. Distrib.
Intl. Church Relief Fund
Intl. Inst. Christian Studies
Iranian Christians Intl.
Island Missionary Society
Issachar Frontier Missions
JAARS, Inc.
JAF Ministries
Japanese Evangelical Msnry Soc
Japanese Evangelization Center
Jews for Jesus
Kids Alive International
Kingdom Building Ministries
Larry Jones International Mins
Latin America Assistance, Inc.
Latin America Mission
Liberty Corner Mission
Liebenzell Mission USA
LIFE Ministries
Lifewater International
LIGHT International, Inc.
Link Care Center
Literacy & Evangelism Intl.

Share International
Shield of Faith Mission Intl.
SIM USA
Slavic Gospel Association
Slavic Missionary Service
Son Shine Ministries Intl.
Source of Light Ministries
South America Mission
Sowers International, The
Spiritual Overseers Service
STEER, Inc.
STEM Ministries
Strategic Ventures Network
TEAM
Teen Missions International
Tele-Missions International
The Master's Mission, Inc.
Things To Come Mission, Inc
TMA Ministries
Training Evangelistic Ldrshp.
Trans World Missions
Trans World Radio
Tribes and Nations Outreach
U.S. Center for World Mission
UFM International
United Evangelical Churches
United World Mission
University Language Service
VELA Ministries International
Venture Middle East
Voice of China and Asia
Voice of the Martyrs, The
Walk Thru The Bible Ministries
WEC International
Word To Russia
World Bible Translation Center
World Concern
World Help
World Horizons
World In Need - USA
World Mission Associates
World Missionary Press, Inc.
World Missions Far Corners
World Missions Fellowship
World Neighbors
World Opportunities Intl.
World Outreach Ministries
World Partners Missionary Ch.

World Reach, Inc.
World Relief Corporation
World Salt Foundation
World Servants
World Team
World Thrust, Inc.
World Vision
World-Wide Missions
Worldwide Discipleship Assoc.
Wycliffe Associates, Inc.
Wycliffe Bible Translators
Young Life
Youth for Christ / USA
Youth With A Mission (YWAM)
YUGO Ministries

FRIENDS

Central Yearly Mtg. of Friends
Evangelical Friends Mission
Friends Church Southwest
Friends United Meeting

FUNDAMENTAL

African Bible Colleges
Baptist International Missions
Baptist Mid-Missions
Baptist World Mission
Berean Mission, Inc.
Biblical Ministries Worldwide
Brazil Gospel Fellowship Msn.
CAM International
CSI Ministries
Fellowship International Msn.
FOM
Fundamental Bapt. Msn Trinidad
Fundamental Bible Missions
Gospel Fellowship Association
Gospel Furthering Fellowship
Gospel Mission of S. America
Have Christ Will Travel Mins.
Independent Board Pres. Msns.
International Partnership Mins
Intl. Discipleship Mission
Liberty Baptist Mission
Missionary Athletes Intl.
Missionary TECH Team
New Tribes Mission

Open Bible Ministries
Pilgrim Fellowship, Inc.
Prison Mission Association
Russian Bible Society, Inc.
Source of Light Ministries
TAM-ICCC
Things To Come Mission, Inc
Trinity Intl. Baptist Mission
UIM International
Voice of China and Asia
World Baptist Fellowship Msn

HOLINESS

Allegheny Wesleyan Meth. Msns.
Bible Missionary Church
Church of God (Anderson, IN)
Church of God (Holiness) Msn.
Church of God of Prophecy
Church of the Nazarene
Churches of Christ in Union
Congregational Holiness Church
Evangelical Bible Mission
Evangelistic Faith Missions
Free Methodist World Missions
Haiti Gospel Mission
Intl. Pentecostal Holiness Ch.
Liberty Corner Mission
Metropolitan Church Assoc.
Missionary Information Exch.
OMS International, Inc.
Pentecostal Free Will Bapt.Ch.
Pillar of Fire Missions Intl.
Salvation Army, U.S.A.
World Gospel Mission

INDEPENDENT

American Tract Society
Bethany Missionary Association
Biblical Ministries Worldwide
Children International
Chinese Christian Mission, Inc
Chosen People Ministries
Christian Literature Bible Ctr
Christian Union Mission
Church of God (Holiness) Msn.

David Livingstone Msny Fndtn
Evangelical Baptist Missions
Evangelize China Fellowship
Fellowship International Msn.
Foundation For His Ministry
Harvesting In Spanish
Hinduism Intl. Ministries
International Missions, Inc.
Mexican Border Missions
Mexican Christian Mission
Ministry of Jesus, Inc.
Mission Possible Foundation
Missionary Crusader, Inc.
Missionary Retreat Fellowship
Network of Intl Christian Schs
New Tribes Mission
Ripe for Harvest, Inc.
Shelter Now International
Shield of Faith Ministries
Spanish World Gospel Mission
Tribes and Nations Outreach
UIM International
Word of Life Fellowship
World Missions Fellowship

LUTHERAN

Advancing Renewal Ministries
American Assoc. Lutheran Chs.
Assoc of Free Lutheran Congs
Concordia Gospel Outreach
Evangelical Lutheran Church
Evangelical Lutheran Synod
Intl. Lutheran Laymen's League
Latin America Lutheran Mission
Lutheran Bible Translators
Lutheran Braille Workers
Lutheran Brethren World Msns.
Lutheran Church-Missouri Synod
Lutheran Lit. Soc. for Chinese
Lutheran World Relief
Lutheran Youth Encounter
Wisconsin Evang. Lutheran Syn.
World Mission Prayer League

MENNONITE

Africa Inter-Mennonite Mission
Children's Haven International
Christian Aid Ministries
Christian Printing Mission
Church of God in Christ, Menn.
Eastern Mennonite Missions
Evangelical Mennonite Church
Franconia Mennonite Conf.
General Conf. Mennonite Church
Mennonite Board of Missions
Mennonite Brethren Msns/Svcs
Mennonite Central Committee
Pacific NW Mennonite Conf.
Rosedale Mennonite Missions
Virginia Mennonite Bd. of Msns

METHODIST

African Methodist Epis. Zion
African Methodist Episcopal Ch
For Haiti with Love Inc.
Mission Soc. for United Meth.
Primitive Methodist Church USA
Self-Help Foundation
Servants in Faith & Technology
United Methodist Church

PENTECOSTAL

All God's Children Intl.
Assemblies of God
Bethel Pentecostal Temple
Children of India Foundation
Christian Advance Intl.
Christian Church of North Am.
Christian Laymen's Msny Evang
Church of God Apostolic Faith
Church of God of Prophecy
Church of God World Missions
Church of God, The
Congregational Holiness Church
Elim Fellowship World Missions
Evangel Bible Translators
FOCAS
Foursquare Missions Intl.
Free Gospel Church Msns. Dept.

Full Gospel Evangelistic Assoc
Full Gospel Grace Fellowship
His Word To The Nations
ICI University
International Leadership Smnrs
Intl. Pentecostal Ch of Christ
Intl. Pentecostal Holiness Ch.
Missionary Action, Inc.
Open Bible Standard Churches
Pentecostal Church of God
Pentecostal Free Will Bapt.Ch.
Rehoboth Ministries, Inc
Romanian Mission of Chicago
Teen World Outreach
United Pentecostal Church Intl

PRESBYTERIAN

African Bible Colleges
Arabic Communication Center
Church Planting International
Cumberland Presbyterian Church
Evangelical Presbyterian Ch.
Independent Board Pres. Msns.
Literacy & Evangelism Intl.
Mission to the World
Orthodox Presbyterian Church
Presb. Center for Msn. Studies
Presb. Evangelistic Fellowship
Presbyterian Church (USA)
Presbyterian Missionary Union
Westminister Biblical Missions
Witnessing Mins. of Christ
World Harvest Mission
World Witness
Worldwide Discipleship Assoc.

REFORMED

Arabic Communication Center
Audio Scripture Ministries
China Ministries International
China Service Coordinating Ofc
Christian Reformed World Msns.
Christian Reformed Wrld Relief
Church Planting International
Dorcas Aid International USA
Evangelical Presbyterian Ch.

International Outreach Mins.
LOGOI/FLET
Luke Society, The
Outreach, Inc.
Presb. Evangelistic Fellowship
Presbyterian Missionary Union
Prison Mission Association
Reformation Translation Flwshp
Reformed Church In America
Reformed Presbyterian Church
United Church Board World Mins
World Harvest Mission
World Witness

WESLEYAN

Allegheny Wesleyan Meth. Msns.
Brethren in Christ World Msns.
Christian Methodist Episcopal
Church of the Nazarene
Congregational Methodist Ch.
Cornerstone, The
Evangelical Congregational Ch.
Evangelical Methodist Church
Evangelistic Faith Missions
Go International
Haiti Gospel Mission
International Gospel Outreach
Primitive Methodist Church USA
Wesleyan World Missions
World Gospel Mission

AGRICULTURAL PROGRAMS

Christian Reformed Wrld Relief
Church World Service & Witness
Dorcas Aid International USA
ECHO
Farms International, Inc.
Floresta USA, Inc.
General Baptists International
Harvesting In Spanish
Heifer Project International
Latin America Assistance, Inc.
Lutheran World Relief
Mazahua Mission
Mennonite Central Committee
Mexican Medical, Inc.
Ministry of Jesus, Inc.
Mission: Moving Mountains
Mustard Seed, Inc.
Prakash Association USA
Red Sea Mission Team
Reformed Church In America
SAND Institutes International
Self-Help Foundation
Shelter Now International
STEER, Inc.
World Concern
World Neighbors
World Relief Corporation

ASSOCIATION OF MISSIONS

AIMS
EFMA
FOM
IFMA
TAM-ICCC

AUDIO RECORDING/DISTRIBUTION

Audio Scripture Ministries
Back to the Bible Intl.
Celebrant Singers
Derek Prince Ministries, Intl.
Emmaus Road, International
European Missions Outreach
Free Will Baptist Association
Gospel Recordings USA

High Adventure Ministries
Hosanna
Impact International
International Bible Institute
John Milton Society for Blind
Lutheran Youth Encounter
M/E International
Mahesh Chavda Ministries Intl.
Middle East Media - USA
Open Doors with Brother Andrew
Overcomer Press, Inc.
Overseas Radio & Television
Pilgrim Fellowship, Inc.
Word To Russia

AVIATION SERVICES

Christian Pilots Association
JAARS, Inc.
Macedonia World Baptist Msns.
Mission Aviation Fellowship
Missionaire International
Missionary Flights Intl.
Missionary Maintenance Svcs.
South America Mission

BIBLE DISTRIBUTION

Advancing Native Missions
Advancing Renewal Ministries
African Methodist Episcopal Ch
Allegheny Wesleyan Meth. Msns.
American Bible Society
AMG International
Armenian Misssionary Assoc.
Asian Outreach U.S.A.
Baptist International Missions
Baptist Missionary Assoc.
Bible League, The
Bible Literature International
Bible Missionary Church
Bibles For The World
Biblical Literature Fellowship
Bright Hope International
Calvary Evangelistic Mission
CAM International
Central Yearly Mtg. of Friends
China Ministries International
Christian Aid Ministries

Christian Broadcasting Network
Christian Life Missions
Christian Literature Crusade
Christian Literature Intl.
Christian Printing Mission
Christian Salvage Mission
Compassion International, Inc.
Concordia Gospel Outreach
Congregational Holiness Church
Cornerstone, The
Evangel Bible Translators
Evangelical Bible Mission
Friends for Missions, Inc.
Gideons International, The
Globe Missionary Evangelism
Go International
Gospel Revival Ministries
Harvesting In Spanish
Heart to Heart Intl Ministries
HOPE Bible Mission, Inc.
In Touch Mission Intl.
Independent Board Pres. Msns.
International Bible Society
Intl. Christian Lit. Distrib.
Intl. Pentecostal Ch of Christ
Ireland Outreach Intl., Inc.
Key Communications
Lutheran Braille Workers
Lutheran Lit. Soc. for Chinese
Middle East Media - USA
Mission 21 India
Missionary Athletes Intl.
Missionary Gospel Fellowship
Muslim Hope
Next Towns Crusade, Inc.
Open Bible Ministries
Open Doors with Brother Andrew
ORA International
Outreach To Asia Nationals
Pentecostal Church of God
Peter Deyneka Russian Mins.
Pocket Testament League
Prakash Association USA
Presbyterian Missionary Union
Progressive Natl Bapt Conv USA
Project Christ International
Red Sea Mission Team
Ripe for Harvest, Inc.

Romanian Mission of Chicago
Russian Bible Society, Inc.
Seed Company, The
SGM International
Slavic Gospel Association
Society for Europe's Evang.
Spanish World Gospel Mission
STEM Ministries
TCM International
Team Expansion, Inc.
The Master's Harvest
Trans World Missions
Tribes and Nations Outreach
Trinity Intl. Baptist Mission
Turkish World Outreach
United Pentecostal Church Intl
Voice of the Martyrs, The
World Bible Translation Center
World Help
World Salt Foundation

BROADCASTING, RADIO AND/OR TV

Alberto Mottesi Evang Assoc
Arab World Ministries
Arabic Communication Center
Asian Outreach U.S.A.
Back to the Bible Intl.
Baptist International Missions
Billy Graham Evang. Assoc.
Calvary Evangelistic Mission
CAM International
Christian Broadcasting Network
Christian Church of North Am.
CMF International
Derek Prince Ministries, Intl.
European Christian Mission
Far East Broadcasting Company
Friends of Israel Gospel Min.
Global Outreach Mission
Good News Productions Intl.
Gospel for Asia
Gospel Mission of S. America
Gospel Missionary Union
Grand Old Gospel Fellowship
HCJB World Radio Msny. Flwshp.
Hermano Pablo Ministries
High Adventure Ministries

Impact International
India Gospel Outreach
International Cooperating Mins
Intl. Board of Jewish Missions
Intl. Lutheran Laymen's League
JAF Ministries
Key Communications
Liberia Christian Mission
Luis Palau Evangelistic Assoc.
Macedonian Missionary Service
Middle East Media - USA
Mission Aides, Inc.
Mission to the Americas
Missionary Revival Crusade
National Religious Broadcaster
Open Doors with Brother Andrew
Overseas Radio & Television
Pocket Testament League
Radio Bible Class
Romanian Missionary Society
RREACH International
SEND International
Seventh-day Adventists
SIM USA
Spanish World Gospel Mission
Trans World Radio
Wisconsin Evang. Lutheran Syn.
Word of Life Fellowship
Word To Russia

CAMPING PROGRAMS

Armenian Misssionary Assoc.
Baptist Faith Missions
Baptist Mid-Missions
BCM International
Brazil Gospel Fellowship Msn.
Child Evangelism Fellowship
CityTeam Ministries
Eastern European Bible Mission
Fellowship International Msn.
Friends in the West
Friendship International
Gospel Fellowship Association
Gospel Missionary Union
Greater Europe Mission
High School Evangelism Flwshp.
Icthus International

International Messengers
International Street Kids Mins
International Students, Inc
Navigators, The
Pioneer Clubs
Teen Missions International
UIM International
Word of Life Fellowship
World Missions Fellowship
Young Life

CHILDCARE/ORPHANAGE

All God's Children Intl.
Armenian Misssionary Assoc.
Assoc of Free Lutheran Congs
Bethany Home, Inc.
Brethren Church Missionary Bd.
Calvary International
Childcare International
Children International
Children of India Foundation
Children's Haven International
Christian Church of North Am.
Christian Dynamics
Church of God of Prophecy
Compassion International, Inc.
Foundation For His Ministry
Free Methodist World Missions
Friends in the West
Haiti Gospel Mission
Harvesting In Spanish
Holt Intl. Children's Services
Hope for the Hungry
India National Inland Mission
India Rural Evangelical Flwshp
International Children's Care
International Needs - USA
Intl. Pentecostal Ch of Christ
Kids Alive International
Larry Jones International Mins
Mexican Medical, Inc.
Mustard Seed, Inc.
New Missions in Haiti
Precious Seed Ministries
Ramabai Mukti Mission
World Missions Fellowship
World Opportunities Intl.

World Vision
World-Wide Missions

CHILDRENS PROGRAMS

Action International Mins.
African Methodist Episcopal Ch
AMG International
Barnabas Ministries, Inc.
Children's Medical Ministries
Christ for the City Intl.
Christian Advance Intl.
Congregational Christian Chs.
East West Ministries
Evangelical Baptist Missions
FOCAS
Go International
Heart to Heart Intl Ministries
Holt Intl. Children's Services
Icthus International
ISOH/Impact
Kids Alive International
Mailbox Club International
Mexican Mission Ministries
Mission 21 India
Mission Ministries, Inc.
Next Towns Crusade, Inc.
Pillar of Fire Missions Intl.
Progressive Natl Bapt Conv USA
Reach Ministries International
Romanian Mission of Chicago
Samaritan's Purse
Trans World Missions

CHURCH CONSTRUCTION

African Leadership
African Methodist Episcopal Ch
AMOR Ministries
Apostolic Christian Church
Armenian Misssionary Assoc.
Christ for the Nations, Inc.
Christian Aid Ministries
Christian Church of North Am.
Christian Fellowship Union
Christian Union Mission
Church Ministries Intl.
Church of God World Missions
Congregational Holiness Church

CSI Ministries
Free Gospel Church Msns. Dept.
Free Will Baptist Association
Fundamental Bapt. Msn Trinidad
Harvest Intl. Christian Outrch
International Cooperating Mins
Macedonian Missionary Service
Men for Missions Intl.
Mennonite Brethren Msns/Svcs
Mexican Border Missions
Mexican Mission Ministries
Mission of Mercy
Missions Outreach Intl.
National Baptist Conv. of Am.
National Baptist Conv. USA
OMS International, Inc.
Oriental Missionary Crusade
Pentecostal Church of God
Pentecostal Free Will Bapt.Ch.
Progressive Natl Bapt Conv USA
Project Partner with Christ
Reciprocal Ministries Intl.
Romanian Mission of Chicago
STEM Ministries
Teen World Outreach

CHURCH ESTABLISHING/PLANTING

ABWE
Action International Mins.
Advent Christian World Msns.
Africa Evangelical Fellowship
Africa Inland Mission Intl
Africa Inter-Mennonite Mission
African Christian Mission
African Mission Evangelism
Agape Gospel Mission
All Peoples Baptist Mission
Allegheny Wesleyan Meth. Msns.
American Baptist Association
American Missionary Fellowship
AmeriTribes
AMG International
Anglican Frontier Missions
Apostolic Team Ministries Intl
Assemblies of God
Assoc of Free Lutheran Congs
BALL World Missions

Baptist Bible Fellowship Intl.
Baptist Faith Missions
Baptist General Conference
Baptist International Missions
Baptist Mid-Missions
Baptist Missionary Assoc.
Baptist Missions to Forgotten
Baptist World Mission
BCM International
Berean Mission, Inc.
Bethany Fellowship Missions
Bethel Pentecostal Temple
Bible Alliance Mission, Inc.
Bible Missionary Church
Biblical Ministries Worldwide
Brazil Gospel Fellowship Msn.
Brethren Assemblies
Brethren Church Missionary Bd.
Brethren in Christ World Msns.
Calvary Commission, Inc.
Calvary International
CAM International
CBInternational
Central Yearly Mtg. of Friends
Childcare International
Chinese Christian Mission, Inc
Christ Community Church
Christ for India, Inc.
Christ for the City Intl.
Christ for the Island World
Christian Aid Mission
Christian and Msny. Alliance
Christian Associates Intl.
Christian Chs. /Chs. of Christ
Christian Church of North Am.
Christian Fellowship Union
Christian Reformed World Msns.
Christians In Action, Inc.
Church of God (Anderson, IN)
Church of God (Holiness) Msn.
Church of God in Christ, Menn.
Church of God of Prophecy
Church of God World Missions
Church of the Nazarene
Church of the United Brethren
Church Planting International
Church Resource Ministries
Churches of Christ in Union

Churches of God General Conf.
CMF International
Congregational Christian Chs.
Congregational Methodist Ch.
Cooperative Baptist Fellowship
Cornerstone, The
Cumberland Presbyterian Church
Dayspring Enterprises Intl.
East West Ministries
East-West Ministries Intl.
Eastern European Outreach
Eastern Mennonite Missions
Elim Fellowship World Missions
European Evangelistic Society
European Missions Outreach
Evangelical Baptist Missions
Evangelical Bible Mission
Evangelical Congregational Ch.
Evangelical Covenant Church
Evangelical Free Church Msn.
Evangelical Friends Mission
Evangelical Lutheran Synod
Evangelical Mennonite Church
Evangelical Methodist Church
Evangelical Presbyterian Ch.
Evangelism Resources
Evangelistic Faith Missions
Evangelize China Fellowship
Every Child Ministries, Inc.
Every Home for Christ
Faith Christian Fellowship
Fellowship International Msn.
Foundation For His Ministry
Foursquare Missions Intl.
Franconia Mennonite Conf.
Free Methodist World Missions
Free Will Baptist Association
French International Mission
Friends Church Southwest
Friends United Meeting
Frontiers
Full Gospel Grace Fellowship
Fundamental Bapt. Msn Trinidad
Fundamental Bible Missions
General Baptists International
General Conf. Mennonite Church
Global Strategy Mission Assoc.
Globe Missionary Evangelism

Gospel Fellowship Association
Gospel for Asia
Gospel Furthering Fellowship
Gospel Mission of S. America
Gospel Missionary Union
Gospel Outreach
Gospel Outreach Mins. Intl.
Gospel Revival Ministries
Grace Brethren Intl. Missions
Grace Ministries International
Greater Europe Mission
Greater Grace World Outreach
Harvest Evangelism, Inc.
Harvesting In Spanish
HBI Global Partners
Hellenic Ministries
His Word To The Nations
Impact International
Independent Board Pres. Msns.
Independent Faith Mission
Independent Gospel Missions
India Evangelical Mission
India Gospel Outreach
India National Inland Mission
India Rural Evangelical Flwshp
InterAct Ministries
International Gospel Outreach
International Messengers
International Missions, Inc.
International Outreach Mins.
International Teams, U.S.A.
Intl. Pentecostal Holiness Ch.
Ireland Outreach Intl., Inc.
Island Missionary Society
Latin America Lutheran Mission
Latin America Mission
Liberty Baptist Mission
Liebenzell Mission USA
LIFE Ministries
Lutheran Brethren World Msns.
Lutheran Church-Missouri Synod
Macedonia World Baptist Msns.
Maranatha Baptist Mission
Mennonite Brethren Msns/Svcs
Metropolitan Church Assoc.
Mexican Border Missions
Mexican Christian Mission
Mexican Mission Ministries

Ministry of Jesus, Inc.
Mission 21 India
Mission Ministries, Inc.
Mission O.N.E., Inc.
Mission Possible Foundation
Mission Soc. for United Meth.
Mission to the Americas
Mission to the World
Mission To Unreached Peoples
Missionary Gospel Fellowship
Missionary Revival Crusade
Mustard Seed, Inc.
National Baptist Conv. USA
New Tribes Mission
Next Towns Crusade, Inc.
North American Baptist Conf.
OC International, Inc.
Omega World Missions
OMF International
OMS International, Inc.
Open Air Campaigners
Open Bible Ministries
Open Bible Standard Churches
Operation Mobilization
Orthodox Presbyterian Church
Pacific NW Mennonite Conf.
Paraclete Mission Group, Inc.
Partners International
PAZ International
Pentecostal Church of God
Pentecostal Free Will Bapt.Ch.
People International
Pilgrim Fellowship, Inc.
Pioneer Bible Translators
Pioneers
Pocket Testament League
Prakash Association USA
Precious Seed Ministries
Presb. Evangelistic Fellowship
Presb. Order for World Evang.
Presbyterian Church (USA)
Primitive Methodist Church USA
Project Christ International
Project Partner with Christ
Reformed Baptist Mission Svcs.
Reformed Church In America
Reformed Episcopal Bd Missions
Reformed Presbyterian Church

Rosedale Mennonite Missions
SEND International
Seventh-day Adventists
Shield of Faith Ministries
Shield of Faith Mission Intl.
SIM USA
South America Mission
South American Missionary Soc.
Southern Baptist Intl. Mission
TEAM
Team Expansion, Inc.
The Master's Harvest
The Master's Mission, Inc.
Things To Come Mission, Inc
Trans World Missions
Turkish World Outreach
UFM International
UIM International
United Evangelical Churches
United Pentecostal Church Intl
United World Mission
WEC International
Wesleyan World Missions
Wisconsin Evang. Lutheran Syn.
Witnessing Mins. of Christ
World Baptist Fellowship Msn
World Gospel Mission
World Harvest Mission
World Help
World Horizons
World Indigenous Missions
World Mission Prayer League
World Missions Far Corners
World Missions Fellowship
World Outreach Ministries
World Partners Missionary Ch.
World Reach, Inc.
World Salt Foundation
World Team
World Witness
World-Wide Missions
Youth With A Mission (YWAM)
YUGO Ministries

CORRESPONDENCE COURSES

African Bible Colleges
AMG International

Arab World Ministries
Assemblies of God
Baptist International Missions
Baptist Mid-Missions
Billy Graham Center, The
Calvary Evangelistic Mission
Christ for India, Inc.
Christian Dynamics
Christian Life Missions
Christian Literature Bible Ctr
Christian Literature Crusade
Churches of God General Conf.
Cook Communications Ministries
Friends of Israel Gospel Min.
Gospel Missionary Union
Grace and Truth, Inc.
Harvestime Intl. Network
India Evangelical Mission
International Missions, Inc.
Intl. Lutheran Laymen's League
Ireland Outreach Intl., Inc.
Macedonian Missionary Service
Mailbox Club International
Prison Mission Association
Project Christ International
Rio Grande Bible Institute
Son Shine Ministries Intl.
Source of Light Ministries
TCM International
Things To Come Mission, Inc
Trans World Radio
WEC International
World Reach, Inc.

DEVELOPMENT, COMMUNITY AND/OR OTHER

Action International Mins.
African Enterprise, Inc.
ALM International
American Baptist Churches USA
AMOR Ministries
Bright Hope International
Calvary International
Christian Reformed Wrld Relief
Church of The Brethren
Church World Service & Witness
CMF International

Dorcas Aid International USA
Eastern Mennonite Missions
Enterprise Development Intl.
Episcopal Church, Msny. Soc.
Evangelical Covenant Church
Evangelical Lutheran Church
Farms International, Inc.
Floresta USA, Inc.
Food for the Hungry
For Haiti with Love Inc.
Free Methodist World Missions
General Conf. Mennonite Church
Global Outreach, Ltd.
Global Reach
Habitat for Humanity Intl
Heifer Project International
International Child Care
International Teams, U.S.A.
InterServe/USA
Intl. Church Relief Fund
Lifewater International
Luke Society, The
Lutheran World Relief
MAP International
Medical Ambassadors Intl.
Mennonite Central Committee
Ministry of Jesus, Inc.
Mission 21 India
Mission: Moving Mountains
Opportunity International
People International
Presbyterian Church (USA)
Self-Help Foundation
Servants in Faith & Technology
Shelter Now International
SIM USA
Sowers International, The
United Church Board World Mins
United Methodist Church
World Concern
World Mission Prayer League
World Neighbors
World Relief Corporation
World Vision

DISABILITY ASSISTANCE PROGRAMS

Christian Blind Mission Intl.
Christian Mission for the Deaf
ComCare International
Deaf Missions International
International Child Care
JAF Ministries
John Milton Society for Blind
Kids Alive International

EDUCATION, CHURCH/SCH. GENERAL CHRISTIAN

African Leadership
Allegheny Wesleyan Meth. Msns.
Assoc of Free Lutheran Congs
Baptist Faith Missions
Barnabas Ministries, Inc.
BCM International
Bethany Home, Inc.
Bethany Missionary Association
Bibles For The World
Bread for the World
Carver Foreign Missions, Inc.
Christian Aid Mission
Christian Methodist Episcopal
Christian Reformed World Msns.
Christian Services, Inc.
Church of God in Christ, Menn.
Church of God World Missions
Church of the United Brethren
Churches of God General Conf.
Compassion International, Inc.
Congregational Christian Chs.
Correll Missionary Ministries
Evangelical Friends Mission
Evangelical Mennonite Church
Faith Christian Fellowship
FOCAS
Free Methodist World Missions
Friends for Missions, Inc.
Friendship Ministries
Fundamental Bible Missions
Gospel Outreach
Grace Ministries International

Greater Grace World Outreach
Haiti Gospel Mission
Harvesting In Spanish
Have Christ Will Travel Mins.
His Word To The Nations
India Rural Evangelical Flwshp
International Bible Institute
International Outreach Mins.
InterServe/USA
John Milton Society for Blind
Kids Alive International
Korea Gospel Mission
Liberia Christian Mission
Liberty Baptist Mission
LIFE Ministries
Lott Carey Baptist Mission
Ministry of Jesus, Inc.
Mission Ministries, Inc.
Mission Possible
Missions To Japan, Inc.
Mustard Seed, Inc.
National Baptist Conv. of Am.
National Baptist Conv. USA
NEED, Inc.
Network of Intl Christian Schs
New Missions in Haiti
OMS International, Inc.
Pillar of Fire Missions Intl.
Prakash Association USA
Reciprocal Ministries Intl.
Reformed Church In America
Rehoboth Ministries, Inc
Schwenkfelder Church in USA
Society of St. Margaret
Son Shine Ministries Intl.
South American Missionary Soc.
The Master's Harvest
United Church Board World Mins
United Evangelical Churches
United Methodist Church
Voice of China and Asia
Walk Thru The Bible Ministries
Wesleyan World Missions
Witnessing Mins. of Christ
World Vision
World-Wide Missions

EDUCATION, EXTENSION (OTHER)

Baptist General Conference
Evangelical Baptist Missions
Handclasp International, Inc.
Heifer Project International
Help for Christian Nationals
ICI University
Mennonite Central Committee
Ministries In Action
Mission Possible Foundation
U.S. Center for World Mission
World Partners Missionary Ch.

EDUCATION, MISSIONARY (CERTIFICATE/DEGREE)

Billy Graham Center, The
Christ for the Nations, Inc.
Christian and Msny. Alliance
Church Ministries Intl.
Elim Fellowship World Missions
Free Will Baptist Association
Literacy & Evangelism Intl.
Overseas Ministries Study Ctr.
Rio Grande Bible Institute
The Master's Mission, Inc.
U.S. Center for World Mission
Wisconsin Evang. Lutheran Syn.

EDUCATION, THEOLOGICAL

ABWE
Advent Christian World Msns.
Africa Evangelical Fellowship
Africa Inland Mission Intl
Africa Inter-Mennonite Mission
African Bible Colleges
African Leadership
African Mission Evangelism
American Baptist Association
American Baptist Churches USA
AMG International
Armenian Misssionary Assoc.
Assemblies of God
Assoc of Free Lutheran Congs
Baptist Bible Fellowship Intl.
Baptist General Conference

Baptist International Missions
Baptist Mid-Missions
Baptist Missionary Assoc.
Baptist World Mission
Berean Mission, Inc.
Bible Missionary Church
Biblical Ministries Worldwide
Brethren in Christ World Msns.
Calvary International
CAM International
China Ministries International
Christian and Msny. Alliance
Christian Reformed World Msns.
Church of God (Holiness) Msn.
Church of God Apostolic Faith
Church of the Nazarene
Church of the United Brethren
Congregational Methodist Ch.
Daystar U.S.
Eastern Mennonite Missions
Elim Fellowship World Missions
European Evangelistic Society
Evangelical Free Church Msn.
Evangelical Lutheran Church
Evangelical Lutheran Synod
Evangelical Mennonite Church
Evangelical Methodist Church
Evangelism Resources
Every Child Ministries, Inc.
Friends Church Southwest
Friends United Meeting
General Conf. Mennonite Church
Globe Missionary Evangelism
Gospel Fellowship Association
Gospel Furthering Fellowship
Gospel Mission of S. America
Gospel Missionary Union
Grace Brethren Intl. Missions
Grace Ministries International
Greater Europe Mission
ICI University
Independent Board Pres. Msns.
India Gospel Outreach
India National Inland Mission
International Gospel Outreach
International Urban Associates
Intl. Inst. Christian Studies

Intl. Pentecostal Ch of Christ
Intl. Pentecostal Holiness Ch.
Latin America Mission
Liberty Baptist Mission
Liebenzell Mission USA
Living Water Teaching Intl.
Lutheran Brethren World Msns.
Lutheran Church-Missouri Synod
Macedonia World Baptist Msns.
Mennonite Board of Missions
Mexican Mission Ministries
Ministry to Eastern Europe
Mission to the Americas
Moravian Church North America
New Tribes Mission
North American Baptist Conf.
OMF International
OMS International, Inc.
Open Bible Standard Churches
Orthodox Presbyterian Church
Outreach, Inc.
Overseas Council for Theol Ed.
Presbyterian Church (USA)
Primitive Methodist Church USA
Rehoboth Ministries, Inc
Rio Grande Bible Institute
Romanian Missionary Society
RREACH International
Seventh-day Adventists
SIM USA
Society for Europe's Evang.
South America Mission
Southern Baptist Intl. Mission
TCM International
Things To Come Mission, Inc
UFM International
United Church Board World Mins
United Pentecostal Church Intl
United World Mission
Virginia Mennonite Bd. of Msns
Wesleyan World Missions
Westminister Biblical Missions
Wisconsin Evang. Lutheran Syn.
World Gospel Mission
World Mission Prayer League
World Partners Missionary Ch.

EDUCATION, THEOLOGICAL BY EXTENSION (TEE)

Advent Christian World Msns.
African Christian Mission
African Leadership
Arab World Ministries
Berean Mission, Inc.
BILD International
Brethren in Christ World Msns.
CBInternational
Christian and Msny. Alliance
Church of God (Anderson, IN)
Church of the Nazarene
Evangelical Free Church Msn.
Evangelical Friends Mission
Evangelical Mennonite Church
Evangelistic Faith Missions
Far East Broadcasting Company
Foursquare Missions Intl.
Friends Church Southwest
Gospel Missionary Union
Grace Ministries International
Greater Europe Mission
Liberia Christian Mission
LOGOI/FLET
Lutheran Brethren World Msns.
Lutheran Church-Missouri Synod
Moravian Church North America
North American Baptist Conf.
Open Bible Standard Churches
Overseas Council for Theol Ed.
Primitive Methodist Church USA
SEND International
TEAM
UFM International
World Gospel Mission
World Witness

EVANGELISM, MASS

AD2000 & Beyond Movement
Advent Christian World Msns.
African Enterprise, Inc.
Alberto Mottesi Evang Assoc
Anis Shorrosh Evang. Assoc.
Baptist World Mission
Bible Literature International

Bible Missionary Church
Billy Graham Evang. Assoc.
Campus Crusade for Christ
Carpenter's Tools
Celebrant Singers
Christian Advance Intl.
Christian and Msny. Alliance
Christian Broadcasting Network
Christian Church of North Am.
Christian Dynamics
Christian Laymen's Msny Evang
Christians In Action, Inc.
Dayspring Enterprises Intl.
Evangelical Bible Mission
Evangelism Resources
Evangelize China Fellowship
Every Home for Christ
Far East Broadcasting Company
Foursquare Missions Intl.
Go International
Gospel for Asia
Gospel Outreach Mins. Intl.
Haiti Gospel Mission
Harvest Evangelism, Inc.
Harvest Intl. Christian Outrch
Hellenic Ministries
Hermano Pablo Ministries
High Adventure Ministries
Hinduism Intl. Ministries
His Word To The Nations
Impact International
In Touch Mission Intl.
Independent Board Pres. Msns.
Independent Faith Mission
Independent Gospel Missions
India Gospel Outreach
India Rural Evangelical Flwshp
INTERCOMM
International Crusades, Inc.
International Gospel Outreach
Intl. Board of Jewish Missions
Ireland Outreach Intl., Inc.
Island Missionary Society
Jews for Jesus
Larry Jones International Mins
Luis Palau Evangelistic Assoc.
Mahesh Chavda Ministries Intl.

Middle East Media - USA
Mission Possible
Missionary Athletes Intl.
Morelli Ministries Intl.
Mutual Faith Ministries Intl.
National Baptist Conv. of Am.
North American Baptist Conf.
On The Go Ministries
Open Air Campaigners
Operation Mobilization
Outreach To Asia Nationals
Partners in Asian Missions
Pocket Testament League
Presb. Evangelistic Fellowship
Ripe for Harvest, Inc.
Samaritan's Purse
Shield of Faith Ministries
Southern Baptist Intl. Mission
STEM Ministries
Teen World Outreach
Training Evangelistic Ldrshp.
Trans World Radio
United Pentecostal Church Intl
Word of Life Fellowship
World Help
World Indigenous Missions
World Reach, Inc.
World Vision
Youth for Christ / USA

EVANGELISM, PERSONAL AND SMALL GROUP

ABWE
Action International Mins.
Africa Evangelical Fellowship
Africa Inland Mission Intl
African Bible Colleges
African Methodist Epis. Zion
Agape Gospel Mission
All Peoples Baptist Mission
Allegheny Wesleyan Meth. Msns.
Ambassadors for Christ Intl.
American Assoc. Lutheran Chs.
American Baptist Association
American Baptist Churches USA
AMF International

Anglican Frontier Missions
Arab World Ministries
BALL World Missions
Baptist Bible Fellowship Intl.
Baptist Faith Missions
Baptist General Conference
Baptist Mid-Missions
Baptist Missionary Assoc.
Baptist Missions to Forgotten
Baptist World Mission
Barnabas Ministries, Inc.
BCM International
Berean Mission, Inc.
Bethel Pentecostal Temple
Bible Alliance Mission, Inc.
Bible Missionary Church
Big World Ventures Inc.
Brazil Gospel Fellowship Msn.
Brethren Church Missionary Bd.
Brethren in Christ World Msns.
Cadence International
Calvary Commission, Inc.
Calvary Evangelistic Mission
CAM International
Campus Crusade for Christ
CBInternational
CEIFA Ministries International
Central Yearly Mtg. of Friends
Child Evangelism Fellowship
Chinese Christian Mission, Inc
Chosen People Ministries
Christ Community Church
Christ for India, Inc.
Christ for the City Intl.
Christ for the Island World
Christian Aid Mission
Christian and Msny. Alliance
Christian Business Men's Comte
Christian Fellowship Union
Christian Medical & Dental Soc
Christian Mission for the Deaf
Christian Outreach Intl.
Christian Reformed World Msns.
Christian Union Mission
Christians In Action, Inc.
Church Ministries Intl.
Church of God (Holiness) Msn.

Church of God in Christ, Menn.
Church of God of Prophecy
Church of the Nazarene
Church Planting International
Churches of Christ in Union
Churches of God General Conf.
CityTeam Ministries
ComCare International
Congregational Methodist Ch.
Cooperative Baptist Fellowship
Cornerstone, The
CSI Ministries
Cumberland Presbyterian Church
East West Ministries
East-West Ministries Intl.
Eastern European Outreach
Eastern Mennonite Missions
Emmanuel Intl. Mission (U.S.)
Episcopal World Mission
European Christian Mission
European Evangelistic Society
Evangelical Baptist Missions
Evangelical Covenant Church
Evangelical Free Church Msn.
Evangelical Friends Mission
Evangelical Lutheran Synod
Evangelical Mennonite Church
Evangelical Methodist Church
Evangelical Presbyterian Ch.
Evangelism Explosion III Intl.
Evangelistic Faith Missions
Every Home for Christ
Faith Christian Fellowship
Farms International, Inc.
Fellowship International Msn.
Fellowship of Assoc. Medical
FOCAS
Food for the Hungry
For Haiti with Love Inc.
Forward Edge International
Foursquare Missions Intl.
Franconia Mennonite Conf.
Free Gospel Church Msns. Dept.
Free Methodist World Missions
Free Will Baptist Association
French International Mission
Friends Church Southwest

Friends of Israel Gospel Min.
Friendship International
Frontiers
Full Gospel Evangelistic Assoc
Full Gospel Grace Fellowship
Fundamental Bapt. Msn Trinidad
Fundamental Bible Missions
General Conf. Mennonite Church
Gideons International, The
Global Outreach Mission
Global Outreach, Ltd.
Global Strategy Mission Assoc.
Globe Missionary Evangelism
Gospel Fellowship Association
Gospel Furthering Fellowship
Gospel Missionary Union
Gospel Recordings USA
Grace Brethren Intl. Missions
Greater Europe Mission
Greater Grace World Outreach
Have Christ Will Travel Mins.
Health Teams International
Heart to Heart Intl Ministries
Hellenic Ministries
High School Evangelism Flwshp.
Hinduism Intl. Ministries
HOPE Bible Mission, Inc.
Hope for the Hungry
Independent Faith Mission
Independent Gospel Missions
India Evangelical Mission
InterAct Ministries
International Crusades, Inc.
International Family Missions
International Gospel League
International Messengers
International Missions, Inc.
International Needs - USA
International Street Kids Mins
International Students, Inc
International Teams, U.S.A.
InterVarsity Mission
Intl. Discipleship Mission
Intl. Inst. Christian Studies
Intl. Pentecostal Ch of Christ
Intl. Pentecostal Holiness Ch.
Iranian Christians Intl.

Island Missionary Society
Japanese Evangelization Center
Jews for Jesus
Korea Gospel Mission
Latin America Lutheran Mission
Latin America Mission
Liberty Baptist Mission
Liberty Corner Mission
Liebenzell Mission USA
LIFE Ministries
Living Water Teaching Intl.
Luke Society, The
Lutheran Church-Missouri Synod
Macedonia World Baptist Msns.
Marriage Ministries Intl.
Medical Ambassadors Intl.
Medical Missions Philippines
Mennonite Brethren Msns/Svcs
Mercy Ships
Metropolitan Church Assoc.
Mexican Border Missions
Mexican Christian Mission
Middle East Christian Outreach
Ministries In Action
Mission O.N.E., Inc.
Mission Soc. for United Meth.
Mission to the World
Mission To Unreached Peoples
Missionary Action, Inc.
Missionary Athletes Intl.
Missionary Dentists
Missionary Gospel Fellowship
Missionary Revival Crusade
Missions To Japan, Inc.
Moravian Church North America
Muslim Hope
Navigators, The
Network of Intl Christian Schs
No Greater Love Ministries
North American Baptist Conf.
OC International, Inc.
OMF International
OMS International, Inc.
Open Bible Ministries
Open Bible Standard Churches
Operation Blessing Intl.
Operation Mobilization

ORA International
Orthodox Presbyterian Church
Outreach To Asia Nationals
Overseas Radio & Television
Pacific NW Mennonite Conf.
Pan American Missions
Pass the Torch Ministries
PAZ International
Pentecostal Free Will Bapt.Ch.
People International
Pioneers
Pocket Testament League
Precious Seed Ministries
Presb. Evangelistic Fellowship
Presb. Order for World Evang.
Presbyterian Church (USA)
Prison Mission Association
Project Care
Project Partner with Christ
Ramabai Mukti Mission
Reach Ministries International
Red Sea Mission Team
Reformed Church In America
Reformed Presbyterian Church
Rehoboth Ministries, Inc
Ripe for Harvest, Inc.
Rosedale Mennonite Missions
Salvation Army, U.S.A.
SEND International
Seventh-day Adventists
Shield of Faith Ministries
Shield of Faith Mission Intl.
Slavic Gospel Association
Society for Europe's Evang.
Son Shine Ministries Intl.
Source of Light Ministries
South America Mission
South American Missionary Soc.
Sowers International, The
Spanish World Gospel Mission
Spiritual Growth Resources
Spiritual Overseers Service
TEAM
Team Expansion, Inc.
Tele-Missions International
The Master's Harvest
Things To Come Mission, Inc

TMA Ministries
Trans World Missions
Trinity Intl. Baptist Mission
Turkish World Outreach
UFM International
UIM International
United Evangelical Churches
United Methodist Church
Venture Middle East
Virginia Mennonite Bd. of Msns
Voice of the Martyrs, The
WEC International
Wesleyan World Missions
Word of Life Fellowship
World Baptist Fellowship Msn
World Gospel Mission
World Harvest Mission
World Indigenous Missions
World Mission Prayer League
World Missions Far Corners
World Missions Fellowship
World Outreach Ministries
World Partners Missionary Ch.
World Salt Foundation
World Team
World Witness
Youth for Christ / USA
Youth With A Mission (YWAM)
YUGO Ministries

EVANGELISM, STUDENT

African Bible Colleges
Ambassadors for Christ, Inc.
Big World Ventures Inc.
Cadence International
Campus Crusade for Christ
Carpenter's Tools
China Outreach Ministries
Christian Outreach Intl.
Crossover Communications Intl.
Eastern European Bible Mission
Evangelism Explosion III Intl.
Greater Europe Mission
High School Evangelism Flwshp.
India Rural Evangelical Flwshp
International Students, Inc

InterVarsity Mission
Japanese Evangelical Msnry Soc
Jews for Jesus
Latin America Assistance, Inc.
Latin America Mission
LIFE Ministries
Mission Ministries, Inc.
Mission to the Americas
Mission To Unreached Peoples
Missions To Japan, Inc.
Navigators, The
Network of Intl Christian Schs
On The Go Ministries
Pioneers
Reach Ministries International
Rosedale Mennonite Missions
Seventh-day Adventists
Teen Missions International
Voice of China and Asia
Worldwide Discipleship Assoc.
Young Life
Youth for Christ / USA

FUNDS TRANSMISSION

Advancing Native Missions
All Peoples Baptist Mission
Ambassadors for Christ Intl.
Apostolic Christian Church
Back to the Bible Intl.
Bible Literature International
Children of India Foundation
China Ministries International
Christ for the Nations, Inc.
Christian Life Missions
Christian Mission for the Deaf
Christian Msns. in Many Lands
Christian Services, Inc.
Church of God (Seventh Day)
CSI Ministries
East West Ministries
East West Missionary Service
European Missions Outreach
Faith Christian Fellowship
Fellowship of Assoc. Medical
Friends for Missions, Inc.
Global Strategy Mission Assoc.

Go Ye Fellowship
Habitat for Humanity Intl
India National Inland Mission
Intl. Foundation for EWHA
Living Water Teaching Intl.
Maranatha Baptist Mission
Mazahua Mission
Medical Missions Philippines
Missionary Revival Crusade
National Baptist Conv. of Am.
NEED, Inc.
Outreach, Inc.
Overseas Council for Theol Ed.
Pilgrim Fellowship, Inc.
Presbyterian Missionary Union
Project Partner with Christ
Reciprocal Ministries Intl.
Red Sea Mission Team
Ripe for Harvest, Inc.
RREACH International
Seed Company, The
Seventh Day Baptist Msny. Soc.
Sowers International, The
Spiritual Growth Resources
STEER, Inc.
VELA Ministries International
World Baptist Fellowship Msn
World Outreach Ministries
World-Wide Missions

FURLOUGHED MISSIONARY SUPPORT

Cedar Lane Missionary Homes
Mission Training International
Missionary Auto-Truck Service
Missionary Retreat Fellowship
Missionary TECH Team
Providence Mission Homes, Inc.

INFORMATION SERVICES

ACMC
AD2000 & Beyond Movement
Adopt-A-People Clearinghouse
ASSIST - Aid to Special Saints
Billy Graham Center, The

China Service Coordinating Ofc
Cities for Christ Worldwide
Episcopal Church Msnry Commun.
Evangelical Missions Info Serv
General Assoc Regular Baptists
Inter-Mission International
Issachar Frontier Missions
LIGHT International, Inc.
Mission Aviation Fellowship
Mission Connection, The
Mission Services Association
Mission Training International
Mission Trng. & Resource Ctr.
Missionary Information Exch.
Missions Resource Center
Overcomer Press, Inc.
Reformed Baptist Mission Svcs.
U.S. Center for World Mission
Worldwide Discipleship Assoc.

LEADERSHIP DEVELOPMENT

ABWE
ACMC
ACTS International Ministries
Advancing Native Missions
Africa Inland Mission Intl
Africa Inter-Mennonite Mission
African Christian Mission
African Enterprise, Inc.
African Leadership
African Mission Evangelism
American Baptist Churches USA
Baptist General Conference
Barnabas International
Berean Mission, Inc.
Bible Alliance Mission, Inc.
Biblical Ministries Worldwide
Big World Ventures Inc.
BILD International
Billy Graham Center, The
Brethren Church Missionary Bd.
CBInternational
China Ministries International
Christ for the City Intl.
Christian Leadership Dev.
Christian Reformed World Msns.

Church of God (Anderson, IN)
Church of the Nazarene
Church Resource Ministries
CityTeam Ministries
CMF International
Crossover Communications Intl.
Cumberland Presbyterian Church
DAWN Ministries
East-West Ministries Intl.
Elim Fellowship World Missions
Episcopal Church, Msny. Soc.
Evangelical Free Church Msn.
Evangelical Friends Mission
Evangelical Lutheran Church
Evangelical Mennonite Church
Evangelical Presbyterian Ch.
Evangelism Resources
Fellowship International Msn.
Foursquare Missions Intl.
Free Methodist World Missions
Friends United Meeting
Global Advance
Globe Missionary Evangelism
Gospel for Asia
Grace Brethren Intl. Missions
Grace Ministries International
Harvest
Help for Christian Nationals
Hinduism Intl. Ministries
His Word To The Nations
IDEA/PROLADES
India Gospel Outreach
Institute Intl Christian Comm
Inter-Mission International
International Leadership Smnrs
International Needs - USA
International Outreach Mins.
International Partnership Mins
International Teams, U.S.A.
International Urban Associates
InterVarsity Mission
Intl. Inst. Christian Studies
Intl. Pentecostal Holiness Ch.
Japan - North American Comm
Kingdom Building Ministries
Latin America Mission
LIFE Ministries

Lion and Lamb Outreach
Luis Palau Evangelistic Assoc.
Lutheran Church-Missouri Synod
Lutheran World Relief
Mennonite Board of Missions
Mennonite Brethren Msns/Svcs
Mission Possible Foundation
Mission to the Americas
Next Towns Crusade, Inc.
OC International, Inc.
Omega World Missions
OMF International
On The Go Ministries
Overseas Council for Theol Ed.
Partners in Asian Missions
Partners International
Pioneers
Presb. Evangelistic Fellowship
Presbyterian Church (USA)
Rehoboth Ministries, Inc
Romanian Missionary Society
RREACH International
SEND International
Society for Europe's Evang.
South American Missionary Soc.
Spiritual Overseers Service
TCM International
Team Expansion, Inc.
UFM International
United Board for Christian Ed.
United Church Board World Mins
United Methodist Church
United World Mission
VELA Ministries International
Venture Middle East
Virginia Mennonite Bd. of Msns
Walk Thru The Bible Ministries
Witnessing Mins. of Christ
World Partners Missionary Ch.
World Reach, Inc.
World Team
World Thrust, Inc.

LINGUISTICS

Africa Inter-Mennonite Mission
Christian Literature Crusade

Evangelical Presbyterian Ch.
Link Care Center
Lutheran Bible Translators
New Tribes Mission
Pioneer Bible Translators
TEAM
Virginia Mennonite Bd. of Msns
Wycliffe Bible Translators

LITERACY

Baptist Mid-Missions
Carver Foreign Missions, Inc.
Christian Dynamics
Christian Literacy Associates
Christian Reformed Wrld Relief
CMF International
General Baptists International
Grace Brethren Intl. Missions
Literacy & Evangelism Intl.
Lutheran Bible Translators
Lutheran Brethren World Msns.
Mission 21 India
New Tribes Mission
Omega World Missions
Pioneer Bible Translators
Salvation Army, U.S.A.
Seed Company, The
WEC International
Witnessing Mins. of Christ
Wycliffe Bible Translators

LITERATURE DISTRIBUTION

African Methodist Epis. Zion
All God's Children Intl.
Allegheny Wesleyan Meth. Msns.
American Tract Society
AMF International
Anis Shorrosh Evang. Assoc.
Arab World Ministries
Asian Outreach U.S.A.
ASSIST - Aid to Special Saints
Back to the Bible Intl.
BALL World Missions
Baptist International Missions
Bethany Fellowship Missions

Bethel Pentecostal Temple
Bible Alliance Mission, Inc.
Bible Literature International
Bible Missionary Church
Brazil Gospel Fellowship Msn.
Calvary Evangelistic Mission
Carver Foreign Missions, Inc.
CBInternational
CEIFA Ministries International
Children's Medical Ministries
China Outreach Ministries
Chosen People Ministries
Christ for India Ministries
Christ for India, Inc.
Christ for the Nations, Inc.
Christian Aid Mission
Christian Broadcasting Network
Christian Laymen's Msny Evang
Christian Leadership Dev.
Christian Life Missions
Christian Literature Bible Ctr
Christian Literature Crusade
Christian Literature Intl.
Christian Printing Mission
Christian Salvage Mission
Christian Union Mission
Christian World Publishers
Church of God (Seventh Day)
Church of God Apostolic Faith
Church of God World Missions
Church of the Nazarene
Concordia Gospel Outreach
Cook Communications Ministries
Derek Prince Ministries, Intl.
Eastern European Bible Mission
European Christian Mission
Evangel Bible Translators
Evangelical Bible Mission
Evangelistic Faith Missions
Evangelize China Fellowship
Every Home for Christ
French International Mission
Friends of Israel Gospel Min.
Friendship International
Full Gospel Evangelistic Assoc
Global Advance
Gospel Mission of S. America

Gospel Revival Ministries
Grace and Truth, Inc.
Grand Old Gospel Fellowship
Harvest Intl. Christian Outrch
Harvestime Intl. Network
Harvesting In Spanish
Heart to Heart Intl Ministries
Help for Christian Nationals
Hermano Pablo Ministries
India Evangelical Mission
India National Inland Mission
International Cooperating Mins
International Gospel League
International Missions, Inc.
International Needs - USA
Intl. Board of Jewish Missions
Intl. Christian Lit. Distrib.
Intl. Discipleship Mission
Intl. Pentecostal Ch of Christ
Iranian Christians Intl.
Ireland Outreach Intl., Inc.
Jews for Jesus
John Milton Society for Blind
Key Communications
Latin America Mission
Lutheran Braille Workers
Lutheran Brethren World Msns.
Lutheran Lit. Soc. for Chinese
Macedonia World Baptist Msns.
Message of Life, Inc.
Mexican Christian Mission
Mexican Mission Ministries
Middle East Christian Outreach
Middle East Media - USA
Mission 21 India
Missionary Crusader, Inc.
Morelli Ministries Intl.
Muslim Hope
New Life League International
Open Bible Ministries
Open Bible Standard Churches
Open Doors with Brother Andrew
Operation Mobilization
Oriental Missionary Crusade
Orthodox Presbyterian Church
Outreach To Asia Nationals
Pan American Missions

Pass the Torch Ministries
Pentecostal Church of God
Peter Deyneka Russian Mins.
Presbyterian Missionary Union
Prison Mission Association
Radio Bible Class
Reformation Translation Flwshp
Reformed Presbyterian Church
Romanian Mission of Chicago
Romanian Missionary Society
Scripture Union (USA)
SGM International
Source of Light Ministries
Spanish World Gospel Mission
TCM International
Tele-Missions International
Training Evangelistic Ldrshp.
Trinity Intl. Baptist Mission
Turkish World Outreach
UIM International
Voice of the Martyrs, The
Walk Thru The Bible Ministries
Word To Russia
World Baptist Fellowship Msn
World Missionary Press, Inc.
World Opportunities Intl.

LITERATURE PRODUCTION

American Tract Society
American Waldensian Society
Arabic Communication Center
Asian Outreach U.S.A.
Assemblies of God
Back to the Bible Intl.
Baptist Mid-Missions
BCM International
Bethany Fellowship Missions
Biblical Literature Fellowship
CAM International
CBInternational
Chinese Christian Mission, Inc
Christ Community Church
Christian Leadership Dev.
Christian Literature Crusade
Christian Printing Mission
Christian Union Mission

Christian World Publishers
Derek Prince Ministries, Intl.
Evangelical Lutheran Synod
Evangelism Explosion III Intl.
Every Home for Christ
Friends of Israel Gospel Min.
Global Evangelization Movement
Global Harvest Ministries
Global Mapping International
Gospel Mission of S. America
Grace and Truth, Inc.
Harvestime Intl. Network
ICI University
Institute of Chinese Studies
International Bible Society
International Cooperating Mins
International Leadership Smnrs
International Outreach Mins.
Intl. Board of Jewish Missions
Iranian Christians Intl.
John Milton Society for Blind
Literacy & Evangelism Intl.
LOGOI/FLET
Luis Palau Evangelistic Assoc.
Lutheran Bible Translators
Lutheran Braille Workers
Lutheran Brethren World Msns.
Lutheran Lit. Soc. for Chinese
Macedonia World Baptist Msns.
Men for Missions Intl.
Mennonite Board of Missions
Message of Life, Inc.
Ministry to Eastern Europe
Mission Possible Foundation
Missionary Crusader, Inc.
Navigators, The
New Life League International
OMF International
Overcomer Press, Inc.
Pioneer Clubs
Radio Bible Class
Reach Ministries International
Reformation Translation Flwshp
Reformed Baptist Mission Svcs.
Romanian Missionary Society
Scripture Union (USA)
SGM International

Source of Light Ministries
Spiritual Growth Resources
Teen Missions International
UIM International
Walk Thru The Bible Ministries
Westminister Biblical Missions
Wisconsin Evang. Lutheran Syn.
World In Need - USA
World Missionary Press, Inc.

MANAGEMENT CONSULTING/TRAINING

ACMC
Barnabas International
Christian Services, Inc.
Enterprise Development Intl.
Global Reach
Media Associates International
Paraclete Mission Group, Inc.
Partners International
Venture Middle East

MEDICAL SUPPLIES

All God's Children Intl.
Blessings International
Children of India Foundation
CHOSEN, Inc.
Christian Advance Intl.
Christian Aid Ministries
Christian Blind Mission Intl.
Christian Pilots Association
Christian Printing Mission
Compassion International, Inc.
Episcopal Church, Msny. Soc.
Flying Doctors of America
For Haiti with Love Inc.
Friends for Missions, Inc.
Grace Ministries International
In Touch Mission Intl.
Interchurch Medical Assistance
International Aid, Inc.
International Child Care
Intl. Christian Leprosy Msn.
ISOH/Impact
Lott Carey Baptist Mission

Ludhiana Christian Medical Col
MAP International
Medical Missions Philippines
Mission of Mercy
Mission Soc. for United Meth.
Missionary Dentists
National Baptist Conv. USA
Operation Blessing Intl.
Presb. Order for World Evang.
Society of St. Margaret
World Concern
World Help

MEDICINE, INCL. DENTAL AND PUBLIC HEALTH

ABWE
Africa Evangelical Fellowship
Africa Inland Mission Intl
ALM International
American Baptist Churches USA
Barnabas Ministries, Inc.
Berean Mission, Inc.
Bibles For The World
Brethren Church Missionary Bd.
Brethren in Christ World Msns.
Children's Medical Ministries
Christian Church of North Am.
Christian Dental Society
Christian Medical & Dental Soc
Christian Reformed Wrld Relief
Church of God in Christ, Menn.
Church of God World Missions
Church of the United Brethren
CMF International
ComCare International
Correll Missionary Ministries
Evangelical Covenant Church
Evangelical Methodist Church
Fellowship of Assoc. Medical
Flying Doctors of America
Foundation For His Ministry
Free Will Baptist Association
Friends United Meeting
General Baptists International
Global Outreach Mission
Global Outreach, Ltd.

Grace Brethren Intl. Missions
HCJB World Radio Msny. Flwshp.
Health Teams International
India Evangelical Mission
International Child Care
InterServe/USA
ISOH/Impact
Larry Jones International Mins
Ludhiana Christian Medical Col
Luke Society, The
MAP International
Medical Ambassadors Intl.
Mennonite Board of Missions
Mennonite Central Committee
Mercy Ships
Mexican Medical, Inc.
Middle East Christian Outreach
Mission Soc. for United Meth.
Missionary Dentists
Moravian Church North America
Mustard Seed, Inc.
NEED, Inc.
North American Baptist Conf.
Operation Blessing Intl.
PAZ International
Presbyterian Church (USA)
Primitive Methodist Church USA
Ramabai Mukti Mission
Reformed Church In America
Reformed Episcopal Bd Missions
Salvation Army, U.S.A.
Seventh-day Adventists
SIM USA
Southern Baptist Intl. Mission
TEAM
The Master's Mission, Inc.
UFM International
United Church Board World Mins
Vellore Christian Medical Col.
WEC International
Wesleyan World Missions
Witnessing Mins. of Christ
World Concern
World Gospel Mission
World Mission Prayer League
World Reach, Inc.
World Relief Corporation

World Witness
World-Wide Missions

NATIONAL CHURCH
NURTURE/SUPPORT

Action International Mins.
Advancing Indigenous Missions
Advancing Native Missions
Africa Evangelical Fellowship
Africa Inter-Mennonite Mission
African Christian Mission
American Baptist Churches USA
American Waldensian Society
Anglican Orthodox Church
Asian Outreach U.S.A.
Assoc of Free Lutheran Congs
Baptist Bible Fellowship Intl.
Baptist General Conference
Baptist World Mission
Barnabas International
Bible Missionary Church
Brethren Church Missionary Bd.
Brethren in Christ World Msns.
Christ Community Church
Christian and Msny. Alliance
Christian Associates Intl.
Christian Church (Disciples)
Christian Methodist Episcopal
Christian Reformed World Msns.
Christians In Action, Inc.
Church of God (Holiness) Msn.
Church of God (Seventh Day)
Church of God, The
Church of The Brethren
Church of the United Brethren
Church Planting International
Churches of Christ in Union
Congregational Christian Chs.
Congregational Holiness Church
Conservative Cong. Christian
Covenant Celebration Church
Cumberland Presbyterian Church
East-West Ministries Intl.
Eastern Mennonite Missions
Emmanuel Intl. Mission (U.S.)
Episcopal Church, Msny. Soc.

Episcopal World Mission
Evangelical Congregational Ch.
Evangelical Covenant Church
Evangelical Lutheran Church
Evangelical Presbyterian Ch.
Every Child Ministries, Inc.
Every Home for Christ
Forward Edge International
Foursquare Missions Intl.
Free Gospel Church Msns. Dept.
Friends United Meeting
Friendship Ministries
Full Gospel Evangelistic Assoc
General Baptists International
General Conf. Mennonite Church
Global Advance
Gospel Furthering Fellowship
Help for Christian Nationals
His Word To The Nations
ICI University
Independent Gospel Missions
India Gospel Outreach
India Rural Evangelical Flwshp
InterAct Ministries
International Gospel Outreach
InterServe/USA
Intl. Pentecostal Holiness Ch.
Iranian Christians Intl.
Island Missionary Society
Japanese Evangelical Msnry Soc
Latin America Lutheran Mission
Liberia Christian Mission
Liberty Corner Mission
LIFE Ministries
Mahesh Chavda Ministries Intl.
Mazahua Mission
Middle East Christian Outreach
Ministries In Action
Mission Possible Foundation
Mission Soc. for United Meth.
Mission to the Americas
Mission To Unreached Peoples
Missions To Japan, Inc.
Moravian Church North America
Morelli Ministries Intl.
Next Towns Crusade, Inc.
OC International, Inc.

OMF International
OMS International, Inc.
Pacific NW Mennonite Conf.
PAZ International
Pentecostal Free Will Bapt.Ch.
Pillar of Fire Missions Intl.
Presbyterian Church (USA)
Presbyterian Missionary Union
Primitive Methodist Church USA
Project Mercy, Inc.
Reciprocal Ministries Intl.
Ripe for Harvest, Inc.
SEND International
Seventh Day Baptist Msny. Soc.
SIM USA
Slavic Gospel Association
Slavic Missionary Service
South America Mission
South American Missionary Soc.
Southern Baptist Intl. Mission
TCM International
Training Evangelistic Ldrshp.
UIM International
United Church Board World Mins
United Methodist Church
United World Mission
Venture Middle East
Virginia Mennonite Bd. of Msns
Wesleyan World Missions
Westminister Biblical Missions
Wisconsin Evang. Lutheran Syn.
World Harvest Mission
World Horizons
World Indigenous Missions
World Mission Associates
World Mission Prayer League
World Missions Fellowship
World Partners Missionary Ch.
World Servants
World Team

PSYCHOLOGICAL COUNSELING

Barnabas International
Friendship Ministries
Link Care Center
Narramore Christian Foundation

PURCHASING SERVICES

Christian Dental Society
Equipping the Saints
Mission Aviation Fellowship
Missionary Auto-Truck Service
Vellore Christian Medical Col.

RECRUITING/MOBILIZING

ACMC
AD2000 & Beyond Movement
Ambassadors for Christ, Inc.
ARISE International
Artists In Christian Testimony
Bethany Fellowship Missions
Bridge Builders International
Caleb Project
China Service Coordinating Ofc
Chinese Christian Mission, Inc
Christian Information Service
Christian Outreach Intl.
Crossover Communications Intl.
Emmaus Road, International
Episcopal Church Msnry Commun.
Episcopal World Mission
Frontiers
Global Opportunities
Global Strategy Mission Assoc.
Go International
Harvest Intl. Christian Outrch
HBI Global Partners
Institute of Hindu Studies
International Messengers
International Teams, U.S.A.
InterVarsity Mission
Intl. Pentecostal Holiness Ch.
Issachar Frontier Missions
Kingdom Building Ministries
Mission Connection, The
Mission To Unreached Peoples
Missionary Action, Inc.
Missions Outreach Intl.
Operation Mobilization
Presb. Center for Msn. Studies
Priority One International
Share International

Shield of Faith Ministries
Strategic Ventures Network
Team Expansion, Inc.
U.S. Center for World Mission
VELA Ministries International
Vellore Christian Medical Col.
World Harvest Mission
World Horizons
World In Need - USA
World Indigenous Missions
World Mission Associates
World Servants
World Team
World Thrust, Inc.
Wycliffe Associates, Inc.

RELIEF AND/OR REHABILITATION

Advent Christian World Msns.
African Enterprise, Inc.
All God's Children Intl.
Apostolic Christian Church
Blessings International
Bright Hope International
CEIFA Ministries International
Childcare International
Children's Medical Ministries
Christian Aid Ministries
Christian and Msny. Alliance
Christian Reformed Wrld Relief
Church of The Brethren
Church World Service & Witness
Dorcas Aid International USA
Eastern European Outreach
Flying Doctors of America
Food for the Hungry
For Haiti with Love Inc.
Foundation For His Ministry
Friends in the West
Globe Missionary Evangelism
Haiti Gospel Mission
International Aid, Inc.
Intl. Church Relief Fund
Larry Jones International Mins
Lutheran World Relief
MAP International
Mennonite Central Committee

Mercy Ships
Mission Ministries, Inc.
Mission of Mercy
Mission Possible
Muslim Hope
Mustard Seed, Inc.
NEED, Inc.
Operation Blessing Intl.
Project Mercy, Inc.
Romanian Mission of Chicago
Samaritan's Purse
Seventh-day Adventists
Shelter Now International
Slavic Gospel Association
Southern Baptist Intl. Mission
Venture Middle East
World Concern
World Opportunities Intl.
World Relief Corporation
World Vision
Youth With A Mission (YWAM)

RESEARCH

AD2000 & Beyond Movement
Advancing Native Missions
Billy Graham Center, The
China Ministries International
China Service Coordinating Ofc
Cooperative Baptist Fellowship
Daystar U.S.
European Evangelistic Society
Global Evangelization Movement
Gospel Outreach Mins. Intl.
Gospel Recordings USA
Handclasp International, Inc.
IDEA/PROLADES
Institute Intl Christian Comm
Institute of Chinese Studies
Institute of Hindu Studies
Issachar Frontier Missions
Japanese Evangelization Center
Kingdom Building Ministries
LIGHT International, Inc.
Link Care Center
MARC
Mission Services Association

Mission Training International
Mission Trng. & Resource Ctr.
Missions Resource Center
OC International, Inc.
Overseas Council for Theol Ed.
Overseas Ministries Study Ctr.
Paraclete Mission Group, Inc.
People International
Peter Deyneka Russian Mins.
Presb. Center for Msn. Studies
Sentinel Group, The
Southern Baptist Intl. Mission
STEM Ministries
U.S. Center for World Mission
VELA Ministries International

Mission Safety International
Mission Training International
Missionaire International
Missionary Auto-Truck Service
Missionary Flights Intl.
Missionary TECH Team
National Religious Broadcaster
Presb. Center for Msn. Studies
Priority One International
Sentinel Group, The
Shelter Now International
STEER, Inc.
TMA Ministries
World Missions Far Corners

SERVICES FOR OTHER AGENCIES

AD2000 & Beyond Movement
Adopt-A-People Clearinghouse
Artists In Christian Testimony
Audio Scripture Ministries
Caleb Project
China Service Coordinating Ofc
Christian Dental Society
Christian Information Service
Christian Salvage Mission
Door of Hope International
East West Missionary Service
ECHO
Global Mapping International
Global Reach
Gospel Literature Intl.
Gospel Recordings USA
Handclasp International, Inc.
Health Teams International
Helps International Ministries
IDEA/PROLADES
Institute of Chinese Studies
Inter-Mission International
Intercristo
INTERDEV
International Aid, Inc.
International Bible Society
International Films, Inc.
Issachar Frontier Missions
Literacy & Evangelism Intl.

SHORT-TERM PROGRAMS COORDINATION

AMOR Ministries
Big World Ventures Inc.
Blossoming Rose
Bridge Builders International
Caleb Project
Calvary International
Celebrant Singers
Childcare International
Christ for the City Intl.
Christian Medical & Dental Soc
Christian Outreach Intl.
Church of God (Anderson, IN)
Conservative Cong. Christian
CSI Ministries
Eastern European Outreach
Emmaus Road, International
Engineering Ministries Intl.
Evangelical Free Church Msn.
Evangelical Lutheran Church
Fellowship of Assoc. Medical
Flying Doctors of America
Forward Edge International
Go International
Habitat for Humanity Intl
Harvest Intl. Christian Outrch
Health Teams International
High School Evangelism Flwshp.
International Crusades, Inc.
International Family Missions

International Messengers
Japanese Evangelical Msnry Soc
Kingdom Building Ministries
Latin America Lutheran Mission
Macedonian Missionary Service
Marriage Ministries Intl.
Men for Missions Intl.
Missionary Athletes Intl.
Missions Outreach Intl.
Mutual Faith Ministries Intl.
New Tribes Mission
Pioneers
Sowers International, The
STEM Ministries
TEAM
Teen Missions International
Teen World Outreach
World Horizons
World Missions Fellowship
World Servants
Wycliffe Associates, Inc.
YUGO Ministries

SUPPLYING EQUIPMENT

Bezalel World Outreach/Galcom
CHOSEN, Inc.
Christian Dental Society
Equipping the Saints
Evangelical Bible Mission
Habitat for Humanity Intl
International Aid, Inc.
Lifewater International
Mission Aviation Fellowship
Progressive Natl Bapt Conv USA
Samaritan's Purse
Vellore Christian Medical Col.

SUPPORT OF NATIONAL WORKERS

Advancing Indigenous Missions
African Methodist Epis. Zion
Ambassadors for Christ Intl.
AmeriTribes
AMG International
Anglican Orthodox Church
Apostolic Christian Church

ARISE International
Assoc of Free Lutheran Congs
Back to the Bible Intl.
BALL World Missions
Bibles For The World
BILD International
Bridge Builders International
Bright Hope International
Carver Foreign Missions, Inc.
Child Evangelism Fellowship
Christ for India Ministries
Christ for India, Inc.
Christ for the Island World
Christian Advance Intl.
Christian Aid Mission
Christian Dynamics
Christian Outreach Intl.
Church of God (Anderson, IN)
Church of God (Holiness) Msn.
Church of God World Missions
Church of the United Brethren
Congregational Holiness Church
Correll Missionary Ministries
Covenant Celebration Church
Cumberland Presbyterian Church
David Livingstone Msny Fndtn
Dayspring Enterprises Intl.
Door of Hope International
East West Ministries
Eastern European Bible Mission
Eastern European Outreach
Episcopal Church, Msny. Soc.
Evangelical Congregational Ch.
Evangelical Friends Mission
Evangelical Presbyterian Ch.
Evangelism Resources
Evangelistic Faith Missions
FOCAS
French International Mission
Friends Church Southwest
Fundamental Bapt. Msn Trinidad
General Baptists International
Gospel for Asia
Gospel Outreach Mins. Intl.
Gospel Recordings USA
Gospel Revival Ministries
Have Christ Will Travel Mins.

Help for Christian Nationals
HOPE Bible Mission, Inc.
Hosanna
In Touch Mission Intl.
Independent Gospel Missions
India Evangelical Mission
India Gospel Outreach
International Gospel League
International Needs - USA
International Partnership Mins
Intl. Christian Leprosy Msn.
Latin America Lutheran Mission
Lion and Lamb Outreach
Lott Carey Baptist Mission
Luke Society, The
Medical Ambassadors Intl.
Mennonite Brethren Msns/Svcs
Metropolitan Church Assoc.
Mexican Border Missions
Mexican Christian Mission
Ministry to Eastern Europe
Mission O.N.E., Inc.
Mission Possible
Mission to the World
Missionaire International
Missionary Action, Inc.
Missionary Gospel Fellowship
National Baptist Conv. of Am.
New Life League International
Omega World Missions
Outreach To Asia Nationals
Partners in Asian Missions
Partners International
PAZ International
Peter Deyneka Russian Mins.
Prakash Association USA
Precious Seed Ministries
Presb. Evangelistic Fellowship
Project Care
Ramabai Mukti Mission
Reach Ministries International
Romanian Mission of Chicago
Salvation Army, U.S.A.
Samaritan's Purse
Schwenkfelder Church in USA
Seed Company, The
Share International

Sowers International, The
Spanish World Gospel Mission
Trans World Missions
VELA Ministries International
Voice of China and Asia
World Missions Far Corners
World Witness
World-Wide Missions

TECHNICAL ASSISTANCE

Bezalel World Outreach/Galcom
Big World Ventures Inc.
Children's Medical Ministries
CHOSEN, Inc.
Christian Blind Mission Intl.
ECHO
Engineering Ministries Intl.
Enterprise Development Intl.
Farms International, Inc.
Global Mapping International
Gospel Recordings USA
Habitat for Humanity Intl
HCJB World Radio Msny. Flwshp.
Heifer Project International
Helps International Ministries
Holt Intl. Children's Services
IDEA/PROLADES
Interchurch Medical Assistance
International Child Care
International Films, Inc.
JAARS, Inc.
JAF Ministries
Lifewater International
M/E International
Media Associates International
Men for Missions Intl.
Mennonite Central Committee
Mission Aides, Inc.
Mission Aviation Fellowship
Mission Safety International
Mission To Unreached Peoples
Missionary Maintenance Svcs.
Missionary TECH Team
Paraclete Mission Group, Inc.
Project Mercy, Inc.
SAND Institutes International

Self-Help Foundation
Servants in Faith & Technology
The Master's Mission, Inc.
TMA Ministries
United Board for Christian Ed.
World Relief Corporation
World Vision
Wycliffe Bible Translators

TRAINING, OTHER

ACTS International Ministries
Advancing Renewal Ministries
African Enterprise, Inc.
Agape Gospel Mission
Ambassadors for Christ Intl.
AMF International
AMOR Ministries
Artists In Christian Testimony
Billy Graham Evang. Assoc.
Calvary Commission, Inc.
Campus Crusade for Christ
Child Evangelism Fellowship
Childcare International
Christ for India, Inc.
Christian Leadership Dev.
Christian Literacy Associates
Church of God of Prophecy
Cities for Christ Worldwide
Cook Communications Ministries
East-West Ministries Intl.
ECHO
Enterprise Development Intl.
Evangelism Explosion III Intl.
Every Child Ministries, Inc.
Global Harvest Ministries
Global Mapping International
Global Opportunities
Global Reach
Habitat for Humanity Intl
Harvest
Harvest Evangelism, Inc.
HBI Global Partners
Heifer Project International
Help for Christian Nationals
Hosanna
InterAct Ministries

INTERDEV
International Crusades, Inc.
International Films, Inc.
International Students, Inc
International Urban Associates
Iranian Christians Intl.
JAF Ministries
Jews for Jesus
Kingdom Building Ministries
Lifewater International
LIGHT International, Inc.
Mahesh Chavda Ministries Intl.
MAP International
Marriage Ministries Intl.
Media Associates International
Mennonite Central Committee
Mercy Ships
Ministry to Eastern Europe
Missionary Maintenance Svcs.
Narramore Christian Foundation
Navigators, The
Oriental Missionary Crusade
Pass the Torch Ministries
Pioneer Clubs
Pocket Testament League
Prison Fellowship Intl.
Progressive Vision
Reciprocal Ministries Intl.
RREACH International
Salvation Army, U.S.A.
SAND Institutes International
Scripture Union (USA)
Self-Help Foundation
Sentinel Group, The
Servants in Faith & Technology
Share International
Shelter Now International
Slavic Gospel Association
Training Evangelistic Ldrshp.
Tribes and Nations Outreach
United Board for Christian Ed.
University Language Service
VELA Ministries International
World Concern
World Mission Associates
Worldwide Discipleship Assoc.
Wycliffe Bible Translators

TRAINING/ORIENTATION, MISSIONARY

Adopt-A-People Clearinghouse
ALM International
Apostolic Team Ministries Intl
Baptist Bible Fellowship Intl.
BCM International
Bethany Fellowship Missions
Bethany Missionary Association
Caleb Project
Calvary International
China Ministries International
Chosen People Ministries
Christian Aid Mission
Christians In Action, Inc.
Church of God of Prophecy
CityTeam Ministries
Deaf Missions International
Emmanuel Intl. Mission (U.S.)
Emmaus Road, International
Episcopal Church Msnry Commun.
Evangelical Covenant Church
Evangelical Lutheran Church
Global Advance
Global Strategy Mission Assoc.
Gospel for Asia
Harvest Intl. Christian Outrch
HBI Global Partners
Hinduism Intl. Ministries
Institute of Hindu Studies
International Family Missions
International Messengers
International Teams, U.S.A.
InterVarsity Mission
Japanese Evangelical Msnry Soc
Liebenzell Mission USA
Link Care Center
Lion and Lamb Outreach
Living Water Teaching Intl.
Lutheran Bible Translators
Lutheran Youth Encounter
Macedonian Missionary Service
Mennonite Board of Missions
Mission O.N.E., Inc.
Mission Soc. for United Meth.

Mission Training International
Mission Trng. & Resource Ctr.
Navigators, The
New Tribes Mission
Next Towns Crusade, Inc.
No Greater Love Ministries
OC International, Inc.
Operation Mobilization
ORA International
Paraclete Mission Group, Inc.
PAZ International
Peoples Mission International
Pioneer Bible Translators
Project Christ International
Reach Ministries International
Shield of Faith Mission Intl.
Team Expansion, Inc.
Teen Missions International
United World Mission
World Indigenous Missions
World Servants
World Team
Wycliffe Bible Translators
Youth With A Mission (YWAM)

TRANSLATION, BIBLE

ABWE
Africa Inter-Mennonite Mission
African Christian Mission
American Bible Society
Baptist Mid-Missions
Churches of Christ in Union
Evangel Bible Translators
Evangelical Baptist Missions
International Bible Society
Lutheran Bible Translators
New Tribes Mission
Pioneer Bible Translators
Reformed Episcopal Bd Missions
Romanian Missionary Society
Russian Bible Society, Inc.
Seed Company, The
WEC International
World Bible Translation Center
Wycliffe Associates, Inc.
Wycliffe Bible Translators

TRANSLATION, OTHER

Biblical Literature Fellowship
Christian Printing Mission
Derek Prince Ministries, Intl.
European Missions Outreach
Gospel Literature Intl.
INTERCOMM
Ministry to Eastern Europe
Radio Bible Class
Reformation Translation Flwshp

VIDEO/FILM
PRODUCTION/DISTRIBUTION

Assemblies of God
Billy Graham Evang. Assoc.
Caleb Project
Campus Crusade for Christ
Celebrant Singers
Christian Broadcasting Network
Dayspring Enterprises Intl.
Derek Prince Ministries, Intl.
Emmaus Road, International
Evangelical Baptist Missions
Good News Productions Intl.
Handclasp International, Inc.
HCJB World Radio Msny. Flwshp.
High Adventure Ministries
Institute of Chinese Studies
INTERCOMM
International Films, Inc.
Intl. Board of Jewish Missions
LOGOI/FLET
Messenger Films, Inc.
Middle East Christian Outreach
Middle East Media - USA
Mission Services Association
Moody Institute of Science
Overseas Radio & Television
Pan American Missions
Priority One International
Progressive Vision
Rio Grande Bible Institute
Servants in Faith & Technology
Tele-Missions International

Walk Thru The Bible Ministries
World Mission Associates

YOUTH PROGRAMS

ABWE
African Enterprise, Inc.
Big World Ventures Inc.
Cadence International
Campus Crusade for Christ
Carpenter's Tools
Christian Services, Inc.
Christian Union Mission
CityTeam Ministries
Compassion International, Inc.
Congregational Christian Chs.
Cornerstone, The
Door of Hope International
Eastern European Bible Mission
Evangelism Explosion III Intl.
Fellowship International Msn.
Friendship International
Have Christ Will Travel Mins.
Hellenic Ministries
High School Evangelism Flwshp.
Hope for the Hungry
Icthus International
International Street Kids Mins
Kids Alive International
Latin America Assistance, Inc.
Lutheran Youth Encounter
Mennonite Central Committee
Mexican Mission Ministries
Pioneer Clubs
Rosedale Mennonite Missions
Scripture Union (USA)
Teen Missions International
Teen World Outreach
Word of Life Fellowship
World Servants
World Witness
Young Life
Youth for Christ / USA
Youth With A Mission (YWAM)
YUGO Ministries

Chapter 6

Countries of activity for U.S. Protestant agencies

In this chapter you will find the countries where agencies reported field personnel in answer to question #12 of the survey questionnaire (see the appendix for details). The few exceptions to this are agencies whose whole program supports—with funds raised in the U.S., but which may not be designated to specific personnel on a regular basis—churches or other initiatives in a country.

Geopolitical shifts and changes continue to occur throughout the world. We have made every attempt to indicate changes of country names since 1992 in a format that is familiar to the North American perspective. For example, due to the recent political changes in the former Zaire, that nation is listed as Congo/Zaire.

All countries are listed in alphabetical order according to the name most commonly recognized in North America. Countries that are part of the Commonwealth of Independent States (most of the former Soviet Union) have been listed separately. Examples of this would

include Armenia, Kyrgyzstan and Belarus. In a few cases we have listed a territory or other administrative district of a country because it is commonly viewed as a separate entity and mission agencies report it that way. An example would be the Azores, located in the Atlantic Ocean 900 miles west of mainland Portugal.

We have separated the personnel totals for all agencies into five categories. Under the "personnel from U.S." heading, the term of expected service has been divided into three categories: 4+ years, 2-4 years and 1-2 years for fully supported personnel. For non-U.S. personnel in the "other countries" heading, the categories are those who are citizens of that ministry country and those who are not citizens, and are fully or partially supported by funds raised in the U.S. by the associated agency. For example, a Korean with specific mission/ministry duties serving in Korea would be included in an agency's "citizens" column of the Korea section. A Korean serving in Russia would be listed in the "not citizen" column of the Russian Federation section.

At the end of each country section, totals of each category for that country are given. Please note that the totals for the "other countries" heading do not necessarily reflect all non-U.S. mission personnel who draw support from U.S. agencies. Some agencies give grants for ongoing institutions and other programs without specifying individual recipients. This may be in addition to U.S. mission personnel based in that country or the agency may not have U.S. personnel living in that country.

COUNTRY Agency	Year Began	Personnel from U.S.			Other Countries	
		4+ Yrs	2-4 Yrs	1-2 Yrs	Citizens	Not Citiz.

AFGHANISTAN

InterServe/USA	1964	15	-	-	-	-
Mennonite Brethren Msns/Svcs	1968	-	2	-	-	-
United Methodist Church		2	-	-	-	-
World Mission Prayer League	1965	3	-	-	-	3
Totals:		20	2	-	-	3

ALBANIA

AMG International	1993	2	-	-	-	1
Assemblies of God	1991	10	-	-	-	-
Baptist Bible Fellowship Intl.	1995	2	-	-	-	-
Baptist International Missions	1996	2	-	-	-	-
Bethany Fellowship Missions	1995	3	-	-	1	1
Brethren Assemblies		6	-	-	-	-
Campus Crusade for Christ	1991	5	-	22	-	-
CBInternational	1992	2	-	3	-	-
CEIFA Ministries International	1991	-	-	-	6	-
Child Evangelism Fellowship	1991	-	-	-	2	3
Christian Aid Mission		-	-	-	2	-
Christian Chs. /Chs. of Christ	1991	-	-	-	-	-
Church of God World Missions	1993	-	-	-	-	2
Church of the Nazarene	1993	4	-	-	-	-
Door of Hope International	1992	4	-	-	-	-
Evangelical Mennonite Church	1995	2	-	-	-	-
Every Home for Christ	1992	-	-	-	6	-
Globe Missionary Evangelism	1995	-	4	-	2	30
Greater Europe Mission	1995	1	-	-	-	-
International Teams, U.S.A.	1992	2	-	-	-	-
Medical Ambassadors Intl.	1995	-	-	-	-	-
Mission Aviation Fellowship	1991	4	-	-	-	-
Paraclete Mission Group, Inc.	1995	2	-	-	-	-
Pioneers	1992	11	-	-	-	-
Presbyterian Church (USA)		7	-	-	-	-
Romanian Mission of Chicago	1995	-	-	-	-	-
SEND International	1993	8	-	-	-	-
Seventh-day Adventists	1992	-	-	-	2	-
Team Expansion, Inc.	1995	6	-	-	-	-
Virginia Mennonite Bd. of Msns	1991	-	2	-	-	-
Wesleyan World Missions	1993	2	-	-	-	-
Wisconsin Evang. Lutheran Syn.	1995	2	-	-	-	-
Youth With A Mission (YWAM)		9	-	-	-	-
Totals:		96	6	25	21	37

COUNTRY Agency	Year Began	Personnel from U.S.			Other Countries	
		4+ Yrs	2-4 Yrs	1-2 Yrs	Citizens	Not Citiz.
AMERICAN SAMOA						
American Baptist Association		2	-	-	-	-
Assemblies of God	1926	2	-	-	-	-
Church of the Nazarene	1960	2	-	-	-	-
Youth for Christ / USA		-	1	-	-	-
Totals:		6	1	-	-	-
ANDORRA						
Elim Fellowship World Missions	1989	2	-	-	-	-
Totals:		2	-	-	-	-
ANGOLA						
Africa Evangelical Fellowship	1914	9	-	-	-	-
Africa Inland Mission Intl	1995	-	-	2	-	-
Assemblies of God	1985	4	-	-	-	-
Christ Community Church	1978	2	-	-	-	-
Church of God World Missions	1938	-	-	-	2	-
Mennonite Brethren Msns/Svcs		-	-	-	1	
Mission to the World	1994	2	-	-	-	-
Seventh-day Adventists	1925	-	-	-	2	-
Southern Baptist Intl. Mission	1968	4	-	-	-	-
United Methodist Church		1	-	-	-	-
World Vision	1970	-	6	1	-	-
Totals:		22	6	3	5	-
ANGUILLA						
Baptist International Missions	1968	2	-	-	-	-
Totals:		2	-	-	-	-
ANTIGUA						
Baptist International Missions	1975	6	-	-	-	-
Habitat for Humanity Intl	1996	-	1	-	-	-
Independent Faith Mission	1950	4	-	-	-	-
Seventh-day Adventists	1944	2	-	-	-	-
Totals:		12	1	-	-	-
ARGENTINA						
ABWE	1978	13	-	-	-	-
Assemblies of God	1910	20	-	-	-	-
Baptist Bible Fellowship Intl.	1959	26	-	-	-	-
Baptist General Conference	1957	14	-	-	-	-
Baptist International Missions	1983	6	-	-	-	-
Baptist Mid-Missions	1987	4	-	-	-	-
Baptist World Mission	1977	4	-	-	-	-
BCM International	1995	-	-	-	2	-

COUNTRY Agency	Year Began	Personnel from U.S.			Other Countries	
		4+ Yrs	2-4 Yrs	1-2 Yrs	Citizens	Not Citiz.
Biblical Ministries Worldwide	1979	9	-	-	-	-
Brethren Assemblies		10	-	-	-	-
Brethren Church Missionary Bd.	1911	1	-	-	-	-
Campus Crusade for Christ	1963	4	-	1	-	-
CBInternational	1947	16	-	2	-	-
Child Evangelism Fellowship	1944	-	-	-	31	1
Chinese Christian Mission, Inc	1992	1	-	-	-	-
Chosen People Ministries	1941	-	-	-	-	3
Christ for the City Intl.	1995	2	-	-	2	-
Christian Aid Mission		-	-	-	9	-
Christian and Msny. Alliance	1897	18	2	-	-	-
Christian Chs. /Chs. of Christ		6	-	-	-	-
Christian Church of North Am.	1975	-	-	-	-	-
Church of God (Anderson, IN)	1927	2	-	-	-	-
Church of God of Prophecy	1955	-	-	-	-	2
Church of the Nazarene	1909	6	-	-	2	-
Elim Fellowship World Missions	1956	2	-	-	-	-
Evangelical Baptist Missions	1974	8	-	-	-	-
Evangelical Lutheran Church	1948	1	-	-	-	-
Evangelical Presbyterian Ch.	1986	3	-	-	-	-
Every Home for Christ	1958	-	-	-	4	-
Full Gospel Grace Fellowship		3	-	-	-	-
Go Ye Fellowship	1968	2	-	-	-	-
Gospel Mission of S. America	1970	6	-	-	-	-
Gospel Missionary Union	1956	13	-	-	1	-
Grace Brethren Intl. Missions	1909	7	-	-	2	-
Harvest Evangelism, Inc.	1985	2	-	-	-	-
Impact International	1975	-	-	-	2	-
International Outreach Mins.	1995	2	-	-	-	-
Latin America Mission	1982	4	2	-	-	-
Maranatha Baptist Mission	1975	4	-	-	-	-
Medical Ambassadors Intl.	1995	-	-	-	6	-
Mennonite Board of Missions	1917	8	-	-	-	-
Mission to the World	1984	2	-	-	-	-
Missionary Revival Crusade	1991	3	-	-	-	-
Navigators, The	1973	4	-	-	-	-
OC International, Inc.	1987	4	-	-	-	-
Presbyterian Church (USA)		13	-	-	-	-
Salvation Army, U.S.A.	1890	6	-	-	-	-
Seventh-day Adventists	1890	2	-	-	6	-
Southern Baptist Intl. Mission	1903	76	5	-	-	-
Spanish World Gospel Mission		-	-	-	1	1
Team Expansion, Inc.	1986	4	-	-	-	-
United Methodist Church		3	-	-	-	-
United Pentecostal Church Intl	1967	8	-	-	-	-
Walk Thru The Bible Ministries	1988	-	-	-	23	-
World Gospel Mission	1970	13	-	-	-	-

COUNTRY	Year	Personnel from U.S.			Other Countries	
Agency	Began	4+ Yrs	2-4 Yrs	1-2 Yrs	Citizens	Not Citiz.
World Salt Foundation		2	-	-	-	-
Youth With A Mission (YWAM)		3	-	-	-	-
Totals:		370	9	3	91	7

ARMENIA

Armenian Misssionary Assoc.	1988	-	-	-	30	1
Christian Aid Mission		-	-	-	1	-
Seventh-day Adventists	1990	2	-	-	-	-
World Vision	1994	-	1	-	-	-
Totals:		2	1	-	31	1

ARUBA

Church of God World Missions	1968	2	-	-	-	-
Totals:		2	-	-	-	-

AUSTRALIA

ABWE	1970	10	-	-	-	-
American Baptist Association	1968	1	-	-	-	-
Apostolic Christian Church	1990	2	-	-	-	-
Back to the Bible Intl.	1957	-	-	-	4	-
Baptist Bible Fellowship Intl.	1954	35	-	-	-	-
Baptist International Missions	1970	21	-	-	-	1
Baptist Mid-Missions	1968	22	-	-	-	-
Baptist World Mission	1984	10	-	-	-	-
BCM International	1995	-	-	-	1	-
Biblical Ministries Worldwide	1981	2	-	-	-	-
Campus Crusade for Christ	1967	6	-	-	-	-
Child Evangelism Fellowship	1944	4	-	-	13	-
China Ministries International	1994	-	-	-	1	-
Christian and Msny. Alliance	1969	2	-	-	-	-
Christian Chs. /Chs. of Christ		14	-	-	-	-
Church of God of Prophecy	1956	2	-	-	-	-
Church of God World Missions	1976	2	-	-	-	-
Church of the Nazarene	1949	2	-	-	2	-
Church Resource Ministries	1988	2	-	-	-	-
Eastern Mennonite Missions	1980	2	-	-	-	-
Elim Fellowship World Missions	1991	2	-	-	-	-
Fellowship International Msn.	1984	8	-	-	-	-
Global Outreach Mission	1994	2	-	-	-	-
Gospel Fellowship Association		6	-	-	-	-
Grace Ministries International	1978	6	-	-	-	-
HCJB World Radio Msny. Flwshp.	1980	-	-	-	3	4
Intl. Pentecostal Holiness Ch.	1995	4	-	-	-	-
Liberty Baptist Mission	1984	4	-	-	-	-
Maranatha Baptist Mission	1964	8	-	-	-	-
Mission to the World	1966	12	4	-	-	-

COUNTRY Agency	Year Began	Personnel from U.S.			Other Countries	
		4+ Yrs	2-4 Yrs	1-2 Yrs	Citizens	Not Citiz.
Navigators, The	1964	10	-	-	-	-
Presbyterian Church (USA)		2	-	-	-	-
Salvation Army, U.S.A.	1880	2	-	-	-	-
Seventh-day Adventists	1885	6	-	-	10	-
Southern Baptist Intl. Mission	1989	6	1	-	-	-
Teen Missions International		-	-	-	4	2
United Evangelical Churches		1	-	-	-	-
United Pentecostal Church Intl	1956	4	-	-	-	-
Walk Thru The Bible Ministries	1980	-	-	-	8	-
Wesleyan World Missions	1945	4	-	-	-	-
World Baptist Fellowship Msn	1995	2	-	-	-	-
Wycliffe Bible Translators	1950	16	-	-	-	-
Youth With A Mission (YWAM)		25	-	-	-	-
Totals:		269	5	-	46	7

AUSTRIA

American Baptist Churches USA	1847	2	-	-	-	-
Assemblies of God	1967	6	-	-	-	-
Baptist International Missions	1984	4	-	-	-	-
Baptist Mid-Missions	1965	2	-	-	-	-
BCM International	1975	1	-	-	-	-
Biblical Ministries Worldwide	1963	2	-	-	-	-
Brethren Assemblies		7	-	-	-	-
Campus Crusade for Christ	1974	4	-	-	-	-
CBInternational	1969	21	2	8	-	-
CEIFA Ministries International	1990	-	-	-	2	-
Child Evangelism Fellowship	1955	1	-	-	6	13
Christian Chs. /Chs. of Christ	1983	-	2	-	-	-
Church of God World Missions	1984	-	-	-	-	2
Elim Fellowship World Missions	1991	1	-	-	-	-
Evangelical Free Church Msn.	1971	2	-	1	-	-
Global Outreach Mission	1986	1	-	-	-	-
Gospel Missionary Union	1966	3	1	-	1	-
Greater Europe Mission	1964	14	4	-	1	1
International Teams, U.S.A.	1973	26	16	1	-	5
InterVarsity Mission	1983	2	-	2	-	-
Mennonite Brethren Msns/Svcs	1953	2	2	-	-	-
Mission to the World	1980	4	2	-	-	-
Navigators, The	1973	7	-	-	-	-
Network of Intl Christian Schs	1995	-	2	-	-	-
Operation Mobilization		3	-	-	-	-
Pocket Testament League	1987	1	-	-	1	1
TEAM	1932	22	3	-	-	-
Trans World Radio	1990	-	-	-	6	-
UFM International	1984	6	-	2	-	-
United Evangelical Churches		1	-	-	-	-
United Methodist Church		2	-	-	-	-

COUNTRY Agency	Year Began	Personnel from U.S.			Other Countries	
		4+ Yrs	2-4 Yrs	1-2 Yrs	Citizens	Not Citiz.
United Pentecostal Church Intl	1971	4	-	-	-	-
World Missions Fellowship	1954	2	-	2	-	-
Young Life	1974	6	9	-	-	-
Youth for Christ / USA		1	-	-	-	-
Youth With A Mission (YWAM)		8	-	-	-	-
	Totals:	168	43	16	17	22

AZERBAIJAN

World Vision	1994	-	2	-	-	-
	Totals:	-	2	-	-	-

AZORES

Baptist Bible Fellowship Intl.	1993	2	-	-	-	-
Baptist Missions to Forgotten		2	-	-	-	-
Gospel Fellowship Association		4	-	-	-	-
	Totals:	8	-	-	-	-

BAHAMAS

AMG International	1993	2	-	-	-	-
Assemblies of God	1942	6	-	-	-	-
Baptist International Missions	1968	7	-	-	-	4
Christian Chs. /Chs. of Christ	1952	2	-	-	-	-
Church of God World Missions	1909	2	-	-	3	-
Global Outreach Mission	1974	1	-	-	-	-
Gospel Missionary Union	1956	4	2	-	-	-
National Baptist Conv. USA	1946	2	-	-	168	-
Salvation Army, U.S.A.	1936	4	-	-	-	-
United Pentecostal Church Intl	1988	2	-	-	-	-
	Totals:	32	2	-	171	4

BAHRAIN

Church of God World Missions	1984	-	-	-	-	2
Reformed Church In America	1889	7	-	-	-	-
	Totals:	7	-	-	-	2

BANGLADESH

ABWE	1954	51	-	4	-	-
American Baptist Churches USA	1976	1	-	-	-	-
Baptist Mid-Missions	1975	3	-	-	-	2
Christian Aid Mission		-	-	-	10	-
Christian Chs. /Chs. of Christ	1990	-	2	-	-	-
Christian Reformed Wrld Relief		2	-	-	-	-
Evangelical Lutheran Church	1993	3	-	1	-	-
Every Home for Christ	1973	-	-	-	18	-
Farms International, Inc.	1996	-	-	-	1	-

COUNTRY / Agency	Year Began	Personnel from U.S. 4+ Yrs	2-4 Yrs	1-2 Yrs	Other Countries Citizens	Not Citiz.
Globe Missionary Evangelism	1981	2	-	-	-	-
International Needs - USA	1974	-	-	-	80	-
InterServe/USA	1971	3	-	-	-	-
Medical Ambassadors Intl.	1988	-	-	-	10	-
Mennonite Central Committee	1970	10	8	-	-	-
Mission to the World	1984	1	-	-	-	-
Partners International	1975	-	-	-	67	-
Presbyterian Church (USA)	1974	6	-	-	-	-
Rosedale Mennonite Missions	1991	-	1	-	-	-
Seventh-day Adventists	1906	12	-	1	-	-
SIM USA	1957	10	-	-	-	-
Southern Baptist Intl. Mission	1957	11	-	-	-	-
World Concern	1975	-	-	-	342	1
World Mission Prayer League	1972	10	-	-	1	9
Youth With A Mission (YWAM)		1	-	-	-	-
Totals:		126	11	6	529	12

BARBADOS

Agency	Year Began	4+ Yrs	2-4 Yrs	1-2 Yrs	Citizens	Not Citiz.
Bible Missionary Church	1960	-	-	-	-	-
Brethren Assemblies		1	-	-	-	-
Christian Chs. /Chs. of Christ	1953	2	-	-	-	-
Church of God World Missions	1936	-	-	-	2	-
National Baptist Conv. USA	1975	-	2	-	3	-
Youth With A Mission (YWAM)		5	-	-	-	-
Totals:		8	2	-	5	-

BELARUS

Agency	Year Began	4+ Yrs	2-4 Yrs	1-2 Yrs	Citizens	Not Citiz.
Baptist International Missions	1993	3	-	-	-	-
Baptist Mid-Missions	1994	2	-	-	-	-
Campus Crusade for Christ	1992	2	-	16	-	-
Childcare International	1992	-	-	-	1	-
Christ for the Nations, Inc.	1992	2	-	-	-	-
Church of God of Prophecy	1996	-	-	-	1	-
Every Home for Christ	1993	-	-	-	6	-
InterVarsity Mission	1992	-	1	-	-	-
Intl. Inst. Christian Studies	1992	1	1	-	-	-
Slavic Gospel Association	1945	-	-	-	8	-
Walk Thru The Bible Ministries	1993	-	-	-	97	-
World Baptist Fellowship Msn	1995	4	-	-	-	-
Totals:		14	2	16	113	-

BELAU(PALAU)

Agency	Year Began	4+ Yrs	2-4 Yrs	1-2 Yrs	Citizens	Not Citiz.
Assemblies of God	1983	2	-	-	-	-
High Adventure Ministries	1991	1	-	-	7	3
Liebenzell Mission USA	1929	-	-	4	-	-
Totals:		3	-	4	7	3

COUNTRY Agency	Year Began	Personnel from U.S.			Other Countries	
		4+ Yrs	2-4 Yrs	1-2 Yrs	Citizens	Not Citiz.
BELGIUM						
Assemblies of God	1949	19	-	-	-	-
Baptist Bible Fellowship Intl.	1962	6	-	-	-	-
Baptist International Missions	1978	2	-	-	-	-
Biblical Literature Fellowship	1958	7	1	1	-	-
CBInternational	1989	10	-	-	-	-
Child Evangelism Fellowship	1955	2	-	-	3	1
Christian Chs. /Chs. of Christ	1956	2	-	-	-	-
Church of God of Prophecy	1983	-	-	-	-	1
Church of God World Missions	1973	4	-	-	-	2
Elim Fellowship World Missions	1991	1	-	-	-	-
Evangelical Free Church Msn.	1977	19	-	2	-	-
Fellowship International Msn.	1991	1	-	-	-	-
Global Outreach Mission	1946	4	-	-	-	-
Global Outreach, Ltd.	1979	1	2	2	-	-
Gospel Missionary Union	1974	7	-	-	2	-
Greater Europe Mission	1971	37	2	-	-	-
International Outreach Mins.	1982	5	-	-	-	-
Mennonite Board of Missions	1950	2	-	-	-	-
Operation Mobilization		8	-	1	-	-
Pilgrim Fellowship, Inc.	1991	-	-	-	1	-
Presbyterian Church (USA)	1973	3	-	-	-	-
UFM International	1991	1	-	-	-	-
United Pentecostal Church Intl	1983	2	-	-	-	-
United World Mission	1970	3	2	-	4	-
World Baptist Fellowship Msn	1991	2	-	-	-	-
Young Life	1984	2	1	-	-	-
Youth With A Mission (YWAM)		4	-	-	-	-
Totals:		154	8	6	10	4
BELIZE						
Assemblies of God	1956	8	-	-	-	-
Baptist Bible Fellowship Intl.	1979	6	-	-	-	-
Calvary Commission, Inc.	1983	1	1	-	-	-
Calvary International	1995	1	-	-	-	-
Christian Advance Intl.	1993	-	2	-	2	-
Christian Reformed World Msns.	1980	1	-	-	-	-
Church of God of Prophecy	1980	-	-	-	1	-
Church of God World Missions	1944	-	-	-	2	-
Church of the Nazarene	1934	1	-	-	-	-
Foursquare Missions Intl.		2	-	-	-	-
Friends United Meeting	1980	1	-	-	-	-
Gospel Missionary Union	1955	4	-	-	4	-
Hope for the Hungry	1990	-	4	-	-	-
International Gospel Outreach	1996	-	-	2	-	-
Living Water Teaching Intl.	1996	-	-	-	-	5

COUNTRY Agency	Year Began	Personnel from U.S.			Other Countries	
		4+ Yrs	2-4 Yrs	1-2 Yrs	Citizens	Not Citiz.
Macedonia World Baptist Msns.	1994	2	-	-	-	-
Mission to the Americas	1960	2	-	-	4	-
Pioneers	1986	4	-	-	-	-
Southern Baptist Intl. Mission	1977	12	5	-	-	-
The Master's Harvest	1990	2	2	-	-	-
TMA Ministries	1994	-	-	2	-	-
United Pentecostal Church Intl	1985	2	-	-	-	-
World Salt Foundation	1979	2	-	-	-	-
Youth With A Mission (YWAM)		6	-	-	-	-
Totals:		57	14	4	13	5

BENIN

Agency	Year Began	4+ Yrs	2-4 Yrs	1-2 Yrs	Citizens	Not Citiz.
Assemblies of God	1937	4	-	-	-	-
Child Evangelism Fellowship	1987	-	-	-	1	2
Christian Chs. /Chs. of Christ	1992	-	4	-	-	-
Church of God of Prophecy	1985	-	-	-	1	-
CMF International	1991	4	-	-	-	-
Evangelical Baptist Missions	1966	1	-	-	-	-
Every Home for Christ	1991	-	-	-	2	-
Foursquare Missions Intl.	1965	2	-	-	-	-
Mennonite Board of Missions	1986	4	-	-	-	-
SIM USA	1946	15	-	3	-	-
Southern Baptist Intl. Mission	1970	21	-	-	-	-
Wycliffe Bible Translators	1984	8	-	-	-	-
Totals:		59	4	3	4	2

BERMUDA

Agency	Year Began	4+ Yrs	2-4 Yrs	1-2 Yrs	Citizens	Not Citiz.
Church of God (Anderson, IN)	1905	2	-	-	-	-
Southern Baptist Intl. Mission	1966	2	-	-	-	-
Totals:		4	-	-	-	-

BHUTAN

Agency	Year Began	4+ Yrs	2-4 Yrs	1-2 Yrs	Citizens	Not Citiz.
Gospel for Asia	1991	-	-	-	28	-
Totals:		-	-	-	28	-

BOLIVIA

Agency	Year Began	4+ Yrs	2-4 Yrs	1-2 Yrs	Citizens	Not Citiz.
American Baptist Churches USA	1986	4	-	1	-	-
Apostolic Team Ministries Intl	1987	2	-	-	-	-
Assemblies of God	1946	16	-	-	-	-
Baptist Bible Fellowship Intl.	1978	2	-	-	-	-
Baptist International Missions	1969	5	-	-	-	-
Baptist Missionary Assoc.	1965	3	-	-	-	-
Brethren Assemblies		17	-	-	-	-
Campus Crusade for Christ	1965	-	-	1	-	-
Central Yearly Mtg. of Friends	1925	5	2	-	-	-

COUNTRY Agency	Year Began	Personnel from U.S.			Other Countries	
		4+ Yrs	2-4 Yrs	1-2 Yrs	Citizens	Not Citiz.
Child Evangelism Fellowship	1943	-	-	-	5	-
Christian Aid Mission		-	-	-	17	-
Church of God (Anderson, IN)	1974	2	-	-	-	-
Church of God (Holiness) Msn.	1945	3	-	-	-	3
Church of God of Prophecy	1974	-	-	-	2	-
Church of God World Missions	1960	-	-	-	2	-
Church of the Nazarene	1945	4	-	-	-	-
Correll Missionary Ministries	1994	-	-	-	9	-
Evangelical Friends Mission	1931	-	-	-	1	-
Evangelical Methodist Church	1978	4	-	-	-	-
Evangelistic Faith Missions	1977	-	2	-	-	-
Every Home for Christ	1971	-	-	-	2	-
Food for the Hungry	1977	2	6	-	-	-
Foursquare Missions Intl.	1928	2	-	-	-	-
Gospel Missionary Union	1937	28	-	3	-	-
Grace Ministries International	1951	6	-	-	-	-
Habitat for Humanity Intl	1984	-	2	-	22	-
Heifer Project International	1957	-	-	-	6	-
ISOH/Impact	1991	-	-	1	-	-
Latin America Mission	1990	-	1	-	-	1
MAP International	1986	-	-	-	-	2
Maranatha Baptist Mission	1963	8	-	-	-	-
Mennonite Central Committee	1959	18	8	-	-	-
New Tribes Mission	1942	97	-	8	2	3
Partners International	1976	-	-	-	12	-
Pioneers	1984	8	-	-	-	-
Primitive Methodist Church USA	1985	2	-	-	-	2
Salvation Army, U.S.A.	1920	1	-	-	-	-
Servants in Faith & Technology	1976	-	-	-	10	-
Seventh-day Adventists	1907	2	-	-	4	-
SIM USA	1907	49	-	4	-	-
South America Mission	1922	30	4	-	-	1
Southern Baptist Intl. Mission	1979	27	-	-	-	-
United Evangelical Churches		2	-	-	-	-
United Methodist Church		9	-	-	-	-
United Pentecostal Church Intl	1974	4	-	-	-	-
United World Mission	1948	11	-	-	2	-
World Concern	1988	2	-	-	19	-
World Gospel Mission	1944	40	-	-	-	1
World Indigenous Missions	1989	4	-	-	-	-
World Mission Prayer League	1938	9	-	-	-	9
World-Wide Missions	1961	-	-	-	1	-
Youth With A Mission (YWAM)		4	-	-	-	-
Totals:		432	25	18	116	22

COUNTRY Agency	Year Began	Personnel from U.S.			Other Countries	
		4+ Yrs	2-4 Yrs	1-2 Yrs	Citizens	Not Citiz.
BOPHUTHATSWANA						
Christian Chs. /Chs. of Christ		4	-	-	-	-
Totals:		4	-	-	-	-
BOSNIA-HERCEGOVINA						
Pioneers	1992	5	-	-	-	-
World Salt Foundation	1987	2	-	-	-	-
World Vision	1994	1	1	2	-	-
Totals:		8	1	2	-	-
BOTSWANA						
Africa Evangelical Fellowship	1973	9	-	-	-	-
Africa Inter-Mennonite Mission	1975	10	-	-	-	-
Assemblies of God	1963	4	-	-	-	-
Child Evangelism Fellowship	1996	1	-	-	-	-
Christian Blind Mission Intl.	1988	-	1	-	-	-
Christian Chs. /Chs. of Christ	1984	2	-	-	-	-
Church of God of Prophecy	1965	-	-	-	-	2
Church of God World Missions	1951	2	-	-	-	-
Church of the Nazarene	1984	2	-	-	2	-
Evangelical Mennonite Church	1988	2	-	-	-	-
Faith Christian Fellowship	1987	2	-	-	-	-
General Conf. Mennonite Church	1975	3	-	-	-	3
Habitat for Humanity Intl	1992	-	6	-	12	-
Intl. Pentecostal Holiness Ch.	1953	2	-	-	-	-
Lutheran Bible Translators	1991	5	-	-	5	-
Lutheran Church-Missouri Synod	1984	4	-	-	-	-
Mennonite Brethren Msns/Svcs	1985	-	2	-	-	-
Mennonite Central Committee	1968	4	4	-	-	-
Seventh-day Adventists	1921	-	-	-	8	-
Southern Baptist Intl. Mission	1968	16	-	-	-	-
United Methodist Church		2	-	-	-	-
United Pentecostal Church Intl	1980	2	-	-	-	-
Totals:		72	13	-	27	5
BRAZIL						
ABWE	1942	100	-	2	-	-
Action International Mins.	1991	4	-	-	-	-
ALM International	1985	-	1	-	-	-
Apostolic Christian Church	1960	23	-	-	-	-
Assemblies of God	1925	15	-	-	-	-
Assoc of Free Lutheran Congs	1964	9	-	-	9	-
Baptist Bible Fellowship Intl.	1952	37	-	-	-	-
Baptist Faith Missions	1923	18	-	-	-	-
Baptist General Conference	1955	8	-	-	-	-
Baptist International Missions	1967	36	-	-	3	-

COUNTRY Agency	Year Began	Personnel from U.S.			Other Countries	
		4+ Yrs	2-4 Yrs	1-2 Yrs	Citizens	Not Citiz.
Baptist Mid-Missions	1935	177	-	-	1	-
Baptist Missionary Assoc.	1953	2	-	-	-	-
Baptist World Mission	1979	13	-	-	-	-
BCM International	1987	-	-	-	4	-
Berean Mission, Inc.	1967	9	-	-	-	-
Bethany Fellowship Missions	1963	33	-	-	2	-
Brazil Gospel Fellowship Msn.	1939	69	-	-	-	-
Brethren Assemblies		14	-	-	-	-
Campus Crusade for Christ	1968	9	-	3	-	-
CBInternational	1946	33	-	6	-	-
Child Evangelism Fellowship	1941	2	-	-	90	2
Christ for the City Intl.	1995	-	-	2	3	-
Christ for the Island World	1991	-	-	-	1	-
Christian Aid Mission		-	-	-	8	-
Christian and Msny. Alliance	1962	22	-	-	-	-
Christian Chs. /Chs. of Christ	1948	49	-	-	-	-
Christian Church of North Am.	1980	-	-	-	-	-
Christians In Action, Inc.	1960	4	-	-	17	-
Church of God (Anderson, IN)	1923	2	-	-	-	-
Church of God of Prophecy	1965	-	-	-	-	2
Church of God World Missions	1951	6	-	-	-	-
Church of the Nazarene	1958	12	-	-	-	-
Churches of God General Conf.	1994	-	2	-	-	-
CMF International	1957	11	-	-	-	-
Cumberland Presbyterian Church		1	-	2	-	-
Evangelical Bible Mission		-	4	-	-	-
Evangelical Free Church Msn.	1986	4	-	-	-	-
Evangelical Lutheran Church	1958	4	-	-	-	-
Every Home for Christ	1963	-	-	-	19	-
Fellowship International Msn.	1964	30	-	-	-	-
Foursquare Missions Intl.	1946	4	-	-	-	-
Free Will Baptist Association	1958	20	-	-	-	-
General Conf. Mennonite Church	1964	1	-	-	1	6
Global Outreach Mission	1973	2	-	-	-	-
Global Outreach, Ltd.	1989	-	1	-	-	-
Go Ye Fellowship	1962	3	-	-	1	-
Gospel Fellowship Association		10	-	-	-	-
Gospel Missionary Union	1911	29	-	-	1	-
Grace Brethren Intl. Missions	1949	8	-	1	-	-
Grace Ministries International	1957	2	-	-	-	-
Habitat for Humanity Intl	1987	-	2	-	7	-
HCJB World Radio Msny. Flwshp.	1985	-	-	-	2	-
International Street Kids Mins	1992	1	-	-	-	-
InterVarsity Mission	1987	-	-	2	-	-
Japanese Evangelical Msnry Soc	1961	1	-	-	-	-
Latin America Mission	1985	-	2	-	4	-
Literacy & Evangelism Intl.	1994	-	-	-	1	-

COUNTRY Agency	Year Began	Personnel from U.S.			Other Countries	
		4+ Yrs	2-4 Yrs	1-2 Yrs	Citizens	Not Citiz.
Lutheran Church-Missouri Synod	1900	-	-	1	-	-
Macedonia World Baptist Msns.	1971	14	-	-	-	-
Maranatha Baptist Mission	1969	8	-	-	-	-
Mennonite Board of Missions	1955	7	-	-	-	-
Mennonite Brethren Msns/Svcs	1946	4	2	-	-	-
Mennonite Central Committee	1968	6	8	-	-	-
Mission Aviation Fellowship	1957	7	-	-	1	-
Mission to the World	1973	3	-	-	-	-
Navigators, The	1963	6	-	-	-	-
New Tribes Mission	1946	160	-	5	3	11
North American Baptist Conf.	1966	6	2	-	-	-
OC International, Inc.	1963	17	-	-	1	-
OMS International, Inc.	1950	7	-	-	-	2
Operation Mobilization		-	1	-	-	-
Partners International	1969	-	-	-	50	-
PAZ International	1976	38	1	1	30	-
Pilgrim Fellowship, Inc.	1948	-	-	-	-	1
Pocket Testament League	1965	-	-	-	2	2
Presbyterian Church (USA)	1859	14	23	7	-	-
Reformed Episcopal Bd Missions	1975	1	-	-	-	-
Salvation Army, U.S.A.	1922	4	-	-	-	-
Seventh-day Adventists	1894	6	-	-	10	-
Shield of Faith Mission Intl.	1970	2	-	-	-	2
SIM USA	1994	2	-	-	-	-
South America Mission	1913	14	1	-	-	-
Southern Baptist Intl. Mission	1881	242	25	-	-	-
TEAM	1972	6	-	-	-	-
Teen Missions International		-	4	-	-	-
Things To Come Mission, Inc	1958	8	-	-	-	-
UFM International	1931	66	-	-	-	-
United Church Board World Mins	1922	-	2	-	-	-
United Methodist Church		7	-	-	-	-
United Pentecostal Church Intl	1956	12	-	-	-	-
United World Mission	1966	2	-	-	-	-
Walk Thru The Bible Ministries	1988	-	-	-	1	-
WEC International	1957	3	-	1	-	-
Wesleyan World Missions	1958	6	-	-	-	-
Wisconsin Evang. Lutheran Syn.	1987	4	-	-	-	-
World Baptist Fellowship Msn	1960	33	-	-	-	-
World Partners Missionary Ch.	1955	11	-	-	-	-
World Team	1957	12	-	-	-	-
World-Wide Missions	1961	2	-	-	-	-
Wycliffe Bible Translators	1956	126	3	1	-	-
Youth for Christ / USA	1950	3	2	-	-	-
Youth With A Mission (YWAM)		29	-	-	-	-
Totals:		1,735	86	34	272	28

COUNTRY Agency	Year Began	Personnel from U.S.			Other Countries	
		4+ Yrs	2-4 Yrs	1-2 Yrs	Citizens	Not Citiz.

BRITISH VIRGIN ISLANDS

Mission to the World	1995	2	-	-	-	-
Totals:		2	-	-	-	-

BULGARIA

All God's Children Intl.	1992	-	-	-	2	-
AMG International	1994	-	-	-	1	-
Baptist Bible Fellowship Intl.	1995	2	-	-	-	-
Baptist General Conference	1994	1	-	-	-	-
Campus Crusade for Christ	1991	10	-	5	-	-
Child Evangelism Fellowship	1976	-	-	-	2	4
Church of God of Prophecy	1991	-	-	-	1	-
Church of God World Missions	1982	1	-	-	1	-
Covenant Celebration Church		-	-	-	1	1
Door of Hope International	1953	-	-	-	8	-
Eastern European Outreach	1992	-	2	1	-	-
Every Home for Christ	1991	-	-	-	2	-
Greater Europe Mission	1986	3	-	-	-	-
International Teams, U.S.A.	1973	1	2	-	-	-
InterVarsity Mission	1991	-	-	1	-	-
Ministry to Eastern Europe	1992	-	-	-	5	-
Mission to the World	1994	2	-	-	-	-
Partners International	1994	-	-	-	12	-
Presb. Evangelistic Fellowship		-	-	-	4	-
SEND International	1992	3	-	-	-	-
United Methodist Church		2	-	-	-	-
Wisconsin Evang. Lutheran Syn.	1992	4	-	-	-	-
Totals:		29	4	7	39	5

BURKINA FASO

Africa Inter-Mennonite Mission	1978	15	-	3	-	-
Assemblies of God	1919	10	-	-	-	-
Baptist Bible Fellowship Intl.	1994	2	-	-	-	-
Child Evangelism Fellowship	1982	-	-	-	4	-
Christian and Msny. Alliance	1923	27	-	-	-	-
Christian Blind Mission Intl.	1988	-	1	-	-	-
Church of God of Prophecy	1987	-	-	-	1	-
Evangelical Mennonite Church	1978	2	-	-	-	-
Every Home for Christ	1995	-	-	-	2	-
General Conf. Mennonite Church	1977	3	-	-	-	4
Gospel Recordings USA	1995	-	-	-	2	-
Mennonite Central Committee	1978	7	5	-	-	-
Mission to the World	1991	2	-	-	-	-
Seventh-day Adventists	1972	-	-	-	6	-
SIM USA	1930	21	-	-	-	-

COUNTRY Agency	Year Began	Personnel from U.S.			Other Countries	
		4+ Yrs	2-4 Yrs	1-2 Yrs	Citizens	Not Citiz.
Southern Baptist Intl. Mission	1971	29	1	-	-	-
Wycliffe Bible Translators	1980	22	3	2	-	-
	Totals:	140	10	5	15	4

BURUNDI

Brethren Assemblies		7	-	-	-	-
Child Evangelism Fellowship	1952	-	-	-	7	-
Mennonite Central Committee	1994	-	6	-	-	-
Seventh-day Adventists	1931	-	-	-	2	-
Southern Baptist Intl. Mission	1978	4	-	-	-	-
World Gospel Mission	1943	3	-	-	-	-
World Vision	1993	-	-	1	-	-
	Totals:	14	6	1	9	-

CAMBODIA

Assemblies of God		20	-	-	-	-
Baptist International Missions	1996	2	-	-	-	-
Campus Crusade for Christ	1989	2	-	-	-	-
Child Evangelism Fellowship	1993	2	-	-	1	-
Christian Aid Mission		-	-	-	26	-
Christian and Msny. Alliance	1923	13	8	-	-	-
Christian Dynamics	1991	-	-	-	12	-
Church of the Nazarene	1992	-	-	-	2	-
Church Resource Ministries	1994	4	-	-	-	-
Elim Fellowship World Missions	1995	1	-	-	-	-
Every Home for Christ	1993	-	-	-	5	-
Mennonite Central Committee	1990	4	8	-	-	-
Mission To Unreached Peoples	1989	-	6	-	-	-
Partners International	1993	-	-	-	2	-
Reformed Church In America		1	-	-	-	-
Seventh-day Adventists	1991	4	-	2	2	-
Tribes and Nations Outreach	1992	-	-	-	1	-
WEC International	1993	-	-	1	-	-
Wesleyan World Missions	1995	2	-	-	-	2
World Concern	1982	5	4	-	56	12
World Relief Corporation	1991	2	1	-	-	2
World Vision	1970	1	4	-	-	-
Youth With A Mission (YWAM)		2	-	-	-	-
	Totals:	65	31	3	107	16

CAMEROON

Assemblies of God	1976	4	-	-	-	-
Baptist General Conference	1982	7	-	-	-	-
Child Evangelism Fellowship	1995	-	-	-	3	-
Church of God of Prophecy	1985	-	-	-	1	-
Church of God World Missions	1969	-	-	-	2	-

COUNTRY Agency	Year Began	Personnel from U.S.			Other Countries	
		4+ Yrs	2-4 Yrs	1-2 Yrs	Citizens	Not Citiz.
Evangelical Lutheran Church	1923	20	-	2	-	-
Gospel Fellowship Association		4	-	-	-	-
Gospel Recordings USA	1994	-	-	-	1	-
Heifer Project International	1974	-	-	-	11	2
Lutheran Bible Translators	1980	6	-	-	12	-
Lutheran Brethren World Msns.		8	-	-	-	-
Navigators, The	1990	4	-	-	-	-
North American Baptist Conf.	1891	20	2	-	-	-
Presbyterian Church (USA)	1879	4	-	-	-	-
Prison Mission Association	1972	-	-	-	1	-
Seventh-day Adventists	1928	6	-	-	11	-
United Pentecostal Church Intl	1971	2	-	-	-	-
Wisconsin Evang. Lutheran Syn.	1969	2	-	-	-	-
World Team	1985	17	-	-	-	5
Wycliffe Bible Translators	1968	105	20	1	-	-
	Totals:	209	22	3	42	7

CANARY ISLANDS

Assemblies of God	1973	10	-	-	-	-
Baptist Bible Fellowship Intl.	1983	1	-	-	-	-
	Totals:	11	-	-	-	-

CAPE VERDE ISLANDS

Church of the Nazarene	1901	2	-	-	-	-
Seventh-day Adventists	1935	-	-	-	4	-
	Totals:	2	-	-	4	-

CARIBBEAN ISLANDS - GENERAL

Assemblies of God	1920	10	-	-	-	-
BCM International	1995	-	-	-	8	-
Calvary Evangelistic Mission	1953	10	3	3	30	2
Church of God World Missions	1924	1	-	-	-	-
Foursquare Missions Intl.	1929	-	-	-	-	-
Macedonia World Baptist Msns.	1983	2	-	-	-	-
Southern Baptist Intl. Mission		58	13	-	-	-
UFM International	1995	2	-	-	-	-
World Baptist Fellowship Msn	1991	10	-	-	-	-
Wycliffe Bible Translators	1996	2	-	-	-	-
	Totals:	95	16	3	38	2

CAYMAN ISLANDS

Assemblies of God		2	-	-	-	-
Baptist International Missions	1960	6	-	-	-	-
Christian Chs. /Chs. of Christ		5	-	-	-	-
Church of God (Holiness) Msn.	1954	2	-	-	2	2
	Totals:	15	-	-	2	2

COUNTRY Agency	Year Began	Personnel from U.S.			Other Countries	
		4+ Yrs	2-4 Yrs	1-2 Yrs	Citizens	Not Citiz.

CENTRAL AFRICA REPUBLIC

Africa Inland Mission Intl	1924	4	-	-	-	-
Baptist Mid-Missions	1920	41	-	-	-	-
Campus Crusade for Christ	1987	2	-	-	-	-
CBInternational		22	-	-	-	-
Child Evangelism Fellowship	1989	-	-	-	16	-
Christian Blind Mission Intl.	1990	-	2	-	-	-
Evangelical Lutheran Church	1974	7	-	1	-	-
Grace Brethren Intl. Missions	1918	17	-	4	-	-
Habitat for Humanity Intl	1991	-	3	-	9	-
SIM USA	1978	1	-	-	-	-
Wycliffe Bible Translators	1989	5	1	-	-	-
	Totals:	99	6	5	25	-

CHAD

Africa Inland Mission Intl	1986	3	-	-	-	-
Baptist Mid-Missions	1925	6	-	-	-	1
Brethren Assemblies		1	-	-	-	-
Church of God World Missions	1968	-	-	-	2	-
Gospel Recordings USA	1995	-	-	-	2	-
Grace Brethren Intl. Missions	1966	2	-	-	-	-
Lutheran Brethren World Msns.		6	-	-	-	-
Mennonite Central Committee	1973	5	3	-	-	-
Southern Baptist Intl. Mission	1994	6	-	-	-	-
TEAM	1969	19	-	-	-	-
WEC International	1962	2	-	-	-	-
Wycliffe Bible Translators	1977	19	3	-	-	-
	Totals:	69	6	-	4	1

CHILE

ABWE	1953	24	-	-	-	-
American Baptist Churches USA	1993	2	-	-	-	-
Assemblies of God	1941	29	-	-	-	-
Baptist Bible Fellowship Intl.	1954	19	-	-	-	-
Baptist International Missions	1996	2	-	-	-	-
Baptist Mid-Missions	1992	6	-	-	-	-
Brethren Assemblies		6	-	-	-	-
Campus Crusade for Christ	1963	-	-	8	-	-
Child Evangelism Fellowship	1942	-	-	-	5	-
Christian and Msny. Alliance	1897	25	-	-	-	-
Christian Chs. /Chs. of Christ	1949	32	-	-	-	-
Christian Church of North Am.	1981	-	-	-	-	-
Church of God of Prophecy	1975	-	-	-	-	2
Church of God World Missions	1954	-	2	-	-	-
Church of the Nazarene	1962	6	-	-	-	-
CMF International	1988	10	-	-	-	-

COUNTRY Agency	Year Began	Personnel from U.S.			Other Countries	
		4+ Yrs	2-4 Yrs	1-2 Yrs	Citizens	Not Citiz.
Evangelical Lutheran Synod	1992	2	-	-	-	-
Foursquare Missions Intl.	1947	1	-	-	-	-
Global Outreach, Ltd.	1989	-	-	2	-	-
Gospel Fellowship Association		6	-	-	-	-
Gospel Mission of S. America	1923	22	-	1	-	4
International Gospel Outreach	1990	-	-	-	2	-
International Partnership Mins	1991	-	-	-	2	-
Macedonia World Baptist Msns.	1996	2	-	-	-	-
Maranatha Baptist Mission	1963	4	-	-	-	-
Mennonite Board of Missions	1970	2	-	-	-	-
Mission to the World	1957	17	4	-	-	-
Navigators, The	1985	4	-	-	-	-
Open Bible Standard Churches	1982	2	-	-	-	-
Operation Blessing Intl.	1990	-	-	-	-	1
Presb. Evangelistic Fellowship		3	-	-	-	-
Presbyterian Church (USA)	1845	7	-	-	-	-
Salvation Army, U.S.A.	1909	8	-	-	-	-
Seventh-day Adventists	1895	4	-	-	1	-
SIM USA	1986	9	-	-	-	-
South American Missionary Soc.	1979	3	-	-	-	-
Southern Baptist Intl. Mission	1917	62	-	-	-	-
Spanish World Gospel Mission	1973	-	-	-	2	-
United Methodist Church		4	-	-	-	-
United Pentecostal Church Intl	1964	6	-	-	-	-
World Team	1982	5	-	-	-	-
Youth With A Mission (YWAM)		6	-	-	-	-
Totals:		340	6	11	12	7

CHINA, PEOPLES REPUBLIC

Agency	Year Began	4+ Yrs	2-4 Yrs	1-2 Yrs	Citizens	Not Citiz.
Advent Christian World Msns.	1897	-	-	-	4	-
All God's Children Intl.	1995	-	-	-	1	-
American Baptist Churches USA	1843	1	-	-	-	-
Anglican Frontier Missions		5	-	-	-	-
Baptist Bible Fellowship Intl.	1950	2	-	-	-	-
Baptist International Missions	1991	12	-	-	-	-
Baptist Mid-Missions	1993	4	-	-	-	-
Bright Hope International		-	-	-	2	-
Christian Aid Mission		-	-	-	329	-
Christian and Msny. Alliance	1900	2	-	-	-	-
Christian Blind Mission Intl.	1985	-	2	-	-	-
Christian Chs. /Chs. of Christ	1990	1	-	4	-	-
Christian Reformed World Msns.	1986	16	8	2	-	-
Church of God World Missions	1992	-	-	-	-	-
Church of The Brethren		-	-	2	-	-
Eastern Mennonite Missions	1982	-	-	3	-	-
Evangelical Lutheran Church	1986	-	-	10	-	-
Evangelize China Fellowship	1947	-	-	-	-	-

COUNTRY Agency	Year Began	Personnel from U.S.			Other Countries	
		4+ Yrs	2-4 Yrs	1-2 Yrs	Citizens	Not Citiz.
Every Home for Christ	1995	-	-	-	-	2
General Conf. Mennonite Church	1909	2	-	-	-	2
Global Strategy Mission Assoc.	1996	-	-	4	-	-
Gospel for Asia	1991	-	-	-	23	-
Heifer Project International	1984	-	-	-	4	-
Holt Intl. Children's Services	1990	-	-	-	6	1
Intl. Pentecostal Holiness Ch.	1911	3	-	-	-	-
Lutheran Church-Missouri Synod	1913	7	-	3	-	-
Macedonia World Baptist Msns.	1996	6	-	-	-	-
Mennonite Board of Missions	1947	2	-	-	-	-
Mennonite Brethren Msns/Svcs		-	-	-	-	2
Mennonite Central Committee	1981	1	7	-	-	-
Mission O.N.E., Inc.	1991	-	-	-	1	-
Mission Soc. for United Meth.	1995	1	-	-	-	-
Mission to the World	1991	2	-	-	-	-
Mission To Unreached Peoples	1986	-	2	-	-	-
Missions To Japan, Inc.		-	-	-	1	-
Partners International	1943	-	-	-	290	-
Presbyterian Church (USA)		4	-	20	-	-
Project Partner with Christ	1987	-	-	-	1	-
Training Evangelistic Ldrshp.	1985	3	-	-	2	-
Tribes and Nations Outreach	1985	-	-	-	-	2
United Church Board World Mins	1830	-	1	-	-	-
United Methodist Church		13	-	-	-	-
Totals:		87	20	48	664	9

COLOMBIA

ABWE	1929	16	-	-	-	-
Action International Mins.	1990	3	1	-	1	-
American Baptist Association	1971	1	-	-	-	-
Assemblies of God	1962	25	-	-	-	-
Baptist Bible Fellowship Intl.	1971	4	-	-	-	-
Baptist International Missions	1990	4	-	-	-	-
Baptist Missions to Forgotten		2	-	-	-	-
BCM International	1995	-	-	-	2	-
Brethren Assemblies		20	-	-	-	-
Brethren in Christ World Msns.	1985	3	3	-	-	-
Calvary International	1996	3	-	-	2	-
Child Evangelism Fellowship	1943	-	-	-	4	-
Christ for the City Intl.	1995	4	2	2	8	2
Christian Aid Mission		-	-	-	24	-
Christian and Msny. Alliance	1923	23	-	-	-	-
Christian Chs. /Chs. of Christ	1962	14	-	-	-	-
Christian Church of North Am.	1970	1	-	-	-	-
Christian Literature Crusade	1973	2	-	-	-	-
Christians In Action, Inc.	1970	3	-	-	28	1
Church of God of Prophecy	1973	-	-	-	2	-

COUNTRY Agency	Year Began	Personnel from U.S.			Other Countries	
		4+ Yrs	2-4 Yrs	1-2 Yrs	Citizens	Not Citiz.
Church of God World Missions	1954	-	-	-	2	-
Cumberland Presbyterian Church	1929	3	-	-	-	-
Deaf Missions International	1970	1	-	-	5	-
Elim Fellowship World Missions	1964	6	-	-	-	-
Enterprise Development Intl.	1989	-	-	-	1	-
Evangelical Covenant Church	1968	7	2	-	-	-
Evangelical Lutheran Church	1944	2	-	-	-	-
Fellowship International Msn.	1991	2	-	-	-	-
General Conf. Mennonite Church	1947	-	-	2	1	4
Gospel Missionary Union	1908	8	-	-	2	-
Habitat for Humanity Intl	1994	-	3	-	2	-
Impact International	1990	-	-	-	1	-
International Needs - USA	1994	-	-	-	9	-
International Outreach Mins.	1986	1	-	-	3	-
International Teams, U.S.A.		2	-	-	-	-
Latin America Mission	1932	13	-	-	8	1
Macedonia World Baptist Msns.	1994	2	-	-	-	-
Maranatha Baptist Mission	1983	4	-	-	-	-
Mennonite Brethren Msns/Svcs	1945	3	2	2	3	-
Mission to the World	1976	23	-	-	-	-
Missionary Revival Crusade	1974	4	-	-	2	-
New Tribes Mission	1944	55	-	2	3	4
OC International, Inc.	1963	-	1	-	2	-
OMS International, Inc.	1943	14	-	-	4	-
Presbyterian Church (USA)	1856	7	-	-	-	-
Reformed Baptist Mission Svcs.	1985	2	-	-	-	-
Seventh-day Adventists	1921	-	-	-	9	-
South America Mission	1934	11	-	1	-	-
Southern Baptist Intl. Mission	1941	41	1	-	-	-
Sowers International, The	1994	-	-	-	1	-
Spanish World Gospel Mission	1974	-	-	-	2	-
TEAM	1923	25	1	-	-	1
Team Expansion, Inc.	1989	2	-	-	-	-
United Pentecostal Church Intl	1936	4	-	-	-	-
Wesleyan World Missions	1941	4	-	-	-	-
Wisconsin Evang. Lutheran Syn.	1974	3	-	-	-	-
World Baptist Fellowship Msn	1968	6	-	-	-	-
Wycliffe Bible Translators	1962	161	10	2	-	-
Youth for Christ / USA		2	-	-	-	-
Youth With A Mission (YWAM)		5	-	-	-	-
Totals:		551	26	11	131	13.

COMOROS ISLANDS

Africa Inland Mission Intl	1975	9	-	-	-	-
Totals:		9	-	-	-	-

COUNTRY Agency	Year Began	Personnel from U.S.			Other Countries	
		4+ Yrs	2-4 Yrs	1-2 Yrs	Citizens	Not Citiz.

CONGO

Assemblies of God	1988	6	-	-	-	-
Christian and Msny. Alliance	1992	9	-	-	-	-
Every Home for Christ	1993	-	-	-	6	-
Global Outreach Mission	1974	2	-	-	-	-
Seventh-day Adventists	1965	-	-	-	2	-
United World Mission	1948	6	-	-	-	-
Wycliffe Bible Translators	1985	17	1	3	-	-
Totals:		40	1	3	8	-

CONGO / ZAIRE

Africa Inland Mission Intl	1912	42	-	8	-	-
Africa Inter-Mennonite Mission	1912	4	-	-	-	-
American Baptist Churches USA	1884	13	-	-	-	1
Assemblies of God	1921	12	-	-	-	-
Baptist Bible Fellowship Intl.	1957	8	-	-	-	-
Berean Mission, Inc.	1938	9	-	3	-	-
Brethren Assemblies		13	-	-	-	-
CBInternational	1946	14	-	-	-	-
Child Evangelism Fellowship	1952	-	-	-	5	-
Christian and Msny. Alliance	1884	2	-	-	-	-
Christian Chs. /Chs. of Christ	1948	34	-	-	-	-
Church of God of Prophecy	1979	-	-	-	-	2
Church of God World Missions	1971	-	-	-	6	-
Episcopal World Mission	1984	3	-	-	-	-
Evangelical Covenant Church	1937	48	19	-	-	-
Evangelical Free Church Msn.	1922	31	-	4	-	-
Evangelical Mennonite Church	1912	2	-	-	-	-
Evangelism Resources	1980	6	-	-	20	2
Every Child Ministries, Inc.	1985	2	-	-	8	-
Every Home for Christ	1965	-	-	-	19	-
General Conf. Mennonite Church	1906	1	-	-	-	1
Grace Ministries International	1928	11	-	2	-	-
Habitat for Humanity Intl	1974	-	1	-	58	-
Independent Faith Mission	1988	15	-	-	-	-
International Outreach Mins.	1986	6	-	-	-	-
Intl. Pentecostal Holiness Ch.	1992	2	-	-	-	-
Literacy & Evangelism Intl.	1989	2	-	-	-	-
Medical Ambassadors Intl.	1987	-	-	-	103	-
Mennonite Central Committee	1960	4	3	-	-	-
Mission Aviation Fellowship	1960	47	-	-	-	2
Mission to the World	1979	2	-	-	-	-
Missionaire International	1995	-	-	-	-	-
Navigators, The	1982	4	-	-	-	-
Operation Blessing Intl.	1991	1	-	-	-	-
Partners International	1969	-	-	-	4	-

COUNTRY Agency	Year Began	Personnel from U.S.			Other Countries	
		4+ Yrs	2-4 Yrs	1-2 Yrs	Citizens	Not Citiz.
Peoples Mission International	1992	-	-	-	1	-
Pioneer Bible Translators	1981	6	-	-	5	-
Presbyterian Church (USA)	1891	12	10	-	-	-
Salvation Army, U.S.A.	1934	3	-	-	-	-
Seventh-day Adventists	1921	10	-	-	5	-
The Master's Mission, Inc.	1980	2	-	-	2	-
UFM International	1931	6	-	2	-	-
United Methodist Church		25	-	-	-	-
World Vision	1960	-	2	-	-	-
World-Wide Missions	1961	1	-	-	3	-
Wycliffe Bible Translators	1977	54	2	-	-	-
Totals:		457	37	19	239	8

COSTA RICA

Agency	Year Began	4+ Yrs	2-4 Yrs	1-2 Yrs	Citizens	Not Citiz.
American Baptist Association	1940	3	-	-	-	-
American Baptist Churches USA	1980	2	-	-	-	-
Assemblies of God	1943	27	-	-	-	-
Baptist Bible Fellowship Intl.	1968	16	-	-	-	-
Baptist International Missions	1968	8	-	-	-	-
Baptist Missionary Assoc.	1961	2	-	-	-	-
Calvary International	1983	6	-	-	-	-
CAM International	1891	20	-	-	1	1
Campus Crusade for Christ	1976	2	-	8	-	-
Chinese Christian Mission, Inc	1982	-	-	-	3	-
Christ for the City Intl.	1995	12	2	4	28	2
Christian Aid Mission		-	-	-	1	-
Christian Chs. /Chs. of Christ		6	-	-	-	-
Christian Leadership Dev.	1973	3	-	-	1	1
Christian Reformed World Msns.	1981	15	-	-	-	-
Church of God (Anderson, IN)	1920	2	-	-	-	-
Church of God of Prophecy	1932	-	-	-	-	2
Church of God World Missions	1935	-	-	-	2	-
Church of the Nazarene	1948	15	-	-	3	-
Deaf Missions International	1986	-	-	-	-	-
Every Home for Christ	1988	-	-	-	2	-
Faith Christian Fellowship	1983	2	-	-	-	-
Foursquare Missions Intl.	1953	2	-	-	-	2
Globe Missionary Evangelism	1996	-	-	2	-	-
Gospel Fellowship Association		2	-	-	-	-
Grace Ministries International	1988	4	-	-	-	-
Habitat for Humanity Intl	1987	-	3	-	-	-
Hope for the Hungry	1990	-	2	-	-	-
IDEA/PROLADES	1982	2	-	-	-	-
International Children's Care	1988	-	1	-	-	-
International Outreach Mins.	1974	2	-	-	-	-
International Teams, U.S.A.	1994	-	2	-	-	-
Intl. Pentecostal Holiness Ch.	1951	2	-	-	-	-

COUNTRY Agency	Year Began	Personnel from U.S.			Other Countries	
		4+ Yrs	2-4 Yrs	1-2 Yrs	Citizens	Not Citiz.
Latin America Assistance, Inc.	1963	1	-	-	2	-
Latin America Mission	1921	45	19	9	6	7
Living Water Teaching Intl.	1994	-	-	-	-	2
Macedonia World Baptist Msns.	1994	2	-	-	-	-
Mennonite Central Committee	1986	2	-	-	-	-
Mission Soc. for United Meth.	1995	8	-	-	-	-
Mission to the Americas	1967	2	-	-	-	-
Navigators, The	1957	2	-	-	-	-
Pentecostal Free Will Bapt.Ch.	1974	-	-	-	2	-
Presbyterian Church (USA)	1970	4	8	2	-	-
Rosedale Mennonite Missions	1961	4	-	-	1	-
Salvation Army, U.S.A.	1907	2	-	-	-	-
Seventh-day Adventists	1903	10	-	1	4	-
South American Missionary Soc.	1982	-	-	-	-	2
Southern Baptist Intl. Mission	1949	34	2	-	-	-
United Methodist Church		3	-	-	-	-
United Pentecostal Church Intl	1975	2	-	-	-	-
Walk Thru The Bible Ministries	1993	-	-	-	1	-
Youth With A Mission (YWAM)		2	-	-	-	-
Totals:		278	39	26	57	19

COTE D'IVOIRE

Assemblies of God	1968	2	-	-	-	-
Baptist Bible Fellowship Intl.	1988	4	-	-	-	-
Baptist General Conference	1977	8	-	-	-	1
Baptist International Missions	1970	14	-	-	-	-
Baptist Mid-Missions	1974	8	-	-	-	-
Calvary International	1989	2	-	-	-	-
Campus Crusade for Christ	1975	2	-	-	-	-
CBInternational	1947	54	6	20	-	-
Child Evangelism Fellowship	1976	-	-	-	22	-
Christian and Msny. Alliance	1930	40	19	-	-	-
Christian Chs. /Chs. of Christ	1985	10	-	-	-	-
Church of God World Missions	1992	2	-	-	-	-
Church of the Nazarene	1987	9	-	-	2	-
Evangelical Baptist Missions	1971	10	-	2	-	-
Every Home for Christ	1991	-	-	-	4	-
Free Will Baptist Association	1958	24	2	1	-	-
Intl. Pentecostal Holiness Ch.	1993	4	-	-	-	-
Liberia Christian Mission	1991	2	-	-	-	-
Lion and Lamb Outreach	1974	1	-	-	3	5
Lutheran Church-Missouri Synod	1991	4	-	4	-	-
Macedonia World Baptist Msns.	1980	2	-	-	-	-
MAP International	1995	-	-	-	1	-
Mission to the World	1976	16	-	-	-	-
Navigators, The	1984	8	-	-	-	-
New Tribes Mission	1982	61	-	7	-	7

COUNTRY Agency	Year Began	Personnel from U.S.			Other Countries	
		4+ Yrs	2-4 Yrs	1-2 Yrs	Citizens	Not Citiz.
Pioneer Bible Translators	1989	2	-	-	-	1
Seventh-day Adventists	1946	4	-	1	14	-
Shield of Faith Mission Intl.	1995	2	-	-	-	-
SIM USA	1968	15	-	-	-	-
Southern Baptist Intl. Mission	1966	28	5	-	-	-
United Methodist Church		1	-	-	-	-
United Pentecostal Church Intl	1973	2	-	-	-	-
Walk Thru The Bible Ministries	1994	-	-	-	2	-
WEC International	1934	8	1	5	-	-
Wycliffe Bible Translators	1970	54	2	-	-	-
	Totals:	403	35	40	48	14

CROATIA

Assemblies of God		5	-	-	-	-
Campus Crusade for Christ	1993	4	-	9	-	-
Child Evangelism Fellowship	1973	-	-	-	1	1
Christian Aid Mission		-	-	-	1	-
Greater Europe Mission	1974	6	-	-	-	-
International Needs - USA	1967	-	-	-	8	-
Mennonite Central Committee	1963	-	1	-	-	-
Navigators, The		2	-	-	-	-
Pioneers	1992	8	-	-	-	-
Presbyterian Church (USA)		2	-	-	-	-
Wesleyan World Missions	1993	2	-	-	-	-
World Salt Foundation	1990	-	2	-	-	-
Youth With A Mission (YWAM)		3	-	-	-	-
	Totals:	32	3	9	10	1

CUBA

Baptist Bible Fellowship Intl.	1955	2	-	-	-	-
Baptist International Missions	1996	-	-	-	2	-
Baptist Mid-Missions	1995	2	-	-	-	-
Christian Aid Mission		-	-	-	74	-
Church of God of Prophecy	1935	-	-	-	1	-
Every Home for Christ	1989	-	-	-	4	-
Partners International	1995	-	-	-	42	1
Presbyterian Church (USA)	1902	-	-	3	-	-
STEM Ministries	1994	-	-	-	-	-
United Methodist Church		2	-	-	-	-
Wisconsin Evang. Lutheran Syn.	1995	1	-	-	-	-
	Totals:	7	-	3	123	1

CYPRUS

AMG International	1974	4	-	-	-	-
Biblical Ministries Worldwide	1971	4	-	-	-	-
Campus Crusade for Christ	1978	2	-	-	-	-

COUNTRY / Agency	Year Began	Personnel from U.S.			Other Countries	
		4+ Yrs	2-4 Yrs	1-2 Yrs	Citizens	Not Citiz.
Child Evangelism Fellowship	1952	6	-	-	-	-
Church of God (Anderson, IN)		1	-	-	-	-
Church of God of Prophecy	1965	-	-	-	2	-
Church of God World Missions	1995	-	-	-	-	2
Episcopal World Mission	1984	-	-	-	2	-
InterServe/USA	1984	2	-	-	-	-
Macedonia World Baptist Msns.	1989	2	-	-	-	-
Orthodox Presbyterian Church	1984	2	-	-	-	-
Seventh-day Adventists	1932	8	-	1	3	-
Venture Middle East	1986	4	-	-	1	1
Youth for Christ / USA		-	2	-	-	-
Youth With A Mission (YWAM)		1	-	-	-	-
Totals:		36	2	1	8	3

CZECH REPUBLIC

Agency	Year Began	4+ Yrs	2-4 Yrs	1-2 Yrs	Citizens	Not Citiz.
American Baptist Churches USA	1995	2	-	-	-	-
Assemblies of God	1981	6	-	-	-	-
Assoc of Free Lutheran Congs	1994	2	-	-	-	-
Baptist International Missions	1994	2	-	-	-	-
Baptist Missionary Assoc.		1	-	-	-	-
Campus Crusade for Christ	1981	12	-	3	-	-
CBInternational	1991	6	-	2	-	-
Child Evangelism Fellowship	1966	1	-	-	4	-
Christian Outreach Intl.	1992	-	5	2	1	2
Church of God World Missions	1991	-	-	-	2	-
Eastern European Bible Mission	1991	-	-	-	10	-
Evangelical Free Church Msn.	1991	11	6	1	-	-
Evangelical Lutheran Synod	1990	3	-	-	-	-
Every Home for Christ	1991	-	-	-	4	-
Grace Brethren Intl. Missions	1993	4	-	-	-	-
HCJB World Radio Msny. Flwshp.	1994	2	-	-	-	-
Hope for the Hungry	1990	-	2	-	-	-
International Messengers	1989	2	-	-	-	2
International Needs - USA	1993	-	-	-	3	-
International Teams, U.S.A.	1973	8	2	-	-	-
InterVarsity Mission	1992	-	2	1	-	-
Intl. Inst. Christian Studies	1995	-	-	1	-	-
Liberty Baptist Mission	1991	2	-	-	-	-
Mission to the World	1991	7	4	2	-	-
Missionary Athletes Intl.	1993	-	3	2	-	2
Salvation Army, U.S.A.	1919	2	-	-	-	-
SEND International	1994	6	-	-	-	-
Seventh-day Adventists	1919	2	-	-	-	-
TEAM	1994	11	2	-	-	-
UFM International	1995	2	-	-	-	-
Wesleyan World Missions	1994	4	-	-	-	-

| COUNTRY | Year | Personnel from U.S. | | | Other Countries | |
Agency	Began	4+ Yrs	2-4 Yrs	1-2 Yrs	Citizens	Not Citiz.
Young Life	1990	4	-	-	-	-
Youth With A Mission (YWAM)		7	-	-	-	-
Totals:		109	26	14	24	6

DENMARK
Bethany Missionary Association		1	-	-	-	-
Child Evangelism Fellowship	1947	2	-	-	9	-
Christian Chs. /Chs. of Christ	1992	-	-	2	-	-
Elim Fellowship World Missions	1995	2	-	-	-	-
Evangelical Lutheran Church		1	-	-	-	-
Global Outreach Mission	1995	2	-	-	-	-
Youth With A Mission (YWAM)		3	-	-	-	-
Totals:		11	-	2	9	-

DJIBOUTI
Church of God World Missions	1995	-	-	-	-	2
Eastern Mennonite Missions	1990	4	1	-	-	-
Seventh-day Adventists	1980	-	-	-	1	-
Totals:		4	1	-	1	2

DOMINICA
Ambassadors for Christ Intl.		-	-	-	4	-
Berean Mission, Inc.	1973	5	-	-	-	-
Churches of Christ in Union		2	-	-	-	-
Gospel Fellowship Association		2	-	-	-	-
Totals:		9	-	-	4	-

DOMINICAN REPUBLIC
American Baptist Churches USA	1980	3	-	-	-	-
Assemblies of God	1922	11	-	-	-	-
Baptist Bible Fellowship Intl.	1996	2	-	-	-	-
Baptist International Missions	1969	12	-	-	-	-
Bethany Fellowship Missions	1968	2	-	-	-	-
Brethren Assemblies		2	-	-	-	-
Child Evangelism Fellowship	1943	-	-	-	16	-
Christian Aid Mission		-	-	-	3	-
Christian and Msny. Alliance	1969	13	-	-	-	-
Christian Chs. /Chs. of Christ		6	-	-	-	-
Christian Reformed World Msns.	1979	21	4	2	-	-
Christian Reformed Wrld Relief		1	-	-	-	-
Church of God World Missions	1940	-	-	-	2	-
Church of the Nazarene	1972	6	-	-	-	-
Floresta USA, Inc.	1985	-	-	-	15	-
Food for the Hungry	1979	1	-	-	-	-
Habitat for Humanity Intl	1987	-	4	-	5	-

COUNTRY Agency	Year Began	Personnel from U.S.			Other Countries	
		4+ Yrs	2-4 Yrs	1-2 Yrs	Citizens	Not Citiz.
Harvest	1982	-	-	-	2	-
Heifer Project International	1962	-	-	-	7	-
International Child Care	1989	-	-	-	12	2
International Children's Care	1987	-	2	-	-	-
Kids Alive International	1989	3	-	-	5	-
Luke Society, The	1991	-	-	-	2	-
Medical Ambassadors Intl.	1988	-	-	-	6	-
Mission Possible	1988	-	1	-	10	-
Mission to the Americas	1981	1	-	-	1	-
Presbyterian Church (USA)		3	-	-	-	-
Seventh-day Adventists	1908	-	-	2	4	-
South American Missionary Soc.	1987	4	-	-	1	-
Southern Baptist Intl. Mission	1962	28	3	-	-	-
STEM Ministries	1994	-	-	-	-	-
UFM International	1943	18	-	2	-	-
United Church Board World Mins	1991	-	1	-	-	-
United Pentecostal Church Intl	1965	6	-	-	-	-
Wisconsin Evang. Lutheran Syn.	1993	2	-	-	-	-
World Indigenous Missions	1987	2	-	-	-	-
World Partners Missionary Ch.	1945	6	-	-	-	-
World Servants	1986	-	-	-	3	-
World Team	1939	4	-	-	-	-
Young Life	1989	4	-	-	-	-
Youth With A Mission (YWAM)		13	-	-	-	-
Totals:		174	15	6	94	2

ECUADOR

Assemblies of God	1962	20	-	-	-	-
Back to the Bible Intl.	1970	-	-	-	6	-
Baptist Bible Fellowship Intl.	1975	14	-	-	-	-
Baptist International Missions	1990	5	-	-	-	-
Baptist Mid-Missions	1988	15	-	-	-	-
Berean Mission, Inc.	1959	17	-	-	-	-
Brethren Assemblies		17	-	-	-	-
Calvary International	1985	8	-	-	1	-
Campus Crusade for Christ	1965	2	-	-	-	-
Child Evangelism Fellowship	1941	-	-	-	4	-
Christian and Msny. Alliance	1897	37	31	-	-	-
Christian Chs. /Chs. of Christ		6	-	-	-	1
Christian Reformed World Msns.	1991	1	-	-	-	1
Christian Reformed Wrld Relief		1	-	-	-	-
Christians In Action, Inc.	1979	2	-	-	8	-
Church of God of Prophecy	1982	-	-	-	-	2
Church of God World Missions	1971	6	-	-	-	2
Church of the Nazarene	1972	15	-	-	-	-
Evangelical Covenant Church	1947	10	-	3	-	-
Fellowship International Msn.	1967	4	-	-	-	-

COUNTRY Agency	Year Began	Personnel from U.S.			Other Countries	
		4+ Yrs	2-4 Yrs	1-2 Yrs	Citizens	Not Citiz.
Foursquare Missions Intl.	1956	2	-	-	-	-
Global Outreach, Ltd.	1989	-	2	-	-	-
Gospel Missionary Union	1896	51	1	2	6	3
HCJB World Radio Msny. Flwshp.	1931	170	-	-	12	45
Heifer Project International	1955	-	-	-	2	-
Holt Intl. Children's Services	1990	-	-	-	10	-
InterVarsity Mission	1992	-	2	-	-	-
Latin America Mission	1975	1	-	-	1	2
Lutheran Bible Translators	1982	2	-	1	3	-
MAP International	1985	3	1	-	1	1
Mission Aviation Fellowship	1948	22	-	3	2	-
Mission to the World	1975	17	7	-	-	-
OMS International, Inc.	1952	21	4	3	-	1
Rosedale Mennonite Missions	1982	10	-	-	-	-
Servants in Faith & Technology	1996	-	-	-	2	-
Seventh-day Adventists	1916	-	-	-	2	-
SIM USA	1989	4	-	-	-	-
Southern Baptist Intl. Mission	1950	55	10	-	-	-
Team Expansion, Inc.	1989	12	-	-	-	-
Trans World Radio	1991	-	2	-	-	-
United Church Board World Mins	1945	-	1	-	1	-
United Pentecostal Church Intl	1957	4	-	-	-	-
Walk Thru The Bible Ministries	1993	-	-	-	7	-
World Baptist Fellowship Msn	1972	16	-	-	-	-
World Mission Prayer League	1951	13	-	-	-	13
World Partners Missionary Ch.	1945	17	-	-	-	-
World Servants	1990	1	-	-	2	-
Youth for Christ / USA	1982	2	-	-	-	-
Totals:		603	61	12	70	70

EGYPT

Ambassadors for Christ Intl.		-	-	-	7	-
Arab World Ministries	1984	9	-	-	-	-
Campus Crusade for Christ	1972	7	-	-	-	-
Christ Community Church	1983	2	-	-	-	-
Christian Aid Mission		-	-	-	1	-
Church of God (Anderson, IN)	1908	4	-	-	-	-
Church of God of Prophecy	1935	-	-	-	2	-
Church of God World Missions	1946	-	-	-	2	-
Eastern Mennonite Missions	1992	2	-	-	-	-
Evangelical Lutheran Church	1967	3	-	-	-	-
Evangelistic Faith Missions	1905	-	-	-	27	-
Habitat for Humanity Intl	1989	-	1	-	1	-
Mennonite Central Committee	1968	6	12	-	-	-
Presbyterian Church (USA)	1954	13	10	-	-	-
Seventh-day Adventists	1879	4	-	-	-	-
Southern Baptist Intl. Mission	1980	10	-	-	-	-

COUNTRY Agency	Year Began	Personnel from U.S.			Other Countries	
		4+ Yrs	2-4 Yrs	1-2 Yrs	Citizens	Not Citiz.
United Pentecostal Church Intl	1960	2	-	-	-	-
Venture Middle East	1994	-	-	-	2	-
Totals:		62	23	-	42	-

EL SALVADOR

All Peoples Baptist Mission	1980	2	-	-	-	-
American Baptist Churches USA	1911	1	-	-	-	-
Assemblies of God	1925	12	-	-	-	-
Brethren Assemblies		4	-	-	-	-
CAM International	1896	9	-	-	-	-
Christian Reformed Wrld Relief		1	-	-	-	-
Church of God World Missions	1940	-	-	-	2	-
Evangelical Lutheran Church	1991	1	-	-	-	-
Evangelistic Faith Missions	1964	-	-	-	-	2
Every Home for Christ	1986	-	-	-	3	-
Foursquare Missions Intl.	1973	2	-	-	-	-
Habitat for Humanity Intl	1992	-	-	-	13	-
Harvesting In Spanish	1980	-	1	2	-	-
Living Water Teaching Intl.	1989	4	-	-	-	-
Medical Ambassadors Intl.	1984	-	-	-	6	-
Mennonite Central Committee	1981	6	5	-	-	-
Operation Blessing Intl.	1985	-	-	-	2	-
Partners International	1989	2	-	-	7	-
Pentecostal Free Will Bapt.Ch.	1994	-	-	-	2	-
Ripe for Harvest, Inc.	1993	-	1	-	-	-
Southern Baptist Intl. Mission	1975	9	-	-	-	-
Trans World Missions	1992	-	-	-	-	2
United Church Board World Mins	1983	-	2	-	-	-
United Pentecostal Church Intl	1975	4	-	-	-	-
Walk Thru The Bible Ministries	1993	-	-	-	1	-
World Reach, Inc.	1996	2	-	-	2	-
Totals:		59	9	2	38	4

EQUATORIAL GUINEA

Assemblies of God	1987	9	-	-	-	-
Every Home for Christ	1994	-	-	-	4	-
Pioneer Bible Translators	1994	2	-	-	-	-
Southern Baptist Intl. Mission	1981	4	-	-	-	-
Totals:		15	-	-	4	-

ERITREA

Evangelistic Faith Missions	1950	-	2	-	12	-
International Needs - USA	1980	-	-	-	3	-
Lutheran Church-Missouri Synod	1975	2	-	-	-	-
SIM USA	1952	5	-	-	-	-
Southern Baptist Intl. Mission	1994	10	2	-	-	-
Totals:		17	4	-	15	-

COUNTRY Agency	Year Began	Personnel from U.S.			Other Countries	
		4+ Yrs	2-4 Yrs	1-2 Yrs	Citizens	Not Citiz.
ESTONIA						
Brethren Assemblies		2	-	-	-	-
Campus Crusade for Christ	1994	1	-	16	-	-
Child Evangelism Fellowship	1968	-	-	-	4	-
Every Home for Christ	1993	-	-	-	-	1
Reformed Church In America		2	-	-	-	-
Walk Thru The Bible Ministries	1993	-	-	-	21	-
	Totals:	5	-	16	25	1
ETHIOPIA						
African Christian Mission	1996	-	-	1	-	-
African Enterprise, Inc.	1996	-	-	-	2	-
Assemblies of God	1968	8	-	-	-	-
Baptist Bible Fellowship Intl.	1960	6	-	-	-	-
Baptist General Conference	1950	5	-	-	-	-
Baptist Mid-Missions	1993	1	-	-	-	1
Christian Blind Mission Intl.	1985	-	2	-	-	-
Church of God of Prophecy	1996	-	-	-	1	-
Church of God World Missions	1994	-	-	-	2	-
Church of the Nazarene	1992	2	-	-	-	-
CMF International	1963	9	-	-	-	-
Eastern Mennonite Missions	1948	2	2	-	-	-
Elim Fellowship World Missions	1995	1	-	-	-	-
Evangelical Lutheran Church	1957	2	-	-	-	-
Every Home for Christ	1991	-	-	-	6	-
Habitat for Humanity Intl	1990	-	5	-	5	-
Helps International Ministries	1992	4	-	-	-	-
Intl. Pentecostal Holiness Ch.	1995	2	-	-	-	-
Medical Ambassadors Intl.	1993	-	-	-	2	-
Mennonite Brethren Msns/Svcs		-	-	-	1	-
Mennonite Central Committee	1975	2	-	-	-	-
Mission O.N.E., Inc.	1991	-	-	-	1	-
Mission to the World	1994	2	2	-	-	-
Mission: Moving Mountains	1995	6	-	1	-	-
Presbyterian Church (USA)	1820	4	18	2	-	-
Reformed Church In America	1963	6	-	-	-	-
Seventh-day Adventists	1907	6	-	1	20	-
SIM USA	1927	87	-	8	-	-
Southern Baptist Intl. Mission	1967	19	6	-	-	-
World Concern	1983	2	-	-	4	-
Wycliffe Bible Translators	1975	17	-	-	-	-
	Totals:	193	35	13	44	1
FIJI						
Ambassadors for Christ Intl.		-	-	-	10	2
Anglican Orthodox Church	1975	-	-	-	1	-

COUNTRY Agency	Year Began	Personnel from U.S.			Other Countries	
		4+ Yrs	2-4 Yrs	1-2 Yrs	Citizens	Not Citiz.
Assemblies of God	1914	8	-	-	-	-
Baptist Bible Fellowship Intl.	1976	2	-	-	-	-
Baptist International Missions	1994	4	-	-	-	-
Biblical Ministries Worldwide	1973	2	-	-	-	4
Child Evangelism Fellowship	1953	2	-	-	1	-
Church of God of Prophecy	1994	-	-	-	1	-
Church of God World Missions	1983	-	-	-	2	-
Church of the Nazarene	1996	2	-	-	-	-
Fellowship International Msn.	1995	1	-	-	1	-
Habitat for Humanity Intl	1991	-	2	2	2	4
International Needs - USA	1987	-	-	-	6	-
Presbyterian Church (USA)	1974	2	-	-	-	-
Seventh-day Adventists	1949	-	-	-	3	-
Youth With A Mission (YWAM)		4	-	-	-	-
Totals:		27	2	2	27	10

FINLAND

Baptist Mid-Missions	1980	2	-	-	-	-
BCM International	1968	-	-	-	2	-
Child Evangelism Fellowship	1961	-	-	-	7	-
Church of God of Prophecy	1981	-	-	-	1	-
Evangelical Lutheran Church	1978	1	-	-	-	-
Faith Christian Fellowship	1982	2	-	-	-	-
Mission Possible Foundation	1985	2	-	-	2	-
Navigators, The		4	-	-	-	-
United Pentecostal Church Intl	1987	2	-	-	-	-
Youth With A Mission (YWAM)		2	-	-	-	-
Totals:		15	-	-	12	-

FRANCE

ABWE	1984	10	-	-	-	-
American Baptist Association	1973	1	-	-	-	-
Apostolic Team Ministries Intl	1980	2	-	-	-	-
Arab World Ministries	1963	39	-	-	-	-
Assemblies of God	1952	11	-	-	-	-
Baptist Bible Fellowship Intl.	1970	8	-	-	-	-
Baptist General Conference	1989	5	-	-	-	-
Baptist International Missions	1969	4	-	-	-	-
Baptist Mid-Missions	1948	26	-	-	-	-
Baptist World Mission	1976	6	-	-	-	-
BCM International	1988	2	-	2	-	-
Bethany Fellowship Missions	1982	7	-	-	1	1
Brethren Assemblies		18	-	-	-	-
Campus Crusade for Christ	1970	28	-	3	-	-
CBInternational	1962	18	-	4	-	-
Child Evangelism Fellowship	1949	2	-	-	12	7

COUNTRY Agency	Year Began	Personnel from U.S.			Other Countries	
		4+ Yrs	2-4 Yrs	1-2 Yrs	Citizens	Not Citiz.
Christian and Msny. Alliance	1962	15	2	-	-	-
Christian Chs. /Chs. of Christ		6	-	-	-	-
Christian Outreach Intl.	1993	1	-	-	1	-
Christian Reformed World Msns.	1989	1	-	-	-	1
Christian World Publishers	1985	2	-	-	-	-
Church of God of Prophecy	1985	-	-	-	1	-
Church of God World Missions	1960	-	-	-	2	-
Church of the Nazarene	1977	4	-	-	-	-
Cornerstone, The	1984	2	-	-	-	-
Eastern Mennonite Missions	1955	-	-	-	3	-
European Missions Outreach	1989	2	-	-	-	-
Evangelical Baptist Missions	1956	26	-	-	-	-
Evangelical Free Church Msn.	1988	12	-	-	-	-
Evangelical Presbyterian Ch.	1992	2	-	-	-	-
Every Home for Christ	1992	-	-	-	4	-
Fellowship International Msn.	1987	1	-	-	-	-
Free Will Baptist Association	1966	9	-	-	-	-
French International Mission	1989	2	-	-	3	-
General Conf. Mennonite Church	1974	2	-	-	-	-
Global Outreach Mission	1946	29	-	-	-	-
Gospel Missionary Union	1960	14	-	-	1	-
Grace Brethren Intl. Missions	1951	19	1	3	-	-
Greater Europe Mission	1949	34	-	-	-	1
Hope for the Hungry	1990	-	2	-	-	-
International Missions, Inc.	1990	6	-	-	-	-
International Teams, U.S.A.	1969	17	3	-	-	1
InterVarsity Mission	1987	1	-	1	-	-
Intl. Pentecostal Holiness Ch.	1981	2	-	-	-	-
Jews for Jesus	1992	-	-	-	1	-
Lion and Lamb Outreach	1991	2	-	-	1	-
Maranatha Baptist Mission	1983	8	-	-	-	-
Mennonite Board of Missions	1953	3	-	-	-	-
Mission Soc. for United Meth.	1991	6	-	-	-	-
Mission to the World	1975	28	1	-	-	-
Navigators, The	1972	10	-	-	-	-
OC International, Inc.	1980	8	-	-	1	-
Operation Mobilization		1	-	-	-	-
Partners International	1983	-	-	-	2	-
Pocket Testament League	1963	-	-	-	2	-
Presbyterian Church (USA)		2	-	-	-	-
Reformed Baptist Mission Svcs.	1992	2	-	-	-	-
Reformed Episcopal Bd Missions	1970	2	-	-	-	-
Society for Europe's Evang.	1956	5	-	-	10	3
Southern Baptist Intl. Mission	1960	50	5	-	-	-
TEAM	1938	53	-	-	-	-
Team Expansion, Inc.	1991	2	-	-	-	-
UFM International	1962	26	-	1	-	-

COUNTRY Agency	Year Began	Personnel from U.S.			Other Countries	
		4+ Yrs	2-4 Yrs	1-2 Yrs	Citizens	Not Citiz.
United Pentecostal Church Intl	1973	4	-	-	-	-
Walk Thru The Bible Ministries	1990	-	-	-	2	-
WEC International	1950	-	1	-	-	-
World Baptist Fellowship Msn	1954	2	-	-	-	-
World Partners Missionary Ch.	1979	6	2	-	-	-
World Team	1980	12	-	-	-	-
Youth for Christ / USA	1949	1	-	-	-	-
Youth With A Mission (YWAM)		9	-	-	-	-
	Totals:	638	17	14	47	14

FRENCH GUIANA

Brethren Assemblies		2	-	-	-	-
Church of God of Prophecy	1991	-	-	-	1	-
Church of the Nazarene	1988	2	-	-	-	-
Seventh-day Adventists	1946	-	-	-	2	-
Southern Baptist Intl. Mission	1982	4	-	-	-	-
	Totals:	8	-	-	3	-

FRENCH POLYNESIA

Baptist Bible Fellowship Intl.	1977	2	-	-	-	-
Seventh-day Adventists	1891	-	-	-	2	-
Youth With A Mission (YWAM)		1	-	-	-	-
	Totals:	3	-	-	2	-

GABON

Child Evangelism Fellowship	1982	-	-	-	8	-
Christian and Msny. Alliance	1934	32	6	-	-	-
InterVarsity Mission	1994	2	-	-	-	-
Medical Ambassadors Intl.	1993	-	-	-	1	-
Seventh-day Adventists	1977	2	-	-	-	-
	Totals:	36	6	-	9	-

GAMBIA

ABWE	1978	17	-	4	-	-
Child Evangelism Fellowship	1986	-	-	-	10	-
Christian Aid Mission		-	-	-	4	-
General Conf. Mennonite Church	1995	2	-	-	-	1
Southern Baptist Intl. Mission	1982	8	4	-	-	-
WEC International	1957	-	-	2	-	-
	Totals:	27	4	6	14	1

GAZA

Southern Baptist Intl. Mission	1954	7	2	-	-	-
	Totals:	7	2	-	-	-

COUNTRY	Year	Personnel from U.S.			Other Countries	
Agency	Began	4+ Yrs	2-4 Yrs	1-2 Yrs	Citizens	Not Citiz.

GEORGIA

Baptist Bible Fellowship Intl.	1995	2	-	-	-	-
	Totals:	2	-	-	-	-

GERMANY

ABWE	1989	5	-	-	-	-
All Peoples Baptist Mission	1980	2	-	-	-	-
American Baptist Association		1	-	-	-	-
Arab World Ministries	1986	3	-	-	-	-
Assemblies of God	1950	35	-	-	-	-
Baptist Bible Fellowship Intl.	1970	24	-	-	-	-
Baptist International Missions	1969	8	-	-	-	-
Baptist Mid-Missions	1952	19	-	-	-	-
Baptist Missions to Forgotten		11	-	-	-	-
BCM International	1969	4	-	-	4	-
Bible Missionary Church	1995	2	-	-	-	-
Biblical Ministries Worldwide	1959	11	-	-	-	-
Brethren Assemblies		4	-	-	-	-
Cadence International	1973	19	33	9	-	-
Campus Crusade for Christ	1966	30	-	-	-	-
Child Evangelism Fellowship	1948	4	-	-	44	1
Christian Chs. /Chs. of Christ	1956	10	-	-	-	-
Christians In Action, Inc.	1972	3	-	-	1	1
Church of God of Prophecy	1959	2	2	1	-	-
Church of God World Missions	1936	6	-	-	-	-
Church of The Brethren	1946	-	-	5	-	-
Church of the Nazarene	1958	18	-	-	2	-
Eastern Mennonite Missions	1957	1	2	-	1	-
European Evangelistic Society	1991	2	-	-	2	-
Evangelical Baptist Missions	1977	6	-	-	-	-
Evangelical Covenant Church	1991	2	-	-	-	-
Evangelical Free Church Msn.	1958	17	3	1	-	-
Evangelical Lutheran Church	1972	2	-	-	-	-
Faith Christian Fellowship	1987	4	-	-	-	-
Fellowship International Msn.	1984	2	-	-	-	-
Foursquare Missions Intl.	1985	2	-	-	-	-
General Conf. Mennonite Church	1994	-	-	-	-	4
Global Outreach Mission	1946	7	-	-	-	-
Globe Missionary Evangelism	1984	2	-	-	-	-
Go Ye Fellowship	1980	2	-	-	-	-
Gospel Fellowship Association		18	-	-	-	-
Gospel Missionary Union	1961	10	2	1	-	-
Grace Brethren Intl. Missions	1969	12	-	-	-	-
Greater Europe Mission	1954	20	2	-	-	2
International Missions, Inc.	1990	4	-	-	-	-
International Teams, U.S.A.	1972	2	1	-	-	-

COUNTRY Agency	Year Began	Personnel from U.S.			Other Countries	
		4+ Yrs	2-4 Yrs	1-2 Yrs	Citizens	Not Citiz.
Intl. Discipleship Mission	1990	2	-	-	-	-
Intl. Pentecostal Holiness Ch.	1987	4	-	-	-	-
Liebenzell Mission USA	1899	-	2	-	-	-
Macedonia World Baptist Msns.	1987	4	-	-	-	-
Maranatha Baptist Mission	1981	4	-	-	-	-
Mennonite Brethren Msns/Svcs	1953	6	6	-	-	-
Mennonite Central Committee	1948	2	-	-	-	-
Mission Possible Foundation	1978	2	1	-	-	-
Mission to the World	1981	8	1	-	-	-
New Tribes Mission	1991	2	-	-	-	-
OC International, Inc.	1981	10	-	-	-	-
Operation Mobilization		4	-	-	-	-
Pocket Testament League	1985	1	-	-	1	-
Presbyterian Church (USA)		2	8	-	-	-
Reformed Episcopal Bd Missions	1950	3	-	-	4	-
Rosedale Mennonite Missions	1952	-	-	2	-	-
Salvation Army, U.S.A.	1886	2	-	-	-	-
SEND International	1980	2	1	-	1	-
Seventh-day Adventists	1875	-	-	-	2	-
Son Shine Ministries Intl.	1986	2	-	-	-	-
Southern Baptist Intl. Mission	1961	46	19	-	-	-
TEAM	1910	16	3	-	-	-
Trans World Radio	1983	1	-	-	3	-
Turkish World Outreach	1988	2	-	-	-	-
UFM International	1976	19	-	4	-	-
United Methodist Church		2	-	-	-	-
United Pentecostal Church Intl	1967	4	-	-	-	-
Walk Thru The Bible Ministries	1988	-	-	-	1	1
WEC International	1948	1	-	-	-	-
Wesleyan World Missions	1988	2	-	-	-	-
World Reach, Inc.	1989	4	-	-	2	-
World Witness	1993	3	-	-	-	-
Young Life	1975	2	8	7	-	-
Youth With A Mission (YWAM)		15	-	-	-	-
Totals:		513	94	30	68	9

GHANA

ABWE	1993	4	-	-	-	-
Advent Christian World Msns.	1993	-	-	-	2	-
African Enterprise, Inc.	1995	-	-	-	3	-
African Methodist Epis. Zion	1896	-	1	-	-	-
African Mission Evangelism	1966	13	-	-	5	-
Agape Gospel Mission	1994	-	-	-	8	3
Ambassadors for Christ Intl.		-	-	-	4	-
Assemblies of God	1931	4	-	-	-	-
Baptist International Missions	1976	-	-	-	-	4
Baptist Mid-Missions	1946	18	-	-	-	-

COUNTRY Agency	Year Began	Personnel from U.S.			Other Countries	
		4+ Yrs	2-4 Yrs	1-2 Yrs	Citizens	Not Citiz.
BCM International	1985	3	-	-	3	-
Bethany Fellowship Missions	1995	2	-	-	-	-
Bible Missionary Church	1984	2	-	-	-	-
Child Evangelism Fellowship	1971	-	-	-	29	2
Christian Aid Mission		-	-	-	1	-
Christian Chs. /Chs. of Christ	1965	7	-	-	-	-
Christians In Action, Inc.	1994	-	-	1	-	-
Church of God of Prophecy	1977	-	-	-	1	-
Church of God World Missions	1965	-	-	-	-	2
Church of the Nazarene	1990	4	-	-	-	-
Evangelical Lutheran Church	1975	2	-	-	-	-
Every Home for Christ	1976	-	-	-	3	-
Foursquare Missions Intl.	1973	2	-	-	-	-
Full Gospel Grace Fellowship		1	-	-	-	-
Global Outreach Mission	1985	-	-	-	2	-
Gospel Recordings USA	1990	-	-	-	2	-
Gospel Revival Ministries	1996	-	-	-	3	-
Habitat for Humanity Intl	1987	-	3	-	16	-
International Bible Institute	1992	-	-	-	-	-
International Needs - USA	1986	-	-	-	25	-
International Partnership Mins	1987	-	-	-	4	-
Intl. Pentecostal Holiness Ch.	1992	3	-	-	-	-
Luke Society, The	1989	-	-	-	2	-
Lutheran Church-Missouri Synod	1960	11	-	5	-	-
Mennonite Board of Missions	1957	6	-	-	-	-
Mission Soc. for United Meth.	1987	6	-	2	-	-
Mission to the World	1991	2	-	-	-	-
National Baptist Conv. of Am.	1980	-	-	-	-	-
Navigators, The	1967	7	-	-	-	-
Partners International	1973	-	-	-	3	-
Pioneers	1984	-	-	-	2	-
Presbyterian Church (USA)	1964	4	-	-	-	-
Salvation Army, U.S.A.	1922	2	-	-	-	-
Self-Help Foundation	1991	1	-	-	1	-
Seventh-day Adventists	1894	2	-	1	4	-
SIM USA	1956	17	-	-	-	-
Southern Baptist Intl. Mission	1947	28	2	-	-	-
United Church Board World Mins	1946	-	1	-	-	-
United Methodist Church		2	-	-	-	-
United Pentecostal Church Intl	1969	5	-	-	-	-
Wycliffe Bible Translators	1962	30	1	-	-	-
Youth With A Mission (YWAM)		2	-	-	-	-
Totals:		190	8	9	123	11

GIBRALTAR

World Salt Foundation		2	-	-	-	-
Totals:		2	-	-	-	-

COUNTRY Agency	Year Began	Personnel from U.S.			Other Countries	
		4+ Yrs	2-4 Yrs	1-2 Yrs	Citizens	Not Citiz.

GREECE

AMG International	1950	2	-	-	11	-
Assemblies of God	1931	10	-	-	-	-
Baptist Bible Fellowship Intl.	1993	2	-	-	-	-
BCM International	1995	-	-	-	2	-
Brethren Assemblies		4	-	-	-	-
Campus Crusade for Christ	1978	3	-	-	-	-
Child Evangelism Fellowship	1971	-	-	-	2	1
Church of God of Prophecy	1931	1	1	1	2	-
Church of God World Missions	1965	-	-	-	2	-
Congregational Christian Chs.		-	-	-	2	-
Eastern Mennonite Missions	1990	2	-	-	-	-
European Christian Mission	1987	7	-	-	-	-
Every Home for Christ	1981	-	-	-	2	-
Global Outreach Mission	1994	2	-	-	-	-
Gospel Missionary Union	1959	6	-	-	3	1
Greater Europe Mission	1966	15	-	-	1	-
Hellenic Ministries	1981	7	-	-	4	5
International Teams, U.S.A.	1990	4	1	-	2	-
OC International, Inc.	1967	2	-	-	-	-
United Pentecostal Church Intl	1975	4	-	-	-	-
Walk Thru The Bible Ministries	1990	-	-	-	2	-
	Totals:	71	2	1	35	7

GREENLAND

Assemblies of God	1989	-	-	-	-	-
New Tribes Mission	1988	1	-	-	-	10
	Totals:	1	-	-	-	10

GRENADA

Baptist International Missions	1979	2	-	-	-	-
Baptist Missions to Forgotten		2	-	-	-	-
Berean Mission, Inc.	1989	3	-	-	-	-
Christian Chs. /Chs. of Christ		4	-	-	-	-
Macedonia World Baptist Msns.	1986	2	-	-	-	-
Maranatha Baptist Mission	1987	2	-	-	-	-
Youth With A Mission (YWAM)		6	-	-	-	-
	Totals:	21	-	-	-	-

GUADELOUPE

Ambassadors for Christ Intl.		-	-	-	7	-
World Team	1947	4	-	-	-	-
	Totals:	4	-	-	7	-

COUNTRY Agency	Year Began	Personnel from U.S.			Other Countries	
		4+ Yrs	2-4 Yrs	1-2 Yrs	Citizens	Not Citiz.
GUAM						
Assemblies of God	1961	3	-	-	-	-
Biblical Ministries Worldwide	1981	4	-	-	-	-
Christian Reformed World Msns.	1962	4	-	-	-	-
Church of the Nazarene	1970	1	-	-	-	-
Evangelical Lutheran Church	1986	-	-	-	-	-
Liebenzell Mission USA	1961	8	-	-	-	-
Mission to the Americas	1957	2	-	-	-	-
Seventh-day Adventists	1930	68	-	9	2	-
Trans World Radio	1975	32	-	3	2	-
Youth With A Mission (YWAM)		1	-	-	-	-
Totals:		123	-	12	4	-
GUATEMALA						
AMG International	1978	2	-	-	5	-
Assemblies of God	1937	11	-	-	-	-
BALL World Missions	1990	-	2	2	-	-
Baptist International Missions	1971	5	-	-	-	-
Baptist Missionary Assoc.		3	-	-	-	-
Brethren Assemblies		6	-	-	-	-
Bright Hope International		-	-	-	2	-
Calvary International	1986	15	-	-	-	-
CAM International	1899	47	-	3	6	2
Child Evangelism Fellowship	1943	-	-	-	3	-
Christian Aid Mission		-	-	-	8	-
Christian and Msny. Alliance	1969	2	-	-	-	-
Christian Chs. /Chs. of Christ	1991	2	4	-	-	-
Christians In Action, Inc.	1970	2	-	69	21	-
Church of God World Missions	1934	2	-	-	-	-
Church of the Nazarene	1904	15	-	-	2	-
Correll Missionary Ministries	1991	-	-	-	4	-
Eastern Mennonite Missions	1967	13	-	-	-	-
Evangelical Lutheran Church	1990	1	-	-	-	-
Evangelistic Faith Missions	1947	-	2	-	-	-
Faith Christian Fellowship	1980	4	-	-	-	-
Friends Church Southwest	1902	4	-	-	-	-
Globe Missionary Evangelism	1983	12	-	2	-	-
Gospel Recordings USA	1994	-	2	-	-	-
Habitat for Humanity Intl	1979	-	2	-	15	-
Heifer Project International	1960	-	-	-	4	-
Help for Christian Nationals	1988	-	-	-	2	-
Holt Intl. Children's Services	1986	-	-	-	25	-
Impact International	1970	-	-	-	7	-
International Children's Care	1990	-	1	5	-	-
Intl. Pentecostal Holiness Ch.	1995	-	2	-	-	-
Kids Alive International	1992	2	-	-	2	-

COUNTRY Agency	Year Began	Personnel from U.S.			Other Countries	
		4+ Yrs	2-4 Yrs	1-2 Yrs	Citizens	Not Citiz.
Latin America Mission	1993	-	2	-	-	-
Living Water Teaching Intl.	1979	9	2	15	5	-
Lutheran Bible Translators	1988	10	-	-	4	-
Lutheran Church-Missouri Synod	1947	9	-	4	-	-
Maranatha Baptist Mission	1991	2	-	-	-	-
Medical Ambassadors Intl.	1983	-	-	-	14	-
Mennonite Brethren Msns/Svcs		-	-	-	2	-
Mennonite Central Committee	1976	4	2	-	-	-
Mission Aviation Fellowship	1977	9	1	-	1	-
Mission Soc. for United Meth.	1987	2	-	-	-	-
Mission to the Americas	1992	-	-	-	14	-
New Life League International	1976	-	-	-	10	5
OC International, Inc.	1979	15	-	1	-	-
Operation Blessing Intl.	1985	-	-	-	6	-
Partners International	1964	-	-	-	7	-
Pentecostal Free Will Bapt.Ch.	1987	-	2	-	2	-
Presbyterian Church (USA)	1822	14	-	20	-	-
Primitive Methodist Church USA	1922	4	-	-	-	4
Southern Baptist Intl. Mission	1948	43	6	-	-	-
Sowers International, The	1994	-	-	-	1	-
United Methodist Church		2	-	-	-	-
United Pentecostal Church Intl	1977	2	-	-	-	-
United World Mission	1952	4	-	-	-	-
Walk Thru The Bible Ministries	1993	-	-	-	1	-
World Baptist Fellowship Msn	1968	2	-	-	-	-
Wycliffe Bible Translators	1952	96	1	-	-	-
Youth With A Mission (YWAM)		17	-	-	-	-
Totals:		392	31	121	173	11

GUINEA

Campus Crusade for Christ	1977	2	-	-	-	-
Christian and Msny. Alliance	1919	2	-	-	-	-
Christian Chs. /Chs. of Christ	1990	1	-	-	-	-
Christian Reformed World Msns.	1984	7	1	2	-	-
Christian Reformed Wrld Relief		1	-	-	-	-
Lutheran Church-Missouri Synod	1990	2	-	-	-	-
Mission Soc. for United Meth.	1995	2	-	-	-	-
National Baptist Conv. USA	1990	-	2	-	11	-
New Tribes Mission	1986	40	-	1	-	8
Open Bible Standard Churches	1988	2	-	-	-	-
Pioneer Bible Translators	1988	20	-	-	-	-
Seventh-day Adventists	1986	2	-	-	-	-
SIM USA	1986	19	-	-	-	-
Southern Baptist Intl. Mission	1989	10	2	-	-	-
WEC International	1986	-	-	1	-	-
World Partners Missionary Ch.	1995	6	-	-	-	-
Totals:		116	5	4	11	8

COUNTRY Agency	Year Began	Personnel from U.S.			Other Countries	
		4+ Yrs	2-4 Yrs	1-2 Yrs	Citizens	Not Citiz.

GUINEA BISSAU

Assemblies of God	1990	4	-	-	-	-
Christians In Action, Inc.	1995	-	2	-	-	-
Seventh-day Adventists	1980	-	-	-	2	-
Southern Baptist Intl. Mission	1989	4	-	-	-	-
WEC International	1939	-	-	5	-	-
Youth With A Mission (YWAM)		1	-	-	-	-
Totals:		9	2	5	2	-

GUYANA

African Methodist Epis. Zion	1911	-	1	-	-	-
Assemblies of God	1953	2	-	-	-	-
Baptist Bible Fellowship Intl.	1993	4	-	-	-	-
Baptist International Missions	1994	1	-	-	1	-
Baptist Mid-Missions	1954	8	-	-	-	-
Bible Missionary Church	1958	4	-	-	-	-
Christian Chs. /Chs. of Christ	1959	2	-	-	-	-
Church of God of Prophecy	1956	-	-	-	1	-
Habitat for Humanity Intl	1995	-	4	-	-	-
Pioneers	1986	1	-	-	1	-
Seventh-day Adventists		-	-	-	2	-
Southern Baptist Intl. Mission	1962	11	-	-	-	-
UFM International	1949	10	-	-	-	-
United Methodist Church		2	-	-	-	-
Virginia Mennonite Bd. of Msns	1988	-	-	-	2	-
Walk Thru The Bible Ministries	1994	-	-	-	-	1
Wesleyan World Missions	1913	1	-	-	-	-
Wycliffe Bible Translators	1974	5	-	-	-	-
Youth With A Mission (YWAM)		5	-	-	-	-
Totals:		56	5	-	7	1

HAITI

Allegheny Wesleyan Meth. Msns.	1969	9	-	-	-	-
American Baptist Churches USA	1923	14	-	-	-	-
Assemblies of God	1945	4	-	-	-	-
Baptist Bible Fellowship Intl.	1982	3	-	-	-	-
Baptist International Missions	1978	4	-	-	-	-
Baptist Mid-Missions	1934	11	-	-	-	-
Baptist World Mission		4	-	-	-	-
Barnabas Ministries, Inc.	1993	-	-	-	8	-
Child Evangelism Fellowship	1946	2	-	-	-	-
Childcare International	1983	-	-	-	30	-
Christian Aid Ministries	1991	-	2	-	-	-
Christian Aid Mission		-	-	-	7	-
Christian Chs. /Chs. of Christ		29	-	-	-	-
Christian Reformed World Msns.	1985	6	1	-	-	-

COUNTRY Agency	Year Began	Personnel from U.S.			Other Countries	
		4+ Yrs	2-4 Yrs	1-2 Yrs	Citizens	Not Citiz.
Church of God of Prophecy	1931	-	-	-	2	-
Church of God World Missions	1933	4	-	-	3	-
Church of The Brethren		-	-	2	-	-
Church of the Nazarene	1950	8	-	-	-	-
Churches of God General Conf.	1967	3	-	2	-	-
CSI Ministries	1963	2	-	-	-	-
ECHO	1993	-	-	1	-	-
Elim Fellowship World Missions	1986	2	-	-	-	-
Evangelical Bible Mission	1943	-	6	-	-	-
Evangelical Free Church Msn.	1993	2	-	-	-	-
FOCAS	1986	-	-	-	25	-
For Haiti with Love Inc.	1969	-	-	-	12	-
Foursquare Missions Intl.	1981	2	-	-	-	-
Friends for Missions, Inc.	1968	1	-	-	15	-
Global Outreach, Ltd.	1979	-	2	2	-	-
Global Strategy Mission Assoc.	1988	2	-	-	-	-
Globe Missionary Evangelism	1989	4	-	-	-	-
Habitat for Humanity Intl	1981	-	3	-	-	-
Haiti Gospel Mission	1972	1	-	-	67	1
Harvest	1982	-	-	-	2	-
Have Christ Will Travel Mins.	1966	-	-	-	31	-
Hope for the Hungry	1983	2	3	-	-	-
International Child Care	1966	2	-	-	270	4
International Partnership Mins	1982	-	-	-	35	-
Intl. Pentecostal Holiness Ch.	1976	5	-	-	-	-
ISOH/Impact		-	1	-	-	-
Macedonia World Baptist Msns.	1967	2	-	-	-	-
Medical Ambassadors Intl.	1981	1	-	-	9	-
Mennonite Central Committee	1958	10	6	-	-	-
Ministries In Action	1970	3	-	-	-	-
Mission Aviation Fellowship	1981	3	2	-	-	-
Mission Possible	1979	4	1	-	80	1
Mission Soc. for United Meth.	1995	1	-	-	-	-
Mission to the Americas	1992	2	-	-	1	-
Mission to the World	1975	2	-	-	-	-
Missionary Flights Intl.	1964	-	-	-	-	-
New Missions in Haiti	1983	-	6	-	-	-
OMS International, Inc.	1958	13	2	2	89	-
Presbyterian Church (USA)	1974	6	-	-	-	-
Reciprocal Ministries Intl.	1988	2	-	-	2	-
Rehoboth Ministries, Inc	1985	2	-	-	-	-
Seventh-day Adventists	1905	6	-	-	6	-
Society of St. Margaret	1927	2	-	-	2	2
Southern Baptist Intl. Mission	1978	4	2	-	-	-
STEM Ministries	1985	-	1	1	-	-
UFM International	1943	35	-	-	-	-
United Methodist Church		2	-	-	-	-

COUNTRY Agency	Year Began	Personnel from U.S.			Other Countries	
		4+ Yrs	2-4 Yrs	1-2 Yrs	Citizens	Not Citiz.
United Pentecostal Church Intl	1966	4	-	-	-	-
Wesleyan World Missions	1948	11	-	-	-	-
World Concern	1987	-	4	-	18	-
World Gospel Mission	1962	2	-	-	-	-
World Partners Missionary Ch.	1954	-	-	-	-	-
World Team	1936	9	-	-	-	6
World-Wide Missions	1960	-	-	2	75	-
Youth With A Mission (YWAM)		10	-	-	-	-
	Totals:	262	42	12	789	14

HONDURAS

Advent Christian World Msns.	1994	-	-	2	-	-
Assemblies of God	1940	17	-	-	-	-
Baptist Bible Fellowship Intl.	1974	1	-	-	-	-
Baptist International Missions	1970	10	-	-	-	-
Baptist Mid-Missions	1959	8	-	-	-	-
Baptist Missionary Assoc.	1976	4	-	-	-	-
Biblical Ministries Worldwide	1954	8	-	-	-	-
Brethren Assemblies		8	-	-	-	-
Brethren in Christ World Msns.		-	2	-	-	2
CAM International	1896	20	-	-	-	-
Child Evangelism Fellowship	1964	1	-	-	1	-
Christian Aid Mission		-	-	-	28	-
Christian Chs. /Chs. of Christ		7	-	-	-	-
Christian Reformed World Msns.	1971	10	5	-	-	-
Christian Reformed Wrld Relief		1	-	-	-	-
Church of God World Missions	1944	8	-	-	1	-
Church of the Nazarene	1970	2	-	-	-	-
Church of the United Brethren	1945	-	-	-	-	-
Congregational Christian Chs.	1975	-	-	-	1	-
Congregational Methodist Ch.	1960	3	-	-	-	-
Deaf Missions International	1991	-	-	-	-	-
Eastern Mennonite Missions	1950	-	2	-	-	-
Evangelistic Faith Missions	1968	-	3	-	-	-
Every Home for Christ	1982	-	-	-	7	-
Foursquare Missions Intl.	1952	2	-	-	-	-
Friends Church Southwest	1915	2	-	-	-	-
General Baptists International	1992	-	4	-	-	-
Global Outreach Mission	1994	2	-	-	-	-
Global Outreach, Ltd.	1979	-	3	2	-	-
Globe Missionary Evangelism	1979	2	-	-	-	-
Habitat for Humanity Intl	1988	-	3	-	13	-
Harvest	1982	-	-	-	1	-
Heifer Project International	1958	-	-	-	-	1
Help for Christian Nationals	1980	-	-	-	1	-
Impact International	1975	-	-	-	3	-
International Gospel Outreach	1993	-	-	1	4	-

COUNTRY Agency	Year Began	Personnel from U.S.			Other Countries	
		4+ Yrs	2-4 Yrs	1-2 Yrs	Citizens	Not Citiz.
Intl. Pentecostal Holiness Ch.	1993	2	-	-	-	-
Living Water Teaching Intl.	1991	5	-	-	-	-
Luke Society, The	1983	-	-	-	4	-
Lutheran Church-Missouri Synod	1961	-	-	2	-	-
Mennonite Central Committee	1981	4	2	-	-	-
Mission Aviation Fellowship	1952	12	-	-	-	2
Mission Soc. for United Meth.	1995	2	-	-	-	-
Mission to the Americas	1951	8	-	-	10	-
Moravian Church North America	1930	-	3	-	1	-
Morelli Ministries Intl.	1996	-	-	-	1	-
Presbyterian Church (USA)	1973	9	-	-	-	-
Reformed Church In America	1985	3	-	-	-	-
Ripe for Harvest, Inc.	1993	-	5	-	-	-
Seventh-day Adventists	1891	4	-	-	-	-
South American Missionary Soc.	1981	14	-	-	-	2
Southern Baptist Intl. Mission	1954	38	4	-	-	-
Spanish World Gospel Mission		-	-	-	2	-
Teen Missions International		-	4	1	-	4
Trans World Missions	1990	-	-	-	-	2
United Church Board World Mins	1921	-	1	-	-	-
United Methodist Church		2	-	-	-	-
United Pentecostal Church Intl	1977	4	-	-	-	-
Wesleyan World Missions	1957	2	-	-	-	-
World Baptist Fellowship Msn	1969	8	-	-	-	-
World Gospel Mission	1944	31	-	-	-	-
World Reach, Inc.	1982	6	-	-	6	-
Youth With A Mission (YWAM)		3	-	-	-	-
Totals:		273	41	8	84	13

HONG KONG

COUNTRY Agency	Year Began	Personnel from U.S.			Other Countries	
		4+ Yrs	2-4 Yrs	1-2 Yrs	Citizens	Not Citiz.
ABWE	1950	11	-	-	-	-
American Baptist Churches USA	1842	2	-	-	1	-
Asian Outreach U.S.A.	1960	-	-	3	1	-
Assemblies of God	1909	26	-	-	-	-
BALL World Missions	1983	2	-	-	-	-
Baptist Bible Fellowship Intl.	1950	11	-	-	-	-
Baptist Mid-Missions	1958	1	-	-	-	-
Biblical Ministries Worldwide	1987	4	-	-	-	-
Brethren Assemblies		2	-	-	-	-
Campus Crusade for Christ	1972	5	-	2	-	-
CBInternational	1963	8	-	-	-	-
Child Evangelism Fellowship	1948	1	-	-	16	4
China Ministries International	1978	-	-	1	30	2
Chinese Christian Mission, Inc	1991	5	-	-	-	-
Christian and Msny. Alliance	1933	10	4	-	-	-
Christian Chs. /Chs. of Christ	1963	18	-	-	-	-
Christian Literature Crusade	1976	2	-	-	-	-

COUNTRY Agency	Year Began	Personnel from U.S.			Other Countries	
		4+ Yrs	2-4 Yrs	1-2 Yrs	Citizens	Not Citiz.
Church of God (Anderson, IN)	1953	2	-	-	-	-
Church of God World Missions	1986	-	-	-	-	2
Church of the Nazarene	1971	6	-	-	-	-
Church of the United Brethren	1949	-	-	-	-	-
Congregational Christian Chs.	1955	-	-	-	1	-
Cumberland Presbyterian Church	1949	1	-	-	-	-
Eastern Mennonite Missions	1965	5	-	-	-	-
Elim Fellowship World Missions	1986	3	-	1	-	-
Evangelical Free Church Msn.	1887	8	4	-	-	-
Evangelical Lutheran Church	1890	6	-	-	-	-
Evangelical Mennonite Church	1993	2	-	-	-	-
General Conf. Mennonite Church	1980	2	-	-	-	2
Holt Intl. Children's Services	1986	-	1	-	3	1
International Missions, Inc.	1949	8	-	-	-	-
International Needs - USA	1992	-	-	-	1	-
Intl. Pentecostal Holiness Ch.	1911	3	-	-	-	-
Kids Alive International	1949	-	-	2	-	-
Lutheran Church-Missouri Synod	1950	40	-	-	-	-
Mission to the World	1983	2	-	-	-	-
Mission To Unreached Peoples	1986	-	2	-	-	-
OC International, Inc.	1993	2	-	-	-	-
OMF International	1951	16	-	-	-	21
OMS International, Inc.	1954	13	2	-	1	-
Partners International	1950	2	-	-	21	-
Presbyterian Church (USA)	1844	9	-	-	-	-
Reach Ministries International		1	-	-	-	-
Reformed Church In America		2	-	-	-	-
Salvation Army, U.S.A.	1930	2	-	-	-	-
Seventh-day Adventists	1888	34	-	5	2	-
Southern Baptist Intl. Mission	1949	63	25	-	-	-
TEAM	1988	4	-	-	-	-
Training Evangelistic Ldrshp.	1987	4	-	-	-	-
United Church Board World Mins	1950	2	2	-	-	-
United Pentecostal Church Intl	1976	4	-	-	-	-
Walk Thru The Bible Ministries	1982	-	-	-	1	-
Wisconsin Evang. Lutheran Syn.	1964	4	-	-	-	-
Youth With A Mission (YWAM)		8	-	-	-	-
Totals:		366	40	14	78	32

HUNGARY

Assemblies of God	1926	4	-	-	-	-
Baptist Bible Fellowship Intl.	1990	10	-	-	-	-
Baptist International Missions	1990	4	-	-	-	-
Baptist World Mission		2	-	-	-	-
BCM International	1994	-	-	-	-	2
Brethren Assemblies		1	-	-	-	-
Campus Crusade for Christ	1978	53	-	29	-	-

COUNTRY / Agency	Year Began	Personnel from U.S.			Other Countries	
		4+ Yrs	2-4 Yrs	1-2 Yrs	Citizens	Not Citiz.
CBInternational	1991	8	1	9	-	-
Child Evangelism Fellowship	1972	1	-	-	12	5
Christian Reformed World Msns.	1990	3	1	2	-	-
Church Resource Ministries	1986	13	-	-	3	-
Faith Christian Fellowship	1987	2	-	-	-	-
Free Methodist World Missions		5	-	-	-	-
Friendship International	1990	-	-	2	-	-
General Conf. Mennonite Church	1993	2	-	-	-	-
Greater Europe Mission	1993	9	1	-	-	1
Habitat for Humanity Intl	1994	2	1	-	-	3
Heart to Heart Intl Ministries		-	-	1	-	-
International Messengers	1989	2	-	-	4	2
International Teams, U.S.A.	1973	3	-	-	-	-
Intl. Pentecostal Holiness Ch.	1989	2	-	-	-	-
Lutheran Church-Missouri Synod	1991	-	-	5	-	-
Mission Soc. for United Meth.	1995	-	2	-	-	-
Mission to the World	1991	4	2	-	-	-
Navigators, The		4	-	-	-	-
OMS International, Inc.	1992	8	6	-	7	4
Pioneers	1992	2	-	-	-	-
Reformed Church In America		2	-	-	-	-
Ripe for Harvest, Inc.	1996	-	1	-	-	-
SEND International	1994	4	-	-	-	-
Team Expansion, Inc.	1995	6	-	-	-	-
United Pentecostal Church Intl	1972	2	-	-	-	-
Westminister Biblical Missions	1991	1	-	-	-	-
World Gospel Mission	1992	5	-	-	-	-
Young Life	1988	2	-	-	-	-
Youth With A Mission (YWAM)		9	-	-	-	-
Totals:		175	15	48	26	17

ICELAND

Assemblies of God		2	-	-	-	-
Baptist Missions to Forgotten		2	-	-	-	-
Globe Missionary Evangelism	1995	-	-	2	-	-
Greater Europe Mission	1985	4	-	-	-	-
Navigators, The	1967	2	-	-	-	-
Totals:		10	-	2	-	-

INDIA

Action International Mins.	1986	4	-	-	-	-
Advent Christian World Msns.	1882	2	-	-	-	1
Ambassadors for Christ Intl.		-	-	-	26	-
American Baptist Churches USA	1836	6	2	-	2	2
AMG International	1968	-	-	-	400	-
Anglican Orthodox Church	1965	-	-	-	2	-

COUNTRY / Agency	Year Began	Personnel from U.S. 4+ Yrs	2-4 Yrs	1-2 Yrs	Other Countries Citizens	Not Citiz.
ARISE International	1993	-	-	-	3	-
Assoc of Free Lutheran Congs	1979	-	-	-	32	-
Back to the Bible Intl.	1970	-	-	-	22	-
Baptist Bible Fellowship Intl.	1952	7	-	-	-	-
Baptist General Conference	1946	-	-	-	3	-
Baptist International Missions	1978	-	-	2	2	-
Baptist Mid-Missions	1935	6	-	-	4	-
Baptist World Mission		2	-	-	-	-
BCM International	1972	-	-	-	181	-
Bibles For The World	1989	-	-	-	-	-
BILD International	1986	-	-	-	-	-
Brethren Assemblies		9	-	-	-	-
Brethren Church Missionary Bd.	1969	-	-	-	2	-
Brethren in Christ World Msns.	1904	-	-	-	-	2
Calvary International	1993	1	-	-	-	-
CBInternational	1945	4	-	4	-	-
Child Evangelism Fellowship	1942	-	-	-	34	-
Childcare International	1981	-	-	-	25	-
Children of India Foundation	1977	-	-	-	2	-
Christ for India, Inc.	1986	-	-	-	500	-
Christian Aid Mission		-	-	-	655	-
Christian Chs. /Chs. of Christ	1928	23	-	-	-	-
Christian Church of North Am.	1965	4	-	-	-	-
Christian Dynamics	1976	-	-	-	36	-
Christians In Action, Inc.	1972	-	-	-	28	-
Church of God of Prophecy	1957	-	-	-	2	-
Church of God World Missions	1936	-	-	-	11	-
Church of the Nazarene	1898	4	-	-	-	-
Church of the United Brethren	1974	-	-	1	2	-
Churches of God General Conf.	1898	-	-	-	1	-
Congregational Christian Chs.	1955	-	-	-	1	-
Congregational Holiness Church	1982	-	-	-	-	-
Correll Missionary Ministries	1978	-	-	-	46	-
Evangelical Free Church Msn.	1995	2	2	-	-	-
Evangelical Friends Mission	1992	2	-	-	-	-
Evangelical Lutheran Church	1842	4	-	-	-	-
Evangelical Presbyterian Ch.	1996	2	-	-	-	-
Evangelism Resources	1993	2	-	-	3	-
Every Home for Christ	1965	-	-	-	674	-
Faith Christian Fellowship	1979	2	-	-	-	-
Farms International, Inc.	1983	-	-	-	2	-
Free Will Baptist Association	1935	2	-	-	-	-
General Conf. Mennonite Church	1900	2	-	-	-	2
Globe Missionary Evangelism	1992	3	-	-	-	-
Gospel for Asia	1979	-	-	-	5,404	-
Gospel Outreach Mins. Intl.	1988	-	-	-	250	-
Gospel Revival Ministries	1995	-	-	-	3	-

COUNTRY Agency	Year Began	Personnel from U.S.			Other Countries	
		4+ Yrs	2-4 Yrs	1-2 Yrs	Citizens	Not Citiz.
Grace Ministries International	1976	-	-	-	-	-
Habitat for Humanity Intl	1983	-	3	-	11	3
Harvest	1990	-	-	-	2	-
Have Christ Will Travel Mins.	1995	-	-	-	5	-
HBI Global Partners	1950	8	-	-	-	-
Heifer Project International	1955	-	-	-	3	-
Help for Christian Nationals	1984	-	-	-	3	-
Holt Intl. Children's Services	1979	-	-	-	60	-
India Evangelical Mission	1970	-	-	-	100	-
India Gospel Outreach	1923	-	-	-	-	-
India National Inland Mission	1964	-	-	-	-	-
India Rural Evangelical Flwshp	1944	-	-	-	127	-
International Gospel Outreach	1993	-	-	-	2	-
International Missions, Inc.	1930	17	-	-	-	-
International Needs - USA	1979	-	-	-	125	-
International Partnership Mins	1988	-	-	-	38	-
InterServe/USA	1852	3	-	-	-	-
Intl. Pentecostal Ch of Christ	1940	1	-	-	-	-
Intl. Pentecostal Holiness Ch.	1911	4	-	-	-	-
Luke Society, The	1982	-	-	-	2	-
Lutheran Church-Missouri Synod	1895	1	-	-	-	-
Medical Ambassadors Intl.	1982	-	-	-	61	-
Mennonite Board of Missions	1899	4	-	-	-	-
Mennonite Brethren Msns/Svcs	1910	-	-	-	100	-
Mennonite Central Committee	1942	1	3	-	-	-
Mission 21 India	1990	-	-	-	-	-
Mission O.N.E., Inc.	1991	-	-	-	58	-
Mission Soc. for United Meth.	1995	-	2	-	-	-
Mission to the World	1957	8	1	-	-	-
Mission To Unreached Peoples	1987	-	2	-	-	-
New Tribes Mission	1945	1	-	-	-	-
OC International, Inc.	1984	-	-	-	4	1
OMS International, Inc.	1941	2	-	-	-	2
Operation Mobilization		3	1	1	-	-
Partners International	1969	-	-	-	466	-
Pocket Testament League	1975	-	-	-	100	-
Prakash Association USA	1968	-	-	-	35	-
Presbyterian Church (USA)	1834	-	-	21	-	-
Project Partner with Christ	1984	-	-	-	1	-
Ramabai Mukti Mission	1929	-	-	-	45	-
Reach Ministries International		2	-	-	-	-
Reformed Church In America	1851	3	-	-	-	-
Reformed Episcopal Bd Missions	1890	-	-	-	6	-
Ripe for Harvest, Inc.	1993	2	-	-	-	-
Salvation Army, U.S.A.	1882	2	-	-	-	-
Seventh-day Adventists	1895	10	-	-	4	-
SIM USA	1893	7	-	-	-	-

COUNTRY Agency	Year Began	Personnel from U.S.			Other Countries	
		4+ Yrs	2-4 Yrs	1-2 Yrs	Citizens	Not Citiz.
Southern Baptist Intl. Mission	1962	11	-	-	-	-
TEAM	1892	2	-	-	-	-
TMA Ministries	1990	-	-	1	-	-
U.S. Center for World Mission	1995	-	-	2	-	-
United Church Board World Mins	1813	4	4	-	3	-
United Methodist Church		10	-	-	-	-
Vellore Christian Medical Col.	1948	-	-	-	-	-
Walk Thru The Bible Ministries	1990	-	-	-	82	-
WEC International	1991	1	-	1	1	1
Wisconsin Evang. Lutheran Syn.	1970	1	-	-	-	-
Witnessing Mins. of Christ	1983	-	-	-	287	-
World Gospel Mission	1937	2	-	-	-	-
World Mission Prayer League	1941	2	-	-	2	-
World Missions Fellowship	1954	4	-	-	4	-
World Partners Missionary Ch.	1924	-	-	-	-	-
World-Wide Missions	1960	-	-	-	5	-
Youth With A Mission (YWAM)		37	-	-	-	-
Totals:		246	20	33	10,100	14

INDONESIA

COUNTRY Agency	Year Began	4+ Yrs	2-4 Yrs	1-2 Yrs	Citizens	Not Citiz.
Advancing Native Missions	1992	1	-	-	1	-
Ambassadors for Christ Intl.		-	-	-	4	-
AMG International	1975	-	-	-	150	-
Assemblies of God	1937	34	-	-	-	-
Baptist Bible Fellowship Intl.	1972	6	-	-	-	-
Baptist International Missions	1971	2	-	-	-	-
Bethany Fellowship Missions	1971	3	-	-	3	-
Bethel Pentecostal Temple	1914	2	-	-	-	-
Brethren Assemblies		3	-	-	-	-
Campus Crusade for Christ	1968	2	-	-	-	-
CBInternational	1961	11	-	4	-	-
Child Evangelism Fellowship	1963	-	-	-	12	1
Christ for the Island World	1983	-	-	-	104	-
Christian Aid Mission		-	-	-	25	-
Christian and Msny. Alliance	1929	55	3	-	-	-
Christian Chs. /Chs. of Christ	1968	24	-	-	-	-
Church of God of Prophecy	1971	-	-	-	2	-
Church of God World Missions	1967	1	-	1	1	1
Church of the Nazarene	1973	8	-	-	-	-
CMF International	1978	9	-	1	-	-
Compassion International, Inc.	1972	2	-	-	-	-
Evangelical Lutheran Church	1970	5	-	-	-	-
Every Home for Christ	1974	-	-	-	52	-
Full Gospel Grace Fellowship		1	-	-	-	-
Globe Missionary Evangelism	1990	2	-	-	-	-
Go Ye Fellowship	1938	1	-	-	1	-
International Needs - USA	1987	-	-	-	16	-

COUNTRY Agency	Year Began	Personnel from U.S.			Other Countries	
		4+ Yrs	2-4 Yrs	1-2 Yrs	Citizens	Not Citiz.
Macedonia World Baptist Msns.	1980	2	-	-	-	-
Mennonite Brethren Msns/Svcs		-	-	-	2	-
Mennonite Central Committee	1948	10	9	-	-	-
Mission Aviation Fellowship	1952	73	-	12	5	2
Mission O.N.E., Inc.	1992	-	-	-	2	-
Mission Soc. for United Meth.	1987	2	-	-	-	-
Mission to the World	1976	9	1	-	-	-
Mission To Unreached Peoples	1991	-	2	-	-	-
Mustard Seed, Inc.	1973	-	-	-	160	-
Navigators, The	1967	10	-	-	-	-
Network of Intl Christian Schs	1995	-	11	-	-	-
New Tribes Mission	1970	70	-	-	2	2
OC International, Inc.	1968	16	4	-	-	-
Omega World Missions	1985	2	-	-	-	-
OMF International	1952	19	-	-	-	40
OMS International, Inc.	1971	11	2	-	-	1
Partners International	1971	-	-	-	302	-
Pioneers	1986	57	-	-	-	-
Pocket Testament League	1972	-	-	-	8	-
Presb. Evangelistic Fellowship		1	-	-	-	-
Presbyterian Church (USA)	1951	14	-	-	-	-
Seventh-day Adventists	1900	6	-	-	-	-
Southern Baptist Intl. Mission	1951	72	7	-	-	-
TEAM	1952	30	-	2	2	-
Things To Come Mission, Inc	1968	2	-	-	-	-
Training Evangelistic Ldrshp.	1974	1	-	-	-	-
Tribes and Nations Outreach	1990	-	-	-	-	1
UFM International	1957	19	-	1	-	-
United Church Board World Mins	1833	-	4	-	-	-
United Methodist Church		2	-	-	-	-
United Pentecostal Church Intl	1938	4	-	-	-	-
Walk Thru The Bible Ministries	1992	-	-	-	1	-
WEC International	1950	5	4	-	-	-
Wesleyan World Missions	1975	5	-	-	-	-
Wisconsin Evang. Lutheran Syn.	1969	1	-	-	-	-
World Baptist Fellowship Msn	1969	7	-	-	-	-
World Indigenous Missions	1992	2	-	-	-	-
World Team	1948	24	-	-	-	17
	Totals:	648	47	21	855	65

IRELAND

Assemblies of God	1979	6	-	-	-	-
Baptist Bible Fellowship Intl.	1977	6	-	-	-	-
Baptist International Missions	1978	14	-	-	-	-
Baptist Mid-Missions	1978	6	-	-	-	2
Baptist World Mission		2	-	-	-	-
BCM International	1965	4	-	2	-	1

COUNTRY Agency	Year Began	Personnel from U.S.			Other Countries	
		4+ Yrs	2-4 Yrs	1-2 Yrs	Citizens	Not Citiz.
Biblical Ministries Worldwide	1975	11	-	-	-	-
Brethren Assemblies		12	-	-	-	-
CBInternational	1991	2	-	-	-	-
Child Evangelism Fellowship	1950	-	-	-	71	-
Christian Associates Intl.	1992	4	-	-	-	-
Christian Chs. /Chs. of Christ	1988	4	-	-	-	-
Church of the Nazarene	1987	-	-	-	2	-
European Christian Mission	1987	1	-	-	-	-
European Missions Outreach	1997	-	-	-	2	-
Evangelical Mennonite Church	1988	2	-	-	-	-
Global Outreach Mission	1965	17	-	-	-	-
Greater Europe Mission	1974	26	-	-	-	-
Habitat for Humanity Intl	1994	1	-	-	1	-
Ireland Outreach Intl., Inc.	1970	3	-	1	-	7
Mennonite Board of Missions	1987	2	-	-	-	-
Mennonite Central Committee	1978	2	-	-	-	-
Mission to the World	1991	3	-	-	-	-
Operation Mobilization		2	-	-	-	-
Seventh-day Adventists	1898	2	-	-	-	-
Team Expansion, Inc.	1988	7	-	-	-	-
UFM International	1980	11	-	-	-	-
United Methodist Church		2	-	-	-	-
Walk Thru The Bible Ministries	1994	-	-	-	2	-
World Baptist Fellowship Msn	1961	2	-	-	-	-
World Harvest Mission	1986	2	-	2	-	-
World Missions Fellowship	1950	4	-	2	2	-
Youth With A Mission (YWAM)		6	-	-	-	-
Totals:		166	-	7	80	10

ISRAEL

AMF International	1978	2	-	-	2	-
Arab World Ministries	1995	4	-	-	-	-
Baptist World Mission	1971	4	-	-	-	-
Child Evangelism Fellowship	1951	2	-	-	2	1
Chosen People Ministries	1951	-	-	-	3	1
Christ for the Nations, Inc.	1969	1	-	-	1	-
Christian and Msny. Alliance	1890	8	-	-	-	-
Christian Chs. /Chs. of Christ		2	-	-	-	-
Church of God of Prophecy	1935	-	-	-	1	-
Church of God World Missions	1964	5	-	-	-	1
Church of The Brethren	1975	-	-	4	-	-
Church of the Nazarene	1921	2	-	-	-	-
Elim Fellowship World Missions	1977	2	-	-	-	-
Episcopal World Mission	1983	2	-	-	-	-
Evangelical Lutheran Church	1967	4	-	1	-	-
General Conf. Mennonite Church	1954	2	-	-	-	-
Helps International Ministries	1994	2	-	-	-	-

COUNTRY Agency	Year Began	Personnel from U.S.			Other Countries	
		4+ Yrs	2-4 Yrs	1-2 Yrs	Citizens	Not Citiz.
High Adventure Ministries	1979	1	-	-	17	1
InterVarsity Mission	1994	-	1	-	-	-
Jews for Jesus	1994	-	-	-	1	-
Maranatha Baptist Mission	1983	2	-	-	-	-
Mennonite Board of Missions	1953	4	-	-	-	-
Presbyterian Church (USA)		4	-	-	-	-
Reformed Baptist Mission Svcs.	1985	-	-	-	2	-
Seventh-day Adventists	1898	2	-	-	2	-
Southern Baptist Intl. Mission	1921	34	16	-	-	-
United Methodist Church		2	-	-	-	-
World Vision	1975	-	1	-	-	-
	Totals:	91	18	5	31	4

ITALY

COUNTRY Agency	Year Began	Personnel from U.S.			Other Countries	
		4+ Yrs	2-4 Yrs	1-2 Yrs	Citizens	Not Citiz.
ABWE	1989	13	-	-	-	-
Assemblies of God	1949	4	-	-	-	-
Back to the Bible Intl.	1961	-	-	-	13	-
Baptist Bible Fellowship Intl.	1978	2	-	-	-	-
Baptist International Missions	1979	1	-	-	-	-
Baptist Mid-Missions	1951	6	-	-	-	-
Baptist Missions to Forgotten		2	-	-	-	-
Baptist World Mission		2	-	-	-	-
BCM International	1967	4	-	-	-	2
Bible Alliance Mission, Inc.	1978	2	-	-	2	4
Biblical Ministries Worldwide	1959	9	-	-	-	-
Brethren Assemblies		7	-	-	-	-
Cadence International	1980	-	4	-	-	-
Campus Crusade for Christ	1969	2	-	-	-	-
CBInternational	1946	21	1	3	-	-
Child Evangelism Fellowship	1956	-	-	-	-	2
Christian Chs. /Chs. of Christ	1947	7	-	-	-	-
Christian Church of North Am.	1927	1	-	-	-	-
Christian Literature Crusade	1956	2	-	-	-	-
Church of God of Prophecy	1996	-	-	-	-	1
Church of God World Missions	1959	2	-	-	-	-
European Christian Mission	1987	2	-	-	-	-
Evangelical Baptist Missions	1983	4	-	-	-	-
Gospel Fellowship Association		2	-	-	-	-
Gospel Missionary Union	1950	7	-	-	2	-
Greater Europe Mission	1954	5	-	-	-	2
Hope for the Hungry	1990	-	2	-	-	-
Independent Faith Mission	1950	7	-	-	-	-
International Teams, U.S.A.	1980	2	2	-	-	-
InterVarsity Mission	1984	3	-	-	-	-
Intl. Pentecostal Holiness Ch.	1987	2	-	-	-	-
Mission to the World	1991	4	-	-	-	-
Navigators, The	1984	2	-	-	-	-

COUNTRY Agency	Year Began	Personnel from U.S.			Other Countries	
		4+ Yrs	2-4 Yrs	1-2 Yrs	Citizens	Not Citiz.
Presbyterian Church (USA)	1972	2	-	-	-	-
Seventh-day Adventists	1877	2	-	-	-	-
SIM USA	1979	2	-	-	-	-
Southern Baptist Intl. Mission	1870	18	-	-	-	-
Spiritual Growth Resources	1984	2	-	-	-	-
TEAM	1950	28	1	-	-	-
UFM International	1974	19	-	-	-	-
Virginia Mennonite Bd. of Msns	1964	8	-	-	-	-
WEC International	1964	3	-	1	-	1
World Team	1970	4	-	-	-	3
Youth With A Mission (YWAM)		1	-	-	-	-
Totals:		216	10	4	17	15

JAMAICA

COUNTRY Agency	Year Began	4+ Yrs	2-4 Yrs	1-2 Yrs	Citizens	Not Citiz.
African Methodist Epis. Zion	1966	-	1	-	-	-
Assemblies of God	1942	14	-	-	-	-
Back to the Bible Intl.	1958	-	-	-	9	-
Baptist Bible Fellowship Intl.	1972	8	-	-	-	-
Baptist International Missions	1974	4	-	-	-	-
Baptist Mid-Missions	1939	2	-	-	-	-
Brethren Assemblies		6	-	-	-	-
Child Evangelism Fellowship	1939	-	-	-	14	-
Christ for the Nations, Inc.	1986	-	-	-	2	-
Christian Blind Mission Intl.	1985	-	2	-	-	-
Christian Chs. /Chs. of Christ	1858	9	-	-	-	-
Church of God of Prophecy	1923	-	-	-	-	1
Church of the United Brethren	1945	-	-	-	-	-
CSI Ministries	1978	3	-	-	-	-
Evangelical Lutheran Church	1990	2	-	-	-	-
Faith Christian Fellowship	1979	4	-	-	-	-
Habitat for Humanity Intl	1993	-	1	-	3	-
Hope for the Hungry	1990	-	2	-	-	-
International Outreach Mins.	1988	2	-	-	-	-
Island Missionary Society	1985	4	-	-	-	-
Lutheran Church-Missouri Synod	1993	4	-	-	-	-
Macedonia World Baptist Msns.	1981	6	-	-	-	-
Mennonite Central Committee	1970	6	8	-	-	-
Mission to the World	1986	2	1	-	-	-
Partners International	1975	-	-	-	-	2
Presbyterian Church (USA)	1981	5	-	-	-	-
Reciprocal Ministries Intl.	1991	1	-	-	1	-
Reformed Baptist Mission Svcs.	1985	-	-	-	2	-
Salvation Army, U.S.A.	1914	5	-	-	-	-
Seventh-day Adventists	1893	10	-	1	3	-
STEM Ministries	1985	-	-	-	-	-
United Church Board World Mins	1987	-	1	-	-	-
United Methodist Church		3	-	-	-	-

COUNTRY Agency	Year Began	Personnel from U.S.			Other Countries	
		4+ Yrs	2-4 Yrs	1-2 Yrs	Citizens	Not Citiz.
World Partners Missionary Ch.	1949	4	-	-	-	-
World Salt Foundation	1990	-	-	2	-	-
World Servants	1989	-	-	-	1	-
Youth With A Mission (YWAM)		9	-	-	-	-
Totals:		113	16	3	35	3

JAPAN

Agency	Year Began	4+ Yrs	2-4 Yrs	1-2 Yrs	Citizens	Not Citiz.
ABWE	1953	15	-	2	-	-
Advent Christian World Msns.	1948	4	1	-	-	-
American Baptist Association	1962	1	-	-	-	-
American Baptist Churches USA	1872	11	1	-	-	-
Anglican Orthodox Church	1993	-	-	-	1	-
Apostolic Christian Church	1988	2	-	-	-	-
Asian Outreach U.S.A.	1988	1	-	-	-	-
Assemblies of God	1913	42	-	-	-	-
Baptist Bible Fellowship Intl.	1950	26	-	-	-	-
Baptist General Conference	1948	16	-	-	-	-
Baptist International Missions	1965	35	-	-	-	-
Baptist Mid-Missions	1949	26	-	-	6	-
Baptist Missionary Assoc.	1953	1	-	-	-	-
Baptist World Mission	1971	14	-	-	-	-
Bethany Fellowship Missions	1980	2	-	-	3	-
Bethany Missionary Association	1959	4	-	-	-	-
Bethel Pentecostal Temple	1930	4	-	-	-	-
Bible Missionary Church	1963	2	-	-	-	-
Biblical Ministries Worldwide	1987	2	-	-	-	-
Brethren Assemblies		11	-	-	-	-
Cadence International	1964	3	4	2	-	-
Campus Crusade for Christ	1962	27	-	3	-	-
CBInternational	1947	8	-	1	-	-
Child Evangelism Fellowship	1948	-	-	-	7	2
Christ Community Church	1951	2	-	-	-	-
Christian and Msny. Alliance	1891	10	-	-	-	-
Christian Chs. /Chs. of Christ	1901	45	-	-	-	-
Christian Reformed World Msns.	1951	16	4	2	-	-
Christians In Action, Inc.	1957	6	-	-	5	2
Church of God (Anderson, IN)	1906	6	-	-	-	-
Church of God of Prophecy	1982	2	-	-	-	-
Church of The Brethren		-	-	2	-	-
Church of the Nazarene	1905	15	-	-	-	-
Evangelical Baptist Missions	1984	4	-	-	-	-
Evangelical Covenant Church	1949	12	2	4	-	-
Evangelical Free Church Msn.	1949	18	-	4	-	-
Evangelical Lutheran Church	1892	14	11	-	-	-
Evangelical Presbyterian Ch.	1988	2	-	-	-	-
Fellowship International Msn.	1980	3	-	-	3	-
Food for the Hungry	1982	-	10	-	-	-

COUNTRY Agency	Year Began	Personnel from U.S.			Other Countries	
		4+ Yrs	2-4 Yrs	1-2 Yrs	Citizens	Not Citiz.
Free Will Baptist Association	1954	14	-	-	-	-
Fundamental Bible Missions		2	-	-	-	-
General Conf. Mennonite Church	1950	3	-	-	-	7
Global Strategy Mission Assoc.	1993	-	2	-	-	-
Gospel Fellowship Association		4	-	-	-	-
Grace Brethren Intl. Missions	1984	6	-	-	-	-
High School Evangelism Flwshp.	1951	6	-	-	12	-
International Missions, Inc.	1966	19	-	-	-	-
International Students, Inc	1979	2	-	-	-	-
Intl. Pentecostal Holiness Ch.	1989	2	2	-	-	-
Japan - North American Comm	1973	-	-	-	-	-
Japanese Evangelical Msnry Soc	1953	-	-	2	6	-
Liberty Corner Mission	1951	2	-	-	1	10
LIFE Ministries	1967	34	7	12	15	-
Lutheran Brethren World Msns.		8	2	6	-	-
Lutheran Church-Missouri Synod	1948	10	20	1	-	-
Macedonia World Baptist Msns.	1996	2	-	-	-	-
Maranatha Baptist Mission	1968	2	-	-	-	-
Mennonite Board of Missions	1949	8	-	-	-	-
Mennonite Brethren Msns/Svcs	1950	2	2	-	-	-
Mission Soc. for United Meth.	1995	2	-	-	-	-
Mission to the World	1961	27	15	3	-	-
Mission To Unreached Peoples	1990	-	2	-	-	-
Navigators, The	1951	24	2	4	-	-
New Life League International	1954	-	-	-	70	7
New Tribes Mission	1949	2	-	-	-	-
Next Towns Crusade, Inc.	1057	2	-	-	-	-
North American Baptist Conf.	1951	9	2	-	-	-
OC International, Inc.	1987	6	-	-	-	-
OMF International	1952	42	-	-	-	80
OMS International, Inc.	1901	11	2	-	-	4
Orthodox Presbyterian Church	1938	7	-	-	-	-
PAZ International	1983	2	2	3	-	-
Pioneers	1988	6	-	-	-	-
Presb. Evangelistic Fellowship		1	-	-	-	-
Presbyterian Church (USA)	1859	4	34	-	-	-
Reformed Church In America	1860	11	-	-	-	-
Reformed Presbyterian Church	1950	5	-	-	-	-
Ripe for Harvest, Inc.	1993	2	-	-	-	-
Salvation Army, U.S.A.	1895	2	-	-	-	-
SEND International	1947	45	1	-	-	-
Seventh-day Adventists	1896	16	-	-	-	-
Southern Baptist Intl. Mission	1889	145	21	-	-	-
TEAM	1891	107	3	-	-	-
United Church Board World Mins	1869	4	17	-	1	-
United Methodist Church		21	-	-	-	-
United Pentecostal Church Intl	1949	2	-	-	-	-

COUNTRY Agency	Year Began	Personnel from U.S.			Other Countries	
		4+ Yrs	2-4 Yrs	1-2 Yrs	Citizens	Not Citiz.
WEC International	1950	1	-	-	-	-
Wesleyan World Missions	1918	2	-	-	-	-
Wisconsin Evang. Lutheran Syn.	1952	6	-	-	-	-
World Gospel Mission	1952	4	-	-	-	-
World Missions Fellowship	1951	-	-	-	2	-
Youth With A Mission (YWAM)		50	-	-	-	-
Totals:		1,106	169	51	132	112

JORDAN

Agency	Year Began	4+ Yrs	2-4 Yrs	1-2 Yrs	Citizens	Not Citiz.
Arab World Ministries	1983	14	-	-	-	-
Calvary International	1989	2	-	-	-	-
CBInternational	1956	8	-	2	-	-
Child Evangelism Fellowship	1991	2	-	-	-	-
Christian Aid Mission		-	-	-	8	-
Christian and Msny. Alliance	1890	2	-	-	-	-
Church of the Nazarene	1950	4	-	-	-	-
InterVarsity Mission	1995	-	-	1	-	-
Mennonite Central Committee	1967	2	-	-	-	-
Southern Baptist Intl. Mission	1952	17	6	-	-	-
Totals:		51	6	3	8	-

KAZAKHSTAN

Agency	Year Began	4+ Yrs	2-4 Yrs	1-2 Yrs	Citizens	Not Citiz.
Campus Crusade for Christ	1991	10	-	-	-	-
Christian Aid Mission		-	-	-	1	-
Church of God of Prophecy	1995	-	-	-	1	-
East-West Ministries Intl.	1994	4	-	-	-	-
Evangelical Presbyterian Ch.	1994	4	-	-	-	-
Every Home for Christ	1994	-	-	-	3	-
International Teams, U.S.A.	1992	-	3	-	-	2
InterVarsity Mission	1993	-	2	3	-	-
Lutheran Bible Translators	1996	-	-	1	-	-
Lutheran Church-Missouri Synod	1993	6	-	1	-	-
Mennonite Brethren Msns/Svcs		-	-	-	1	-
Mission to the World	1991	4	6	-	-	-
Presbyterian Church (USA)		4	-	-	-	-
Slavic Gospel Association	1945	-	-	-	31	-
Walk Thru The Bible Ministries	1994	-	-	-	28	-
Totals:		32	11	5	65	2

KENYA

Agency	Year Began	4+ Yrs	2-4 Yrs	1-2 Yrs	Citizens	Not Citiz.
ABWE	1983	4	-	-	-	-
Africa Inland Mission Intl	1895	253	-	59	-	-
African Christian Mission	1996	5	-	-	-	-
African Enterprise, Inc.	1975	-	-	-	8	-
Ambassadors for Christ Intl.		-	-	-	3	-
American Baptist Association		3	-	-	-	-

COUNTRY Agency	Year Began	Personnel from U.S.			Other Countries	
		4+ Yrs	2-4 Yrs	1-2 Yrs	Citizens	Not Citiz.
Anglican Orthodox Church	1972	-	-	-	1	-
Assemblies of God	1967	29	-	-	-	-
BALL World Missions	1979	-	2	2	-	-
Baptist Bible Fellowship Intl.	1962	41	-	-	-	-
Baptist Faith Missions		-	-	2	-	-
Baptist International Missions	1991	6	-	-	-	-
Bright Hope International		-	-	-	5	-
Campus Crusade for Christ	1972	43	-	-	-	-
CBInternational	1972	20	-	3	-	-
Child Evangelism Fellowship	1966	7	-	-	17	1
Childcare International	1904	-	-	-	60	-
Christian Aid Mission		-	-	-	99	-
Christian Blind Mission Intl.	1976	5	-	-	-	-
Christian Chs. /Chs. of Christ	1960	69	-	-	-	-
Christian Reformed World Msns.	1986	1	-	-	-	-
Christian Reformed Wrld Relief		2	-	-	-	-
Christian Services, Inc.	1977	1	-	-	-	-
Church of God (Anderson, IN)	1905	8	-	-	-	-
Church of God of Prophecy	1978	-	-	-	-	1
Church of God World Missions	1977	8	2	-	-	2
Church of the Nazarene	1984	20	-	-	2	-
CMF International	1977	42	-	3	-	-
Compassion International, Inc.	1979	-	2	-	-	2
Daystar U.S.	1963	7	-	-	3	-
Eastern Mennonite Missions	1964	10	-	-	2	-
Elim Fellowship World Missions	1940	24	-	1	-	-
Evangelical Lutheran Church	1969	2	-	-	-	-
Evangelical Presbyterian Ch.	1996	2	-	-	-	-
Food for the Hungry	1976	1	6	-	-	-
Foursquare Missions Intl.	1982	2	-	-	-	-
Friends in the West	1990	-	-	-	59	-
Friends United Meeting	1902	-	2	2	-	-
General Conf. Mennonite Church	1990	4	-	-	-	-
Globe Missionary Evangelism	1979	6	-	-	-	-
Go International	1992	-	-	2	-	-
Gospel Furthering Fellowship	1935	3	-	-	1	-
Habitat for Humanity Intl	1985	-	4	-	8	1
Handclasp International, Inc.	1988	2	-	-	5	-
Heifer Project International	1981	-	-	-	3	-
Independent Faith Mission	1973	16	-	-	-	-
International Gospel League	1978	5	-	-	-	-
International Gospel Outreach	1990	2	-	1	4	-
International Missions, Inc.	1956	23	-	-	-	-
International Outreach Mins.	1990	2	2	-	-	-
InterVarsity Mission	1981	-	2	1	-	-
Intl. Pentecostal Ch of Christ	1938	3	-	-	-	-
Intl. Pentecostal Holiness Ch.	1972	11	-	-	-	-

COUNTRY / Agency	Year Began	Personnel from U.S. 4+ Yrs	2-4 Yrs	1-2 Yrs	Other Countries Citizens	Not Citiz.
Lutheran World Relief	1989	2	-	-	-	-
M/E International	1990	2	-	-	-	-
MAP International	1992	3	-	-	-	3
Medical Ambassadors Intl.	1987	-	-	-	8	-
Mennonite Central Committee	1962	7	3	-	-	-
Mission O.N.E., Inc.	1991	-	-	-	29	-
Mission Soc. for United Meth.	1991	5	-	-	-	-
Mission to the World	1961	20	2	-	-	-
Mission: Moving Mountains	1992	10	-	6	3	3
Navigators, The	1968	5	-	-	-	-
OC International, Inc.	1985	8	-	-	2	-
Open Bible Standard Churches	1983	2	-	-	-	-
Orthodox Presbyterian Church	1979	2	-	-	-	-
Partners International	1972	-	-	-	22	-
Presb. Evangelistic Fellowship	1987	-	-	-	-	2
Presbyterian Church (USA)	1955	11	6	4	-	-
Presbyterian Missionary Union	1985	2	-	-	-	-
Reformed Baptist Mission Svcs.	1985	2	-	-	-	-
Reformed Church In America	1977	10	-	-	-	-
Salvation Army, U.S.A.	1896	1	-	-	-	-
Scripture Union (USA)		1	-	-	-	-
Seventh-day Adventists	1906	40	-	3	27	-
Share International	1995	-	-	-	2	-
SIM USA	1977	23	-	-	-	-
Source of Light Ministries	1991	1	-	-	-	-
Southern Baptist Intl. Mission	1956	76	27	-	-	-
The Master's Mission, Inc.	1980	16	-	-	2	-
Things To Come Mission, Inc	1975	7	-	-	-	-
United Church Board World Mins	1974	-	3	-	-	-
United Methodist Church		11	-	-	-	-
United Pentecostal Church Intl	1972	6	-	-	-	-
Walk Thru The Bible Ministries	1990	-	-	-	16	-
World Concern	1984	4	7	-	16	-
World Gospel Mission	1932	67	-	-	-	4
World Mission Associates	1986	2	-	-	-	-
World Mission Prayer League	1968	12	-	-	-	12
World Reach, Inc.	1983	-	-	-	18	-
World Salt Foundation	1991	-	-	2	-	-
World Servants	1992	-	-	-	2	-
World-Wide Missions	1962	-	-	-	2	-
Wycliffe Bible Translators	1978	76	5	3	-	-
Young Life	1984	4	-	2	-	-
Youth for Christ / USA		-	2	-	-	-
Youth With A Mission (YWAM)		9	-	-	-	-
Totals:		1,139	77	96	429	31

COUNTRY Agency	Year Began	Personnel from U.S.			Other Countries	
		4+ Yrs	2-4 Yrs	1-2 Yrs	Citizens	Not Citiz.

KIRIBATI

Elim Fellowship World Missions	1991	2	-	-	-	-
	Totals:	2	-	-	-	-

KOREA, SOUTH

Assemblies of God	1928	5	-	-	-	-
Baptist Bible Fellowship Intl.	1950	21	-	-	-	-
Baptist World Mission	1977	2	-	-	-	-
BCM International	1995	-	-	-	3	-
Brethren Assemblies		2	-	-	-	-
Cadence International	1975	2	2	-	-	-
Child Evangelism Fellowship	1957	-	-	-	141	-
China Ministries International	1994	-	-	-	3	-
Christian Chs. /Chs. of Christ	1925	4	-	-	-	-
Church of God World Missions	1965	-	2	-	-	-
Church of the Nazarene	1948	6	-	-	-	-
Evangelical Lutheran Church	1986	2	-	-	-	-
Evangelistic Faith Missions	1971	-	-	-	7	-
Every Home for Christ	1958	-	-	-	5	-
Far East Broadcasting Company	1976	-	2	-	2	-
Gospel Fellowship Association		6	-	-	-	-
Habitat for Humanity Intl	1994	1	-	-	-	1
Holt Intl. Children's Services	1956	-	-	-	300	-
Intl. Lutheran Laymen's League	1965	1	-	-	-	-
Lutheran Church-Missouri Synod	1958	6	-	-	-	-
Mission to the World	1957	4	2	-	-	-
Navigators, The	1966	2	-	-	-	-
Network of Intl Christian Schs	1983	-	110	-	-	-
New Tribes Mission	1993	2	-	-	2	-
OMF International	1960	6	-	-	-	13
OMS International, Inc.	1907	7	-	-	-	-
Orthodox Presbyterian Church	1946	2	-	-	-	-
Partners International	1976	-	-	-	90	-
Pocket Testament League	1952	-	-	-	2	-
Presbyterian Church (USA)	1884	6	19	-	-	-
Salvation Army, U.S.A.	1908	2	-	-	-	-
Seventh-day Adventists	1904	8	-	-	-	-
Southern Baptist Intl. Mission	1950	71	8	-	-	-
TEAM	1953	5	-	-	-	-
United Church Board World Mins	1983	-	2	-	-	-
United Methodist Church		11	-	-	-	-
United Pentecostal Church Intl	1965	3	-	-	-	-
Voice of China and Asia	1955	1	-	-	150	-
Walk Thru The Bible Ministries	1988	-	-	-	10	-
Westminister Biblical Missions	1974	1	-	-	-	-

COUNTRY Agency	Year Began	Personnel from U.S.			Other Countries	
		4+ Yrs	2-4 Yrs	1-2 Yrs	Citizens	Not Citiz.
World-Wide Missions	1963	-	-	-	3	-
Worldwide Discipleship Assoc.	1991	3	-	-	-	-
Totals:		192	147	-	718	14

KUWAIT

Reformed Church In America	1900	2	-	-	-	-
Totals:		2	-	-	-	-

KYRGYZSTAN

Campus Crusade for Christ	1992	4	-	4	-	-
Christian Aid Mission		-	-	-	4	-
Every Home for Christ	1995	-	-	-	-	1
Habitat for Humanity Intl	1996	1	-	-	-	1
Mennonite Brethren Msns/Svcs		-	1	-	1	-
Pioneers	1994	7	-	-	-	-
Presbyterian Church (USA)		6	-	-	-	-
Venture Middle East	1995	-	-	-	2	1
Walk Thru The Bible Ministries	1993	-	-	-	7	-
Totals:		18	1	4	14	3

LAOS

Assemblies of God	1990	3	-	-	-	-
Christian Aid Mission		-	-	-	3	-
Christian and Msny. Alliance	1929	8	-	-	-	-
Food for the Hungry	1990	4	-	-	-	-
Mennonite Central Committee	1975	2	-	-	-	-
Mission O.N.E., Inc.	1994	-	-	-	4	-
Partners International		-	-	-	1	-
Seventh-day Adventists	1919	2	-	-	-	-
Tribes and Nations Outreach	1989	-	-	-	1	-
World Concern	1990	4	-	-	21	4
World Vision	1969	1	1	1	-	-
Totals:		24	1	1	30	4

LATVIA

Calvary International	1989	12	-	-	1	-
Campus Crusade for Christ	1995	-	-	16	-	-
Christian Associates Intl.	1992	-	-	-	2	-
Evangelical Lutheran Church	1991	1	-	-	-	-
Greater Europe Mission	1992	3	1	2	-	8
International Messengers	1991	2	-	-	-	2
Navigators, The		2	-	-	-	-
Walk Thru The Bible Ministries	1993	-	-	-	29	-
World Baptist Fellowship Msn	1995	2	-	-	-	-
Youth With A Mission (YWAM)		4	-	-	-	-
Totals:		26	1	18	32	10

COUNTRY Agency	Year Began	Personnel from U.S.			Other Countries	
		4+ Yrs	2-4 Yrs	1-2 Yrs	Citizens	Not Citiz.
LEBANON						
Child Evangelism Fellowship	1947	-	-	-	2	-
Christian and Msny. Alliance	1890	2	-	-	-	-
Every Home for Christ	1995	-	-	-	2	1
Kids Alive International	1951	-	-	-	-	3
Mennonite Central Committee	1976	2	-	-	-	-
Presbyterian Church (USA)	1823	3	-	-	-	-
Seventh-day Adventists	1970	-	-	-	6	-
Venture Middle East	1994	-	-	-	1	-
Youth for Christ / USA	1960	2	-	-	-	-
Youth With A Mission (YWAM)		1	-	-	-	-
	Totals:	10	-	-	11	4
LESOTHO						
Africa Inland Mission Intl	1986	8	-	1	-	-
Africa Inter-Mennonite Mission	1972	2	-	-	-	-
Assemblies of God	1950	2	-	-	-	-
Campus Crusade for Christ	1979	8	-	-	-	-
Church of the Nazarene	1994	2	-	-	-	-
Mennonite Central Committee	1973	2	4	-	-	-
Mission Aviation Fellowship	1979	12	-	-	-	-
National Baptist Conv. USA	1961	2	-	-	6	-
Presbyterian Church (USA)	1977	2	-	-	-	-
United Church Board World Mins	1984	-	3	-	-	-
Youth With A Mission (YWAM)		1	-	-	-	-
	Totals:	41	7	1	6	-
LIBERIA						
Advent Christian World Msns.	1988	-	-	-	1	-
African Bible Colleges	1976	-	4	-	-	-
African Methodist Epis. Zion	1876	-	1	-	-	-
Agape Gospel Mission	1994	-	-	-	2	1
ALM International	1989	-	2	-	-	-
Anglican Orthodox Church	1980	-	-	-	1	-
Assemblies of God	1908	8	-	-	-	-
Baptist International Missions	1985	-	-	-	2	-
Baptist Mid-Missions	1938	17	-	-	-	-
Carver Foreign Missions, Inc.	1955	1	6	2	7	-
Child Evangelism Fellowship	1955	-	-	-	8	-
Christian Chs. /Chs. of Christ	1971	1	-	-	-	-
Christian Reformed World Msns.	1978	2	-	-	-	-
Christian Services, Inc.	1967	1	-	-	-	-
Christian Union Mission	1968	3	-	-	-	-
Church of God of Prophecy	1979	-	-	-	1	-
Church of God World Missions	1974	-	-	-	-	2
Church of the Nazarene	1988	-	-	-	2	-

COUNTRY Agency	Year Began	Personnel from U.S.			Other Countries	
		4+ Yrs	2-4 Yrs	1-2 Yrs	Citizens	Not Citiz.
Evangelical Lutheran Church	1862	2	-	-	-	-
Gospel Recordings USA	1994	-	-	-	2	-
Have Christ Will Travel Mins.	1966	-	-	-	31	-
Lutheran Bible Translators	1969	10	-	1	25	-
Lutheran Church-Missouri Synod	1978	-	-	2	-	-
Mennonite Board of Missions	1988	3	-	-	-	-
National Baptist Conv. USA	1882	2	-	-	-	-
Partners International	1964	-	-	-	347	-
Presb. Evangelistic Fellowship		-	-	-	2	-
Reformed Episcopal Bd Missions	1990	-	-	-	3	-
Scripture Union (USA)		-	-	-	2	-
Seventh-day Adventists	1927	2	-	-	-	-
SIM USA	1952	26	-	2	-	-
Source of Light Ministries	1979	2	-	-	-	-
Southern Baptist Intl. Mission	1960	13	-	-	-	-
United Methodist Church		7	-	-	-	-
United Pentecostal Church Intl	1924	2	-	-	-	-
World Relief Corporation		-	2	-	-	-
World Vision	1984	-	1	-	-	-
World-Wide Missions	1964	-	-	-	4	-
Youth for Christ / USA	1978	2	-	-	-	-
Youth With A Mission (YWAM)		1	-	-	-	-
	Totals:	105	16	7	440	3

LITHUANIA

Agency	Year Began	4+ Yrs	2-4 Yrs	1-2 Yrs	Citizens	Not Citiz.
Baptist Bible Fellowship Intl.	1991	4	-	-	-	-
Campus Crusade for Christ	1991	5	-	5	-	-
CBInternational	1996	2	-	1	-	-
European Evangelistic Society	1990	2	-	-	-	-
Mennonite Brethren Msns/Svcs	1994	4	2	2	-	-
Mennonite Central Committee	1993	-	1	-	-	-
Navigators, The		2	-	-	-	-
Presbyterian Church (USA)		2	-	-	-	-
United Methodist Church		4	-	-	-	-
Walk Thru The Bible Ministries	1995	-	-	-	3	-
	Totals:	25	3	8	3	-

LUXEMBOURG

Agency	Year Began	4+ Yrs	2-4 Yrs	1-2 Yrs	Citizens	Not Citiz.
Assemblies of God	1981	2	-	-	-	-
Biblical Ministries Worldwide	1973	2	-	-	-	-
Greater Europe Mission	1990	2	-	-	-	2
	Totals:	6	-	-	-	2

MACAO

Agency	Year Began	4+ Yrs	2-4 Yrs	1-2 Yrs	Citizens	Not Citiz.
CBInternational	1986	8	-	-	-	-
Chinese Christian Mission, Inc	1990	4	-	-	-	-

COUNTRY Agency	Year Began	Personnel from U.S.			Other Countries	
		4+ Yrs	2-4 Yrs	1-2 Yrs	Citizens	Not Citiz.
Christians In Action, Inc.	1976	2	-	-	1	-
Church of the United Brethren	1987	3	4	-	-	-
Evangelical Free Church Msn.	1993	3	-	-	-	-
Lutheran Church-Missouri Synod	1988	4	-	-	-	-
OMF International	1995	-	-	-	-	2
Partners International	1962	-	-	-	2	1
Southern Baptist Intl. Mission	1910	16	4	-	-	-
TEAM	1994	3	-	-	-	-
	Totals:	43	8	-	3	3

MACEDONIA

Child Evangelism Fellowship	1975	-	-	-	2	-
Christian Aid Mission		-	-	-	5	-
Door of Hope International	1994	2	-	-	-	-
Partners International	1991	-	-	-	25	5
Pioneers	1994	2	-	-	-	-
SEND International	1993	11	-	-	-	-
	Totals:	15	-	-	32	5

MADAGASCAR

Africa Inland Mission Intl	1979	4	-	-	-	-
Anglican Orthodox Church	1967	-	-	-	2	-
Assemblies of God	1990	6	-	-	-	-
CBInternational	1966	6	-	2	-	-
Child Evangelism Fellowship	1988	-	-	-	5	2
Church of the Nazarene	1994	6	-	-	-	-
Episcopal World Mission	1991	2	-	-	-	-
Evangelical Lutheran Church	1888	17	-	-	-	-
Presbyterian Church (USA)		3	-	-	-	-
Seventh-day Adventists	1926	4	-	-	3	-
Southern Baptist Intl. Mission	1986	9	5	-	-	-
United Pentecostal Church Intl	1970	10	-	-	-	-
	Totals:	67	5	2	10	2

MALAWI

Africa Evangelical Fellowship	1906	2	-	-	-	-
African Bible Colleges	1989	16	-	-	-	-
African Enterprise, Inc.	1980	-	-	-	5	-
Assemblies of God	1944	10	-	-	-	-
Baptist International Missions	1992	4	-	-	-	-
Brethren in Christ World Msns.	1987	2	-	-	-	-
Child Evangelism Fellowship	1988	-	-	-	6	-
Christian Aid Mission		-	-	-	4	-
Christian Chs. /Chs. of Christ		7	-	-	-	-
Christian Reformed Wrld Relief		1	-	-	-	-
Church of God of Prophecy	1977	-	-	-	1	-

COUNTRY Agency	Year Began	Personnel from U.S.			Other Countries	
		4+ Yrs	2-4 Yrs	1-2 Yrs	Citizens	Not Citiz.
Church of God World Missions	1951	-	-	-	-	2
Church of the Nazarene	1957	13	-	-	-	-
Cities for Christ Worldwide	1996	-	-	2	-	-
Every Home for Christ	1995	-	-	-	5	-
Foursquare Missions Intl.	1985	2	-	-	-	-
Habitat for Humanity Intl	1986	-	6	-	65	-
Intl. Pentecostal Holiness Ch.	1950	6	-	-	-	-
Mission to the World	1994	-	2	-	-	-
National Baptist Conv. USA	1900	-	2	-	52	-
Navigators, The	1986	4	-	-	-	-
Presbyterian Church (USA)		9	20	-	-	-
Seventh-day Adventists	1902	20	-	2	20	-
Southern Baptist Intl. Mission	1959	41	-	-	-	-
Teen Missions International		-	1	3	2	1
United Pentecostal Church Intl	1979	4	-	-	-	-
Wisconsin Evang. Lutheran Syn.	1963	7	-	-	-	-
	Totals:	148	31	7	160	3

MALAYSIA

Advent Christian World Msns.	1959	-	-	-	4	-
Assemblies of God	1928	2	-	-	-	-
Brethren Church Missionary Bd.	1974	-	-	-	2	-
Campus Crusade for Christ	1968	2	-	-	-	-
Christian and Msny. Alliance	1969	10	26	-	-	-
Church of God of Prophecy	1983	-	-	-	2	-
Elim Fellowship World Missions	1983	2	-	-	-	-
Every Home for Christ	1983	-	-	-	9	-
Globe Missionary Evangelism	1980	2	-	-	-	-
Intl. Pentecostal Holiness Ch.	1995	2	-	-	-	-
New Tribes Mission	1993	-	-	-	2	-
OMF International	1952	1	-	-	-	19
Partners International	1954	-	-	-	43	-
Seventh-day Adventists	1911	4	-	-	4	-
Southern Baptist Intl. Mission	1951	17	2	-	-	-
United Methodist Church		1	-	-	-	-
United Pentecostal Church Intl	1981	2	-	-	-	-
Youth With A Mission (YWAM)		11	-	-	-	-
	Totals:	56	28	-	66	19

MALDIVES

Evangelical Mennonite Church	1991	2	-	-	-	-
	Totals:	2	-	-	-	-

MALI

African Christian Mission	1988	4	-	3	-	-
Assemblies of God	1988	8	-	-	-	-

COUNTRY Agency	Year Began	Personnel from U.S.			Other Countries	
		4+ Yrs	2-4 Yrs	1-2 Yrs	Citizens	Not Citiz.
Campus Crusade for Christ	1972	2	-	-	-	-
Child Evangelism Fellowship	1993	-	-	-	2	-
Christian and Msny. Alliance	1923	33	-	-	-	-
Christian Blind Mission Intl.	1991	-	2	-	-	-
Christian Chs. /Chs. of Christ	1985	2	-	-	-	-
Christian Reformed World Msns.	1984	8	-	-	-	-
Evangelical Baptist Missions	1951	18	-	-	-	-
Gospel Missionary Union	1919	17	2	1	-	-
Mission Aviation Fellowship	1985	8	-	2	-	-
Pioneers	1988	-	-	-	-	2
Seventh-day Adventists	1982	2	-	-	-	-
Southern Baptist Intl. Mission	1983	17	9	-	-	-
United World Mission	1954	5	-	-	-	-
Walk Thru The Bible Ministries	1994	-	-	-	3	-
World Vision	1975	-	2	-	-	-
Wycliffe Bible Translators	1979	21	-	-	-	-
Youth With A Mission (YWAM)		2	-	-	-	-
	Totals:	147	15	6	5	2

MALTA
Assemblies of God	1985	2	-	-	-	-
Baptist Bible Fellowship Intl.	1983	2	-	-	-	-
Intl. Pentecostal Holiness Ch.	1988	2	-	-	-	-
	Totals:	6	-	-	-	-

MARSHALL ISLANDS
Assemblies of God	1964	5	-	-	-	-
Gospel Fellowship Association		4	-	-	-	-
Seventh-day Adventists	1930	4	-	-	-	-
	Totals:	13	-	-	-	-

MAURITANIA
World Vision	1984	2	1	2	-	-
	Totals:	2	1	2	-	-

MAURITIUS
Child Evangelism Fellowship	1979	-	-	-	2	-
Presbyterian Church (USA)	1982	2	-	-	-	-
	Totals:	2	-	-	2	-

MEXICO
ABWE	1991	2	-	-	-	-
Action International Mins.	1991	2	-	-	2	-
Advent Christian World Msns.	1987	-	-	-	7	-
All Peoples Baptist Mission	1984	4	-	2	-	-

COUNTRY Agency	Year Began	Personnel from U.S.			Other Countries	
		4+ Yrs	2-4 Yrs	1-2 Yrs	Citizens	Not Citiz.
American Baptist Churches USA	1870	6	-	-	-	-
AmeriTribes		-	-	-	6	-
AMF International	1991	-	-	-	2	-
AMG International	1958	4	-	-	-	-
AMOR Ministries	1980	11	-	-	5	-
Apostolic Christian Church	1978	1	-	-	-	-
Apostolic Team Ministries Intl	1988	-	1	-	-	-
Assemblies of God	1915	68	-	-	-	-
Assoc of Free Lutheran Congs	1979	6	-	-	4	-
Baptist Bible Fellowship Intl.	1950	62	-	-	-	-
Baptist General Conference	1955	11	2	-	-	-
Baptist International Missions	1965	44	-	-	1	-
Baptist Mid-Missions	1960	20	-	-	-	-
Baptist Missionary Assoc.	1953	5	-	-	-	-
Baptist Missions to Forgotten		2	-	-	-	-
Baptist World Mission	1971	13	-	-	-	-
BCM International	1960	-	-	-	4	-
Bethany Fellowship Missions	1971	18	-	-	-	-
Bethany Missionary Association	1959	4	-	-	-	-
Bible Missionary Church	1963	2	-	-	-	-
Biblical Ministries Worldwide	1951	11	-	-	-	-
Brethren Assemblies		32	-	-	-	-
Brethren Church Missionary Bd.	1979	2	-	-	-	-
Brethren in Christ World Msns.	1990	2	-	-	-	-
Calvary Commission, Inc.	1982	7	3	-	-	-
Calvary International	1986	12	-	-	2	1
CAM International	1955	47	-	4	3	1
Campus Crusade for Christ	1961	4	-	-	-	-
Child Evangelism Fellowship	1939	1	-	-	12	-
Childcare International	1983	-	-	-	5	-
Children's Haven International	1977	-	2	1	-	-
Christ for the City Intl.	1995	10	4	-	6	2
Christian Advance Intl.	1985	4	-	-	26	1
Christian Aid Mission		-	-	-	8	-
Christian and Msny. Alliance	1954	10	-	-	-	-
Christian Chs. /Chs. of Christ	1902	53	-	-	-	-
Christian Fellowship Union	1947	2	-	-	-	-
Christian Reformed World Msns.	1953	13	-	-	-	-
Christian Union Mission	1976	2	-	-	-	-
Christians In Action, Inc.	1972	2	-	-	15	-
Church of God Apostolic Faith	1950	2	-	2	-	-
Church of God World Missions	1932	2	-	-	15	-
Church of the Nazarene	1903	10	-	-	-	-
CMF International	1980	8	-	-	-	-
Congregational Christian Chs.	1960	-	-	-	3	-
Congregational Methodist Ch.	1963	9	-	-	-	-
Elim Fellowship World Missions	1962	15	-	-	-	-

COUNTRY Agency	Year Began	Personnel from U.S.			Other Countries	
		4+ Yrs	2-4 Yrs	1-2 Yrs	Citizens	Not Citiz.
Evangelical Covenant Church	1946	15	-	6	-	-
Evangelical Free Church Msn.	1987	5	2	-	-	-
Evangelical Friends Mission	1978	4	-	-	-	-
Evangelical Lutheran Church	1956	2	-	-	-	-
Evangelical Mennonite Church	1993	1	-	-	-	-
Evangelical Methodist Church	1946	2	-	-	-	-
Evangelical Presbyterian Ch.	1993	2	-	-	-	-
Every Home for Christ	1963	-	-	-	5	-
Fellowship International Msn.	1984	8	-	-	-	-
Foundation For His Ministry	1967	-	-	-	-	-
Full Gospel Grace Fellowship		2	-	-	-	-
General Conf. Mennonite Church	1946	-	-	-	-	6
Global Strategy Mission Assoc.	1986	4	1	-	1	-
Globe Missionary Evangelism	1979	-	16	-	-	-
Gospel Fellowship Association		14	-	-	-	-
Gospel Missionary Union	1956	5	-	-	-	-
Gospel Recordings USA	1970	-	2	-	2	-
Grace Brethren Intl. Missions	1951	9	-	-	-	-
Habitat for Humanity Intl	1987	-	5	-	26	-
Heifer Project International	1959	-	-	-	3	-
Hope for the Hungry	1987	-	2	-	-	-
Impact International	1990	-	-	-	2	-
In Touch Mission Intl.		-	-	-	2	-
Independent Faith Mission	1985	4	-	-	-	-
International Family Missions	1996	4	-	-	-	-
International Gospel Outreach	1992	2	-	-	-	-
International Outreach Mins.	1986	2	-	-	4	-
International Partnership Mins	1991	-	-	-	-	2
International Teams, U.S.A.	1968	-	5	-	-	2
Intl. Discipleship Mission	1951	2	-	-	-	-
Intl. Pentecostal Ch of Christ	1950	1	-	-	-	-
Intl. Pentecostal Holiness Ch.	1930	2	-	-	-	-
Kids Alive International	1990	-	-	-	1	-
Latin America Lutheran Mission	1943	-	-	-	-	-
Latin America Mission	1965	19	7	1	5	-
Liberty Baptist Mission	1987	2	-	-	-	-
Living Water Teaching Intl.	1995	-	-	-	1	-
Lutheran Church-Missouri Synod	1940	6	-	-	-	-
Macedonia World Baptist Msns.	1983	10	-	-	-	-
Maranatha Baptist Mission	1966	12	-	-	-	-
Mazahua Mission	1986	1	-	-	-	-
Medical Ambassadors Intl.	1990	-	-	1	-	-
Mennonite Brethren Msns/Svcs	1905	4	3	-	-	-
Mennonite Central Committee	1981	3	9	-	-	-
Metropolitan Church Assoc.	1930	1	-	-	-	-
Mexican Border Missions	1961	2	-	-	5	-
Mexican Christian Mission	1963	4	-	-	5	-

COUNTRY Agency	Year Began	Personnel from U.S.			Other Countries	
		4+ Yrs	2-4 Yrs	1-2 Yrs	Citizens	Not Citiz.
Mexican Medical, Inc.	1967	2	-	2	-	-
Mexican Mission Ministries	1954	10	-	-	12	-
Mission Aviation Fellowship	1946	3	-	-	1	-
Mission Ministries, Inc.	1983	2	-	-	-	-
Mission Soc. for United Meth.	1995	4	-	-	-	2
Mission to the Americas	1952	8	-	-	8	2
Mission to the World	1973	41	7	-	-	-
Missionary Gospel Fellowship	1973	-	-	-	2	2
Missionary Revival Crusade	1949	24	-	-	-	-
Navigators, The	1966	4	-	-	-	-
New Tribes Mission	1975	84	-	-	4	1
Next Towns Crusade, Inc.	1964	3	-	1	-	-
North American Baptist Conf.	1992	6	-	-	-	-
OC International, Inc.	1967	4	-	-	-	-
OMS International, Inc.	1990	13	4	1	-	1
Open Bible Standard Churches	1964	3	-	-	-	-
Operation Mobilization		6	-	-	-	-
Partners International	1968	-	-	-	2	-
Pentecostal Free Will Bapt.Ch.	1960	-	-	-	2	-
Pocket Testament League	1984	-	-	-	2	-
Precious Seed Ministries	1985	-	-	-	8	-
Presb. Evangelistic Fellowship	1980	4	-	-	6	-
Presbyterian Church (USA)	1872	4	23	7	-	-
Primitive Methodist Church USA	1995	2	-	-	-	2
Project Partner with Christ	1964	-	-	-	1	-
Reach Ministries International	1983	2	-	-	-	-
Reformed Church In America	1924	10	-	-	-	-
Rio Grande Bible Institute	1946	51	2	6	-	-
Ripe for Harvest, Inc.	1995	-	-	1	-	-
Salvation Army, U.S.A.	1937	3	-	-	-	-
Seventh-day Adventists	1893	26	-	1	14	-
Shield of Faith Mission Intl.	1972	7	-	-	-	-
Source of Light Ministries	1962	2	-	-	-	-
Southern Baptist Intl. Mission	1880	91	10	-	-	-
Spanish World Gospel Mission	1970	-	-	-	3	1
TEAM	1988	13	-	-	-	-
The Master's Harvest	1992	2	-	-	-	-
The Master's Mission, Inc.	1995	2	-	-	-	-
Trans World Missions	1949	-	-	-	-	-
Trinity Intl. Baptist Mission	1975	2	-	-	-	-
UFM International	1971	14	-	-	-	-
UIM International	1960	20	-	-	-	-
United Evangelical Churches		2	-	-	-	-
United Methodist Church		7	-	-	-	-
United Pentecostal Church Intl	1979	12	-	-	-	-
VELA Ministries International	1984	1	-	-	9	-
Walk Thru The Bible Ministries	1995	-	-	-	2	-

COUNTRY Agency	Year Began	Personnel from U.S.			Other Countries	
		4+ Yrs	2-4 Yrs	1-2 Yrs	Citizens	Not Citiz.
WEC International	1990	4	2	3	-	1
Wesleyan World Missions	1920	5	-	-	-	-
Westminister Biblical Missions	1974	1	-	-	-	-
Wisconsin Evang. Lutheran Syn.	1968	2	-	-	-	-
World Baptist Fellowship Msn	1953	26	-	-	-	-
World Gospel Mission	1945	15	-	-	-	-
World Indigenous Missions	1981	35	-	-	-	-
World Mission Prayer League	1945	5	-	-	-	5
World Partners Missionary Ch.	1982	1	-	-	-	-
World Salt Foundation	1983	6	-	-	-	-
World Servants	1992	-	-	-	3	-
World Team	1990	-	-	1	-	2
World Witness	1878	13	-	-	100	-
World-Wide Missions	1962	-	-	-	14	-
Wycliffe Bible Translators	1936	206	3	-	-	-
Youth for Christ / USA		2	-	-	-	-
Youth With A Mission (YWAM)		19	-	-	-	-
YUGO Ministries	1964	13	-	-	12	-
	Totals:	1,546	115	40	393	34

MICRONESIA

Baptist Bible Fellowship Intl.	1972	2	-	-	-	-
Baptist International Missions	1974	4	-	-	-	-
Baptist Mid-Missions	1981	4	-	-	-	-
Child Evangelism Fellowship	1957	2	-	-	-	-
Conservative Cong. Christian	1984	2	-	2	-	-
Global Outreach Mission	1988	2	-	-	-	-
Independent Faith Mission	1990	2	-	-	-	-
Liebenzell Mission USA	1907	5	-	-	-	-
Mission to the World	1986	2	-	-	-	-
United Church Board World Mins	1852	-	2	-	-	-
United Pentecostal Church Intl	1981	4	-	-	-	-
Youth With A Mission (YWAM)		1	-	-	-	-
	Totals:	30	2	2	-	-

MOLDAVA

Baptist International Missions	1993	2	-	-	-	-
CEIFA Ministries International	1990	-	-	-	1	-
Macedonia World Baptist Msns.	1992	6	-	-	-	-
Walk Thru The Bible Ministries	1994	-	-	-	16	-
	Totals:	8	-	-	17	-

MONACO

Trans World Radio	1960	18	-	-	10	-
UFM International	1995	2	-	-	-	-
	Totals:	20	-	-	10	-

COUNTRY Agency	Year Began	Personnel from U.S.			Other Countries	
		4+ Yrs	2-4 Yrs	1-2 Yrs	Citizens	Not Citiz.
MONGOLIA						
Action International Mins.		2	-	-	-	-
Asian Outreach U.S.A.	1992	-	-	-	-	2
Assemblies of God		14	-	-	-	-
Campus Crusade for Christ	1991	5	-	-	-	-
Christian Aid Mission		-	-	-	9	-
Evangelical Free Church Msn.	1993	4	2	-	-	-
Mission to the World	1994	-	1	-	-	-
New Tribes Mission	1993	7	-	-	-	2
World Concern	1983	2	4	-	-	-
World Mission Prayer League	1993	-	4	-	-	4
	Totals:	34	11	-	9	8
MOROCCO						
Fellowship International Msn.	1950	8	-	-	2	-
Southern Baptist Intl. Mission	1966	12	-	-	-	-
U.S. Center for World Mission	1984	2	-	-	-	-
	Totals:	22	-	-	2	-
MOZAMBIQUE						
Africa Evangelical Fellowship	1936	8	-	-	-	-
Africa Inland Mission Intl	1985	18	-	3	-	-
Assemblies of God	1974	8	-	-	-	-
Brethren Assemblies		2	-	-	-	-
Christian Chs. /Chs. of Christ	1992	2	-	4	-	-
Christian Reformed Wrld Relief		1	-	-	-	-
Church of the Nazarene	1922	6	-	-	2	-
Elim Fellowship World Missions	1995	1	-	1	-	-
General Conf. Mennonite Church	1994	2	-	-	-	-
Heifer Project International	1996	-	1	-	-	-
Mennonite Central Committee	1971	7	3	-	-	-
Mission Aviation Fellowship	1991	2	-	-	-	-
OMS International, Inc.	1994	3	-	-	-	1
Operation Mobilization		-	-	2	-	-
PAZ International	1994	-	-	-	2	-
Presbyterian Church (USA)		2	-	-	-	-
Southern Baptist Intl. Mission	1973	13	-	-	-	-
TEAM	1988	-	-	-	-	1
Teen Missions International		-	-	-	-	3
United Church Board World Mins	1883	-	3	-	-	-
United Methodist Church		2	-	-	-	-
Wesleyan World Missions	1916	2	-	-	-	-
World Vision	1984	1	4	-	-	-
Wycliffe Bible Translators	1994	9	-	-	-	-
Youth With A Mission (YWAM)		1	-	-	-	-
	Totals:	90	11	10	4	5

COUNTRY Agency	Year Began	Personnel from U.S.			Other Countries	
		4+ Yrs	2-4 Yrs	1-2 Yrs	Citizens	Not Citiz.

MYANMAR / BURMA

Agency	Year Began	4+ Yrs	2-4 Yrs	1-2 Yrs	Citizens	Not Citiz.
Ambassadors for Christ Intl.		-	-	-	6	-
Baptist World Mission		2	-	-	-	-
BCM International	1991	-	-	-	53	-
Child Evangelism Fellowship	1980	-	-	-	15	-
Christian Aid Mission		-	-	-	135	-
Church of God World Missions	1981	-	-	-	2	-
Every Home for Christ	1981	-	-	-	23	-
Gospel for Asia	1988	-	-	-	442	-
Mission O.N.E., Inc.	1991	-	-	-	3	-
Partners International	1978	-	-	-	165	1
Pass the Torch Ministries	1988	-	-	-	3	-
Seventh-day Adventists	1919	4	-	-	-	-
Tribes and Nations Outreach	1985	-	-	-	2	-
World Concern	1993	-	2	-	7	-
Youth for Christ / USA		2	-	-	-	-
Totals:		8	2	-	856	1

NAMIBIA

Agency	Year Began	4+ Yrs	2-4 Yrs	1-2 Yrs	Citizens	Not Citiz.
Africa Evangelical Fellowship	1970	-	-	2	-	-
Africa Inland Mission Intl	1981	8	-	5	-	-
Assemblies of God	1979	4	-	-	-	-
Child Evangelism Fellowship	1996	-	-	-	2	-
Church of the Nazarene	1973	2	-	-	-	-
Evangelical Lutheran Church	1983	3	-	1	-	-
Every Home for Christ	1995	-	-	-	1	-
Lutheran Bible Translators	1996	3	-	-	-	-
Southern Baptist Intl. Mission	1968	16	-	-	-	-
United Pentecostal Church Intl	1986	2	-	-	-	-
Totals:		38	-	8	3	-

NEPAL

Agency	Year Began	4+ Yrs	2-4 Yrs	1-2 Yrs	Citizens	Not Citiz.
Anglican Frontier Missions		2	-	-	-	-
BCM International	1995	-	-	-	7	-
Bible Missionary Church	1994	-	-	-	-	-
BILD International	1986	-	-	-	-	-
Child Evangelism Fellowship	1988	-	-	-	2	-
Christian Aid Mission		-	-	-	133	-
Christian Blind Mission Intl.	1988	-	2	-	-	-
Church of God World Missions	1994	-	-	-	-	-
Evangelical Friends Mission	1993	-	-	-	2	2
Evangelical Lutheran Church	1974	2	-	-	-	-
Every Home for Christ	1982	-	-	-	38	-
Foursquare Missions Intl.	1985	2	-	-	-	-
General Conf. Mennonite Church	1983	2	-	-	-	-
Gospel for Asia	1984	-	-	-	182	-

COUNTRY Agency	Year Began	Personnel from U.S.			Other Countries	
		4+ Yrs	2-4 Yrs	1-2 Yrs	Citizens	Not Citiz.
Gospel Recordings USA	1982	-	-	-	4	-
International Needs - USA	1975	-	-	-	40	-
InterServe/USA	1952	8	-	-	-	-
Medical Ambassadors Intl.	1984	-	-	-	2	-
Mennonite Board of Missions	1957	12	-	-	-	-
Mennonite Central Committee	1957	4	4	-	-	-
Mission O.N.E., Inc.	1995	-	-	-	2	-
Mission To Unreached Peoples	1985	-	2	-	-	-
Pioneers	1988	2	-	-	-	-
Presbyterian Church (USA)	1954	10	13	-	-	-
Seventh-day Adventists	1957	-	-	-	9	-
SIM USA	1995	2	-	-	-	-
Southern Baptist Intl. Mission	1983	8	-	-	-	-
TEAM	1892	15	2	-	-	-
Tribes and Nations Outreach	1994	-	-	-	1	-
United Church Board World Mins	1979	-	3	-	-	-
United Methodist Church		6	-	-	-	-
Wesleyan World Missions	1950	1	-	-	-	-
World Concern	1980	6	-	2	-	1
World Mission Prayer League	1954	9	-	-	-	9
World-Wide Missions	1964	1	-	-	2	-
Totals:		92	26	2	424	12

NETHERLANDS

Assemblies of God	1965	4	-	-	-	-
Baptist Bible Fellowship Intl.	1979	2	-	-	-	-
Baptist Mid-Missions	1954	6	-	-	-	-
BCM International	1948	2	1	-	7	-
Biblical Ministries Worldwide	1959	7	-	-	-	-
Brethren Assemblies		4	-	-	-	-
CBInternational	1985	3	-	2	-	-
Child Evangelism Fellowship	1949	2	-	-	4	5
Christian Associates Intl.	1987	6	-	-	3	2
Church of God World Missions	1982	-	-	-	1	-
Church of The Brethren		-	-	2	-	-
European Missions Outreach	1989	2	-	-	-	-
Greater Europe Mission	1983	10	-	-	-	-
Habitat for Humanity Intl	1994	1	-	-	1	-
International Missions, Inc.	1976	3	-	-	-	-
Trans World Radio	1983	3	-	1	-	-
United Pentecostal Church Intl	1962	2	-	-	-	-
Walk Thru The Bible Ministries	1991	-	-	-	1	-
World Harvest Mission	1990	7	-	-	2	-
Youth With A Mission (YWAM)		48	-	-	-	-
Totals:		112	1	5	19	7

COUNTRY Agency	Year Began	Personnel from U.S.			Other Countries	
		4+ Yrs	2-4 Yrs	1-2 Yrs	Citizens	Not Citiz.
NETHERLANDS ANTILLES						
Child Evangelism Fellowship		2	-	-	-	-
Global Outreach Mission	1994	2	-	-	-	-
Grace Ministries International	1953	-	-	-	-	-
Seventh-day Adventists	1926	2	-	-	2	-
Southern Baptist Intl. Mission	1983	6	-	-	-	-
TEAM	1931	10	-	-	-	-
Trans World Radio	1964	57	-	7	29	-
United Pentecostal Church Intl	1974	4	-	-	-	-
	Totals:	83	-	7	31	-
NEW CALEDONIA						
Assemblies of God	1969	2	-	-	-	-
Baptist International Missions	1995	2	-	-	-	-
Wycliffe Bible Translators	1986	2	2	-	-	-
Youth With A Mission (YWAM)		2	-	-	-	-
	Totals:	8	2	-	-	-
NEW ZEALAND						
Advent Christian World Msns.	1995	-	-	2	-	-
American Baptist Association		2	-	-	-	-
Baptist Bible Fellowship Intl.	1971	12	-	-	-	-
Baptist International Missions	1979	4	-	-	-	-
Baptist Mid-Missions	1973	8	-	-	-	-
Baptist World Mission		3	-	-	-	-
Berean Mission, Inc.	1983	-	2	-	2	-
Biblical Ministries Worldwide	1968	8	-	-	-	-
Campus Crusade for Christ	1972	6	-	-	-	-
Child Evangelism Fellowship	1951	-	-	-	6	-
Christian and Msny. Alliance	1972	4	-	-	-	-
Christian Chs. /Chs. of Christ		4	-	-	-	-
Church of God World Missions	1987	-	-	-	2	-
Elim Fellowship World Missions	1964	2	-	-	-	-
Fellowship International Msn.	1995	2	-	-	-	-
Navigators, The	1953	2	-	-	-	-
Presbyterian Church (USA)		4	-	-	-	-
Southern Baptist Intl. Mission	1994	2	-	-	-	-
Teen Missions International		-	-	-	2	-
United Pentecostal Church Intl	1969	2	-	-	-	-
Walk Thru The Bible Ministries	1982	-	-	-	6	-
World Baptist Fellowship Msn	1979	4	-	-	-	-
Youth With A Mission (YWAM)		12	-	-	-	-
	Totals:	81	2	2	18	-

COUNTRY Agency	Year Began	Personnel from U.S.			Other Countries	
		4+ Yrs	2-4 Yrs	1-2 Yrs	Citizens	Not Citiz.
NICARAGUA						
American Baptist Churches USA	1917	7	-	-	-	-
Assemblies of God	1936	8	-	-	-	-
Baptist International Missions	1965	2	-	-	-	-
Brethren in Christ World Msns.	1965	2	-	-	-	-
Child Evangelism Fellowship	1969	-	-	-	4	-
Christian Reformed Wrld Relief		1	-	-	-	-
Church of God World Missions	1950	2	-	-	2	-
Church of the Nazarene	1937	2	-	-	-	-
Church of the United Brethren	1965	-	-	-	-	-
Enterprise Development Intl.	1990	-	1	-	-	-
Evangelical Lutheran Church	1980	2	-	2	-	-
Every Home for Christ	1965	-	-	-	5	-
Habitat for Humanity Intl	1984	-	2	-	21	-
Latin America Assistance, Inc.	1988	1	-	-	2	-
Living Water Teaching Intl.	1988	-	-	-	1	1
Mennonite Central Committee	1979	3	7	-	-	-
Mission Aviation Fellowship	1972	2	-	2	-	-
Missionary Action, Inc.	1989	-	-	-	2	-
National Baptist Conv. USA	1958	2	-	-	3	-
Pentecostal Free Will Bapt.Ch.	1970	-	-	-	2	-
Presbyterian Church (USA)	1973	4	5	6	-	-
Reformed Church In America		1	-	-	-	-
Rosedale Mennonite Missions	1972	1	-	-	1	-
Seventh-day Adventists	1928	2	-	1	-	-
Southern Baptist Intl. Mission	1989	6	7	-	-	-
Trans World Missions	1966	-	-	-	-	2
United Church Board World Mins	1972	-	2	-	-	-
United Methodist Church		2	-	-	-	-
World Relief Corporation		1	-	-	-	-
Young Life	1988	3	-	-	-	-
Youth With A Mission (YWAM)		2	-	-	-	-
	Totals:	56	24	11	43	3
NIGER						
Agape Gospel Mission	1995	-	-	-	-	2
Assemblies of God	1991	6	-	-	-	-
Baptist International Missions	1966	2	-	-	-	-
Elim Fellowship World Missions	1991	2	-	-	-	-
Evangelical Baptist Missions	1929	10	-	-	-	-
Fellowship International Msn.	1971	3	-	-	-	-
Lutheran World Relief	1990	2	-	-	-	-
Mission to the World	1994	2	-	-	-	-
Seventh-day Adventists	1987	4	-	-	4	-
SIM USA	1924	65	-	2	-	-
Southern Baptist Intl. Mission	1969	12	4	-	-	-

COUNTRY Agency	Year Began	Personnel from U.S.			Other Countries	
		4+ Yrs	2-4 Yrs	1-2 Yrs	Citizens	Not Citiz.
World Vision	1973	-	-	1	-	-
Wycliffe Bible Translators	1980	9	-	-	-	-
Youth With A Mission (YWAM)		1	-	-	-	-
	Totals:	118	4	3	4	2

NIGERIA

Advent Christian World Msns.	1967	-	-	-	2	-
Agape Gospel Mission	1984	-	-	-	17	-
Ambassadors for Christ Intl.		-	-	-	2	-
Assemblies of God	1939	8	-	-	-	-
Baptist Bible Fellowship Intl.	1987	4	-	-	-	-
Baptist International Missions	1982	12	-	-	2	-
Baptist Missions to Forgotten		2	-	-	-	-
Baptist World Mission		2	-	-	-	-
Bible Missionary Church	1971	2	-	-	-	-
Brethren Assemblies		6	-	-	-	-
Calvary International	1987	5	-	-	-	-
Campus Crusade for Christ	1969	11	-	-	-	-
Child Evangelism Fellowship	1982	-	-	-	60	-
Christian Aid Mission		-	-	-	42	-
Christian and Msny. Alliance	1983	2	-	-	-	-
Christian Chs. /Chs. of Christ	1955	2	-	-	-	-
Christian Methodist Episcopal		1	-	-	-	-
Christian Mission for the Deaf	1960	-	-	-	3	-
Christian Reformed World Msns.	1940	37	4	2	1	-
Christian Reformed Wrld Relief		2	-	-	-	-
Church of God (Holiness) Msn.	1988	2	-	-	-	2
Church of God of Prophecy	1971	-	-	-	5	1
Church of God World Missions	1951	-	-	-	2	-
Church of The Brethren	1922	-	6	2	-	-
Church of the Nazarene	1977	3	-	-	-	-
Congregational Christian Chs.	1965	-	-	-	2	-
Elim Fellowship World Missions	1975	3	-	-	-	-
Evangelical Baptist Missions	1985	-	-	-	2	-
Evangelical Lutheran Church	1913	4	-	1	-	-
Evangelism Resources	1994	-	-	-	2	-
Every Home for Christ	1976	-	-	-	3	-
Faith Christian Fellowship	1983	-	-	-	-	-
Fellowship International Msn.	1975	4	-	-	-	-
Gospel Revival Ministries	1990	-	-	-	5	-
InterVarsity Mission	1995	-	1	-	-	-
Intl. Inst. Christian Studies	1988	1	1	-	-	-
Ireland Outreach Intl., Inc.	1994	-	-	-	4	-
Lutheran Church-Missouri Synod	1936	21	-	3	-	-
Mennonite Central Committee	1963	5	3	-	-	-
Mission to the World	1975	8	-	-	-	-
Navigators, The	1976	2	-	-	-	-

COUNTRY Agency	Year Began	Personnel from U.S.			Other Countries	
		4+ Yrs	2-4 Yrs	1-2 Yrs	Citizens	Not Citiz.
North American Baptist Conf.	1961	4	-	-	-	-
Partners International	1963	-	-	-	67	-
Pentecostal Free Will Bapt.Ch.	1988	-	-	-	2	-
Pioneers	1988	-	-	-	2	-
Presb. Evangelistic Fellowship		1	-	-	2	-
Seventh-day Adventists	1914	-	-	-	3	-
SIM USA	1893	72	-	2	-	-
Southern Baptist Intl. Mission	1850	86	9	-	-	-
The Master's Mission, Inc.	1980	-	-	-	5	-
United Methodist Church		9	-	-	-	-
United Pentecostal Church Intl	1970	6	-	-	-	-
United World Mission	1990	2	-	-	-	-
Walk Thru The Bible Ministries	1984	-	-	-	17	-
World Partners Missionary Ch.	1905	10	4	-	-	-
Wycliffe Bible Translators	1963	25	-	-	-	-
	Totals:	364	28	10	252	3

NORTHERN MARIANA ISLANDS

Far East Broadcasting Company	1974	-	7	-	-	-
General Baptists International	1947	-	2	-	-	-
Macedonia World Baptist Msns.	1996	2	-	-	-	-
Pioneers	1983	1	-	-	-	1
Seventh-day Adventists	1930	2	-	-	-	-
Youth With A Mission (YWAM)		2	-	-	-	-
	Totals:	7	9	-	-	1

NORWAY

ABWE	1978	8	-	-	-	-
Baptist International Missions	1973	1	-	-	-	-
Child Evangelism Fellowship	1947	-	-	-	-	2
Evangelical Lutheran Church		2	-	-	-	-
Intl. Pentecostal Holiness Ch.	1992	2	-	-	-	-
Maranatha Baptist Mission	1983	2	-	-	-	-
Seventh-day Adventists	1931	2	-	-	-	-
United Pentecostal Church Intl	1978	2	-	-	-	-
Walk Thru The Bible Ministries	1994	-	-	-	8	-
Youth With A Mission (YWAM)		3	-	-	-	-
	Totals:	22	-	-	8	2

PAKISTAN

Ambassadors for Christ Intl.		-	-	-	4	-
Anglican Orthodox Church	1967	-	-	-	2	-
Baptist Bible Fellowship Intl.	1959	4	-	-	-	-
BCM International	1991	1	-	-	1	-
CBInternational	1954	14	2	2	-	-
Christian Aid Mission		-	-	-	11	-

COUNTRY Agency	Year Began	Personnel from U.S.			Other Countries	
		4+ Yrs	2-4 Yrs	1-2 Yrs	Citizens	Not Citiz.
Christian Reformed World Msns.	1993	2	-	-	-	-
Church of God of Prophecy	1991	-	-	-	1	-
Church of God World Missions	1977	-	-	-	2	-
Episcopal World Mission	1990	2	-	-	-	-
Globe Missionary Evangelism	1992	2	-	-	-	-
Gospel for Asia	1983	-	-	-	1	-
International Missions, Inc.	1954	10	-	-	-	-
InterServe/USA	1852	7	-	-	-	-
Key Communications	1960	-	-	-	2	-
Literacy & Evangelism Intl.	1989	2	-	-	-	-
Mennonite Brethren Msns/Svcs		-	2	-	-	-
Mission O.N.E., Inc.	1994	-	-	-	30	-
OMF International	1988	2	-	-	-	4
Partners International	1975	-	-	-	3	-
Presbyterian Church (USA)	1834	12	8	-	-	-
Seventh-day Adventists	1914	12	-	-	3	-
Shield of Faith Mission Intl.	1983	1	-	-	-	2
SIM USA	1957	2	-	-	-	-
Southern Baptist Intl. Mission	1984	4	-	-	-	-
TEAM	1946	49	1	-	-	-
United Pentecostal Church Intl	1971	4	-	-	-	-
Wesleyan World Missions	1992	-	-	-	2	-
Westminister Biblical Missions	1974	2	-	-	1	-
World Mission Prayer League	1946	3	-	-	-	3
World Relief Corporation		1	-	-	-	-
World Witness	1905	16	1	-	400	-
Totals:		152	14	2	463	9

PANAMA

Assemblies of God	1967	10	-	-	-	-
Baptist Bible Fellowship Intl.	1976	9	-	-	-	-
Baptist International Missions	1980	2	-	-	-	-
Cadence International	1958	-	2	-	-	-
CAM International	1944	7	-	-	1	-
Christian Chs. /Chs. of Christ		4	-	-	-	-
Church of God of Prophecy	1946	-	-	-	1	-
Church of God World Missions	1935	-	-	-	2	2
Evangelical Lutheran Church		2	-	-	-	-
Every Home for Christ	1995	-	-	-	1	-
Foursquare Missions Intl.	1928	2	-	-	-	-
Free Will Baptist Association	1971	6	-	-	-	-
Gospel Missionary Union	1953	6	2	-	1	-
HCJB World Radio Msny. Flwshp.	1980	2	-	-	-	-
Latin America Mission	1978	-	-	-	2	-
Lutheran Church-Missouri Synod	1941	6	-	6	-	-
Mennonite Brethren Msns/Svcs		-	-	-	4	-
New Tribes Mission	1953	80	-	1	-	3

COUNTRY Agency	Year Began	Personnel from U.S.			Other Countries	
		4+ Yrs	2-4 Yrs	1-2 Yrs	Citizens	Not Citiz.
Southern Baptist Intl. Mission	1975	24	3	-	-	-
Trans World Missions	1990	-	-	-	-	2
United Methodist Church		3	-	-	-	-
United Pentecostal Church Intl	1980	4	-	-	-	-
Wycliffe Bible Translators	1970	5	-	-	-	-
Youth With A Mission (YWAM)		3	-	-	-	-
Totals:		175	7	7	12	7

PAPUA NEW GUINEA

ABWE	1967	18	-	-	-	-
Apostolic Christian Church	1961	5	4	-	-	-
Baptist Bible Fellowship Intl.	1961	16	-	-	-	-
Baptist International Missions	1968	10	-	-	-	-
Baptist World Mission	1978	2	-	-	-	-
Bible Missionary Church	1963	8	-	-	-	-
Brethren Assemblies		6	-	-	-	-
Child Evangelism Fellowship	1992	-	-	-	6	-
Christian Aid Mission		-	-	-	9	-
Christian Chs. /Chs. of Christ		28	-	-	-	-
Church of the Nazarene	1954	48	-	-	18	-
Churches of Christ in Union		6	-	-	-	-
Evangelical Bible Mission	1948	-	55	-	-	-
Evangelical Lutheran Church	1886	6	-	1	-	-
Every Home for Christ	1987	-	-	-	8	-
Foursquare Missions Intl.	1956	2	-	-	-	-
Habitat for Humanity Intl	1983	-	9	-	7	9
International Outreach Mins.	1993	2	-	-	-	-
Kids Alive International	1992	1	-	-	-	-
Liebenzell Mission USA	1914	6	-	-	-	-
Lutheran Church-Missouri Synod	1948	9	-	8	-	-
Maranatha Baptist Mission	1975	4	-	-	-	-
Mission Soc. for United Meth.	1995	2	-	-	-	-
Mission to the World	1975	6	-	-	-	-
Mustard Seed, Inc.	1971	-	-	1	26	4
New Tribes Mission	1950	339	-	35	-	52
Open Bible Standard Churches	1974	2	-	-	-	-
Operation Mobilization		2	-	-	-	-
Pioneer Bible Translators	1978	29	-	-	35	-
Pioneers	1980	14	-	-	1	-
Presbyterian Church (USA)		3	-	-	-	-
Seventh-day Adventists	1908	2	-	-	2	-
Walk Thru The Bible Ministries	1991	-	-	-	3	-
Wesleyan World Missions	1961	9	-	-	-	1
Wycliffe Bible Translators	1956	415	31	6	-	-
Youth With A Mission (YWAM)		4	-	-	-	-
Totals:		1,004	99	51	115	66

| COUNTRY | Year | Personnel from U.S. | | | Other Countries | |
Agency	Began	4+ Yrs	2-4 Yrs	1-2 Yrs	Citizens	Not Citiz.
PARAGUAY						
ABWE	1976	15	-	-	-	-
Apostolic Christian Church	1991	1	-	-	-	-
Assemblies of God	1945	23	-	-	-	-
Baptist Bible Fellowship Intl.	1980	6	-	-	-	-
Brethren Assemblies		14	-	-	-	-
Child Evangelism Fellowship	1972	-	-	-	6	-
Christian Aid Mission		-	-	-	27	-
Christian Church of North Am.	1982	-	-	-	-	-
Church of God of Prophecy	1977	-	-	-	-	2
Church of God World Missions	1954	2	-	-	-	2
Congregational Methodist Ch.	1990	2	-	-	-	-
Every Home for Christ	1977	-	-	-	2	-
Full Gospel Grace Fellowship		2	-	-	-	-
General Conf. Mennonite Church	1952	2	-	-	-	-
Global Outreach Mission	1994	2	-	-	-	-
Habitat for Humanity Intl	1996	-	2	-	-	-
International Partnership Mins	1995	-	-	-	1	1
Living Water Teaching Intl.	1991	-	2	-	-	-
Lutheran Church-Missouri Synod	1938	-	-	2	-	-
Mennonite Brethren Msns/Svcs		-	-	-	4	-
Mennonite Central Committee	1930	2	3	-	-	-
Mission Soc. for United Meth.	1988	6	-	-	-	-
New Tribes Mission	1946	67	-	2	1	-
Seventh-day Adventists	1900	-	-	-	2	-
SIM USA	1987	15	-	-	-	-
South America Mission	1991	4	3	-	-	2
Southern Baptist Intl. Mission	1945	39	2	-	-	-
STEM Ministries	1992	-	-	-	-	-
United Pentecostal Church Intl	1973	2	-	-	-	-
World Gospel Mission	1986	8	-	-	-	-
World Salt Foundation	1979	2	-	-	-	-
Wycliffe Bible Translators	1992	4	-	-	-	-
Youth With A Mission (YWAM)		2	-	-	-	-
	Totals:	220	12	4	43	7
PERU						
ABWE	1929	39	-	-	-	-
Allegheny Wesleyan Meth. Msns.	1972	2	-	-	-	-
AMG International	1994	2	-	-	-	-
Assemblies of God	1919	13	-	-	-	-
Baptist Bible Fellowship Intl.	1958	11	-	-	-	-
Baptist Faith Missions	1935	2	-	-	-	-
Baptist International Missions	1968	9	-	-	-	-
Baptist Mid-Missions	1937	34	-	-	-	-
BCM International	1995	-	-	-	2	2

COUNTRY Agency	Year Began	Personnel from U.S.			Other Countries	
		4+ Yrs	2-4 Yrs	1-2 Yrs	Citizens	Not Citiz.
Bible Missionary Church	1988	2	-	-	-	-
Brethren Assemblies		16	-	-	-	-
Childcare International	1984	-	-	-	12	1
Christ for the City Intl.	1995	1	-	-	4	-
Christian Aid Mission		-	-	-	26	-
Christian and Msny. Alliance	1925	19	1	-	-	-
Christian Leadership Dev.	1986	-	-	-	3	-
Christians In Action, Inc.	1980	2	-	-	1	-
Church of God World Missions	1947	-	-	-	2	-
Church of the Nazarene	1914	9	-	-	-	-
Eastern Mennonite Missions	1986	7	1	-	1	-
Elim Fellowship World Missions	1964	2	-	-	-	-
Evangelical Free Church Msn.	1975	5	3	-	-	-
Evangelical Lutheran Church	1966	1	-	-	-	-
Evangelical Lutheran Synod	1968	3	-	-	-	-
Every Home for Christ	1963	-	-	-	2	-
Food for the Hungry	1981	-	4	-	-	-
Habitat for Humanity Intl	1982	-	2	-	46	-
Heifer Project International		-	-	-	6	-
Kids Alive International	1991	2	-	1	-	-
Latin America Mission	1975	2	-	-	2	-
Luke Society, The	1988	-	-	-	2	-
Lutheran Church-Missouri Synod	1995	2	-	-	-	-
Lutheran World Relief	1994	-	-	-	1	-
Macedonia World Baptist Msns.	1987	12	-	-	-	-
Maranatha Baptist Mission	1964	2	-	-	-	-
Mennonite Brethren Msns/Svcs	1944	6	2	-	4	-
Mission to the World	1957	20	2	-	-	-
Scripture Union (USA)		2	-	-	-	-
Seventh-day Adventists	1898	-	-	-	2	-
SIM USA	1965	7	-	-	-	-
South America Mission	1921	25	-	-	-	5
South American Missionary Soc.	1979	2	-	-	-	-
Southern Baptist Intl. Mission	1950	52	11	-	-	-
Spanish World Gospel Mission		-	-	-	2	-
TEAM	1962	10	-	-	-	-
United Pentecostal Church Intl	1962	4	-	-	-	-
Wesleyan World Missions	1903	6	-	-	-	-
World Concern	1995	-	1	-	-	-
World Mission Prayer League	1985	2	-	1	-	3
World Team	1906	10	-	-	-	8
Wycliffe Bible Translators	1946	181	10	5	-	-
Youth With A Mission (YWAM)		2	-	-	-	-
Totals:		528	37	7	118	19

COUNTRY Agency	Year Began	Personnel from U.S.			Other Countries	
		4+ Yrs	2-4 Yrs	1-2 Yrs	Citizens	Not Citiz.

PHILIPPINES

Agency	Year Began	4+ Yrs	2-4 Yrs	1-2 Yrs	Citizens	Not Citiz.
ABWE	1927	46	-	4	-	-
Action International Mins.	1974	37	-	-	1	-
Advent Christian World Msns.	1950	-	-	2	-	1
Ambassadors for Christ Intl.		-	-	-	2	-
American Baptist Churches USA	1900	3	-	-	-	-
AMG International	1976	-	-	-	22	-
Anglican Orthodox Church	1975	-	-	-	1	-
Assemblies of God	1925	54	-	-	-	-
Back to the Bible Intl.	1957	-	-	-	25	-
Baptist Bible Fellowship Intl.	1950	52	-	-	-	-
Baptist General Conference	1949	18	-	2	-	-
Baptist International Missions	1970	32	-	-	2	-
Baptist Missionary Assoc.	1974	5	-	-	-	-
Baptist Missions to Forgotten		2	-	-	-	-
Barnabas International	1994	2	-	-	-	-
BCM International	1981	-	-	-	15	-
Berean Mission, Inc.	1952	2	-	-	-	-
Bethany Fellowship Missions	1971	7	-	-	-	-
Bethany Home, Inc.	1946	1	-	-	-	-
Bible Missionary Church	1978	2	-	-	-	-
Brethren Assemblies		18	-	-	-	-
Cadence International	1950	-	2	-	-	-
Calvary International	1988	14	-	-	-	-
Campus Crusade for Christ	1965	44	-	3	-	-
CBInternational	1955	57	4	8	-	-
Child Evangelism Fellowship	1952	-	-	-	64	-
Childcare International	1996	-	-	-	3	-
China Ministries International	1995	-	-	-	2	-
Christian Aid Mission		-	-	-	268	-
Christian and Msny. Alliance	1902	43	6	-	-	-
Christian Blind Mission Intl.	1988	-	1	-	-	-
Christian Chs. /Chs. of Christ	1901	46	-	-	-	-
Christian Church of North Am.	1970	2	-	-	-	-
Christian Reformed World Msns.	1961	27	4	2	3	-
Christians In Action, Inc.	1977	2	-	-	8	-
Church of God of Prophecy	1952	-	-	-	2	-
Church of God World Missions	1947	9	-	-	2	2
Church of the Nazarene	1946	34	-	-	-	-
Congregational Christian Chs.	1960	-	-	-	2	-
Correll Missionary Ministries	1978	-	-	-	12	-
Covenant Celebration Church	1974	-	-	-	3	-
Eastern Mennonite Missions	1971	2	-	-	2	-
Emmanuel Intl. Mission (U.S.)	1979	1	-	-	-	-
Enterprise Development Intl.	1991	2	-	-	-	-
Evangelical Free Church Msn.	1951	28	-	-	-	-
Evangelical Friends Mission	1978	-	-	-	2	-

COUNTRY Agency	Year Began	Personnel from U.S.			Other Countries	
		4+ Yrs	2-4 Yrs	1-2 Yrs	Citizens	Not Citiz.
Every Home for Christ	1960	-	-	-	21	-
Faith Christian Fellowship	1979	8	-	-	-	-
Far East Broadcasting Company	1948	-	11	-	3	-
Farms International, Inc.	1984	-	-	-	2	-
Foursquare Missions Intl.	1927	2	-	-	-	-
Free Gospel Church Msns. Dept.	1920	5	-	-	-	-
General Baptists International	1957	-	5	-	-	-
Globe Missionary Evangelism	1985	4	-	-	-	-
Gospel Fellowship Association		14	-	-	-	-
Gospel for Asia	1984	-	-	-	41	-
Gospel Recordings USA	1984	-	-	-	6	-
Gospel Revival Ministries	1994	-	-	-	5	-
Grace Brethren Intl. Missions	1984	9	-	-	-	-
Grace Ministries International	1978	4	-	2	-	-
Habitat for Humanity Intl	1986	-	2	-	22	2
Harvest	1995	-	1	-	-	-
Heifer Project International	1954	-	-	-	10	-
Help for Christian Nationals	1982	-	-	-	2	-
Holt Intl. Children's Services	1975	-	-	-	40	-
Independent Faith Mission	1991	2	-	-	-	-
International Bible Institute	1979	-	-	-	1	-
International Missions, Inc.	1951	24	-	-	-	-
International Needs - USA	1977	-	-	-	29	-
International Teams, U.S.A.	1965	7	-	-	18	-
Intl. Pentecostal Holiness Ch.	1975	4	-	-	-	-
Luke Society, The	1980	-	-	-	6	-
Lutheran Church-Missouri Synod	1946	5	-	2	-	-
Medical Ambassadors Intl.	1975	2	-	-	47	-
Mennonite Central Committee	1977	6	1	-	-	-
Mission Ministries, Inc.	1983	-	-	-	-	2
Mission Soc. for United Meth.	1987	2	-	-	-	-
Mission to the World	1975	14	3	-	-	-
Mission To Unreached Peoples	1987	-	2	-	-	-
Missions To Japan, Inc.		-	-	-	1	3
Navigators, The	1961	10	-	-	-	-
New Tribes Mission	1951	104	-	4	2	2
North American Baptist Conf.	1986	6	-	-	-	-
OC International, Inc.	1952	12	-	-	4	-
Omega World Missions	1979	5	-	-	15	-
OMF International	1952	33	-	-	-	106
OMS International, Inc.	1982	6	-	-	32	-
Open Bible Standard Churches	1978	5	-	-	-	-
Oriental Missionary Crusade	1958	2	-	-	-	-
Partners International	1968	-	-	-	514	-
Pass the Torch Ministries	1992	-	-	-	1	1
Pentecostal Free Will Bapt.Ch.	1962	-	-	-	2	-
Pocket Testament League	1972	-	-	-	12	-

COUNTRY Agency	Year Began	Personnel from U.S.			Other Countries	
		4+ Yrs	2-4 Yrs	1-2 Yrs	Citizens	Not Citiz.
Presbyterian Church (USA)	1899	4	14	-	-	-
Reach Ministries International	1976	-	-	-	5	-
Reformed Church In America	1950	4	-	-	-	-
Salvation Army, U.S.A.	1937	1	-	-	-	-
SEND International	1947	35	-	-	-	-
Seventh-day Adventists	1906	19	-	1	16	-
SIM USA	1984	5	-	-	-	-
Southern Baptist Intl. Mission	1948	127	17	-	-	-
Sowers International, The	1993	-	-	-	4	-
TEAM	1987	21	-	-	-	-
Teen Missions International		-	-	1	2	-
Things To Come Mission, Inc	1958	2	-	-	-	-
Tribes and Nations Outreach	1985	-	-	-	2	-
UFM International	1985	15	-	-	-	-
United Evangelical Churches		6	-	-	-	-
United Methodist Church		8	-	-	-	-
United Pentecostal Church Intl	1957	8	-	-	-	-
Walk Thru The Bible Ministries	1982	-	-	-	2	-
Wesleyan World Missions	1932	2	-	-	-	-
World Indigenous Missions	1986	6	-	-	-	-
World Mission Prayer League	1985	4	-	-	-	4
World Team	1981	18	-	-	-	9
World-Wide Missions	1965	-	-	-	1	-
Wycliffe Bible Translators	1953	201	14	-	-	-
Youth With A Mission (YWAM)		12	-	-	-	-
Totals:		1,385	87	31	1,309	132

POLAND

Back to the Bible Intl.	1993	-	-	-	5	-
Baptist International Missions	1991	2	-	-	-	-
Baptist Mid-Missions	1990	2	-	-	-	-
BCM International	1997	-	-	1	-	1
Campus Crusade for Christ	1977	14	-	-	-	-
CBInternational	1991	12	-	-	-	-
Child Evangelism Fellowship	1970	-	-	-	8	1
Christian Aid Mission		-	-	-	3	-
Christian and Msny. Alliance	1993	4	-	-	-	-
Church of God World Missions	1989	-	-	-	2	-
Church of The Brethren		-	-	2	-	-
Church Resource Ministries	1993	4	-	-	-	-
Evangelical Free Church Msn.	1993	4	2	-	-	-
Evangelical Lutheran Church		2	-	-	-	-
Every Home for Christ	1981	-	-	-	2	-
Fellowship International Msn.	1995	1	-	-	-	-
Friendship Ministries	1996	-	2	-	-	-
Greater Europe Mission	1992	2	-	-	-	-
Habitat for Humanity Intl	1995	1	-	-	1	-

COUNTRY / Agency	Year Began	Personnel from U.S.			Other Countries	
		4+ Yrs	2-4 Yrs	1-2 Yrs	Citizens	Not Citiz.
International Messengers	1985	7	-	-	5	7
International Teams, U.S.A.	1973	2	1	-	-	-
InterVarsity Mission	1991	-	1	1	-	-
Ministry to Eastern Europe	1993	-	-	-	4	-
Mission to the World	1994	2	-	-	-	-
Mission To Unreached Peoples	1989	-	2	-	-	-
Pocket Testament League	1986	-	-	-	2	-
Presbyterian Church (USA)		2	-	-	-	-
Project Care	1991	-	-	-	2	-
SEND International	1991	12	-	-	-	-
United Church Board World Mins	1986	-	2	-	-	-
Walk Thru The Bible Ministries	1992	-	-	-	1	-
Young Life	1990	1	-	-	-	-
Youth With A Mission (YWAM)		6	-	-	-	-
Totals:		80	10	4	35	9

PORTUGAL

COUNTRY / Agency	Year Began	4+ Yrs	2-4 Yrs	1-2 Yrs	Citizens	Not Citiz.
ABWE	1978	29	-	2	-	-
Africa Evangelical Fellowship	1979	2	-	-	-	-
Assemblies of God	1967	11	-	-	-	-
Baptist Bible Fellowship Intl.	1987	4	-	-	-	-
Baptist World Mission		2	-	-	-	-
Brethren Assemblies		4	-	-	-	-
CBInternational	1945	6	-	1	-	-
CEIFA Ministries International	1990	-	-	-	1	-
Child Evangelism Fellowship	1949	-	-	-	10	1
Christian Chs. /Chs. of Christ		5	-	-	-	-
Church of God of Prophecy	1976	-	-	-	1	-
Church of God World Missions	1965	-	-	-	-	2
Church of the Nazarene	1973	5	-	-	-	-
Correll Missionary Ministries	1978	-	-	-	2	-
Grace Brethren Intl. Missions	1990	5	-	-	-	-
Greater Europe Mission	1971	13	-	-	-	-
Mennonite Brethren Msns/Svcs	1986	2	2	-	-	-
Mission to the World	1979	7	2	-	-	-
PAZ International	1995	-	-	-	-	4
Pocket Testament League	1986	-	-	-	-	2
Presbyterian Church (USA)	1972	2	-	-	-	-
Southern Baptist Intl. Mission	1959	20	3	-	-	-
TEAM	1936	17	-	-	-	-
United Pentecostal Church Intl	1972	2	-	-	-	-
WEC International	1980	1	-	-	-	-
World Partners Missionary Ch.	1992	4	-	-	-	-
Youth for Christ / USA	1966	2	1	-	-	-
Totals:		143	8	3	14	9

COUNTRY Agency	Year Began	Personnel from U.S.			Other Countries	
		4+ Yrs	2-4 Yrs	1-2 Yrs	Citizens	Not Citiz.

PUERTO RICO

COUNTRY Agency	Year Began	4+ Yrs	2-4 Yrs	1-2 Yrs	Citizens	Not Citiz.
Apostolic Christian Church	1989	2	-	-	-	-
Baptist Bible Fellowship Intl.	1955	6	-	-	-	-
Baptist International Missions	1965	16	-	-	-	-
Baptist Mid-Missions	1959	6	-	-	-	-
Baptist World Mission		4	-	-	-	-
Biblical Ministries Worldwide	1968	2	-	-	-	-
Brethren Assemblies		2	-	-	-	-
Child Evangelism Fellowship	1946	-	-	-	3	-
Christian Chs. /Chs. of Christ	1976	14	-	16	-	-
Church of God World Missions	1944	-	-	-	2	-
Church of the Nazarene	1944	2	-	-	-	-
Evangelical Lutheran Church		2	-	-	-	-
Gospel Fellowship Association		4	-	-	-	-
Grace Ministries International	1963	6	-	-	-	-
InterVarsity Mission	1992	-	2	-	-	-
Lutheran Church-Missouri Synod	1993	2	-	2	-	-
Macedonia World Baptist Msns.	1981	14	-	-	-	-
Maranatha Baptist Mission	1983	2	-	-	-	-
Mennonite Board of Missions	1945	2	-	-	-	-
Seventh-day Adventists	1901	16	-	-	-	-
UFM International	1986	-	-	2	-	-
United Pentecostal Church Intl	1964	2	-	-	-	-
Wesleyan World Missions	1952	4	-	-	-	-
Wisconsin Evang. Lutheran Syn.	1963	4	-	-	-	-
World Indigenous Missions	1996	2	-	-	-	-
	Totals:	114	2	20	5	-

ROMANIA

COUNTRY Agency	Year Began	4+ Yrs	2-4 Yrs	1-2 Yrs	Citizens	Not Citiz.
All God's Children Intl.	1991	-	-	-	2	-
AMG International	1994	-	-	-	12	-
Assemblies of God	1989	12	-	-	-	-
Baptist Bible Fellowship Intl.	1990	14	-	-	-	-
Baptist International Missions	1990	10	-	-	-	-
Baptist Mid-Missions	1993	2	-	-	-	-
Baptist Missions to Forgotten		2	-	-	-	-
Baptist World Mission		2	-	-	-	-
Brethren Assemblies		4	-	-	-	-
Bright Hope International		-	-	-	30	-
Calvary Commission, Inc.	1990	-	-	-	-	-
Calvary International	1995	2	-	-	-	-
Campus Crusade for Christ	1980	20	-	-	-	-
CBInternational	1991	10	1	2	-	-
CEIFA Ministries International	1990	-	-	1	3	-
Child Evangelism Fellowship	1974	-	-	-	22	3
Christ for the Nations, Inc.	1992	-	-	-	8	-

COUNTRY Agency	Year Began	Personnel from U.S.			Other Countries	
		4+ Yrs	2-4 Yrs	1-2 Yrs	Citizens	Not Citiz.
Christian Aid Ministries	1992	-	2	-	-	-
Christian Aid Mission		-	-	-	4	-
Christian Reformed World Msns.	1993	-	-	3	-	-
Church of God World Missions	1922	-	-	-	5	-
Church of the Nazarene	1992	4	-	-	-	-
Church Resource Ministries	1990	6	-	-	-	-
Eastern European Bible Mission	1991	-	-	-	9	-
Eastern European Outreach	1992	-	6	-	-	-
Evangelical Baptist Missions	1990	4	-	-	-	-
Evangelical Free Church Msn.	1991	8	17	6	-	-
Food for the Hungry	1991	2	-	-	-	-
Friends in the West	1990	-	-	1	-	-
Friends United Meeting	1995	-	1	-	-	-
Greater Europe Mission	1988	2	2	-	-	-
Habitat for Humanity Intl	1995	1	-	1	1	1
Heart to Heart Intl Ministries	1994	-	2	1	-	1
Holt Intl. Children's Services	1991	-	2	-	30	-
International Children's Care	1991	-	1	-	-	-
International Messengers	1989	-	-	1	2	1
International Needs - USA	1992	-	-	-	3	-
International Teams, U.S.A.	1973	4	2	-	1	-
InterVarsity Mission	1993	-	2	2	-	-
Intl. Inst. Christian Studies	1991	2	-	-	-	-
Luke Society, The	1991	-	-	-	2	-
Macedonia World Baptist Msns.	1994	2	-	-	-	-
Ministry to Eastern Europe	1989	-	-	-	4	-
Mission to the World	1994	-	2	-	-	-
Navigators, The		3	-	-	-	-
Open Bible Standard Churches	1992	-	-	-	-	-
Operation Blessing Intl.	1990	-	-	-	1	-
Presbyterian Church (USA)		5	-	-	-	-
Romanian Mission of Chicago	1990	-	-	-	-	-
Romanian Missionary Society	1968	4	-	-	3	1
SEND International	1993	2	-	-	-	-
Shield of Faith Mission Intl.	1995	2	-	-	-	-
Source of Light Ministries	1991	1	-	-	-	-
UFM International	1995	4	-	-	-	-
United World Mission	1991	1	-	-	-	-
Walk Thru The Bible Ministries	1991	-	-	-	5	-
World Mission Prayer League	1994	2	-	-	-	2
World Vision	1977	-	-	2	-	-
Worldwide Discipleship Assoc.	1995	1	-	-	-	-
Totals:		138	40	20	147	9

RUSSIAN FEDERATION

American Baptist Churches USA	1864	2	-	-	-	-
AMG International	1990	-	-	-	2	-

COUNTRY Agency	Year Began	Personnel from U.S.			Other Countries	
		4+ Yrs	2-4 Yrs	1-2 Yrs	Citizens	Not Citiz.
Baptist Bible Fellowship Intl.	1993	14	-	-	-	-
Baptist International Missions	1991	22	-	-	-	-
Baptist Mid-Missions	1992	9	-	-	-	-
Baptist Missions to Forgotten		3	-	-	-	-
BCM International	1993	-	1	-	3	-
Bible Missionary Church	1992	4	-	-	-	-
Bright Hope International		-	-	-	8	-
Calvary International	1990	15	-	-	-	-
Campus Crusade for Christ	1991	77	-	107	-	-
CBInternational	1991	3	-	-	-	-
CEIFA Ministries International	1991	-	-	-	2	-
Child Evangelism Fellowship	1968	2	-	-	20	4
Chosen People Ministries	1989	-	-	-	-	2
Christ for the Island World	1995	-	-	-	6	-
Christian Aid Mission		-	-	-	19	-
Christian and Msny. Alliance	1993	26	4	-	-	-
Christian Associates Intl.	1992	1	-	-	-	-
Christian Chs. /Chs. of Christ		2	-	-	-	-
Christian Reformed World Msns.	1994	1	-	-	1	-
Church of God World Missions	1992	3	-	-	-	2
Church of the Nazarene	1992	10	-	-	2	-
Church Resource Ministries	1992	13	-	-	-	-
Door of Hope International	1954	-	-	-	2	-
East-West Ministries Intl.	1993	8	-	-	-	-
Eastern European Outreach	1994	-	2	5	-	-
Evangelical Baptist Missions	1994	2	-	2	-	-
Evangelical Free Church Msn.	1993	4	1	3	-	-
Evangelical Presbyterian Ch.	1993	2	-	-	-	-
Evangelism Resources	1992	-	-	-	3	1
Every Home for Christ	1991	-	-	-	13	-
General Conf. Mennonite Church	1993	-	-	-	-	3
Global Outreach Mission	1994	2	-	-	-	-
Global Strategy Mission Assoc.	1991	2	28	5	1	-
Globe Missionary Evangelism	1990	5	-	-	-	-
Gospel for Asia	1992	-	-	-	19	-
Grace Brethren Intl. Missions	1993	2	-	2	-	-
Greater Europe Mission	1993	1	-	-	-	-
Help for Christian Nationals	1995	-	-	-	1	-
High School Evangelism Flwshp.	1993	1	-	-	5	-
InterAct Ministries	1991	8	-	-	-	1
International Gospel Outreach	1993	-	2	-	-	-
International Outreach Mins.	1992	1	-	-	-	-
International Teams, U.S.A.	1991	-	5	-	-	1
InterVarsity Mission	1991	2	2	10	-	-
Intl. Inst. Christian Studies	1991	1	-	-	-	2
Intl. Pentecostal Holiness Ch.	1992	2	-	-	-	-
Jews for Jesus	1991	-	-	-	4	5

COUNTRY Agency	Year Began	Personnel from U.S.			Other Countries	
		4+ Yrs	2-4 Yrs	1-2 Yrs	Citizens	Not Citiz.
Lutheran Bible Translators	1996	1	-	-	-	-
Lutheran Church-Missouri Synod	1992	12	-	21	-	-
Mennonite Brethren Msns/Svcs	1995	-	2	-	4	-
Mennonite Central Committee	1990	1	4	-	-	-
Mission Aviation Fellowship	1993	4	-	-	-	-
Mission Soc. for United Meth.	1995	10	1	14	-	-
Mission to the World	1991	3	-	-	-	-
Mission To Unreached Peoples	1993	-	4	-	-	-
Missionaire International	1994	-	-	-	4	-
New Tribes Mission	1992	18	-	-	-	2
OMS International, Inc.	1993	7	6	70	-	5
Partners International	1992	-	-	-	1	-
Peter Deyneka Russian Mins.		2	1	-	28	-
Pioneers	1993	6	-	-	-	-
Presbyterian Church (USA)		7	-	-	-	-
Project Partner with Christ	1991	-	-	-	1	-
Ripe for Harvest, Inc.	1995	-	4	-	-	-
Salvation Army, U.S.A.	1913	-	23	-	-	-
SEND International	1990	15	-	8	-	-
Seventh-day Adventists	1886	26	-	2	10	-
Shield of Faith Mission Intl.		2	-	-	-	-
Slavic Gospel Association	1945	-	-	-	36	-
TEAM	1904	16	-	2	-	-
UFM International	1995	6	-	-	-	-
United Methodist Church		11	-	-	-	-
Walk Thru The Bible Ministries	1993	-	-	-	297	-
Wesleyan World Missions	1993	8	-	-	-	-
Wisconsin Evang. Lutheran Syn.	1991	5	-	-	-	-
World Help	1991	-	-	-	4	-
World Indigenous Missions	1992	4	-	-	-	-
World Reach, Inc.	1992	4	-	-	3	-
World Servants	1994	-	-	-	1	-
World Team	1993	14	-	-	-	2
World Vision	1990	-	-	1	-	-
World Witness	1993	4	-	-	-	-
Young Life	1990	4	-	-	-	-
Youth With A Mission (YWAM)		33	-	-	-	-
Totals:		473	90	252	500	30

RWANDA

African Enterprise, Inc.	1984	-	-	-	8	-
Assemblies of God		2	-	-	-	-
CBInternational	1967	7	-	-	-	-
Child Evangelism Fellowship	1987	-	-	-	3	-
Christian Aid Mission		-	-	-	16	-
Church of God (Anderson, IN)		2	-	-	-	-
Church of God of Prophecy	1982	-	-	-	1	-

COUNTRY Agency	Year Began	Personnel from U.S.			Other Countries	
		4+ Yrs	2-4 Yrs	1-2 Yrs	Citizens	Not Citiz.
Church of God World Missions	1980	-	-	-	2	-
Church of the Nazarene	1986	2	-	-	-	-
Evangelical Friends Mission	1987	6	-	-	-	-
Seventh-day Adventists	1920	16	-	-	9	-
Southern Baptist Intl. Mission	1977	3	-	-	-	-
World Concern	1995	-	-	1	5	-
World Relief Corporation		-	-	1	-	-
World Vision	1994	-	2	-	-	-
	Totals:	38	2	2	44	-

SENEGAL

Assemblies of God	1956	10	-	-	-	-
Baptist International Missions	1975	4	-	-	-	-
Brethren Assemblies		3	-	-	-	-
Campus Crusade for Christ	1985	4	-	-	-	-
CBInternational	1962	12	2	12	-	-
Evangelical Lutheran Church	1976	11	-	-	-	-
Mission to the World	1991	6	3	-	-	-
Mission: Moving Mountains	1995	6	-	-	-	-
New Tribes Mission	1954	63	-	8	-	20
Pioneers	1991	6	-	-	-	-
Seventh-day Adventists	1952	-	-	-	4	-
SIM USA	1984	7	-	1	-	-
Southern Baptist Intl. Mission	1969	22	11	-	-	-
United Methodist Church		6	-	-	-	-
United World Mission	1948	7	3	5	3	-
Walk Thru The Bible Ministries	1994	-	-	-	1	-
WEC International	1936	1	-	-	-	-
Youth With A Mission (YWAM)		4	-	-	-	-
	Totals:	172	19	26	8	20

SERBIA

Church of God World Missions	1968	-	-	-	5	-
Mennonite Central Committee	1963	-	2	-	-	-
	Totals:	-	2	-	5	-

SIERRA LEONE

Assemblies of God	1920	2	-	-	-	-
Child Evangelism Fellowship	1987	-	-	-	3	-
Christian Aid Mission		-	-	-	4	-
Christian Blind Mission Intl.	1976	-	4	-	-	-
Christian Mission for the Deaf	1987	-	-	-	-	1
Christian Reformed World Msns.	1980	4	-	-	-	-
Christians In Action, Inc.	1969	-	-	-	32	-
Church of the United Brethren	1855	-	-	-	-	-
Every Home for Christ	1993	-	-	-	7	-

COUNTRY Agency	Year Began	Personnel from U.S.			Other Countries	
		4+ Yrs	2-4 Yrs	1-2 Yrs	Citizens	Not Citiz.
Free Gospel Church Msns. Dept.	1927	6	-	-	-	-
Gospel Recordings USA	1990	-	-	-	2	-
Lutheran Bible Translators	1973	4	-	-	11	-
National Baptist Conv. USA	1950	2	-	-	52	-
Seventh-day Adventists	1905	2	-	-	5	-
Southern Baptist Intl. Mission	1984	8	-	-	-	-
United Pentecostal Church Intl	1975	2	-	-	-	-
World Partners Missionary Ch.	1945	2	-	-	-	-
World Vision	1978	-	1	-	-	-
Totals:		32	5	-	116	1

SINGAPORE

Agency	Year Began	4+ Yrs	2-4 Yrs	1-2 Yrs	Citizens	Not Citiz.
ABWE	1991	4	-	-	-	-
Ambassadors for Christ Intl.		-	-	-	4	-
Anglican Frontier Missions		2	-	-	-	-
Assemblies of God	1926	15	-	-	-	-
Baptist Bible Fellowship Intl.	1967	4	-	-	-	-
Baptist International Missions	1982	4	-	-	-	-
Baptist Mid-Missions	1983	4	-	-	-	-
Baptist World Mission		2	-	-	-	-
Campus Crusade for Christ	1969	12	-	2	-	-
CBInternational	1985	2	-	-	-	-
Child Evangelism Fellowship	1970	-	-	-	2	2
Christian Chs. /Chs. of Christ		6	-	-	-	-
Church of God World Missions	1989	-	-	-	-	2
CMF International	1990	2	-	-	-	-
Evangelical Free Church Msn.	1957	10	1	-	-	-
Evangelical Lutheran Church	1966	8	-	-	-	-
Foursquare Missions Intl.	1982	-	2	-	-	-
Global Strategy Mission Assoc.	1984	2	-	-	-	-
Gospel Recordings USA	1980	-	-	-	2	-
International Gospel Outreach	1995	-	-	2	-	-
Intl. Pentecostal Holiness Ch.	1985	2	-	-	-	-
Mission Soc. for United Meth.	1995	2	-	-	-	-
Mission To Unreached Peoples	1995	-	2	-	-	-
Navigators, The	1962	2	-	-	-	-
Network of Intl Christian Schs	1995	-	7	-	-	-
New Tribes Mission	1994	4	-	-	-	-
OC International, Inc.	1987	6	-	-	2	2
OMF International	1865	12	-	-	-	35
Partners International	1952	2	-	-	3	-
Reformed Church In America	1987	2	-	-	-	-
Seventh-day Adventists	1904	30	-	-	10	-
Southern Baptist Intl. Mission	1956	10	1	-	-	-
Trans World Radio	1991	2	3	-	-	-
United Methodist Church		2	-	-	-	-
United Pentecostal Church Intl	1981	2	-	-	-	-

COUNTRY Agency	Year Began	Personnel from U.S.			Other Countries	
		4+ Yrs	2-4 Yrs	1-2 Yrs	Citizens	Not Citiz.
Walk Thru The Bible Ministries	1982	-	-	-	6	-
World Baptist Fellowship Msn	1987	2	-	-	-	-
Youth for Christ / USA	1982	3	-	-	-	-
Youth With A Mission (YWAM)		10	-	-	-	-
Totals:		170	16	4	29	41

SLOVAKIA

Assemblies of God	1981	4	-	-	-	-
Baptist General Conference	1992	2	-	-	-	-
Baptist Mid-Missions	1992	4	-	-	-	-
Campus Crusade for Christ	1993	7	-	8	-	-
Child Evangelism Fellowship	1966	-	-	-	6	-
Eastern European Bible Mission	1993	-	-	-	5	-
Evangelical Lutheran Church	1991	3	3	-	-	-
Greater Europe Mission	1988	8	-	-	-	-
International Messengers	1989	2	-	-	-	2
International Needs - USA	1993	-	-	-	3	-
InterVarsity Mission	1994	-	2	-	-	-
Lutheran Church-Missouri Synod	1991	-	-	7	-	-
Ministry to Eastern Europe	1992	-	-	-	5	-
Navigators, The		4	-	-	-	-
Presbyterian Church (USA)		4	-	-	-	-
UFM International	1995	3	-	2	-	-
Totals:		41	5	17	19	2

SLOVENIA

Assemblies of God		4	-	-	-	-
Bethany Fellowship Missions	1995	4	-	-	-	-
CBInternational	1991	4	-	1	-	-
Habitat for Humanity Intl	1995	1	-	-	-	1
Navigators, The		4	1	-	-	-
Totals:		17	1	1	-	1

SOLOMON ISLANDS

American Baptist Association	1969	1	-	-	-	-
Assemblies of God	1977	4	-	-	-	-
Campus Crusade for Christ	1975	2	-	-	-	-
Child Evangelism Fellowship	1975	-	-	-	10	1
Episcopal World Mission	1984	2	-	-	3	-
Every Home for Christ	1986	-	-	-	10	-
Maranatha Baptist Mission	1983	2	-	-	-	-
Mission Soc. for United Meth.	1987	2	-	-	-	-
Wycliffe Bible Translators	1977	21	1	-	-	-
Totals:		34	1	-	23	1

COUNTRY Agency	Year Began	Personnel from U.S.			Other Countries	
		4+ Yrs	2-4 Yrs	1-2 Yrs	Citizens	Not Citiz.

SOMALIA

Eastern Mennonite Missions	1981	1	-	-	-	-
Mennonite Central Committee	1975	-	1	-	-	-
World Concern	1995	-	-	3	23	2
Totals:		1	1	3	23	2

SOUTH AFRICA

ABWE	1980	38	-	2	-	-
Africa Evangelical Fellowship	1906	17	-	-	-	-
Africa Inland Mission Intl	1994	1	-	-	-	-
Africa Inter-Mennonite Mission	1982	2	-	-	-	-
African Christian Mission	1996	2	-	-	-	-
African Enterprise, Inc.	1962	4	-	-	60	-
Ambassadors for Christ Intl.		-	-	-	2	-
American Baptist Churches USA	1990	-	2	-	-	1
Assemblies of God	1917	28	-	-	-	-
Baptist Bible Fellowship Intl.	1980	18	-	-	-	-
Baptist International Missions	1968	15	-	-	-	-
Baptist Missions to Forgotten		2	-	-	-	-
Biblical Ministries Worldwide	1976	15	-	-	-	-
Brethren Assemblies		7	-	-	-	-
Calvary International	1996	2	-	-	-	-
Campus Crusade for Christ	1971	8	-	-	-	-
Child Evangelism Fellowship	1947	1	-	-	41	2
Christ Community Church	1907	4	-	-	-	-
Christian Chs. /Chs. of Christ	1920	24	-	-	-	-
Church of God of Prophecy	1967	-	-	-	3	-
Church of the Nazarene	1933	21	-	-	7	-
Cornerstone, The	1995	2	-	-	-	-
Eastern Mennonite Missions	1990	-	-	1	-	-
Elim Fellowship World Missions	1975	1	-	-	-	-
Evangelical Baptist Missions	1981	14	-	-	-	-
Evangelical Lutheran Church	1844	3	-	-	-	-
Foursquare Missions Intl.	1929	2	-	-	-	-
General Conf. Mennonite Church	1982	2	-	-	-	-
Gospel Fellowship Association		4	-	-	-	-
Habitat for Humanity Intl	1987	-	2	-	5	-
Independent Faith Mission	1975	11	-	-	-	-
International Bible Institute	1996	-	-	-	-	-
International Outreach Mins.	1992	2	-	-	-	-
Intl. Pentecostal Holiness Ch.	1911	14	2	-	5	-
Jews for Jesus	1989	-	-	-	2	-
Lutheran Church-Missouri Synod	1982	-	-	2	-	-
Maranatha Baptist Mission	1991	2	-	-	-	-
Mennonite Central Committee	1990	2	4	-	-	-
Metropolitan Church Assoc.	1930	1	-	-	-	-

COUNTRY Agency	Year Began	Personnel from U.S.			Other Countries	
		4+ Yrs	2-4 Yrs	1-2 Yrs	Citizens	Not Citiz.
Mission to the World	1994	-	2	-	-	-
National Baptist Conv. USA	1897	-	2	-	51	-
Navigators, The		6	-	-	-	-
Open Bible Ministries	1969	2	-	-	-	-
Operation Mobilization		1	-	-	-	-
Partners International	1980	-	-	-	43	-
Presbyterian Church (USA)		-	2	4	-	-
Salvation Army, U.S.A.	1883	2	-	-	-	-
Seventh-day Adventists	1887	12	-	-	10	-
SIM USA	1992	1	-	-	-	-
Southern Baptist Intl. Mission	1977	69	7	-	-	-
TEAM	1892	29	-	-	-	2
UFM International	1979	4	-	1	-	-
United Church Board World Mins	1835	-	3	-	-	-
United Pentecostal Church Intl	1948	2	-	-	-	-
Walk Thru The Bible Ministries	1990	-	-	-	31	-
Wesleyan World Missions	1901	14	-	-	-	-
World Thrust, Inc.	1993	-	-	-	3	-
World Vision	1963	-	1	-	-	-
Young Life	1985	2	2	-	-	-
Youth for Christ / USA	1977	5	6	-	-	-
Youth With A Mission (YWAM)		4	-	-	-	-
Totals:		422	35	10	263	5

SPAIN

ABWE	1968	17	-	-	-	-
Ambassadors for Christ Intl.		-	-	-	2	-
AMG International	1991	7	-	-	-	2
Arab World Ministries	1984	4	-	-	-	-
Assemblies of God	1923	33	-	-	-	-
Baptist Bible Fellowship Intl.	1970	18	-	-	-	-
Baptist International Missions	1965	4	-	-	-	-
Baptist Mid-Missions	1979	8	-	-	-	-
Baptist World Mission	1980	4	-	-	-	-
BCM International	1962	3	-	-	6	3
Bethany Fellowship Missions	1990	2	-	-	-	-
Biblical Ministries Worldwide	1959	6	-	-	-	-
Brethren Assemblies		8	-	-	-	-
Brethren in Christ World Msns.		2	-	-	-	-
Cadence International	1974	-	2	-	-	-
CAM International	1971	14	-	2	1	3
Campus Crusade for Christ	1970	4	-	-	-	-
CBInternational	1984	8	-	1	-	-
Child Evangelism Fellowship	1967	-	-	-	3	2
Christ for the City Intl.	1995	2	-	-	1	-
Christian and Msny. Alliance	1978	8	-	-	-	-
Christian Associates Intl.	1991	4	-	-	-	-

COUNTRY Agency	Year Began	Personnel from U.S.			Other Countries	
		4+ Yrs	2-4 Yrs	1-2 Yrs	Citizens	Not Citiz.
Christian Chs. /Chs. of Christ		1	-	-	-	-
Church of God of Prophecy	1981	-	-	-	1	2
Church of God World Missions	1937	3	-	-	-	2
Church of the Nazarene	1981	2	-	-	-	-
Correll Missionary Ministries	1993	-	-	-	2	-
Elim Fellowship World Missions	1966	4	-	-	-	-
European Christian Mission	1983	8	-	-	-	-
Evangelical Free Church Msn.	1994	4	-	-	-	-
Evangelical Mennonite Church	1991	2	-	-	-	-
Every Home for Christ	1977	-	-	-	2	-
Fellowship International Msn.	1991	3	-	-	-	-
Free Will Baptist Association	1974	5	-	-	-	-
Gospel Fellowship Association		4	-	-	-	-
Gospel Furthering Fellowship	1992	2	-	-	-	-
Gospel Missionary Union	1976	13	-	-	1	-
Grace Brethren Intl. Missions	1984	4	-	-	-	-
Greater Europe Mission	1960	27	-	-	-	-
Help for Christian Nationals	1988	1	-	-	-	-
International Teams, U.S.A.	1972	2	2	-	-	-
InterVarsity Mission	1985	-	1	1	-	-
Intl. Pentecostal Holiness Ch.	1988	2	-	-	-	-
Latin America Mission	1989	2	2	-	-	-
Maranatha Baptist Mission	1987	2	-	-	-	-
Mennonite Board of Missions	1976	2	-	-	-	-
Mission Soc. for United Meth.	1987	2	-	-	-	-
Mission to the World	1991	10	4	-	-	-
Navigators, The	1970	10	-	-	-	-
OMS International, Inc.	1972	7	-	1	9	7
Operation Mobilization		4	-	-	-	-
Pocket Testament League	1969	-	-	-	2	-
Presbyterian Church (USA)		4	-	-	-	-
Primitive Methodist Church USA	1979	3	-	-	-	3
Salvation Army, U.S.A.	1971	2	-	-	-	-
SEND International	1987	7	-	-	-	2
South American Missionary Soc.	1991	2	-	-	-	-
Southern Baptist Intl. Mission	1921	47	7	-	-	-
Spanish World Gospel Mission	1959	-	-	-	1	1
TEAM	1934	28	-	-	-	-
UFM International	1991	8	-	2	-	-
United Methodist Church		2	-	-	-	-
United Pentecostal Church Intl	1979	2	-	-	-	-
United World Mission	1948	2	-	-	-	-
Walk Thru The Bible Ministries	1984	-	-	-	2	-
WEC International	1968	3	1	2	-	-
World Baptist Fellowship Msn	1955	4	-	-	-	-
World Indigenous Missions	1985	2	-	-	-	-
World Partners Missionary Ch.	1985	14	-	-	-	-

COUNTRY Agency	Year Began	Personnel from U.S.			Other Countries	
		4+ Yrs	2-4 Yrs	1-2 Yrs	Citizens	Not Citiz.
World Salt Foundation	1987	2	-	-	-	-
World Team	1972	15	-	-	-	-
Youth for Christ / USA	1982	2	-	-	-	-
Youth With A Mission (YWAM)		12	-	-	-	-
Totals:		443	19	9	33	27

SRI LANKA

AMG International	1978	-	-	-	2	-
Back to the Bible Intl.	1955	-	-	-	30	-
Baptist Bible Fellowship Intl.	1989	2	-	-	-	-
BCM International	1985	-	-	-	5	-
Childcare International	1989	-	-	-	1	1
Christian Aid Mission		-	-	-	7	-
Every Home for Christ	1970	-	-	-	11	-
Farms International, Inc.	1971	-	-	-	2	-
Foursquare Missions Intl.	1976	1	-	-	-	-
Gospel for Asia	1983	-	-	-	251	-
Habitat for Humanity Intl	1994	-	2	-	2	2
International Needs - USA	1976	-	-	-	18	-
Lutheran Church-Missouri Synod	1927	-	-	2	-	-
Presbyterian Church (USA)		2	-	-	-	-
Seventh-day Adventists	1922	8	-	-	-	-
Southern Baptist Intl. Mission	1977	4	-	-	-	-
TEAM	1955	2	-	-	-	-
Trans World Radio	1978	20	-	-	-	-
United Church Board World Mins	1816	-	1	-	-	-
Wesleyan World Missions	1993	-	-	-	4	-
Totals:		39	3	2	333	3

ST CHRISTOPHER AND NEVIS

Baptist International Missions	1994	2	-	-	-	-
Totals:		2	-	-	-	-

ST LUCIA

Macedonia World Baptist Msns.	1994	2	-	-	-	-
Wycliffe Bible Translators	1984	6	-	-	-	-
Totals:		8	-	-	-	-

ST VINCENT

Ambassadors for Christ Intl.		-	-	-	5	-
Baptist Mid-Missions	1946	7	-	-	-	-
Bible Missionary Church	1960	-	-	-	-	-
Christian Chs. /Chs. of Christ		6	-	-	-	-
World Team	1951	2	-	-	-	-
Totals:		15	-	-	5	-

COUNTRY Agency	Year Began	Personnel from U.S.			Other Countries	
		4+ Yrs	2-4 Yrs	1-2 Yrs	Citizens	Not Citiz.
SUDAN						
Africa Inland Mission Intl	1949	1	-	-	-	-
Ambassadors for Christ Intl.		-	-	-	5	-
Assemblies of God	1980	2	-	-	-	-
Church of The Brethren	1983	2	2	-	-	-
Mennonite Central Committee	1975	5	3	-	-	-
Mission O.N.E., Inc.	1991	-	-	-	16	-
Partners International	1973	-	-	-	18	-
Presbyterian Church (USA)	1900	10	5	-	-	-
Reformed Church In America	1949	3	-	-	-	-
Seventh-day Adventists	1978	6	-	-	9	-
SIM USA	1938	6	-	-	-	-
	Totals:	35	10	-	48	-
SURINAME						
Assemblies of God	1959	2	-	-	-	-
Biblical Ministries Worldwide		2	-	-	-	-
Christian and Msny. Alliance	1987	2	-	-	-	-
Church of God of Prophecy	1992	-	-	-	1	-
Church of God World Missions	1982	-	-	-	2	-
Church of the Nazarene	1984	2	-	-	-	-
Fellowship International Msn.	1972	2	-	-	-	-
Full Gospel Grace Fellowship		2	-	-	-	-
Independent Faith Mission	1967	21	-	-	-	-
International Missions, Inc.	1961	7	-	-	-	-
Mennonite Board of Missions	1985	2	-	-	-	-
Mission Aviation Fellowship	1964	8	-	-	-	-
Orthodox Presbyterian Church	1987	4	-	-	-	-
Seventh-day Adventists	1945	-	-	-	2	-
Southern Baptist Intl. Mission	1971	7	1	-	-	-
Wesleyan World Missions	1945	2	-	-	-	-
World Team	1957	9	-	-	-	-
Wycliffe Bible Translators	1967	28	-	-	-	-
	Totals:	100	1	-	5	-
SWAZILAND						
Assemblies of God	1985	10	-	-	-	-
Campus Crusade for Christ	1973	4	-	-	-	-
Church of God of Prophecy	1977	-	-	-	1	-
Church of the Nazarene	1910	21	-	-	5	-
Eastern Mennonite Missions	1971	2	-	-	-	-
Mennonite Central Committee	1971	3	3	-	-	-
Metropolitan Church Assoc.	1936	2	-	-	-	-
National Baptist Conv. USA	1971	-	2	-	19	-
OC International, Inc.	1987	6	-	3	-	3
Southern Baptist Intl. Mission	1983	12	2	-	-	-

COUNTRY Agency	Year Began	Personnel from U.S.			Other Countries	
		4+ Yrs	2-4 Yrs	1-2 Yrs	Citizens	Not Citiz.
Trans World Radio	1974	18	-	-	8	-
United Pentecostal Church Intl	1982	6	-	-	-	-
Wesleyan World Missions	1910	4	-	-	-	-
World Relief Corporation	1988	1	-	-	-	-
	Totals:	89	7	3	33	3

SWEDEN

COUNTRY Agency	Year Began	4+ Yrs	2-4 Yrs	1-2 Yrs	Citizens	Not Citiz.
Child Evangelism Fellowship	1946	-	-	-	-	2
Christian Associates Intl.	1992	1	-	-	-	1
Evangelical Baptist Missions	1974	4	-	-	-	-
Faith Christian Fellowship	1982	2	-	-	-	-
Fellowship International Msn.	1972	3	-	-	-	-
Greater Europe Mission	1956	1	-	-	-	-
HCJB World Radio Msny. Flwshp.	1992	-	-	-	2	2
Operation Mobilization		1	-	-	-	-
Salvation Army, U.S.A.	1880	1	-	-	-	-
UFM International	1984	2	-	-	-	-
Walk Thru The Bible Ministries	1989	-	-	-	1	-
Youth for Christ / USA	1982	1	-	-	-	-
Youth With A Mission (YWAM)		6	-	-	-	-
	Totals:	22	-	-	3	5

SWITZERLAND

COUNTRY Agency	Year Began	4+ Yrs	2-4 Yrs	1-2 Yrs	Citizens	Not Citiz.
Baptist Bible Fellowship Intl.	1987	2	-	-	-	-
Child Evangelism Fellowship	1950	4	-	-	17	17
Christ for the City Intl.	1995	-	-	-	-	2
Church of The Brethren		-	-	2	-	-
Church of the Nazarene	1978	3	-	-	-	-
InterVarsity Mission	1985	-	1	-	-	-
Mennonite Central Committee	1942	4	3	-	-	-
Seventh-day Adventists	1870	2	-	-	-	-
United Methodist Church		1	-	-	-	-
Youth for Christ / USA	1964	3	5	-	-	-
Youth With A Mission (YWAM)		12	-	-	-	-
	Totals:	31	9	2	17	19

SYRIA

COUNTRY Agency	Year Began	4+ Yrs	2-4 Yrs	1-2 Yrs	Citizens	Not Citiz.
Christian Aid Mission		-	-	-	2	-
Mennonite Central Committee	1990	1	1	-	-	-
	Totals:	1	1	-	2	-

TAIWAN, REPUBLIC OF CHINA

COUNTRY Agency	Year Began	4+ Yrs	2-4 Yrs	1-2 Yrs	Citizens	Not Citiz.
Assemblies of God	1948	13	-	-	-	-
Baptist Bible Fellowship Intl.	1950	14	-	-	-	-
Baptist Mid-Missions	1972	6	-	-	-	-

COUNTRY Agency	Year Began	Personnel from U.S.			Other Countries	
		4+ Yrs	2-4 Yrs	1-2 Yrs	Citizens	Not Citiz.
Baptist Missionary Assoc.	1953	1	-	-	-	-
Brethren Assemblies		2	-	-	-	-
Campus Crusade for Christ	1964	6	-	-	-	-
CBInternational	1952	21	7	10	-	-
Child Evangelism Fellowship	1951	2	-	-	13	-
China Ministries International	1988	2	-	-	10	-
Christian and Msny. Alliance	1952	18	-	-	-	-
Christian Chs. /Chs. of Christ		10	-	-	-	-
Christian Reformed World Msns.	1953	5	-	-	1	-
Christians In Action, Inc.	1979	2	-	-	-	-
Church of God World Missions	1982	-	-	-	2	-
Church of the Nazarene	1956	2	-	-	-	-
Evangelical Covenant Church	1952	9	-	-	-	-
Evangelical Lutheran Church	1951	5	-	-	-	-
Evangelical Presbyterian Ch.	1985	2	-	-	-	-
Foursquare Missions Intl.	1988	2	-	-	-	-
General Conf. Mennonite Church	1954	5	-	-	1	4
Go Ye Fellowship	1951	1	-	-	-	-
Gospel Fellowship Association		2	-	-	-	-
Kids Alive International	1970	2	-	-	2	-
Liberty Baptist Mission		2	-	-	-	-
Liberty Corner Mission	1952	2	-	-	-	5
Lutheran Brethren World Msns.		6	-	1	-	-
Lutheran Church-Missouri Synod	1951	6	14	-	-	-
Macedonia World Baptist Msns.	1981	2	-	-	-	-
Mission to the World	1974	7	2	-	-	-
Mustard Seed, Inc.	1948	-	-	-	130	-
Navigators, The	1984	8	-	-	-	-
OC International, Inc.	1950	8	-	-	-	-
OMF International	1952	23	-	-	-	63
OMS International, Inc.	1917	15	5	-	13	2
Partners International	1959	-	-	-	50	2
Presbyterian Church (USA)	1952	9	-	-	-	-
Reformed Church In America	1952	3	-	-	-	-
SEND International	1967	19	-	-	-	6
Seventh-day Adventists	1902	8	-	-	1	-
Southern Baptist Intl. Mission	1948	84	6	-	-	-
Sowers International, The	1994	-	-	-	1	-
TEAM	1951	37	-	-	-	-
Team Expansion, Inc.	1995	8	-	-	-	-
United Church Board World Mins	1960	-	4	-	-	-
United Methodist Church		4	-	-	-	-
United Pentecostal Church Intl	1978	4	-	-	-	-
Voice of China and Asia	1946	-	-	-	50	-
Walk Thru The Bible Ministries	1995	-	-	-	1	-
Wisconsin Evang. Lutheran Syn.	1968	3	-	-	-	-

COUNTRY Agency	Year Began	Personnel from U.S.			Other Countries	
		4+ Yrs	2-4 Yrs	1-2 Yrs	Citizens	Not Citiz.
World Gospel Mission	1953	2	-	-	-	-
Youth With A Mission (YWAM)		15	-	-	-	-
	Totals:	407	38	11	275	82

TANZANIA

COUNTRY Agency	Year Began	4+ Yrs	2-4 Yrs	1-2 Yrs	Citizens	Not Citiz.
Africa Evangelical Fellowship	1990	2	-	-	-	-
Africa Inland Mission Intl	1909	38	-	4	-	-
African Christian Mission	1995	-	2	-	-	-
African Enterprise, Inc.	1974	-	-	-	6	-
Assemblies of God	1940	16	-	-	-	-
Baptist Bible Fellowship Intl.	1988	14	-	-	-	-
Campus Crusade for Christ	1977	6	-	1	-	-
Christian Aid Mission		-	-	-	8	-
Christian Blind Mission Intl.	1976	4	-	-	-	-
Church of God (Anderson, IN)	1968	6	-	-	-	-
Church of God of Prophecy	1978	-	-	-	1	-
Church of God World Missions	1971	-	-	-	2	-
Church of the Nazarene	1990	4	-	-	-	-
Eastern Mennonite Missions	1934	21	1	2	1	-
Elim Fellowship World Missions	1955	10	-	2	-	-
Evangelical Free Church Msn.	1993	2	-	-	-	-
Evangelical Lutheran Church	1924	26	-	1	-	-
Gospel Furthering Fellowship	1949	2	-	-	2	-
Grace Ministries International	1954	12	-	-	-	-
Habitat for Humanity Intl	1986	-	4	-	47	-
Heifer Project International	1974	2	-	-	5	1
Medical Ambassadors Intl.	1987	-	-	-	7	-
Mennonite Central Committee	1962	3	-	-	-	-
Mission to the World	1991	6	-	-	-	-
Mission: Moving Mountains	1993	12	-	1	-	-
Navigators, The		2	-	-	-	-
Partners International	1986	-	-	-	15	-
Seventh-day Adventists	1903	8	-	-	5	-
Southern Baptist Intl. Mission	1956	76	10	-	-	-
Team Expansion, Inc.	1995	10	-	-	-	-
Teen Missions International		-	-	-	1	-
United Pentecostal Church Intl	1980	6	-	-	-	-
Walk Thru The Bible Ministries	1994	-	-	-	14	-
World Gospel Mission	1985	8	-	-	-	-
	Totals:	296	17	11	114	1

THAILAND

COUNTRY Agency	Year Began	4+ Yrs	2-4 Yrs	1-2 Yrs	Citizens	Not Citiz.
ABWE	1993	2	-	-	-	-
American Baptist Churches USA	1833	25	2	-	-	1
AMG International	1981	-	-	-	-	3
Assemblies of God	1968	26	-	-	-	-

COUNTRY Agency	Year Began	Personnel from U.S.			Other Countries	
		4+ Yrs	2-4 Yrs	1-2 Yrs	Citizens	Not Citiz.
Baptist Bible Fellowship Intl.	1983	8	-	-	-	-
Baptist General Conference	1990	3	-	-	1	-
Baptist International Missions	1979	2	-	-	-	-
Baptist World Mission	1979	4	-	-	-	-
Campus Crusade for Christ	1971	4	-	4	-	-
Child Evangelism Fellowship	1957	-	-	-	6	1
Chinese Christian Mission, Inc	1991	-	-	-	1	-
Christian Aid Mission		-	-	-	9	-
Christian and Msny. Alliance	1929	29	3	-	-	-
Christian Chs. /Chs. of Christ	1949	47	-	-	-	-
Church of God of Prophecy	1968	-	-	-	2	-
Church of God World Missions	1977	-	-	-	2	-
Church of the Nazarene	1989	8	-	-	2	-
CMF International	1994	6	-	-	-	-
Covenant Celebration Church		-	-	-	-	1
Evangelical Covenant Church	1971	8	-	-	-	-
Evangelical Lutheran Church	1975	3	-	-	-	-
Every Home for Christ	1971	-	-	-	11	-
Food for the Hungry	1978	1	4	-	-	-
Globe Missionary Evangelism	1985	4	-	2	-	-
Gospel for Asia	1982	-	-	-	12	-
Heifer Project International	1974	-	-	-	4	-
Holt Intl. Children's Services	1976	-	-	-	60	-
Lutheran Church-Missouri Synod	1986	8	-	4	2	-
Mennonite Brethren Msns/Svcs	1992	2	2	-	2	-
Mennonite Central Committee	1978	1	-	-	-	-
Mission O.N.E., Inc.	1991	-	-	-	3	-
Mission To Unreached Peoples	1988	-	4	-	-	-
Network of Intl Christian Schs	1993	-	48	-	-	-
New Tribes Mission	1951	66	-	1	-	4
OMF International	1952	62	-	-	-	113
Partners International	1955	-	-	-	70	-
Pass the Torch Ministries	1987	-	-	-	5	2
Pioneers	1985	9	-	-	-	-
Pocket Testament League	1981	-	-	-	3	-
Presbyterian Church (USA)	1840	10	20	-	-	-
Seventh-day Adventists	1919	14	-	-	11	-
Southern Baptist Intl. Mission	1949	60	13	-	-	-
Tribes and Nations Outreach	1985	-	-	-	-	2
United Church Board World Mins	1832	-	4	-	-	-
Walk Thru The Bible Ministries	1988	-	-	-	5	-
WEC International	1947	3	-	3	-	1
Wisconsin Evang. Lutheran Syn.	1993	2	-	-	-	-
World Concern	1995	2	2	-	24	3
World Partners Missionary Ch.	1992	4	2	-	-	-
Youth With A Mission (YWAM)		12	-	-	-	-
Totals:		435	104	14	235	131

COUNTRY Agency	Year Began	Personnel from U.S.			Other Countries	
		4+ Yrs	2-4 Yrs	1-2 Yrs	Citizens	Not Citiz.

TOGO

ABWE	1973	48	-	4	-	-
Assemblies of God	1937	11	-	-	-	-
Child Evangelism Fellowship	1983	-	-	-	2	-
Christian Blind Mission Intl.	1985	-	3	1	-	-
Church of God of Prophecy	1991	-	-	-	1	-
Church of God World Missions	1992	-	-	-	2	-
Every Home for Christ	1991	-	-	-	17	-
International Partnership Mins	1991	2	-	-	6	-
Lutheran Bible Translators	1992	-	-	-	3	-
Lutheran Church-Missouri Synod	1980	9	-	-	-	-
Ministry of Jesus, Inc.	1984	6	-	-	35	-
Seventh-day Adventists	1964	2	-	-	4	-
Southern Baptist Intl. Mission	1964	35	3	-	-	-
Wycliffe Bible Translators	1967	20	-	1	-	-
Youth With A Mission (YWAM)		3	-	-	-	-
	Totals:	136	6	6	70	-

TONGA

Ambassadors for Christ Intl.		-	-	-	2	-
Assemblies of God	1975	2	-	-	-	-
Youth With A Mission (YWAM)		5	-	-	-	-
	Totals:	7	-	-	2	-

TRINIDAD & TOBAGO

Baptist International Missions	1974	-	-	-	2	-
Baptist Missions to Forgotten		2	-	-	-	-
Campus Crusade for Christ	1977	2	-	-	-	-
Church of God of Prophecy	1954	-	-	-	1	-
Church of God World Missions	1956	-	-	-	2	-
Church of the Nazarene	1926	4	-	-	2	-
Fundamental Bapt. Msn Trinidad	1921	7	-	-	6	4
Habitat for Humanity Intl	1996	-	2	-	-	-
His Word To The Nations	1982	-	-	-	2	-
Intl. Pentecostal Holiness Ch.	1993	2	-	-	-	-
Seventh-day Adventists	1893	14	-	-	4	-
Southern Baptist Intl. Mission	1962	12	-	-	-	-
STEM Ministries	1986	-	-	-	-	-
TEAM	1964	10	-	-	-	-
United Pentecostal Church Intl	1980	2	-	-	-	-
Virginia Mennonite Bd. of Msns	1971	1	2	-	-	-
World Team	1953	7	-	-	-	2
	Totals:	63	4	-	19	6

COUNTRY Agency	Year Began	Personnel from U.S.			Other Countries	
		4+ Yrs	2-4 Yrs	1-2 Yrs	Citizens	Not Citiz.
TURKEY						
Calvary International	1991	2	-	-	-	-
Christian Aid Mission		-	-	-	4	-
Evangelical Mennonite Church	1995	2	-	-	-	-
Pioneers	1989	3	-	-	-	-
Presbyterian Church (USA)		2	-	-	-	-
Rosedale Mennonite Missions	1984	-	6	2	-	-
Seventh-day Adventists	1889	-	-	-	2	-
Shield of Faith Mission Intl.		1	-	-	-	-
TEAM	1960	2	-	-	-	-
Turkish World Outreach	1965	8	-	-	-	-
United Church Board World Mins	1819	4	9	-	1	-
World Horizons	1990	2	-	-	-	-
World Witness	1993	2	-	-	-	-
World-Wide Missions	1963	-	-	-	2	-
	Totals:	28	15	2	9	-
UGANDA						
Africa Inland Mission Intl	1918	4	-	2	-	-
African Enterprise, Inc.	1971	-	-	-	18	-
AMG International	1995	-	-	-	2	-
Baptist Bible Fellowship Intl.	1986	2	-	-	-	-
Baptist International Missions	1994	10	-	-	-	-
Brethren Assemblies		2	-	-	-	-
Campus Crusade for Christ	1971	3	-	-	-	-
CBInternational	1961	11	-	2	-	-
Child Evangelism Fellowship	1965	-	-	-	8	-
Childcare International	1984	-	-	-	5	-
Christian Aid Mission		-	-	-	2	-
Christian Blind Mission Intl.	1990	-	2	-	-	-
Christian Reformed Wrld Relief		1	-	-	-	-
Church of God (Anderson, IN)	1983	3	-	-	-	-
Church of God of Prophecy	1981	-	-	-	1	-
Church of God World Missions	1982	-	-	-	2	-
Elim Fellowship World Missions	1962	3	-	-	-	-
Fellowship International Msn.	1991	-	-	-	2	-
Friends in the West	1978	-	-	4	-	-
Friends United Meeting	1983	1	-	-	-	-
Global Outreach, Ltd.	1979	-	4	5	-	-
Habitat for Humanity Intl	1984	-	3	-	43	-
Heifer Project International	1982	-	-	-	6	1
International Gospel League	1979	5	-	-	-	-
International Needs - USA	1994	-	-	-	15	-
Literacy & Evangelism Intl.	1992	2	-	-	-	-
Luke Society, The	1984	-	-	-	1	-
Medical Ambassadors Intl.	1990	-	-	-	8	-

COUNTRY Agency	Year Began	Personnel from U.S.			Other Countries	
		4+ Yrs	2-4 Yrs	1-2 Yrs	Citizens	Not Citiz.
Mennonite Central Committee	1962	4	4	-	-	-
Mission Ministries, Inc.	1994	-	-	-	1	-
Mission O.N.E., Inc.	1992	-	-	-	-	1
Mission to the World	1991	1	-	-	-	-
Mission: Moving Mountains	1992	2	-	1	-	-
Morelli Ministries Intl.	1996	-	-	-	1	-
Navigators, The	1972	4	-	-	-	-
Presb. Evangelistic Fellowship	1986	-	-	-	5	-
Reformed Episcopal Bd Missions	1958	2	-	-	-	-
Seventh-day Adventists	1926	-	-	-	9	-
Southern Baptist Intl. Mission	1962	26	2	-	-	-
Teen Missions International		-	-	-	1	-
United Methodist Church		2	-	-	-	-
Walk Thru The Bible Ministries	1990	-	-	-	8	-
World Concern	1985	3	3	-	-	4
World Gospel Mission	1992	5	-	-	-	-
World Harvest Mission	1983	4	2	1	-	-
Wycliffe Bible Translators	1989	2	-	-	-	-
Youth for Christ / USA		1	-	-	-	-
Youth With A Mission (YWAM)		1	-	-	-	-
Totals:		104	20	15	138	6

UKRAINE

Allegheny Wesleyan Meth. Msns.	1993	3	-	-	-	-
Baptist International Missions	1996	2	-	-	-	-
Baptist Missions to Forgotten		2	-	-	-	-
Barnabas International	1992	2	-	-	-	-
BCM International	1993	-	2	-	2	-
Campus Crusade for Christ	1991	19	-	47	-	-
CBInternational	1991	14	-	3	-	-
Child Evangelism Fellowship	1968	1	-	-	6	6
Christian Aid Mission		-	-	-	131	-
Christian Chs. /Chs. of Christ	1991	-	-	4	-	-
Christian Outreach Intl.	1990	-	9	-	5	-
Church of God (Holiness) Msn.	1996	-	-	2	-	2
Church of God of Prophecy	1973	2	-	-	-	-
Church of God World Missions	1992	-	-	-	2	-
Church of the Nazarene	1992	2	-	-	-	-
CMF International	1994	4	-	-	-	-
Eastern European Bible Mission	1993	-	-	-	44	-
Eastern European Outreach	1994	-	2	1	-	-
Evangelical Free Church Msn.	1993	6	-	-	-	-
Evangelical Lutheran Synod	1992	2	-	-	-	-
Every Home for Christ	1991	-	-	-	6	-
Fellowship International Msn.	1995	2	-	-	-	-
Globe Missionary Evangelism	1996	-	-	4	-	-
Greater Europe Mission	1994	4	-	-	-	1

COUNTRY Agency	Year Began	Personnel from U.S.			Other Countries	
		4+ Yrs	2-4 Yrs	1-2 Yrs	Citizens	Not Citiz.
HCJB World Radio Msny. Flwshp.	1995	2	-	-	-	-
International Messengers	1994	2	-	-	-	2
International Teams, U.S.A.	1995	2	-	-	-	-
InterVarsity Mission	1989	-	-	3	-	-
Intl. Pentecostal Holiness Ch.	1990	2	-	-	-	-
Luke Society, The	1992	-	-	-	1	-
Mennonite Central Committee	1990	-	1	-	-	-
Mission Possible Foundation		-	2	-	-	-
Mission to the World	1994	6	5	35	-	-
Muslim Hope	1993	2	-	-	-	2
Operation Blessing Intl.	1992	-	-	-	2	-
Reformed Church In America		1	-	-	-	-
SEND International	1990	18	-	-	-	-
Slavic Gospel Association	1945	-	-	-	16	-
Team Expansion, Inc.	1991	16	-	-	-	-
Walk Thru The Bible Ministries	1993	-	-	-	698	-
World Concern	1993	-	-	-	31	-
Youth With A Mission (YWAM)		14	-	-	-	-
Totals:		130	21	99	944	13

UNITED ARAB EMIRATES

Church of God World Missions	1992	-	-	-	-	2
Macedonia World Baptist Msns.	1991	2	-	-	-	-
TEAM	1960	31	2	2	-	-
Totals:		33	2	2	-	2

UNITED KINGDOM

ABWE	1984	11	-	-	-	-
Ambassadors for Christ Intl.		-	-	-	12	-
Apostolic Team Ministries Intl	1987	-	2	-	-	-
Arab World Ministries	1986	15	-	-	-	-
Back to the Bible Intl.	1954	-	-	-	13	-
Baptist Bible Fellowship Intl.	1971	46	-	-	-	-
Baptist International Missions	1965	26	-	-	-	-
Baptist Mid-Missions	1972	18	-	-	-	4
Baptist Missions to Forgotten		2	-	-	-	-
Baptist World Mission	1975	12	-	-	-	-
BCM International	1947	6	-	-	14	3
Berean Mission, Inc.	1982	4	2	-	-	2
Biblical Ministries Worldwide	1970	2	-	-	-	-
Brethren in Christ World Msns.	1980	2	-	-	-	-
Cadence International	1981	2	2	-	-	-
Calvary International	1988	2	-	-	-	-
Campus Crusade for Christ	1967	20	-	-	-	-
CBInternational	1994	2	-	-	-	-
Child Evangelism Fellowship	1947	4	-	-	11	11

COUNTRY Agency	Year Began	Personnel from U.S.			Other Countries	
		4+ Yrs	2-4 Yrs	1-2 Yrs	Citizens	Not Citiz.
China Ministries International	1987	-	-	-	2	-
Christian and Msny. Alliance	1975	8	-	-	-	-
Christian Chs. /Chs. of Christ	1958	55	2	-	-	-
Christian Literature Crusade	1941	2	-	-	-	-
Christians In Action, Inc.	1965	2	-	-	10	-
Church of God World Missions	1955	4	-	-	-	2
Church of The Brethren		-	-	6	-	-
CMF International	1989	14	-	2	-	-
Elim Fellowship World Missions	1979	2	-	-	-	-
European Christian Mission	1987	2	-	-	-	-
Evangelical Baptist Missions	1976	6	-	-	-	-
Evangelical Free Church Msn.	1993	3	2	-	-	-
Evangelical Lutheran Church	1973	1	-	-	-	-
Faith Christian Fellowship	1978	16	-	-	-	-
Fellowship International Msn.	1986	4	-	-	-	-
Global Outreach Mission	1978	10	-	-	-	-
Globe Missionary Evangelism	1979	10	-	-	-	-
Gospel Fellowship Association		12	-	-	-	-
Gospel Missionary Union	1984	8	-	-	1	-
Gospel Recordings USA	1970	-	2	-	-	-
Grace Brethren Intl. Missions	1982	6	-	-	-	-
Habitat for Humanity Intl	1994	2	1	-	2	1
HCJB World Radio Msny. Flwshp.	1980	-	-	-	4	-
Helps International Ministries	1988	6	-	-	-	-
His Word To The Nations	1991	-	-	-	1	-
Independent Faith Mission	1984	2	-	-	-	-
INTERDEV	1993	2	-	-	-	-
International Missions, Inc.	1966	10	-	-	-	-
International Teams, U.S.A.	1986	17	4	-	5	1
Intl. Pentecostal Holiness Ch.	1978	4	2	1	-	-
Jews for Jesus	1992	-	-	-	2	-
Maranatha Baptist Mission	1983	11	-	-	-	-
Mennonite Board of Missions	1974	5	-	-	-	-
Mission Soc. for United Meth.	1995	2	-	-	-	-
Mission to the World	1985	3	-	-	-	-
Missionary Athletes Intl.	1990	9	-	-	-	-
Operation Mobilization		20	3	15	-	-
Pillar of Fire Missions Intl.	1960	-	5	-	-	-
Presbyterian Church (USA)		11	68	-	-	-
Reformed Baptist Mission Svcs.	1985	2	-	-	-	-
Salvation Army, U.S.A.	1865	7	-	2	-	-
Seventh-day Adventists	1902	10	-	-	25	-
Son Shine Ministries Intl.	1985	2	-	-	-	-
Southern Baptist Intl. Mission	1977	17	9	-	-	-
Things To Come Mission, Inc	1965	2	-	-	-	-
Trans World Radio	1983	4	-	-	1	-
United Pentecostal Church Intl	1965	4	-	-	-	-

COUNTRY Agency	Year Began	Personnel from U.S.			Other Countries	
		4+ Yrs	2-4 Yrs	1-2 Yrs	Citizens	Not Citiz.
United World Mission	1967	6	-	-	-	-
Walk Thru The Bible Ministries	1984	-	-	-	10	-
WEC International	1913	4	1	-	1	1
World Baptist Fellowship Msn	1972	2	-	-	-	-
World Harvest Mission	1994	2	-	6	-	-
World Salt Foundation		2	-	-	-	-
World Team	1986	4	-	-	-	2
Wycliffe Associates, Inc.	1993	-	1	-	-	-
Youth for Christ / USA	1983	4	-	-	-	-
Youth With A Mission (YWAM)		62	-	-	-	-
Totals:		577	106	32	114	27

URUGUAY

COUNTRY Agency	Year Began	Personnel from U.S.			Other Countries	
		4+ Yrs	2-4 Yrs	1-2 Yrs	Citizens	Not Citiz.
Assemblies of God	1946	14	-	-	-	-
Baptist Bible Fellowship Intl.	1958	2	-	-	-	-
Baptist General Conference	1991	2	-	2	-	-
Baptist Missionary Assoc.		1	-	-	-	-
Baptist World Mission	1968	5	-	-	-	-
Biblical Ministries Worldwide	1965	12	-	-	-	-
Brethren Assemblies		1	-	-	-	-
Christian Aid Mission		-	-	-	9	-
Christian Chs. /Chs. of Christ		8	-	-	-	-
Christian Church of North Am.	1970	-	-	-	-	-
Church of God (Anderson, IN)	1984	2	-	-	-	-
Church of God of Prophecy	1957	-	-	-	-	2
Church of God World Missions	1945	2	-	-	2	-
Every Home for Christ	1978	-	-	-	1	-
Free Will Baptist Association	1961	7	-	-	-	-
Globe Missionary Evangelism	1996	-	-	1	-	-
Gospel Mission of S. America	1970	6	-	-	-	-
Grace Ministries International	1982	-	-	-	-	-
Mennonite Brethren Msns/Svcs	1950	-	2	-	-	-
Salvation Army, U.S.A.	1917	2	-	-	-	-
Seventh-day Adventists	1895	-	-	-	2	-
SIM USA	1995	2	-	-	-	-
South American Missionary Soc.	1984	2	-	-	-	-
Southern Baptist Intl. Mission	1911	39	-	-	-	-
United Methodist Church		2	-	-	-	-
United Pentecostal Church Intl	1930	2	-	-	-	-
Walk Thru The Bible Ministries	1993	-	-	-	2	-
Totals:		111	2	3	16	2

UZBEKISTAN

COUNTRY Agency	Year Began	Personnel from U.S.			Other Countries	
		4+ Yrs	2-4 Yrs	1-2 Yrs	Citizens	Not Citiz.
Bright Hope International		-	-	-	2	-
Campus Crusade for Christ	1991	4	-	10	-	-
Christian Aid Mission		-	-	-	11	-

| COUNTRY | Year | Personnel from U.S. | | | Other Countries | |
Agency	Began	4+ Yrs	2-4 Yrs	1-2 Yrs	Citizens	Not Citiz.
Every Home for Christ	1994	-	-	-	1	-
International Outreach Mins.	1996	2	-	-	-	-
Macedonia World Baptist Msns.	1996	2	-	-	-	-
Pioneers	1995	4	-	-	-	-
Presbyterian Church (USA)		-	-	3	-	-
Walk Thru The Bible Ministries	1994	-	-	-	31	-
World Concern	1993	-	2	-	4	3
	Totals:	12	2	13	49	3

VANUATU

Assemblies of God	1967	4	-	-	-	-
Wycliffe Bible Translators	1981	6	-	-	-	-
	Totals:	10	-	-	-	-

VENEZUELA

Assemblies of God	1920	17	-	-	-	-
Baptist Bible Fellowship Intl.	1958	4	-	-	-	-
Baptist International Missions	1980	10	-	-	-	-
Baptist Mid-Missions	1924	5	-	-	-	-
Bible Missionary Church	1984	2	-	-	-	-
Brethren Assemblies		1	-	-	-	-
Brethren in Christ World Msns.	1980	2	-	1	-	-
CBInternational	1986	15	-	4	-	-
Child Evangelism Fellowship	1942	-	-	-	2	-
Christian and Msny. Alliance	1972	13	-	-	-	-
Christian Chs. /Chs. of Christ		10	-	-	-	-
Christian Church of North Am.	1960	-	-	-	-	-
Christian Outreach Intl.	1994	-	6	4	2	-
Church of God (Anderson, IN)	1980	2	-	-	-	-
Church of God of Prophecy	1968	2	-	-	-	-
Church of God World Missions	1966	-	-	-	2	2
Church of the Nazarene	1982	4	-	-	-	-
Church Resource Ministries	1993	4	-	-	-	-
Eastern Mennonite Missions	1978	4	-	-	-	-
Evangelical Free Church Msn.	1920	36	2	2	-	-
Evangelical Mennonite Church	1978	6	-	-	-	-
Fellowship International Msn.	1968	4	-	-	-	-
Harvest	1982	-	-	-	1	-
Impact International	1989	-	-	-	2	-
Intl. Pentecostal Holiness Ch.	1978	2	-	-	-	-
Latin America Mission	1989	5	1	-	-	-
Lutheran Church-Missouri Synod	1951	24	-	3	-	-
Maranatha Baptist Mission	1983	7	-	-	-	-
Medical Ambassadors Intl.	1995	-	-	-	3	-
Mennonite Brethren Msns/Svcs	1951	-	2	-	-	-
Mission Aviation Fellowship	1965	8	-	-	-	-

COUNTRY Agency	Year Began	Personnel from U.S.			Other Countries	
		4+ Yrs	2-4 Yrs	1-2 Yrs	Citizens	Not Citiz.
Mission Ministries, Inc.	1990	3	-	-	-	-
Navigators, The	1975	6	-	-	-	-
New Tribes Mission	1946	111	-	6	16	6
Pentecostal Free Will Bapt.Ch.	1979	-	2	-	2	-
Presbyterian Church (USA)	1897	2	8	-	-	-
Reformed Church In America		4	-	-	-	-
Servants in Faith & Technology	1994	-	-	-	8	-
Seventh-day Adventists	1910	2	-	-	-	-
Southern Baptist Intl. Mission	1949	68	8	-	-	-
Spanish World Gospel Mission		-	-	-	3	-
TEAM	1906	89	1	4	-	-
Team Expansion, Inc.	1986	7	-	-	-	-
United Pentecostal Church Intl	1956	4	-	-	-	-
United World Mission	1947	4	-	-	-	-
WEC International	1954	2	-	-	-	-
	Totals:	489	30	24	41	8

VIETNAM

Assemblies of God	1971	9	-	-	-	-
Baptist Mid-Missions	1995	2	-	-	-	-
Bright Hope International		-	-	-	-	3
Christian Aid Mission		-	-	-	39	-
Christian and Msny. Alliance	1911	2	-	-	-	-
Church of the Nazarene	1995	3	-	-	-	-
Covenant Celebration Church		-	-	-	1	-
Gospel for Asia	1994	-	-	-	36	-
Holt Intl. Children's Services	1972	-	3	-	15	1
International Teams, U.S.A.	1995	-	2	-	-	3
Lutheran Church-Missouri Synod	1995	2	-	-	-	-
Mennonite Central Committee	1990	4	4	-	-	-
Mission Soc. for United Meth.	1995	2	-	-	-	-
Paraclete Mission Group, Inc.	1995	2	-	-	-	-
Partners International	1991	-	-	-	334	-
Presbyterian Church (USA)		4	-	-	-	-
Seventh-day Adventists	1937	2	-	-	2	-
Tribes and Nations Outreach	1988	-	-	-	1	1
World Concern	1989	1	-	-	-	2
World Relief Corporation		-	1	-	-	-
World Vision	1960	2	1	-	-	-
	Totals:	35	11	-	428	10

VIRGIN ISLANDS - USA

Baptist International Missions	1963	6	-	-	-	2
Brethren Assemblies		2	-	-	-	-
Christian Chs. /Chs. of Christ	1986	2	-	-	-	-

COUNTRY Agency	Year Began	Personnel from U.S.			Other Countries	
		4+ Yrs	2-4 Yrs	1-2 Yrs	Citizens	Not Citiz.
Church of God World Missions	1967	2	-	-	-	-
Youth With A Mission (YWAM)		9	-	-	-	-
	Totals:	21	-	-	-	2

WEST BANK
Christian Aid Mission		-	-	-	2	-
Evangelical Lutheran Church	1967	2	-	-	-	-
Friends United Meeting	1889	-	1	-	-	-
Kids Alive International	1950	-	-	-	1	-
Mennonite Central Committee	1950	2	6	-	-	-
Southern Baptist Intl. Mission	1989	4	1	-	-	-
	Totals:	8	8	-	3	-

WESTERN SAMOA
Church of God of Prophecy	1981	2	-	-	-	-
Church of God World Missions	1987	-	-	-	2	-
	Totals:	2	-	-	2	-

YEMEN
InterServe/USA	1991	2	-	-	-	-
Southern Baptist Intl. Mission	1964	34	7	-	-	-
	Totals:	36	7	-	-	-

YUGOSLAVIA
Bright Hope International		-	-	-	1	-
Campus Crusade for Christ	1979	6	-	-	-	-
Child Evangelism Fellowship	1973	4	-	-	2	-
Pocket Testament League	1968	-	-	-	8	-
	Totals:	10	-	-	11	-

ZAMBIA
Africa Evangelical Fellowship	1910	25	-	8	-	-
Ambassadors for Christ Intl.		-	-	-	6	-
Baptist Bible Fellowship Intl.	1989	13	-	-	-	-
Baptist Mid-Missions	1990	10	-	-	-	-
Brethren Assemblies		25	-	-	-	-
Brethren in Christ World Msns.	1906	7	2	-	-	-
Campus Crusade for Christ	1975	-	-	2	-	-
CBInternational	1981	2	-	-	-	-
Child Evangelism Fellowship	1970	-	-	-	3	-
Christian Chs. /Chs. of Christ	1962	16	-	-	-	-
Christian Reformed Wrld Relief		1	-	-	-	-
Church of God (Anderson, IN)	1990	2	-	-	-	-
Church of God World Missions	1965	2	-	-	2	-
Church of the Nazarene	1961	4	-	-	-	-

COUNTRY Agency	Year Began	Personnel from U.S.			Other Countries	
		4+ Yrs	2-4 Yrs	1-2 Yrs	Citizens	Not Citiz.
Every Home for Christ	1967	-	-	-	6	-
Habitat for Humanity Intl	1982	-	2	-	17	-
International Needs - USA	1985	-	-	-	16	-
Intl. Pentecostal Holiness Ch.	1950	4	-	-	-	-
Mennonite Central Committee	1962	6	3	-	-	-
Mission Aviation Fellowship	1995	4	-	-	-	-
Mission O.N.E., Inc.	1992	-	-	-	1	-
National Baptist Conv. USA	1993	2	-	-	16	-
Navigators, The	1985	2	1	-	-	-
Pioneers	1995	2	-	-	-	-
Presbyterian Church (USA)		5	-	-	-	-
Salvation Army, U.S.A.	1922	2	-	-	-	-
Seventh-day Adventists	1905	8	-	-	16	-
Southern Baptist Intl. Mission	1959	23	-	-	-	-
Teen Missions International		-	-	-	1	-
United Church Board World Mins	1962	-	2	-	-	-
United Pentecostal Church Intl	1980	4	-	-	-	-
Walk Thru The Bible Ministries	1994	-	-	-	1	-
Wesleyan World Missions	1930	15	-	-	-	-
Wisconsin Evang. Lutheran Syn.	1953	14	-	-	-	-
Youth With A Mission (YWAM)		2	-	-	-	-
Totals:		200	10	10	85	-

ZIMBABWE

Africa Evangelical Fellowship	1906	9	-	-	-	-
African Enterprise, Inc.	1978	-	-	-	10	-
Assemblies of God	1964	4	-	-	-	-
Baptist Mid-Missions	1996	2	-	-	-	-
Brethren Assemblies		5	-	-	-	-
Brethren in Christ World Msns.	1896	5	-	3	-	-
Campus Crusade for Christ	1978	8	-	-	-	-
Child Evangelism Fellowship	1951	-	-	-	2	-
Christian Aid Mission		-	-	-	37	-
Christian Blind Mission Intl.	1990	-	1	-	-	-
Christian Chs. /Chs. of Christ	1956	59	-	-	-	-
Church of God of Prophecy	1976	-	-	-	2	-
Church of the Nazarene	1963	4	-	-	-	-
Elim Fellowship World Missions	1995	1	-	-	-	-
Every Home for Christ	1995	-	-	-	26	-
Habitat for Humanity Intl	1996	-	4	-	-	-
Heifer Project International	1984	-	-	-	4	-
Independent Faith Mission	1992	3	-	-	-	-
Intl. Pentecostal Holiness Ch.	1950	1	-	-	2	-
Mennonite Central Committee	1980	-	1	-	-	-
Mission Aviation Fellowship	1964	6	-	-	-	-
Mission to the World	1991	2	-	-	-	-
Presbyterian Church (USA)		2	-	-	-	-

COUNTRY Agency	Year Began	Personnel from U.S.			Other Countries	
		4+ Yrs	2-4 Yrs	1-2 Yrs	Citizens	Not Citiz.
Salvation Army, U.S.A.	1891	5	-	-	-	-
Seventh-day Adventists	1894	14	-	2	22	-
Southern Baptist Intl. Mission	1956	23	-	-	-	-
TEAM	1942	16	2	4	-	-
Teen Missions International		2	-	-	3	-
United Church Board World Mins	1893	1	4	-	-	-
United Methodist Church		12	-	-	-	-
Youth for Christ / USA		-	2	-	-	-
Totals:		184	14	9	108	-

Chapter 7

Canadian Protestant agencies

T his chapter is the basic information directory of Canadian Protestant agencies engaged in mission ministries outside Canada and the U.S. The comprehensive coverage includes the agencies that directly support the work of such ministries or the work of overseas national churches/workers. The agencies supplied the information; the survey questionnaire used to gather the information is reproduced in the appendix.

The *Handbook* covers an agency's overseas ministry and support activities but not its mission work in Canada. Much cross-cultural mission work takes place in Canada, but due to the additional complexity of reporting such activities we have not undertaken the task for this publication. Agencies with both overseas and Canadian mission ministries, however, were asked to include Canada-based ministry personnel in the total that appears in the "Home ministry & office staff" line of the "Other Personnel" section.

Each agency will have at least seven of the basic categories of information listed below, with others included as applicable.

Agency name

Agencies are listed alphabetically. If the article "the" is in an agency's name, it will appear at the end of the name so the agency is in the most commonly referenced alphabetical order. Rare exceptions occur where the Christian public commonly uses the article "the" as the first word in the name.

Agencies that have changed their name since the previous *Handbook* have their prior name listed, with a cross-reference to the current or new name. A subdivision of a larger organization may be listed separately if it is organized to also serve the larger mission community rather than just its parent organization.

Telephone and fax number

The common format of showing the area code in parentheses is used throughout.

E-Mail address

This is the first time electronic mail addresses appear in the directory. The Internet format and emerging standards for capitalization are used. For example, upper case letters are used to the left of the @ sign when meaningful, but all characters to the right are lower case. Acronyms are upper case, and if a second word is also in the name it is all lower case. For example, MARC Publications' address is MARCpubs@wvi.org in this format.

In some cases, agencies have a general e-mail address, such as Info@xxxx.org. Others have supplied an individual person's address within the organization. In cases where only a Web address is given, it generally means a Web page provides access to several e-mail addresses so an inquiry can be immediately directed to the relevant department or person.

Instead of providing a general e-mail address, an agency may indicate the format to be used to contact individuals within the agency. This usually takes the form of something like Firstname.Lastname@xxxx.org and would be used by the sender when the individual is known.

Mission agencies began to use e-mail on a fairly broad scale by 1995, and over 60 percent of the agencies listed now use e-mail on a regular basis.

Web address

Since 1996 a good number of mission organizations have established a presence on the World Wide Web portion of the Internet. This is the first time a request for a Web address (technically called a uniform resource locator or URL) was included in the survey. Unlike e-mail addresses, Web addresses are case sensitive and must be entered exactly as given.

Because the Web is so new, changes in Web addresses are still taking place as agencies consider different options for a Web presence. Therefore, some addresses may have been added or changed since the *Handbook* database was finalized. The full Web address is given, including the required "http://" prefix, except in cases where including the prefix would have caused the address to spill over to a second line.

Over 30 percent of the agencies provide information about themselves and their work on the Web. A few include audio recordings that can be heard by those with the appropriate sound card and speakers on their personal computers (PCs). Some agencies are starting to include full-motion video clips to take advantage of the Web's multimedia capabilities. This requires a more sophisticated PC and a faster connection to the Internet.

Postal mailing address

A post office box number appears whenever the agency has one, since it is unlikely to change over time.

Chief executive officer

In a few cases where there are multiple primary contacts, two names are listed.

Short descriptive paragraph

A brief description appears based on the denominational orientation and primary activities information supplied by the agency. It always has the same general order so the reader is presented with a format that is consistent across all agencies. Additional specific information, such as name changes, mergers, or other unique aspects may also be included.

Quotation from the agency's mission or purpose statement

This is the first time the survey invited agencies to include their board-adopted short mission or purpose statement in their survey responses. Some of the statements are concise and are shown in their entirety. For most, however, such common or similar phrases as "exists for the purpose of" are replaced by ellipses to present a more concise statement.

Year founded in Canada

This is the year the agency or overseas mission component of a larger organization was founded in Canada. In some cases the denomination or organization may have existed earlier in another country. For some organizations, the founding date of the missionary-sending component may be later than the founding of the larger organization. For denominations and other organizations that have experienced mergers, the founding date is generally that of the oldest component involved in the merger.

Income for overseas ministries

This is the part of an agency's overall income used for ministry activities outside Canada and the USA or in activities that directly facilitate overseas ministries. "NA" indicates that income in this sense is not applicable, and usually applies to specialized service agencies or agencies whose income is reported under a sister or parent organization. "NR" indicates that income for overseas ministries was not reported by the agency for the survey, but may make this information available on request.

Amount of gifts-in-kind

If applicable, this is the portion of the income that was received in the form of donated gifts-in-kind commodities and/or services used for overseas ministries. Please note that some agencies do not include gifts-in-kind as part of their financial audit process, so the value of such gifts is not included in their income for overseas ministries. Gifts-in-kind amounts that were an insignificant percentage are not shown as a separate item.

Fully supported USA personnel overseas

Not all agencies have overseas personnel in the following categories, so the above heading will not always appear. If applicable, the following lines will appear with the appropriate numbers:

- ◆ "Expecting to serve more than 4 years" for persons from Canada who are fully supported by the agency.
- ◆ "Expecting to serve 1 up to 4 years" for persons from Canada who are fully supported by the agency.
- ◆ "Nonresidential mission personnel" for fully supported Canadian mission personnel not residing in the country or countries of their ministry, but assigned to work and travel overseas at least 12 weeks per year on operational aspects of the overseas ministry.

Other personnel

If applicable for the agency, the following lines will appear:

- ◆ "Non-Canadian serving in own/other country" for persons with either citizenship in their country of service or another non-Canadian country, who are fully or partially supported from Canada.
- ◆ "Bivocational/Tentmaker from Canada" for persons sponsored or supervised by the agency, but who support themselves partially or fully through non-church/mission vocations and live overseas for the purpose of Christian witness, evangelism and/or encouraging believers.
- ◆ "Short-Term less than 1 year from Canada" for persons who went on overseas projects or mission trips that lasted less than 1 year but at least 2 weeks through the agency, either fully or partially supported, including those raising their own support.
- ◆ "Home ministry and office staff in Canada" for persons assigned to ministry and/or office duties in Canada either as full-time or part-time paid staff/associates.

Countries

These are the countries where the agency sends Canadian personnel or regularly supports national or other non-Canadian personnel. Following the name of the country is the number of Canadian personnel with terms of service of one year or more. In some cases a continent or other general area instead of a country is shown. This may be due to several reasons, such as mission personnel whose ministry covers several countries.

Where an agency's work is maintained either by nationals of countries other than Canada or the U.S., by personnel serving less than one year, or by those serving on a nonresidential basis, the country of activity is listed without a personnel total. Please refer to chapter 9 for detailed country personnel totals of all categories for each agency.

ABWE (Association of Baptists for World Evangelism) - Canada

(519)759-3400   Fax: **(519)759-2271**
222 Fairview Dr., # 203, Brantford, ON N3R 2W9
Mr. Frank Bale, Director

An independent Baptist sending agency engaged in church planting, theological education, TEE, evangelism, and medical work.

Year Founded in Canada 1940
Income for Overseas Ministries . $ 630,984
Amount of Gifts-In-Kind . . . . $ 77,839
Fully Supported Canada Personnel Overseas:
 Expecting to serve more than 4 years 15
 Expecting to serve 1 up to 4 years 8
 Nonresidential mission personnel 4
Other Personnel:
 Short-Term less than 1 year from Canada . . 5
 Home ministry & office staff in Canada . . . 7
Countries: Argentina 2, Asia 2, Bangladesh 3, Brazil 5, Chile 1, Peru 2, Portugal 4, S Africa 2, Ukraine 2.

Action International Ministries

(403)443-2221   Fax: **(403)443-7455**
E-Mail: 75342.663@compuserve.com
Web: http://www.supernet.ab.ca/~action/
P.O. Box 280, Three Hills, AB T0M 2A0
Mr. Doug W. Fearn, Canadian Director

An interdenominational sending agency of evangelical tradition engaged in evangelism, camping programs, church planting, and training. Overseas personnel totals from 1992 report.

Year Founded in Canada 1980
Income for Overseas Ministries . $ 864,326
Fully Supported Canada Personnel Overseas:
 Expecting to serve more than 4 years 17
Other Personnel:
 Short-Term less than 1 year from Canada . . 15
 Home ministry & office staff in Canada . . . 3
Countries: Colombia 4, Philippines 13.

Africa Community Technical Service

(604)339-1212   Fax: **(604)339-1300**
E-Mail: Moore@nicad3.nic.bc.ca
2064 Comox Ave., Comox, BC V9M 3S5
Mr. David Moore, Director

An interdenominational service agency of evangelical tradition engaged in technical

assistance and development in several countries of Africa. Income amount from 1992 report.

Year Founded in Canada 1972
Income for Overseas Ministries . $ 117,355
Personnel:
 Short-Term less than 1 year from Canada . . 3

Africa Evangelical Fellowship

(519)622-7818   Fax: **(519)622-7129**
E-Mail: 102653.410@compuserve.com
51 Cambridge St., Cambridge, ON N1R 3R8
Rev. John Pomeroy, Exec. Director

An interdenominational sending agency of evangelical tradition engaged in evangelism, church planting, Christian education, theological education, TEE, and medical work.

".. evangelizing unbelievers, discipling believers .. and developing spiritually mature fellowships of local churches equipped to fulfill the Great Commission."

Year Founded in Canada 1930
Income for Overseas Ministries $ 1,712,519
Fully Supported Canada Personnel Overseas:
 Expecting to serve more than 4 years 45
 Expecting to serve 1 up to 4 years 3
Other Personnel:
 Bivocational/Tentmaker from Canada 2
 Short-Term less than 1 year from Canada . . 7
 Home ministry & office staff in Canada . . 8
Countries: Angola 5, Botswana 3, Malawi 1, Mozambique 2, S Africa 13, Zambia 18, Zimbabwe 6.

Africa Inland Mission (Canada)

(416)751-6077   Fax: **(416)751-3467**
E-Mail: AIM-CAN@aimint.org
Web: http://www.goshen.net/aim-ca/
1641 Victoria Park Ave., Scarborough, ON M1R 1P8
Dr. John Brown, Director

An interdenominational sending agency of evangelical tradition engaged in leadership development, church planting, Christian education, medical work, and technical assistance.

"to plant maturing churches .. through the evangelization of unreached people groups and the effective preparation of church leaders."

Year Founded in Canada 1953
Income for Overseas Ministries $ 1,815,000
Fully Supported Canada Personnel Overseas:

Expecting to serve more than 4 years 57
Expecting to serve 1 up to 4 years 38
Nonresidential mission personnel 1
Other Personnel:
Short-Term less than 1 year from Canada . . 31
Home ministry & office staff in Canada . . . 11
Countries: Cen Africa Rep 2, Chad 1, Congo/Zaire 17, Kenya 66, Lesotho 4, Sudan 1, Tanzania 4.

African Enterprise Association of Canada

(604)228-0930   Fax: (604)228-0936
E-Mail: 74667.3105@compuserve.com
4509 W. 11th Ave., Vancouver, BC V6R 2M5
Mr. David Richardson, Exec. Director

An interdenominational service agency of evangelical tradition engaged in evangelism and support of national churches in over 30 countries of Africa. Income amount from 1992 report.

"... To evangelise the cities of Africa through Word and Deed in Partnership with the Church."

Year Founded in Canada 1964
Income for Overseas Ministries . . $ 45,600
Personnel:
Short-Term less than 1 year from Canada . . 2
Home ministry & office staff in Canada . . . 2

Anglican Church of Canada, Partners in Mission

(416)924-9192   Fax: (416)924-3483
600 Jarvis St., Toronto, ON M4Y 2J6
Dr. Eleanor Johnson, Director

A denominational sending agency of Anglican tradition engaged in support of national churches, development, theological education, evangelism, relief aid. Statistical information from 1992.

Year Founded in Canada 1885
Income for Overseas Ministries . . $ 6,000,000
Fully Supported Canada Personnel Overseas:
Expecting to serve more than 4 years 19
Other Personnel:
Home ministry & office staff in Canada . . . 31
Countries: Unspecified 19.

Apostolic Church In Canada, The

(416)489-0453
27 Castlefield Ave., Toronto, ON M4R 1G3
Rev. J. Karl Thomas, Gen. Secretary

A denominational sending agency of Pentecostal tradition engaged in evangelism, Bible distribution, church planting, and support of national workers.

Year Founded in Canada 1930
Income for Overseas Ministries . $ 117,000
Fully Supported Canada Personnel Overseas:
Expecting to serve more than 4 years 4
Other Personnel:
Bivocational/Tentmaker from Canada 1
Short-Term less than 1 year from Canada . . 2
Home ministry & office staff in Canada . . . 9
Countries: Brazil 4.

Apostolic Church of Pentecost of Canada, Missionary Department

(403)273-5777   Fax: (403)273-8102
E-Mail: 102024.3341@compuserve.com
Web: http://www.illuminart.com/acop
809 Manning Rd NE, #200, Calgary, AB T2E 7M9
Rev. Rick Parkyn, Missions Director

A denominational sending agency of Pentecostal tradition engaged in evangelism, church planting, and literature production.

Year Founded in Canada 1921
Income for Overseas Ministries . $ 850,700
Fully Supported Canada Personnel Overseas:
Expecting to serve more than 4 years 27
Other Personnel:
Home ministry & office staff in Canada . . . 5
Countries: Burkina Faso 3, Guatemala 6, Malawi 2, Mexico 6, Poland 4, S Africa 4, Zimbabwe 2.

Arab World Ministries (Canada)

(519)653-3170   Fax: (519)653-3002
P.O. Box 3398, Cambridge, ON N3H 4T3
Mr. Norm Leduc, Canadian Director

An interdenominational sending agency of evangelical tradition engaged in church planting, audio recording/distribution, correspondence courses, TEE, and evangelism.

Year Founded in Canada 1967
Income for Overseas Ministries . $ 576,000
Fully Supported Canada Personnel Overseas:
Nonresidential mission personnel 28
Other Personnel:
Bivocational/Tentmaker from Canada 20
Short-Term less than 1 year from Canada . . 8
Home ministry & office staff in Canada . . . 7

Associated Gospel Churches

(905)634-8184   Fax: (905)634-6283
E-Mail: AGC@ftn.net
Web: http://www.ftn.net/~agc/
3228 S. Service Rd., Burlington, ON L7N 3H8
Dr. Donald Hamilton, President

A support agency of evangelical and Baptistic tradition encouraging mission mobilization for evangelism and church planting.

".. to assist member churches in their obedience to the Great Commission of Jesus Christ."

Year Founded in Canada 1922
Income for Overseas Ministries . . . . NA
Personnel:
Home ministry & office staff in Canada   . . . 6

Association of Baptists for World Evangelism - Canada

See: ABWE - Canada

Association of Regular Baptist Churches (Canada)

(416)925-3261   Fax: (416)925-8305
130 Gerrard, Street E., Toronto, ON M5A 3T4
Rev. Stephen Kring, Chairman

A denominational sending agency of Baptist tradition engaged in church planting and missionary training.

".. to support by prayer and finance, the establishing of local churches in other countries or in the homeland which are pioneer or weak..."

Year Founded in Canada 1957
Income for Overseas Ministries . . . . NR
Personnel:
Home ministry & office staff in Canada   . . . 1
Countries: Caribbean Isls, France, Spain.

Barry Moore Ministries

(519)661-0205   Fax: (519)661-0206
Box 9100, London, ON N6E 1V0
Rev. John Laari, Exec. Director

An interdenominational service agency of evangelical tradition engaged in evangelism and literature production/distribution.

Year Founded in Canada 1960
Income for Overseas Ministries . . $ 76,107
Amount of Gifts-In-Kind . . . . $ 43,739

Fully Supported Canada Personnel Overseas:
Nonresidential mission personnel   1
Other Personnel:
Short-Term less than 1 year from Canada   . . 2
Home ministry & office staff in Canada   . . . 3

BCM International (Canada), Inc.

(905)549-9810   Fax: (905)549-7664
798 Main St., E., Hamilton, ON L8M 1L4
Miss Chloe Chamberlain, Exec. Secretary

A nondenominational support agency of evangelical tradition engaged in Christian education, childrens camping programs, and correspondence courses.

Year Founded in Canada 1942
Income for Overseas Ministries . . . . NR
Fully Supported Canada Personnel Overseas:
Expecting to serve more than 4 years   4
Other Personnel:
Home ministry & office staff in Canada   . . . 1
Countries: Netherlands 1, Pakistan 1, Spain 2.

BGCC Global Ministries

(604)448-1242   Fax: (604)448-1241
E-Mail: BGCC@datanet.ab.ca
313 - 3851 Francis Rd., Richmond, BC V7C 1J6
Dann Pantoja, Director of Global Ministries

A denominational sending agency of Baptist tradition engaged in church planting, community and leadership development, evangelism, and support of national churches. The mission agency of the Baptist General Conference of Canada.

Year Founded in Canada 1995
Income for Overseas Ministries . $ 275,000
Amount of Gifts-In-Kind . . . . $ 50,000
Fully Supported Canada Personnel Overseas:
Expecting to serve more than 4 years   2
Expecting to serve 1 up to 4 years   6
Other Personnel:
Bivocational/Tentmaker from Canada   3
Short-Term less than 1 year from Canada   . . 32
Home ministry & office staff in Canada   . . . 2
Countries: Asia 3, Hungary 2, Ireland 1, Macedonia 1, Portugal 1.

Bible Holiness Movement

(250)498-3895
P.O. Box 223, Postal Station A, Vancouver, BC V6C 2M3
Evangelist Wesley H. Wakefield, Bishop-General

A denominational support agency of Holiness and Wesleyan tradition engaged in evangelism, church planting, literature production/distribution, support of national churches, and workers.

Year Founded in Canada 1949
Income for Overseas Ministries . . $ 28,966
Amount of Gifts-In-Kind . . . . $ 2,026
Personnel:
Non-Canadian serving in own/other country 47
Home ministry & office staff in Canada . . . 11
Countries: Ghana, India, Kenya, Malawi, Nigeria, Philippines, Tanzania, Uganda, Zambia.

Bible League of Canada, The
(905)319-9500   Fax: (905)319-0484
E-Mail: BibLeag@worldchat.com
P.O. Box 5037, Burlington, ON L7R 3Y8
Rev. John G. Klomps, Exec. Director

A nondenominational service agency of evangelical tradition engaged in Bible and literature distribution, evangelism, and translation work.

".. to provide Scriptures that bring individuals into the fellowship of Christ and His Church."

Year Founded in Canada 1949
Income for Overseas Ministries $ 2,612,735
Personnel:
Home ministry & office staff in Canada . . . 16

Brethren Assemblies (Canada)
(No central office)

The Brethren Assemblies are also known as "Christian Brethren" or "Plymouth Brethren". Missionaries are sent from each local assembly (church) and not through a central agency. Personnel totals are summaries from the "Workers Abroad" reference booklet published by MSC Canada.

Income for Overseas Ministries . . . . NA
Fully Supported Canada Personnel Overseas:
Expecting to serve more than 4 years . . . 207
Expecting to serve 1 up to 4 years 2
Nonresidential mission personnel 2
Other Personnel:
Short-Term less than 1 year from Canada . . 6
Countries: Angola 1, Argentina 2, Austria 10, Belgium 6, Bolivia 8, Botswana 2, Brazil 3, Chile 12, Colombia 1, Congo/Zaire 4, Costa Rica 4, Dominican Rep 2, Ecuador 6, Egypt 2, El Salvador 2, Finland 5, France 20, Grenada 2, Guatemala 2, Hong Kong 2, India 6, Ireland 6, Italy 3, Japan 4, Kenya 4, Madagascar 2, Mexico 8, Netherlands 2, Nigeria 2, Pakistan 1, Peru 3,

Philippines 2, Poland 4, Portugal 4, Spain 9, St Chris-Nevis 2, St Vincent 1, UK 2, Unspecified 10, Uruguay 7, Venezuela 6, Zambia 27.

Calcutta Mission of Mercy
(604)929-1330   Fax: (604)253-6167
P.O. Box 65599, Vancouver, BC V5N 5K5
Rev. Mohan Maharaj, Exec. Director

A denominational service agency of Pentecostal and evangelical tradition engaged in relief feeding programs, children/youth programs, Christian education, evangelism, and medical work. Affiliated with the Pentecostal Assemblies of Canada and the Assemblies of God USA. Additional financial support sent directly to India by churches and others not included in total.

Year Founded in Canada 1978
Income for Overseas Ministries . $ 510,127
Fully Supported Canada Personnel Overseas:
Expecting to serve more than 4 years 1
Other Personnel:
Bivocational/Tentmaker from Canada 6
Home ministry & office staff in Canada . . . 3
Countries: India 1.

Campus Crusade for Christ of Canada
(604)582-3100   Fax: (604)588-7582
Web: http://www.crusade.org/
P.O. Box 300, Vancouver, BC V6C 2X3
Mr. Marvin Kehler, President

An interdenominational sending agency of evangelical tradition engaged in evangelism, leadership development, literature distribution, and support of national churches.

".. helping to fulfill the Great Commission in Canada and around the world, by developing a movement of evangelism and discipleship."

Year Founded in Canada 1967
Income for Overseas Ministries $ 4,368,563
Fully Supported Canada Personnel Overseas:
Expecting to serve more than 4 years 5
Expecting to serve 1 up to 4 years 7
Nonresidential mission personnel 14
Other Personnel:
Short-Term less than 1 year from Canada . 327
Home ministry & office staff in Canada . . 216
Countries: Japan 1, Nigeria 2, Philippines 2, Russia 3, S Africa 2, Ukraine 2.

Canadian Baptist Ministries

(905)821-3533   Fax: (905)826-3441
E-Mail: CBMadmin@inforamp.net
Web: http://www.cbmin.org/
7185 Millcreek Dr., Mississauga, ON L5N 5R4
Rev. David Phillips, Gen. Secretary

A denominational sending agency of Baptist tradition engaged in leadership development, theological education, and support of natl. churches.

Year Founded in Canada 1874
Income for Overseas Ministries $ 5,450,000
Fully Supported Canada Personnel Overseas:
   Expecting to serve more than 4 years 51
   Expecting to serve 1 up to 4 years 26
   Nonresidential mission personnel 30
Other Personnel:
   Short-Term less than 1 year from Canada . . 75
   Home ministry & office staff in Canada . . . 30
Countries: Albania 2, Angola 2, Asia 7, Belgium 11, Bolivia 5, China (PRC) 2, Congo/Zaire 8, Croatia 2, France 2, Guyana 6, India 4, Indonesia 4, Kenya 12, Latvia 2, Slovakia 2, Ukraine 4, Venezuela 2.

Canadian Bible Society / La Societe Biblique Canadienne

(416)757-4171   Fax: (416)757-3376
10 Carnforth Rd., Toronto, ON M4A 2S4
Rev. Dr. Floyd C. Babcock, Gen. Secretary

A transdenominational agency serving churches of all confessions through Scripture translation/production/distribution, linguistics, literacy work, and services for other agencies.

".. to promote and encourage the wider circulation throughout Canada of the Scriptures, without note or comment, and to cooperate with the United Bible Societies in its worldwide work."

Year Founded in Canada 1904
Income for Overseas Ministries $ 4,000,000
Personnel:
   Home ministry & office staff in Canada . . 130

Canadian Churches' Forum for Global Ministries

(416)924-9351   Fax: (416)924-5356
E-Mail: CCForum@web.net
230 St. Clair Ave., West, Toronto, ON M4V 1R5
Robert Faris, Coord. Outreach/Communication

An affiliated interdenominational service institution of The Canadian Council of Churches engaged in missionary orientation and re-entry programs, leadership development, and services for other agencies.

".. an agency through which the Canadian churches reflect and work together on global mission issues through programs of education, dialogue and training."

Year Founded in Canada 1921
Income for Overseas Ministries . . . . NA
Personnel:
   Home ministry & office staff in Canada . . . 3

Canadian Convention of Southern Baptists

(403)932-5688   Fax: (403)932-4937
E-Mail: 70420.2230@compuserve.com
Postal Bag 300, Cochrane, AB T0L 0W0
Rev. Allen Schmidt, Exec. Director

A denominational sending agency of Baptist tradition engaged in church planting, agricultural programs, Christian education, evangelism, leadership development, and relief aid.

Year Founded in Canada 1985
Income for Overseas Ministries . $ 303,412
Fully Supported Canada Personnel Overseas:
   Expecting to serve more than 4 years 6
Other Personnel:
   Home ministry & office staff in Canada . . . 8
Countries: Chile 2, Malaysia 2, Nigeria 2.

Canadian Food for the Hungry

(604)853-4262   Fax: (604)853-4332
E-Mail: CFH@mindlink.bc.ca
Web: http://www.cfh.ca
005-2580 Cedar Pk. Pl., Abbotsford, BC V2T 3S5
David Collins, Exec. Director

A nondenominational service agency engaged in development, agricultural programs, support of national churches, and relief aid.

".. speaking out to all people about physical and spiritual hunger, sending people to share Christ's love, and facilitating emergency relief and sustainable development."

Year Founded in Canada 1988
Income for Overseas Ministries $ 6,400,000
Amount of Gifts-In-Kind . . . $ 6,000,000
Fully Supported Canada Personnel Overseas:
   Expecting to serve more than 4 years 2
   Expecting to serve 1 up to 4 years 3

Other Personnel:
Home ministry & office staff in Canada . . . 8
Countries: Unspecified 5.

Canadian Friends Service Committee

(416)920-5213 **Fax: (416)920-5214**
60 Lowther Ave., Toronto, ON M5R 1C7
Mr. Peter Chapman, Coordinator

An interdenominational service agency of Friends tradition engaged in agricultural programs, medical work, and relief aid.

Year Founded in Canada 1931
Income for Overseas Ministries . $ 100,000

Canadian South America Mission

(403)443-2250 **Fax: (403)443-2099**
E-Mail: 75457.2247@compuserve.com
Box 716, Three Hills, AB T0M 2A0
Dan C. Wiebe, Exec. Director

An interdenominational sending agency of fundamentalist and evangelical tradition engaged in leadership development, agricultural programs, disability assistance programs, evangelism, and support of national churches.

".. to establish the church of Jesus Christ in South America by planting and nurturing churches, training church leaders, [and] developing church associations."

Year Founded in Canada 1983
Income for Overseas Ministries . $ 150,000
Fully Supported Canada Personnel Overseas:
Expecting to serve more than 4 years 4
Expecting to serve 1 up to 4 years 1
Nonresidential mission personnel 5
Other Personnel:
Short-Term less than 1 year from Canada . . 3
Home ministry & office staff in Canada . . . 1
Countries: Brazil 1, Colombia 2, Peru 2.

Centre for World Mission - British Columbia

(604)854-3818 **Fax: (604)854-3818**
P.O. Box 2436, Clearbook, BC V2T 4X3
Mr. John Burman, Director

An interdenominational support agency of evangelical and fundamental tradition engaged in mobilization for mission, and information, research and training services for other agencies.

"to promote information on 'Hidden Peoples' of Canada and the world... to help churches by providing resource material and information to aid in their missions program outreach."

Year Founded in Canada 1981
Income for Overseas Ministries . . . . NA
Personnel:
Home ministry & office staff in Canada . . . 2

Child Evangelism Fellowship of Canada

(204)943-2774
E-Mail: 103442.1544@compuserve.com
P.O. Box 165, Winnipeg, MB R3C 2G9
Rev. Don Collins, Natl. Director

An interdenominational sending agency of evangelical tradition engaged in childrens programs, evangelism, literature production/distribution, and training.

".. to assist and promote the evangelizing and discipling of children through leadership, coordination and administrative support to CEF ministries across Canada and overseas."

Year Founded in Canada 1963
Income for Overseas Ministries . $ 555,000
Fully Supported Canada Personnel Overseas:
Expecting to serve more than 4 years 10
Expecting to serve 1 up to 4 years 4
Other Personnel:
Non-Canadian serving in own/other country 17
Home ministry & office staff in Canada . . . 65
Countries: Albania 1, Argentina 1, Austria, Brazil 2, France 1, Hong Kong, Hungary 2, Ireland, Italy 1, Japan 2, S Africa 2, St Vincent, Sweden 2, Switzerland, UK.

Christian Aid Mission

(800)871-0882 **Fax: (905)871-5165**
E-Mail: info@christianaid.ca
Web: http://www.christianaid.ca
201 Stanton St., Fort Erie, ON L2A 3N8
Mr. James S. Eagles, President

A nondenominational service agency of evangelical tradition engaged in support of national workers, funds transmission, missions information/research services, and literature production.

"To aid, encourage, and strengthen indigenous new testament Christianity, particularly where Christians are impoverished, few or persecuted..."

Year Founded in Canada 1953

Income for Overseas Ministries . $ 508,024
Personnel:
Non-Canadian serving in own/other country   311
Home ministry & office staff in Canada . . . 16
Countries: Africa, Asia, CIS, China (PRC), Europe-E, India, Latin America, Philippines.

Christian and Missionary Alliance in Canada, The

(905)771-6747   Fax: (905)771-9874
E-Mail: NationalOffice@cmacan.org
P.O. Box 7900, Thornhill, ON L3T 1A7
Rev. Wallace C.E. Albrecht, Vice President

A denominational sending agency of evangelical tradition engaged in church planting, TEE, and evangelism. Statistical data from 1992..

Year Founded in Canada 1981
Income for Overseas Ministries $ 8,290,327
Fully Supported Canada Personnel Overseas:
Expecting to serve more than 4 years   . . . 189
Expecting to serve 1 up to 4 years   21
Nonresidential mission personnel   2
Other Personnel:
Bivocational/Tentmaker from Canada 11
Short-Term less than 1 year from Canada . . 20
Home ministry & office staff in Canada . . . 17
Countries: Argentina 6, Australia 6, Brazil 5, Burkina Faso 2, Cambodia 1, Chile 4, Colombia 8, Congo/Zaire 11, Cote d'Ivoire 11, Ecuador 8, Europe-E 1, France 6, Gabon 12, Germany 6, Guatemala 2, Guinea 12, Hong Kong 2, India 2, Indonesia 23, Japan 4, Jordan 2, Korea-S 2, Laos 1, Mali 7, Mexico 8, Pakistan 4, Peru 10, Philippines 22, Spain 3, Taiwan (ROC) 7, Thailand 6, UK 2, Venezuela 4.

Christian Blind Mission International (Canada)

(905)640-6464   Fax: (905)640-4332
E-Mail: 102001.3725@compuserve.com
P.O. Box 800, Stouffville, ON L4A 7Z9
Mr. Art Brooker, Natl. Director

An interdenominational service agency of evangelical tradition engaged in disability assistance programs, community development, medical work, and relief aid.

".. serving the blind and handicapped in the developing world, irrespective of nationality, race, sex, or religion .. [with] the ultimate aim .. to show the love of Christ..."

Year Founded in Canada 1978
Income for Overseas Ministries $ 4,968,922

Amount of Gifts-In-Kind   . . . $ 568,000
Fully Supported Canada Personnel Overseas:
Expecting to serve more than 4 years   6
Other Personnel:
Home ministry & office staff in Canada   . . . 30
Countries: Bangladesh 2, Kenya 2, Philippines 2.

Christian Indigenous Development Overseas

(403)286-0611   Fax: (403)247-4686
E-Mail: 74401.3712@compuserve.com
142 Dalhousie Rd., NW, Calgary, AB T3A 2H1
Mr. H.A. McLean, President

A transdenominational service agency of evangelical tradition engaged in development, funds transmission, and technical assistance.

Year Founded in Canada 1977
Income for Overseas Ministries . $ 173,000

Christian Literature Crusade
See: Croisade du Livre Chretien

Christian Reformed World Relief Committee of Canada

(905)336-2920   Fax: (905)336-8344
P.O. Box 5070, Burlington, ON L7R 3Y8
Mr. Wayne DeJong, Director

A denominational ministry service agency of Reformed tradition engaged in community development, relief/rehabilitation, literacy work, and management consulting/training in more than 30 countries worldwide.

Year Founded in Canada 1969
Income for Overseas Ministries $ 4,149,890
Fully Supported Canada Personnel Overseas:
Expecting to serve more than 4 years   18
Other Personnel:
Short-Term less than 1 year from Canada . . 10
Home ministry & office staff in Canada . . . 6
Countries: Belize 2, Haiti 4, Mali 1, Philippines 4, Sierra Leone 1, Tanzania 4, Uganda 2.

Church of God (Anderson, IN), Canadian Board of Missions

(403)672-0772   Fax: (403)672-6888
E-Mail: WCDNChurchofGod@wildrose.net
4717-56th St., Camrose, AB T4V 2C4
Rev. John D. Campbell, Mission Coordinator

A denominational support agency of Holiness and Wesleyan tradition engaged in funds transmission, church construction, Christian education, and support of national churches.

Year Founded in Canada 1946
Income for Overseas Ministries . $ 174,934
Personnel:
Non-Canadian serving in own/other country . 6
Short-Term less than 1 year from Canada . . 2
Home ministry & office staff in Canada . . . 3
Countries: Australia, Uganda, Zambia.

CNEC - Partners International
See: Partners International Canada

Compassion Canada
(519)668-0224   **Fax: (519)685-1107**
E-Mail: CompCan@web.net
Web: http://www.web.net/compassion
P.O. Box 5591, London, ON N6A 5G8
Rev. Barry Slauenwhite, President

A transdenominational service agency of evangelical tradition engaged in childcare programs, child and community development, and literacy work in over 20 countries.

Year Founded in Canada 1964
Income for Overseas Ministries $ 5,615,868
Fully Supported Canada Personnel Overseas:
Expecting to serve more than 4 years 1
Nonresidential mission personnel 1
Other Personnel:
Short-Term less than 1 year from Canada . . 10
Home ministry & office staff in Canada . . . 24
Countries: Africa 1.

Croisade du Livre Chretien / Christian Literature Crusade
(514)933-9466   **Fax: (514)933-7629**
4257 ouest Ste-Catherine, Montreal, PQ H3Z 1P7
Mr. Rod Fowler, Director

An interdenominational service agency of evangelical tradition engaged in literature production/distribution and Bible distribution.

Year Founded in Canada 1977
Income for Overseas Ministries . . . . NR
Personnel:
Home ministry & office staff in Canada . . . 8

Czechoslovak Evangelical Mission
(905)822-8808
1601 Bramsey Dr., Mississauga, ON L5J 2H8
Rev. Joseph R. Novak, President

An interdenominational support agency of Baptist tradition engaged in Gospel tract production for distribution in the Czech and Slovakia Republics.

Year Founded in Canada 1984
Income for Overseas Ministries . . $ 30,000
Personnel:
Short-Term less than 1 year from Canada . . 1
Home ministry & office staff in Canada . . . 1

Door of Hope International (Canada)
(604)430-1747
E-Mail: 104461.166@compuserve.com
P.O. Box 65959, Vancouver, BC V5N 5L3
Rev. E. Culley, Chairman

An interdenominational service agency of evangelical tradition engaged in Bible distribution, literature distribution, literature production, support of national churches, and relief aid.

Year Founded in Canada 1972
Income for Overseas Ministries . . $ 36,458
Fully Supported Canada Personnel Overseas:
Expecting to serve more than 4 years 2
Other Personnel:
Short-Term less than 1 year from Canada . . 1
Home ministry & office staff in Canada . . . 1
Countries: Albania 1, Russia 1.

Emmanuel International
(905)640-2111   **Fax: (905)640-2186**
E-Mail: Info@e-i.org
Web: http://www.e-i.org
P.O. Box 4050, Stouffville, ON L4A 8B6
Mr. Andrew Atkins, Gen. Director

An interdenominational sending agency of evangelical tradition engaged in support of national churches, development, TEE, relief aid, missionary training, and youth programs.

".. to encourage, strengthen and assist churches worldwide to meet the spiritual and physical needs of the poor in accordance with Holy Scriptures..."

Year Founded in Canada	1975
Income for Overseas Ministries	$ 3,077,000

Fully Supported Canada Personnel Overseas:

Expecting to serve more than 4 years 5
Expecting to serve 1 up to 4 years 5
Nonresidential mission personnel 9

Other Personnel:

Non-Canadian serving in own/other country 26
Short-Term less than 1 year from Canada . . 1
Home ministry & office staff in Canada . . 17

Countries: Brazil, Haiti 1, Jamaica, Malawi 4, Philippines 2, Sudan 2, Tanzania, Uganda 1.

European Christian Mission

(604)943-0211   **Fax: (604)943-0212**
E-Mail: 74663.3176@compuserve.com
1077 56th St., Ste 226, Delta, BC V4L 2A2
Rev. Vincent Price, Dir. for N. America

An interdenominational sending agency of evangelical tradition engaged in evangelism, broadcasting, and literature distribution.

Year Founded in Canada 1960
Income for Overseas Ministries . $ 181,191

Eurovangelism

(905)821-6301   **Fax: (905)821-6311**
207-2476 Argentia Rd., Missisauga, ON L5N 6M1
Mr. John Murray, Exec. Director

A nondenominational agency of evangelical tradition supporting national workers and churches, TEE, evangelism, and relief aid.

"...to serve the Church across Europe by envisioning, encouraging, and equipping national Christian workers."

Year Founded in Canada 1976
Income for Overseas Ministries . $ 145,000
Personnel:

Non-Canadian serving in own/other country 30
Home ministry & office staff in Canada . . . 2

Countries: Austria, Poland, Romania, Russia.

Evangelical Covenant Church of Canada

(403)934-5845   **Fax: (403)934-5847**
E-Mail: 104415.3677@compuserve.com
630 Westchester Rd., Strathmore, AB T1P 1H8
Jerome K. Johnson, Superintendent

A denominational conference of covenantal and evangelical tradition engaged in funds transmission and mission mobilization for evangelism and church planting.

Year Founded in Canada 1904
Income for Overseas Ministries . . $ 52,280
Personnel:

Short-Term less than 1 year from Canada . . 1
Home ministry & office staff in Canada . . . 3

Evangelical Lutheran Church in Canada, World Mission

(204)786-6707
1512 St. James Street, Winnipeg, MB R3H 0L2
Rev. Peter Mathiasen, Asst. to the Bishop

A denominational sending agency of Lutheran tradition engaged in church planting, development, and training.

Year Founded in Canada 1967
Income for Overseas Ministries . $ 496,715
Fully Supported Canada Personnel Overseas:

Expecting to serve more than 4 years 3
Expecting to serve 1 up to 4 years 10

Other Personnel:

Short-Term less than 1 year from Canada . . 5
Home ministry & office staff in Canada . . . 3

Countries: Argentina 2, Cameroon 2, Colombia 2, El Salvador 1, Papua New Guin 5, Peru 1.

Evangelical Mennonite Conference Board of Missions

(204)326-6401   **Fax: (204)326-1613**
E-Mail: EMConf@mts.net
P.O. Box 1268, Steinbach, MB R0A 2A0
Rev. Henry Klassen, Exec. Secretary

A denominational sending agency of Mennonite tradition engaged in church planting, broadcasting, TEE, evangelism, leadership development, and literature distribution.

Year Founded in Canada 1953
Income for Overseas Ministries $ 1,000,000
Fully Supported Canada Personnel Overseas:

Expecting to serve more than 4 years 35

Other Personnel:

Non-Canadian serving in own/other country . 6
Short-Term less than 1 year from Canada . . 15
Home ministry & office staff in Canada . . . 32

Countries: Africa 4, Mexico 13, Paraguay 18.

Evangelical Mennonite Mission Conf. Board of Missions & Service

(204)253-7929   **Fax: (204)256-7384**
Box 52059 Niakwa P.O., Winnipeg, MB R2M 5P9
Mr. Len Sawatzky, Director

A denominational sending agency of Mennonite tradition engaged in church planting, development, Christian education, evangelism, and support of national workers.

Year Founded in Canada 1959
Income for Overseas Ministries . $ 301,171
Fully Supported Canada Personnel Overseas:
    Expecting to serve more than 4 years 6
    Expecting to serve 1 up to 4 years 5
Other Personnel:
    Non-Canadian serving in own/other country . 9
    Short-Term less than 1 year from Canada . . 7
    Home ministry & office staff in Canada . . . 1
Countries: Bolivia 2, Burkina Faso 5, Mexico 4.

Evangelical Tract Distributors

(403)477-1538
P.O. Box 146, Edmonton, AB T5J 2G9
Mr. John Harder, President

An interdenominational specialized service agency of evangelical tradition publishing gospel tracts in 60 languages/dialects for missionaries and national workers engaged in evangelism.

Year Founded in Canada 1935
Income for Overseas Ministries . . . . NA
Personnel:
    Home ministry & office staff in Canada . . . 9

Everyday Publications, Inc.

(416)291-9411
E-Mail: 102604.1530@compuserve.com
421 Nugget Ave., #2, Scarborough, ON M1S 4L8
Dr. R. E. Harlow, Board Chair
Mr. Patrick N. Long, President

A nondenominational service agency of Christian/Plymouth Brethren tradition publishing Christian books in simplified English, Swahili, Spanish, French, and Portuguese and supplying them at no cost or subsidized rates for developing countries.

Year Founded in Canada 1964
Income for Overseas Ministries . $ 102,971
Personnel:

Home ministry & office staff in Canada . . . 5

FAIR (Fellowship Agency for International Relief)

(519)821-4830   **Fax: (519)821-9829**
E-Mail: 103227.1367@compuserve.com
679 Southgate Dr., Guelph, ON N1G 4S2
Rev. Colin Butcher, Coordinator

A denominational service agency of Baptist and evangelical tradition engaged in relief aid, development, and medical work. The relief arm of FEBInternational.

Year Founded in Canada 1974
Income for Overseas Ministries . . $ 93,729

Far East Broadcasting Associates of Canada

(604)430-8439   **Fax: (604)430-5272**
E-Mail: KenReeve@bc.sympatico.com
Web: http://www.febc.org/febchome.html
6850 Antrim Ave., Burnaby, BC V5J 4M4
Mr. Don Patterson, Dir.- Intl. Broadcast Support
Mr. Ken Reeve, Dir. - Administration/Controller

An interdenominational specialized service agency of evangelical tradition engaged in broadcasting, audio recording/distribution, and literature distribution for evangelism and national church nurture.

Year Founded in Canada 1964
Income for Overseas Ministries $ 1,092,000
Fully Supported Canada Personnel Overseas:
    Expecting to serve more than 4 years 3
    Expecting to serve 1 up to 4 years 3
Other Personnel:
    Short-Term less than 1 year from Canada . . 3
    Home ministry & office staff in Canada . . . 19
Countries: Cambodia 1, Hong Kong 1, N Mariana Isls 1, Philippines 1, Thailand 1, UK 1.

FEBInternational

(519)821-4830   **Fax: (519)821-9829**
E-Mail: 103227.1367@compuserve.com
679 Southgate Dr., Guelph, ON N1G 4S2
Rev. Paul S. Kerr, Director

A denominational sending agency of Baptist and evangelical tradition engaged in church planting, extension education, TEE, and evangelism.

Year Founded in Canada   1964
Income for Overseas Ministries $ 2,721,000
Fully Supported Canada Personnel Overseas:
  Expecting to serve more than 4 years   80
  Expecting to serve 1 up to 4 years   9
Other Personnel:
  Bivocational/Tentmaker from Canada   6
  Short-Term less than 1 year from Canada   . . 12
  Home ministry & office staff in Canada   . . .   6
Countries: Asia 4, Belgium 10, Colombia 9, France 8,
Germany 2, Italy 2, Japan 10, Latin America 2, Nigeria
2, Pakistan 22, Singapore 2, Spain 6, Switzerland 2,
Venezuela 8.

Frontiers Canada
(604)275-7592   Fax: (604)275-7785
6240 London Rd., Richmond, BC V73 3S4
Mr. Bob Grandholm, Director

An interdenominational sending agency of
evangelical tradition engaged in church planting,
evangelism, support of national workers, and
missionary training.

".. working in close cooperation with local
churches to see vital, worshipping witnessing
churches established..."

Year Founded in Canada   1984
Income for Overseas Ministries   . $ 450,000
Fully Supported Canada Personnel Overseas:
  Expecting to serve more than 4 years   22
  Nonresidential mission personnel   3
Other Personnel:
  Non-Canadian serving in own/other country   .   3
  Bivocational/Tentmaker from Canada   2
  Home ministry & office staff in Canada   . . .   8
Countries: Africa 2, Asia 3, Central Asia 10, Europe 3,
Indonesia 4.

Fundamental Baptist Mission of Trinidad and Tobago (Canada)
(905)385-1503
38 Elora Dr., Unit #41, Hamilton, ON L9C 7L6
Mr. Ted R. Smith, Director

An independent support agency of Baptist and
fundamental tradition engaged in funds
transmission for national worker support.
Financial data included in USA sister agency.

Year Founded in Canada   1990
Income for Overseas Ministries   . . . .   NA
Personnel:
  Non-Canadian serving in own/other country   .   1

Countries: Trinidad & Tobg.

Galcom International
(905)574-4626   Fax: (905)574-4633
E-Mail: Galcom@galcom.org
65 Nebo Rd., Hamilton, ON L8W 2C9
Rev. Allan T. McGuirl, Intl. Director

An interdenominational support agency of
evangelical and fundamental tradition engaged in
designing, building and distributing hi-tech communications equipment for other agencies used in
evangelism and other ministries in 15 countries.

"To provide durable technical equipment for
communicating the Gospel worldwide .. at the
lowest possible price."

Year Founded in Canada   1989
Income for Overseas Ministries   . $ 213,845
Personnel:
  Home ministry & office staff in Canada   . . . 14

Glad Tidings Missionary Society
(604)873-3621   Fax: (604)876-1558
3456 Fraser St., Vancouver, BC V5V 4C4
Pastor Ernest C. Culley, President

A nondenominational sending agency of
independent tradition engaged in evangelism and
church planting.

Year Founded in Canada   1948
Income for Overseas Ministries   . $ 151,809
Fully Supported Canada Personnel Overseas:
  Expecting to serve more than 4 years   5
  Expecting to serve 1 up to 4 years   4
Other Personnel:
  Non-Canadian serving in own/other country   .   4
  Short-Term less than 1 year from Canada   . . 24
Countries: Mexico 4, Taiwan (ROC) 2, Uganda 3.

Global Outreach Mission
(905)684-1401
P.O. Box 1210, St. Catharines, ON L2R 7A7
Dr. James O. Blackwood, President

A transdenominational sending agency of
evangelical and independent tradition engaged in
church planting, broadcasting, evangelism,
medical work, and supplying equipment.

Year Founded in Canada   1943
Income for Overseas Ministries $ 1,192,883
Fully Supported Canada Personnel Overseas:

Expecting to serve more than 4 years 25
Other Personnel:
Home ministry & office staff in Canada . . . 8
Countries: Belgium 2, Brazil 1, Congo 1, France 3, Germany 2, Guatemala 4, Haiti 2, India 4, Ireland 4, S Africa 2.

Gospel for Asia
(905)574-8800   **Fax: (905)574-1849**
E-Mail: 104017.2011@compuserve.com
120 Lancing Dr. #6, Hamilton, ON L8W 3A1
Pastor Wendell Leytham, Canadian Director

A nondenominational support agency of evangelical tradition engaged in funds transmission for support of national workers and churches, Bible distribution, and training.

Year Founded in Canada 1985
Income for Overseas Ministries . $ 755,000
Personnel:
Home ministry & office staff in Canada . . . 3

Gospel Missionary Union of Canada
(204)338-7831   **Fax: (204)339-3321**
E-Mail: 76726.2126@compuserve.com
2121 Henderson Hwy., Winnipeg, MB R2G 1P8
Grant Morrison, VP Canadian Ministries

An interdenominational sending agency of Baptist and evangelical tradition engaged in church planting, church construction, correspondence courses, development, theological education, and youth programs.

Year Founded in Canada 1949
Income for Overseas Ministries $ 2,679,361
Fully Supported Canada Personnel Overseas:
Expecting to serve more than 4 years 85
Expecting to serve 1 up to 4 years 27
Other Personnel:
Short-Term less than 1 year from Canada . . 12
Home ministry & office staff in Canada . . . 11
Countries: Argentina 2, Austria 10, Bahamas 4, Belgium 3, Belize 4, Bolivia 38, Brazil 4, Colombia 1, Ecuador 6, Italy 1, Mali 14, Panama 3, Russia 15, Spain 5, UK 2.

Greater Europe Mission (Canada)
(905)728-8222   **Fax: (905)728-8958**
E-Mail: 74064.2661@compuserve.com
100 Ontario St., Oshawa, ON L1G 4Z1
Rev. Neil Rempel, Canadian Director

An interdenominational sending agency of evangelical tradition engaged in theological education, camping programs, church planting, TEE, evangelism, and literature distribution.

".. to assist the peoples of Europe in building up the Body of Christ so every person in Europe is within reach of a witnessing fellowship."

Year Founded in Canada 1959
Income for Overseas Ministries . $ 708,104
Fully Supported Canada Personnel Overseas:
Expecting to serve more than 4 years 11
Expecting to serve 1 up to 4 years 11
Other Personnel:
Short-Term less than 1 year from Canada . . 5
Home ministry & office staff in Canada . . . 4
Countries: Austria 2, France 3, Germany 2, Italy 2, Latvia 8, Luxembourg 2, Netherlands 2, Ukraine 1.

HCJB World Radio Missionary Fellowship in Canada
(905)821-6313   **Fax: (905)821-6314**
E-Mail: HCJBcan@mhs.wrmf.org
2476 Argentia Rd., Suite 201, Mississauga, ON L5N 6M1
Mr. Craig Cook, Director for Canada

An interdenominational sending agency of evangelical tradition engaged in broadcasting, correspondence courses, evangelism, medical work, and technical assistance.

Year Founded in Canada 1967
Income for Overseas Ministries $ 1,203,993
Fully Supported Canada Personnel Overseas:
Expecting to serve more than 4 years 32
Other Personnel:
Short-Term less than 1 year from Canada . . 5
Home ministry & office staff in Canada . . . 1
Countries: Ecuador 32.

High Adventure Gospel Communication Ministries

(905)898-5447   Fax: (905)898-5447
E-Mail: HiAdvCan@rogers.wave.ca
Web: http://www.highadventure.org
P.O. Box 425, Station E, Toronto, ON M6H 4E3
Mr. George K. Otis, President

An interdenominational support agency of charismatic and evangelical tradition engaged in broadcasting and Bible and literature distribution.

Year Founded in Canada 1979
Income for Overseas Ministries . . . . NR
Fully Supported Canada Personnel Overseas:
  Expecting to serve more than 4 years 1
Other Personnel:
  Home ministry & office staff in Canada . . . 3
Countries: Asia 1.

HOPE International Development Agency

(604)525-5481   Fax: (604)525-3471
E-Mail: Hope@web.apc.org
Web: http://web.idirect.com/~hope/index.html
P.O. Box 608, New Westminster, BC V3L 4Z3
Mr. David McKenzie, Exec. Director

An interdenominational service agency of independent tradition engaged in agricultural programs, relief aid, and technical assistance.

".. founded on Christian principles [to] provide alternate technological and educational support to people in developing countries where environmental, economic and/or social circumstances have interfered with the ability of local communities to sustain themselves..."

Year Founded in Canada 1975
Income for Overseas Ministries $ 9,500,000
Amount of Gifts-In-Kind . . . $ 6,000,000
Fully Supported Canada Personnel Overseas:
  Expecting to serve more than 4 years 2
  Expecting to serve 1 up to 4 years 7
  Nonresidential mission personnel 8
Other Personnel:
  Non-Canadian serving in own/other country   33
  Short-Term less than 1 year from Canada . . 24
  Home ministry & office staff in Canada . . . 15
Countries: Bangladesh, Cambodia 3, Dominican Rep, Ethiopia 2, Honduras, India, Namibia 2, Nepal, Philippines, Rwanda, S Africa 2, Sri Lanka, Sudan.

Inter-Varsity Christian Fellowship of Canada

(905)884-6880   Fax: (905)884-6550
E-Mail: National@ivcf.dar.com
Web: http://www.dar.com/ivcf
40 Vogell Road #17, Richmond Hill, ON L4B 3N6
Mr. James E. Berney, Gen. Director

An interdenominational support agency of evangelical tradition with the primary goal of fostering evangelism, spiritual development and missionary service among students and faculty in universities and other schools. Financial and personnel data from 1992.

Year Founded in Canada 1928
Income for Overseas Ministries . $ 200,297
Personnel:
  Short-Term less than 1 year from Canada . . 6
  Home ministry & office staff in Canada . . 120

International Child Care (Canada)

(905)821-6318   Fax: (905)821-6319
E-Mail: ICC.Canada@sympatico.ca
Web: http://www.intlchildcare.org
2476 Argentia Rd., #113, Mississauga, ON L5N 6M1
Mr. Dana Osburn, Natl. Director

An interdenominational sending agency of evangelical tradition engaged in childcare programs and providing medical supplies.

Year Founded in Canada 1972
Income for Overseas Ministries . $ 998,040
Amount of Gifts-In-Kind . . . $ 144,756
Fully Supported Canada Personnel Overseas:
  Expecting to serve more than 4 years 2
  Expecting to serve 1 up to 4 years 4
Other Personnel:
  Short-Term less than 1 year from Canada . . 4
  Home ministry & office staff in Canada . . . 1
Countries: Haiti 6.

International Children's Haven (Canada)

(604)794-3844
8169 Annis Road, Chilliwack, BC V2P 6H3
Mr. William Baerg, President

An interdenominational service agency of evangelical tradition engaged in childcare programs. Income amount from 1992.

Year Founded in Canada 1984
Income for Overseas Ministries . . $ 60,000

International Christian Aid Canada
(905)632-5703 **Fax: (905)632-5176**
P.O. Box 5090, Burlington, ON L7R 4G5
Mr. Kenneth D. Roe, Exec. Director

A nondenominational support agency of evangelical tradition engaged in relief aid, agricultural programs, development, and providing medical supplies. Statistical data from 1992.

Year Founded in Canada 1979
Income for Overseas Ministries $ 1,312,180
Personnel:
Home ministry & office staff in Canada . . . 6

International Missions in Ontario
(905)646-0228 **Fax: (905)646-8707**
P.O. Box 20164, St. Catharines, ON L2M 7W7
Rev. Robert Brown, Canadian Representative

An interdenominational sending agency of evangelical and independent tradition engaged in church planting, evangelism, literature distribution, and medical work.

"To .. proclaim the Gospel and .. establish local indigenous churches, primarily among unreached Asian communities worldwide."

Year Founded in Canada 1953
Income for Overseas Ministries . $ 308,564
Fully Supported Canada Personnel Overseas:
Expecting to serve more than 4 years 12
Other Personnel:
Short-Term less than 1 year from Canada . . 1
Home ministry & office staff in Canada . . . 3
Countries: Kenya 2, Pakistan 4, Philippines 4, UK 2.

International Needs - Canada
(403)340-0882 **Fax: (403)340-0882**
Web: http://www.ualberta.ca/~dharapnu/intlneed/
52 Harvey Close, Red Deer, AB T4N 6C4
Rev. Glenn Fretz, Exec. Director

A transdenominational service agency of evangelical tradition engaged in support of natl. workers, literature distribution, and youth programs.

".. to link Canadian Christians and churches with overseas ministries of INC that seek to inte-grate evangelism, discipleship, and fulfillment of human needs through effective development."

Year Founded in Canada 1976
Income for Overseas Ministries . $ 259,306
Personnel:
Non-Canadian serving in own/other country 53
Short-Term less than 1 year from Canada . . 2
Home ministry & office staff in Canada . . . 2
Countries: Ghana, Nepal, Philippines, Zambia.

International Teams of Canada
(604)437-8000
E-Mail: 72072.3310@compuserve.com
Web: http://www.iteams.org
5059 SE Marine Dr., Burnaby, BC V5J 3G5
Neil Ostrander, President

A nondenominational sending agency of evangelical tradition engaged in church planting, development, evangelism, relief aid, missionary training, and youth programs.

Year Founded in Canada 1966
Income for Overseas Ministries . $ 894,456
Fully Supported Canada Personnel Overseas:
Expecting to serve more than 4 years 17
Expecting to serve 1 up to 4 years 14
Other Personnel:
Non-Canadian serving in own/other country 27
Short-Term less than 1 year from Canada . 200
Home ministry & office staff in Canada . . . 23
Countries: Albania 1, Australia 1, Austria 7, Czech Rep 2, France 1, Germany 6, Hungary 2, Italy 2, Jamaica 1, Philippines 4, Poland 2, Romania, Russia, UK 2.

INTERSERVE (Canada)
(416)499-7511 **Fax: (416)499-4472**
E-Mail: 74140.3626@compuserve.com
10 Huntingdale Blvd, Scarborough, ON M1W 2S5
Mr. Craig Shugart, Exec. Director

An interdenominational service agency of evangelical tradition engaged in evangelism, church planting, correspondence courses, and extension education.

".. an international fellowship of Christian professionals .. discipling people in countries where traditional missionaries can't go."

Year Founded in Canada 1908
Income for Overseas Ministries . . . . NA
Fully Supported Canada Personnel Overseas:
Expecting to serve more than 4 years 16

Expecting to serve 1 up to 4 years 8
Other Personnel:
Bivocational/Tentmaker from Canada 8
Short-Term less than 1 year from Canada . . 12
Home ministry & office staff in Canada . . . 5
Countries: Asia 24.

Janz Team Ministries
(204)334-0055   Fax: (204)339-3321
E-Mail: JTMwpq@aol.com
2121 Henderson Hwy., Winnipeg, MB R2G 1R7
Mr. Marvin Thiessen, North American Director

An interdenominational sending agency of
evangelical tradition engaged in evangelism,
audio recording/distribution, camping programs,
Christian ed., and support of national churches.

Year Founded in Canada 1954
Income for Overseas Ministries $ 1,984,903
Fully Supported Canada Personnel Overseas:
Expecting to serve more than 4 years 58
Expecting to serve 1 up to 4 years 5
Nonresidential mission personnel 2
Other Personnel:
Non-Canadian serving in own/other country . 3
Bivocational/Tentmaker from Canada 1
Short-Term less than 1 year from Canada . . 9
Home ministry & office staff in Canada . . . 8
Countries: Brazil 6, Germany 53, Hungary 3, Portugal
1, Russia.

Japan Evangelistic Band (Canada)
(604)266-5772
3841 W. 38th Ave., Vancouver, BC V6N 2Y5
Mr. William F. Philip, Secy./Treasurer

An interdenominational support agency of
Holiness tradition engaged in theological
education and funds transmission. Information
from 1992.

Year Founded in Canada 1903
Income for Overseas Ministries . . $ 1,000
Personnel:
Home ministry & office staff in Canada . . . 1
Countries: Japan.

Language Recordings International
(905)574-8220   Fax: (905)574-6843
E-Mail: LRIcdn@inforamp.net
1059 Upper James St., Ste. 210, Hamilton, ON
L9C 3A6
Rev. Roy Grant, Exec. Director

An interdenominational service agency of
evangelical tradition engaged in audio recording
and distribution of Gospel messages in the
languages of unreached people groups.

Year Founded in Canada 1967
Income for Overseas Ministries . . $ 91,400
Fully Supported Canada Personnel Overseas:
Expecting to serve more than 4 years 4
Other Personnel:
Non-Canadian serving in own/other country . 4
Short-Term less than 1 year from Canada . . 2
Home ministry & office staff in Canada . . . 3
Countries: Kenya 4.

Latin America Mission (Canada)
(905)569-0001
3075 Ridgeway Dr. Unit #14, Mississauga, ON
L5L 5M6
Dr. Garth Wilson, Interim Director

An interdenominational service agency of
evangelical tradition engaged in evangelism,
theological ed., funds transmission, leadership
development, and support of national churches.

Year Founded in Canada 1961
Income for Overseas Ministries . . $ 513,142
Fully Supported Canada Personnel Overseas:
Expecting to serve more than 4 years 23
Other Personnel:
Non-Canadian serving in own/other country . 4
Short-Term less than 1 year from Canada . . 12
Home ministry & office staff in Canada . . . 3
Countries: Colombia 8, Costa Rica 10, Guatemala 2,
Mexico 3.

Leprosy Mission Canada, The
(416)441-3618   Fax: (416)441-0203
E-Mail: TLM@tlmcanada.org
Web: http://www.tlmcanada.org
75 The Donway West, Suite 1410, North York, ON
M3C 2E9
Rev. Peter Derrick, Exec. Director

An interdenominational service agency of evangelical tradition engaged in medical work, disability assistance programs, evangelism, and specialized missionary training.

Year Founded in Canada 1892
Income for Overseas Ministries . . . . NR
Fully Supported Canada Personnel Overseas:
Expecting to serve more than 4 years 3
Other Personnel:
Home ministry & office staff in Canada . . . 9
Countries: Unspecified 3.

Liebenzell Mission of Canada
(519)822-9748   Fax: (519)767-1069
E-Mail: LMCanada@sentex.net
R.R. 1,, Moffat, ON L0P 1J0
Rev. Karl-Heinz Dimmer, Exec. Director

An interdenominational sending agency of evangelical tradition engaged in church planting, theological education, evangelism, and leadership development.

Year Founded in Canada 1966
Income for Overseas Ministries . $ 260,000
Fully Supported Canada Personnel Overseas:
Expecting to serve more than 4 years 3
Other Personnel:
Short-Term less than 1 year from Canada . . 3
Home ministry & office staff in Canada . . . 2
Countries: Ecuador 2, Namibia 1.

Lutheran Bible Translators of Canada, Inc.
(519)742-3361   Fax: (519)742-5989
Box 934, Kitchener, ON N2G 4E3
Mrs. Carol Martin, Director

A denominational sending agency of Lutheran tradition engaged in Bible translation, funds transmission, and literacy work. Financial and personnel information from 1992.

Year Founded in Canada 1974
Income for Overseas Ministries . . $ 33,995
Fully Supported Canada Personnel Overseas:
Expecting to serve more than 4 years 2
Countries: Cameroon 2.

Mennonite Brethren Missions/ Services
(204)669-6575   Fax: (204)654-1865
E-Mail: 74577.332@compuserve.com
Web: http://www.mobynet.com/mbms/mbms.html
2-169 Riverton Ave., Winnipeg, MB R2L 2E5
Dave Dyck, Director of Programs

A denominational support agency of Mennonite and evangelical tradition engaged in church planting, agricultural programs, development, theological education, evangelism, and medical work. Financial and personnel totals combined in U.S. sister agency of the same name.

Year Founded in Canada 1878
Income for Overseas Ministries $ 3,270,964
Personnel:
Short-Term less than 1 year from Canada . . 9
Home ministry & office staff in Canada . . . 9

Mennonite Central Committee Canada
(204)261-6381   Fax: (204)269-9875
E-Mail: MCC@mennonitecc.ca
Web: http://www.mennonitecc.ca/mcc/
134 Plaza Dr., Winnipeg, MB R3T 5K9
Mr. Marvin Frey, Exec. Director

A denominational service agency of Mennonite tradition engaged in community development, agricultural programs, support of natl. churches, relief aid, and technical assistance. Financial and overseas personnel totals are consolidated in the Mennonite Central Comte. Intl. report.

Year Founded in Canada 1963
Income for Overseas Ministries . . . . NA
Personnel:
Home ministry & office staff in Canada . . . 53

Mennonite Economic Development Associates
(204)956-6430   Fax: (204)942-4001
E-Mail: 74260.125@compuserve.com
302-280 Smith St., Winnipeg, MB R3C 1K2
Dr. Ben Sprunger, President

A denominational service agency of Mennonite tradition engaged in technical assistance, agricultural programs, and management consulting/training.

Year Founded in Canada 1953
Income for Overseas Ministries $ 2,254,000
Fully Supported Canada Personnel Overseas:
   Expecting to serve 1 up to 4 years 4
   Nonresidential mission personnel 4
Other Personnel:
   Non-Canadian serving in own/other country 141
   Home ministry & office staff in Canada . . . 14
Countries: Bolivia, Cuba 1, Haiti, Nicaragua, Paraguay, Russia 1, Tanzania 2, Zimbabwe.

Middle East Christian Outreach - Canada

(905)453-5790　　　　**Fax: (905)453-5790**
P.O. Box 23555, Brampton, ON L6V 4J4
Mr. Don Joshua, Canadian Director

An interdenominational service agency of evangelical Christians engaged in evangelism, theological education, literature distribution, and support of national churches.

Year Founded in Canada 1976
Income for Overseas Ministries . . $ 28,000
Fully Supported Canada Personnel Overseas:
   Expecting to serve more than 4 years 1
Other Personnel:
   Short-Term less than 1 year from Canada . . 1
   Home ministry & office staff in Canada . . . 1
Countries: Asia 1.

Mission Aviation Fellowship of Canada

(519)821-3914　　　　**Fax: (519)823-1650**
E-Mail: Info@mafc.ccmail.compuserve.com
P.O. Box 368, Guelph, ON N1H 6K5
Mr. Eugene R. Parkins, President

A nondenominational specialized service agency of evangelical tradition engaged in aviation services, development, and technical assistance.

Year Founded in Canada 1972
Income for Overseas Ministries $ 2,500,000
Fully Supported Canada Personnel Overseas:
   Expecting to serve more than 4 years 59
   Expecting to serve 1 up to 4 years 7
Other Personnel:
   Short-Term less than 1 year from Canada . . 2
   Home ministry & office staff in Canada . . . 8
Countries: Angola 22, Botswana 4, Brazil 4, Congo/Zaire 2, Ethiopia 2, Germany 4, Indonesia 8, Kenya 2, Lesotho 2, Namibia 2, Papua New Guin 11, Tanzania 2, UK 1.

Mission Possible Canada

(519)285-2644
E-Mail: MissionPossible@odyssey.on.ca
Web: http://www.odyssey.on.ca/~missionpossible
P.O. Box 46047, London, ON N5W 3A1
James McKeegan, Board Vice-Chair

An interdenominational service agency of charismatic and evangelical tradition engaged in Christian education, medical work, and relief aid.

Year Founded in Canada 1994
Income for Overseas Ministries . . $ 56,071
Countries: Dominican Rep, Haiti.

Missionary Health Institute, Inc.

(416)494-7512　　　　**Fax: (416)492-3740**
E-Mail: MissHi@msn.com
4000 Leslie St., North York, ON M2K 2R9
Dr. K. L. Gamble, Exec. Director

An interdenominational service agency of evangelical tradition engaged in health care services, psychological counseling, mission-related health care research, and missionary orientation and re-entry workshops.

Year Founded in Canada 1936
Income for Overseas Ministries . . . . NR
Personnel:
   Home ministry & office staff in Canada . . . 9

Missionary Ventures of Canada

(519)824-5311　　　　**Fax: (519)824-9452**
E-Mail: Javco@in.on.ca
336 Speedvale Ave. W., Guelph, ON N1H 7M7
Mr. John Verdone, President

An interdenominational service agency of evangelical tradition engaged in short-term programs coordination for church and school construction, agricultural programs, and evangelism.

Year Founded in Canada 1991
Income for Overseas Ministries . $ 250,000
Personnel:
   Short-Term less than 1 year from Canada . . 50
   Home ministry & office staff in Canada . . . 2

MSC Canada

(416)920-4391   Fax: (416)920-7793
E-Mail: MSCCan@ican.net
27 Charles St., E., Toronto, ON M4Y 1R9
Mr. William Yuille, President

A service agency for Brethren assemblies missionaries sent by their local assemblies. Overseas personnel totals included in the Brethren Assemblies (Canada) report. Income total from 1992 report.

Year Founded in Canada   1940
Income for Overseas Ministries $ 3,846,315

Navigators of Canada, The

(519)666-0301   Fax: (519)666-2004
E-Mail: 71744.755@compuserve.com
Box 27070, London, ON N5X 3X5
Mr. Ross Rains, Canadian Director

An interdenominational sending agency of evangelical tradition engaged in evangelism and literature production/distribution. Financial and personnel information from 1992.

Year Founded in Canada   1960
Income for Overseas Ministries . $ 672,188
Fully Supported Canada Personnel Overseas:
   Expecting to serve more than 4 years   23
   Expecting to serve 1 up to 4 years   5
Countries: Argentina 2, Chile 2, Europe-E 3, UK 1, Unspecified 20.

New Tribes Mission of Canada

(519)369-2622   Fax: (519)369-5828
E-Mail: 74104.1576@compuserve.com
P.O. Box 707, Durham, ON N0G 1R0
Raymond Jones, Chairman

A nondenominational support agency of fundamental and independent tradition engaged in church planting, linguistics, literacy work, Bible translation, and missionary training.

".. to assist the ministry of the local church through the mobilizing, equipping, and coordinating of missionaries to evangelize unreached people groups, translate the Scriptures, and see indigenous New Testament churches established..."

Year Founded in Canada   1950
Income for Overseas Ministries $ 3,183,599

Fully Supported Canada Personnel Overseas:
   Expecting to serve more than 4 years   . . . 171
Other Personnel:
   Home ministry & office staff in Canada   . . . 30
Countries: Bolivia 11, Brazil 13, Colombia 4, Cote d'Ivoire 7, Guinea 8, Indonesia 7, Mexico 12, Panama 3, Papua New Guin 52, Paraguay 5, Philippines 2, Russia 2, Senegal 20, Thailand 4, Venezuela 21.

OMF Canada

(905)568-9971   Fax: (905)568-9974
Web: http://www.omf.org/world/ca/
5759 Coopers Ave., Mississauga, ON L4Z 1R9
Rev. William Fietje, National Director

An interdenominational sending agency of evangelical tradition engaged in church planting, theological education, evangelism, and literature distribution/production.

Year Founded in Canada   1888
Income for Overseas Ministries $ 1,251,905
Fully Supported Canada Personnel Overseas:
   Expecting to serve more than 4 years   73
   Expecting to serve 1 up to 4 years   9
Other Personnel:
   Bivocational/Tentmaker from Canada   5
   Short-Term less than 1 year from Canada   . . 58
   Home ministry & office staff in Canada   . . . 29
Countries: Asia 1, Hong Kong 1, Indonesia 6, Japan 12, Korea-S 2, Malaysia 4, Philippines 17, Singapore 4, Taiwan (ROC) 8, Thailand 27.

OMS International - Canada

(905)528-8723   Fax: (905)528-8148
P.O. Box 33522, Dundurn P.O., Hamilton, ON L8P 4X4
Dr. Stanley R. Dyer, Exec. Director

A nondenominational sending agency of Wesleyan and evangelical tradition engaged in theological education, church planting, evangelism, and support of national churches.

Year Founded in Canada   1944
Income for Overseas Ministries . . . .   NR
Fully Supported Canada Personnel Overseas:
   Expecting to serve more than 4 years   3
   Expecting to serve 1 up to 4 years   14
Other Personnel:
   Short-Term less than 1 year from Canada   . . 70
   Home ministry & office staff in Canada   . . 6
Countries: Ecuador 2, Estonia 3, Haiti 3, Hong Kong 1, Indonesia 2, Japan 2, Korea-S 1, Mexico 1, Russia 2.

Open Doors With Brother Andrew
(905)567-1303   Fax: (905)567-9398
P.O. Box 597, Streetsville, ON L5M 2C1
Rev. Paul W. Johnson, Director for Canada

A nondenominational support agency of
evangelical tradition engaged in literature and
Bible distribution, broadcasting, and training.

Year Founded in Canada 1977
Income for Overseas Ministries . $ 339,264
Fully Supported Canada Personnel Overseas:
Expecting to serve more than 4 years 4
Other Personnel:
Short-Term less than 1 year from Canada . . 60
Home ministry & office staff in Canada . . . 3
Countries: Asia 4.

Operation Mobilization - Canada
(905)835-2546   Fax: (905)835-2533
E-Mail: Info@omcdn.om.org
Web: http://www.om.org/
212 West St., Port Colborne, ON L3K 4E3
Gordon Abraham, Exec. Director

An interdenominational sending agency of
evangelical tradition engaged in evangelism,
Bible distribution, church planting, leadership
development, literature distribution, support of
national workers, mobilization for mission, and
missionary training.

".. to motivate, develop and equip people for
world evangelization, and to strengthen and help
plant churches, especially among the unreached
in the Middle East, South and Central Asia, and
Europe."

Year Founded in Canada 1966
Income for Overseas Ministries $ 1,200,000
Fully Supported Canada Personnel Overseas:
Expecting to serve more than 4 years 28
Expecting to serve 1 up to 4 years 43
Nonresidential mission personnel 1
Other Personnel:
Non-Canadian serving in own/other country . 2
Bivocational/Tentmaker from Canada 5
Short-Term less than 1 year from Canada . . 39
Home ministry & office staff in Canada . . . 14
Countries: Africa 4, Asia 8, Austria 2, Belgium 1,
Central Asia 4, Czech Rep 1, Finland 2, Germany 4,
Hungary 4, India 2, Malaysia 2, Mexico 1, Pakistan 3,
S Africa 4, Sudan 2, Sweden 2, UK 3, Ukraine 2,
Unspecified 17, Uruguay 3.

Outreach Canada
(604)272-0732   Fax: (604)272-2744
E-Mail: Info@outreach.ca
Web: http://www.outreach.ca
16-12240 Horseshoe Way, Richmond, BC
V7A 4X9
Dr. Gerald Kraft, Exec. Director

An interdenominational support agency of
evangelical tradition engaged in mission-related
research and information services, management
consulting/training, and support of natl. churches.

Year Founded in Canada 1977
Income for Overseas Ministries . . $ 50,000
Personnel:
Home ministry & office staff in Canada . . . 8

Overseas Missionary Fellowship
See: OMF Canada

Partners International Canada
(905)458-1202   Fax: (905)458-4339
8500 Torbram Rd. #48, Brampton, ON L6T 5C6
Rev. Grover Crosby, President

A nondenominational support agency of evangelical tradition engaged in support of national
workers and churches, and funds transmission.
Previously CNEC - Partners International.

Year Founded in Canada 1959
Income for Overseas Ministries . $ 830,000
Personnel:
Home ministry & office staff in Canada . . . 6

Pentecostal Assemblies of Canada, Overseas Missions
(905)542-7400   Fax: (905)542-7313
E-Mail: OMD@paoc.org
Web: http://www.epbc.edu/paoc/
6745 Century Ave., Mississauga, ON L5N 6P7
Rev. Stewart Hunter, Director Overseas Missions

A denominational sending agency of
Pentecostal tradition engaged in church planting,
theological education, TEE, literature distribution, support of national churches, and relief
aid. Financial and personnel data from 1992.

Year Founded in Canada 1919
Income for Overseas Ministries $ 7,956,594

Fully Supported Canada Personnel Overseas:
Expecting to serve more than 4 years . . . 167
Expecting to serve 1 up to 4 years 8
Other Personnel:
Bivocational/Tentmaker from Canada 10
Short-Term less than 1 year from Canada . 416
Home ministry & office staff in Canada . . . 15
Countries: Brazil 12, China (PRC) 2, Cote d'Ivoire 2, Estonia 2, Greece 4, Guinea 6, Hong Kong 7, Iceland 2, India 1, Indonesia 4, Israel 2, Kenya 34, Liberia 3, Macao 2, Malawi 10, Mozambique 4, Netherlands 2, S Africa 6, Senegal 2, Seychelles 2, Spain 4, Sri Lanka 5, Taiwan (ROC) 4, Tanzania 12, Thailand 17, Uganda 6, Zambia 6, Zimbabwe 12.

Persecuted Church Fellowship

(604)278-0692   Fax: (604)279-9080
15620 Westminster Hwy, Richmond, BC V6V 1A6
Mr. Michael S. Lapka, President

An interdenominational service agency of evangelical tradition supporting national workers in evangelism and Bible/literature distribution.

Year Founded in Canada 1976
Income for Overseas Ministries . . $ 75,000
Personnel:
Non-Canadian serving in own/other country   30
Short-Term less than 1 year from Canada . . 3
Countries: Russia, Ukraine.

Pioneers

(519)268-8778   Fax: (519)268-2787
E-Mail: pi.canada@onlinesys.com
Web: http://www.pioneers.org
P.O. Box 220, Dorchester, ON N0L 1G0
Mr. Neale Unruh, Canadian Managing Director

A nondenominational service agency of evangelical tradition engaged in church planting, evangelism, and mobilization for mission.

".. mobilizes teams to glorify God among unreached peoples by initiating church planting movements in partnership with local churches."

Year Founded in Canada 1981
Income for Overseas Ministries . $ 510,627
Fully Supported Canada Personnel Overseas:
Expecting to serve more than 4 years 9
Expecting to serve 1 up to 4 years 1
Other Personnel:
Non-Canadian serving in own/other country . 1
Short-Term less than 1 year from Canada . . 45
Home ministry & office staff in Canada . . . 3

Countries: Asia 1, Belize 2, Bolivia 5, Brazil 2.

Presbyterian Church in Canada, Life and Mission Agency

(416)441-1111   Fax: (416)441-2825
50 Wynford Dr., North York, ON M3C 1J7
Rev. Ian Morrison, Gen. Secretary

A denominational sending agency of Presbyterian and Reformed tradition engaged in support of national churches, development, theological education, leadership development, and medical work. Income amount from 1992.

Year Founded in Canada 1875
Income for Overseas Ministries $ 2,600,000
Fully Supported Canada Personnel Overseas:
Expecting to serve more than 4 years 32
Expecting to serve 1 up to 4 years 15
Countries: Asia 1, Congo/Zaire 2, Guatemala 1, Hong Kong 1, India 5, Japan 3, Kenya 4, Latin America 1, Malawi 6, Mauritius 6, Mozambique 1, Nepal 5, Nicaragua 3, Nigeria 4, S Africa 1, Taiwan (ROC) 3.

RBMU International
See: World Team

Salvation Army, The

(416)425-2111   Fax: (416)422-6102
E-Mail: RJBowles@sallynet.org
Web: http://www.sallynet.org
2 Overlea Blvd., Toronto, ON M4H 1P4
Donald Kerr, Commissioner

A denominational sending agency of Holiness and evangelical tradition engaged in evangelism, childcare programs, development, Christian education, relief aid, and youth programs. Financial and personnel information from 1992.

Year Founded in Canada 1882
Income for Overseas Ministries $ 6,172,171
Fully Supported Canada Personnel Overseas:
Expecting to serve more than 4 years 51
Expecting to serve 1 up to 4 years 6
Other Personnel:
Bivocational/Tentmaker from Canada 6
Short-Term less than 1 year from Canada . . 19
Home ministry & office staff in Canada . . . 14
Countries: Argentina 1, Bangladesh 2, Barbados 2, Brazil 4, Congo/Zaire 1, France 4, Germany 2, Hungary 4, Indonesia 1, Jamaica 2, Japan 1, Kenya 3, New Zealand 2, Pakistan 5, Papua New Guin 2, Portugal 1, Russia 2, S Africa 9, Zambia 4, Zimbabwe 5.

Samaritan's Purse - Canada
(403)250-6565   **Fax: (403)250-6567**
E-Mail: Canada@samaritan.org
Web: http://www.samaritan.org/
Box 20100, Calgary Pl., Calgary, AB T2P 4J2
Rev. Sean P. Campbell, Exec. Director
Franklin Graham, President

A nondenominational support agency of
evangelical tradition engaged in relief aid,
evangelism, funds transmission, childrens
programs, and providing medical supplies.

".. specializing in meeting the needs of victims
of war, poverty, natural disasters, and disease
while sharing the Good News of Jesus Christ."

Year Founded in Canada 1973
Income for Overseas Ministries $ 5,200,000
Amount of Gifts-In-Kind . . . $ 3,310,000
Fully Supported Canada Personnel Overseas:
  Nonresidential mission personnel 1
Other Personnel:
  Short-Term less than 1 year from Canada . 135
  Home ministry & office staff in Canada . . . 8

Scripture Gift Mission (Canada)
(905)475-0521   **Fax: (905)475-8643**
#32-300 Steelcase Rd., Markham, ON L3R 2W2
Rev. Jim Wright, Exec. Director

A nondenominational support agency of evangelical tradition providing Scripture leaflets for
evangelism and edification in many languages.

Year Founded in Canada 1947
Income for Overseas Ministries . . $ 10,000
Personnel:
  Home ministry & office staff in Canada . . . 3

SEND International of Canada
(519)657-6775   **Fax: (519)657-7027**
E-Mail: 74741.1220@compuserve.com
22423 Jefferies Rd., Unit 7, R.R.#3, Komoka, ON
N0L 1R0
Rev. Leander Rempel, Director

An interdenominational sending agency of
Baptist and evangelical tradition engaged in
church planting, broadcasting, theological
education, evangelism, leadership development,
and support of national churches.

".. to glorify God through establishing the
Church of Jesus Christ where it does not exist
and serving it where it does exist."

Year Founded in Canada 1963
Income for Overseas Ministries $ 1,256,630
Fully Supported Canada Personnel Overseas:
  Expecting to serve more than 4 years 33
  Expecting to serve 1 up to 4 years 1
Other Personnel:
  Short-Term less than 1 year from Canada . . 25
  Home ministry & office staff in Canada . . . 14
Countries: CIS 3, Hong Kong 3, Japan 5, Philippines
19, Spain 4.

SIM Canada
(416)497-2424   **Fax: (416)497-2444**
E-Mail: postmast@sim.ca
Web: http://www.sim.org
10 Huntingdale Blvd, Scarborough, ON M1W 2S5
Dr. Arnell Motz, Exec. Director

An interdenominational sending agency of
evangelical and Baptist tradition engaged in
church planting, broadcasting, theological ed.,
medical work, relief aid, and Bible translation.

".. evangelizing the unreached and ministering
to human need, discipling believers into churches
equipped to fulfill Christ's Commission."

Year Founded in Canada 1893
Income for Overseas Ministries $ 6,544,949
Fully Supported Canada Personnel Overseas:
  Expecting to serve more than 4 years 65
  Expecting to serve 1 up to 4 years 17
  Nonresidential mission personnel 2
Other Personnel:
  Non-Canadian serving in own/other country 17
  Short-Term less than 1 year from Canada . . 63
  Home ministry & office staff in Canada . . . 62
Countries: Bangladesh, Benin 15, Bolivia 4, Burkina
Faso 10, Chile 1, Cote d'Ivoire 3, Ecuador 1, Ethiopia
13, Ghana 6, India 3, Kenya 1, Niger 12, Nigeria 6,
Pakistan 3, Paraguay 1, Peru 3.

Slavic Gospel Assoc. of Canada
(905)821-6321   **Fax: (905)821-6322**
P.O. Box 250, Mississauga, ON L5M 2B8
Rev. Robert W. Irvin, Canadian Director

An interdenominational service agency of
evangelical tradition engaged in Bible
distribution and correspondence courses.

Year Founded in Canada 1947

Income for Overseas Ministries . . . . NR

South American Missionary Society in Canada

(705)728-7151   Fax: (705)728-6703
E-Mail: DStock@central.georcoll.on.ca
Box 21082, Barrie, ON L4M 6JI
Dr. C.P.S. Taylor, Chairman

A denominational sending agency of Anglican and evangelical tradition engaged in mobilization for mission, leadership development, evangelism, and support of national workers.

".. to find and send those whom God is calling to the mission field, and to widen and deepen the missionary vision of Canadian Anglicans."

Year Founded in Canada 1979
Income for Overseas Ministries . . $ 93,824
Fully Supported Canada Personnel Overseas:
    Expecting to serve more than 4 years 2
    Expecting to serve 1 up to 4 years 1
Other Personnel:
    Non-Canadian serving in own/other country . 6
    Short-Term less than 1 year from Canada . . 30
    Home ministry & office staff in Canada . . . 3
Countries: Honduras 3.

Student Mission Advance

(905)572-6992   Fax: (905)572-6518
E-Mail: SMA@netaccess.on.ca
Web: http://www.netaccess.on.ca/fingertip
Box 91051 Effort Sq., Hamilton, ON L8N 4G3
Sam Aragones, Exec. Director

An interdenominational support agency of evangelical tradition engaged in mobilization for cross-cultural mission involvement.

Year Founded in Canada 1984
Income for Overseas Ministries . . . . NA
Personnel:
    Home ministry & office staff in Canada . . . 4

TEAM - The Evangelical Alliance Mission of Canada

(403)250-2140   Fax: (403)291-2857
E-Mail: 72102.440@compuserve.com
Airways P.O. Box 56030, Calgary, AB T2E 8K5
Lorne Strom, Director

A nondenominational sending agency of evangelical tradition engaged in church planting, camping programs, theological education, evangelism, linguistics, and medical work.

".. to help [local] churches send missionaries to plant reproducing churches in other nations."

Year Founded in Canada 1890
Income for Overseas Ministries $ 2,580,794
Fully Supported Canada Personnel Overseas:
    Expecting to serve more than 4 years 75
    Expecting to serve 1 up to 4 years 4
Other Personnel:
    Bivocational/Tentmaker from Canada 2
    Short-Term less than 1 year from Canada . . 9
    Home ministry & office staff in Canada . . 9
Countries: Brazil 2, Chad 5, France 5, Germany 2, India 3, Indonesia 2, Italy 5, Japan 13, Nepal 2, Neth Antilles 3, Pakistan 7, Peru 3, S Africa 3, Spain 2, Taiwan (ROC) 2, Trinidad & Tobg 2, United Arab Emr 4, Unspecified 1, Venezuela 9, Zimbabwe 4.

Trinitarian Bible Society (Canada)

(905)454-4688   Fax: (905)454-1788
E-Mail: TBSC@mail.ica.net
Web: http://www.trinitarian.com
39 Caldwell Crescent, Brampton, ON L6W 1A2
Dr. Robert A. Baker, General Director

A nondenominational service agency of evangelical and fundamental tradition engaged in Bible distribution and translation. Financial information from 1992.

Year Founded in Canada 1968
Income for Overseas Ministries . $ 169,969
Personnel:
    Home ministry & office staff in Canada . . . 2

UFM International In Canada

(905)238-0904   Fax: (905)629-8439
E-Mail: UFMCan@mail.ican.net
Web: http://www.ufm.org
1020 Matheson Blvd. E. #11, Mississauga, ON L4W 4J9
Mr. Dale Losch, Managing Director

An interdenominational sending agency of evangelical and Baptist tradition engaged in church planting, missionary education, TEE, evangelism, and medical work. Financial and personnel information from 1992.

Year Founded in Canada 1931

Income for Overseas Ministries $ 1,200,000
Fully Supported Canada Personnel Overseas:
   Expecting to serve more than 4 years   44
   Expecting to serve 1 up to 4 years   2
Other Personnel:
   Short-Term less than 1 year from Canada   . .   6
   Home ministry & office staff in Canada   . . .   5
Countries: Brazil 17, Congo/Zaire 1, Dominican Rep 2,
   France 3, Germany 2, Guyana 2, Haiti 6, Indonesia 6,
   Ireland 6, Japan 1.

United Church of Canada, Division of World Outreach

(416)231-5931   **Fax: (416)232-6008**
E-Mail: UCCDWO@uccan.org
Web: http://www.uccan.org
3250 Bloor St. West, Etobicoke, ON M8X 2Y4
Ms. Rhea M. Whitehead, Gen. Secretary

A denominational sending agency of
ecumenical tradition engaged in development,
agricultural programs, extension education, funds
transmission, and missionary training. Financial
and personnel information from 1992.

Year Founded in Canada   1925
Income for Overseas Ministries $ 9,000,000
Fully Supported Canada Personnel Overseas:
   Expecting to serve more than 4 years   96
Countries: Africa, Asia, Caribbean Isls, Latin America,
   Oceania, Unspecified 96.

Venture Teams International

(403)777-2970   **Fax: (403)777-2973**
E-Mail: VTI@spots.ab.ca
Web: www.netaccess.on.ca/~sma/gallery/
vti/display/display.htm
#3A, 3023 - 21st St. NE, Calgary, AB T2E 7T1
Mr. Len Lane, Exec. Director

An interdenominational service agency of
evangelical tradition engaged in evangelism,
youth programs, and other forms of ministry
outreach through short-term internship teams.
Financial and personnel information from 1992.

Year Founded in Canada   1978
Income for Overseas Ministries   . . $ 53,295
Personnel:
   Short-Term less than 1 year from Canada   . . 18
   Home ministry & office staff in Canada   . . . 15

Voice of The Martyrs, The

(905)602-4832   **Fax: (905)602-4833**
E-Mail: VOM@planeteer.com
Box 117, Port Credit, Mississauga, ON L5G 4L5
Mr. Klaas Brobbel, Exec. Director

A nondenominational service agency of
evangelical tradition engaged in Bible distribution, broadcasting, and literature production/
distribution. Statistical information from 1992.

Year Founded in Canada   1971
Income for Overseas Ministries   . $ 250,000
Fully Supported Canada Personnel Overseas:
   Expecting to serve 1 up to 4 years   2
   Nonresidential mission personnel   2
Other Personnel:
   Home ministry & office staff in Canada   . . .   3
Countries: Costa Rica 2.

WEC International (Canada)

(905)529-0166   **Fax: (905)529-0630**
E-Mail: 76604.1246@compuserve.com
Web: http://www.netaccess.on.ca/fingertip/
37 Aberdeen Ave., Hamilton, ON L8P 2N6
Drs. Philip & Nancy Wood, Canadian Directors

An interdenominational sending agency of
evangelical tradition engaged in church planting,
TEE, evangelism, medical work, and Bible
translation.

".. to evangelize the unreached peoples .. to
establish fully discipled, self governing, self
supporting and reproducing churches able to
fulfill their part in the Great Commission."

Year Founded in Canada   1936
Income for Overseas Ministries   . $ 913,416
Fully Supported Canada Personnel Overseas:
   Expecting to serve more than 4 years   76
Other Personnel:
   Short-Term less than 1 year from Canada   . .   7
   Home ministry & office staff in Canada   . . . 23
Countries: Africa 6, Asia 31, Belgium 2, Brazil 2,
   Cambodia 2, Central Asia 8, Congo/Zaire 4, Cote
   d'Ivoire 4, Equat Guinea 2, Gambia 3, Ghana 2, Mexico
   2, Senegal 2, Singapore 2, Thailand 1, UK 3.

Western Tract Mission, Inc.

(306)244-0446
104 - 33rd St., West, Saskatoon, SK S7L 0V5
David Wolfrom, Chairman of the Board

An interdenominational service agency of evangelical tradition engaged in literature production/distribution for evangelistic efforts and correspondence courses.

Year Founded in Canada 1941
Income for Overseas Ministries . . . . NA
Personnel:
Home ministry & office staff in Canada . . . 13

World Gospel Mission (Canada)
(506)468-2116   **Fax: (506)468-2118**
E-Mail: Doxa@mi.net
P.O. Box 58, Pennfield, NB E0G 2R0
Rev. Brian Murray, Board Chair

An interdenominational support agency of Wesleyan tradition engaged in evangelism, church planting, and theological education. Income amount from 1992. Personnel totals consolidated in U.S. report.

Year Founded in Canada 1982
Income for Overseas Ministries . . $ 91,525

World Mission Prayer League
(403)672-0464   **Fax: (403)672-0464**
E-Mail: wmpl_canada@wildrose.net
5408 49th Ave., Camrose, AB T4V 0N7
Rev. Rob Lewis, Exec. Director

A denominational sending agency of Lutheran tradition engaged in evangelism, agricultural programs, and Christian education. Financial and personnel information from 1992.

Year Founded in Canada 1969
Income for Overseas Ministries . $ 121,823
Fully Supported Canada Personnel Overseas:
Expecting to serve more than 4 years 8
Expecting to serve 1 up to 4 years 2
Other Personnel:
Home ministry & office staff in Canada . . . 2
Countries: Bolivia 2, Ecuador 2, Kenya 1, Mexico 2, Pakistan 3.

World Radio Missionary Fellowship in Canada (HCJB)
See: HCJB World Radio Msnry. Flwshp

World Relief Canada
(905)415-8181   **Fax: (905)415-0287**
E-Mail: 71102.1204@compuserve.com
600 Alden Rd., Suite 310, Markham, ON L3R 0E7
Rev. Doug Stiller, President

An interdenominational service agency of evangelical tradition engaged in relief aid and community development. Financial and personnel information from 1992.

Year Founded in Canada 1982
Income for Overseas Ministries $ 5,593,254
Fully Supported Canada Personnel Overseas:
Expecting to serve more than 4 years 7
Countries: Angola 6, Lebanon 1.

World Team
(905)821-6300   **Fax: (905)821-6325**
E-Mail: 74071.203@compuserve.com
Web: http://www.worldteam.org/
2476 Argentia Road, Suite 203, Mississauga, ON L5N 6M1
Rev. Kenneth Bennett, Canadian Director

A nondenominational sending agency of evangelical tradition engaged in church planting, theological education, evangelism, and Bible translation. Merger of Worldteam and RBMU International in 1995.

".. to establish reproducing churches among the least-evangelized peoples of the world."

Year Founded in Canada 1948
Income for Overseas Ministries . $ 783,430
Fully Supported Canada Personnel Overseas:
Expecting to serve more than 4 years 49
Expecting to serve 1 up to 4 years 11
Other Personnel:
Non-Canadian serving in own/other country . 2
Bivocational/Tentmaker from Canada 2
Short-Term less than 1 year from Canada . . 8
Home ministry & office staff in Canada . . . 13
Countries: Brazil 1, Cameroon 5, Cen Africa Rep, Cuba 2, Haiti 6, Indonesia 15, Italy 3, Mexico 2, Peru 8, Philippines 14, Russia 2, Trinidad & Tobg 2.

World Vision Canada

(905)821-3030   **Fax: (905)821-1825**
E-Mail: Info@worldvision.ca
Web: http://www.worldvision.ca
6630 Turner Valley Road, Mississauga, ON
L5N 2S4
Dave Toycen, President

A transdenominational service agency of evangelical and ecumenical tradition engaged in childcare programs, community development, medical work, leadership development, relief aid, and rehabilitation.

".. a Christian humanitarian relief and development organization inviting Canadians to share their resources to empower people living in poverty."

Year Founded in Canada 1954
Income for Overseas Ministries $ 65,183,000
Amount of Gifts-In-Kind . . . $ 463,000
Fully Supported Canada Personnel Overseas:
  Expecting to serve more than 4 years 3
  Expecting to serve 1 up to 4 years 13
Other Personnel:
  Home ministry & office staff in Canada . . 303
Countries: Angola, Armenia, Azerbaijan, Bangladesh, Belarus, Bolivia, Botswana, Brazil, Burundi 1, Cambodia 1, Chad, Chile, China (PRC), Colombia, Congo/Zaire, Costa Rica, Croatia, Cyprus, Dominican Rep, Ecuador, Egypt, El Salvador, Eritrea, Ethiopia 2, Fiji, Gaza, Georgia, Guatemala, Haiti, Honduras, Hungary, India, Indonesia, Israel, Jamaica, Jordan, Kenya, Laos, Lebanon, Lesotho, Liberia, Malawi 2, Mali, Mauritania, Mexico, Mozambique 1, Myanmar/Burma, Nepal, Nicaragua, Niger, Nigeria, Panama, Peru, Philippines, Romania, Russia 2, Rwanda 3, S Africa, Senegal 1, Sierra Leone, Somalia, Sri Lanka, Sudan 1, Suriname, Swaziland, Tanzania 2, Thailand, Tonga, Turkey, Uganda, Ukraine, Vietnam, West Bank, Zambia, Zimbabwe.

Wycliffe Bible Translators of Canada

(403)250-5411   **Fax: (403)250-2623**
E-Mail: general_CAD_delivery@wycliffe.org
Web: http://www.wbtc.org
P.O. Box 3068, Station B, Calgary, AB T2M 4L6
Mr. Jack Popjes, Exec. Director

An interdenominational sending agency of evangelical tradition engaged in Bible translation, literacy work, community development, linguistics, and training for mission personnel.

"[To] challenge, train and assist Canadians to serve indigenous peoples through Bible translation and literacy-based development."

Year Founded in Canada 1968
Income for Overseas Ministries $ 5,000,000
Fully Supported Canada Personnel Overseas:
  Expecting to serve more than 4 years . . . 385
  Expecting to serve 1 up to 4 years 20
Other Personnel:
  Short-Term less than 1 year from Canada . . 30
Countries: Africa 4, Asia 16, Australia 4, Benin 2, Bolivia 1, Brazil 13, Burkina Faso 7, Cameroon 24, Cen Africa Rep 2, Chad 2, Colombia 15, Congo 4, Congo/Zaire 5, Cote d'Ivoire 3, Ecuador 2, Europe-W 10, Ghana 6, Guatemala 10, Guyana 2, India 3, Indonesia 9, Kenya 6, Malaysia 3, Mexico 14, Mozambique 5, New Zealand 4, Nigeria 1, Panama 2, Papua New Guin 40, Peru 11, Philippines 29, Suriname 5, Thailand 6, Togo 1, Unspecified 134.

Young Life of Canada

(604)688-7622   **Fax: (604)688-3125**
E-Mail: YLife@alternatives.com
Web: www.alternatives.com/groups/ylife/index.htm
1155 W. Pender, #610, Vancouver, BC V6E 2P4
Mr. Harold J. Merwald, Natl. Director

A transdenominational ministry of evangelical tradition engaged in evangelism, youth programs, leadership development, and camping programs.

Year Founded in Canada 1954
Income for Overseas Ministries . . $ 75,000
Amount of Gifts-In-Kind . . . . $ 35,000
Personnel:
  Non-Canadian serving in own/other country . 1
  Home ministry & office staff in Canada . . . 60
Countries: Brazil.

Youth for Christ - Canada

(403)291-1197   **Fax: (403)291-1197**
E-Mail: YFCCan@cadvision.com
1212 - 31 Ave. N.E., #540, Calgary, AB T2E 7S8
Randy Steinwand, National Director

A transdenominational support agency of evangelical tradition engaged in student evangelism and short-term programs coordination.

Year Founded in Canada 1944
Income for Overseas Ministries . $ 150,000
Personnel:
  Bivocational/Tentmaker from Canada . . . 50
  Short-Term less than 1 year from Canada . . 40

Home ministry & office staff in Canada   .   .   200

Youth With A Mission (Canada)
(250)766-3838   Fax: (250)766-2387
E-Mail: 102636.432@compuserve.com
Box 922, Winfield, BC 4OH 2C0
Loren Cunningham, Intl. Director
Paul Martinson, Canadian Director

A sending agency of charismatic and
evangelical tradition engaged in evangelism,
missionary education, mobilization for mission,
relief aid, and youth programs.

Year Founded in Canada   1966
Income for Overseas Ministries . . . . NR
Fully Supported Canada Personnel Overseas:
   Expecting to serve more than 4 years   . . .   350
Other Personnel:
   Short-Term less than 1 year from Canada   .   400
Countries: Albania 1, Argentina 2, Australia 9, Belize 2,
   Brazil 11, Costa Rica 1, Fiji 3, France 1, Greece 1,
   Greenland 3, Grenada 3, Guinea Bissau 1, Guyana 3,
   Haiti 1, Hong Kong 1, Hungary 2, India 6, Ireland 1,
   Japan 2, Mexico 4, Mozambique 1, Netherlands 16,
   New Zealand 4, Paraguay 1, Philippines 5, S Africa 2,
   Sierra Leone 1, Singapore 2, Spain 1, Sweden 6,
   Thailand 3, UK 11, Ukraine 5, Unspecified 234.

Chapter 8

Indices to Canadian Protestant agencies

Many *Handbook* users find it valuable to locate agencies by particular categories of church tradition or ministry activity. This chapter provides the user with those indices. Agency responses on the *Mission Handbook* survey questionnaire helped define the categories that are listed. The organizations in each category appear in alphabetical order by organization name.

Index by church tradition

If an agency needed more than one generic or denominational category to describe its traditional doctrinal and/or ecclesiastical stance, the agency may appear under as many as two of the given categories. We have arranged the list alphabetically by category and within each category by agency name. See question #7 of the survey questionnaire reproduced in the appendix for the actual wording of the question and the check-off list of choices.

Index by ministry activity

Almost all agencies are involved in several types of ministry activities. Each agency may be listed under as many as six primary categories of activity. We asked those with more than six primary activities to indicate the six activities toward which they had committed the largest amount of resources.

We have divided the broad activities of education and evangelism into subcategories. For example, the evangelism category appears as "evangelism, mass" and "evangelism, student," and so on. See question #8 of the survey questionnaire in the appendix for the actual wording of the question and the check-off list of activities.

Agencies often convey new categories under the "other" choice in the previous survey, so we usually add or reword three or four categories for the new survey. Sometimes we drop categories because of lack of use. The most-used categories, however, have remained the same over the years.

ANGLICAN

Anglican Church of Canada
South American Missionary Soc.

BAPTIST

ABWE - Canada
Assoc. of Regular Baptist Chs.
Associated Gospel Churches
BGCC Global Ministries
Canadian Baptist Ministries
Canadian Conv. of So. Baptists
Czechoslovak Evangelical Msn.
FAIR
FEBInternational
Fundamental Baptist Mission
Gospel Missionary Union Canada
SEND International of Canada
SIM Canada
UFM International In Canada

CHARISMATIC

High Adventure Ministries
Mission Possible Canada

CHRISTIAN/PLYMOUTH BRETHREN

Brethren Assemblies (Canada)
Everyday Publications, Inc.
MSC Canada

ECUMENICAL

Canadian Bible Society
Canadian Churches' Forum
United Church of Canada
World Vision Canada

EVANGELICAL

Action International Mins.
Africa Community Technical Svc
Africa Evangelical Fellowship
Africa Inland Mission (Canada)
African Enterprise Association
Arab World Ministries (Canada)
Associated Gospel Churches

Barry Moore Ministries
BCM International (Canada)
Bible League of Canada, The
Calcutta Mission of Mercy
Campus Crusade for Christ
Canadian S. American Mission
Centre for World Mission B.C.
Child Evangelism Fellowship
Christian Aid Mission
Christian and Msny. Alliance
Christian Blind Mission Intl.
Christian Indigenous Dev.
Compassion Canada
Croisade du Livre Chretien
Door of Hope Intl. (Canada)
Emmanuel International
European Christian Mission
Eurovangelism
Evangelical Covenant Ch Canada
Evangelical Tract Distributors
FAIR
Far East Broadcasting Assocs.
FEBInternational
Frontiers Canada
Galcom International
Global Outreach Mission
Gospel for Asia
Gospel Missionary Union Canada
Greater Europe Mission
HCJB World Radio Msnry. Flwshp
High Adventure Ministries
Inter-Varsity Christian Flwshp
International Child Care
International Children's Haven
International Christian Aid
International Missions Ontario
International Needs - Canada
International Teams of Canada
INTERSERVE (Canada)
Janz Team Ministries
Language Recordings Intl.
Latin America Mission (Canada)
Leprosy Mission Canada
Liebenzell Mission of Canada
Mennonite Brethren Missions
Middle East Christian Outreach
Mission Aviation Flwshp Canada
Mission Possible Canada

Missionary Health Institute
Missionary Ventures of Canada
Navigators of Canada, The
OMF Canada
OMS International - Canada
Open Doors With Brother Andrew
Operation Mobilization Canada
Outreach Canada
Partners International Canada
Persecuted Church Fellowship
Pioneers
Salvation Army, The
Samaritan's Purse - Canada
Scripture Gift Mission
SEND International of Canada
SIM Canada
Slavic Gospel Assoc.
South American Missionary Soc.
Student Mission Advance
TEAM of Canada
Trinitarian Bible Society
UFM International In Canada
Venture Teams International
Voice of The Martyrs, The
WEC International (Canada)
Western Tract Mission, Inc.
World Relief Canada
World Team
World Vision Canada
Wycliffe Bible Translators
Young Life of Canada
Youth for Christ - Canada
Youth With A Mission (Canada)

FRIENDS

Canadian Friends Service Comte

FUNDAMENTAL

Canadian S. American Mission
Centre for World Mission B.C.
Fundamental Baptist Mission
Galcom International
New Tribes Mission of Canada
Trinitarian Bible Society

HOLINESS

Bible Holiness Movement
Church of God (Anderson, IN)
Japan Evangelistic Band
Salvation Army, The

INDEPENDENT

Glad Tidings Missionary Soc.
Global Outreach Mission
HOPE Intl. Development Agency
International Missions Ontario
New Tribes Mission of Canada

LUTHERAN

Evangelical Lutheran Church
Lutheran Bible Translators
World Mission Prayer League

MENNONITE

Evangelical Mennonite Conf.
Evangelical Mennonite Msn Conf
Mennonite Brethren Missions
Mennonite Central Committee
Mennonite Economic Development

PENTECOSTAL

Apostolic Church In Canada
Apostolic Church of Pentecost
Calcutta Mission of Mercy
Pentecostal Assemblies Canada

PRESBYTERIAN

Presbyterian Church in Canada

REFORMED

Christian Reformed Wld. Relief
Presbyterian Church in Canada

WESLEYAN

Bible Holiness Movement
Church of God (Anderson, IN)
OMS International - Canada
World Gospel Mission (Canada)

AGRICULTURAL PROGRAMS

Canadian Conv. of So. Baptists
Canadian Food for the Hungry
Canadian Friends Service Comte
Canadian S. American Mission
Christian Reformed Wld. Relief
HOPE Intl. Development Agency
International Christian Aid
Mennonite Brethren Missions
Mennonite Central Committee
Mennonite Economic Development
Missionary Ventures of Canada
United Church of Canada
World Mission Prayer League

ASSOCIATION OF MISSIONS

Canadian Churches' Forum

AUDIO RECORDING/DISTRIBUTION

Arab World Ministries (Canada)
Far East Broadcasting Assocs.
Janz Team Ministries
Language Recordings Intl.

AVIATION SERVICES

Mission Aviation Flwshp Canada

BIBLE DISTRIBUTION

Apostolic Church In Canada
Bible League of Canada, The
Canadian Bible Society
Croisade du Livre Chretien
Door of Hope Intl. (Canada)
Gospel for Asia
High Adventure Ministries
Open Doors With Brother Andrew
Operation Mobilization Canada
Persecuted Church Fellowship
Slavic Gospel Assoc.
Trinitarian Bible Society
Voice of The Martyrs, The

BROADCASTING, RADIO AND/OR TV

European Christian Mission
Evangelical Mennonite Conf.
Far East Broadcasting Assocs.
Global Outreach Mission
HCJB World Radio Msnry. Flwshp
High Adventure Ministries
Open Doors With Brother Andrew
SEND International of Canada
SIM Canada
Voice of The Martyrs, The

CAMPING PROGRAMS

Action International Mins.
BCM International (Canada)
Greater Europe Mission
Inter-Varsity Christian Flwshp
Janz Team Ministries
TEAM of Canada
Venture Teams International
Young Life of Canada

CHILDCARE/ORPHANAGE

Compassion Canada
International Child Care
International Children's Haven
Salvation Army, The
World Vision Canada

CHILDRENS PROGRAMS

BCM International (Canada)
Calcutta Mission of Mercy
Child Evangelism Fellowship
Compassion Canada
Samaritan's Purse - Canada

CHURCH CONSTRUCTION

Church of God (Anderson, IN)
Gospel Missionary Union Canada
Missionary Ventures of Canada

CHURCH ESTABLISHING/PLANTING

ABWE - Canada
Action International Mins.
Africa Evangelical Fellowship
Africa Inland Mission (Canada)
Apostolic Church In Canada
Apostolic Church of Pentecost
Arab World Ministries (Canada)
Assoc. of Regular Baptist Chs.
Associated Gospel Churches
BGCC Global Ministries
Bible Holiness Movement
Canadian Conv. of So. Baptists
Christian and Msny. Alliance
Evangelical Lutheran Church
Evangelical Mennonite Conf.
Evangelical Mennonite Msn Conf
FEBInternational
Frontiers Canada
Glad Tidings Missionary Soc.
Global Outreach Mission
Gospel Missionary Union Canada
Greater Europe Mission
International Missions Ontario
International Teams of Canada
INTERSERVE (Canada)
Liebenzell Mission of Canada
Mennonite Brethren Missions
New Tribes Mission of Canada
OMF Canada
OMS International - Canada
Operation Mobilization Canada
Pentecostal Assemblies Canada
Pioneers
SEND International of Canada
SIM Canada
TEAM of Canada
UFM International In Canada
Venture Teams International
WEC International (Canada)
World Gospel Mission (Canada)
World Team

CORRESPONDENCE COURSES

Arab World Ministries (Canada)
BCM International (Canada)

Everyday Publications, Inc.
Gospel Missionary Union Canada
HCJB World Radio Msnry. Flwshp
INTERSERVE (Canada)
Slavic Gospel Assoc.

DEVELOPMENT, COMMUNITY AND/OR OTHER

Africa Community Technical Svc
Africa Inland Mission (Canada)
Anglican Church of Canada
BGCC Global Ministries
Canadian Food for the Hungry
Christian Blind Mission Intl.
Christian Indigenous Dev.
Christian Reformed Wld. Relief
Compassion Canada
Emmanuel International
Evangelical Lutheran Church
Evangelical Mennonite Msn Conf
FAIR
Gospel Missionary Union Canada
International Christian Aid
International Teams of Canada
Mennonite Brethren Missions
Mennonite Central Committee
Mission Aviation Flwshp Canada
Presbyterian Church in Canada
Salvation Army, The
United Church of Canada
World Relief Canada
World Vision Canada
Wycliffe Bible Translators

DISABILITY ASSISTANCE PROGRAMS

Canadian S. American Mission
Christian Blind Mission Intl.
Leprosy Mission Canada

EDUCATION, CHURCH/SCH. GENERAL CHRISTIAN

Africa Evangelical Fellowship
Africa Inland Mission (Canada)
BCM International (Canada)

Calcutta Mission of Mercy
Canadian Conv. of So. Baptists
Church of God (Anderson, IN)
Evangelical Mennonite Msn Conf
Janz Team Ministries
Mission Possible Canada
Salvation Army, The
World Mission Prayer League

EDUCATION, EXTENSION (OTHER)

FEBInternational
INTERSERVE (Canada)
United Church of Canada

EDUCATION, MISSIONARY (CERTIFICATE/DEGREE)

UFM International In Canada
Wycliffe Bible Translators
Youth With A Mission (Canada)

EDUCATION, THEOLOGICAL

ABWE - Canada
Africa Evangelical Fellowship
Anglican Church of Canada
Canadian Baptist Ministries
Gospel Missionary Union Canada
Greater Europe Mission
Japan Evangelistic Band
Latin America Mission (Canada)
Liebenzell Mission of Canada
Mennonite Brethren Missions
Middle East Christian Outreach
OMF Canada
OMS International - Canada
Pentecostal Assemblies Canada
Presbyterian Church in Canada
SEND International of Canada
SIM Canada
TEAM of Canada
World Gospel Mission (Canada)
World Team

EDUCATION, THEOLOGICAL BY EXTENSION (TEE)

ABWE - Canada
Africa Evangelical Fellowship
Arab World Ministries (Canada)
Christian and Msny. Alliance
Emmanuel International
Eurovangelism
Evangelical Mennonite Conf.
FEBInternational
Greater Europe Mission
Pentecostal Assemblies Canada
UFM International In Canada
WEC International (Canada)

EVANGELISM, MASS

African Enterprise Association
Barry Moore Ministries
FEBInternational
Janz Team Ministries
OMS International - Canada
Operation Mobilization Canada
Samaritan's Purse - Canada
Venture Teams International
WEC International (Canada)

EVANGELISM, PERSONAL AND SMALL GROUP

ABWE - Canada
Action International Mins.
Africa Evangelical Fellowship
Anglican Church of Canada
Apostolic Church In Canada
Apostolic Church of Pentecost
Arab World Ministries (Canada)
Associated Gospel Churches
BGCC Global Ministries
Bible Holiness Movement
Bible League of Canada, The
Calcutta Mission of Mercy
Campus Crusade for Christ
Canadian Conv. of So. Baptists
Canadian S. American Mission
Child Evangelism Fellowship

Christian and Msny. Alliance
European Christian Mission
Evangelical Covenant Ch Canada
Evangelical Mennonite Conf.
Evangelical Mennonite Msn Conf
Frontiers Canada
Galcom International
Glad Tidings Missionary Soc.
Global Outreach Mission
Greater Europe Mission
HCJB World Radio Msnry. Flwshp
International Missions Ontario
International Teams of Canada
INTERSERVE (Canada)
Latin America Mission (Canada)
Leprosy Mission Canada
Liebenzell Mission of Canada
Mennonite Brethren Missions
Middle East Christian Outreach
Missionary Ventures of Canada
Navigators of Canada, The
OMF Canada
OMS International - Canada
Persecuted Church Fellowship
Pioneers
Salvation Army, The
SEND International of Canada
South American Missionary Soc.
TEAM of Canada
UFM International In Canada
Western Tract Mission, Inc.
World Gospel Mission (Canada)
World Mission Prayer League
World Team
Youth for Christ - Canada
Youth With A Mission (Canada)

EVANGELISM, STUDENT

Eurovangelism
Inter-Varsity Christian Flwshp
International Missions Ontario
Latin America Mission (Canada)
Young Life of Canada
Youth for Christ - Canada

FUNDS TRANSMISSION

Christian Aid Mission
Christian Indigenous Dev.
Church of God (Anderson, IN)
Evangelical Covenant Ch Canada
Fundamental Baptist Mission
Gospel for Asia
Japan Evangelistic Band
Latin America Mission (Canada)
Lutheran Bible Translators
Partners International Canada
Samaritan's Purse - Canada
United Church of Canada

INFORMATION SERVICES

Centre for World Mission B.C.
Christian Aid Mission
Outreach Canada

LEADERSHIP DEVELOPMENT

Africa Inland Mission (Canada)
BGCC Global Ministries
Campus Crusade for Christ
Canadian Baptist Ministries
Canadian Churches' Forum
Canadian Conv. of So. Baptists
Canadian S. American Mission
Christian Reformed Wld. Relief
Evangelical Mennonite Conf.
Latin America Mission (Canada)
Liebenzell Mission of Canada
Operation Mobilization Canada
Presbyterian Church in Canada
SEND International of Canada
South American Missionary Soc.
World Vision Canada
Young Life of Canada

LINGUISTICS

Canadian Bible Society
New Tribes Mission of Canada
TEAM of Canada
Wycliffe Bible Translators

LITERACY

Canadian Bible Society
Christian Reformed Wld. Relief
Compassion Canada
Lutheran Bible Translators
New Tribes Mission of Canada
Wycliffe Bible Translators

LITERATURE DISTRIBUTION

Barry Moore Ministries
Bible Holiness Movement
Bible League of Canada, The
Campus Crusade for Christ
Child Evangelism Fellowship
Croisade du Livre Chretien
Czechoslovak Evangelical Msn.
Door of Hope Intl. (Canada)
European Christian Mission
Evangelical Mennonite Conf.
Evangelical Tract Distributors
Everyday Publications, Inc.
Far East Broadcasting Assocs.
Greater Europe Mission
High Adventure Ministries
International Missions Ontario
International Needs - Canada
Middle East Christian Outreach
Navigators of Canada, The
OMF Canada
Open Doors With Brother Andrew
Operation Mobilization Canada
Pentecostal Assemblies Canada
Persecuted Church Fellowship
Scripture Gift Mission
Voice of The Martyrs, The
Western Tract Mission, Inc.

LITERATURE PRODUCTION

Apostolic Church of Pentecost
Barry Moore Ministries
Bible Holiness Movement
Child Evangelism Fellowship
Christian Aid Mission
Croisade du Livre Chretien
Czechoslovak Evangelical Msn.

Door of Hope Intl. (Canada)
Evangelical Tract Distributors
Everyday Publications, Inc.
Navigators of Canada, The
OMF Canada
Scripture Gift Mission
Voice of The Martyrs, The
Western Tract Mission, Inc.

MANAGEMENT CONSULTING/TRAINING

Christian Reformed Wld. Relief
Mennonite Economic Development
Outreach Canada

MEDICAL SUPPLIES

Christian Blind Mission Intl.
International Child Care
International Christian Aid
Samaritan's Purse - Canada

MEDICINE, INCL. DENTAL AND PUBLIC HEALTH

ABWE - Canada
Africa Evangelical Fellowship
Africa Inland Mission (Canada)
Calcutta Mission of Mercy
Canadian Friends Service Comte
Christian Blind Mission Intl.
FAIR
Global Outreach Mission
HCJB World Radio Msnry. Flwshp
International Missions Ontario
Leprosy Mission Canada
Mennonite Brethren Missions
Mission Possible Canada
Presbyterian Church in Canada
SIM Canada
TEAM of Canada
UFM International In Canada
WEC International (Canada)

NATIONAL CHURCH NURTURE/SUPPORT

African Enterprise Association
Anglican Church of Canada
Associated Gospel Churches
BGCC Global Ministries
Bible Holiness Movement
Campus Crusade for Christ
Canadian Baptist Ministries
Canadian Food for the Hungry
Canadian S. American Mission
Church of God (Anderson, IN)
Door of Hope Intl. (Canada)
Emmanuel International
Eurovangelism
Gospel for Asia
Janz Team Ministries
Latin America Mission (Canada)
Mennonite Central Committee
Middle East Christian Outreach
OMS International - Canada
Outreach Canada
Partners International Canada
Pentecostal Assemblies Canada
Presbyterian Church in Canada
SEND International of Canada

PSYCHOLOGICAL COUNSELING

Missionary Health Institute

RECRUITING/MOBILIZING

Associated Gospel Churches
Centre for World Mission B.C.
Evangelical Covenant Ch Canada
Operation Mobilization Canada
Pioneers
South American Missionary Soc.
Student Mission Advance
Youth With A Mission (Canada)

RELIEF AND/OR REHABILITATION

Anglican Church of Canada
Calcutta Mission of Mercy
Canadian Conv. of So. Baptists

Canadian Food for the Hungry
Canadian Friends Service Comte
Christian Blind Mission Intl.
Christian Reformed Wld. Relief
Door of Hope Intl. (Canada)
Emmanuel International
Eurovangelism
FAIR
HOPE Intl. Development Agency
International Christian Aid
International Teams of Canada
Mennonite Central Committee
Mission Possible Canada
Pentecostal Assemblies Canada
Salvation Army, The
Samaritan's Purse - Canada
SIM Canada
World Relief Canada
World Vision Canada
Youth With A Mission (Canada)

RESEARCH

Centre for World Mission B.C.
Christian Aid Mission
Missionary Health Institute
Outreach Canada

SERVICES FOR OTHER AGENCIES

Canadian Bible Society
Canadian Churches' Forum
Centre for World Mission B.C.
Missionary Health Institute

SHORT-TERM PROGRAMS COORDINATION

Missionary Ventures of Canada
Youth for Christ - Canada

SUPPLYING EQUIPMENT

Galcom International
Global Outreach Mission

SUPPORT OF NATIONAL WORKERS

Apostolic Church In Canada
Bible Holiness Movement
Christian Aid Mission
Eurovangelism
Evangelical Mennonite Msn Conf
Frontiers Canada
Fundamental Baptist Mission
Gospel for Asia
International Needs - Canada
Operation Mobilization Canada
Partners International Canada
Persecuted Church Fellowship
South American Missionary Soc.

TECHNICAL ASSISTANCE

Africa Community Technical Svc
Africa Inland Mission (Canada)
Christian Indigenous Dev.
Galcom International
HCJB World Radio Msnry. Flwshp
HOPE Intl. Development Agency
Mennonite Central Committee
Mennonite Economic Development
Mission Aviation Flwshp Canada

TRAINING, OTHER

Action International Mins.
Centre for World Mission B.C.
Child Evangelism Fellowship
Evangelical Lutheran Church
Gospel for Asia
Open Doors With Brother Andrew

TRAINING/ORIENTATION, MISSIONARY

Assoc. of Regular Baptist Chs.
Canadian Churches' Forum
Emmanuel International
Frontiers Canada
International Teams of Canada
Leprosy Mission Canada
Missionary Health Institute
New Tribes Mission of Canada
Operation Mobilization Canada

United Church of Canada
Venture Teams International

TRANSLATION, BIBLE

Canadian Bible Society
Lutheran Bible Translators
New Tribes Mission of Canada
SIM Canada
Trinitarian Bible Society
WEC International (Canada)
World Team
Wycliffe Bible Translators

TRANSLATION, OTHER

Bible League of Canada, The
Everyday Publications, Inc.

YOUTH PROGRAMS

Calcutta Mission of Mercy
Emmanuel International
Gospel Missionary Union Canada
International Needs - Canada
International Teams of Canada
Salvation Army, The
Venture Teams International
Young Life of Canada
Youth With A Mission (Canada)

Chapter 9

Countries of activity for Canadian Protestant agencies

In this chapter you will find the countries where agencies reported field personnel in answer to question #12 of the survey questionnaire (see the appendix for details). The few exceptions to this are agencies whose whole program supports—with funds raised in Canada, but which may not be designated to specific personnel on a regular basis—churches or other initiatives in a country.

Geopolitical shifts and changes continue to occur throughout the world. We have made every attempt to indicate changes of country names since 1992 in a format that is familiar to the North American perspective. For example, due to the recent political changes in the former Zaire, that nation is listed as Congo/Zaire.

All countries are listed in alphabetical order according to the name most commonly recognized in North America. Countries that are part of the Commonwealth of Independent States (most of the former Soviet Union) have been listed separately. Examples of this would

include Armenia, Kyrgyzstan and Belarus. In a few cases we have listed a territory or other administrative district of a country because it is commonly viewed as a separate entity and mission agencies report it that way. An example would be Greenland, located many miles from Denmark.

We have separated the personnel totals for all agencies into five categories. Under the "personnel from Canada" heading, the term of expected service has been divided into three categories: 4+ years, 2-4 years and 1-2 years for fully supported personnel. For non-Canadian personnel in the "other countries" heading, the categories are those who are citizens of that ministry country and those who are not citizens, and are fully or partially supported by funds raised in Canada by the associated agency. For example, a Kenyan with specific mission/ministry duties serving in Kenya would be included in an agency's "citizens" column of the Kenya section. A Kenyan serving in Russia would be listed in the "not citizen" column of the Russian Federation section.

At the end of each country section, totals of each category for that country are given. Please note that the totals for the "other countries" heading do not necessarily reflect all non-Canadian mission personnel who draw support from Canadian agencies. Some agencies give grants for ongoing institutions and other programs without specifying individual recipients. This may be in addition to Canadian mission personnel based in that country or the agency may not have Canadian personnel living in that country.

COUNTRY Agency	Year Began	Personnel from Canada			Other Countries	
		4+ Yrs	2-4 Yrs	1-2 Yrs	Citizens	Not Citiz.
ALBANIA						
Canadian Baptist Ministries	1993	2	-	-	-	-
Child Evangelism Fellowship	1995	1	-	-	-	-
Door of Hope Intl. (Canada)	1993	1	-	-	-	-
International Teams of Canada	1991	-	1	-	-	2
Youth With A Mission (Canada)		1	-	-	-	-
	Totals:	5	1	-	-	2
ANGOLA						
Africa Evangelical Fellowship	1917	5	-	-	-	-
Brethren Assemblies (Canada)		1	-	-	-	-
Canadian Baptist Ministries	1956	2	-	-	-	-
Mission Aviation Flwshp Canada	1989	19	1	2	-	-
World Relief Canada	1989	6	-	-	-	-
	Totals:	33	1	2	-	-
ARGENTINA						
ABWE - Canada	1950	2	-	-	-	-
Brethren Assemblies (Canada)		2	-	-	-	-
Child Evangelism Fellowship	1956	-	-	1	1	-
Christian and Msny. Alliance		6	-	-	-	-
Evangelical Lutheran Church	1992	-	2	-	-	-
Gospel Missionary Union Canada	1955	2	-	-	-	-
Navigators of Canada, The		2	-	-	-	-
Salvation Army, The		1	-	-	-	-
Youth With A Mission (Canada)		2	-	-	-	-
	Totals:	17	2	1	1	-
AUSTRALIA						
Christian and Msny. Alliance		4	2	-	-	-
Church of God (Anderson, IN)		-	-	-	-	2
International Teams of Canada	1976	1	-	-	-	-
Wycliffe Bible Translators	1950	4	-	-	-	-
Youth With A Mission (Canada)		9	-	-	-	-
	Totals:	18	2	-	-	2
AUSTRIA						
Brethren Assemblies (Canada)		10	-	-	-	-
Child Evangelism Fellowship	1971	-	-	-	-	1
Eurovangelism	1992	-	-	-	2	-
Gospel Missionary Union Canada	1966	9	-	1	-	-
Greater Europe Mission	1963	1	1	-	-	-
International Teams of Canada	1974	7	-	-	-	8
Operation Mobilization Canada	1962	-	2	-	-	-
	Totals:	27	3	1	2	9

COUNTRY Agency	Year Began	Personnel from Canada			Other Countries	
		4+ Yrs	2-4 Yrs	1-2 Yrs	Citizens	Not Citiz.

BAHAMAS
Gospel Missionary Union Canada	1956	2	2	-	-	-
Totals:		2	2	-	-	-

BANGLADESH
ABWE - Canada	1968	2	1	-	-	-
Christian Blind Mission Intl.	1994	2	-	-	-	-
Salvation Army, The		2	-	-	-	-
SIM Canada	1957	-	-	-	-	11
Totals:		6	1	-	-	11

BARBADOS
Salvation Army, The		2	-	-	-	-
Totals:		2	-	-	-	-

BELGIUM
Brethren Assemblies (Canada)		6	-	-	-	-
Canadian Baptist Ministries	1985	6	-	5	-	-
FEBInternational	1977	10	-	-	-	-
Global Outreach Mission	1976	2	-	-	-	-
Gospel Missionary Union Canada	1966	3	-	-	-	-
Operation Mobilization Canada	1962	-	-	1	-	-
WEC International (Canada)	1989	2	-	-	-	-
Totals:		29	-	6	-	-

BELIZE
Christian Reformed Wld. Relief	1986	2	-	-	-	-
Gospel Missionary Union Canada	1955	4	-	-	-	-
Pioneers	1986	2	-	-	1	-
Youth With A Mission (Canada)		2	-	-	-	-
Totals:		10	-	-	1	-

BENIN
SIM Canada	1946	10	1	4	-	1
Wycliffe Bible Translators	1993	2	-	-	-	-
Totals:		12	1	4	-	1

BOLIVIA
Brethren Assemblies (Canada)		8	-	-	-	-
Canadian Baptist Ministries	1898	5	-	-	-	-
Evangelical Mennonite Msn Conf	1969	2	-	-	-	1
Gospel Missionary Union Canada	1937	29	6	3	-	-
Mennonite Economic Development	1978	-	-	-	2	1
New Tribes Mission of Canada	1942	11	-	-	-	-

COUNTRY Agency	Year Began	Personnel from Canada			Other Countries	
		4+ Yrs	2-4 Yrs	1-2 Yrs	Citizens	Not Citiz.
Pioneers	1984	5	-	-	-	-
SIM Canada	1907	3	-	1	-	-
World Mission Prayer League	1938	2	-	-	-	-
Wycliffe Bible Translators	1955	1	-	-	-	-
Totals:		66	6	4	2	2

BOTSWANA

Africa Evangelical Fellowship	1973	3	-	-	-	-
Brethren Assemblies (Canada)		2	-	-	-	-
Mission Aviation Flwshp Canada	1990	4	-	-	-	-
Totals:		9	-	-	-	-

BRAZIL

ABWE - Canada	1936	5	-	-	-	-
Apostolic Church In Canada	1970	4	-	-	-	-
Brethren Assemblies (Canada)		3	-	-	-	-
Canadian S. American Mission	1913	-	-	1	-	-
Child Evangelism Fellowship	1995	2	-	-	-	-
Christian and Msny. Alliance		5	-	-	-	-
Emmanuel International	1981	-	-	-	4	-
Global Outreach Mission	1974	1	-	-	-	-
Gospel Missionary Union Canada	1911	4	-	-	-	-
Janz Team Ministries	1975	6	-	-	2	-
Mission Aviation Flwshp Canada	1972	4	-	-	-	-
New Tribes Mission of Canada	1946	13	-	-	-	-
Pentecostal Assemblies Canada	1970	12	-	-	-	-
Pioneers	1990	2	-	-	-	-
Salvation Army, The		4	-	-	-	-
TEAM of Canada	1983	2	-	-	-	-
UFM International In Canada	1931	15	-	2	-	-
WEC International (Canada)	1957	2	-	-	-	-
World Team	1957	1	-	-	1	-
Wycliffe Bible Translators	1956	13	-	-	-	-
Young Life of Canada	1991	-	-	-	1	-
Youth With A Mission (Canada)		11	-	-	-	-
Totals:		109	-	3	8	-

BURKINA FASO

Apostolic Church of Pentecost		3	-	-	-	-
Christian and Msny. Alliance		2	-	-	-	-
Evangelical Mennonite Msn Conf	1986	4	-	1	-	-
SIM Canada	1930	7	3	-	-	-
Wycliffe Bible Translators	1983	7	-	-	-	-
Totals:		23	3	1	-	-

COUNTRY Agency	Year Began	Personnel from Canada			Other Countries	
		4+ Yrs	2-4 Yrs	1-2 Yrs	Citizens	Not Citiz.
BURUNDI						
World Vision Canada		-	-	1	-	-
Totals:		-	-	1	-	-
CAMBODIA						
Christian and Msny. Alliance		-	1	-		
Far East Broadcasting Assocs.	1996	1	-	-		
HOPE Intl. Development Agency	1991	-	2	1		1
WEC International (Canada)	1993	2	-	-	-	-
World Vision Canada	1970	-	-	1	-	-
Totals:		3	3	2	-	1
CAMEROON						
Evangelical Lutheran Church	1967	2	-	-	-	-
Lutheran Bible Translators	1984	2	-	-	-	-
World Team	1984	4	-	1	-	-
Wycliffe Bible Translators	1968	20	-	4	-	-
Totals:		28	-	5	-	-
CENTRAL AFRICA REPUBLIC						
Africa Inland Mission (Canada)	1924	-	2	-	-	-
World Team	1983	-	-	-	-	1
Wycliffe Bible Translators	1989	2	-	-	-	-
Totals:		2	2	-	-	1
CHAD						
Africa Inland Mission (Canada)	1986	1	-	-	-	-
TEAM of Canada	1969	5	-	-	-	-
Wycliffe Bible Translators	1990	2	-	-	-	-
Totals:		8	-	-	-	-
CHILE						
ABWE - Canada	1950	1	-	-	-	-
Brethren Assemblies (Canada)		12	-	-	-	-
Canadian Conv. of So. Baptists	1994	2	-	-	-	-
Christian and Msny. Alliance		4	-	-	-	-
Navigators of Canada, The		2	-	-	-	-
SIM Canada	1986	1	-	-	-	1
Totals:		22	-	-	-	1
CHINA, PEOPLES REPUBLIC						
Canadian Baptist Ministries	1990	-	2	-	-	-
Christian Aid Mission		-	-	-	50	-
Pentecostal Assemblies Canada	1919	2	-	-	-	-
Totals:		2	2	-	50	-

COUNTRY Agency	Year Began	Personnel from Canada			Other Countries	
		4+ Yrs	2-4 Yrs	1-2 Yrs	Citizens	Not Citiz.
COLOMBIA						
Action International Mins.	1987	4	-	-	-	-
Brethren Assemblies (Canada)		1	-	-	-	-
Canadian S. American Mission	1934	2	-	-	-	-
Christian and Msny. Alliance		7	1	-	-	-
Evangelical Lutheran Church	1967	-	-	2	-	-
FEBInternational	1969	6	-	3	-	-
Gospel Missionary Union Canada	1908	1	-	-	-	-
Latin America Mission (Canada)		8	-	-	4	-
New Tribes Mission of Canada	1944	4	-	-	-	-
Wycliffe Bible Translators	1962	15	-	-	-	-
	Totals:	48	1	5	4	-
CONGO						
Global Outreach Mission	1974	1	-	-	-	-
Wycliffe Bible Translators	1985	4	-	-	-	-
	Totals:	5	-	-	-	-
CONGO / ZAIRE						
Africa Inland Mission (Canada)	1912	10	-	7	-	-
Brethren Assemblies (Canada)		2	-	-	-	-
Canadian Baptist Ministries	1961	8	-	-	-	-
Christian and Msny. Alliance		11	-	-	-	-
Mission Aviation Flwshp Canada	1973	2	-	-	-	-
Presbyterian Church in Canada	1987	2	-	-	-	-
Salvation Army, The		1	-	-	-	-
UFM International In Canada	1931	1	-	-	-	-
WEC International (Canada)	1913	4	-	-	-	-
Wycliffe Bible Translators	1985	3	-	2	-	-
	Totals:	44	-	9	-	-
COSTA RICA						
Brethren Assemblies (Canada)		4	-	-	-	-
Latin America Mission (Canada)		10	-	-	-	-
Voice of The Martyrs, The	1988	-	2	-	-	-
Youth With A Mission (Canada)		1	-	-	-	-
	Totals:	15	2	-	-	-
COTE D'IVOIRE						
Christian and Msny. Alliance		9	2	-	-	-
New Tribes Mission of Canada	1982	7	-	-	-	-
Pentecostal Assemblies Canada	1986	2	-	-	-	-
SIM Canada	1968	3	-	-	-	-
WEC International (Canada)	1936	4	-	-	-	-
Wycliffe Bible Translators	1970	3	-	-	-	-
	Totals:	28	2	-	-	-

COUNTRY Agency	Year Began	Personnel from Canada			Other Countries	
		4+ Yrs	2-4 Yrs	1-2 Yrs	Citizens	Not Citiz.
CROATIA						
Canadian Baptist Ministries	1991	-	2	-	-	-
Totals:		-	2	-	-	-
CUBA						
Mennonite Economic Development	1995	-	1	-	-	-
World Team	1928	2	-	-	-	-
Totals:		2	1	-	-	-
CZECH REPUBLIC						
International Teams of Canada	1974	-	2	-	-	-
Operation Mobilization Canada		-	1	-	-	-
Totals:		-	3	-	-	-
DOMINICAN REPUBLIC						
Brethren Assemblies (Canada)		2	-	-	-	-
Mission Possible Canada	1996	-	-	-	-	-
UFM International In Canada	1949	2	-	-	-	-
Totals:		4	-	-	-	-
ECUADOR						
Brethren Assemblies (Canada)		6	-	-	-	-
Christian and Msny. Alliance		8	-	-	-	-
Gospel Missionary Union Canada	1896	6	-	-	-	-
HCJB World Radio Msnry. Flwshp	1967	32	-	-	-	-
Liebenzell Mission of Canada	1989	2	-	-	-	-
OMS International - Canada	1946	-	-	2	-	-
SIM Canada	1989	-	-	1	-	-
World Mission Prayer League	1951	2	-	-	-	-
Wycliffe Bible Translators	1953	2	-	-	-	-
Totals:		58	-	3	-	-
EGYPT						
Brethren Assemblies (Canada)		2	-	-	-	-
Totals:		2	-	-	-	-
EL SALVADOR						
Brethren Assemblies (Canada)		2	-	-	-	-
Evangelical Lutheran Church	1988	-	1	-	-	-
Totals:		2	1	-	-	-
EQUATORIAL GUINEA						
WEC International (Canada)	1933	2	-	-	-	-
Totals:		2	-	-	-	-

COUNTRY Agency	Year Began	Personnel from Canada			Other Countries	
		4+ Yrs	2-4 Yrs	1-2 Yrs	Citizens	Not Citiz.
ESTONIA						
OMS International - Canada	1995	-	-	3	-	-
Pentecostal Assemblies Canada	1991	2	-	-	-	-
Totals:		2	-	3	-	-
ETHIOPIA						
HOPE Intl. Development Agency	1983	-	2	-	2	-
Mission Aviation Flwshp Canada		2	-	-	-	-
SIM Canada	1927	11	2	-	-	2
World Vision Canada	1971	-	-	2	-	-
Totals:		13	4	2	2	2
FIJI						
Youth With A Mission (Canada)		3	-	-	-	-
Totals:		3	-	-	-	-
FINLAND						
Brethren Assemblies (Canada)		5	-	-	-	-
Operation Mobilization Canada		2	-	-	-	-
Totals:		7	-	-	-	-
FRANCE						
Brethren Assemblies (Canada)		20	-	-	-	-
Canadian Baptist Ministries	1992	2	-	-	-	-
Child Evangelism Fellowship	1955	-	-	1	-	-
Christian and Msny. Alliance		4	2	-	-	-
FEBInternational	1985	8	-	-	-	-
Global Outreach Mission	1969	3	-	-	-	-
Greater Europe Mission	1959	2	1	-	-	-
International Teams of Canada	1969	1	-	-	-	2
Salvation Army, The		4	-	-	-	-
TEAM of Canada	1952	5	-	-	-	-
UFM International In Canada	1962	3	-	-	-	-
Youth With A Mission (Canada)		1	-	-	-	-
Totals:		53	3	1	-	2
GABON						
Christian and Msny. Alliance		10	-	2	-	-
Totals:		10	-	2	-	-
GAMBIA						
WEC International (Canada)	1957	3	-	-	-	-
Totals:		3	-	-	-	-

COUNTRY Agency	Year Began	Personnel from Canada			Other Countries	
		4+ Yrs	2-4 Yrs	1-2 Yrs	Citizens	Not Citiz.

GERMANY

Christian and Msny. Alliance		6	-	-	-	-
FEBInternational	1996	-	-	2	-	-
Global Outreach Mission	1970	2	-	-	-	-
Greater Europe Mission	1959	-	2	-	-	-
International Teams of Canada	1989	2	2	2	-	-
Janz Team Ministries	1954	50	-	3	1	-
Mission Aviation Flwshp Canada	1989	-	4	-	-	-
Operation Mobilization Canada	1962	2	1	1	-	-
Salvation Army, The		2	-	-	-	-
TEAM of Canada	1994	2	-	-	-	-
UFM International In Canada		2	-	-	-	-
Totals:		68	9	8	1	-

GHANA

Bible Holiness Movement	1961	-	-	-	12	-
International Needs - Canada	1995	-	-	-	15	-
SIM Canada	1956	4	2	-	-	-
WEC International (Canada)	1940	2	-	-	-	-
Wycliffe Bible Translators	1962	6	-	-	-	-
Totals:		12	2	-	27	-

GREECE

Pentecostal Assemblies Canada	1982	4	-	-	-	-
Youth With A Mission (Canada)		1	-	-	-	-
Totals:		5	-	-	-	-

GREENLAND

Youth With A Mission (Canada)		3	-	-	-	-
Totals:		3	-	-	-	-

GRENADA

Brethren Assemblies (Canada)		2	-	-	-	-
Youth With A Mission (Canada)		3	-	-	-	-
Totals:		5	-	-	-	-

GUATEMALA

Apostolic Church of Pentecost	1975	6	-	-	-	-
Brethren Assemblies (Canada)		-	2	-	-	-
Christian and Msny. Alliance		2	-	-	-	-
Global Outreach Mission	1983	4	-	-	-	-
Latin America Mission (Canada)		2	-	-	-	-
Presbyterian Church in Canada	1985	1	-	-	-	-
Wycliffe Bible Translators	1991	9	-	1	-	-
Totals:		24	2	1	-	-

COUNTRY Agency	Year Began	Personnel from Canada			Other Countries	
		4+ Yrs	2-4 Yrs	1-2 Yrs	Citizens	Not Citiz.

GUINEA

Christian and Msny. Alliance		12	-	-	-	-
New Tribes Mission of Canada	1986	8	-	-	-	-
Pentecostal Assemblies Canada	1988	6	-	-	-	-
Totals:		26	-	-	-	-

GUINEA BISSAU

Youth With A Mission (Canada)		1	-	-	-	-
Totals:		1	-	-	-	-

GUYANA

Canadian Baptist Ministries	1992	-	-	6	-	-
UFM International In Canada	1949	2	-	-	-	-
Wycliffe Bible Translators	1991	2	-	-	-	-
Youth With A Mission (Canada)		3	-	-	-	-
Totals:		7	-	6	-	-

HAITI

Christian Reformed Wld. Relief	1986	4	-	-	-	-
Emmanuel International	1978	-	-	1	2	2
Global Outreach Mission	1982	2	-	-	-	-
International Child Care	1986	2	3	1	-	-
Mennonite Economic Development	1983	-	-	-	19	-
Mission Possible Canada	1995	-	-	-	-	-
OMS International - Canada	1964	1	-	2	-	-
UFM International In Canada	1943	6	-	-	-	-
World Team	1936	6	-	-	-	-
Youth With A Mission (Canada)		1	-	-	-	-
Totals:		22	3	4	21	2

HONDURAS

South American Missionary Soc.	1991	2	-	1	6	-
Totals:		2	-	1	6	-

HONG KONG

Brethren Assemblies (Canada)		2	-	-	-	-
Child Evangelism Fellowship	1991	-	-	-	-	2
Christian and Msny. Alliance		2	-	-	-	-
Far East Broadcasting Assocs.	1986	-	-	1	-	-
OMF Canada	1954	1	-	-	-	-
OMS International - Canada	1950	-	-	1	-	-
Pentecostal Assemblies Canada	1949	7	-	-	-	-
Presbyterian Church in Canada	1987	1	-	-	-	-
SEND International of Canada	1989	2	-	1	-	-
Youth With A Mission (Canada)		1	-	-	-	-
Totals:		16	-	3	-	2

COUNTRY Agency	Year Began	Personnel from Canada			Other Countries	
		4+ Yrs	2-4 Yrs	1-2 Yrs	Citizens	Not Citiz.
HUNGARY						
BGCC Global Ministries	1996	-	2	-	-	-
Child Evangelism Fellowship	1995	2	-	-	-	-
International Teams of Canada	1989	2	-	-	-	-
Janz Team Ministries	1991	1	2	-	-	-
Operation Mobilization Canada		2	-	2	-	-
Salvation Army, The		-	4	-	-	-
Youth With A Mission (Canada)		2	-	-	-	-
	Totals:	9	8	2	-	-
ICELAND						
Pentecostal Assemblies Canada	1986	2	-	-	-	-
	Totals:	2	-	-	-	-
INDIA						
Bible Holiness Movement	1991	-	-	-	3	-
Brethren Assemblies (Canada)		6	-	-	-	-
Calcutta Mission of Mercy	1954	1	-	-	-	-
Canadian Baptist Ministries	1870	4	-	-	-	-
Christian Aid Mission		-	-	-	50	-
Christian and Msny. Alliance		2	-	-	-	-
Global Outreach Mission	1972	4	-	-	-	-
HOPE Intl. Development Agency	1981	-	-	-	30	-
Operation Mobilization Canada	1963	-	2	-	-	-
Pentecostal Assemblies Canada	1987	1	-	-	-	-
Presbyterian Church in Canada	1900	5	-	-	-	-
SIM Canada	1893	1	2	-	-	-
TEAM of Canada	1894	3	-	-	-	-
Wycliffe Bible Translators	1966	3	-	-	-	-
Youth With A Mission (Canada)		6	-	-	-	-
	Totals:	36	4	-	83	-
INDONESIA						
Canadian Baptist Ministries	1973	3	-	1	-	-
Christian and Msny. Alliance		20	3	-	-	-
Frontiers Canada	1990	4	-	-	-	-
Mission Aviation Flwshp Canada	1972	8	-	-	-	-
New Tribes Mission of Canada	1970	7	-	-	-	-
OMF Canada	1954	4	2	-	-	-
OMS International - Canada	1978	2	-	-	-	-
Pentecostal Assemblies Canada	1989	4	-	-	-	-
Salvation Army, The		1	-	-	-	-
TEAM of Canada	1950	2	-	-	-	-
UFM International In Canada	1957	6	-	-	-	-

COUNTRY Agency	Year Began	Personnel from Canada			Other Countries	
		4+ Yrs	2-4 Yrs	1-2 Yrs	Citizens	Not Citiz.
World Team	1949	15	-	-	-	-
Wycliffe Bible Translators	1971	9	-	-	-	-
Totals:		85	5	1	-	-
IRELAND						
BGCC Global Ministries	1996	-	1	-	-	-
Brethren Assemblies (Canada)		6	-	-	-	-
Child Evangelism Fellowship	1995	-	-	-	4	-
Global Outreach Mission	1972	4	-	-	-	-
UFM International In Canada	1980	6	-	-	-	-
Youth With A Mission (Canada)		1	-	-	-	-
Totals:		17	1	-	4	-
ISRAEL						
Pentecostal Assemblies Canada	1981	2	-	-	-	-
Totals:		2	-	-	-	-
ITALY						
Brethren Assemblies (Canada)		3	-	-	-	-
Child Evangelism Fellowship	1990	1	-	-	-	-
FEBInternational	1985	2	-	-	-	-
Gospel Missionary Union Canada	1967	1	-	-	-	-
Greater Europe Mission	1959	2	-	-	-	-
International Teams of Canada	1980	-	2	-	-	-
TEAM of Canada	1981	5	-	-	-	-
World Team	1970	1	2	-	-	-
Totals:		15	4	-	-	-
JAMAICA						
Emmanuel International	1982	-	-	-	2	-
International Teams of Canada	1995	-	1	-	-	-
Salvation Army, The		2	-	-	-	-
Totals:		2	1	-	2	-
JAPAN						
Brethren Assemblies (Canada)		4	-	-	-	-
Campus Crusade for Christ		1	-	-	-	-
Child Evangelism Fellowship	1962	-	2	-	-	-
Christian and Msny. Alliance		4	-	-	-	-
FEBInternational	1965	8	-	2	-	-
OMF Canada	1951	10	2	-	-	-
OMS International - Canada	1901	-	1	1	-	-
Presbyterian Church in Canada	1927	3	-	-	-	-
Salvation Army, The		1	-	-	-	-
SEND International of Canada	1945	5	-	-	-	-

COUNTRY Agency	Year Began	Personnel from Canada			Other Countries	
		4+ Yrs	2-4 Yrs	1-2 Yrs	Citizens	Not Citiz.
TEAM of Canada	1891	12	1	-	-	-
UFM International In Canada		1	-	-	-	-
Youth With A Mission (Canada)		2	-	-	-	-
	Totals:	51	6	3	-	-
JORDAN						
Christian and Msny. Alliance		2	-	-	-	-
	Totals:	2	-	-	-	-
KENYA						
Africa Inland Mission (Canada)	1895	42	2	22	-	-
Bible Holiness Movement	1980	-	-	-	1	-
Brethren Assemblies (Canada)		4	-	-	-	-
Canadian Baptist Ministries	1970	6	4	2	-	-
Christian Blind Mission Intl.	1985	2	-	-	-	-
International Missions Ontario	1956	2	-	-	-	-
Language Recordings Intl.	1977	4	-	-	4	-
Mission Aviation Flwshp Canada	1972	2	-	-	-	-
Pentecostal Assemblies Canada	1919	26	-	8	-	-
Presbyterian Church in Canada	1983	2	2	-	-	-
Salvation Army, The		3	-	-	-	-
SIM Canada	1977	1	-	-	-	-
World Mission Prayer League	1968	1	-	-	-	-
Wycliffe Bible Translators	1978	6	-	-	-	-
	Totals:	101	8	32	5	-
KOREA, SOUTH						
Christian and Msny. Alliance		2	-	-	-	-
OMF Canada	1968	-	2	-	-	-
OMS International - Canada	1907	-	-	1	-	-
	Totals:	2	2	1	-	-
LAOS						
Christian and Msny. Alliance		-	1	-	-	-
	Totals:	-	1	-	-	-
LATVIA						
Canadian Baptist Ministries	1995	2	-	-	-	-
Greater Europe Mission	1992	3	4	1	-	-
	Totals:	5	4	1	-	-
LEBANON						
World Relief Canada		1	-	-	-	-
	Totals:	1	-	-	-	-

COUNTRY Agency	Year Began	Personnel from Canada			Other Countries	
		4+ Yrs	2-4 Yrs	1-2 Yrs	Citizens	Not Citiz.

LESOTHO
Africa Inland Mission (Canada)	1986	-	2	2	-	-
Mission Aviation Flwshp Canada		2	-	-	-	-
	Totals:	2	2	2	-	-

LIBERIA
Pentecostal Assemblies Canada	1908	3	-	-	-	-
	Totals:	3	-	-	-	-

LUXEMBOURG
Greater Europe Mission	1994	2	-	-	-	-
	Totals:	2	-	-	-	-

MACAO
Pentecostal Assemblies Canada	1949	2	-	-	-	-
	Totals:	2	-	-	-	-

MACEDONIA
BGCC Global Ministries	1996	-	1	-	-	-
	Totals:	-	1	-	-	-

MADAGASCAR
Brethren Assemblies (Canada)		2	-	-	-	-
	Totals:	2	-	-	-	-

MALAWI
Africa Evangelical Fellowship	1900	1	-	-	-	-
Apostolic Church of Pentecost	1947	2	-	-	-	-
Bible Holiness Movement	1992	-	-	-	1	-
Emmanuel International	1986	2	2	-	-	2
Pentecostal Assemblies Canada	1978	10	-	-	-	-
Presbyterian Church in Canada	1962	1	1	4	-	-
World Vision Canada	1975	-	-	2	-	-
	Totals:	16	3	6	1	2

MALAYSIA
Canadian Conv. of So. Baptists	1993	2	-	-	-	-
OMF Canada	1928	2	-	2	-	-
Operation Mobilization Canada		-	2	-	-	-
Wycliffe Bible Translators	1978	3	-	-	-	-
	Totals:	7	2	2	-	-

COUNTRY Agency	Year Began	Personnel from Canada			Other Countries	
		4+ Yrs	2-4 Yrs	1-2 Yrs	Citizens	Not Citiz.

MALI
Christian and Msny. Alliance		7	-	-	-	-
Christian Reformed Wld. Relief	1988	1	-	-	-	-
Gospel Missionary Union Canada	1919	14	-	-	-	-
Totals:		22	-	-	-	-

MAURITIUS
Presbyterian Church in Canada	1981	4	2	-	-	-
Totals:		4	2	-	-	-

MEXICO
Apostolic Church of Pentecost	1963	6	-	-	-	-
Brethren Assemblies (Canada)		8	-	-	-	-
Christian and Msny. Alliance		8	-	-	-	-
Evangelical Mennonite Conf.	1954	13	-	-	3	-
Evangelical Mennonite Msn Conf	1982	-	4	-	4	4
Glad Tidings Missionary Soc.		2	-	2	-	-
Latin America Mission (Canada)		3	-	-	-	-
New Tribes Mission of Canada	1975	12	-	-	-	-
OMS International - Canada	1985	-	-	1	-	-
Operation Mobilization Canada	1957	1	-	-	-	-
WEC International (Canada)	1990	2	-	-	-	-
World Mission Prayer League	1943	-	-	2	-	-
World Team		2	-	-	-	-
Wycliffe Bible Translators	1936	12	-	2	-	-
Youth With A Mission (Canada)		4	-	-	-	-
Totals:		73	4	7	7	4

MOZAMBIQUE
Africa Evangelical Fellowship	1937	2	-	-	-	-
Pentecostal Assemblies Canada	1934	4	-	-	-	-
Presbyterian Church in Canada	1988	1	-	-	-	-
World Vision Canada	1984	-	-	1	-	-
Wycliffe Bible Translators	1994	5	-	-	-	-
Youth With A Mission (Canada)		1	-	-	-	-
Totals:		13	-	1	-	-

NAMIBIA
HOPE Intl. Development Agency	1991	-	2	-	-	-
Liebenzell Mission of Canada	1994	1	-	-	-	-
Mission Aviation Flwshp Canada		2	-	-	-	-
Totals:		3	2	-	-	-

COUNTRY Agency	Year Began	Personnel from Canada			Other Countries	
		4+ Yrs	2-4 Yrs	1-2 Yrs	Citizens	Not Citiz.
NEPAL						
International Needs - Canada	1984	-	-	-	20	-
Presbyterian Church in Canada	1965	5	-	-	-	-
TEAM of Canada	1968	2	-	-	-	-
	Totals:	7	-	-	20	-
NETHERLANDS						
BCM International (Canada)		1	-	-	-	-
Brethren Assemblies (Canada)		2	-	-	-	-
Greater Europe Mission	1983	-	-	2	-	-
Pentecostal Assemblies Canada	1989	2	-	-	-	-
Youth With A Mission (Canada)		16	-	-	-	-
	Totals:	21	-	2	-	-
NETHERLANDS ANTILLES						
TEAM of Canada	1931	3	-	-	-	-
	Totals:	3	-	-	-	-
NEW ZEALAND						
Salvation Army, The		2	-	-	-	-
Wycliffe Bible Translators	1991	4	-	-	-	-
Youth With A Mission (Canada)		4	-	-	-	-
	Totals:	10	-	-	-	-
NICARAGUA						
Mennonite Economic Development	1988	-	-	-	50	-
Presbyterian Church in Canada	1985	-	3	-	-	-
	Totals:	-	3	-	50	-
NIGER						
SIM Canada	1924	12	-	-	-	1
	Totals:	12	-	-	-	1
NIGERIA						
Bible Holiness Movement	1959	-	-	-	20	-
Brethren Assemblies (Canada)		2	-	-	-	-
Campus Crusade for Christ	1987	-	2	-	-	-
Canadian Conv. of So. Baptists	1991	2	-	-	-	-
FEBInternational	1979	2	-	-	-	-
Presbyterian Church in Canada	1955	2	2	-	-	-
SIM Canada	1893	5	-	1	-	1
Wycliffe Bible Translators	1983	1	-	-	-	-
	Totals:	14	4	1	20	1

COUNTRY Agency	Year Began	Personnel from Canada			Other Countries	
		4+ Yrs	2-4 Yrs	1-2 Yrs	Citizens	Not Citiz.

NORTHERN MARIANA ISLANDS

Far East Broadcasting Assocs.	1992	1	-	-	-	-
Totals:		1	-	-	-	-

PAKISTAN

BCM International (Canada)		1	-	-	-	-
Brethren Assemblies (Canada)		1	-	-	-	-
Christian and Msny. Alliance		4	-	-	-	-
FEBInternational	1969	20	-	2	-	-
International Missions Ontario	1954	4	-	-	-	-
Operation Mobilization Canada	1978	3	-	-	-	-
Salvation Army, The		5	-	-	-	-
SIM Canada	1957	3	-	-	-	-
TEAM of Canada	1946	5	2	-	-	-
World Mission Prayer League	1945	3	-	-	-	-
Totals:		49	2	2	-	-

PANAMA

Gospel Missionary Union Canada	1953	3	-	-	-	-
New Tribes Mission of Canada	1953	3	-	-	-	-
Wycliffe Bible Translators	1970	2	-	-	-	-
Totals:		8	-	-	-	-

PAPUA NEW GUINEA

Evangelical Lutheran Church	1967	-	2	3	-	-
Mission Aviation Flwshp Canada	1987	11	-	-	-	-
New Tribes Mission of Canada	1950	52	-	-	-	-
Salvation Army, The		2	-	-	-	-
Wycliffe Bible Translators	1956	32	1	7	-	-
Totals:		97	3	10	-	-

PARAGUAY

Evangelical Mennonite Conf.	1957	18	-	-	3	-
Mennonite Economic Development	1991	-	-	-	-	1
New Tribes Mission of Canada	1946	5	-	-	-	-
SIM Canada	1987	1	-	-	-	-
Youth With A Mission (Canada)		1	-	-	-	-
Totals:		25	-	-	3	1

PERU

ABWE - Canada	1945	2	-	-	-	-
Brethren Assemblies (Canada)		3	-	-	-	-
Canadian S. American Mission	1926	2	-	-	-	-
Christian and Msny. Alliance		10	-	-	-	-
Evangelical Lutheran Church	1976	1	-	-	-	-

COUNTRY Agency	Year Began	Personnel from Canada			Other Countries	
		4+ Yrs	2-4 Yrs	1-2 Yrs	Citizens	Not Citiz.
SIM Canada	1965	3	-	-	-	-
TEAM of Canada	1961	3	-	-	-	-
World Team	1981	8	-	-	-	-
Wycliffe Bible Translators	1946	11	-	-	-	-
Totals:		43	-	-	-	-

PHILIPPINES

Action International Mins.	1980	13	-	-	-	-
Bible Holiness Movement	1961	-	-	-	4	-
Brethren Assemblies (Canada)		2	-	-	-	-
Campus Crusade for Christ	1991	2	-	-	-	-
Christian Aid Mission		-	-	-	30	-
Christian and Msny. Alliance		21	1	-	-	-
Christian Blind Mission Intl.	1992	2	-	-	-	-
Christian Reformed Wld. Relief	1988	4	-	-	-	-
Emmanuel International	1979	2	-	-	4	-
Far East Broadcasting Assocs.	1996	-	1	-	-	-
International Missions Ontario	1955	4	-	-	-	-
International Needs - Canada	1984	-	-	-	10	-
International Teams of Canada	1984	2	2	-	7	-
New Tribes Mission of Canada	1951	2	-	-	-	-
OMF Canada	1951	16	1	-	-	-
SEND International of Canada	1945	19	-	-	-	-
World Team	1981	10	2	2	-	-
Wycliffe Bible Translators	1953	29	-	-	-	-
Youth With A Mission (Canada)		5	-	-	-	-
Totals:		133	7	2	55	-

POLAND

Apostolic Church of Pentecost	1990	4	-	-	-	-
Brethren Assemblies (Canada)		4	-	-	-	-
Eurovangelism	1980	-	-	-	9	-
International Teams of Canada	1974	-	2	-	-	-
Totals:		8	2	-	9	-

PORTUGAL

ABWE - Canada	1976	-	2	2	-	-
BGCC Global Ministries	1996	-	1	-	-	-
Brethren Assemblies (Canada)		4	-	-	-	-
Janz Team Ministries	1988	1	-	-	-	-
Salvation Army, The		1	-	-	-	-
Totals:		6	3	2	-	-

ROMANIA

Eurovangelism	1974	-	-	-	8	-

COUNTRY Agency	Year Began	Personnel from Canada			Other Countries	
		4+ Yrs	2-4 Yrs	1-2 Yrs	Citizens	Not Citiz.
International Teams of Canada	1971	-	-	-	-	4
Totals:		-	-	-	8	4

RUSSIAN FEDERATION

Campus Crusade for Christ	1991	-	2	1	-	-
Door of Hope Intl. (Canada)	1978	1	-	-	-	-
Eurovangelism	1985	-	-	-	11	-
Gospel Missionary Union Canada	1992	-	3	12	-	-
International Teams of Canada	1990	-	-	-	-	2
Janz Team Ministries	1992	-	-	-	-	-
Mennonite Economic Development	1989	-	1	-	11	2
New Tribes Mission of Canada	1992	2	-	-	-	-
OMS International - Canada	1991	-	-	2	-	-
Persecuted Church Fellowship	1976	-	-	-	15	-
Salvation Army, The		2	-	-	-	-
World Team	1992	-	2	-	-	-
World Vision Canada		-	-	2	-	-
Totals:		5	8	17	37	4

RWANDA

World Vision Canada		-	3	-	-	-
Totals:		-	3	-	-	-

SENEGAL

New Tribes Mission of Canada	1954	20	-	-	-	-
Pentecostal Assemblies Canada	1989	2	-	-	-	-
WEC International (Canada)	1936	2	-	-	-	-
World Vision Canada	1975	1	-	-	-	-
Totals:		25	-	-	-	-

SEYCHELLES

Pentecostal Assemblies Canada	1985	2	-	-	-	-
Totals:		2	-	-	-	-

SIERRA LEONE

Christian Reformed Wld. Relief	1982	1	-	-	-	-
Youth With A Mission (Canada)		1	-	-	-	-
Totals:		2	-	-	-	-

SINGAPORE

FEBInternational	1994	2	-	-	-	-
OMF Canada	1951	4	-	-	-	-
WEC International (Canada)	1980	2	-	-	-	-
Youth With A Mission (Canada)		2	-	-	-	-
Totals:		10	-	-	-	-

COUNTRY Agency	Year Began	Personnel from Canada			Other Countries	
		4+ Yrs	2-4 Yrs	1-2 Yrs	Citizens	Not Citiz.
SLOVAKIA						
Canadian Baptist Ministries	1989	2	-	-	-	-
Totals:		2	-	-	-	-
SOUTH AFRICA						
ABWE - Canada	1978	1	-	1	-	-
Africa Evangelical Fellowship	1889	11	2	-	-	-
Apostolic Church of Pentecost		4	-	-	-	-
Campus Crusade for Christ	1987	2	-	-	-	-
Child Evangelism Fellowship	1995	2	-	-	-	-
Global Outreach Mission	1976	2	-	-	-	-
HOPE Intl. Development Agency	1983	2	-	-	-	-
Operation Mobilization Canada		-	4	-	-	2
Pentecostal Assemblies Canada	1908	6	-	-	-	-
Presbyterian Church in Canada	1985	1	-	-	-	-
Salvation Army, The		9	-	-	-	-
TEAM of Canada	1892	3	-	-	-	-
Youth With A Mission (Canada)		2	-	-	-	-
Totals:		45	6	1	-	2
SPAIN						
BCM International (Canada)		2	-	-	-	-
Brethren Assemblies (Canada)		9	-	-	-	-
Christian and Msny. Alliance		3	-	-	-	-
FEBInternational	1985	6	-	-	-	-
Gospel Missionary Union Canada	1967	5	-	-	-	-
Pentecostal Assemblies Canada	1985	4	-	-	-	-
SEND International of Canada	1988	4	-	-	-	-
TEAM of Canada	1952	2	-	-	-	-
Youth With A Mission (Canada)		1	-	-	-	-
Totals:		36	-	-	-	-
SRI LANKA						
Pentecostal Assemblies Canada	1982	5	-	-	-	-
Totals:		5	-	-	-	-
ST CHRISTOPHER AND NEVIS						
Brethren Assemblies (Canada)		2	-	-	-	-
Totals:		2	-	-	-	-
ST VINCENT						
Brethren Assemblies (Canada)		1	-	-	-	-
Child Evangelism Fellowship	1991	-	-	-	2	-
Totals:		1	-	-	2	-

COUNTRY Agency	Year Began	Personnel from Canada			Other Countries	
		4+ Yrs	2-4 Yrs	1-2 Yrs	Citizens	Not Citiz.
SUDAN						
Africa Inland Mission (Canada)	1949	-	1	-	-	-
Emmanuel International	1985	-	2	-	-	1
Operation Mobilization Canada	1978	2	-	-	-	-
World Vision Canada	1972	-	-	1	-	-
	Totals:	2	3	1	-	1
SURINAME						
Wycliffe Bible Translators	1967	5	-	-	-	-
	Totals:	5	-	-	-	-
SWEDEN						
Child Evangelism Fellowship	1985	2	-	-	-	-
Operation Mobilization Canada		-	2	-	-	-
Youth With A Mission (Canada)		6	-	-	-	-
	Totals:	8	2	-	-	-
SWITZERLAND						
Child Evangelism Fellowship	1950	-	-	-	-	4
FEBInternational	1995	2	-	-	-	-
	Totals:	2	-	-	-	4
TAIWAN, REPUBLIC OF CHINA						
Christian and Msny. Alliance		7	-	-	-	-
Glad Tidings Missionary Soc.	1963	-	2	-	-	-
OMF Canada	1952	8	-	-	-	-
Pentecostal Assemblies Canada	1951	4	-	-	-	-
Presbyterian Church in Canada	1880	3	-	-	-	-
TEAM of Canada	1951	2	-	-	-	-
	Totals:	24	2	-	-	-
TANZANIA						
Africa Inland Mission (Canada)	1909	4	-	-	-	-
Bible Holiness Movement	1995	-	-	-	1	-
Christian Reformed Wld. Relief	1978	4	-	-	-	-
Emmanuel International	1985	-	-	-	-	1
Mennonite Economic Development	1986	-	2	-	49	-
Mission Aviation Flwshp Canada	1987	2	-	-	-	-
Pentecostal Assemblies Canada	1913	12	-	-	-	-
World Vision Canada	1970	2	-	-	-	-
	Totals:	24	2	-	50	1
THAILAND						
Christian and Msny. Alliance		2	4	-	-	-

COUNTRY Agency	Year Began	Personnel from Canada			Other Countries	
		4+ Yrs	2-4 Yrs	1-2 Yrs	Citizens	Not Citiz.
Far East Broadcasting Assocs.	1987	1	-	-	-	-
New Tribes Mission of Canada	1951	4	-	-	-	-
OMF Canada	1952	27	-	-	-	-
Pentecostal Assemblies Canada	1961	17	-	-	-	-
WEC International (Canada)	1947	1	-	-	-	-
Wycliffe Bible Translators	1987	6	-	-	-	-
Youth With A Mission (Canada)		3	-	-	-	-
Totals:		61	4	-	-	-

TOGO
Wycliffe Bible Translators	1967	1	-	-	-	-
Totals:		1	-	-	-	-

TRINIDAD & TOBAGO
Fundamental Baptist Mission	1990	-	-	-	1	-
TEAM of Canada	1963	2	-	-	-	-
World Team	1953	-	2	-	-	-
Totals:		2	2	-	1	-

UGANDA
Bible Holiness Movement	1980	-	-	-	3	-
Christian Reformed Wld. Relief	1986	2	-	-	-	-
Church of God (Anderson, IN)	1983	-	-	-	-	2
Emmanuel International	1983	1	-	-	-	8
Glad Tidings Missionary Soc.		3	-	-	4	-
Pentecostal Assemblies Canada	1948	6	-	-	-	-
Totals:		12	-	-	7	10

UKRAINE
ABWE - Canada	1986	-	2	-	-	-
Campus Crusade for Christ	1991	-	-	2	-	-
Canadian Baptist Ministries	1987	4	-	-	-	-
Greater Europe Mission	1994	1	-	-	-	-
Operation Mobilization Canada		-	-	2	-	-
Persecuted Church Fellowship	1976	-	-	-	15	-
Youth With A Mission (Canada)		5	-	-	-	-
Totals:		10	2	4	15	-

UNITED ARAB EMIRATES
TEAM of Canada	1960	3	1	-	-	-
Totals:		3	1	-	-	-

UNITED KINGDOM
Brethren Assemblies (Canada)		2	-	-	-	-
Child Evangelism Fellowship	1986	-	-	-	2	1

COUNTRY Agency	Year Began	Personnel from Canada			Other Countries	
		4+ Yrs	2-4 Yrs	1-2 Yrs	Citizens	Not Citiz.
Christian and Msny. Alliance		-	2	-	-	-
Far East Broadcasting Assocs.	1996	-	1	-	-	-
Gospel Missionary Union Canada	1985	2	-	-	-	-
International Missions Ontario	1971	2	-	-	-	-
International Teams of Canada	1987	2	-	-	2	-
Mission Aviation Flwshp Canada		1	-	-	-	-
Navigators of Canada, The		1	-	-	-	-
Operation Mobilization Canada	1962	-	-	3	-	-
WEC International (Canada)	1913	3	-	-	-	-
Youth With A Mission (Canada)		11	-	-	-	-
Totals:		24	3	3	4	1

URUGUAY

	Year Began	4+ Yrs	2-4 Yrs	1-2 Yrs	Citizens	Not Citiz.
Brethren Assemblies (Canada)		7	-	-	-	-
Operation Mobilization Canada	1990	2	-	1	-	-
Totals:		9	-	1	-	-

VENEZUELA

	Year Began	4+ Yrs	2-4 Yrs	1-2 Yrs	Citizens	Not Citiz.
Brethren Assemblies (Canada)		6	-	-	-	-
Canadian Baptist Ministries	1992	2	-	-	-	-
Christian and Msny. Alliance		4	-	-	-	-
FEBInternational	1990	8	-	-	-	-
New Tribes Mission of Canada	1946	21	-	-	-	-
TEAM of Canada	1906	9	-	-	-	-
Totals:		50	-	-	-	-

ZAMBIA

	Year Began	4+ Yrs	2-4 Yrs	1-2 Yrs	Citizens	Not Citiz.
Africa Evangelical Fellowship	1910	17	1	-	-	-
Bible Holiness Movement	1992	-	-	-	2	-
Brethren Assemblies (Canada)		27	-	-	-	-
Church of God (Anderson, IN)		-	-	-	-	2
International Needs - Canada	1984	-	-	-	8	-
Pentecostal Assemblies Canada	1950	6	-	-	-	-
Salvation Army, The		2	2	-	-	-
Totals:		52	3	-	10	2

ZIMBABWE

	Year Began	4+ Yrs	2-4 Yrs	1-2 Yrs	Citizens	Not Citiz.
Africa Evangelical Fellowship	1897	6	-	-	-	-
Apostolic Church of Pentecost	1951	2	-	-	-	-
Mennonite Economic Development	1993	-	-	-	5	1
Pentecostal Assemblies Canada	1948	12	-	-	-	-
Salvation Army, The		5	-	-	-	-
TEAM of Canada	1939	4	-	-	-	-
Totals:		29	-	-	5	1

Chapter 10

U.S. Catholic overseas mission

Anthony J. Gittins

L et me begin with two dis-
claimers: one cannot do justice to this topic in a few
words, and whatever is said about
something as elusive or evolving as
trends will depend on one's point of
view. In this brief space I will identify five trends, mention certain
corollaries and candidly acknowl-
edge existing tensions as the mission of Jesus continues to unfold
among us.

This text is not supported by statistics (but see Allan Scheid's "U.S.
Catholic overseas missionaries,"
chapter 12 of the *1993-95 Mission
Handbook*), but nor is it simply
impressionistic: it results from a
broad and deep engagement over
the years with the theoretical and
practical issues discussed.

1. The wider implications of "local church"

It is sometimes said that the Vati-

can II Council (1962-65) "rediscovered" the local church: the integrity
and responsibility of each diocesan
community under its local bishop
was seen in a new light after the
Council. But the process leading to
this rediscovery is perhaps less
widely understood.

From the seventeenth century,
the global mission of the Roman
Catholic Church was centrally
organized by the Congregation for
the Society for the Propagation of
the Faith in Rome. Through *jus
commissionis*, the Holy See con-
fided particular geographical territories to particular missionary
societies. Every place on earth thus
came within a designated canonical
territory. Each missionary society
was then uniquely responsible for
recruiting priests for its respective
territories, and the society in question normally appointed the bishop

Anthony J. Gittins, C.S.Sp., a member of the Congregation of the Holy Ghost (Spiritans), is a professor of theological anthropology at the Catholic Theological Union in Chicago, Illinois. Professor Gittins was a missionary in Sierra Leone, where he did his doctoral work in anthropology among the Mende people. His most recent books include *Gifts and Strangers* and *Bread for the Journey*.

of each territory from among its members. Because of the preponderance of European and North American missionaries, by 1965 most bishops of Africa, Asia and Oceania were European or American.

In 1969 *jus commissionis* was abolished. Each local bishop became responsible for staffing and evangelizing the local church in his care. No longer could he rely on a particular (overseas) missionary society for personnel. Moreover, from now on bishops would normally be appointed from among the indigenous clergy—secular or diocesan, rather than regular or from the missionary societies. Fortunately the numbers of local clergy were increasing just as the West saw an unprecedented drop in its clerical missionary recruits.

After 1969 there was a proliferation of dioceses in the non-Western world, with a corresponding increase in the number of indigenous bishops and a decrease in expatriate missionaries generally and expatriate bishops in particular. Local bishops had to cast their nets as widely as possible if they were to find expatriate missionaries.

Twenty years after the abolition of *jus commissionis* the contours of Catholic mission had clearly changed. Where many local churches had been heavily dependent on expatriate missionaries, now many parts of the southern hemisphere, while not entirely self-sufficient in terms of clergy, had nevertheless produced them in significant numbers. Where before large territories in the south had been evangelized by missionaries who were homogeneous in terms of ethnicity and membership of particular societies, now the same large territories not only had far fewer expatriate missionaries but were also much more diverse, both ethnically and in their membership of missionary societies.

So the local church was produced, or rediscovered, typically led by an indigenous bishop, assisted by a small cadre of expatriate clerical missionaries, and with increasing numbers of local clergy and women religious (sisters). Not only did this open the door to the further development of local churches, but it became possible to identify a Providential matching of bishops seeking new missionary personnel with the proliferation of laity seeking placements in missions overseas.

Inculturation—the process whereby local churches become authentically local and authentically Christian through a subtle integration of the gospel and particular cultures (or through the incarnation of the gospel in a particular cultural milieu)—was now much more possible, at least in theory.

The evangelizing armies of the north (priests, brothers and nuns) had been significantly reduced; the evangelized churches of the south were now maturing. A multifaceted Christianity refracting the light of many cultures could now be held up as an authentic model of the body of Christ, the church. The growing ultramontanism (the centralization of authority in the hands of the pope) of Pope John Paul II, however, may inhibit the fuller development of local churches worldwide.

2. The wider implications of lay missionaries

There was a time when to say "missionary work" in a Roman Catholic context implied pioneering sacramental ministry (chiefly baptism and confirmation, with long lines of penitents at the sacrament of reconciliation and a smattering of church marriages). Thus, to say "missionary" was to imply "ordained priest" (with lay brothers and sisters serving as auxiliaries, not to say lesser missionaries).

By the end of the 1960s a new trend was noticeable: a growing number of laity seeking—even demanding—involvement in the wider mission of the church. This is well known, and was the subject of a report in a previous edition of this *Handbook*. But now within the Roman Catholic church, numbers of laity recruited for overseas mission exceed prospective clerical recruits, and a new institutionalization is apparent.

Many people join organizations that were formed specifically for the laity, created by those missionary societies of men (and also of women) that were once the mainstay of Catholic missionary activity. Some, however, join specifically lay-founded and lay-led groups like the Volunteer Missionary Movement (VMM). The former find they are absorbing a long history and often a rich tradition of ministry; nevertheless there may be lingering traces, or less subtle indications, of clerical or hierarchical control. The latter, while free to develop their own lay character, lack a history or tradition. Both kinds of organizations attract recruits, though individual organizations wax and wane. We may need another generation before we can discern real trends.

One point to note: despite contemporary centralizing tendencies, and despite Roman control over religious and missionary societies, the lay missionary organizations continue to develop in varied ways and with varying degrees of success. At this point, such organizations remain free-standing and autonomous. Perhaps they are not yet perceived as ecclesially significant.

Three things are becoming clear. First, the increase in the numbers of lay missionaries has underlined the urgent need for appropriate and intensive theological and practical training. Second, the trend away from a missionary commitment that is characteristically for a lifetime, to one that is characteristically for three years or less, calls for a careful reappraisal of what we think the missionary presence can and should accomplish. And third, the presence of two contrasting models of missionary commitment—one clerical, sacramental and long-term; the other lay, non-sacramental and short-term—is creating a range of effects, from openness, collaboration and real mutuality on the one hand, to less wholesome responses on the other.

3. Eucharist, ministry and Christian unity

The decline in clergy is particularly noticeable in the richer countries of the First World. But the impact of declining numbers has been felt acutely (and will probably be felt chronically) in the Third World, where the rising numbers of the baptized are more than the rising numbers that indigenous clergy can adequately serve. The outcome is what has been called a "Eucharistic famine": many communities deprived of the Eucharist for long periods, with no real hope of an improved situation unless radical changes are made in Roman Catholic practice.

Currently, Rome is emphasizing the values of unity and universality. Yet this creates many tensions in missionary circles, both in theological discussion and for the practical implementation of inculturation. Critical pastoral needs remain unresolved.

For all its promise, the increase in laity in mission cannot alleviate the Eucharistic famine, and currently all signs point to an ever-deteriorating pastoral situation. At a local level, "priestless parishes" are increasing, with certain obvious effects: Mass and Holy Communion become rarer, while Liturgies of the Word and Communion Services increase. This represents a major change in Roman Catholic practice. Vatican II acclaimed the Eucharist as the center and the source of the Christian life. For some Roman Catholics this phrase has become less a reality, less even than a pious hope, and more a nostalgic memory.

A further trend concerns ecumenical relations. Official Roman Catholic dialogue seems less than animated and creative at times. A hopeful trend is noticeable at the grassroots, and among theologians and missionaries. Deep and lasting commitment to ecumenical collaboration is palpable. Many local-level initiatives are being taken, such as the agreement, in 1995, between the U.S. Catholic Mission Association and the Committee on Common Witness of the World Council of Churches. In relation to preparation courses for overseas missionary personnel, the agreement pledged "never again to do separately what can be done together." This pledge ratified what was increasingly the practice, and Roman Catholics are now regularly part of common orientations with the Lutheran Church (ELCA), the Presbyterian Church (USA), the United Church of Christ (UCC) and others. The place of the Eucharist remains paramount. The practical question—whether we gather in unity or gather to be united—continues to challenge ecumenically-minded Christians.

4. Christology, pneumatology and interreligious dialogue

As the dialogue with world religions continues, its effect on missionary deployment and policy is increasingly felt. "Outside the church, no salvation" is a slogan that has already been reinterpreted by Roman Catholics in relation to their understanding of "church" in the context of ecumenism. Now it is being reexamined more explicitly in the broader context of the world's religions.

In 1990 Pope John Paul II issued a lengthy encyclical, *Redemptoris Missio*, on the subject of mission. A few months later, also from Rome, from a different but official Roman congregation, came *Dialogue and Proclamation*. While the former document displays papal thought which is both conservative and wary of dialogue in a theological and missiological sense, the general tenor of the latter is considerably more open to other perspectives and to the necessity of real, respectful and mutual dialogue. So while one discernible trend is toward retrenchment and proclamation, a complementary trend espouses greater openness and exchange.

From the dialogue in progress, one can identify further trends in missiological thinking. For some, a classical Christocentric understanding remains in place and is the starting point for further discussion. A theocentric model that would look to discern the workings of God, but not explicitly Christ, in people's lives now exists alongside the Christocentric view. As interreligious dialogue continues, and one hears the voices of those with a variety of experiences of God, a new and increasingly animated discussion of pneumatology or the place of the Holy Spirit in the world is taking place. The Catholic Theological Society of America devoted its annual meeting of 1996 to the topic of the Holy Spirit, and for many Catholics it is becoming increasingly helpful to see the Spirit at work in the wider world, where it is difficult to see how Jesus or the Christ can be said to be central, much less indispensable.

For others, to speak only of God the Creator or God the Holy Spirit (rather than explicitly of Jesus the Christ) as the focal point of interreligious dialogue is deeply disturbing and threatens age-old understandings. The debate continues.

5. Reconciliation and conflict resolution

The belated understanding of the implications of the Holocaust has brought in its train awareness of many other unspeakable acts of atrocity, both from before World War II and also more recently in places like Romania, Rwanda and Bosnia. Because of this increasing sensitization to human brutality and the urge to vengeance, a new paradigm of mission seems to be emerging more and more clearly: mission as reconciliation.

One senses in the Roman Catholic community that while the agenda for contextualization and inculturation is unfinished and perhaps even at an impasse, another agenda may be claiming priority. The agenda of reconciliation has hardly been addressed yet it promises much. Truth Commissions have been established by several nations as a means of discovering raw facts about brutality and offering amnesty to some guilty parties.

Conferences, discussions and publications have proliferated almost overnight within the Roman Catholic context and certainly beyond. Of all the trends that one might identify, none is more palpable than this. "Mission as reconciliation" is now not merely a slogan but a rallying cry. It represents something distinctly possible amid a sea of daunting challenges.

At the end of his wonderful *Transforming Mission* (Orbis, 1991), David Bosch describes thirteen models or paradigms of mission: mission as reconciliation is not among them. Yet in the past few years this phrase may have been uttered more often than any of the thirteen. It has magnetic appeal. It seems to have caught the Roman Catholic imagination. But it is certainly not limited to the Roman Catholic community, and may become a focus both of ecumenical mission and collaboration. Reconciliation, after all, is not only a subject that may galvanize missionaries from many denominations within the Christian tradition: it may even become the road to real unity.

Countries served by
U.S. Catholic sending communities, 1996
(Listed by country, gender and sending community)

Albania
Women (1): Missionaries of Charity - 1

American Samoa
Men (1): Maryknoll Fathers & Brothers - 1
Women (3): Los Angeles Archdiocese - 2; Marist Missionary Sisters (MA) - 1

Angola
Women (3): Daughters of Charity (CA) - 2; Daughters of Charity (NY) - 1

Antigua
Men (1): Franciscan Sisters of Philadelphia - 1

Argentina
Men (6): Divine Word, Society (IL) - 1; Jesuits (WI) - 1; Marian Fathers (IL) - 2; Maryknoll Fathers & Brothers - 1; Maryknoll Mission Assoc of the Faithful - 1
Women (14): Cabrini Mission Corps - 3; Christian Charity, Sisters (IL) - 1; Christian Charity, Sisters (NJ) - 1; Maryknoll Mission Assoc of the Faithful - 1; Mercy, Sisters (CA) - 1; Mercy, Sisters (MI) - 1; Mission Srs of Sacred Heart - 1; Resurrection, Sisters - 1; St. Casimir, Sisters (IL) - 4

Australia
Men (10): Divine Word, Society (IL) - 7; Franciscan OFM Cap (St Joseph Prov) - 2; Gallup Diocese - 1
Women (12): Cabrini Mission Corps - 1; Franciscan Missionaries of Mary - 1; Holy Family of Nazareth, Srs (IL) - 5; Little Sisters of Jesus - 1; Marist Missionary Sisters (MA) - 2; Missionary Sr Servs of Holy Spirit - 2

Bahamas
Men (17): Benedictine - Am Cassinese Cong (MN) - 6; Cong. of the Sacred Hearts (MA) - 6; Jesuits (New England) - 2; Passionists (NJ) - 3
Women (8): Charity, Sisters (NY) - 3; Dominican Sisters (Caldwell, NJ) - 2; Franciscan Sisters of Clinton, IA - 1; Mercy, Sisters (ME) - 2

Bangladesh
Men (23): Holy Cross Brothers (IN) - 6; Holy Cross Fathers (CT) - 1; Holy Cross Fathers (IN) - 10; Marianists (MO) - 1; Maryknoll Fathers & Brothers - 4; Pontifical Institute for Foreign Missions - 1
Women (13): Holy Cross, Cong. of Sisters (IN) - 7; Maryknoll Sisters - 6

Belgium
Men (3): Evansville Diocese - 1;

Lansing Diocese - 1; New York Archdiocese - 1

Women (2): Franciscan Sisters of Atonement - 1; Religious of the Assumption (N Am Prov) - 1

Belize

Men (28): Benedictine - Swiss Am Fed (AR) - 4; Jesuit Volunteers: International - 2; Jesuits (LA) - 1; Jesuits (MO) - 13; Jesuits (WI) - 2; O.L. Most Holy Trinity, Society - 5; St. Louis Archdiocese - 1

Women (19): Charity of Nazareth, Sisters (KY) - 2; Dominican Sisters (St. Katharine, KY) - 1; Holy Family, Sisters (LA) - 3; Jesuit Volunteers: International - 5; Mercy, Sisters (CT) - 1; Mercy, Sisters (MD) - 1; O.L. Most Holy Trinity, Society - 2; Pallottine Sisters (MO) - 4

Benin

Women (3): Daughters of Charity/Sac. Hrt. of Jesus - 1; Rel Hospitalieres de St Joseph - 1; Religious Venerini Sisters - 1

Bermuda

Women (4): Charity of SVP, Sisters (Halifax) - 4

Bolivia

Men (80): Allentown Diocese - 1; Bridgeport Diocese - 1; Chicago Archdiocese - 1; Christian Brothers, De La Salle (MD) - 1; Des Moines Diocese - 1; Dominican Friars (IL) - 6; Galveston-Houston Diocese - 1; Kansas City-St Joseph (MO) Diocese - 1; LaCrosse Diocese - 3; Maryknoll Fathers & Brothers - 29; Maryknoll Mission Assoc of the Faithful - 5; Oblates of Mary

Immaculate (NH) - 2; Order of Friars Minor (Holy Name Prov) - 7; Portland (OR) Archdiocese - 2; Salesian Lay Missioners (NY) - 7; Springfield (MA) Diocese - 1; St. Louis Archdiocese - 6; Xaverian Brothers (MD) - 5

Women (75): Adorers of the Blood of Christ (IL) - 5; Daughters of Charity (MO) - 1; Daughters of Charity (NY) - 1; Dominican Sisters (Sinsinawa, WI) - 6; Franciscan Mission Service - 1; Franciscan Sisters of Allegany - 3; Maryknoll Mission Assoc of the Faithful - 5; Maryknoll Sisters - 29; Mercy, Sisters (Merion, PA) - 1; Most Precious Blood, Sisters (MO) - 6; Our Lady Victory Mission Sisters - 2; Presentation, Sisters (Dubuque, IA) - 4; Presentation, Sisters (NY) - 1; Salesian Lay Missioners (NY) - 9; School Sisters of Notre Dame (MD) - 1

Botswana

Women (1): Ursulines (NY) - 1

Brazil

Men (175): Benedictine - Am Cassinese Cong (KS) - 4; Benedictine - Am Cassinese Cong (PA) - 3; Camden Diocese - 2; Cistercians (NY) - 2; Columbans - 3; Comboni Lay Missionary Program - 1; Davenport Diocesan Volunteer Prog - 4; Detroit Archdiocese - 1; Franciscan OFM Conv (NY) - 5; Holy Cross Brothers (TX) - 13; Jesuits (CA) - 1; Jesuits (LA) - 9; Jesuits (New England) - 3; Kansas City (KS) Archdiocese - 1; Legionaries of Christ - 3; Maryknoll Fathers & Brothers - 5; Maryknoll Mission Assoc of the

Faithful - 4; Missionhurst - 2; Oblates of Mary Immaculate (DC) - 15; Oblates of Mary Immaculate (MN) - 8; Oblates of Mary Immaculate (NH) - 1; Oblates of the Virgin Mary - 1; Order of Friars Minor (Holy Name Prov) - 14; Order of Friars Minor (S Heart Prov) - 21; Pontifical Institute for Foreign Missions - 2; Redemptorists (Brasil) - 21; Redemptorists (CO) - 16; Saginaw Diocese - 1; St. Francis de Sales, Oblates (DE) - 3; St. Francis de Sales, Oblates (OH) - 1; Stigmatine Fathers - 2; Xaverian Missionaries - 3

Women (98): Benedictine Sisters (Atchison, KS) - 1; Benedictine Sisters (St. Joseph, MN) - 2; Columbus Diocese - 1; Comboni Lay Missionary Program - 1; Davenport Diocesan Volunteer Prog - 4; Divine Savior, Sisters (WI) - 1; Dominican Sisters (San Rafael, CA) - 1; Felician Sisters (IL) - 2; Felician Sisters (MI) - 1; Felician Sisters (NY) - 1; Franciscan Sisters (Wheaton) - 3; Franciscan Sisters of Allegany - 5; Franciscan Sisters of Atonement - 1; Franciscan Sisters of Joliet, IL - 7; Franciscan Sisters of Mary - 3; Franciscan Sisters of Sacred Heart - 3; Franciscan Sisters of St. George - 2; Franciscan Sisters of the Holy Eucharist - 1; Franciscan Sisters of the Poor - 1; Holy Cross, Cong. of Sisters (IN) - 10; IHM Sisters of Monroe - 2; Imm Heart of Mary, Servs (ME) - 3; Kansas City (KS) Archdiocese - 1; Maryknoll Mission Assoc of the Faithful - 4; Maryknoll Sisters - 2; Medical Missionaries of Mary - 1; Mission Srs Imm Concept (NJ) - 2; Mission Srs Imm Heart of Mary - 1; Mission Srs of Sacred Heart - 1; Notre Dame de Namur, Srs (CA) - 1; Notre Dame de Namur, Srs (CT) - 1; Notre Dame de Namur, Srs (OH) - 4; Order of St. Clare (OH) - 3; Poor Handmaids of Jesus Christ - 1; St Joseph, Sisters, TOSF - 1; St. Joseph of Lyons, Srs - 1; St. Joseph, Cong of Srs (Concordia) - 2; St. Joseph, Cong of Srs (Rockville Ctr) - 1; St. Joseph, Sisters (Rochester) - 11; St. Mary of Namur, Sisters (NY) - 2; St. Mary of Namur, Sisters (TX) - 1; Ursuline Sisters (MO) - 1

Cambodia

Men (6): Maryknoll Fathers & Brothers - 3; Maryknoll Mission Assoc of the Faithful - 3
Women (6): Maryknoll Mission Assoc of the Faithful - 3; Maryknoll Sisters - 3

Cameroon

Men (2): Claretian Missionaries (IL) - 1; Xaverian Missionaries - 1
Women (14): Daughters of Mary and Joseph - 1; Daughters of the Holy Spirit - 1; Holy Union Sisters (MA) - 3; Los Angeles Archdiocese - 2; Notre Dame, Cong of Srs (CT) - 1; Presentation of Mary, Srs (NH) - 2; Servants of Mary, Srs - 1; St. Mary of Namur, Sisters (NY) - 1; Ursuline Sisters (MO) - 2

Canada

Men (37): Augustinians of the Assumption - 2; Buffalo Diocese - 1; Camden Diocese - 2; Dominican

Friars (LA) - 2; El Paso Diocese - 1; Fort Wayne-South Bend Diocese - 1; Franciscan Friars of Atonement - 9; Holy Family, Missionaries of - 1; Lafayette (IN) Diocese - 1; Lansing Diocese - 1; LaSalette Fathers (WI) - 1; Legionaries of Christ - 1; Louisville Diocese - 1; Oblates of Mary Immaculate (MN) - 3; Oblates of Mary Immaculate (NH) - 3; Providence Diocese - 1; Salesians (NY) - 4; San Bernardino Diocese - 1; Springfield (IL) Diocese - 1
Women (44): Benedictine Sisters (Mt. Angel, OR) - 1; Franciscan Mission Srs O.L. Sorrows - 2; Franciscan Sisters of Atonement - 6; Little Sisters of the Poor (NY) - 6; Mission de N D des Anges, Srs (Quebec) - 2; Mission Srs Imm Concept (Quebec) - 13; Missionaries of Charity (NE Region) - 1; Missionary Srs of Our Lady of Africa - 2; Sacred Heart, Society - 2; Scalabrini Sisters (IL) - 2; Sisters of St Chretienne - 1; St. Joseph of Peace, Sisters - 5; St. Mary of Namur, Sisters (NY) - 1

Central African Republic
Men (1): Franciscan OFM (ME) - 1
Women (1): Missionaries of Charity - 1

Chad
Men (1): Missionaries of Africa 1

Chile
Men (59): Columbans - 4; Holy Cross Associates - 2; Holy Cross Brothers (IN) - 1; Holy Cross Brothers (NY) - 1; Holy Cross Fathers (IN) - 11; Jesuits (MD) - 6;

Maryknoll Fathers & Brothers - 18; Maryknoll Mission Assoc of the Faithful - 6; Oblates of the Virgin Mary - 2; Precious Blood, Society (OH) - 7; Salesians (NY) - 1
Women (49): Daughters of the Holy Spirit - 2; Franciscan Sisters of Allegany - 1; Holy Child Jesus, Society (PA) - 4; Holy Cross Associates - 3; Maryknoll Mission Assoc of the Faithful - 4; Maryknoll Sisters - 13; Mercy, Sisters (MI) - 1; Owensboro Diocese - 1; Precious Blood, Sisters (OH) - 5; Providence, Sisters (MA) - 1; School Sisters of Notre Dame (CT) - 5; School Sisters of St. Francis of Bethlehem, PA - 1; School Sisters of St. Francis of Pgh, PA - 1; St. Columban, Sisters - 2; St. Joseph Carondelet, Srs (CA) - 2; St. Joseph Carondelet, Srs (MN) - 2; St. Joseph Carondelet, Srs (NY) - 1

China
Men (12): Benedictine - Am Cassinese Cong (MN) - 1; Jesuits (OR) - 1; Marist Brothers (NY) - 2; Maryknoll Fathers & Brothers - 4; Maryknoll Mission Assoc of the Faithful - 1; Order of Friars Minor (S Heart Prov) - 2; Salesians (NY) - 1
Women (7): Daughters of Charity (MO) - 1; Maryknoll Mission Assoc of the Faithful - 1; Maryknoll Sisters - 2; Missionary Benedictine Sisters - 1; Providence, Sisters (IN) - 1; St. Columban, Sisters - 1

Colombia
Men (15): Basilian Fathers (Toronto) - 2; Boise Diocese - 2; Consolata Missionary Fathers - 2; Denver Archdiocese - 1; Divine

Word, Society (IL) - 1; Lexington Diocese - 1; Oblates of Mary Immaculate (DC) - 1; Sacred Heart Missionaries (IL) - 3; Scalibrini Fathers (IL) - 1; Viatorians (IL) - 1 **Women** (18): Denver Archdiocese - 2; Dominican Sisters (NY) - 2; Franciscan Sisters (Rochester, MN) - 7; Grey Nuns (MA) - 2; Little Sisters of the Poor (NY) - 1; Manchester Diocese - 1; Marist Missionary Sisters (MA) - 2; Portland (ME) Diocese - 1

Congo

Women (1): Little Sisters of the Poor (NY) - 1

Cook Islands

Men (1): Cong. of the Sacred Hearts (CA) - 1

Costa Rica

Men (11): Christian Foundation for Children & Aging - 1; Franciscan OFM Cap (St Joseph Prov) - 2; Franciscan OFM Cap (St Mary Prov) - 1; Franciscan OFM Conv (NY) - 2; Missionary Servants/Most Holy Trinity - 4; New Orleans Archdiocese - 1
Women (6): Missionary Cenacle Volunteers - 2; Oblate Sisters of Providence - 3; School Sisters of St. Francis (Milwaukee, WI) - 1

Cote D'Ivoire

Men (5): African Missions, Society of - 2; Christian Brothers, Cong. - 1; Marianists (MO) - 1; SMA Lay Missionaries - 1
Women (2): Bernardine Franciscan Sisters - 1; SMA Lay Missionaries - 1

Cuba

Men (1): Franciscan OFM Cap (St Mary Prov) - 1

Cyprus

Men (2): Franciscan OFM (DC) - 2

Czech Republic

Men (1): Philadelphia Archdiocese - 1
Women (3): Good Shepherd Sisters (DC) - 1; Mercy, Sisters (Dallas, PA) - 1; St. Joseph of Chambery, Srs - 1

Denmark

Men (4): Oblates of Mary Immaculate (MN) - 4

Dominica

Men (4): Redemptorists (MD) - 4

Dominican Republic

Men (24): Arlington Diocese - 2; Brooklyn Diocese - 2; Green Bay Diocese - 2; Milwaukee Archdiocese - 2; Missionhurst - 5; Montfort Missionaries (NY) - 1; New York Archdiocese - 1; Redemptorists (PR) - 8; Scarboro Missions - 1
Women (22): Divine Providence, Sisters (PA) - 1; Dominican Sisters (Adrian, MI) - 7; Franciscan Sisters of Millvale, PA - 1; Franciscan Sisters of Philadelphia - 2; Holy Child Jesus, Society (PA) - 1; Oblate Sisters of Providence - 1; Orlando Diocese - 1; Our Lady Christian Doctrine, Sisters - 1; Rel Hospitalieres de St Joseph - 2; Response-Ability Program - 1; Schoenstatt Sisters of Mary (WI) - 1; St. Joseph, Cong of Srs (Rockville Ctr) - 2; St. Mary of Namur, Sisters (NY) - 1

East Timor

Women (3): Maryknoll Sisters - 3

Ecuador

Men (19): Bridgeport Diocese - 1; Comboni Missionaries - 1; Family Unity International, Inc. - 2; Gallup Diocese - 1; Indianapolis Archdiocese - 1; Jesuits (CA) - 1; Jesuits (NY) - 1; Joliet Diocese - 1; Metuchen Diocese - 1; New York Archdiocese - 1; Providence Diocese - 1; Rostro de Cristo Mission Vol Program - 6; Salesian Lay Missioners (NY) - 1

Women (20): Charity of Leavenworth, Sisters - 2; Charity, Sisters (OH) - 1; Davenport Diocesan Volunteer Prog - 2; Divine Providence, Congregation (KY) - 2; Dominican Sisters (Kenosha, WI) - 1; Family Unity International, Inc. - 1; Franciscan Sisters of Little Falls - 3; Maryknoll Sisters - 1; Rostro de Cristo Mission Vol Program - 3; Scarboro Missions - 1; Sisters of Charity, BVM (IA) - 3

Egypt

Men (7): Franciscan OFM (DC) - 1; Indianapolis Archdiocese - 1; Jesuits (New England) - 1; Maryknoll Fathers & Brothers - 4

Women (1): Little Sisters of the Assumption - 1

El Salvador

Men (17): Cleveland Diocese - 5; Davenport Diocese - 1; Franciscan Mission Service - 1; Gary Diocese - 1; Jesuits (MD) - 1; Jesuits (NY) - 1; Maryknoll Fathers & Brothers - 3; Missionaries of Pastoral Charity

Society - 1; Order of Friars Minor (Imm Conc Prov) - 2; Richmond Diocese - 1

Women (25): Cleveland Diocese - 4; Dominican Sisters (Sinsinawa, WI) - 1; Franciscan Sisters of Holy Family (IA) - 2; Franciscan Srs Perpetual Adoration - 1; Maryknoll Mission Assoc of the Faithful - 3; Maryknoll Sisters - 6; Mercy, Sisters (CA) - 1; Notre Dame, Cong of Srs (CT) - 1; Providence, Sisters (WA) - 2; School Sisters of Notre Dame (MD) - 1; Society of Helpers (IL) - 1; St. Joseph, Cong of Srs (Orange) - 1; Volunteer Missionary Movement - 1

England

Men (10): Christian Brothers, De La Salle (CA) - 1; Columbans - 1; Divine Word, Society (IL) - 1; Franciscan Friars of Atonement - 3; Legionaries of Christ - 1; O.L. Most Holy Trinity, Society - 2; Wilmington Diocese - 1

Women (5): Franciscan Sisters of Philadelphia - 1; Missionaries of Charity (NE Region) - 2; Missionary Sr Servs of Holy Spirit - 1; Religious of the Assumption (N Am Prov) - 1

Estonia

Women (1): Most Precious Blood, Sisters (MO) - 1

Ethiopia

Men (9): Christian Brothers, De La Salle (Midwest) - 1; Christian Brothers, De La Salle (NY) - 2; Christian Brothers, De La Salle (RI) - 2; Jesuits (New England) - 1; Mary-

knoll Fathers & Brothers - 1; Spiritans (PA) - 1; Vincentians (PA) - 1
Women (13): Comboni Missionary Sisters (VA) - 1; Daughters of Charity (MD) - 1; Daughters of Charity (MO) - 1; Franciscan Missionaries of Mary - 1; Franciscan Sisters of Philadelphia - 1; Good Shepherd Sisters (OH) - 1; Medical Mission Sisters - 2; Medical Missionaries of Mary - 4; Religious Teachers Filippini - 1

Fiji

Men (4): Columbans - 3; Jesuits (CA) - 1
Women (2): Marist Missionary Sisters (MA) - 2

Finland

Women (4): Most Precious Blood, Sisters (MO) - 4

France

Women (8): Daughters of Charity (MO) - 2; Daughters of the Holy Spirit - 1; Jesus and Mary, Rel (MD) - 1; Religious of the Assumption (N Am Prov) - 4

Gambia

Women (2): Presentation of Mary, Srs (MA) - 1; School Sisters of Notre Dame (MO) - 1

Germany

Men (9): Lansing Diocese - 1; Legionaries of Christ - 3; Richmond Diocese - 1; Saginaw Diocese - 1; Savannah Diocese - 1; Servite Friars (IL) - 1; Sioux City Diocese - 1
Women (3): Dominican Sisters (Mission San Jose) - 1; School Sisters of Notre Dame (WI) - 2

Ghana

Men (35): Divine Word, Society (IL) - 10; Franciscan OFM Conv (MD) - 6; Holy Cross Brothers (IN) - 5; Holy Cross Fathers (IN) - 1; Jesuits (NY) - 4; Los Angeles Archdiocese - 1; Missionaries of Africa - 3; SMA Lay Missionaries - 4; Spiritan Associates - 1
Women (44): Divine Providence, Congregation (KY) - 5; Franciscan Missionaries of Mary - 2; Holy Cross, Cong. of Sisters (IN) - 2; IHM Sisters of Monroe - 2; Loretto, Sisters (CO) - 2; Medical Mission Sisters - 7; Missionary Sr Servs of Holy Spirit - 4; Missionary Srs of Our Lady of Africa - 1; School Sisters of Notre Dame (CT) - 3; School Sisters of Notre Dame (MO) - 4; School Sisters of Notre Dame (TX) - 5; School Sisters of Notre Dame (WI) - 1; Sisters of Charity, BVM (IA) - 1; SMA Lay Missionaries - 4; Spiritan Associates - 1

Greece

Men (1): Order of Friars Minor (St John Bapt Prov) - 1

Greenland

Men (1): Oblates of Mary Immaculate (MN) - 1

Guam

Men (13): Franciscan OFM Cap (GU) - 1; Franciscan OFM Cap (St Mary Prov) - 8; Great Falls-Billings Diocese - 1; Jesuit Volunteers: International - 1; Jesuits (NY) - 2
Women (3): Franciscan Sisters of Joliet, IL - 1; Mercedarian Missionaries of Berriz - 2

Guatemala

Men (59): Benedictine - Swiss Am Fed (IL) - 3; Benedictine - Swiss Am Fed (LA) - 1; Christian Brothers, De La Salle (MD) - 1; Christian Brothers, De La Salle (Midwest) - 1; Christian Foundation for Children & Aging - 2; Claretian Missionaries (IL) - 2; Claretian Vol & Lay Missionaries - 1; Comboni Missionaries - 1; Dominican Friars (CA) - 1; Dubuque Archdiocese - 1; Franciscan Mission Service - 2; Galveston-Houston Diocese - 1; God's Child Project - 1; Greensburg Diocese - 1; Helena Diocese - 1; Jesuits (NY) - 2; Maryknoll Fathers & Brothers - 15; Missionhurst - 2; New Ulm Diocese 3; Oblates of Mary Immaculate (MN) - 1; Oblates of Mary Immaculate (TX) - 3; Oklahoma City Archdiocese - 1; Order of Friars Minor (Imm Conc Prov) - 6; Passionists (NJ) - 1; Precious Blood, Society (OH) - 2; Spokane Diocese - 1; Volunteer Missionary Movement - 2

Women (84): Adorers of the Blood of Christ (IL) - 1; Benedictine Sisters (Ferdinand, IN) - 3; Benedictine Sisters (Watertown, SD) - 1; Cabrini Mission Corps - 1; Charity, Sisters (NY) - 3; Charity, Sisters (OH) - 1; Christian Foundation for Children & Aging - 4; Claretian Vol & Lay Missionaries - 2; Daughters of Charity (IN) - 1; Daughters of Charity (MD) - 1; Daughters of Charity (MO) - 1; Dominican Sisters (Akron, OH) - 1; Dominican Sisters (Houston, TX) - 2; Franciscan Mission Service - 2; Franciscan Sisters of Little Falls - 1; Franciscan Sisters of Peace - 2; Franciscan Sisters of Philadelphia - 3; Helena Diocese - 2; IHM Sisters of Scranton - 1; Maryknoll Mission Assoc of the Faithful - 1; Maryknoll Sisters - 19; Mercy, Sisters (CT) - 2; Mercy, Sisters (Dallas, PA) - 1; Mercy, Sisters (Pgh, PA) - 1; Mission Srs Imm Heart of Mary - 1; Notre Dame, Cong of Srs (CT) - 2; Order of St. Clare (TN) - 2; Precious Blood, Sisters (OH) - 3; Presentation, Sisters (CA) - 1; Presentation, Sisters (Dubuque, IA) - 1; School Sisters of Notre Dame (MN) - 4; School Sisters of Notre Dame (TX) - 1; School Sisters of Notre Dame (WI) - 1; School Sisters of St. Francis (Milwaukee, WI) - 3; Sisters of Charity Incarnate Word - 3; Sisters of Charity, BVM (IA) - 1; Spokane Diocese - 2; Volunteer Missionary Movement - 2

Guyana

Men (1): Catholic Medical Mission Board - 1

Women (1): Ursuline Nuns of the Roman Union - 1

Haiti

Men (28): Christian Foundation for Children & Aging - 1; Christian Instruction, Brothers (ME) - 2; Jesuits (NY) - 1; Missionhurst - 2; O.L. Most Holy Trinity, Society - 1; Oblates of Mary Immaculate (NH) - 17; St. Francis de Sales, Oblates (DE) - 1; Xaverian Brothers (MA) - 1; Xaverian Brothers (MD) - 2

Women (27): Blessed Sacrament Sisters - 2; Dominican Sisters

(Edmonds, WA) - 1; Franciscan Missionaries of O. L. (N Am Prov) - 2; Hands Together, Inc. - 4; Holy Cross, Sisters (NH) - 3; Hospital Sisters of St. Francis (Am Prov) - 4; Imm Heart of Mary, Servs (ME) - 2; Little Sisters of Jesus - 1; Mercy, Sisters (CT) - 1; Missionaries of Charity - 1; Missionaries of Charity (NE Region) - 2; O.L. Most Holy Trinity, Society - 1; Sisters of St Joseph (IN) - 1; St. Anne, Sisters (MA) - 2

Honduras

Men (32): Dominican Friars (IL) - 2; Franciscan OFM Cap (St Joseph Prov) - 1; Franciscan OFM Cap (St Mary Prov) - 2; Franciscan OFM Conv (MD) - 1; Jesuits (CA) - 4; Jesuits (MO) - 8; Jesuits (New England) - 1; Jesuits (WI) - 3; Maryknoll Fathers & Brothers - 5; Order of Friars Minor (Imm Conc Prov) - 4; Rostro de Cristo Mission Vol Program - 1
Women (22): Franciscan Sisters - 4; IHM Sisters of Monroe - 2; Mercy, Sisters (Dallas, PA) - 1; Mercy, Sisters (IL) - 2; Rostro de Cristo Mission Vol Program - 1; School Sisters of Notre Dame (MO) - 5; School Sisters of Notre Dame (TX) - 1; School Sisters of Notre Dame (WI) - 2; School Sisters of St. Francis (Milwaukee, WI) - 2; St. Agnes, Cong. of Sisters (WI) - 2

Hong Kong

Men (35): Columbans - 2; Hartford Archdiocese - 1; Jesuits (CA) - 1; Jesuits (MD) - 1; Maryknoll Fathers & Brothers - 29; Maryknoll Mission Assoc of the Faithful - 1
Women (34): Franciscan Mission Srs O.L. Sorrows - 6; Good Shepherd Sisters (MO) - 1; Good Shepherd Sisters (NY) - 2; Maryknoll Sisters - 23; Mission de N D des Anges, Srs (Quebec) - 1; St. Columban, Sisters - 1

Hungary

Women (5): Sacred Heart, Society Devoted (CA) - 3; School Sisters of Notre Dame - (TX) - 1; St. Joseph, Cong of Srs (Orange) - 1

India

Men (52): Adorno Fathers - 1; Cong. of the Sacred Hearts (MA) - 3; Davenport Diocesan Volunteer Prog - 1; Divine Word, Society (IL) - 2; Duluth Diocese - 1; Jesuits (IL) - 22; Jesuits (MD) - 9; Marianists (MD) - 1; Marianists (MO) - 4; Passionists (IL) - 1; Philadelphia Archdiocese - 1; Pontifical Institute for Foreign Missions - 1; Sacred Heart, Priests of the (WI) - 1; St. Francis de Sales, Oblates (DE) - 1; St. Francis de Sales, Oblates (OH) - 2; Trinitarians (USA) - 1
Women (20): Charity of Nazareth, Sisters (KY) - 3; Christian Foundation for Children & Aging - 1; Franciscan Missionaries of Mary - 1; Holy Cross, Cong. of Sisters (IN) - 1; Little Sisters of the Poor (NY) - 4; Mary Immaculate, Sisters (PA) - 1; Missionaries of Charity - 1; Missionaries of Charity (NE Region) - 1; Sisters of Notre Dame (Chardon, OH) - 5; Sisters of the Sacred Hearts (HI) - 2

Indonesia

Men (21): Crosier Fathers & Brothers - 6; Divine Word, Society (IL) - 8; Jesuits (New England) - 1; Maryknoll Fathers & Brothers - 2; Oblates of Mary Immaculate (NH) - 1; Sacred Heart, Priests of the (WI) - 2; Xaverian Missionaries - 1
Women (3): Franciscan Sisters - 1; Sacred Heart, Society - 2

Ireland

Men (10): Atlanta Archdiocese - 1; Legionaries of Christ - 2; Marianists (OH) - 6; San Antonio Archdiocese - 1
Women (11): Franciscan Sisters of Philadelphia - 5; Medical Missionaries of Mary - 3; Religious of the Assumption (N Am Prov) - 3

Israel

Men (23): Augustinians of the Assumption - 1; Christian Brothers, De La Salle (CA) - 2; Christian Brothers, De La Salle (Midwest) - 5; Christian Brothers, De La Salle (NY) - 1; Christian Brothers, De La Salle (RI) - 1; Franciscan OFM (DC) - 7; Jesuits (New England) - 1; Knoxville Diocese - 1; Maryknoll Fathers & Brothers - 2; Order of Friars Minor (Assumption Prov) - 1; Sioux Falls Diocese - 1
Women (6): Daughters of Charity (IN) - 2; Holy Cross, Cong. of Sisters (IN) - 2; St. Joseph, Cong of Srs (Orange) - 1; Ursulines (NY) - 1

Italy

Men (25): Christian Brothers, De La Salle (Midwest) - 1; Divine Word, Society (IL) - 6; Franciscan Friars of Atonement - 3; Jesuits (NY) - 1; Legionaries of Christ - 5; Marianists (OH) - 1; Metuchen Diocese - 1; O.L. Most Holy Trinity, Society - 1; Oblates of Mary Immaculate (TX) - 1; Order of Friars Minor (S Heart Prov) - 3; Salesians (NY) - 2
Women (25): Christian Charity, Sisters (IL) - 1; Comboni Missionary Sisters (VA) - 1; Daughters of Wisdom - 1; Divine Savior, Sisters (WI) - 2; Holy Family of Nazareth, Srs (Pgh, PA) - 1; Holy Union Sisters (MA) - 1; Jesus and Mary, Rel (MD) - 1; Marist Missionary Sisters (MA) - 1; Missionaries of Charity (NE Region) - 3; Missionary Benedictine Sisters - 2; Missionary Srs of Our Lady of Africa - 3; Notre Dame de Namur, Srs (CT) - 1; O.L. Most Holy Trinity, Society - 1; Religious of the Assumption (N Am Prov) - 3; Scalabrini Sisters (IL) - 1; School Sisters of Notre Dame (WI) - 2

Jamaica

Men (31): Franciscan Friars of Atonement - 1; Jesuit Volunteers: International - 1; Jesuits (MD) - 1; Jesuits (New England) - 24; Passionists (NJ) - 4
Women (32): Dominican Sisters (Blauvelt, NY) - 1; Franciscan Mission Service - 1; Franciscan Sisters - 1; Franciscan Sisters of Allegany - 10; Lamp Ministries - 1; Marist Missionary Sisters (MA) - 3; Mercy, Sisters (OH) - 8; Mission Srs Imm Heart of Mary - 1; Servants of Mary (NE) - 2; St. Joseph, Cong of Srs (Pittsburgh) - 4

Japan

Men (125): Augustinians (IL) - 1; Augustinians (PA) - 7; Benedictine - Am Cassinese Cong (MN) - 4; Columbans - 6; Cong. of the Sacred Hearts (MA) - 7; Divine Word, Society (IL) - 11; Franciscan Friars of Atonement - 4; Franciscan OFM Cap (St Joseph Prov) - 1; Franciscan OFM Cap (St Mary Prov) - 2; Franciscan OFM Conv (MD) - 3; Jesuits (CA) - 5; Jesuits (MD) - 4; Jesuits (New England) - 1; Jesuits (NY) - 4; Marianists (MO) - 1; Marianists (OH) - 3; Marist Brothers (NY) - 5; Maryknoll Fathers & Brothers - 25; Maryknoll Mission Assoc of the Faithful - 1; Missionhurst - 1; Oblates of Mary Immaculate (DC) - 6; Oblates of Mary Immaculate (MN) - 3; Oblates of Mary Immaculate (NH) - 1; Order of Friars Minor (Assumption Prov) - 1; Order of Friars Minor (Holy Name Prov) - 2; Order of Friars Minor (Imm Conc Prov) - 1; Order of Friars Minor (St John Bapt Prov) - 1; Passionists (IL) - 8; Pontifical Institute for Foreign Missions - 3; Salesians (NY) - 1; Xaverian Missionaries - 2

Women (49): Columbans - 1; Company of Mary - 1; Daughters of Charity (IN) - 1; Daughters of Charity (MO) - 4; Franciscan Missionaries of Mary - 2; Franciscan Sisters of Atonement - 1; Hospital Sisters of St. Francis (Am Prov) - 1; Maryknoll Mission Assoc of the Faithful - 2; Maryknoll Sisters - 14; Notre Dame de Namur, Srs (MA) - 2; Notre Dame de Namur, Srs (MD) - 1; Order of St. Clare (MA) - 1; Passionist Nuns (PA) - 2; Presentation of Mary, Srs (MA) - 1; School Sisters of Notre Dame (IL) - 1; School Sisters of Notre Dame (MO) - 7; St. Joseph Carondelet, Srs (CA) - 2; St. Joseph Carondelet, Srs (NY) - 2; St. Joseph, Cong of Srs (Wichita) - 3

Jordan

Men (3): Franciscan OFM (DC) - 1; Jesuits (New England) - 2

Kazakhstan

Men (1): Order of Friars Minor (Assumption Prov) - 1

Kenya

Men (118): African Missions, Society of - 1; Augustinians of the Assumption - 2; Catholic Medical Mission Board - 2; Christian Brothers, De La Salle (CA) - 3; Christian Brothers, De La Salle (MD) - 2; Christian Brothers, De La Salle (Midwest) - 5; Christian Brothers, De La Salle (NY) - 4; Christian Brothers, De La Salle (RI) - 4; Comboni Lay Missionary Program - 2; Consolata Missionary Fathers - 6; Divine Word, Society (IL) - 1; Dominican Friars (CA) - 1; Dominican Friars (NY) - 6; Holy Cross Brothers (NY) - 1; Holy Cross Fathers (IN) - 4; Jesuits (IL) - 1; Jesuits (MD) - 1; Jesuits (NY) - 1; Jesuits (OR) - 2; Jesuits (WI) - 3; Los Angeles Archdiocese - 2; Marianists (OH) - 11; Maryknoll Fathers & Brothers - 24; Maryknoll Mission Assoc of the Faithful - 6; Mill Hill Missionaries - 1; O.L. Most Holy Trinity, Society - 4; Order of Friars

Minor (Holy Name Prov) - 3; Order of Friars Minor (St John Bapt Prov) - 1; Passionists (NJ) - 1; Rochester Diocese - 1; Sacred Heart, Brothers (NY) - 2; Spiritans (PA) - 1; Steubenville Diocese -1; Vincentians (PA) - 4; Xaverian Brothers (MA) - 4

Women (76): Bismark Diocese - 1; Catholic Medical Mission Board - 2; Comboni Missionary Sisters (VA) - 2; Consolata Missionary Fathers - 1; Consolata Missionary Sisters - 6; Dominican Sisters (Racine, WI) - 2; Franciscan Mission Srs for Africa - 2; Franciscan Missionaries of Mary - 2; Franciscan Sisters (Buffalo, NY) - 2; Franciscan Sisters of Philadelphia - 4; Incarnate Word Bl. Sacrament, Srs. - 2; Lasallian Volunteers - 2; Little Sisters of the Poor (NY) - 1; Los Angeles Archdiocese - 2; Maryknoll Mission Assoc of the Faithful - 5; Maryknoll Sisters - 4; Medical Mission Sisters - 4; Missionary Srs of Our Lady of Africa - 3; Notre Dame de Namur, Srs (CA) - 2; Notre Dame de Namur, Srs (MA) - 5; Sacred Heart of Jesus & Poor, Serv - 3; Sacred Heart, Society - 2; School Sisters of Notre Dame (MN) - 4; School Sisters of Notre Dame (MO) - 3; School Sisters of Notre Dame (WI) - 1; Sisters of Charity Incarnate Word - 7; St. Joseph, Sisters (Springfield) - 1; Volunteer Missionary Movement - 1

Korea

Men (34): Augustinians of the Assumption - 1; Cistercians (NY) -

1; Columbans - 6; Divine Word, Society (IL) - 1; Jesuits (WI) - 1; Maryknoll Fathers & Brothers - 21; Metuchen Diocese - 1; Salesians (NY) - 2

Women (30): Adorers of the Blood of Christ (KS) - 2; Charity of Seton Hill, Sisters (PA) - 4; Franciscan Missionaries of Mary - 1; Good Shepherd Sisters (MO) - 1; Good Shepherd Sisters (NY) - 1; Little Sisters of the Poor (NY) - 2; Maryknoll Sisters - 13; Order of St. Clare (MN) - 2; Sacred Heart, Society - 1; St. Columban, Sisters - 2; St. Joseph, Cong of Srs (Orange) - 1

Lebanon

Men (3): Jesuits (New England) - 3
Women (1): Jesus and Mary, Rel (MD) - 1

Lesotho

Men (4): Sacred Heart, Brothers (RI) - 4
Women (3): Holy Child Jesus, Society (PA) - 2; Imm Heart of Mary, Servs (ME) - 1

Liberia

Men (9): African Missions, Society of - 5; Holy Cross Brothers (IN) - 1; Salesian Lay Missioners (NY) - 1; Salesians (NY) - 2
Women (1): St. Joseph of Chambery, Srs - 1

Lithuania

Men (1): Dominican Friars (NY) - 1
Women (3): Franciscan Sisters of Providence of God - 3

Madagascar

Men (3): LaSalette Fathers (MO) - 3

Women (2): Christian Foundation for Children & Aging - 1; Daughters of Charity (NY) - 1

Malawi

Men (10): Comboni Missionaries - 1; Jesuits (OR) - 1; Marianists (MD) - 1; Marianists (OH) - 3; Missionaries of Africa - 2; Order of Friars Minor (Holy Name Prov) - 1; Order of Friars Minor (St John Bapt Prov) - 1

Women (6): Daughters of Wisdom - 3; Mission Srs Imm Concept (Quebec) - 1; Missionary Srs of Our Lady of Africa - 2

Malaysia

Women (1): Little Sisters of the Poor (NY) - 1

Mali

Women (3): Holy Cross, Sisters (NH) - 3

Marshall Islands

Men (6): Jesuit Volunteers: International 1; Jesuits (NY) - 5

Women (3): Jesuit Volunteers: International - 3

Mexico

Men (147): Augustinians of the Assumption - 4; Austin Diocese - 1; Basilian Fathers (Toronto) 5; Benedictine - Swiss Am Fed (WI) - 1; Chicago Archdiocese - 2; Christian Brothers, De La Salle (CA) - 1; Christian Brothers, De La Salle (NY) - 1; Comboni Missionaries - 2; Davenport Diocesan Volunteer Prog - 1; Divine Word, Society (IL) - 6; Dominican Friars (CA) - 4; (Unknown) - 1; Fort Worth Diocese - 1; Franciscan OFM Conv (CA) - 1; Franciscan OFM Conv (IL) - 2; Green Bay Diocese - 1; Holy Cross Fathers (IN) - 5; Holy Family, Missionaries of - 2; Jackson Diocese - 1; Jesuits (CA) - 2; Jesuits (MD) - 1; Jesuits (MO) - 1; Lay Mission Oblates of Mary Imm - 1; Legionaries of Christ - 8; Marianists (MO) - 7; Marist Brothers (NY) - 2; Maryknoll Fathers & Brothers - 21; Maryknoll Mission Assoc of the Faithful - 4; Miami Archdiocese - 1; Missionary Servants/Most Holy Trinity - 6; Missionhurst - 1; New York Archdiocese - 1; Nuestros Pequenos Hermanos - 1; O.L. Most Holy Trinity, Society - 2; Oblates of Mary Immaculate (CA) - 5; Oblates of Mary Immaculate (DC) - 1; Oblates of Mary Immaculate (MN) - 1; Oblates of Mary Immaculate (NH) - 2; Oblates of Mary Immaculate (TX) - 8; Order of Friars Minor (Assumption Prov) - 1; Order of Friars Minor (OL Guadalupe Prov) - 4; Order of Friars Minor (St Barbara Prov) - 6; Order of Friars Minor (St John Bapt Prov) - 1; Pueblo Diocese - 1; Quest 2; Redemptorists (PR) - 1; Resurrection Congregation - 2; Saginaw Diocese - 1; San Francisco Archdiocese - 2; Spiritans (PA) - 2; St. Francis de Sales, Oblates (DE) - 2; St. Francis de Sales, Oblates (OH) - 1; St. Joseph, Congregation of - 2; Xaverian Missionaries - 1

Women (94): Carmelite Sisters (Corpus Christi) - 1; Daughters of Mary and Joseph - 2; Daughters of St Mary of Providence - 1; Daven-

port Diocesan Volunteer Prog - 4;
Dominican Sisters (Edmonds, WA)
- 1; Dominican Sisters (Mission San
Jose) - 3; Dominican Sisters (San
Rafael, CA) - 1; (UNKNOWN) - 4;
Felician Franciscan Sisters
(Assumpt Prov) - 2; Franciscan Sisters of Chicago - 1; Franciscan Sisters of Penance - 1; Franciscan
Sisters of Tiffin, OH - 1; Holy Child
Jesus, Society (PA) - 1; Holy
Spirit/Mary Imm, Srs (TX) - 6;
Humility of Mary, Cong (IA) - 1;
Humility of Mary, Sisters - 1; IHM
Sisters of Monroe - 2; Lalmba
Association - 1; Marianites of Holy
Cross, Cong. - 1; Marist Sisters - 1;
Maryknoll Mission Assoc of the
Faithful - 4; Maryknoll Sisters - 8;
Mercedarian Missionaries of Berriz
- 1; Mercy, Sisters (IL) - 1; Mercy,
Sisters (NE) - 2; Mission Sisters,
Sacred Heart (PA) - 2; Missionaries
of Charity - 2; Missionaries of
Charity (NE Region) - 1; Missionary Servants/Most Blessed Trinity -
3; Missionary Sr Servs of Holy
Spirit - 1; Nuestros Pequenos Hermanos - 2; Poor Clare Missionary
Sisters - 1; Poor Handmaids of
Jesus Christ - 5; Presentation, Sisters (Sioux Falls, IA) - 4; Quest - 3;
Sacred Heart of Jesus, Sisters (TX) -
3; Sacred Heart, Society - 1; Scalabrini Sisters (IL) - 1; Social Service, Sisters (CA) - 1; St Francis
Mission Community (TX) - 1; St.
Joseph, Cong of Srs (Orange) - 3;
Ursuline Nuns of the Cong. of Paris
- 2; Ursuline Sisters (MO) - 3; Ursulines (NY) - 1; Xaverian Mission
Soc of Mary (MA) - 2

Micronesia

Men (23): Jesuit Volunteers:
International - 6; Jesuits (LA) - 1;
Jesuits (NY) - 14; Los Angeles
Archdiocese - 2
Women (12): Jesuit Volunteers:
International - 1; Los Angeles Archdiocese - 1; Maryknoll Sisters - 9;
Mercedarian Missionaries of Berriz
- 1

Montserrat

Women (1): Mission Srs Imm
Heart of Mary - 1

Morocco

Men (1): Order of Friars Minor
(Assumption Prov) - 1

Mozambique

Men (2): Jesuits (New England) - 1;
Jesuits (OR) - 1

Namibia

Men (2): Sacred Heart Missionaries
(IL) - 1; St. Francis de Sales,
Oblates (OH) - 1
Women (5): Maryknoll Sisters - 2;
Mission Sisters, Sacred Heart (PA) -
1; Missionary Benedictine Sisters - 2

Nepal

Men (13): Holy Cross Brothers (IN)
- 1; Jesuit Volunteers: International
- 2; Jesuits (IL) - 9; Jesuits (New
England) - 1
Women (4): Jesuit Volunteers:
International - 1; Maryknoll Sisters
- 2; School Sisters of Notre Dame
(MO) - 1

Netherlands

Men (3): Legionaries of Christ - 1;
New York Archdiocese - 1;

Philadelphia Archdiocese - 1

New Caledonia

Men (1): Marist Fathers & Brothers (MA) - 1

New Zealand

Men (1): Redemptorists (MD) - 1

Nicaragua

Men (23): Blessed Sacrament, Cong. of (OH) - 1; Christian Brothers, De La Salle (Midwest) - 1; Franciscan OFM Cap (St Joseph Prov) - 14; Gallup Diocese - 1; Jesuits (MD) - 1; Jesuits (MI) - 1; Jesuits (MO) - 1; Maryknoll Fathers & Brothers - 1; Montfort Missionaries (NY) - 2

Women (42): Cabrini Mission Corps 1; Charity of Nazareth, Sisters (KY) 1; Franciscan Sisters of Little Falls 2; Franciscan Sisters of Philadelphia 1; Franciscan Sisters of the Holy Cross 3; Holy Names, Sisters (CA) 3; Marianites of Holy Cross, Cong. 1; Maryknoll Sisters 10; Mission Sisters, Sacred Heart (PA) 1; Missionaries of Charity (NE Region) 1; Notre Dame de Namur, Srs (CA) 1; Notre Dame de Namur, Srs (CT) 1; Notre Dame de Namur, Srs (OH) 1; Sacred Heart, Society 1; St. Agnes, Cong. of Sisters (WI) 10; St. Joseph Carondelet, Srs (CA) 1; St. Joseph of Medaille, Sisters 2; St. Teresa of Jesus, Soc - 1

Niger

Men (1): Missionaries of Africa - 1

Nigeria

Men (26): Christian Brothers, De La Salle (Midwest) - 1; Dominican Friars (IL) - 8; Jesuits (MD) - 6; Jesuits (NY) - 10; Jesuits (WI) - 1

Women (26): Daughters of the Holy Spirit - 2; Dominican Sisters (Great Bend, KS) - 3; Franciscan Sisters (Wheaton) - 1; Franciscan Sisters of Millvale, PA - 1; Holy Child Jesus, Society (African Prov) - 3; Holy Child Jesus, Society (PA) - 1; Medical Missionaries of Mary - 1; Notre Dame de Namur, Srs (CA) - 1; Notre Dame de Namur, Srs (OH) - 1; Parish Visitors of Mary Imm - 2; Sacred Heart Lay Missioners (SCJs) - 1; School Sisters of Notre Dame (MD) - 7; School Sisters of Notre Dame (WI) - 2

Okinawa

Men (8): Franciscan OFM Cap (St Mary Prov) - 8

Pakistan

Men (10): Christian Brothers, De La Salle (Midwest) - 1; Dominican Friars (NY) - 8; Mill Hill Missionaries - 1

Women (9): Dominican Sisters (Sparkhill, NY) - 3; Franciscan Missionaries of Mary - 1; Jesus and Mary, Rel (MD) - 1; Medical Mission Sisters - 4

Palau

Men (3): Jesuit Volunteers: International - 2; Jesuits (NY) - 1

Panama

Men (22): Franciscan OFM Cap (St Joseph Prov) - 4; Holy Cross Fathers (IN) - 1; Jesuits (MO) - 1; Vincentians (PA) - 16

Women (8): Humility of Mary, Cong (IA) - 1; Maryknoll Sisters - 7

Papua New Guinea

Men (61): Capuchin Franciscan Volunteer Corps - 2; Divine Word, Society (IL) - 22; Franciscan OFM Cap (Mid-America Prov) - 6; Franciscan OFM Cap (St Augustine Prov) - 12; Marist Fathers & Brothers (DC) - 3; O.L. Most Holy Trinity, Society - 1; Order of Friars Minor (Assumption Prov) - 1; Passionists (NJ) - 1; Pontifical Institute for Foreign Missions - 1; Sacred Heart Missionaries (IL) - 12

Women (23): Charity Sisters of Ottowa (St Joseph Prov) - 1; Dominican Sisters (Adrian, MI) - 1; Humility of Mary, Cong (IA) - 1; Marist Missionary Sisters (MA) - 3; Mission Sisters, Sacred Heart (PA) - 2; Missionary Sr Servs of Holy Spirit - 3; Salesian Lay Missioners (NY) - 1; Sisters of Notre Dame (Toledo, OH) - 11

Paraguay

Men (9): Brooklyn Diocese - 1; Divine Word, Society (IL) - 2; Jesuits (LA) - 3; Oblates of Mary Immaculate (NH) - 1; Redemptorists (MD) - 2

Women (3): Missionary Sr Servs of Holy Spirit - 1; School Sisters of Notre Dame (IL) - 2

Peru

Men (142): Augustinians (IL) - 6; Augustinians (PA) - 5; Bridgeport Diocese - 1; Carmelite Friars (IL) - 9; Charleston Diocese - 1; Christian Brothers, Cong. - 1; Christian Brothers, Cong. (NY) - 11; Comboni Missionaries - 1; Davenport Diocesan Volunteer Prog - 1; Dominican Friars (NY) - 4; Dubuque Archdiocese - 1; Fargo Diocese - 1; Holy Cross Brothers (IN) - 1; Holy Cross Fathers (CT) - 5; Holy Cross Fathers (IN) - 3; Jefferson City Diocese - 5; Jesuit Volunteers: International - 1; Jesuits (CA) - 1; Jesuits (IL) - 16; LaCrosse Diocese - 1; Louisville Diocese - 1; Marianists (MD) - 1; Marianists (MO) - 2; Marist Fathers & Brothers (MA) - 2; Maryknoll Fathers & Brothers - 24; Maryknoll Mission Assoc of the Faithful - 5; Miami Archdiocese - 1; Mobile Archdiocese - 2; Norbertines (PA) - 1; Norbertines (WI) - 6; Ogdensburg Diocese - 2; Order of Friars Minor (Holy Name Prov) - 4; Order of Friars Minor (OL Guadalupe Prov) - 2; Order of Friars Minor (St Barbara Prov) - 1; Philadelphia Archdiocese - 1; Pittsburgh Diocese - 1; Precious Blood, Society (OH) - 8; Richmond Diocese - 1; Springfield (IL) Diocese - 1; Worcester Diocese - 1

Women (137): Benedictine Sisters (Ferdinand, IN) - 4; Charity of Leavenworth, Sisters - 7; Charity of SVP, Sisters (Halifax) - 3; Daughters of the Holy Spirit - 2; Davenport Diocesan Volunteer Prog - 4; Divine Providence, Sisters (MO) - 1; Divine Providence, Sisters (PA) - 1; Dominican Sisters (Adrian, MI) - 2; Dominican Sisters (Columbus, OH) - 2; Dominican Sisters (Springfield, IL) - 5; Franciscan Missionaries of Mary - 1; Franciscan Sisters (Rochester, MN) - 2; Franciscan Sisters of Christian Charity - 5;

Franciscan Sisters T.O.R. (Syracuse) - 4; Holy Cross, Cong. of Sisters (IN) - 4; Holy Cross, Sisters (NH) - 2; IHM Sisters of Scranton - 4; Jefferson City Diocese - 6; Jesuit Volunteers: International - 2; Marist Missionary Sisters (MA) - 5; Maryknoll Mission Assoc of the Faithful - 6; Maryknoll Sisters - 19; Medical Mission Sisters - 3; Mercy, Sisters (CA) - 1; Mercy, Sisters (IA) - 1; Mercy, Sisters (Merion, PA) - 6; Mercy, Sisters (Pgh, PA) - 2; Most Precious Blood, Sisters (MO) - 1; Notre Dame de Namur, Srs (CA) - 1; Notre Dame de Namur, Srs (CT) - 1; Notre Dame de Namur, Srs (OH) - 1; Presentation of Mary, Srs (MA) - 1; Presentation Sisters (ND) - 1; Presentation, Sisters (CA) - 1; School Sisters of Notre Dame (MO) - 1; School Sisters of St. Francis (Milwaukee, WI) - 2; St Joseph, Sisters, TOSF - 2; St. Columban, Sisters - 4; St. Joseph Carondelet, Srs (CA) - 1; St. Joseph Carondelet, Srs (MN) - 2; St. Joseph Carondelet, Srs (NY) - 5; St. Joseph, Sisters (Nazareth) - 1; St. Joseph, Sisters (Philadelphia) - 1; Ursuline Nuns of the Cong. of Paris - 4; Ursuline Sisters (MO) - 1; Ursulines of Toledo - 1; Vincentian Sisters of Charity (PA) - 1

Philippines

Men (170): Alexian Brothers (IL) - 2; Anchorage Diocese - 1; Blessed Sacrament, Cong. of (OH) - 5; Carmelites, Discalced (WI) - 4; Christian Brothers, De La Salle (CA) - 1; Christian Brothers, De La Salle (MD) - 3; Christian Brothers, De La Salle (Midwest) - 3; Columbans - 14; Comboni Missionaries - 1; Cong. of the Sacred Hearts (MA) - 1; Divine Word, Society (IL) - 18; Dominican Friars (NY) - 1; Franciscan OFM Conv (MD) - 1; Jesuits (CA) - 2; Jesuits (MD) - 2; Jesuits (NY) - 47; Jesuits (WI) - 1; LaSalette Fathers (MA) - 3; Marist Brothers (NY) - 1; Maryknoll Fathers & Brothers - 21; Missionhurst - 1; O.L. Most Holy Trinity, Society - 2; Oblates of Mary Immaculate (DC) - 1; Oblates of Mary Immaculate (MN) - 4; Oblates of Mary Immaculate (NH) - 2; Order of Friars Minor (Assumption Prov) - 2; Order of Friars Minor (St Barbara Prov) - 3; Order of Friars Minor (St John Bapt Prov) - 10; Passionists (IL) - 1; Passionists (NJ) - 6; Pontifical Institute for Foreign Missions - 2; Sons of Mary, Health of the Sick - 2; Vincentians (PA) - 1; Xaverian Missionaries - 1

Women (41): Christian Charity, Sisters (NJ) - 2; Daughters of St Mary of Providence - 2; Dominican Nuns (Summit, NJ) - 1; Holy Family of Nazareth, Srs (Pgh, PA) - 1; Holy Family of Nazareth, Srs (Phil, PA) - 2; Little Sisters of Jesus - 1; Maryknoll Sisters - 10; Mercy, Sisters (NE) - 1; Mercy, Sisters (NY) - 1; Mission Srs of Sacred Heart - 1; Missionary Benedictine Sisters - 1; Missionary Sr Servs of Holy Spirit - 1; O.L. Most Holy Trinity, Society - 1; Presentation of Mary, Srs (NH) - 1; Providence, Sisters (WA) - 4;

Salesian Lay Missioners (NY) - 1; Scalabrini Sisters (IL) - 1; Sisters of the Sacred Hearts (HI) - 2; Social Service, Sisters (CA) - 2; St. Columban, Sisters - 4; St. Joseph, Sisters (Philadelphia) - 1

Poland

Men (1): Christian Brothers, De La Salle (NY) - 1

Women (5): Bernardine Franciscan Sisters - 1; Charity of Nazareth, Sisters (KY) - 1; Dominican Sisters (Edmonds, WA) - 1; Franciscan Sisters of Holy Family (IA) - 1; Sacred Heart, Society - 1

Portugal

Men (2): Philadelphia Archdiocese - 1; San Francisco Archdiocese - 1

Puerto Rico

Men (53): Franciscan OFM Cap (St Augustine Prov) - 6; Franciscan OFM Cap (St Mary Prov) - 1; Hartford Archdiocese - 1; Jesuits (NY) - 8; Marianists (MD) - 7; Missionary Servants/Most Holy Trinity - 3; Oblates of Mary Immaculate (DC) - 3; Redemptorists (PR) - 20; Spiritans (PA) - 4

Women (23): Charity, Sisters (NY) - 1; Divine Providence, Sisters (PA) - 3; Dominican Sisters (Adrian, MI) - 2; Franciscan Sisters of Philadelphia - 4; IHM Sisters of Monroe - 2; Missionary Servants/Most Blessed Trinity - 1; Social Service, Sisters (NY) - 1; St Joseph, Sisters, TOSF - 1; St. Joseph, Cong of Srs (Rockville Ctr) - 8

Romania

Women (3): Bernardine Franciscan

Sisters - 2; Divine Providence, Sisters (MO) - 1

Russia

Men (6): Anchorage Diocese - 1; Augustinians of the Assumption - 1; Corpus Christi Diocese - 1; Divine Word, Society (IL) - 1; Dominican Friars (NY) - 1; Jesuits (MD) - 1

Women (4): Salesian Lay Missioners (NY) - 1; St. Agnes, Cong. of Sisters (WI) - 3

Rwanda

Men (1): Marist Brothers (NY) - 1

Women (1): St. Mary of Namur, Sisters (NY) - 1

Saipan

Men (1): Jesuits (NY) - 1

Women (2): Mercedarian Missionaries of Berriz - 1; Mercy, Sisters (NY) - 1

Scotland

Women (1): Missionaries of Charity - 1

Senegal

Men (1): Marist Fathers & Brothers (MA) - 1

Women (2): Marist Sisters - 1; St. Joseph of Lyons, Srs - 1

Seychelles

Men (2): Christian Instruction, Brothers (ME) - 2

Siberia

Men (1): Order of Friars Minor (Assumption Prov) - 1

Sierra Leone

Men (10): Salesians (NY) - 4; Xaverian Missionaries - 6

Women (6): Poor Clare Missionary Sisters - 1; School Sisters of Notre Dame (MO) - 3; Xaverian Mission Soc of Mary (MA) - 2

Singapore

Women (2): Little Sisters of the Poor (NY) - 2

Slovakia

Men (1): Sacred Heart Missionaries (IL) - 1
Women (1): Providence, Sisters (IN) - 1

Slovenia

Men (1): Blessed Sacrament, Cong. of (OH) - 1

Solomon Islands

Men (4): Dominican Friars (NY) - 1; Marist Fathers & Brothers (MA) - 2; Vincentians (PA) - 1
Women (4): Marist Missionary Sisters (MA) - 4

South Africa

Men (29): Charity, Brothers of (PA) - 1; Franciscan Third Order Regular (FL) - 1; Jesuits (MD) - 1; Jesuits (MO) - 2; Order of Friars Minor (Assumption Prov) - 2; Order of Friars Minor (Holy Name Prov) - 1; Order of Friars Minor (St John Bapt Prov) - 1; Richmond Diocese - 1; Sacred Heart, Priests of the (WI) - 3; Servite Friars (IL) - 6; Spiritans (PA) - 2; St. Francis de Sales, Oblates (DE) - 8
Women (21): Dominican Sisters (Adrian, MI) - 4; Holy Names, Sisters (CA) - 1; IHM Sisters of Monroe - 8; Missionary Benedictine Sisters - 2; Missionary Srs of Pre-

cious Blood - 1; Notre Dame de Namur, Srs (MA) - 1; School Sisters of St. Francis of Pgh, PA - 2; St Joseph, Sisters, TOSF - 1; Ursulines (NY) - 1

Spain

Men (5): Legionaries of Christ - 1; Metuchen Diocese - 2; Miami Archdiocese - 1; Missionaries of Africa - 1
Women (4): Religious of the Assumption (N Am Prov) - 3; Sacred Heart, Society - 1

Sri Lanka

Men (8): Christian Brothers, De La Salle (MD) - 1; Jesuits (LA) - 7
Women (3): Franciscan Missionaries of Mary - 2; Little Sisters of the Poor (NY) - 1

St. Kitts-Nevis

Men (1): Miami Archdiocese - 1

St. Lucia

Men (6): Davenport Diocesan Volunteer Prog - 1; Redemptorists (MD) - 5
Women (1): Davenport Diocesan Volunteer Prog - 1

St. Vincent

Men (4): Christian Brothers, De La Salle (MD) - 1; Christian Brothers, De La Salle (Midwest) - 1; Lasallian Volunteers - 2
Women (1): Inst. of the Blessed Virgin Mary - 1

Sudan

Men (6): Comboni Missionaries - 3; Jesuits (LA) - 1; Jesuits (MI) - 1; Mill Hill Missionaries - 1

Women (7): Maryknoll Mission Assoc of the Faithful - 1; Maryknoll Sisters - 5; Medical Missionaries of Mary - 1

Swaziland

Women (3): Mantellate Sr. Servants of Mary - 3

Sweden

Men (5): Oblates of Mary Immaculate (MN) - 4; Passionists (IL) - 1
Women (2): Missionaries of Charity (NE Region) - 1; Sacred Heart, Society - 1

Syria

Men (1): Order of Friars Minor (S Heart Prov) - 1

Tahiti

Men (1): Oblates of Mary Immaculate (NH) - 1

Taiwan

Men (65): Benedictine - Am Cassinese Cong (IL) - 1; Benedictine - Am Cassinese Cong (PA) - 1; Columbans - 2; Divine Word, Society (IL) - 7; Jesuits (CA) - 9; Jesuits (MO) - 1; Maryknoll Fathers & Brothers - 34; Order of Friars Minor (S Heart Prov) - 1; Viatorians (IL) - 1; Vincentians (PA) - 8
Women (40): Daughters of Charity (IN) - 2; Daughters of Charity (MD) - 4; Daughters of Charity (MO) - 5; Daughters of Charity (NY) - 2; Divine Savior, Sisters (WI) - 4; Franciscan Mission Srs O.L. Sorrows - 3; Franciscan Sisters - 1; Hospital Sisters of St. Francis (Am Prov) - 2; Maryknoll Sisters - 7; Missionary Sr Servs of Holy Spirit -

1; Providence, Sisters (IN) - 4; Sacred Heart, Society Devoted (CA) - 4; Social Service, Sisters (CA) - 1

Tanzania

Men (65): Jesuits (IL) - 1; Jesuits (MI) - 3; Maryknoll Fathers & Brothers - 36; Maryknoll Mission Assoc of the Faithful - 7; Missionaries of Africa - 1; Order of Friars Minor (Holy Name Prov) - 1; Order of Friars Minor (S Heart Prov) - 1; Precious Blood, Society (MO) - 1; Salesians (NY) - 1; San Jose Diocese - 1; Society of the Divine Savior - 4; Spiritan Associates - 1; Spiritans (PA) - 6; Volunteer Missionary Movement - 1
Women (37): Franciscan Sisters - 1; Franciscan Sisters of Sylvania, OH - 1; Jesuit Volunteers: International - 2; Maryknoll Mission Assoc of the Faithful - 7; Maryknoll Sisters - 17; Medical Missionaries of Mary - 3; Missionary Benedictine Sisters - 2; Missionary Srs of Our Lady of Africa - 2; Spiritan Associates - 1; St. Joseph, Sisters (Springfield) - 1

Thailand

Men (31): Christian Brothers, De La Salle (Midwest) - 1; Franciscan Mission Service - 1; Jesuits (CA) - 2; Jesuits (MD) - 1; Maryknoll Fathers & Brothers - 8; Maryknoll Mission Assoc of the Faithful - 4; Redemptorists (CO) - 12; Stigmatine Fathers - 2
Women (14): Franciscan Sisters (Rochester, MN) - 1; Maryknoll Mission Assoc of the Faithful - 4; Maryknoll Sisters - 2; Ursuline Sis-

ters (MO) - 1; Ursulines (CA) - 2;
Ursulines (NY) - 4

Tunisia
Men (1): Missionaries of Africa - 1

Turkey
Women (1): Little Sisters of the
Poor (NY) - 1

Uganda
Men (35): Comboni Lay Missionary Program - 1; Comboni Missionaries - 2; Holy Cross Brothers (IN) -
1; Holy Cross Brothers (NY) - 9;
Holy Cross Fathers (CT) - 2; Holy
Cross Fathers (IN) - 8; Jesuits (MI)
- 3; Jesuits (WI) - 2; Mill Hill Missionaries - 1; Missionaries of Africa
- 2; Sacred Heart, Brothers (LA) - 1;
Sacred Heart, Brothers (RI) - 1;
Volunteer Missionary Movement -
1; Xaverian Brothers (MA) - 1
Women (33): Comboni Lay Missionary Program - 3; Daughters of
Mary and Joseph - 2; Franciscan
Mission Srs for Africa - 2; Franciscan Sisters (Rochester, MN) - 1;
Holy Cross, Cong. of Sisters (IN) -
10; Mary of the Presentation, Srs
(ND) - 4; Medical Mission Sisters -
4; Medical Missionaries of Mary -
2; Missionary Srs of Our Lady of
Africa - 1; Sacred Heart, Society -
3; Volunteer Missionary Movement
- 1

Uruguay
Men (1): Jesuits (CA) - 1

Vanuatu
Men (2): Marist Fathers & Brothers
(MA) - 2

Venezuela
Men (17): Lincoln Diocese - 3;
Maryknoll Fathers & Brothers - 3;
Maryknoll Mission Assoc of the
Faithful - 2; Philadelphia Archdio-
cese - 1; San Diego Diocese - 1;
Society of St. Edmund - 2; St. Paul-
Minneapolis Archdiocese - 3;
Wichita Diocese - 2
Women (8): Maryknoll Mission
Assoc of the Faithful - 4; Medical
Mission Sisters - 3; Ursulines (NY) - 1

Vietnam
Men (6): Divine Word, Society (IL)
- 1; Maryknoll Fathers & Brothers -
3; Maryknoll Mission Assoc of the
Faithful - 1; Washington Archdio-
cese - 1
Women (1): Maryknoll Mission
Assoc of the Faithful - 1

Virgin Islands
Men (6): Charlotte Diocese - 1;
Redemptorists (MD) - 5
Women (5): Charity of St. Eliza-
beth, Sisters - 2; Marist Missionary
Sisters (MA) - 2; Missionaries of
Charity (NE Region) - 1

West Indies
Men (4): Cincinnati Archdiocese -
1; Divine Word, Society (IL) - 3
Women (6): Carmelite Sisters (Corpus Christi) - 3; Dominican Sisters
(Sinsinawa, WI) - 1; Franciscan Sisters of Philadelphia - 2

Western Samoa
Men (4): Marist Fathers & Brothers
(DC) - 1; Maryknoll Fathers &
Brothers - 2; Monterey Diocese - 1

Zaire

Men (16): Adorno Fathers - 1;
Crosier Fathers & Brothers - 2;
Divine Word, Society (IL) - 1;
Jesuits (MI) - 1; Jesuits (OR) - 1;
Missionhurst - 1; Order of Friars
Minor (S Heart Prov) - 3; Order of
Friars Minor (St John Bapt Prov) -
1; Sacred Heart, Priests of the (WI)
- 2; Xaverian Brothers (MA) - 1;
Xaverian Missionaries - 2
Women (11): Daughters of Charity
(MD) - 1; Daughters of Charity
(MO) - 2; Mission Srs Imm Heart of
Mary - 1; Sacred Heart, Society - 1;
St. Mary of Namur, Sisters (NY) -
1; St. Mary of Namur, Sisters (TX) -
3; St. Ursula, Society - 1; Ursuline
Sisters (Tildonk) - 1

Zambia

Men (49): Albany Diocese - 1;
Franciscan OFM Conv (IL) - 1;
Franciscan OFM Conv (IN) - 9;
Jesuits (LA) - 2; Jesuits (NY) - 2;
Jesuits (OR) - 7; Lay Mission
Oblates of Mary Imm - 2; Marianists
(MD) - 5; Marianists (OH) - 1; Mis-
sionaries of Africa - 2; Oblates of
Mary Immaculate (TX) - 7; Sacred
Heart, Brothers (NY) - 1; Sacred
Heart, Brothers (RI) - 3; San Jose
Diocese - 1; Sulpicians (MD) - 5
Women (11): Comboni Missionary
Sisters (VA) - 2; Franciscan Mis-
sion Srs for Africa - 1; Holy
Spirit/Mary Imm, Srs (TX) - 5; Lay
Mission Oblates of Mary Imm - 1;
Missionary Srs of Our Lady of
Africa - 1; Presentation Sisters (ND)
- 1

Zimbabwe

Men (13): Jesuits (LA) - 3; Jesuits
(MD) - 1; Jesuits (MI) - 1; Jesuits
(NY) - 1; Marianhill Missionaries -
3; Toledo Diocese - 1; Volunteer
Missionary Movement - 3
Women (19): Franciscan Mission
Srs for Africa - 2; Franciscan Srs
Perpetual Adoration - 2; IHM Sis-
ters of Monroe - 2; Maryknoll Sis-
ters - 3; Missionary Srs of Precious
Blood - 1; Notre Dame de Namur,
Srs (CA) - 1; Notre Dame de
Namur, Srs (MA) - 1; Notre Dame
de Namur, Srs (OH) - 1; Sacred
Heart of Mary, Rel - 3; Toledo Dio-
cese - 1; Volunteer Missionary
Movement - 2

Chapter 11

The Orthodox Christian Mission Center

Dimitrios Couchell

In January 1994, the former Mission Center of the Greek Orthodox Archdiocese, established originally in January 1985, became the Orthodox Christian Mission Center (OCMC). The OCMC now functions as the official mission and evangelism agency of all the Canonical Orthodox churches in North America.

The Standing Conference of Canonical Orthodox Bishops in the Americas (SCOBA) hierarchs appoint the OCMC's 40-member board of trustees. Board members meet twice a year to formulate the program that the OCMC staff implements.

The Mission Center is located in a modest house in Saint Augustine, Florida, just a ten-minute walk from the historic Saint Photios Greek Orthodox National Shrine. There are six full-time and two part-time staff at the center. What follows are descriptions of programs implemented during 1995-96.

Support of missionaries from the U.S.

1. Fr. Martin and Presbytera Renee Ritsi and their two children have begun their fourth year of service in Albania.

2. Fr. Luke and Presbytera Faith Veronis have begun their second year of service in Albania.

3. Iconographer Demetri and Sandra Leussis completed a very successful second year of service in Slovakia.

4. Sister Makaria Lambros, an Orthodox nun from New York, continues her service in South Korea as Abbess of the Holy Transfiguration

---

Dimitrios Couchell is executive director of the Orthodox Christian Mission Center in Saint Augustine, Florida.

Monastery and assistant to Bishop Sotirios.

5. Penny Deligiannis of Illinois completed one year of service in Albania. She has been in charge of establishing a publishing house for the Orthodox church in Albania. She has just been appointed director of Diakonia Agapes, the Orthodox church's development agency, in Albania. We expect her to serve one more year in Albania.

6. Christine Kouros of Indiana served seven months in Uganda in 1995 to help reorganize the central office there.

7. Jimmy Nakos of Texas served eight months in Albania. He is a CPA and helped establish a bookkeeping system for the Orthodox church in Albania.

8. Fr. John and Isabel Anderson of Montana served for one semester in 1995 at the Makarios Seminary in Nairobi, Kenya.

9. Nicholas Chakos of Pittsburgh departed in January 1996 for longterm service in Tanzania, where he will help develop the religious education program of the Orthodox church.

10. Anastasia Bradford of Florida has begun her second year of service in San Ramon, Costa Rica, where she is principal at a school for the deaf.

11. Fr. Anastasios Gonzales-Garaboa has been serving in Mexico City, Mexico, since December 1995.

12. Fr. Jose Angel Velez-Carde and his family began in August 1996 to establish Puerto Rico's first Greek Orthodox parish.

13. Fr. Michael Graves is in his tenth year of service in Haiti and the Dominican Republic.

Mission teams

The concept of short-term mission teams was first implemented in 1987. Since then 31 teams comprised of approximately 450 Orthodox Christians from North America, ages 18 to 70, have participated on teams to Africa, Asia, Eastern Europe and Central America.

The members of these teams have contributed greatly to the expansion of our program. The enthusiasm and zeal they exhibit on their return have alerted thousands to the critical need for mission and evangelism.

In 1995, mission teams served in the following countries:

- Israel: A fourteen-member team to the Holy Land helped an Arab Orthodox community in northern Galilee.
- India: A four-member teaching team was sent to help a missionary in Calcutta, India.
- Slovakia: A nine-member team helped construct a church in the town of Humene.

◆ Mexico: A five-member team built a home for a poor family in Tijuana and assisted in developing an orphanage.

Mission teams for 1996 have served in Israel, India, Kenya and Haiti.

Scholarships and financial aid

The OCMC has provided scholarships and financial aid for 16 mission students preparing to serve as missionaries in their own nations.

◆ Holy Cross School of Theology (Brookline, Massachusetts): Students from Albania, Chile, Ethiopia, Georgia, Indonesia, Korea, Puerto Rico, Romania, Russia and Uganda.

◆ Saint Vladimir's Theological Seminary (Crestwood, New York): A student from Russia.

◆ Saint Tikhon's Theological Seminary (South Canaan, Pennsylvania): A student from the Ukraine.

Development projects

The Agape Canister program has supported the following projects:

◆ Saint Herman's Seminary, Kodiak, Alaska

◆ Haiti Cottage Industries

◆ Makarios Seminary, Kenya

◆ Chavogere Medical Clinic, Kenya

◆ Theotokos Day Care Center, Masbate, Philippines

◆ Arab Rehabilitation Center, Israel

◆ Ethiopian Orphanages, Ethiopia

◆ Adeiso Pig Farm, Ghana

◆ Holy Cross Hospital, Uganda

◆ Food and medical resources, India

Support of indigenous priests

Through the Support A Mission Priest program, indigenous priests in Africa and Asia have received monthly financial support.

In Asia: Indonesia - 4, Philippines - 2.

In Africa: Cameroon - 5, Chad - 1, Congo/Brazzaville - 1, Ghana - 13, Kenya - 75, Nigeria - 11, Tanzania - 10, Uganda - 17.

Education and public relations

◆ Newsletter: Two issues are published each year and mailed to every Orthodox parish and priest in North America, plus the members of the Ss. Cyril & Methodios Orthodox Mission Society.

◆ Mission lecture tours: A three-week tour was made by Fr. Martin Ritsi and family during November and December 1996. Fr. Michael Graves of Haiti was sponsored for a three-week tour of Orthodox parishes in 1995.

◆ The First International Mission and Evangelism Conference was co-sponsored with Holy Cross Theological School in Brookline,

Massachusetts, on August 6-11, 1995. One hundred five people from 13 nations participated. His Beatitude Archbishop Anastasios of Albania was the keynote speaker.

♦ In February 1995 we completed production of a 26-minute public relations video. This was distributed to over 1,000 Orthodox parishes, priests and hierarchs to make the OCMC and its programs known.

Conclusion

The total income of the OCMC during 1995 was $997,965.51; expenditures totaled $975,694.43. We are so grateful to be engaged cooperatively in the never ending task and responsibility passed on to us by our Lord and Savior Jesus Christ as he ascended into the heavens, directing his followers to "Go therefore and make disciples of all nations, baptizing them in the name of the Father and of the Son and of the Holy Spirit, teaching them to observe all that I have commanded you; and lo, I am with you always, to the close of the age" (Matt. 28:19-20, RSV).

Bibliography

Selection has been made for general usefulness to the typical reader of the *Mission Handbook*, with emphasis on empirical or reasonably objective data, and with global or regional coverage. The perspective is mainly North Atlantic/Pacific.

BOOKS

Barrett, David B., ed. *World Christian Encyclopedia*. New York: Oxford University Press, 1982.

Bedell, Kenneth B., ed. *Yearbook of American & Canadian Churches*. Nashville: Abingdon Press, 1992-1997. http://www.ncccusa.org/

Brierley, Peter W., ed. *World Churches Handbook: Based on the Operation World Database by Patrick Johnstone, 1993*. London: Christian Research, 1997.

Engel, James F. *A Clouded Future? Advancing North American World Missions*. Milwaukee: Christian Stewardship Association, 1996.

Goddard, Burton L., ed. *The Encyclopedia of Modern Christian Missions*. Camden: Thomas Nelson & Sons, 1967.

Johnstone, Patrick. *Operation World*. Grand Rapids: Zondervan Publishing House, 1993.

Latourette, Kenneth Scott. *A History of the Expansion of Christianity*. New York: Harper & Row, 1937, plus updates.

———. *Christianity in a Revolutionary Age*, Vols. IV & V. New York: Harper & Row, 1962.

MARC (Mission Advanced Research & Communications Center). *Mission Handbook: North American Protestant Ministries Overseas (1980-89), Mission Handbook: A Guide to USA/Canadian Christian Ministries Overseas (1993)*. Monrovia: MARC, four editions, 1980-1993.

Missionary Research Library (MRL). *North American Protestant Foreign Mission Agencies*. New York: MRL, seven editions, 1953-1966.

Missionary Research Library and MARC. *North American Protestant Ministries Overseas Directory (1968-70), Mission Handbook: North American Protestant Ministries Overseas (1973-76)*. New York and Monrovia: MRL & MARC, four editions, 1968-1976.

Neill, Stephen. *A History of Christian Missions*. New York: Penguin Books, 1964.

———. Gerald Anderson and John Goodwin, eds. *Concise Dictionary of the Christian World Mission*. Nashville: Abingdon Press, 1971.

Phillips, James M. and Robert T. Coote, eds. *Toward the Twenty-First Century in Christian Mission*. Grand Rapids: Wm. B. Eerdmans Publishing Co.

U.S. Catholic Mission Association (USCMA). *Annual Report on U.S. Catholic Overseas Mission*. Washington, D.C.: USCMA, 1992.

JOURNALS/PERIODICALS

Evangelical Missions Quarterly. Published by EMIS, Box 794, Wheaton, IL 60189.

International Bulletin of Missionary Research. Published quarterly by the Overseas Ministries Study Center, 490 Prospect St., New Haven, CT 06511. http://www.ospelcom. net/omsc/

International Review of Mission. Published quarterly by the Commission on World Mission and Evangelism, WCC, 150 Route de Ferney, 1211 Geneva 2, Switzerland.

Missiology: An International Review. Published quarterly by the American Society of Missiology, 616 Walnut Ave., Scottdale, PA 15683.

Mission Studies. Published twice a year by International Association for Mission Studies, Normannenweg 17-21, D-20537 Hamburg, Germany. http://www.iams.org.uk/

Appendix

Survey questionnaire

Shown on these pages is the full questionnaire used for this version of the *Handbook*. For agencies that had previously appeared in the *Handbook*, their name, address, etc., information covered by questions 1-8 was also printed in *Handbook* format with an option to review it and make any needed updates or fill in questions 1-8. Every agency was asked to fill in questions 9-16 with their current statistical information as applicable. The questionnaire for Canadian agencies had "Canada" or "Canadian" instead of "USA" in the relevant places.

MISSION HANDBOOK
USA/CANADIAN PROTESTANT MINISTRIES OVERSEAS QUESTIONNAIRE FOR THE SEVENTEENTH EDITION

Questionnaire for the 1996 survey of USA organizations involved in overseas ministries.

1. What is your organization's name as you are known and would like to be listed in the *Mission Handbook*?

    _____

2. Mailing Address:

    _____
    (P.O. Box or Street)   (City)   (State)   (Zip Code)

3. Telephone number: (_____)_____
    Fax number: (_____)_____
    Please indicate if your organization has either or both of the following and would like them listed:
    Electronic-mail address: _____
    Internet WorldWide Web site: _____

4. Chief Executive Officer in the USA:

    _____
            (Name)   (Title of Position)

5. Year organization founded in USA: _____

6. Which one of the following is most used in describing your organization's denominational orientation?

   ❑ Denominational   ❑ Interdenominational   ❑ Nondenominational
   ❑ Transdenominational   ❑ Prefer that a denominational orientation not be used
   ❑ Other: _____

7. Which one (or two if needed) of the following terms describes the traditional doctrinal and/or ecclesiastical stance of your organization?

   ❑ Adventist   ❑ Episcopal   ❑ Methodist
   ❑ Baptist   ❑ Evangelical   ❑ Pentecostal
   ❑ Brethren   ❑ Friends   ❑ Presbyterian
   ❑ Christian ("Restoration Mvmnt.")   ❑ Fundamentalist   ❑ Reformed
   ❑ Christian/Plymouth Brethren   ❑ Holiness   ❑ Wesleyan
   ❑ Charismatic   ❑ Independent   ❑ Other: _____
   ❑ Congregational   ❑ Lutheran
   ❑ Ecumenical   ❑ Mennonite

8. Select up to six descriptors from the following list which are primary activities of your organization. If actively involved in more than six, please indicate only the six for which the most resources are currently committed.

   ❑ Agricultural programs   ❑ Education, theological   ❑ Psychological counseling
   ❑ Audio recording/distrib.   ❑ Evangelism, mass   ❑ Purchasing services
   ❑ Aviation services   ❑ Evangelism, pers. & sm. grp.   ❑ Recruiting/Mobilizing
   ❑ Bible distribution   ❑ Evangelism, student   ❑ Relief and/or rehabilitation
   ❑ Broadcstg., radio and/or TV ❑ Funds transmission   ❑ Research (missions related)
   ❑ Camping programs   ❑ Furloughed missionary support ❑ Services for other agencies
   ❑ Childcare/orphanage   ❑ Info. service (msn. related)   ❑ Short-term programs. coord.
   ❑ Children's programs   ❑ Leadership development   ❑ Supplying equipment
   ❑ Church constr./financing   ❑ Linguistics   ❑ Technical assistance
   ❑ Church estab./planting   ❑ Literacy   ❑ Training/Orientation, msny.
   ❑ Correspondence courses   ❑ Literature distribution   ❑ Training, other
   ❑ Dev., comm. and/or other   ❑ Literature production   ❑ Translation, Bible
   ❑ Disability assist. programs ❑ Mgt. consulting/training   ❑ Translation, other
   ❑ Ed., ch./sch. gen. Chrstn.   ❑ Medical supplies   ❑ Video/Film prod./distrib.
   ❑ Ed., missionary (certificate) ❑ Med., incl. dntl. & pub. health ❑ Youth programs
   ❑ Ed., theo. by extn. (TEE)   ❑ Natl. church nurture/support   ❑ Other: _____
   ❑ Ed., extension (other)   ❑ National worker support

   Which one of the above activities is most commonly associated with your organization? _____

FINANCIAL DATA (Note: if some of the financial categories do not apply, please indicate "NA" for not applicable.)

9. What was your organization's grand total income for all ministries in the USA and overseas, raised in the USA in calendar or fiscal 1995 or 1996? (Denominations should report their board total) $_____

10. Of the grand total for all ministries reported in Question 9, what was the amount of income for overseas ministries? $_____

11. Of the amount reported in Question 10, what, if any, was the dollar amount of gifts-in-kind commodities and/or services that were donated for overseas activities to you organization? $ _____

12. COUNTRIES OF SERVICE AND FIELD PERSONNEL

For personnel from USA: Include those engaged in **cross-cultural ministry** and **fully supported** under your organization. Include those on furlough and those on loan to another organization if they are fully supported by your organization. Include those on loan to your organization only if fully supported by you. Include spouses, even if they don't have "official" ministry status but serve in a ministry or support role.

For personnel from countries other than the USA: Include personnel with specific mission/ministry duties who are fully or partially supported on a regular basis by/through your organization from funds raised in the USA.

(Note: Indicate a region only if a specific country is not suitable) Country of Service	Year Work Began	From USA: Fully supported personnel with length of service expected to be:			From countries other than USA: Fully or partially supported personnel. Show the number on appropriate country of service line.	
		1, up to 2 Years	2 to 4 Years	More than 4 Years	Citizens of their country of service	Not citizens of their country of service

Please make additional copies of this page if needed.

OTHER PERSONNEL (Categories other than those reported in Question 12)

13. Number of **nonresidential USA mission personnel** (persons not residing in the country or countries of their ministry but assigned to work and travel overseas at least 12 weeks per year on operational aspects of the ministry) who are part of your organization:

_____ Fully supported by your organization _____Partially supported

14. Number of **short-term personnel** from the USA who went on overseas service projects or mission trips **less than 1 year, but at least 2 weeks**, in 1995 or 1996 through your organization, either fully or partially supported including those raising their own support: _____

15. Number of **bi-vocational or "tentmaker" missionaries sponsored or supervised by your organization** from the USA (persons who support themselves partially or fully through non-church/mission vocations and live overseas for the purpose of Christian witness, evangelism and/or encouraging believers): _____

16. Number of **staff** and/or other employees assigned to ministry and/or office duties **in the USA**:

_____ Full-time paid staff _____ Part-time paid staff/associates
_____ Volunteer (ongoing) helpers

17. If your organization has a board-adopted short (less than 60 words) purpose or **mission statement, please enclose a copy** from a brochure, letterhead, newsletter, or other copy that you share with others.

If you have **additional comments** about your organization or this survey which you would like us to be aware of, please indicate below or enclose on a separate sheet.

THANK YOU for filling out this form! We appreciate it.

Submitted by: _____ Date: _____

MARC

Bringing you key resources on the world mission of the church

MARC books and other publications support the work of MARC (Mission Advanced Research and Communications Center), which is to inspire vision and empower Christian mission among those who extend the whole gospel to the whole world.

Recent MARC titles:

▸ *Directory of Schools and Professors of Mission in the U.S.A. and Canada*, John A. Siewert, editor. Puts you in contact with the institutions that offer mission courses and the professors who teach them. Contact information is included for each institution and faculty member, including phone numbers and e-mail addresses. $11.95

▸ *Serving With the Poor in Latin America*, T. Yamamori, B. Myers, C. René Padilla and Greg Rake, editors. Real cases and analysis of Christian ministry are presented from throughout Latin America that broaden our understanding of holism in action. $12.95

▸ *Serving With the Poor in Africa*, T. Yamamori, B. Myers, K. Bediako & L. Reed, editors. Actual cases from different African countries contextualize holistic ministry. Commentary and analysis highlights such topics as holistic healing, AIDS, evangelism and more. $15.95

▸ *Serving With the Poor in Asia*, T. Yamamori, B. Myers & D. Conner, editors. Cases and commentary from seven different Asian contexts reveal how holism impacts anthropology, theology and other disciplines. $15.95

▸ *The New Context of World Mission*, Bryant L. Myers. A thorough yet concise visual portrayal of the entire sweep of Christian mission. Full-color graphics and up-to-date statistics reveal the history and future of world mission.

Book	$ 8.95
Slides	$149.95
Overheads	$149.95
Presentation Set *(one book, slides, overheads)*	$249.00

▸ *With an Eye on the Future: Development and Mission in the 21st Century*, Duane Elmer & Lois McKinney, editors. Cutting-edge thinkers present essays in the fields of mission, development, education and church leadership that propose new strategies in the areas that will be vital to mission in the next century. $24.95

▶ *Street Children: A Guide to Effective Ministry*, Phyllis Kilbourn, editor. Uniquely designed to orient workers among street children, this volume gives several examples that depict the plight of street children around the world. Explains who they are, where they can be found, why they are on the streets and how we can respond in biblical ways to this global crisis. $23.95

▶ *Healing the Children of War*, Phyllis Kilbourn, editor. A practical handbook for ministry to children who have suffered deep traumas. Examines the impact of war on children; the grieving child; forgiveness; restoring hope to the child; and many other important issues that surround children who have been victimized by war. $21.95

▶ *Children in Crisis*, Phyllis Kilbourn, editor. Alerts us to the multiple ways in which children are suffering around the world—AIDS, abandonment, abuse, forced labor, girl-child discrimination—and equips us to respond in biblical ways. $21.95

▶ *God So Loves the City*, Jude Tiersma and Charles Van Engen, editors. An international team of urban practitioners explore the most urgent issues facing those who minister in today's cities. Their new methodology reveals the first steps toward a theology for urban mission. $21.95

▶ *Caring for the Whole Person*, E. Anthony Allen. The author merges the spiritual, psychological and social aspects of life to challenge Christian health workers to address the total needs of the whole person. Also reveals the author's personal journey to integrate his Christian faith with his profession as a psychiatrist. $9.95

▶ *Ministry in Islamic Contexts*, The Lausanne Committee for World Evangelization. This informative booklet concisely sets the scene for accomplishing effective Christian ministry in Islamic contexts. $6.50

Contact us toll free in the U.S.: 1-800-777-7752
Direct: (626) 301-7720

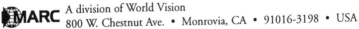

MARC A division of World Vision
800 W. Chestnut Ave. • Monrovia, CA • 91016-3198 • USA

Ask for the MARC Newsletter and complete publications list